LET'S TRAVEL
PATHWAYS THROUGH
MINNESOTA

An insider's guide to lodging,
specialty shops, restaurants,
bed & breakfasts, museums and
historic sites. Also includes state,
regional, community and corporate
profiles, and much more!

CLARK & MILES PUBLISHING INC., SAINT PAUL, MINNESOTA

Published by:
Clark & Miles Publishing, Inc.
1670 S. Robert St. Suite 315
Saint Paul, Minnesota 55118
(612) 454-8212
(800) 728-9972 (outside the Twin Cities metro area)

Although the author and publisher have exhaustively researched all sources to ensure the accuracy and completeness of the information contained in this book, readers are advised that conditions of the businesses and attractions profiled can change over a period of time. We therefore assume no responsibility for errors, inaccuracies, omissions or any other inconsistency herein.

Printed and bound in Minnesota, U.S.A.

Publisher's Cataloging in Publication
(Prepared by Quality Books Inc.)

Marshall, Alex B.
    Let's travel pathways through Minnesota / Alex B. Marshall. --
2nd ed.
    p. cm.
    New ed. of: Pathways through Minnesota.
    Includes index.
    ISBN 0-9626647-1-5

    1. Minnesota--Description and travel.   I. Title.

F604.3.M37 1994   917.76'0453
                           QBI94-1492

PREFACE

The inspiration for this guide was simple. We felt there was a real need to probe deeper into the unlimited number of travel and sight-seeing opportunities available in Minnesota, and bring the entire state to life in a single publication.

What separates us from other travel guides?

We don't just compile information. We highlight the very best. We have based the selections in this book on interviews we've done with people throughout Minnesota and research we've conducted all over the state. We've asked them to give us their recommendations, to tell us which businesses and attractions are unique to their community and worthy of a visit. The profiles and listings are not designed as critiques in any way but rather to help travelers select what is of special interest to them.

While we have made every effort to ensure that this book is complete, there are bound to be some unavoidable exclusions. We would love to hear about any of your favorite places that merit consideration for our next edition.

We are thrilled to bring you the best Minnesota has to offer. Every member of our staff has found this to be a most enlightening experience and we will not forget all of the wonderful people we have met along the way. We sincerely hope your experience with this publication is as fantastic as ours.

Many of the businesses and communities profiled here have shown us tremendous support by providing information and granting interviews as well as making books available for their customers and visitors. Once again, special thanks to all of the staff and participants who, together, helped make this Minnesota's newest and most complete travel guide.

Tell them you read about their place in *Let's Travel Pathways Through Minnesota.*

LET'S TRAVEL PATHWAYS THROUGH MINNESOTA

Publisher's Representatives
Anne Arthur
Debra Bank
Jamey Gonzalez
Carl Hornburg
Ken Kozitza
Gary Larson
Ellen Magratten
Bill Magratten
Vicki Mickelson
Burt Patwell
Randy Thiel

Contributing Writers
Grant McGinnis
Bob Waldridge
Carla Waldemar
Ken Kuczynski
Larry Keltto
Alex B. Marhsall

Artwork
Martiena Richter
Bob Negaard

Layout
Irene Waldridge

Special Projects
Teresa Fudenberg
Norma Schwartz

Cover Design & Graphics
Joseph Crowley

Director of Marketing
Ross P. Bird

Editorial
Grant McGinnis
Claudia Debner

Publisher
Randall C. Bird

*Cover photos provided
by the Minnesota
Office of Tourism*

CONTENTS

Arrowhead

Bluff Country

Heartland

Metroland

Prairieland & Southern Lakes

Heartland

Lake of
the Woods

Arrowhead

Int'l
Falls

Crookston
Red Lake

Lake
Winnibigoshish

Ely

Grand Marais

Mississippi
River

Fargo/Moorhead
Leech Lake

Detroit Lakes

Brainerd

Aitkin

Duluth

Fergus Falls

Mille
Lacs
Lake

Metroland

Alexandria

St.
Cloud

Willmar

Montevideo

Minneapolis/
St. Paul

New
Ulm

Mankato

Rochester

Worthington   Windom

Albert Lea

Prairieland
& Southern Lakes

Bluff
Country

Minnesota

People have always travelled to Minnesota.

And why not? With more than 10,000 lakes and more shoreline than Florida, California and Hawaii combined, the country's best fishing, excellent outdoor opportunities, a rich history and plenty else going for it, the reasons are obvious.

But something happened along the way that's changed all that. Oh sure, they still travel to Minnesota for vacation, more in fact every year. Some even fly in from all over the country just for the day. The reason?

To shop.

Welcome to the Mall of America, symbolic of all that is the new Minnesota, symbolic of the '90s kind of place that has hosted the Super Bowl, the World Series, the U.S. Open Golf Championships, the NCAA Final Four, the Olympic Sports Festival and just about every other big sporting event you'd care to name in recent years.

Welcome to the new Minnesota.

Some 16 million people passed through the doors of Mall of America in the first six months of operation. At 4.2 million square feet, it is the largest shopping and entertainment complex in America. And in so many ways that all that nature couldn't, it has put Minnesota on the map.

You can't see it all in a afternoon but the tourists try. Oh, how they try. This is the Melting Pot personified, the ultimate conglomeration of all things American.

They come in special chartered buses from the entire upper midwest. Major airlines offer special shopping fares so visitors from Japan, Europe and every state in America can experience the Mall.

The attractions are obvious.

• Four major department stores, including Bloomingdale's, Macy's, and the much-revered Nordstrom.

• A seven-acre indoor amusement park, Knott's Camp Snoopy, named in honor of Peanuts creator and Minnesota native Charles Schulz.

• An entertainment area commonly known as the Fourth-Floor Stroll, the 23,000-square foot Gatlin Brothers Music City Grill where you can find live music and line dancing on a weekday afternoon and a virtual orgy of sports at America's Original Sports Bar.

• The 70,000-square foot Oshman's, where you can shoot hoops on a real basketball court, try out a hockey stick on plastic ice, hit golf balls in a driving range, box 12 rounds in a real ring, ski on a mechanical hill, shoot your new crossbow at a target or try out the batting cage. No purchase necessary.

• Then there's the 15,000-square feet of childhood creativity at the Lego Imagination Center.

• A ton of great eating spots.

• Plus stores. Lots of stores. Of all sizes, shapes and descriptions. Toss in 12,750 parking spaces, all gratis, none more than 300 feet from the door and you've got the Mother of all Malls.

Do you think developer Victor Gruen could have imagined all this when he opened America's first enclosed shopping mall just down the freeway in Edina in 1956? Southdale, still going strong, has spawned 38,000 imitators, the latest and greatest of which draws 90-100,000 people each and every weekday and between 150- and 170,000 people a day on weekends.

The Mall hands out some 750,000 of their handy-dandy map guides every week. Ten thousand people hold full-time jobs there.

And the best part? It's only a very small slice of what the Twin Cities and the rest of Minnesota has to offer. Minneapolis-St. Paul itself has to be what you'd call a model metropolis. In poll after poll, year after year, it has come to represent everything great about America. It's safe, it's trendy, and it's fun.

If specialty shopping is your thing, you'll love the Conservatory, Calhoun Square and Gaviidae Common. Nicollet Mall, a thoroughfare long-since closed to traffic, is still going strong with stores like Dayton's, Saks Fifth Avenue and Neiman Marcus. It has a sophisti-cated air about it, like being in London or Sydney but missing the stuffiness of those bigger places.

Throw in the usual dash of fine dining and cultural attractions, a riverfront now rejuvenated on both sides, the finest arena in the United States (Target Center), the Metrodome and Major League Baseball and you have a downtown alive after five. Don't let the Mall's magnetism keep you away from it.

For many an afterthought, for others a bonus, downtown St. Paul offers a change of pace.

The presence of "Phantom of the Opera" at the Ordway Music Theatre has brought renewed attention to the long-suffering little sis-ter. So, too, the restoration of the stately Saint Paul Hotel, a classic hotel in every sense. St. Paul has a charm all its own, from the State

Capitol to the mansions of Summit Avenue to the eclectic shops of Grand Avenue.

And if your entourage includes the kids, the obvious answer is Valleyfair. Opened in 1976 in Shakopee, it is the largest amusement park in the Upper Midwest and every year they seem to add something new and enticing.

If you're looking for something with a tad more educational value, try the Minnesota Children's Museum in St. Paul or the Minnesota Zoo in Apple Valley. Both are excellent.

For adults only, the pleasures of Mystic Lake Casino are nearby with more than $100 million in winnings having been distributed thus far from some 60 Vegas-style blackjack tables, 600 video slots and a 1,200-seat bingo palace.

All of this, together, is the new Minnesota.

Yet there's still so much more.

There is still the serene beauty of the Boundary Waters, the stunning bluffs of the Mississippi River, the gorgeous resorts of the Brainerd Lakes area and the rich history of the Prairieland. Stretching some 400 miles from north to south and encompassing everything from tiny hamlets to a major metropolis, there truly is something for everyone in this great state.

In autumn, the dazzling hues of Minnesota's hardwood forests are a visual symphony of color. With the maple's showy reds and rich golds and the rusts of the oaks, September and October are magnificent months for hiking, biking or boating. Hunters still find forests, fields and wetlands abundant with wild turkeys, deer, bear, moose and game birds.

Then comes winter, when the landscape is transformed into a pristine adventureland for skiers, dog sledders, snowmobilers and ice fisherman. Minnesota's ski areas, from Lutsen and Giants Ridge in the north to Afton Alps in the east to Mount Kato in the west, are among the best in the Midwest.

Throw in the diverse ethnic traditions of Minnesota's settlers, the rich past of Minnesota's Natives, the many attractions both man-made and natural, and this is a state with much to offer.

And then there is the one factor that endures, Mall or no Mall, lakes or no lakes, tradition and history and commerce aside. It is the tradition of "Minnesota Nice" and even though it may be a source of sheepish embarrassment to the locals, it is your assurance of a good time in the North Star state.

After all, this is what you came for, isn't it?

Golfing Minnesota

Driving winds. Blowing snow. Frozen lakes. And snowmobile trails galore. Chances are, that's the kind of image the word "Minnesota" conjures up in the minds of the uninitiated, those who haven't had the good fortune to visit. Or haven't been paying attention.

For those who have, the picture is very, very different. Lush, tree-lined fairways. Gorgeous water holes. Top-notch resorts. And a state that's gone golf crazy. That's right, golf crazy.

There may be legendary winters in these parts but there's also seven months of glorious golf weather and a couple of million people who have fallen in love with the game. In fact, the 1991 U.S. Open set new attendance standards at the Hazeltine National Golf Club in Chaska. The 1993 Burnett Senior Classic established an all-time attendance mark in its first edition at the Bunker Hills Golf Course in Coon Rapids. And the LPGA Minnesota Classic continues to draw hordes to the fabulous Edinburgh USA course in Brooklyn Park.

Throw in a hugely successful 1993 Walker Cup, pitting the best American amateurs against their counterparts from Great Britain, at Interlachen Country Club and a boom in resort golf development and you have facilities and players to rival the world's best. Oh yes, one more trivia note. The 1993 U.S. Amateur Champion hails from Minnesota. He is John Harris of Edina.

Yes, Minnesotans love their golf. And the good news is there are plenty of places to play to challenge champions and chumps alike.

It wasn't always that way. For generations, Minnesotans have played resort golf throughout the state. But for the most part, it was mom 'n pop golf, a few flags in a pasture with a little mowing thrown in for good measure. Very little mowing actually.

But things change.

It really began in the Brainerd Lakes area at a resort called Grand

View Lodge, where they took the plunge and built a world-class golf facility. The results were almost instantaneous. The Pines at Grand View was recognized by *Golf Digest* as one of the country's finest new resort courses. It is hailed as Minnesota's best public play facility in the company of Edinburgh USA in Brooklyn Park, Bunker Hills in Coon Rapids, Willinger's at Northfield and Majestic Oaks in Ham Lake. In 1994, a third nine opened and an 8,000-square foot clubhouse was added to an already spectacular facility.

With its national recognition and instantaneous regional acclaim, The Pines at Grand View spawned a pile of imitators. Like Superior National on the North Shore of Lake Superior at Lutsen. Like Wildflower at Fair Hills Resort in Detroit Lakes and The Lakes at Ruttger's Bay Lake Lodge in Deerwood.

For decades, when you mentioned resort golf in Minnesota, there was one name that came to mind: Madden's.

Located just up the road from Grand View, Madden's had 45 holes of golf when Grand View had just nine. Madden's has constantly upgraded and expanded and improved and enhanced but it always held true to the original philosophy of sending guests home in a good mood with a low score, preferably their lowest score ever.

Today's golfers want the opposite approach.

They want spectacular scenery, major challenges, lots of water and the kind of stuff they see on television. Now Madden's, like its competitors, is going to give it to them. By 1997, a 7,000-yard championship course will be open for business, carved out of 212 wooded, rolling acres.

Madden's is not alone. Designed by internationally acclaimed course architects Tom Weiskopf and Jay Morrish, The Wilds in Shakopee promises to be top drawer all the way. Developers have spent $7 million on the course adjacent to the Mystic Lake Casino with a resort hotel to follow in the near future.

It was actually Izaty's Golf & Yacht Club on Lake Mille Lacs that started the trend. By transforming a very average resort course into a contemporary challenge, Izaty's built the only Pete Dye-style course in Minnesota. It offers water-logged target golf (bring balls by the dozen and pray lots) with facilities to match. The trend continues with another new challenge being christened near Grand Rapids with the opening of Sugarbrooke.

Still, some prefer the old standbys, places like Peter's Sunset Beach in Glenwood, which boasts the Pezhekee National Golf Course on Lake Minnewaska and Arrowwood Resort near Alexandria. Then there's Breezy Point Resort, McGuire's Irish Hills, Mille Lacs Golf Resort, Whitefish Golf Club and several others, all in the Brainerd Lakes region, and any number of nine- and 18-hole layouts available for public play and scattered throughout the state.

The development shows no signs of waning. Hey, there may be snow and ice in Minnesota. But don't let the reputation fool you. It may not be long before this neck of the woods is known as the "Land of 10,000 Links"!

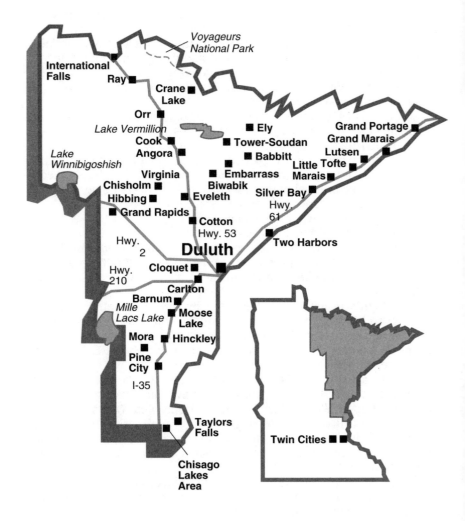

Arrowhead

It is the essence of Minnesota. The unmistakable aroma of a crackling campfire. The smell of pines. The pristine beauty of a serene lake. Nature at your feet.

It is largely as it has always been, relatively untouched by the modern world, a place to seek solitude, to unwind, to relax, to explore, to savor. It is Minnesota's Arrowhead region, so-named for its unusual shape, and unique in so many ways.

From the rugged beauty of the North Shore to the rich history and culture of the Iron Range to the solemn beauty of the Boundary Waters Canoe Area and Voyageur's National Forest, the Arrowhead has long drawn visitors to partake of its rich resources and to escape the world beyond.

The Arrowhead is a land comprised largely of wilderness.

There are more than 4,000 lakes in all, more than 2,000 streams and rivers. There are countless numbers of tranquil resorts that thrive on nature's bounty and a bustling city thrown in for good measure. Throughout the glacial lakes and spring-fed streams of the region, you'll find walleye, northern pike, trout, steelhead, bass and panfish. In the Boundary Waters, explore a true national treasure, one of the world's finest areas for fishing and canoeing. And at Voyageurs National Park, you'll find 30 lakes and hundreds of islands to be explored by motorboat, canoe, kayak and sailboat. But not by car because there is not a single mile of roadway within its boundaries.

Of course, there's a little larger body of water in this region, too.

It is mighty Lake Superior, the world's largest freshwater lake. Drive the North Shore to the resort towns of Lutsen and Tofte and Grand Marais. Explore Duluth and its many attractions. Or just stand and stare at the awesome beauty and power that is Superior.

There's something about this unique part of the world that makes

you want to draw on associations with other parts of the globe. The
woods, thick with pine and underlaid by rugged bedrock, lead you to
look north, to Canada and Alaska. The towns that blossomed here in
the early parts of the 20th Century, spurred on by iron ore and the
wealth below, attracted workers by the hundreds from the Old World.
The rich, ethnic traditions they carried with them continue to thrive.
And Lake Superior itself is hardly a lake at all, more like an ocean
and all that entails.

Still, this is Minnesota.

At the center of the Arrowhead's economic engine is Duluth, a
city of 85,000 with a long history tied to the lake. When the St.
Lawrence Seaway went through, Duluth became the westernmost
Atlantic seaport in North America, connecting the city and the region
around it to the rest of the world.

Today, its economy is much more diverse. It has undergone a
transformation, the kind of downtown revival most cities can only
dream of. Its culture is rich. Its attractions are many. And it is a city
that knows how to celebrate with festivals and parks and recreational
opportunities galore.

But not far afield, the real Arrowhead awaits, an Arrowhead that
is a year-round destination for sportsmen and outdoor enthusiasts, a
destination for fishermen and hikers, canoeists and skiers, cyclists
and those who'd prefer a relaxing round of golf.

Perhaps the most challenging part of the Arrowhead is deciding
where to go and what to explore first. The choice is yours.

The history of the Arrowhead is closely bound up with the wealth
of natural resources that have fueled its economy since the Europeans
discovered the region more than 300 years ago. Native Ojibwa bands
began trading furs with the French and French-Canadian voyageurs
in an enterprise that eventually grew to continental proportions and
nearly wiped out the beaver altogether. Grand Portage National
Monument, found at the Arrowhead's most northeasterly tip, was the
hub of such activity and is today an outstanding place to gain an
appreciation of the past. The reconstructed North West Company fur
trading post near Pine City gives yet another glimpse of life as it was.

The loggers and the miners came afterwards and left their indeli-
ble impressions on the land, as well. There are excellent historical
sites throughout the region relating to logging and mining, including
Chisholm's Ironworld USA, in the deep passages of the Soudan
Underground mine at Tower and on the slopes of the Hill Annex
open-pit mine near Calument.

Come for the past. Come for the present. But do come. The
Arrowhead calls as it has called generations before.

BIWABIK

Incorporated in 1892, Biwabik now greets visitors with a delightful Bavarian-style theme. Its name in Ojibwa means "valuable," and indeed it is today. As the gateway to *Giants Ridge Recreation Area,* it is the center for many winter activities. Each year, thousands of cross-country skiers descend on the area to participate in the *Pepsi Challenge Cross-Country Ski Race,* which kicks off in Biwabik the night before with spaghetti dinners served up to racers, visitors and townspeople alike. At the end of the race, everyone finds other ethnic foods waiting to warm them up.

Weihnachtsfest is celebrated in December with a magnificent Christmas lighting display and a wonderland art fair of crafts, displays, music and entertainment.

For further information, contact:
City of Biwabik
P.O. Box 529, Biwabik, MN 55708
Phone: 218-865-4183

RESORT

The Laurentian Resort	Box 350, County Road 138, Biwabik, MN 55708 Phone: 800-843-7434 Hrs: Open year-round. Visa, MasterCard and Discover accepted.

The Laurentian Resort is a unique year-round family resort offering all the best in Minnesota vacations. That's because it's located on beautiful Wynne Lake right next to Giants Ridge Ski Area, one of the state's best ski areas. And that means fun and sun for the whole family any time of the year.

In their lakeside, three and four-bedroom villas, you'll find some of the finest accommodations in the Midwest. They also offer one and two bedroom condominium suites. All units are professionally decorated and most offer fireplaces and kitchens. Some even include a jacuzzi and sauna. In the summer, boats, bikes and rollerblades can be rented and there is a supervised children's program for ages 3-9.

Guests also enjoy the heated swimming pool, hot tubs, tennis court and hiking trails. Of course, in winter, Giants Ridge Ski Area dominates the scene. Sleep and ski packages are quite popular because of the excellent skiing here. Restaurants are nearby, so you don't have to worry about a thing—except having fun!

CHISAGO LAKES AREA

Encompassing the communities of Chisago City, Center City, Lindstrom, Shafer and North Branch, the Chisago Lakes area is a land of tranquil waters and rolling farmland. The region was settled almost exclusively by Swedish immigrants, and this heritage is reflected in traditional craft and antique shops, ethnic eateries, and historic monuments and buildings.

Center City, along with Chisago City, also is known for its antique and craft shops, and charter companies in the Twin Cities regularly offer antique-shopping tours to the Chisago Lakes area. Shafer, meanwhile, is home of the intriguing farm museum *Yesterfarm of Memories.* The historical roots of these cities are celebrated in area festivals, including Lindstrom's *Karl Oscar Days,* the *Center City Days,* and the *Ki-Chi-Sago Days* in Chisago City during the third weekend in September.

For further information, contact:
Lindstrom Chamber of Commerce
P.O. Box 283, Lindstrom, MN 55045   Phone: 612-257-2282

SPECIALTY SHOP

| *Eichten's Hidden Acres Cheese & Buffalo Farm* | Highway 8, (2.2 miles East of) Center City, MN 55021. **Phone for Retail: 612-257-1566, Mail Order: 612-257-4752.** Hrs: Daily 9 a.m.-6 p.m. Visa and MasterCard accepted. |

Eichten's Hidden Acres is not only unique as a cheese shop and factory, but the newest addition is a herd of Bison (buffalo). It is one of just a few herds of its size privately owned. Joe and Mary Eichten and their family have been in the cheese business since 1976, specializing in European style cheese including Dutch gouda, Danish tilsit, baby Swiss and many more.

Along with the buffalo meat and the nationally acclaimed award winning cheeses sold, imported candies and jams, maple syrup, honey, unique gifts and other speciality foods have been added to the gift shop.

The American public likes the buffalo meat because it is lower in cholesterol, fat and calories than chicken and higher in protein than beef. For your convenience, all items can also be purchased through the Cheese Factory mail order department.

SPECIALTY SHOPS

Gustaf's Fine Gifts & Collectibles and Gustaf's World of Christmas	P.O. Box 722, 13045 Lake Blvd., Lindstrom, MN 55045 **Phone: 612-257-6688 or 800-831-8413.** Hrs: Mon.-Sat. 9:30 a.m.-5:30 p.m., Fri. to 8:30 p.m., Sun. 12-5 p.m. Extended Holiday hours. Major credit cards accepted.

Built in 1879 by Gustaf Anderson, known as "Guldgubben" (old gold man, or man of gold), this historic house is now the home of Gustaf's Fine Gifts and Collectibles and Gustaf's World of Christmas.

Gustaf's has a magnificent display of gifts that will be of interest even to the youngest member in your family. Gustaf's is an authorized dealer of the new Disney Classics and has a very large inventory of Hummel figurines. There is crystal by Swarovski and Iris Arc, Russian boxes, music boxes, men's gifts, Cherished Teddies, Lowell Davis, Afghans, gifts and much more.

Gustaf's World of Christmas is a Showcase Dealer for Department 56. Gustaf's carries Snow Village, New England Village, North Pole, Dickens Village, Christmas in the City, Alpine Village and all accessories. There is a large collection of Christopher Radko ornaments, Old World glass German ornaments, Byers' Choice Carolers, Annalee dolls, Madame Alexander dolls, over 300 santas, nativities, angels, toys, collector cars, Coca Cola collectibles, and Fitz & Floyd.

◆ ◆ ◆ ◆ ◆ ◆ ◆

Sven's Swedish Clogs & Quality Footware	10,000 Lake Boulevard, Chisago City, MN 55013 **Phone: 612-257-4598.** Hrs: Mon.-Fri. 10 a.m.-6 p.m.; Sat. 9 a.m.-5 p.,m.; Sun. 11 a.m.-5 p.m. Visa, MasterCard and AmEx accepted.

Service and top quality are Sven Carlsson's priorities. He has been making clogs for close to 50 years, and customers are assured of obtaining the absolute finest when they stop at Sven's Swedish Clogs and Quality Footwear. With a factory outlet right on the premises, customers are also assured of finding the best possible prices.

An authentic Swedish windmill greets all who enter the comfortable shop. The main attraction is Sven's handcrafted Swedish clogs, but other items are also on hand. Sven offers a line of very soft Romika shoes, sheepskin boots and Bout Clarks of England liners, Weinbrenner workboots, SAS shoes, and Minnetonka moccasins.

Sven's handmade clogs are created with wooden bases imported from Sweden. He prepares the bases and attaches all leather uppers, cut and sewn right in Chisago City and available in a variety of colors.

Sven makes clogs for men, women, and children and welcomes custom orders at no extra charge.

CHISHOLM

Chisholm became a village in 1901, was completely destroyed by fire in 1908 and was rebuilt within a year. This is a testimony to the tenacity and pride of the diverse groups who began the city. Today this tradition lives on as the town is famous for its ethnic foods, entertainment and unique ways it celebrates its mining heritage.

ATTRACTIONS & EVENTS

Chisholm is the home of *IRONWORLD USA,* a living tribute to the early Iron Trail settlers and a celebration of their ethnic heritage. This theme park brings history alive with imaginative hands-on exhibits, music, dancing, specialty foods and craft demonstrations. Visitors travel back to a time gone by on a scenic trolley ride to see old mining locations and learn from costumed narrators how miners and their families lived during that era. A 1,600-seat amphitheater offers entertainment, often by top performers.

A close-up view of the mines and the men who worked them can be found at the *Minnesota Museum of Mining,* located on Chisholm's main street. Housed here is the equipment used during the early days of the *Mesabi Range,* including a steam locomotive and a 1910 Atlantic steam shovel. A replica of an old mining town completes a fascinating stroll through history.

Antique car buffs will delight in the old automotive treasures at the *Classic Cars Museum* where 45 beautifully restored vintage automobiles are displayed. These include a 1924 Star, a model built only for a few years, and a 1935 Ford rumble seat coupe.

Winter in Chisholm means it's not only time to get outside and enjoy the tranquil beauty of the surrounding winter wonderland, but to also take part in exhilarating festivities like *Polar Bear Days* and the *Polar Bear Kitty Cat World Series Snowmobile Races.*

Summertime is a continuous celebration, highlighted with the 5-day *International Polkafest* and *Minnesota Ethnic Days*. *Chisholm Fire Days* are held in September.

For further information, contact:
Chisholm Chamber of Commerce
327 W. Lake St.
Chisholm, MN 55719
Phone: 800-422-0806

ANTIQUES

Dream Cottage Antiques	300 N.W. First Street, Chisholm, MN 55719 **Phone 218-254-2153.** Hrs: (Summer) Tues.-Thur. 4 p.m.-7 p.m.; Sat.-Sun.11 a.m.-4 p.m. (Winter) Thur. 4-7 p.m.; Sat. 11 a.m.-4 p.m.

Dream Cottage Antiques truly is a collector's dream—an entire house filled with old treasures and collectibles. The Dream Cottage itself also is an antique. Look for a cozy turn-of-the-century stucco house on the corner of First Street N.W. and Highway 73 in Chisholm.

As Millie Muhar, life-long collector and owner, says, there is "something for the collector in all of us." Two floors and a basement of Dream Cottage Antiques are carefully arranged to show items as they might actually be used. Glass and kitchenware are displayed in the kitchen; pictures are displayed on the walls.

Browse through the rooms of furniture, jewelry, books, magazines, old records, sporting collectibles and dolls, including an extensive Barbie doll collection.

Early mining memorabilia and handcrafted items from the Iron Range also are available. They can provide shipping for your purchase, if needed.

INTERPRETIVE CENTER

IRONWORLD USA	P.O. Box 392, Chisholm, MN 55719 **Phone: 218-254-3321 or 800-372-6437 (In MN)** Hrs: Seasonally from 10 a.m. to 7 p.m. daily

In the heart of the Iron Range is a theme park, IRONWORLD USA, dedicated to the preservation and celebration of the region's cultural heritage. From the Interpretive and Research Centers to the flag-lined walkways of Festival Park, one can see exhibits, visit the library and archives, or enjoy the ethnic crafts, strolling musicians and delicious foods of Festival Park.

Ride the electric trolley along the edge of an open pit mine, or have the children enjoy the Carousel and remote control boats. Enjoy a meal in the ethnic restaurant and see top-name stars in the outdoor amphitheater.

COOK/LAKE VERMILION

A resort community located two hours north of Duluth, Cook is your gateway to the famed Boundary Waters Canoe Area, the remote, untouched home to timberwolves, black bear, and bald eagles. Camping and fishing expeditions routinely start out from Cook, which offers a wide variety of resort accommodations that range from rustic cabins to luxurious rooms. Many offer top-notch outfitting services and boat rentals designed to make the visitor's wilderness experience an exciting yet comfortable adventure.

ATTRACTIONS & EVENTS

However, Cook offers more than just resorts. It's a complete rustic community with gift shops, supper clubs, grocery stores, and auto services, all carefully geared to the traveler's needs. Located just off *Lake Vermilion* with its 40,000 acres of sky-blue waters, 365 islands, and 1,200 miles of scenic shoreline, Cook is a fisherman's dream-come-true.

The *Minnesota Department of Natural Resources* has maintained a hatchery and stocking service at Lake Vermilion since 1969. This, together with sport fishing "catch and release" practices, have made the lake one of the premier walleye lakes in Minnesota.

For those who want a break from fishing, the Cook/Vermilion area also offers fine golf courses, tennis courts, horseback riding, and miles of hiking trails in the quiet woods.

The *Ashawa Ski Trail* around the west end of Lake Vermilion offers groomed ski trails.

The *Vermilion Fairways Golf Course* offers a challenging 9-hole course complete with club house offering short orders and a pro shop.

Check out the *Harvest Moon Festival* in September with an antique car show, parade, food booths, pet shows, pancake breakfast, arts and crafts show and more.

Whatever the size of your group or whatever time of year, Lake Vermilion hosts the perfect vacation. You'll meet friendly people, have unlimited fun, and relax in natural beauty.

Experience Lake Vermilion and take advantage of its "good nature."

For further information, contact:
Cook Visitors Information Center
P.O. Box 155
Cook, MN 55723   Phone: 218-666-5850

RESORTS

Life of Riley **Resort**	Box 1167, Cook, MN 55723 **Phone: 218-666-5453 or 800-777-4479** Hrs: Seasonally, 6 a.m.-10:30 p.m. Visa, MasterCard and Discover accepted.

'Life of Riley'— an appropriate name for a memorable vacation on beautiful Lake Vermilion and secluded Norwegian Bay. Here, fishermen are surrounded by the Superior National Forest, abundant wildlife and prosperous, sky-blue fishing waters.

Nineteen fully furnished vacation homes come complete with walk-out decks and a private, panoramic lakeshore view. Each has been remodeled with the comfort and convenience of the family in mind. The restaurant serves meals prepared from scratch and with generous portions. The game room comes with pool table, ping-pong, video games and is open 24 hours. A safe sandy beach, boats, motors, canoes and waterfront toys are available.

Riley's qualified staff provides superior service. The waterfront and protected harbor are well managed and efficient. Fish cleaning, daily fish records and seminars are provided. The Naturalist Program, in conjunction with the U.S. Forest Service, offers an exceptional opportunity to explore, learn about and appreciate the wilderness.

◆ ◆ ◆ ◆ ◆ ◆ ◆

Pehrson Lodge **Resort**	2246 Vermilion Drive, Cook, MN 55723 **Phone: 800-543-9937** Hrs: Open May 15-Sept. 30. Visa and MasterCard accepted.

Pehrson Lodge Resort on scenic Lake Vermilion features 21 carpeted, well-furnished cabins complete with linens and microwaves. The resort is situated on 68 wooded acres with 1,800 feet of shoreline and a 650-foot natural sand beach. All cabins are either located directly on the lake or include a good view of the lake and have sundecks and BBQ grills. Some cabins even have fireplaces.

This resort was chosen by *Midwest Living* magazine as one of the Midwest's "outstanding small resorts." A children's program is offered during summer months for children ages 4 to 12.

Lake Vermilion is a stunning northwoods lake with 1,200 miles of wooded shoreline, 40,000 acres of water and enough fish to satisfy the most avid angler. That's because it's stocked each year with millions of walleye fry to maintain a healthy supply of trophy fish! A weekly seminar is presented by a professional guide that will give valuable insights on fishing for walleye, northern pike, large and small mouth bass and crappie.

RESORT

Ludlow's Island Lodge	Lake Vermilion, Cook, MN 55723 **Phone: 218-666-5407 or 800-537-5308** Hrs.: Daily, May through Oct. Visa, MasterCard and AmEx accepted.

Ludlow's Island Lodge offers outstanding service for a pampering getaway. This 19-cottage resort situated on an island and two adjacent shorelines of Lake Vermilion in northern Minnesota is the highest rated AAA and Mobil Guide resort of its type in the state. Ludlow's Island is also the only resort in Minnesota to receive *Family Circle* magazine's "Family Resort of the Year" award for 1990. Furthermore, *USA Today* featured Ludlow's as one of five "hotspots" from around the world to visit in 1993.

Each cabin is nestled privately among the pine and birch with an excellent view of the lake and surrounding woods. Spend your time relaxing or enjoy a variety of activities. The cottages, which range in size from one to five bedrooms, all have fireplaces, decks, knotty pine or cedar interiors and Weber grills on spacious decks. Kitchens are completely equipped with dishwashers, microwaves, blenders, drip coffee makers and popcorn poppers.

The resort facilities include a camping island for kids, tennis and racquetball courts, canoes, paddleboats, power boats, kayaks, sailboats, a waterslide, a playground with treehouse, sauna, protected sandy beach swimming area, lodge and game rooms. Golf is nearby. Fishing clinics provide up-to-the-minute tips on the best strategies for walleye, bass and northern pike. Guides are available, as is the best in rental fishing equipment.

RESORT

Vermilion Beach Village Resort

Lake Vermilion, P.O. Box 249, Cook, MN 55723
Phone: 218-666-5440 or 800-833-0036
Open May 13th-Sept 25th.
Major credit cards and checks accepted.

Sandcastles and footprints wash away, but memories last forever at Vermilion Beach, a unique resort on Lake Vermilion that is a community all its own. Everything you need for a memorable vacation is there—completely modern cottages, fully carpeted and just steps away from a wonderful natural sand beach. This is the last resort on the lake—the road goes no farther—so you can be sure you're away from the busy world. It's a very secluded family retreat.

Ten furnished housekeeping cottages grace this lovely resort. Each comes with deck, picnic table, BBQ, microwave, coffeemakers and electric toasters. Monday is get acquainted day with a bonfire on the beach. The atmosphere is casual and good fellowship prevails. Here, lasting friendships are made and renewed year after year.

Pamper yourself in the Garden Restaurant. Enjoy the renowned Sunday Champagne brunch, Wednesday Mexican Fiesta or one of many delightful lunches or dinners. Have a cocktail or "mocktail" in the Fish Tales Lounge. There's even a ladies only Champagne pontoon ride on Lake Vermilion!

Catch the latest news via TV satellite, then step outside and marvel at the unspoiled beauty of wilderness surroundings. Many species of birds and animals inhabit this area. There's hiking trails, berry picking and bird watching. Water ski, sail, canoe and explore the natural sights and sounds. Turn the kids loose in the playground or the games room.

And when you're ready, the naturally clear waters of Lake Vermilion offer a variety of wonderful fishing for all ages. Walleyes, crappies, bass, northern, muskie and panfish abound in this pristine water.

There's no crowding here. The spacious grounds extend from the beach to the forest. Your hosts, Zeke and Bev Stinson, are beginning

their third decade at Vermilion Beach Village Resort and they extend their northwoods hospitality to business groups, too.

When you want to get away from a busy world and relax and unwind in a natural setting, you'll especially enjoy the wonderful warmth at Vermilion Beach Village Resort.

RESORT

Vermilion Dam Lodge

Lake Vermilion, P.O. Box 1105-P, Cook, MN 55723. **Phone: 218-666-5418 or 800-325-5780** FAX: **218-666-5693.** Hrs: Open year-round. Major credit cards accepted.

All the comforts of city dwelling amidst the tranquility and beauty of a wilderness setting. That's what you'll find at Vermilion Dam Lodge. Lake Vermilion has been classified as one of the three most beautiful lakes in the world by a journalist for *Redbook* magazine. Vermilion spans 40 miles from east to west and encompasses some 1,200 miles of shoreline, including 365 islands.

Twenty one miles north of Cook, MN, Vermilion Dam Lodge has much to offer guests who come to unwind in the northwoods. Visitors can fish, hunt, hike, canoe, sail, swim, water ski, or just enjoy nature. In other words, there's something for everyone at Vermilion Dam Lodge, a 3 diamond, AAA resort. It's the ideal place to get away from it all.

They staff a full-time naturalist to help you explore this pristine wilderness. And if fishing is your thing, count on Lake Vermilion to deliver an eye-popping catch. Millions of walleye fry are added to the lake every year and there is no major industry nearby to pollute the waters. The conscientious dock boys will help you dock and tie up your boat. If you wish, they also clean your daily catch.

Clean, comfortable cabins that are close to the lake accommodate from 2 to 12 persons. The knotty-pine elegance and efficiency of the vacation homes make visitor stays a pleasure. Try the Chalet or the Honeymooner, each with one bedroom, queen-sized bed, fireplace and two person Jacuzzi. Or, try the three-bedroom Morningside with an outstanding view of the lake.

At the end of a busy, fun-filled day, relax and soothe muscles in the sauna or heated swimming pool. Then head for the main lodge to socialize, or retire to the luxury of your cabin to rest up for the next day's adventure!

COTTON

Although the early settlers of northeastern Minnesota were used to living in remote areas, Cotton was going too far for most of them. Originally settled in 1897 by a dogged individualist known as "Charlie in the brush," Cotton did not have a paved road connection with the rest of Minnesota until 1922.

Although Cotton, located 40 miles north of Duluth, boasts three restaurants, a bakery, motel and a handful of other service businesses, its 600 residents zealously guard its peaceful atmosphere. However, the calm is shattered on the fourth weekend of each August with the annual *Minnesota State Old Time Fiddle Championship,* which attracts top fiddlers from across the United States and Canada. As a companion to the fiddle event, Cotton arranges an *Old Time Scandinavian Dance* on the first weekend of each month from June through October. For further information on Cotton, contact:

Minnesota State Old Time Fiddle Championship
P.O. Box 205, Cotton, MN 55724
Phone: 218-482-3430 or 218-482-5549

SPECIALTY SHOP

Sue's Sweet Shop	Highway 53, Cotton, MN 55724 **Phone: 218-482-3281** Hrs.: Summer, Mon.-Sun. 7 a.m.-8 p.m. Winter, Mon.-Sun. 7 a.m. 7 p.m.

What began as an idea for a coffee shop opened in May of 1985 as a restaurant where everything on the menu is home cooked. Built by the owner and her family, it's a place where Sue Wudinich and her crew serve up a menu featuring roast turkey, baked ham and roast beef with "real" mashed potatoes and gravy in a warm country atmosphere. Several kinds of pies, made from scratch daily, are offered on the menu, as well as bread pudding, cookies, sandwiches and breakfast items. Coffee here is a favorite in the area, especially when accompanied by a homemade cinnamon or pecan roll. Treats from the soda fountain include sundaes, malts, floats and cones.

Sue is planning to share her home cooking secrets in a cookbook to be available soon. Visitors may not find the standard hamburger and fries fare at Sue's Sweet Shop, but they will find good home cooking and tasty desserts. Remember to ask about the daily specials for meals and soup. The restaurant is open for breakfast, lunch and dinner.

CRANE LAKE

Once part of the great fur trade route, Crane Lake today is a modern northwoods resort community. A host of wilderness lodges, marinas, outfitters, and campgrounds make the town an ideal starting point for a journey into the serene lakes and rivers abutting the U.S.-Canada border. Crane Lake provides a genuine wilderness experience for those looking for a few days of solitude. The Crane Lake area also offers intriguing glimpses into history. First came the Indians, who left behind the *Painted Rocks* at Lac La Croix and Namakan. Painted hundreds of years ago, these pictographs are the last traces of the first people of this vast lake area. By *Crane Lake Gorge,* visitors can see the remnants of a late 18th-century voyageurs wintering camp, while the *Kettle Falls Motel* is a memory of the logging boom of the early 20th century.

For further information, contact:
Crane Lake Commercial Club
Crane Lake, MN 55725
Phone: 218-993-2346

RESORT

Nelson's Resort	94 PM Nelson Road, Crane Lake, MN 55725 **Phone: 218-993-2295** Hours: Open May 13-Oct. 2 Visa and MasterCard accepted.

Located on the Minnesota-Ontario border waters at Crane Lake, Nelson's Resort is a haven in the wilderness reachable by plane or car. Boating enthusiasts delight in over 40 miles of continuous waters from Crane Lake into Sand Point and Namakan and up to Kabetogama Lake, all without a portage.

Nelson's can arrange all types of boat trips, from fishing and camping to fly-in or wildlife camera excursions. Boat rides with shore lunch are especially popular. Nelson's will furnish everything you need and the border waters are teeming with walleye, lake trout, crappie and bass. Or try snorkling, waterskiing, swimming and canoeing. Miles of nature trails, a games room, sauna and fireplace provide other diversions. A range of accommodations is available and the food is outstanding, with a homestyle menu including home baked breads and pastries. Vegetables are grown in an organic garden. Babysitting available. European or American plan. Airport shuttle service. Store, gift shop and laundromat.

DULUTH

It was not so long ago that Duluth's waterfront was hardly a tourist attraction. Then something changed.

The city, long driven by its ties to Great Lakes shipping, turned its attention to life's finer things. The result, after a $150 million investment, is one of the truly great downtown renaissances in North America, a fantastic waterfront, a thriving business and entertainment sector and all the ingredients to draw folks from far and wide, just for fun. The turnaround has been so great that the city won a national City Livability Award for Outstanding Achievement plus an All-America Cities award. The hotels, restaurants, unique shops, boardwalks, horse-drawn carriage paths and festivals make this restored port area a hub of activity during the summer months and a natural starting point to explore the city's many attractions.

Of course, Duluth is still a worldclass seaport, with 49 miles of docks shipping 40 million metric tons annually, the largest volume of any port on the Great Lakes. Duluth's airport boasts the longest runway in Minnesota and the aerial lift bridge, one of only two of its kind in the world, still rises to 138 feet in less than a minute.

Duluth has always been a gateway to the world.

Originally occupied by the Sioux and Chippewa and claimed for the French in 1679 by the explorer Daniel duLuth, the city passed a couple of centuries as a fur trading post. In 1871 the Duluth ship canal was cut, firmly establishing it as a major shipping center. When the St. Lawrence Seaway opened almost a century later, Duluth became the United States' westernmost Atlantic Seaport. Ship watching remains a favorite pastime and there's even a Boatwatcher's Hotline (218-772-6489) you can call for up-to-the-minute information on arrivals and departures.

Add all of that up and you may reach the conclusion that Duluth, with 85,000 citizens and a whole lot going for it, just might be the best-kept secret in all of Minnesota.

ATTRACTIONS

Where to begin? At the harbor, of course.

The harbor area offers a variety of attractions, including the ***Corps of Engineers Canal Park Marine Museum,*** with exhibits related to the rich marine history of Lake Superior. The ***William A. Irvin,*** former flagship of the U.S. Steel Great Lakes Fleet, is now a 610-foot floating museum. For a view from the water, the ***Vista Fleet Harbor Cruises*** are an excellent choice. If you're a true landlubber, stick to the ***Downtown Lake Walk,*** a two-mile, landscaped pathway that takes you from *Leif Erikson Park* to *Canal Park* and provides you with a stunning view along the way. Visit *Bayfront Festival Park* and the *Duluth Entertainment Convention Center,* home to major sporting events, entertainment and conventions. A little further into town is *The Depot,* a restored train station in the Chateau style that houses three museums, a visual arts institute and three performing arts organizations and *Fitger's,* a brewery now transformed into a hotel and shops.

Be sure and explore the *International Sculpture Garden* in *Lake Place* as well as the *Waterfront Sculpture Walk.* At the new *Lake Superior Zoological Gardens,* you'll find more than 500 species of animals from nearly every place on earth.

"Glensheen", a 39-room Jacobean revival mansion on the shores of Lake Superior, is a fun place to visit. Or take in a professional baseball game with the *Duluth Dukes* of the Northern League. Or place a wager at the *Fond-du-Luth Gaming Casino.* The skiing is great at *Spirit Mountain* in the winter months, the golfing fine at *Enger Park* and *Lester Park* during the spring, summer and fall. Or take a ride on the *North Shore Scenic Railroad.* For more natural pursuits, check out the spring salmon run or the fall hawk migration as seen from *Skyline Drive.*

EVENTS

Perhaps the *Grandma's Marathon* is the best-known of the many festivals and events that grace Duluth's calendar each year.

"Grandma's", as it's known among serious runners, attracts a worldwide field of more than 6,000 each June who come to race and partake of everything Duluth has to offer. In winter, the *John Beargrease Sled Dog Marathon,* the premiere sled dog race in the Lower 48, is an attraction as is the *Duluth Winter Sports Festival.* In August, the *Bayport Blues Festival* draws music lovers from all over as does the *International Folk Festival* later in the month.

The *Duluth Aviation Expo, Taste North,* and *Fourth-Fest* are among the other events worth exploring plus there's wonderful hiking, camping and fishing, too. Need we say more?

For further information, contact:
Duluth Convention and Visitors Bureau
100 Lake Place Drive
Duluth, MN 55802
Phone 218-722-4011 or 800-4-DULUTH

BED & BREAKFAST

The Mansion

3600 London Road, Duluth, MN 55804
Phone: 218-724-0739
Hrs: Open seasonally and winter weekends.

This magnificent home was built between 1928 and 1930 by Marjorie Congdon Dudley and her husband Harry C. Dudley. The construction is of steel and concrete with an exterior of stone and leaded windows.

In 1983, Warren and Sue Monson opened the Mansion as Duluth's first bed and breakfast inn. The seven acre estate is nestled on 525 feet of Lake Superior beach with manicured lawns, woods and beautiful gardens. The Mansion is being preserved just as it was when built by the Dudleys.

The main house has 10 bedrooms and pricing is reflective of room sizes and amenities. The Peach Room and the Beige Room are lakeside, offering a queen size bed. They share a bathroom with a shower.

The Yellow Room and the Houseman's Room are pondside, have queen size beds, private bath and tub.

Also pondside is the Pink Room with queen size bed and private bath with tub and shower.

Lakeside again, the Green Room and the Blue Room both offer king size beds, share a bathroom with both a tub and walk-in shower.

The Anniversary Suite and the South Guest Room both provide a lake view, king size beds, and private bath with tub and shower. These rooms are very large. The South Guest Room has a large bay window overlooking the lake.

The Master Suite offers a king size bed, private bath with a tub and large, original, marble walk-in shower. This is the largest suite in The Mansion.

There is also a carriage house with a one-bedroom apartment. It includes a TV and a refrigerator but no cooking facilities.

Guests are encouraged to make themselves at home on the grounds and inside the mansion. The common rooms include the Library, Living Room, Summer Room, Gallery, Dining Room and Trophy Room. Guests enjoy a large country-style breakfast as part of their stay.

CHARTER FISHING

Deep Secret Charters

5254 Albert Olson Road
Duluth, MN 55804
Phone: 218-525-6733
Hrs: May-Oct. Daily trips.

Serious fishermen now and then are afflicted with an irresistible itch to troll the depths of Lake Superior. They "scratch" that itch by arranging a charter with Deep Secret Charters and going after the truly big ones on the largest freshwater lake in the world and brimming with trout, steelhead, and coho, chinook, and Atlantic salmon.

Deep Secret Charters operates out of the beautiful port of Knife River, just 15 minutes northeast of Duluth on Old Highway 61. It's run by Captain Gordon Olson, licensed by the U.S. Coast Guard. He is a Minnesota state licensed guide (#16) and he is a member of the North Shore Charter Captains Association.

Deep Secret sports a flying bridge, heated cabin, and large fishing deck and it is furnished with all the necessary deep-sea trolling gear. Also provided is the latest in electronics, including radar, Loran C navigational device, and a color videograph-depth finder. The *Deep Secret* is fitted with U.S. Coast Guard-approved safety equipment, and she can accommodate up to six people. Children are welcome.

CULTURAL CENTER

The Depot

506 W. Michigan Street, Duluth, MN 55802
Phone: 218-727-8025. Hrs: May-mid-Oct. daily 10 a.m.-5 p.m.; Mid-Oct.-April Mon.-Sat. 10 a.m.-5 p.m., Sun. 1 p.m.-5 p.m.

Built in 1892 as a train station, the Depot is now one of Duluth's favorite attractions. The Chateuesque-style building, listed on the National Register of Historic Places, has become the cultural center of the northland. Eight organizations are housed in the historic landmark, including three museums, a visual arts agency and four performing arts organizations. The Depot's museum complex offers a variety of experiences for visitors—train, historical and children's museum as well as art galleries.

The A.M. Chisholm Museum, featuring educational displays and one of the largest train museums in North America, is housed in the Lake Superior Museum of Transportation. See the past come alive in the St. Louis County Historical Society's exhibits and catch a glimpse of 1910 Duluth by strolling or taking a vintage trolley through Depot Square. The museum complex also houses Duluth Art Institute's galleries, featuring exhibits by local and regional artists. The performing arts wing offers performances on a regular schedule.

LODGING

***Park Inn
International***

Duluth Lakeshore, 250 Canal Park Drive
Duluth, MN 55802. **Phone: 218-727-8821 or
800-777-8560.** Visa, MasterCard, AmEx,
Discover and Diners accepted.

Park Inn International is located on the lakeshore in downtown Duluth. Situated in the heart of beautiful Canal Park, it is only steps away from the aerial lift bridge, ship canal and the Marine Museum. There is easy access to I-35 and the scenic North Shore Drive.

The two-story hotel has 145 recently remodeled guest rooms. Guests have the choice of a luxury whirlpool suite, executive "king" quarters, or rooms with a view of the city or lake. The lakeshore deck is available for cocktails or lunch.

Indoors, the hot tub and sauna will prove relaxing and a dip in the pool totally refreshing. The restaurant, at street level, offers a casual yet elegant dining experience. Fresh seafood, ribs, homestyle dinners and gourmet soups are served by friendly staff.

The days end with music at the Schooners Beach Club Lounge. Seven nights a week live jazz, rhythm and blues, variety and Top 40 bands can be heard there. Special services offered by Park Inn include discount ski weekends, group rates and Schooner's Charter packages for fishing on Lake Superior.

The Inn is convenient to Duluth's downtown business district, shopping, the Depot Train Museum, Fond-du-Luth Gaming Casino and the Duluth Civic Center.

LODGING

Fitger's Inn

Fitger's Brewery Complex
600 East Superior Street, Duluth, MN 55802
Phone: 218-722-8826 or 800-726-2982
Hrs: Open year-round.

For over 100 years the Fitger's Brewery Complex in Duluth was home for the A. Fitger's Brewing Company. Ten years ago, the entire complex was preserved and redesigned to include the beautiful Fitger's Inn.

Each of the 48 rooms is unique and luxurious. Many rooms offer breathtaking views of Lake Superior and the two-room suites feature 20 foot-high ceilings and huge skylights. Rooms and suites are individually decorated and come complete with all of the modern amenities including Jacuzzis and big fluffy robes.

The lobby is a Victorian Wonder with a grand piano and large palms. The service is reminiscent of more gracious times. The Fitger's Inn staff will cater to your every need including free shoe shines and free hot chocolate with your bed turndown, and more.

Fitger's Inn is the star of the Lakewalk in Duluth, located right on the shores of Lake Superior. There is an interesting shopping mall located in the brewery complex as well as free covered parking.

◆ ◆ ◆ ◆ ◆ ◆ ◆

Radisson Hotel Duluth— Harborview

505 West Superior Street, Duluth, MN 55802
Phone: 800-333-3333 or 218-727-8981
Hrs: Open year-round.
Major credit cards accepted.

This beautiful circular hotel is one of Duluth's largest first class hotels and towers over Lake Superior, providing a spectacular view of the bay as freighters of the world come and go.

"Friendly hospitality..." these are the words visitors use most often to describe the Radisson Hotel Duluth-Harborview. You'll feel the warm welcome the moment you enter, too.

The hotel offers 268 guest rooms and suites comfortably furnished with king-size, queen or full beds and cable television. With eight versatile and attractive meeting rooms they can accommodate groups from 15 to 400.

After a busy day of business or sightseeing, relax in the sauna, whirlpool or on the patio with spacious heated indoor pool.

A spectacular dining experience awaits you in the revolving rooftop restaurant with a dramatic panoramic view of the city and the world's busiest inland seaport. Located in the heart of downtown Duluth, the Radisson is convenient to everything.

RESTAURANT

Minnesota Steakhouse

325 Lake Ave. & Canal Park, Duluth, MN
Phone: 218-722-4486
Hrs: Sun.-Thurs. 4 p.m.-10 p.m.; Fri.-Sat. 4 p.m.-midnight. Major credit cards accepted.

Minnesota Steakhouse is a down-home, family restaurant and proud of it. From the rustic exterior and the crackling fire that greets visitors to the knotty pine interior, visitors will feel like a part of the northwoods experience. It's just like going up north to your frontier cabin lodge!

This "Land of 10,000 Steaks" specializes in USDA choice and aged beef. The steaks are uniquely seasoned and grilled to create a delicious taste experience. The beef comes in a dozen shapes and sizes at Minnesota Steakhouse, from top sirloin to prime rib or a 20-ounce Porterhouse, with plenty of choices in between. These fabulous dinners are served with a huge baked-potato, a generous salad and fast service.

Let's just say it has big portions at a mid-range price. Even the utensils are big here, sized for lumberjacks and other big eaters.

The restaurant also serves fresh seafood, baby back ribs, chicken and pasta. You can begin your dinner with a Paul Bunyan onion, a great big onion that's slivered, fried and served with an out-of-this-world sauce. Or, try the potato canoes, loaded with cheese and other good stuff.

The entrées are served with a large order of wonderfully soft Bob's bread, seasoned with Parmesan, butter and chervil. It arrives at your table too hot to touch for a minute or two, but it's worth the wait.

There's a full-service bar overlooking the fireplace from which you can order your favorite beverage or fine wine.

RESTAURANTS

Augustino's *Restaurant*	Fitger's Brewery Complex, 600 East Superior Street, Duluth, MN 55802. **Phone: 218-722-2787 or 218-722-8826.** Hrs: Daily-Breakfast, Lunch, and Dinner, Sunday Brunch. All major credit cards accepted.

You are always welcome at Augustino's. This Italian Ristorante and Lounge offers delicious Italian and American regional food, along with a casual atmosphere and magnificent view of Lake Superior—all add to the great ambience of this marvelous restaurant.

The food here is prepared simply, but with the greatest of skill. The pastas, soups, sauces and entrées are all made fresh daily. A recommended chef specialty is the Fettuccine Alfredo with smoked salmon. Other seafood specialties are also available.

Seasonal favorites include a variety of salads; the Viking Ship Salad which looks just like it sounds, the Flaming Spinach Salad (they really set this one on fire), and an assortment of Caesar Salads.

Daily specials, hand-made individual 'personal' pizzas and great sandwiches and burgers round out the menu. Award winning desserts feature temptations like Death By Chocolate (Morte Del Cioccolato), Amaretto Cheesecake, real Italian Cannoli and more.

Full lounge service with the best wine list in the northland.

◆ ◆ ◆ ◆ ◆ ◆

Grandma's *Saloon & Deli*	522 Lake Ave. S., Duluth, MN 55802 **Phone: 218-727-4192** Hrs: Hours vary, call ahead. Major credit cards accepted.

Vintage decor, Italian pasta, overstuffed sandwiches and fresh wild rice entrées headline the bill of fare at Grandma's Saloon & Deli. Specialty drinks and desserts, including award-winning cheesecake, are enjoyed at this popular restaurant and night spot. (There is a second location next to the bustling Miller Hill Mall in Duluth.)

Grandma's Original Saloon & Deli is joined by Mickey's Grill in a lively old time complex on Lake Avenue. Mickey's Grill is known for its choice steaks, plump poultry and fresh seafood, hot off the grill.

Grandma's Sports Garden, right across the street, dishes up pizza, sandwiches and burgers along with live sports in an indoor gym. At night, the gym becomes Duluth's largest dance hall!

Meanwhile, the Original Grandma's at Canal Park is kept jumping with a full service bar and a variety of activities. One of the largest decks overlooking Lake Superior gives a great view of the beach for outdoor drinks and dining, in the daytime or evening.

RESTAURANT

Lakeview Castle	5135 North Shore Scenic Drive, Duluth, MN 55804. **Phone: 218-525-1014** Hrs.: Restaurant, 8 a.m.-10 p.m. Lounge, open until 1 a.m. All major credit cards accepted.

The Lakeview Castle offers a fine dining experience and quiet, comfortable lodging along the scenic North Shore drive, just minutes from downtown Duluth. The restaurant and lounge area were built 15 years ago, staying true to the stone and woodwork material and maintaining the look of a castle.

In 1914, Lakeview Castle began as a fish stand and coffee shop. Over the years it has evolved into a nightclub, with cottages available in the summer. Steaks, seafood and Greek specialties such as dolmades, spanakopeta and swordfish stavros highlight the menu. The Castle's seafood platter combines scallops, shrimp, Lake Superior trout and king crab to bring together a feast to satisfy any seafood lover. Breakfast and lunch are served, too.

For a more intimate setting, the lounge offers both lunch and dinner menus every day. For weekend entertainment, a disc jockey and dancing are offered in a friendly, spacious atmosphere. Their castle is your castle.

SPECIALTY SHOP

Canelake's Candy	Holiday Center, Duluth, MN 55802 **Phone: 218-722-4609** Hrs.: Mon.-Sat. 10 a.m.-9 p.m. Sun. noon-5 p.m.

Need your sweet tooth satisfied? Come to Canelake's Candy—a real tradition in candy. Originally started in 1905, the founder of Canelake's Candy Kitchen believed in making his candies with the freshest and best ingredients possible. Grade AA butter, real whipped cream and hand-roasted nuts were used. Chocolates were hand-dipped on marble tables, hand-rolled, hand-decorated and the Canelake boxes were hand-packed. Today this art and tradition are still carried on at Canelake's Candy by Jim Cina using the same wonderful recipes the founder created.

An original Canelake secret candy recipe is known as "Hot Air." Crisp, fluffy, light and airy, this old-time sensation is an all time best seller! Other selected candies include caramels, dipped nuts, toffee, creams, brittles and bars.

Canelake's has another candy store in Virginia. Mail orders are accepted.

SPECIALTY SHOPS

| *Catherine Imports/Of Nations* | 394 Lake Ave. S., Duluth, MN 55802. **Phone: 218-722-3444 (Of Nations)** 218-722-7514 **(Catherine Imports)** Hrs: M-F 10 a.m.-9 p.m., Sat. 10-6, Sun 11-5. Winter hours vary. Major credit cards accepted. |

Six years ago, Catherine Wehseler opened Catherine Imports in the historic Dewitt-Seitz Marketplace in Duluth. Since then, she has wisely separated her inventory and opened another shop, Of Nations, in the same building. The Dewitt-Seitz Marketplace, built as a warehouse and manufacturing site in 1909, now houses a variety of interesting specialty shops.

Of Nations carries unusual beads from Africa, India, China and other countries. Also, there is a variety of tribal art and musical instruments such as thumb pianos, Jamaican drums, Kenyan one-armed harps and drums from Taos, New Mexico. Other items include sculpture, art, rugs and jewelry from around the world and Native American art as well.

Catherine Imports carries 14k gold and sterling silver items from Italy, bath products from France, nesting dolls and lacquer boxes from Russia and German anniversary clocks. Catherine Imports offers a cup of tea in a relaxing environment to shop for unique gifts.

◆ ◆ ◆ ◆ ◆ ◆ ◆

| *Dewitt-Seitz Marketplace* | 394 Lake Ave. S. Duluth, MN 55802 **Phone: 218-722-0047** |

The DeWitt-Seitz Marketplace is a collection of 15 unique shops and restaurants located in the renovated DeWitt-Seitz Building on the Duluth waterfront. This building is on the National Register of Historic Places and was home of the DeWitt-Seitz Company, a furniture jobber and mattress manufacturer.

The 1909 warehouse's renovation began in 1985. The first and second floors were turned into The DeWitt-Seitz Marketplace, while offices were constructed on the lower and on the third and fourth floors. The renovation complemented the building's post and beam construction; the original hardwood floors were kept while a wooden staircase was added. An adjacent building was purchased in 1987 and became part of the complex in 1988.

The marketplace is located in Canal Park, conveniently near the Aerial Lift Bridge, the canal, and the new Lake Walk.

TOURS

Glensheen	3300 London Road, Duluth, MN 55804 **Phone: 218-724-8864 for reservations or 218-724-8863 for recorded info. Call ahead for tour times, admission fees and reservations.**

Near the turn of the century, the iron mining industry played an important part in transforming Duluth into a prosperous city with a sophisticated lifestyle. Beautiful, stately homes were crafted for the financially successful. Glensheen was built in the style of an early 17th century English country estate with a 39-room Jacobean-style manor house. It was completed in 1908 for Chester Adgate Congdon, an attorney, legislative member, philanthropist and self-made millionaire.

Set on 22.7 acres, Glensheen took three years to complete, at a cost of nearly $1 million. In 1968, members of the Congdon family gave the priceless estate to the University of Minnesota so that it would be preserved for public use and educational purposes. Glensheen was opened to the public in July 1979. Children and adults enjoy visiting the manor house, where the Congdon family and their six children once resided. A tour of the estate, including the bowling green, coach house, boat house, formal gardens and gardener's cottage shows the intricate attention to detail that brings students of architecture, interior design, art history and horticulture to Glensheen. Reservations are recommended. Special tours can be arranged for schools and groups of 20 or more.

ELY

Charles Kurault, the famed CBS correspondent, once selected Ely as his favorite summer vacation destination. How could anyone disagree?

Many people love Ely because it's the perfect place to find peace and quiet. The fresh air and sparkling clean water wash away the pressures of life.

Nature's nearby bounty offers a wide variety of fabulous options. If you want to fish, there's smallmouth bass, trophy-sized northern pike, walleye, lake trout, largemouth bass, crappie, bluegill and stream trout. When it comes to accommodations, take your pick of everything from luxury villas to peaceful lodges. Many Ely resorts offer a variety of experiences that include sailing, paddle boats, water-skiing, private beaches, hiking trails, indoor games and other activities.

ATTRACTIONS & EVENTS

Ely is considered the "Canoe Capital of the World" because it offers the best access to the famed *Boundary Waters Canoe Area Wilderness and Quetico Provincial Park.* The canoe country is a two-million acre designated wilderness where a unique network of portage trails between pristine lakes creates a paradise for the canoe camper.

Ely also sits in the midst of the largest concentration of timberwolves in the lower 48 states and has been a center of scientific wolf research for more than 50 years. *The International Wolf Center* houses the $1 million "Wolves and Humans" exhibit and features a 1.5 acre enclosure for a pack of four wolves now being raised by the staff.

Fall offers the chance to wander through miles of beautiful colors. Enjoy the vivid shades, from red maples to yellow birches to green pines, or hunt for the ruffed grouse, black bear or deer.

Winter is a time for solitude and fun. Many resorts offer cozy cabins for cross-country skiers and snowmobilers taking advantage of the hundreds of miles of trails in the area.

For further information, contact:
Ely Chamber of Commerce
1600 East Sheridan Street
Ely, MN 55731
Phone: 218-365-6123 or 800-777-7281

ART GALLERY

Bois Fort Gallery

130 E. Sheridan St.
Ely, MN 55731
Phone: 218-365-5066
Hrs.: 9 a.m.-8 p.m. Sun. 9 a.m.-5 p.m.

A faction of the Ojibwa Indian tribe native to northern Minnesota was dubbed by their fellow tribesmen the "Sagwadagawiniwag," or "Men of the Thick Fir Woods." Early French explorers shortened the title and put it into their own language, calling the band "Bois Forts" or "Strong Woods." So is named the rustic fine arts gallery started by Carl Gawboy, himself a member of the Bois Fort tribe. Gawboy, an Ely native, opened the gallery in 1973, 14 miles east of Ely on the Fernberg Road. Relocated in 1975, the gallery now sits in downtown Ely and welcomes the visitors and natives who are drawn to its selection of quality artwork.

Gawboy began the gallery to provide an outlet for his art and that of other fine artists of the area. Currently owned by Judy Fredrickson, the gallery continues to house the quality work of northwoods residents, while also drawing pieces from other areas of Minnesota and the rest of the country. A variety of media and artists is displayed here.

Among some of the current artists displayed are Gawboy, a regional painter; Gerald Brimacombe, a photographer and painter; and Ray Plantz, a pastel artist. Many limited-edition prints are available by such noted artists as Les Kouba, Terry Redlin, Carl Brenders and Robert Bateman. Stoneware by Pat and Ken Larson and jewelry by Wildbryde and others grace the shelves and walls. The gallery's structure and decor, like the art it displays, remain in the tradition of the rustic northwoods. Its wood-frame structure was built in the 1890's and restored hardwood floors in the loft display area and warm-wood shelving throughout create a fitting backdrop for the work displayed.

A recent addition to the gallery is a room called "Creations for Kids." This section features quality activity toys and books for children, uniquely designed to nurture their creative spirit. A full-service custom frame shop stocks more than 300 molding samples and offers museum mounting. All this is done in keeping with the Bois Fort Gallery motto: "Because you like your ordinary things to be special!"

INTERPRETIVE CENTER

The International Wolf Center

1396 Highway 169, Ely, MN 55731
Phone: 800-359-9653. Hrs: May, June, Sept, mid
Oct. 9-5 p.m. daily. July, Aug. 9-7 daily. Mid
Oct.-April, 10-5, Tues., Fri., Sat. 10-5. Sun. 10-3.

Perhaps the most maligned creature in history, the wolf is finally gaining some awareness and praise through the efforts of organizations like The International Wolf Center. Their mission, as a non-profit educational organization, is to be a focal point for worldwide environmental education about wolves. It supports the survival of the wolf by teaching about the wolf's life, its interrelationships with other species and its role within human cultures.

It all started in 1985 when the Science Museum of Minnesota created the "Wolves and Humans" exhibit to provide public education about the wolf and its relationship with other species. The award winning exhibit received wide public acclaim and was viewed by 2.5 million people as it toured the United States and Canada.

Private, public and professional groups concerned with wolf research, education and preservation came together to support the wolf project and became the nucleus for the development of the International Wolf Center (IWC), a tax-exempt, non-profit organization. Beginning in 1985, the IWC developed the ambitious mission and programmatic goals in response to international needs for a comprehensive center promoting public education about wolves. The search for an ideal location to permanently house the "Wolves and Humans" exhibit ended in Ely, located adjacent to Minnesota's Boundary Waters area. Ely sits at the center of the largest wolf population remaining in the lower 48 states.

The International Wolf Center opened its doors to the $1 million "Wolves and Humans" exhibits and its $3 million facility in 1993. Here, guests learn about the natural history of wolves by observing the Center's captive pack and touring the exhibits. Howling and communications programs, flights over territory, winter treks and summer family day programs offer the visitor a glimpse into the life of the elusive wolf.

RESORT

Burntside Lodge

2755 Burntside Lodge Road, Ely, MN 55731
Phone: 218-365-3894
Hrs.: Late May to mid-September.
Visa, MasterCard, AmEx, and Discover accepted.

Burntside Lodge, originally known as Brownell Outing Company, was established as a hunting camp in the early 1900s. The Chippewa Indian tribe lived on the lake and gave it the name "Burntside" after the north shore of this glacier-made lake was devastated by a forest fire. Burntside has been a resort since 1913 and is listed on the National Register of Historic Places. Its designation is due to the high integrity and large collection of log buildings that remain in a remarkable state of preservation.

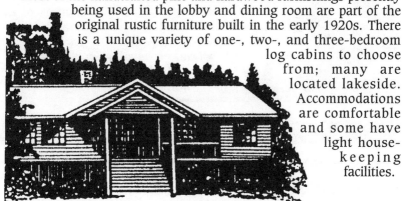

Most of the handcrafted pine and hardwood furnishings presently being used in the lobby and dining room are part of the original rustic furniture built in the early 1920s. There is a unique variety of one-, two-, and three-bedroom log cabins to choose from; many are located lakeside. Accommodations are comfortable and some have light housekeeping facilities.

Burntside Lodge also offers a dining experience unmatched in the area. A full menu includes over 20 entrées and an excellent choice of homemade desserts. Chef-prepared walleye pike, lake trout, seafood, steaks and barbecued ribs are popular selections. Chef specials include Saturday night prime rib, Steak au Poivre, Steak Neptune, as well as other specials.

Launching and dock space are generally available to all guests, along with boat and motor, canoe, pontoon and paddleboat rentals. Burntside Lake is an exceptional lake trout and small-mouth bass lake. Guided day trips into the Boundary Waters on Basswood Lake, Burntside or other lakes are also available. Other resort activities include a sandy swimming beach; children's playground; shuffleboard; and a recreation building with a pool table, ping pong and video games.

Burntside Lodge is a place where families have come for over 80 years to share a good time in the beauty and quiet of the Minnesota northwoods. For many, the annual return to Burntside is a tradition.

RESORT

Superior Forest Lodge & Outfitters

HC1, Box 3199, Ely, MN 55731
Phone: 800-777-7503
Hrs: May-Oct. 7 a.m.-9 p.m.
Major credit cards accepted.

For a family-style vacation in the true northwoods, you can't beat Superior Forest Lodge & Outfitters. They are located on Farm Lake with easy access to the Boundary Waters Canoe Area.

Hosts Tim and Nancy Krugman have carved out of this pristine wilderness a unique resort, campsite, canoe area for anyone who wants to "get away from it all." Cabins sleep from two to eight and there's even a private log cabin on an island. If you want to camp, there's plenty of sites on a beautiful peninsula. Day trips to the B.W.C.A. with a return to the comfort of the resort at day's end is a popular activity for guests. That's why they say you get the best of both worlds at Superior Forest Lodge.

Specializing in northwoods family vacations.

RESTAURANT

Sir G's Italian Restaurant

520 E. Sheridan Street, Ely, MN 55731. **Phone: 218-365-3688.** Hrs: (Summer) daily 11:30 a.m.-11 p.m. (Winter) daily 4 p.m.-9 p.m.
Visa and MasterCard accepted.

The exquisite Italian foods served in this restaurant are big in flavor and big in portions. The present owner purchased the restaurant in 1982 from a native of Italy. Authentic Italian recipes were part of the acquisitions from Sir G.

Over the years, chef-owner Neil has expanded the menu and added several of his own specialty creations. The homemade pastas of ravioli, cannelloni, lasagne, and spaghetti are just the beginning of some delicious dishes. His flair for delicate seasonings is also carried forth in the Italian gravies, sauces, and dressings.

The pizza rollers and ovens are in plain view to patrons of the restaurant, so they can watch the chef prepare their order. Generous garnishments and toppings abound. Beer and wines are available with meals. Carry-out service also is available.

Sir G's Italian Restaurant continually receives high ratings from tourists and locals alike. Service is always quick and courteous.

OUTFITTERS

Boundary Waters Canoe Outfitters, Inc.

1323 E. Sheridan Street, Ely, MN 55731. **Phone: 218-365-3201 or 800-544-7736.** Hrs: (Summer) May 1-Oct. 1, daily 7 a.m.-8 p.m.; Office phone answered all year 7 a.m.-8 p.m. Visa, MasterCard and Discover accepted.

It's best to be prepared if you plan to spend some time paddling through the wilderness and Boundary Waters Canoe Outfitters provides personal service for the novice as well as for the experienced. Family-owned and operated, the headquarters and motel are conveniently located on the main street of Ely. It is one of the largest canoe outfitters serving the Boundary Waters Canoe Area.

Five types of trips are offered, including the deluxe complete outfitting canoe trip, deluxe lightweight, econo-canoe trip, partial outfitting, and fly-in canoe trips. The company has private landings at three major entry points, Moose, Mudro, and Lake One. Staff members with years of experience on the trails plan trips well-suited to your capabilities and desires. Points of interest, fishing spots, and campsites can be incorporated into your route.

An orientation session explains each piece of equipment and how to use it. Only high quality, trail-tested equipment canoes and camping gear can be found at Boundary Waters Canoe Outfitters.

◆ ◆ ◆ ◆ ◆ ◆ ◆

Tom & Wood's Moose Lake Wilderness Canoe Trips

P.O. Box 358, Ely, MN 55731
Phone: 218-365-5837 or 800-322-5837
Hrs: May 1-Sept. 25, daily 24-hours-a-day
Visa and MasterCard accepted.

Whether you're a novice or experienced canoeist, Tom, Woods, and their staff will cater to your every need. This is the Boundary Waters Canoe Area. And, nowhere in North America can such a variety of freshwater gamefish be found.

As North America's only outfitter specializing in ultra-lightweight outfitting, the canoes, tents, sleeping bags, packs, and food are custom-made to their own specifications. Every detail of the trip is discussed prior to embarking. All camping equipment is reviewed. Techniques of outdoor cooking and food preparation are given. Map work and routes are selected, and an orientation is held on how to correctly handle a canoe, choose a good tent site, and erect the tent. Before the trip and after the return, guests may enjoy overnight accommodations of private double bedrooms as well as private bunk rooms, showers, and a family-style guest dining room overlooking Moose Lake. Reservations are necessary because a permit is required to get into the Boundary Waters Canoe Area. Call early.

EMBARRASS

The tiny Iron Range community of Embarrass has gained more national acclaim than cities 10 times its size. Primarily a Finnish farming settlement until the early 1950s, the town now is celebrated in architectural circles for its numerous original log buildings. The cold climate has preserved the century-old buildings remarkably well, and when the mining industry took a downturn in the early 1980s, the town's residents set out to rejuvenate their heritage.

The local *SISU Heritage* organization has saved seven of the log buildings from demolition and has listed them on the National Register of Historic Places. For visitors, the organization offers *Heritage Homestead Tours* of restored homesteads, saunas, and a rare housebarn. SISU also sponsors the *Summer Festival,* complete with music, Finnish foods, dancing, and arts and crafts.

For further information, contact:
Town of Embarrass
7503 Levander Road
Embarrass, MN 55732   Phone: 218-984-2672

HISTORICAL SOCIETY

SISU Heritage   P.O. Box 127
                           Embarrass, MN 55732
                           Phone: 218-984-2672

SISU is an organization started by townspeople to promote and preserve their Finnish heritage. The log buildings constructed by Finnish settlers, many now on the National Register of Historic Places, are the primary focus of these efforts. Through the work of SISU, many derelict farmsteads have been stabilized, saved from demolition and are now available for touring. The SISU Tori ethnic craft shop offers finely crafted items for sale.

In addition, SISU sponsors the Summer Festival, an entertainment packed event with fun for all, including dancing, ethnic foods, arts and crafts. In December, the organization arranges a Finnish Christmas with Finnish cooking, carols and a horse-drawn sleigh ride to the cemetery where lighted candles are placed along the way in memory of those who once inhabited this place.

Also, Embarrass hosts the Embarrass Region Fair in August, offering visitors even more fun. Every year the fair gets bigger as more entertainment and events are added.

BED & BREAKFAST

Finnish Heritage Homestead

4776 Waisanen Road
Embarrass, MN 55732
Phone: 218-984-3318

This unique bed & breakfast offers historic buildings, farm animals, gardens and loads of tranquility. It has a long tradition of hospitality, having been established in 1891 and serving as a boarding house for loggers and railroad workers. Today, its country comforts and sprawling setting offer relaxation with a charming blend of Finnish-American architecture and history.

Four guest rooms are furnished with family antiques of specially selected items. Three rooms have queen-sized beds, the other room has two twin-sized beds. A cozy parlor and a breezy gazebo offer respite to the spirit and warmth to the heart.

In season, you can pick delicious wild or domestic berries or gather a bouquet of wild flowers from the meadow. Stroll past the vegetable garden and the carefully tended flower beds. They will pack a picnic lunch for your venture to the many sight-seeing and recreational activities in the area where you'll enjoy the rural atmosphere and friendly hospitality of the people.

Excellent fishing, winter sports and outstanding scenery and many tours are available nearby. Over 3,000 miles of snowmobile trails start at the driveway of Finnish Heritage Homestead. The Boundary Waters Canoe Area is just 1/2 an hour away.

Finnish Heritage Homestead is one of the homesteads featured on the SISU Heritage Pioneer Homestead Tour offered in Embarrass, Minnesota. The onsite historic buildings, farm animals, gardens and Finnish sauna represent the heritage of the Finnish settlers who first built housing on this land.

EVELETH

A fascinating mixture of natural beauty and small-town American charm, Eveleth offers the visitor a wonderful variety of things to see and do. Eveleth is the perfect spot for boating, swimming and fishing. Public boat access, sandy beaches, city parks, tennis courts, dining and live entertainment offer endless recreational opportunities for visitors.

Cyclists can take advantage of easy riding along the Fayal Pond Trail System. Walking trails lead you through forests, around lakes and reveal spectacular views of Eveleth's mining area. Golfers can tee-off for a challenging nine holes along beautiful Saint Mary's Lake while boaters set their sails or launch fishing and pleasure crafts on nearby Ely Lake.

ATTRACTIONS & EVENTS

Known as the "Hockey Capital of the Nation," Eveleth is home to the *U.S. Hockey Hall of Fame,* where visitors have a chance to relive some of the great moments in a sport that numbers Iron Range athletes among its greats. A favorite is the videotape of the winning game of the 1980 Winter Olympics, when the U.S. Olympic Gold Medal team defeated the USSR.

Leonidas Overlook, the highest point on the *Mesabi Range,* offers a breathtaking panoramic view of current taconite operations and area mines.

To get a jump on the snowmobiling season, the cities of Eveleth and Virginia co-host the annual *Snowmobile Grass Drag Races* on Labor Day weekend. This popular event attracts thousands of spectators who come to see racers from around the country test the speed of their "sleds" on a 600-foot, 5-lane grass track.

Every October, outstanding individuals, chosen for their contribution to the sport of hockey, are inducted into the U.S. Hockey Hall of Fame during "Enshrinement" ceremonies which include a special exhibition hockey game.

For further information, contact:
Eveleth Chamber of Commerce
P.O. Box 657
Eveleth, MN 55734
Phone: 218-744-1940

MUSEUM

Hockey Hall of Fame	Off Highway 53 on Hat Trick Ave. Eveleth, MN 55734 **Phone: 218-744-5167** Hrs: Mon.-Sat. 9-5; Sun. 11-5

When sports are classified according to skill, hockey is rated by most experts as the most skilled of all. Its requirements of speed, strength and coordination will take a cruel measure of even the best-toned physique—and all these qualities must be found in a man who is also a championship skater!

As hockey moved south from Canada in the first years of this century, one of its early strongholds was the town of Eveleth, Minnesota. Town records show that the first hockey game was played in Eveleth in 1903.

By 1920, the city's team was playing throughout the nation, as a member of the American Amateur Hockey Association, which later developed into the Amateur Hockey Association of the United States. Hockey fever has never died down in Eveleth. The town supports an active school hockey program and has provided a lion's share of the "greats" in U.S. Hockey History, from players like Mike Karakas and Frank Brimsek to coaches like John Mariucci. It is for these reasons that Eveleth, Minnesota—often called the "amateur hockey capital of the U.S.A."—was chosen as the site of the United States Hockey Hall of Fame.

The entrance houses the Zamboni display, theater and gift shop. In the Great Hall are the pylons of all the enshrinees and an art display. The Mezzanine level hosts the 1960-1980 Olympic Champions display and film library. On the 2nd floor are amateur, International College and Olympic and Pro displays along with old artifacts, a slide presentation, shooting rink and more.

Through documentation of the game's history and development in the United States—including historical literature, records, photos, equipment, cups, educational materials for player training and films of the greatest games—the United States Hockey Hall of Fame serves as a gathering place for both scholars and practitioners of the sport—for coaches, players, hockey promoters.

It also serves as a Mecca for hockey lovers the world over and a place of recognition for the hockey "greats" of the United States. It serves as a center for encouraging young people in the immense dedication it will take to become the hockey "greats" of the future.

The United States Hockey Hall of Fame Inc. is a non-profit organization established in 1973 and dedicated to the sport of hockey—"That memories may never fade of flying puck and flashing blade."

Contributions and donations to the Hall are greatly appreciated and tax deductible.

SPECIALTY SHOPS

The Garden Cottage	Junction of Highway 53 and 16E, Eveleth, MN 55734. **Phone: 218-744-5199.** Hrs: (Summer) Mon.-Sat. 10 a.m.-6 p.m.; Sun. noon-5 p.m. (Winter) Dec. 25-April 1, Call for hours. Visa, MasterCard and Discover accepted.

A retired banker, Eileen Mickelson, fulfilled a lifetime dream when she transformed a vine-covered guesthouse into an antique and gift shop. This quaint cottage has an everchanging variety of antiques, art, handcrafts, and books in all price ranges. It is ideal for those who are looking for unique decorating ideas for their homes.

On any day you might find a Maxfield Parrish print hung next to the bright collection of depression glass, a Raggedy Ann nestled among the chintz pillows on the antique oak rocker, contemporary metal and stone sculptures intermingled with the handcarved Minnesota woodland creatures. In the farm kitchen, the old iron cookstove is covered with antique kitchen gadgets between the yellowware bowls and the Griswold pots. Contrasts abound, with exquisite porcelain and antique dolls surrounded by handmade quilts and rugs on the rustic twig loveseat. You will also find books for gardeners, cooks, nature lovers, and collectors everywhere. Books, too, are in the children's corner along with antique and handcrafted toys.

◆ ◆ ◆ ◆ ◆ ◆ ◆

Paul's Italian Market	623 Garfield Street, Eveleth, MN 55734 **Phone: 218-744-1244** Hrs: Mon. 8 a.m.-6 p.m.; Sat. 8 a.m.-4 p.m.; Sun. 9 a.m.-2 p.m.

In the early 1900's, Paul's Italian Market moved to its present location in a three-story stucco building over 100 years old that was once the Rex Reed Hotel. As they walk over the wooden floors, visitors can see that the market carries imported bulk pasta in the same way it has for many years.

The little market has a steady clientele which enjoys the many Italian foods sold here. Among these are a large selection of domestic and imported cheeses, homemade antipasto and Italian breads along with muffins that are baked fresh in the store.

In the meat section, customers are assisted by a butcher in choosing from the selection of fresh and imported meats, homemade sausages and especially Italian sausage, porketta and beefetta products. Holiday roasts are also available.

The market has recently introduced its line of Famous Fonti Family homemade pasta. Paul's Italian Market also offers shipping in addition to full service groceries.

GRAND MARAIS

Today a center for Lake Superior fishing, Grand Marais was only officially incorporated as a village in 1903. Originally, the Ojibwa Indians (also known as Chippewa) lived in the area and called the natural harbor along Lake Superior Gitch-be-to-beek (Big Pond).

In the 1700s, French fur trappers passing through the region took on the Ojibwa name for the bay, calling it Grand Marais (Big Marsh in French). In 1854, fur trader Richard B. Godfrey erected a rough shelter and became the first postmaster for the area. But times were hard, so he soon returned to the East. About 20 years later, more settlers came and put down roots, finally founding a real community.

At the turn of the century, Grand Marais was a small, bustling town dependent on logging, commercial fishing, and farming. Settlers with dreams of wealth continued to move into the area, and the town flourished despite the relative isolation of the North Shore. Although logging and lumbering still are economically important to Grand Marais and its population of 1,500, tourism has become the backbone of the town's economy.

ATTRACTIONS & EVENTS

Comfortable, quaint accommodations welcome visitors, who can choose from a variety of eating establishments that serve everything from homemade pizza to blueberry buttermilk pancakes. Grand Marais also has intriguing shops that sell items ranging from paintings by local artists to fresh smoked fish.

No matter what the season, the surrounding northwoods always beckon those who love the outdoors. Hiking trails abound in summer, and in winter, cross-country ski trails and snowmobile trails offer an alternative to those cold-weather blahs.

Of course, there's always plenty of fishing in rivers, small lakes, and Lake Superior, as well as berry picking throughout the summer, camping, rock hunting and canoeing. The nearby *Boundary Waters Canoe Area* holds 1,100 lakes within its one million acres, truly a canoeist's paradise.

Within Grand Marais's city limits, visitors can camp, hike or golf at the nine-hole course on the outskirts of town, or swim in the Olympic-size municipal pool, with adjacent sauna and whirlpool.

For further information, contact:
Grand Marais Chamber of Commerce
P.O. Box 1048, Grand Marais, MN 55604
Phone: 800-622-4014

OUTFITTER

Gunflint Northwoods Outfitters	HC 64 750 Gunflint Trail, Grand Marais, MN 55604. **Phone: 218-388-2296 or 800-362-5251** FAX 218-388-9429. Hrs: May 1-Oct. 15, Mon.-Sun 7-7. Major credit cards accepted.

It was 1927 when the Kerfoot family first arrived in Gunflint. Since building their homestead on remote Gunflint Lake, which borders Canada, the family has weathered the Depression, two wars, and decades without electricity, telephones or roads. By the 1950's, the modern world began to encroach, attracted to the beauty of the largest canoe area in the world.

Thus, the Kerfoots built an outfitting post to accommodate these adventures. The family is still at it and over the years they've built bigger and better facilities, expanded the services offered to their visitors and accumulated top quality equipment and first-hand knowledge about the wilderness.

Gunflint Northwoods Outfitters makes the logistics of canoe adventuring easy for Boundary Waters Canoe Area visitors. A large outfitting headquarters includes a room for trip planning and equipment packing. Bunkhouses with showers and a sauna accommodate overnight guests before and after trips, plus vans and busses are available for transportation to various canoe landings. There is also a lodge with stone fireplaces and open-beam ceilings for more modern accommodations and delicious home-cooked meals. A full-time naturalist is on staff to review paddling and portaging skills with guests. A trading post supplies fishing tackle, clothing, gifts, etc.

The Kerfoots are experts in the canoe area and help visitors plan their trips from beginning to end. The outfitters educate their visitors about the U.S. Forest Service rules, brief them on wildlife they're likely to see and on campsite clean-up.

Several specialized packaged trips are available through the outfitters, including air transportation packages, wilderness-skills workshops, and deluxe trips including lodge stays and guides. Whatever level of comfort and attention you prefer, a Boundary Waters trip is an experience of a lifetime and Gunflint Northwoods Outfitters provides the service and the knowledge to make it the best it can possibly be.

OUTFITTERS

| *Bear Track Outfitting Company* | Box 937, Grand Marais, MN 55604
Phone: 218-387-1162. Reservations: 800-795-8068. Hrs: 8 a.m.-8 p.m., every day.
Visa and MasterCard accepted. |

A wilderness experience is yours to enjoy with complete confidence through the expertise and personalized trip planning you'll receive from David and Cathi Williams at Bear Track Outfitting. They specialize in complete, deluxe canoe outfitting for the magnificent Boundary Waters Canoe Area, Quetico Provincial Park, and for backpacking and kayaking on Isle Royale National Park.

They cater to families and novice outdoorspeople and are happy to give you any level of service you need. They even have cozy wilderness cabins nestled deep in the Superior National Forest and available year-round with superbly groomed cross-country ski trails right out the door.

Or rent one of their new luxurious 28' motorhomes and change your nightly destination to suit your mood while enjoying the incredible wilderness in elegance and comfort. They'll even plan your menu and stock the fridge so all you have to do is relax and have a good time! Their motto? "Nobody does it better!"

◆ ◆ ◆ ◆ ◆ ◆ ◆

| *Hungry Jack Canoe Outfitters and Cabins* | 434 Gunflint Trail, Grand Marais, MN 55604
Phone: 218-388-2275 or 800-648-2922 (for reservations). Hrs.: May-October, daily 7 a.m.-8 p.m. Visa and MasterCard accepted |

The Boundary Waters Canoe Area draws refugees from the fast lane to its silent and serene labyrinth of lakes. Ready with carefully prepared staples, canoes, packs, tents and sound advice, Dave and Nancy Seaton outfit and shelter adventurers.

Located on the shores of Hungry Jack Lake, the Seatons' outfitter operation offers individualized service. Complete meal packages with various menus, top equipment, orientation courses and extensive trip routing combine with personal attention to ensure unforgettable experiences. Several models of ultra lightweight Kevlar canoes are available. In addition, the outfitters handle all the necessary permits. A head-start tow service is available across Saganaga Lake for those entering Quetico Provincial Park in Ontario or traveling the border.

Hungry Jack Outfitters also boasts two lakeside cabins for those who prefer day trips and a bunkhouse is available for canoeists to rest up both before and after expeditions.

RESORT

Bearskin Lodge

275 Gunflint Trail, Grand Marais, MN 55604
Phone: 218-388-2292 or 800-338-4170
Hrs: 7:30 a.m.-9:30 p.m. year-round.
Major credit cards accepted.

Along a secluded bay of East Bearskin Lake on the border of the Boundary Waters Canoe Area Wilderness is a modern, quiet, family resort called Bearskin Lodge. Originally built in 1925, this rustic fishing camp has grown and prospered into a lovely year-round resort. Its reputation for comfortable, quality accommodations and equipment combined with hospitality and service in a wilderness setting are known by many travelers and vacationers.

Guests have a choice of accommodations, either one of the beautiful lakeside, housekeeping cabins or lodge townhouses. The cabins are strategically positioned along the bay and set back into the woods for privacy and the true northwoods experience. Amenities include fully equipped kitchens, private baths, dining and living area and free-standing fireplace.

The main lodge has a comfortable lounge area with a massive granite fireplace. Meals are served in the dining room with all the service you would wish, delicious food and a relaxed atmosphere. A gift shop, hot tub hus and private sauna are available for guests.

East Bearskin is a 440-acre lake with 14 miles of shoreline and is excellent for swimming and fishing. Smallmouth bass, walleye and northern pike are standard fare for fishermen. Guide service, tackle and live bait are also available.

A full-time naturalist coordinates summer activities for people of all ages, including special nature hikes, environmental games and slide presentations. "Kid's Korner" is the children's activities program for ages 3-13. It's guaranteed to keep kids busy with supervised activities and plenty of fun.

In winter, 58 kilometers of well-groomed and marked wilderness ski trails offer excellent cross-country skiing and snowshoeing.

RESORT

Gunflint Lodge

HC 64 750 Gunflint Trail, Grand Marais, MN
55604. **Phone: 218-388-2294 or 800-328-3325**
FAX 218-388-9429. Open year-round, Mon.-
Sun 7 a.m.-10 p.m. Major credit cards accepted.

In northeastern Minnesota along the Canadian border and right
next to the Boundary Waters Wilderness, Gunflint Lodge is a world of
serene beauty for hiking, fishing, canoeing, cross-country skiing or
just relaxing.

The main lodge, built in 1953, is decorated with Voyageur artifacts, carved birds and Indian crafts. Accommodations vary from one
to four bedrooms in size and are comfortably furnished with a fireplace in each living room. Many of the cabins have complete kitchens,
private saunas and whirlpool tubs. The deluxe two-bedroom units
also include a microwave, CD music system and VCR.

Fishing and the northwoods seem to go together. Fishermen travel to Gunflint Lake for its walleye, smallmouth bass and for what is
probably the finest inland trout fishing in Minnesota. Top quality
boats and motors, canoes, kayaks and rafts are available. The lodge's
Gunflint guides are the best in the area to help guests become
acquainted with the lakes and fishing styles. A day with a guide also
includes a complete fish fry for a shore lunch. Children will enjoy
swimming, the recreation area, half-day fishing trips, nature hikes
and other family fun. The dining room is open for three meals a day,
offering a different menu each night. Enjoy a picnic lunch to take
fishing or while exploring the wilderness and wildlife, or visit any of
the secluded beaches.

Winter enthusiasts come to the Gunflint for outstanding cross-
country skiing and dog sledding trips. Over 100 km of tracked ski
trails lace through the Gunflint back basin and up into the highlands
and into Canada. One trail goes into the moose feeding yards while
another is in an area frequented by a pack of timber wolves. Dog sled
rides are offered by the hour, 1/2 day and
full day. Dog sled expeditions are offered
into the Boundary Waters Wilderness
for multi-night camping trips.

RESORTS

Naniboujou Lodge & Restaurant	HC1, P.O. Box 505, Grand Marais, MN 55604. **Phone:** **218-387-2688.** Hrs: (Restaurant) Mon.-Sat. 8 a.m.-10:30 a.m. and 11:30 a.m.-2:30 p.m.; Tea 3-5 p.m. and 5:30 p.m.-8:30 p.m.; Sunday brunch 8 a.m.-2:30 p.m. Visa, MasterCard and Discover accepted.

Built in 1928 as an exclusive private resort, the unique Naniboujou Lodge has served such members as Babe Ruth, Jack Dempsey and Ring Lardner.

Naniboujou is on the National Register of Historic Places. Minnesota's largest native stone fireplace made with 200 tons of lake rocks and decorated in Cree Indian design stands in the dining room.

A variety of queen, double, and twin beds in guest rooms and connecting suites are available. Fireplace rooms are also available for an additional charge. No televisions or telephones are in the rooms, providing a truly natural experience. Breakfast and luncheons provide wholesome, northwoods selections. Dinner entrées include an exquisite selection of fresh Lake Superior fish, chicken breasts sauteed with fresh tomatoes, and boneless barbecued pork ribs.

With the area's reputation of unspoiled forest, guests can enjoy scenic drives and nature walks through the Boundary Waters Canoe Area, the Gunflint Trail, or Superior National Forest.

◆ ◆ ◆ ◆ ◆ ◆

The Nor'Wester	550 Gunflint Trail, Grand Marais, MN 55604 **Phone: 218-388-2252 or 800-992-4FUN** Hrs: Open Year-round Visa, MasterCard and Discover accepted.

Dreaming of a cozy cabin on the shore of a sun-dappled, spring fed lake? That's just what you'll find at The Nor'Wester on the shore of Poplar Lake. It's a resort and canoe outfitter that's been family owned and operated for over 50 years! Carl and Luana Brandt give every guest a personal welcome to a blend of rustic warmth and modern conveniences. The lodge features both American Plan and Housekeeping accommodations, two level villas and Cabins that have either 2 or 3 bedrooms. The new Nor'Wester Dining Room was recently added to the main lodge and features various selections from a half-century tradition of country cooking, served in a charming antique setting. Of course, you can combine your stay with a trip to the Boundary Waters Canoe area, since The Nor'Wester is set up for outfitting, too.

LODGING

East Bay Hotel-Restaurant and Lounge	P.O. Box 220, Grand Marais, MN 55604 **Phone: 218-387-2800 or 800-414-2807** Hrs: 7 a.m.-9 p.m. Visa, MasterCard and Discovery accepted.

Located in downtown Grand Marais, the East Bay Hotel-Restaurant and Lounge is housed in an historic building built circa 1910. Though the building has been refurbished and updated, it still retains its old fashion charm and elegance.

And why not? Third generation owners have made this a very friendly, family oriented place to stay. They offer a wide range of accommodations, from economy to moderate and luxury. A new addition to the building offers guests a lake view, private balconies, two-person jacuzzi, king-size bed and refrigerator. Family suites with fireplaces are also offered.

There's a conference room available for your meeting needs and a hot tub and sauna area, too. An outdoor deck is perfect for meeting someone special, as they offer food and beverage service. The dining rooms serve three meals a day, every day, along with your favorite cocktail. Traditional meals and bakery items are made from scratch and fresh fish is offered in season. Pets are allowed!

RESTAURANT

Blue Water Cafe/Upper Deck	Wisconsin and First, P.O. Box 302, Grand Marais, MN 55604. **Phone: 218-387-1597.** Hrs: Summer, 5 a.m.-9 p.m. daily. Winter, 6 a.m.-8 p.m. Closed holidays. Visa and MasterCard accepted.

The Blue Water Cafe is truly "the meeting place in Grand Marais." It is a popular place for local residents as well as tourists. It comprises the first floor of a corner building located on the harbor of downtown Grand Marais. The walls of the cafe are decorated with interesting pictures of early settlers in the area.

Dinner entrées feature house specialties such as walleye, chicken and steak. The second floor is called the Upper Deck. It has a nautical decor and allows diners to enjoy a fantastic view of the harbor and town of Grand Marais.

While in the area, don't forget to enjoy the great scenery and hiking that Cascade River State park—located nine miles south of Grand Marais—has to offer.

SPECIALTY SHOP

Lake Superior Trading Post

On the Harbor, Grand Marais, MN 55604
Phone: 218-387-2020
Hrs: Summer, 9 a.m.-8 p.m., Sun. 9-5. Winter,
Mon.-Sat. 9-5. Major credit cards accepted.

A trip to the North Shore of Lake Superior would not be complete without visiting the renowned Lake Superior Trading Post in Grand Marais—the touchstone of the North Shore. In 1988, a fire destroyed the original Lake Superior Trading Post, but its hard-won spirit survived and within one year, a new building of similar design was re-opened on the site of the old.

The building itself is fun to explore as it is built of logs and timbers from the northwoods and provides an atmosphere that enhances the shopping experience. The gifts, clothing, toys, books, footwear, jewelry, food and everything else are relevant to the beauty and adventure of the North Shore.

There are unique gifts from all over the world, functional and well made clothing, books about the North Shore and Minnesota, rugged footwear suitable for hiking or canoeing, gourmet foods—there's even baby clothes! In other words, there's something for everyone.

Many product names will be recognizable to visitors: Patagonia, Columbia, Woolrich, North Face, Timberland, Old Town Canoes, W.A. Fisher maps, Slumberjack sleeping bags, Henschel hats, Iverson Snowshoes, Cascade Designs, Therma-Rest, Tilley hats.

Visitors can find everything from greeting cards to bird feeders. Aside from the wide selection in clothing, they can also choose from many other gift items such as dolls, baskets, wild-life prints, Scandinavian Jewelry, crystal, wood boxes, rugs and candles.

For some of the best gift selections in the Grand Marais area, Lake Superior Trading Post is a must.

GRAND RAPIDS

Mississippi River navigation begins below a series of turbulent rapids near Grand Rapids, once the rugged home of lumberjacks and today the heart of one of the most popular fishing and camping resort areas in Minnesota. Soon after its founding in 1877, Grand Rapids became a center for the logging industry, serving as the starting point for the historic log drives to Minneapolis. Iron mining and processing eventually superceded logging, and dams soon tamed the rapids that had given the city its name decades earlier.

Today, iron processing still is a major industry, but the city also is a retail center with a wide selection of shops, hotels, restaurants, parks, and wide, tree-lined streets.

ATTRACTIONS & EVENTS

Grand Rapids was founded on the resources of the surrounding forests, and several attractions celebrate this natural heritage. The *Chippewa National Forest* includes 1,312 lakes, with excellent swimming, boating, canoeing, and even bald eagle viewing sites. *The Forest History Interpretive Center* features an authentically reconstructed logging camp from 1900, complete with costumed guides and a "wanagan," a combination cook shack and store that floated along with the loggers on the log drives to Minneapolis.

Pokegama Golf Course is an 18-hole championship course on Pokegama Lake, two miles west of Grand Rapids. *Wendigo Golf Club* is a challenging course amid rolling terrain and hardwood forests—beautiful! *Sugarbrooke Golf Club* at Ruttger's Sugar Lake Lodge is a completely new 18-hole par 72 course.

During the *Tall Timber Days* in August, modern-day lumberjacks compete in wood chopping, buck sawing, and pole climbing along with other lumberjack events.

Grand Rapids is also the hometown of Judy Garland and celebrates its famous daughter with the *Judy Garland Museum* and the *Judy Garland Festival* in June.

The *Mississippi Melodie Showboat* is a riverboat presenting 19th century song and dance along with comedy during summer weekends. In January, *The Grand Vinterslass* holds snowmobiles races, curling tournaments and other family fun events.

For further information, contact:

1000 Grand Lakes Visitor and Convention Bureau
1 Third Street N.W.
Grand Rapids, MN 55744
Phone: 218-326-1281 or 800-472-6366

HISTORIC SITE

Forest History Center	A Minnesota Historical Society Site. Near highways 169 and 2, Grand Rapids. Mailing Address: 2609 County Road 76, Grand Rapids, MN 55744. **Phone: 218-327-4482**. Hrs: May 28-Oct. 15 (logging camp and visitors center) Mon.-Sat. 10 a.m.-5 p.m. Sun. noon-5 p.m. Admission charge.

At the end of the 19th century, the mighty white pine ruled the forests of northern Minnesota and lumberjacks came to harvest them. Through the long, cold winters, the lumberjacks felled trees and prepared them for the spring log drive down the rivers to the sawmills. The Forest History Center offers visitors the chance to experience the life of these turn-of-the-century lumberjacks at its authentic reproduction of a logging camp. At the camp, costumed staff recreate the lifestyles of the camp blacksmith, saw filer, clerk, cook, and the lumberjacks themselves. Down a short path near the logging camp, visitors also will find a river wanigan floating in the Mississippi River. This boat, used in log drives, is the ticket to the river's past. Board the wanigan, and listen to the exciting tales of log jams, fast water, and the history of the mighty Mississippi.

A visit to the Forest History Center is a great introduction to the fascinating life cycle of forests and ways people have used this resource throughout the centuries.

HISTORICAL SOCIETY

The Itasca County Historical Society	10 5th St. NW, P.O. Box 664, Grand Rapids, MN 55744 **Phone: (218) 326-6431**. Hrs.: Summer: M-F, 9:30 a.m.- 5 p.m.; Sat. 9:30 a.m.-4 p.m.; Sun. 11 a.m.-4 p.m. Winter: M-F, 9:30 a.m.-5 p.m.; Sat. 9:30 a.m.-4 p.m.; Closed Sunday.

If you're a Judy Garland fan, then there's no place like the Itasca County Historical Society. The Society features the Judy Garland Historical Center, the only Judy Garland museum in the world. Items include rare photographs and recordings, movie stills, video documentaries, lobby cards, taped interviews and other items that highlight the beloved actress's career.

But there's more than just Judy Garland memorabilia. The Society's educational displays emphasize origins, the area's Ojibwa Indian heritage, the early loggers and settlers and papermaking. The Society maintains an extensive collection of early photographs, artwork, maps and written material, all depicting the area's rich past.

The Museum Store offers a wide selection of quality books and other materials on Minnesota, regional and local history. The store is also an outlet for Ojibwa Indian birchbark crafts and beadwork and features a treasure of Garland music and "Oz" items.

RESORT

Ruttger's Sugar Lake Lodge

P.O. Box 847. Grand Rapids, MN 55744-0847
Phone: 218-327-1462 or 1-800-450-4555
Hrs: Open year-round.
Major credit cards accepted.

Whether you're looking for the classic northwoods vacation or a meeting center amid the pristine wilderness, Ruttger's Sugar Lake Lodge will not disappoint. The Ruttger's tradition of providing superior lodging, meals and service is now offered in Grand Rapids on the shores of beautiful Sugar Lake. It's a wonderful, new lodge with cozy accommodations and a spectacular golf course, as well.

Sugarbrooke is the new 18-hole course adjacent to the lodge area. This par 71, 6,500 yard course was designed by Joel Goldstrand to be one of the finest courses available in northern Minnesota. Every detail has been thought through in order to make this course truly the way golfing should be. For avid golfers, this is a "must play" course!

Accommodations are also exceptional. The Lakeside Cottages are one- and two-bedroom cottages with a spectacular view of the lake. Amenities include gas fireplace, knotty pine interior, custom made log furniture, small refrigerator, microwave and coffeemaker. Forty-eight three-bedroom golf course villas offer fully-equipped kitchens, fireplaces, T.V. and walkout patio.

Of course what would Ruttger's be without their outstanding conference facilities? They can accommodate groups up to 300. Naturally, they offer full service event planning, as well. It's all part of the Ruttger's experience.

They have two restaurants, Otis's and Jack's. Otis's is known for its char-grilled atlantic salmon, tender steaks, pastas and Italian specialties. Jack's delights the palate with fresh walleye, steak and specialty entrées.

Your stay entitles you to a 50% discount on green fees at the Sugarbrooke Golf Club and a 15% discount at their restaurants. KidsKamp programs for ages 4-12 are included, as well as continental breakfast, use of canoes, paddleboats and rowboats, tennis courts, outdoor pool, sand beach, weekly activities, towel service—in short, all the things Ruttger's has come to be known for in resort excellence.

LODGING

Sawmill Inn	2301 So. Pokegama Ave., Grand Rapids, MN 55744. **Phone: 218-326-8501 or (800) 804-8006.** Hrs.: Open year-round All major credit cards accepted.

The area's largest full-service hotel, The Sawmill Inn of Grand Rapids offers ideal accommodations for vacationers as well as business travelers

The Sawmill Inn is widely known for its unique decor and excellent customer service. You will experience the rugged north country atmosphere from the moment you walk into the lobby. The hotel is tastefully decorated with stone fireplaces, exposed wood beam ceilings, log walls, antique logging tools and photographs of the old north country. Choose from 124 suites and rooms, half of which are located adjacent to the pool. With two saunas, whirlpool and heated swimming pool, the indoor domed pool and recreation area is the perfect place for lounging and relaxing.

At mealtime, savor the Walleye Pike ala Ritz, homemade soups and seasonal menus in the Cedars Dining room. For more casual dining, relax in the Cedars Lounge. The Sawmill Inn offers facilities for up to 500 people for business meetings, banquets and catering.

RESTAURANT

The First Grade Restaurant	10 NW Fifth Street, Grand Rapids, MN 55744. **Phone:** 218-326-9361. Hrs: Summer; Mon. - Sat. 7 a.m.-5 p.m., Sun. 9 a.m.-4 p.m. Winter; Mon.-Sat. 7 a.m.-4 p.m. Visa, MasterCard, AmEx, Discover and Diners accepted

If only the food in school had really been this good, we'd all still be in the first grade! That's how you'll feel after eating at Mary Jo Hendricks's establishment in Grand Rapids, formerly classrooms, kindergarten, Principal's office and third grade.

Surrounded by flashcards, chalkboards, *Dick and Jane* books, teddy bears, dolls and, of course, apples for the teacher, this restaurant is the star pupil in a turn-of-the-century school now converted into a gallery of shops. Hendricks offers glorious soups, sandwiches, quiche, salads, whole-grain breads, muffins and desserts. To quote *Minneapolis-St. Paul Magazine,* "The wild-rice salad alone is worth the drive from the Twin Cities." We agree.

Daily specials dot the menu and the desserts (try cranberry raspberry pie or bread pudding with rum or custard sauce for a real treat) are famous. And nobody is in a hurry to leave, either, as they reminisce about the first grade and savor the many delicious dishes. Reservations are recommended.

CORPORATE PROFILE

Blandin Paper Company

Blandin Paper Company, currently the fifth-largest producer in North America of publication papers for magazines and catalogs, has been a part of the city of Grand Rapids for nearly 100 years.

Before the turn of the century, a dam was built across the Mississippi River and the Grand Rapids Water, Power and Boom Company began. Several years later, Itasca Paper Company was formed at the site. With the purchase of the company in 1927 by Charles K. Blandin came reinvestment and growth.

Originally, Blandin Paper Company produced newsprint, primarily for the St. Paul Pioneer Press. Today, its lightweight coated paper is shipped all over North America to be used in magazines and catalogs.

Its paper is valued for its low cost, strength and ability to be mailed economically.

In 1977, British Columbia Forest Products purchased Blandin Paper Company. In 1987, BCFP was purchased by Fletcher Challenge Ltd., New Zealand, and Blandin became a subsidiary of the newly formed Fletcher Challenge Canada. Today Blandin is the primary pulp and paper operation of Fletcher Challenge, which is the world's seventh-largest forest products company and one of Fortune's Global 500-ranking companies.

Blandin Paper occupies approximately 50 acres in the downtown business district of Grand Rapids and includes four modern paper machines.

The No. 6 paper machine, built in 1989 and featured in the Blandin Mill Tour, is the most recently constructed paper machine of its kind in North America. Its off-line coaters are reputed to be the fastest in the world, and its papermaking capacity makes it a world leader in coated publication paper production.

Since Blandin's paper is used by major magazine and catalog publishers throughout the United States and Canada, it can be found in such well-known magazine titles as *Time, Forbes, Newsweek* and *Sports Illustrated.* Catalogue merchandisers, like L.L. Bean and J.C. Penney, like Blandin's lightweight paper for mailing purposes, as well.

Recently, Blandin began making a recycled paper for customers who request it for their publications. Following the opening of Superior Recycled Fiber Industries in Duluth, in which Blandin is a participating partner, Blandin receives regular shipments of recycled office pulp for use in producing recycled paper on all four of its paper machines.

Blandin Mill Tours, which run from Memorial Day to Labor Day, start from the Blandin Tour and Information Center at 116 Third St.

NW, in Grand Rapids. The tour includes a video on the corporation and on papermaking at Blandin. Interpretive information is included.

Tour guides take groups of 10 or fewer as the groups assemble and go through the mill on a continuous basis. The papermaking process is explained thoroughly, along with important facts about forestry. It's a fascinating look at the paper business.

For Blandin, the area's forest resources are of utmost importance and the company plants some 90,000 trees annually.

Most of the wood for paper production comes from within an 80-mile radius of Grand Rapids, and Blandin works with private landowners as well as government landowners to ensure that the resource continues to increase and thrive in the area.

In its papermaking process Blandin uses primarily aspen, which regenerates quickly. Spruce and balsam are also used. In addition, Blandin is involved in extensive aspen research through a cooperative program with the University of Minnesota.

Its own hybrid seed and tree-planting operations ensure that intensive reforestation occurs. The self-guided Blandin Forest Tour starts nine miles south of Grand Rapids and runs from June into October.

Blandin Paper Company has been a part of the Grand Rapids community for nearly 100 years. It's the community's largest employer with 1,100 people on the payroll.

Blandin has employed generations of Itasca County families in its ranks throughout its history, further cementing the relationship between the community and the company.

Distant ownership with a multinational perspective has brought technological and competitive advantages to this northern Minnesota paper mill, but it remains an integral part of Minnesota's forest industry and a progressive leader in forestry, labor relations and paper-making world-wide.

BLANDIN PAPER

HIBBING

For nearly a century, the city of Hibbing and iron ore mining have been synonymous. Hibbing's Hull Rust Mahoning Mine has been called the "Grand Canyon of the North." The village of Hibbing sprang up near the mine in 1893, so close in fact that in 1918, the whole town had to be moved to accommodate Hull Rust's expansion. While steeped in its mining tradition, this bustling town is a center of community activities, but close enough to the serenity of the northwoods that it's possible to have the "best of both worlds."

ATTRACTIONS & EVENTS

The *Greyhound Bus Origin Center* commemorates the 1914 founding of the country's major bus lines. When the town of Hibbing was moved in 1918, miners who previously walked to work now needed transportation, spawning the growth of a shuttle service into a nationwide bus company. *Hibbing High School's* magnificent 1,800-seat auditorium, designed after the old Capital Theater in New York, is complete with Czechoslovakian crystal chandeliers, giving this historic structure an architectural beauty seldom found in a school building.

Hull Rust Mahoning Mine, the first open pit mine on the *Mesabi Range,* offers a spectacular view of the pit measuring more than three miles long, up to two miles wide and 535 feet deep. It took the removal of more than 1.4 billion tons of earth to create such a pit. Current day taconite mining operations can also be seen from the observation deck at this site.

A world away from history and mining is the *Paulucci Space Theatre,* a planetarium featuring a Cinema 360 movie projection system and multi-media programs on astronomy, space exploration and the environment.

The Hibbing World Classic Rodeo ropes spectators into town in October. After the snow flies, it's the *Winter Frolic Celebration* or *Last Chance Curling Bonspiel,* which draws avid curling fans and competitors from around the country and Canada. *The Mines & Pines Jubilee* highlights the summer with a myriad of activities from one end of town to the other. Stock car racing and the *St. Louis County Fair* add to the summer fun.

For further information, contact:
Hibbing Chamber of Commerce
P.O. Box 727
Hibbing, MN 55746   Phone: 800-444-2246

ENTERTAINMENT

Paulucci Space Theatre	Highway 169 and E. Twenty-Third Street Hibbing, MN 55746. **Phone: 218-262-6720** Hrs: Summer, 1, 2, 4 & 7 p.m. Sept.-May, Fri. 7 p.m., Sat. 11, 2, 3; Sun, 2 & 3 p.m.

"Come voyage with us!" beckon the brochures. Voyage to the landscapes of pre-history when only dinosaurs stalked the earth. Voyage through the dark, mysterious reaches of the solar system and outer space. Voyage dangerously near jagged, sea-side cliffs on the soundless wings of a hang-glider. Voyage to the Paulucci Space Theatre, located on the campus of Arrowhead Hibbing Community College.

The center was co-founded by Jeno F. Paulucci and the Paulucci Family Foundation, the Upper Great Lakes Regional Commission, the U.S. Department of Commerce and Energy and the Iron Range Resources and Rehabilitation Board. Underneath its vaulted dome await the marvels of the earth and sky brought breathtakingly close by thrilling visual illusions.

Catering to the curious of all ages, the theatre offers both educational and entertaining multi-media shows. An astronomy curriculum sequence teaches the wonders of the heavens to students in kindergarten through ninth grade. First grade classes are introduced to easily identifiable constellations, while ninth graders come away talking about neutron stars, white dwarfs, pulsars and black holes. The theatre, crowned with a 40-foot diameter dome, features a C 360 movie projection system. Using a fish-eye lens, films are projected over most of the dome's interior surface, an effect which totally immerses audiences in spectacular cinematography. A central computer console controls all the shows and utilizes 25 slide projectors and a dynamic multi-track sound to whisk audiences away on unforgettable journeys.

In addition to its regular programs, the theatre schedules a wide variety of special workshops and symposiums, offers money-saving memberships and houses a gift shop filled with unusual educational items and novelty toys. A visit to the Paulucci Space Theatre is like a visit to another world!

HISTORICAL SOCIETY

Hibbing Historical Society Museum | 400 East 23rd Street, Hibbing, MN 55746
Phone: 218-263-8522
Hrs: Mon.-Sat 9 a.m.-5 p.m., Sun. 1 p.m.-5 p.m.

Want a glimpse into Hibbing's past? The **Hibbing Historical Society Museum** will provide it. The Hibbing Almanac takes the visitor through the important events that took place in Hibbing from the 1880's to the present. Artifacts from those early pioneer days help illustrate the various tools and utensils that were used by early settlers. Logging and mining tools, along with pictorial displays, show how the tools were used in logging and mining operations.

A large 1913 model of North Hibbing depicts the growth of the town and illustrates why Hibbing was forced to move to accommodate mining after the discovery of rich iron ore deposits beneath the town. The audio-visual and pictorial displays, along with the many artifacts shown are well arranged and make it easy to understand the history and background of this great Iron Range town.

MUSEUM

Greyhound Bus Origin Center | 400 East 23rd Street, Hibbing, MN 55746
Phone: 218-263-5814
Hrs: Mon.-Sat 9 a.m.-5 p.m.

Located in the same building as the Historical Society, **The Greyhound Origin Center,** explains to visitors why Hibbing is recognized as the birthplace of the bus industry in the U.S. Here, visitors can see the story of the men and machines that created Greyhound Bus Lines as told through pictorial displays, hundreds of artifacts and memorabilia, audio-visual presentations plus a taped show of "The Greyhound Story—from Hibbing to everywhere."

Visitors start their tour by passing through a tunnel that comes alive with auto sounds of 1914, when it all began and continues on to show how Greyhound grew to be the largest bus company in the world. They also have on display a 1914 Hupmobile, a 1927 white bus and a 1936 super coach.

LODGING

Kahler Park Hotel	1402 East Howard, Hibbing, MN 55746 **Phone: 800-262-3481** Hrs: Open year-round. Major credit cards accepted.

If you expect the usual at the Kahler Park Hotel in Hibbing, you won't get it. But you will get a lot more than that!

This Hotel is the premier establishment of its kind for the Iron Range and travelers looking for the best should note it well. For example, it's the only facility in Hibbing or the surrounding area with swimming pool, whirlpool and sauna.

The Hotel provides a comfortable, "country inn" look, having recently undergone a complete 2.1 million dollar renovation. Some 124 rooms are offered including three elegant suites. A relaxing decor combines with such room amenities as remote-controlled cable television, computer dataport phone jack and video movie rentals. A state-of-the-art key card system provides added privacy and security. Naturally, room service is available.

Pleasurable dining is a hallmark of the Kahler, too. A casual atmosphere in elegant surroundings sets the tone at Reflections restaurant, known as Hibbing's finest. A varied American menu features everything from sandwiches to delicate seafood, choice steaks and gourmet delights. Breakfast, lunch and dinner are served daily, but the Sunday brunch is a particular favorite with locals and visitors alike.

The Crystal Lounge is also a favorite as a piano bar with weekend entertainment and several televisions. Here, you can find your favorite cocktail in a friendly, relaxed atmosphere.

Service goes a long way at the Kahler. You'll find the staff ready and willing to meet your every need. They welcome all groups including motorcoach groups, athletic teams, corporate conventions, wedding parties and the like. They'll even provide special breakfasts or dinners for your group—whatever it takes to have a memorable stay.

In fact, they're well equipped to handle your group; three rooms are offered. The Arrowhead Ballroom handles 350 theater-style or 250 banquet-style, with complete audio/visual capabilities and an optional dance floor. Whispering Pines accommodates 65. It opens onto the patio, so it's perfect for receptions. The Northern Lights room is designed for more intimate gatherings of 35 or fewer.

The Kahler Park Hotel is surrounded by lakes, forests, beautiful scenery and a rich ethnic heritage. Recreational opportunities are the best of Minnesota with hunting, fishing, boating, skiing, snowmobiling and golf—all within minutes of the hotel.

No wonder, then, the Kahler Park Hotel is northern Minnesota's top choice for lodging, dining and meeting on the Iron Range.

HINCKLEY

On Saturday, September 1, 1894, one of the worst fires in history ravaged the young railroad town of Hinckley and five other surrounding communities in eastern Minnesota. Four hundred people died in the flames. But Hinckley recovered and grew into a successful, prosperous industrial and agricultural city of 1,000 inhabitants. The city also benefits from its convenient location just off Interstate 35 halfway between Duluth and the Twin Cities, and numerous restaurants and motels have been built to serve motorists.

The Fire Museum, housed in the rebuilt St. Paul and Duluth Railroad Depot, leads Hinckley's many attractions. Listed on the National Register of Historic Places, the depot burned in the 1894 fire. Exhibits relate the events connected with that great tragedy, but the museum also features agricultural and logging artifacts from the period before the fire. A recent attraction, *Grand Casino Hinckley,* boasts everything from video slots to its famous all-you-can-eat buffet. For further information, contact: *Hinckley Area Chamber of Commerce,* P.O. Box 189, Hinckley, MN 550378. Phone: 612-384-7837

RESTAURANT

Cassidy's Restaurant	I-35 and Hwy 48, Hinckley, MN 55037 **Phone:** 612-384-6129 Hrs: 6 a.m.-10 p.m. Open year-round. Visa and MasterCard accepted.

What makes a restaurant prosper for more than a generation? Most would tell you a good location, great service, a nice atmosphere and wonderful food. Take Cassidy's for example.

Since 1964, they've been serving hearty, wholesome food in a rustic, comfortable setting where people are warm and friendly and the conversation is always good. They've become known for their salad bar, a vegetarian delight that features two homemade soups daily, seven kinds of bread made in their own bakery, several varieties of muffins plus a wide array of salad items. Their Saturday morning breakfast buffet is every bit as good and includes all you can eat from three breakfast bars.

Dinner entrées range from liver 'n onions and meatloaf to jumbo butterfly shrimp and filet mignon. Try the deli croissants for lunch, the hot fudge brownie delight for dessert. A good selection of beer and wine is offered. Hosts Sybil and Willy Welcher also have a gift shop, take-out bakery and daily specials. Banquet room available.

RESTAURANT

Tobie's

I-35 and Highway 48, Hinckley, MN 55037
Phone: 612-384-6175
Hrs: Open daily
Major credit cards accepted.

Whether it's because Tobie's is the half-way point between the Twin Cities and the Twin Ports or because of the outstanding food served by second generation owners, Tobie's in Hinckley has become a traditional stop for anyone traveling to the Duluth area.

It was first started in the 1940's and became famous for serving up tantalizing baked goods with plenty of fresh, hot coffee. John and Esther Schrade bought Tobie's Restaurant in 1966 and moved it to its present location on the freeway. Now, the second generation of Schrades have expanded to offer a unique blend of food, lodging, shopping, entertainment and fun.

Tobie's Restaurant, the convenience store/self-service gas, ice cream shoppe and dining and lounge facilities continue to be a welcome stop for tourists, business people, truck drivers, high school teams and local folk. The fine menu selections, fresh bakery goods, 24-hour welcome, live music, dancing and renowned summer breakfast buffets keep generations coming back for more.

Tobie's Express is a fast food spot near Tobie's Restaurant with seating for 50 and a drive-through. Highlights of the menu include breakfast, sandwiches, chicken, pizza by the slice and, of course, the famous Tobie's pastries.

The caramel rolls baked fresh in the bakery section are reason enough to stop and visit. But then, any of the home cooked meals on the menu are worth the exit off of I-35. The lounge offers live evening entertainment and a chance to unwind and socialize.

Just walk across the parking lot for a good night's sleep at Tobie's Motor Lodge. The ice cream shoppe rounds out the Tobie's experience!

Tobie's takes parties, meetings and weddings for groups up to 400 people and they can cater for groups with as many as 5,000, as they did for the M.S. Bikeathon.

INTERNATIONAL FALLS

As the final outpost on the edge of great boreal forests and lakes stretching to the high Arctic, International Falls offers a rare glimpse of untamed nature. The city was long known as a stopping place on a route traveled by voyageurs in search of beaver furs, but it was not incorporated as a village until 1901.

At that time it was named Koochiching, but this was changed to International Falls in 1903 to reflect its location on the Canadian border and to celebrate the waterfalls cascading down Rainy River. However, the town might as well have kept its original name, because as early as 1905, the falls were dammed to create water power for the paper industry, which still is the city's largest employer. The city's name eventually became the inspiration for "Frostbite Falls," the hometown of itinerant cartoon characters Rocky and Bullwinkle, which is appropriate considering International Falls routinely registers the lowest winter temperatures in the country.

ATTRACTIONS & EVENTS

The city is an excellent starting point for excursions into *Voyageurs National Park*—219,000 acres of wilderness, islands, and water, which is dominated by four lakes, three of which form the border with Canada. Unlike the Boundary Waters Canoe Area, motor-boating is allowed on the 83,000 acres of water and 2,000 miles of shoreline in Voyageurs National Park, and visitors can rent, or bring their own boats, or take a naturalist tour with *Ride The Pride Boat Tours.*

At visitor centers on nearby *Rainy or Kabetogama Lakes,* exhibits and orientation films on Voyageurs National Park are available for viewing, along with maps and information on other naturalist programs, such as the popular, free *North Canoe Voyages.* The *Koochiching County Historical Museum* shows a pictorial history, and the *Giant Thermometer* (one of the most popular attractions in town) gives visitors and locals a chance to spot a new record-breaking low. The *Bronko Nagurski Museum* is a lasting tribute to this outstanding man, athlete and citizen.

For further information, contact:
International Falls Visitors and Convention Bureau
P.O. Box 169
International Falls, MN 56649
Phone: 218-283-9400

BOAT TOURS

Voyageurs National Park Boat Tours, Inc.	Route 8, Box 303, International Falls, MN 56649 **Phone: 218-286-5470** Hrs: Open mid-May to mid-Oct. Visa and MasterCard accepted.

The Pride of Rainy Lake offers naturalist-guided and other narrated sight-seeing tours in Voyageurs National Park. A 49-passenger vessel, the Pride is the largest jet-powered passenger boat in the Midwest and operates from the Park's Rainy Lake Visitor Center.

Passengers will see many interesting sites such as bald eagles and their nests, or a herring gull and cormorant rookery. Tour Little American Island with its century-old gold mine, or take a day-long outing to historic Kettle Falls Hotel. Special trips such as dinner cruises, buffet supper trips and starwatches are also scheduled throughout the summer.

This boat is designed to move quickly across open expanses and can cruise quietly into shallow bays and coves other boats this size cannot navigate. Tours truly offer a first-class experience in the waters of this national park.

HISTORIC SITE

Grand Mound	A Minnesota Historical Society Site. 17 miles west of International Falls on Hwy 11. R.R. 7, P.O. Box 453, International Falls, MN 56649. **Phone: 218-285-3332.** Hrs: May 1-Labor Day, Mon.-Sat. 10 a.m.-5 p.m., Sun. noon-5 p.m.; Sept. 6-Oct. 31 Sat. 10 a.m.-4 p.m.; Sun. noon-4 p.m. Free.

The Upper Midwest's largest ancient burial mound, Grand Mound was created by the Laurel Indians who lived in the area from 200 B.C. to about 800 A.D. Archaeologists have dated the oldest artifacts found to Archaic Indians who camped here as long ago as 7,000 years. Adjacent to the mounds are former Indian camps of other eras arranged in distinct layers that give clues to the peoples who once inhabited these lands.

The Laurel Indians were adaptable people who fit weapons and tools to their environment. They borrowed such weapons as the toggle-headed harpoon from people of the Sub-Arctic, yet they also took up mound building, a tradition found in Woodland Indian cultures.

The first archaeological excavation was started in 1933 and research continues today. A nearby history center offers an audio-visual program that covers past Indian cultures and the mounds they built, as well as the nature trails surrounding the area. In winter, cross-country skiing and special programs are offered.

HOUSEBOAT RENTALS

Rainy Lake Houseboats

Route 8, Box 408, International Falls, MN 56649
Phone: 800-554-9188 or 218-286-5391
Hrs: Open mid-May through September
Visa, MasterCard and AmEx accepted.

Imagine spending your vacation in the unparalleled peace and serenity of a national park. But not just any national park. How about one without roads, where the only means of getting around is on the water? Now that's a vacation!

The only place that fills that bill is Voyageurs National Park and the only way to experience all it has to offer is on a houseboat vacation with Rainy Lake Houseboats.

Voyageurs National Park, the only inland water-based park in the national park system, was established in 1971. It is located near the center of the greatest system of interconnected waterways on earth and no roads exist within its boundaries. The natural features here are fascinating, from the exposed outcropping of age-old granite to the ancient pines struggling for existence on rugged cliffs. Glacier scarred islands dot the landscape. Endless forests of pine, spruce, birch and aspen soften the harshness and provide haven for the abundant wildlife. This is a timeless land. It is a place to rest and wander, to fish and sightsee. It is a place to renew one's spirit.

Every houseboat is fully appointed and completely modern giving you the total freedom to explore as the mood moves you. You can probe hidden bays and intimate islands. The captain of a Rainy Lake Houseboat has no schedule but his own, no deadlines and no stress.

Established in 1976, Rainy Lake Houseboats carries on the traditions of the Dougherty family which has been serving the Rainy Lake Country since 1918. Exceptional service is their hallmark, the kind of special touches that make the difference between a good vacation and a great one. Send your grocery list ahead and they'll have the houseboat fully stocked and ready to go when you arrive.

"The Chairman II" is the latest addition to the fleet, a 62-foot long, 16-foot wide V.I.P. craft with the best of everything. Rates include food, linens, boats, motors, guides, cooks and just about anything else you could need. The only items not included are fuel, bait, licenses and refreshments. The fishing (smallmouth bass, northern pike, crappie and walleye) is superb. And the pristine wilderness of Voyageurs National Park, with its abundant bald eagles, loons and black bear, is unmatched.

Even if you don't know bow from stern, all the houseboats are set up for easy operation. You'll get a course in reading charts and marking buoys and you'll be on your way to complete relaxation.

RESORT

Thunderbird Lodge

Rt. 8, Box 407, International Falls, MN 56649
Phone: 218-286-3151
Hrs: 7 a.m.-10 p.m. every day.
Major credit cards accepted.

Thunderbird Lodge offers a perfect opportunity to explore and enjoy the 218,000 acre Voyageurs National Park—without giving up the comforts of home. The allure of Rainy Lake is mystery, with its endless succession of rocky shoreline, the countless pine-clad islands, cliffs, forests and rivers. Wildlife abounds: deer, bear, moose, wolf, otter, eagle and beaver all share this beautiful land. And, of course, fishing is superb! Those who visit are refreshed in body and renewed in spirit.

In the midst of this pristine wilderness lies Thunderbird Lodge, waiting to service those who cannot resist this wonderful land. A Thunderbird vacation offers year-round recreational opportunities. Water ski, cross-country ski, snowmobile, fish, hike, explore, sun-bathe, or relax—there's something for everyone.

The lodge is AAA rated and has all the conveniences including color TV's, private baths, electric heat, air conditioning, phones and carpeting. Cabins are the same but are spaced widely for privacy and located nearer the docks for your convenience.

Try the Thunderbird Restaurant. It, too, is AAA rated and serves up fine food and beverages with a spectacular view of the lake. Specialty dinners include steak 'n lobster, steak 'n shrimp and Chicken Oscar, a sautéed chicken breast with crab meat, asparagus and hollandaise sauce.

Outside, enjoy paddle boats, canoes and tennis. Don't miss the guided fishing trips to Ontario or Minnesota waters—unforgettable fishing.

If that's not enough, there are boat tours of Voyageurs National Park, miles of hiking trails and even an historic gold mine to visit. Fort Francis, Ontario, offers a unique shopping experience.

Thunderbird Lodge is a 1994 site of the Minnesota Governor's Fishing Opener.

RESTAURANT

The Spot Supper Club & Fireside Lounge

Hwy. 53 and 18th Street
International Falls, MN 56649
Phone: 218-283-2440
Hrs: Major credit cards accepted.

Three generations of the same family have served up wonderfully delicious food from The Spot in International Falls. It began in 1936 with Carl and Isabelle Olson and is now expertly operated by their grandson, Rick—a trained chef—and wife Sue. Rick has won many awards and trophies for his culinary skills.

Many things have changed over the years, but one thing remains the same—The Spot is dedicated to providing a pleasurable dining experience.

The Spot offers a wide variety of menu selections, including their specials, Prime Rib and Spot's famous BBQ Ribs. Other favorites include Walleye Pike, shrimp, choice steaks, chicken and salmon. A well-rounded wine list is also offered.

A new feature at The Spot is their classic dinners, a full seven-course dinner offered periodically. The Spot also offers banquet facilities for up to 50.

SPECIALTY SHOP

The Border

200 2nd Ave., International Falls, MN 56649
Phone: 218-283-4414
Hours vary, please call.
Major credit cards accepted.

The last building in the U.S., that's The Border in International Falls. This wonderfully eclectic business offers just about anything you can imagine from a Northwoods border town.

A unique gift gallery includes original art and limited edition prints by well-known artists, hand-carved decoys, porcelain and crystal items, collector plates, music boxes and jewelry. You'll also find Hudson Bay blankets, Finnish and Norwegian woolen throws, sheepskin slippers, designer sweatshirts, fur-lined boots and In-Fisherman jackets.

If you're hungry, there's a host of gourmet goodies and delectable delights. For the kids, they have stuffed animals, books, tapes, toys, dolls and games. Indian arts, crafts and unique clothing are also featured. And after all that, they offer one of the world's finest taxidermy studios!

IRON TRAIL REGION

Just an hour's drive from Duluth or Ely and 3½ hours from Minneapolis/St. Paul, the Iron Trail region blends the quiet, rustic beauty of the northwoods with the fascinating history of the great iron ore mining era. Immigrants from more than 40 countries came to work the mines of the Mesabi Range, producing ore for the nation's steel mills for more than a half century. These hard-working people left behind a rich ethnic culture and one of the most unique historical areas in the country. Visitors to this region of Northeastern Minnesota can get off the beaten path to discover beautiful lakes, scenic vistas, dramatic mine views, fish stocked mine pits and enjoy exhilarating outdoor activities in any season. The Iron Trail stretches from Hibbing on the west to Hoyt Lakes on the east and boasts over 20 attractions within 45 minutes of each other. Travelers will find a wide selection of lodging accommodations, from luxury villas to economically priced motels.

Looking for the "Trail"? It's actually a collection of wonderfully diverse communities that form this very special region, rather than a trail. But if it's trails you're seeking, there are plenty in the area for hiking, biking, mountain biking, snowmobiling, downhill and cross-country skiing. They wind through the woods, past pristine lakes and streams into a world of natural, unspoiled beauty. Snowmobilers can ride over 2,000 miles of well-marked, groomed snowmobile trails from numerous access points originating in the Iron Trail communities. Summertime festivals abound, especially on the Fourth of July.

Leonidas Merritt, who discovered the first iron ore in the area, used the named "Missabe" to characterize this mining territory and to name the Missabe Railroad. It was an adaptation of the Chippewa Indian word "Missabay," meaning "Giant's Range." The spelling has since been changed to Mesabi and Mesaba, both of which are now used to describe the region.

The Iron Trail is home to two major attractions, IRONWORLD USA, located in Chisholm and Giants Ridge Recreation Area, situated in the Town of White. Within a short drive of the area is the Soudan Underground Mine State Park, in Soudan, where visitors can experience the thrill of descending half a mile beneath the earth to see Minnesota's first underground mine.

Then, if you feel lucky, you can stop by Fortune Bay Casino in nearby Tower. In the opposite direction is a large scale view of early open pit mining at the Hill Annex Mine State Park in Calumet. Take a trolley ride 500 feet down into the heart of the open pit mine. Numerous other attractions are listed separately under the Iron Trail towns where they are located.

Aurora was established in 1905 and maintains the ethnic traditions so typical of other Iron Trail communities. Surrounded by the Superior National Forest, it enjoys the scenic beauty of both forest and lakes.

Biwabik is the gateway to Giants Ridge Recreation Area and is the center for many winter activities. Biwabik hosts thousands of alpine and nordic skiers, snowmobilers and other outdoor enthusiasts.

The home of IRONWORLD USA, *Chisholm* is famous for its ethnic foods, entertainment and unique ways it celebrates its mining heritage. At one time, there were 45 mines operating in the area.

Eveleth displays an interesting mixture of natural beauty and small town charm. It's an excellent place for boating, swimming and fishing. Cyclists can take advantage of easy riding along the Fayal Pond trail system. Walking trails lead through forests, around lakes and reveal spectacular views of Eveleth's mining area.

The U.S. Hockey Hall of Fame is located in Eveleth and the city is known as the "Hockey Capital of the Nation" because of its interest in the sport.

Hibbing remains another city with deep roots in the mining tradition. In fact, the whole town once had to move to accommodate expansion of the local mine! Hibbing's Hull Rust Mahoning Mine has been called the "Grand Canyon of the North." The open-pit mine is three miles long, two miles wide and 535 feet deep.

Hibbing's Greyhound Bus Origin Center commemorates the 1914 founding of the country's major bus line.

Hoyt Lakes combines all the charm of a small town with the adventures of an exclusive resort. Tennis, bike trails, hiking trails, golf, boating and swimming are offered in summer. In winter, visitors enjoy great ice fishing, ice hockey, snowshoeing and snowmobiling. Some 53 miles of well-maintained ski trails with slopes are graded for every level of expertise from beginner to pro.

Mountain Iron might be called the birthplace of the Mesabi Range, for it was here that iron ore was first discovered by Leonidas Merritt. The Mountain Iron Mine and Minntac Overlook is designated as a National Historic Monument and offers a spectacular view.

Virginia has been called the "Queen City of the North," as it lies at the heart of the Mesabi Range. Area lakes make the perfect setting for boating and anglers rarely set their sights too high. The Virginia Heritage Museum preserves the logging and mining heritage.

The *Town of White* is the official home of Giants Ridge Recreation Area, a winter mecca of downhill and cross-country skiing, snowboarding and snowmobiling, or hiking and biking in summer or fall. The Pepsi Challenge Cross-Country Ski Race is held here.

For further information, contact:
Iron Trail Convention and Visitors Bureau
P.O. Box 559, Eveleth, MN 55734
Phone: 800-777-8497

LUTSEN/TOFTE/LITTLE MARAIS

Nestled away in one of Minnesota's most spectacular corners is the North Shore. Known for its stunning beauty and fabulous outdoor attractions, it is home to a string of charming communities: Lutsen, Tofte and Little Marais.

The towns were first settled by prospectors in search of mineral riches as well as lumbermen, fishermen and a few hardy farmers who carved a living out of the rocky landscape. After a few tough winters, the dreams of riches diminished but the awesome beauty of the region did not. It remains the chief attraction.

ATTRACTIONS & EVENTS

The name "Lutsen" has long been synonymous with skiing thanks to the *Lutsen Mountain Ski Area.* Rich in skiing tradition and buoyed by the Olympic success of area native Cindy Nelson, it has recently undergone a massive expansion and upgrading which makes it the Midwest's most comprehensive skiing facility. Lutsen Mountain boasts 1,500 acres and a vertical rise of more than 800 feet. A gondola operates year-round. But there's more here than just skiing.

The *Bluefin Bay Resort* offers fine accommodations and food to match. The area is also home to a number of other resorts, hotels and bed & breakfast homes including the *Mountain Inn, Lutsen Resort* and, located at the foot of the ski hills, the *Village Inn Resort.*

Of course, fishing, hiking and camping are well-known attraction in the area, too. The cross-country skiing is among the best in Minnesota, including the well-groomed *North Shore Mountains Ski Trail,* the *Superior Hiking Trail,* and the *Sawbill Trail. Tettegouche State Park* offers camping and spectacular scenery for hiking. The latest recreational addition to the region is the *Superior National Golf Course,* one of Minnesota's best new resort courses. Carved out of the *Sawtooth Mountains,* it has drawn rave reviews.

During the winter, two very different races buzz through the area: the *John Beargrease Sled Dog Marathon* and the *International 500* snowmobile race. For the more sedate, this magnificent area has inspired artists for generations and the many studios and galleries are well worth a visit.

For further information, contact:
Lutsen/Tofte Tourism Association
P.O. Box 2248, Tofte, MN 55615   Phone: 218-663-7804

BED & BREAKFAST

Lindgren's Bed & Breakfast	County Road 35, P.O. Box 56, Lutsen, MN 55612-0056. **Phone: 218-663-7450** Hrs: Open year-round. Visa and MasterCard accepted.

A successful Bed & Breakfast inn is one that makes guests feel right at home and, judging by the long guest list, Lindgren's B&B is one of the most successful. You'll find it along the North Shore at Lutsen, amid the pristine wilderness of lake and forest.

Located on the "Lake Superior Circle Tour," this B&B provides a year-round haven for travelers and vacationers alike. All year 'round, you're greeted by the warmth of a magnificent stone fireplace, a coziness complemented by the log cabin style interior. Built in the 1920's, the home has been extensively remodeled and decorated with all manner of creatures that inhabit the lands of Superior National Forest. Along one wall is a row of grand picture windows looking out over the endless waters of Lake Superior. In one corner is a baby grand piano, which guests are welcome to play. An assortment of books, games, CD's and a stereo is available as well.

Outside, guests enjoy horseshoes, volleyball, relax in the old-fashioned porch swing on the water's edge or toast marshmallows at a beach bonfire. Skiers especially like the area because of the hundreds of miles of groomed trails and downhill skiing nearby. At Lindgren's, guests are just a few feet away from their 480 feet of walkable Lake Superior shoreline and a short drive from Lutsen's new championship golf course and countless miles of unspoiled hiking trails. Nearby, there is access to the Boundary Waters Canoe Area wilderness.

The four rooms offered at Lindgren's provide great views of the lake. Three have king-sized beds and one comes with a two-person whirlpool. Another has a fireplace, can accommodate a group and has a private entrance. All rooms have a color television.

But whichever room you choose, the soothing waves of Lake Superior lapping the rocky shore will lull you into excellent slumber. In the morning, you are treated to a magnificent breakfast. Keep a sharp eye for special homemade treats, too!

BED & BREAKFAST

The Stone Hearth Inn on Lake Superior	1118 Highway 61 East, Little Marais, MN 55614 **Phone: 218-226-3020** Hrs.: Open year around. Visa and MasterCard accepted.

The hummingbirds visible from the veranda can tell you: the Stone Hearth Inn is a place you can't resist. The fully renovated 1920s inn cast its spell on Susan and Charlie Michels, too.

She was a guest the first month that Charlie opened the Inn; they were married a year later. Now, year-round, the Michels bring the refined comforts of a classic bed and breakfast.

Nestled at the base of a steep hill, the Inn has a superb setting. Charlie "always dreamed of living on big water" and bought the run-down property in 1989. During the next year he gave the existing architecture a thorough facelift, carefully preserving original details. "All it needed was a porch and a fireplace," he says.

The veranda, with its inviting Adirondack furniture, spans the breadth of the Inn. Relaxing there, visitors can look out through the stately black spruce to the "big water" beyond. Only a gentle curve of green separates you from Superior's rocky shoreline.

"Sometimes the lake comes up to greet us," Susan says. Storms occasionally have sprinkled the lawn with beach stones, the same kind Charlie used to build the splendid hearth.

Sigh contentedly as you sink into the fireside easy chairs for a chat or a read. Well-thumbed reading material as well as furnishings were chosen for comfort. Delicate English pieces keep company with mission oak antiques and primitive pine reproductions, a warmth without pretense that makes you feel entirely at home.

There are five rooms at the Inn: four are furnished with full-sized, antique beds; one with king or twin beds. All have reading chairs. Three face the lake; two look out on the rocky shore. All have private baths. The Boathouse, which features units with double whirlpool tubs and gas fireplaces, sits literally on the water's edge.

Inn guests receive a full breakfast. Menus vary, but Charlie's specialty is blueberry wildrice pancakes; Susan's is delicately spiced french toast, stuffed with cream cheese, nuts and fruits of the season. Guests in the lakefront room receive a complimentary continental breakfast. Superior suite guests are on their own for meals.

After breakfast, you're soon ready to ski from the door to 20 kilometers of groomed, private cross country trails. There's also shuttle service to the Superior Hiking Trail.

Complimentary evening treats frequently appear, including cookies and spiced cider, venison sausage and cheese.

RESORT

Bluefin Bay On Lake Superior	Highway 61, Tofte, MN 55615 **Phone: 800-258-3346 or 218-663-7296** Hrs: Open year-round. Visa, MasterCard and Discover accepted.

"New England Close to Home" is a valid description of Bluefin Bay Resort on Lake Superior. In the early 1900's, Lake Superior provided a bounty of fresh fish which in turn was sent to markets in Duluth, Minneapolis, St. Paul and Chicago. Lake Superior trout and bluefin gained a reputation for their unique flavor and freshness. The modern day Bluefin follows in that North Shore tradition of good food, cozy accommodations and friendly service.

The *Twin Cities Reader* named Bluefin Bay "...the most romantic resort in Minnesota." Nestled on the shores of Lake Superior, all of the suites, townhomes and condominiums offer a spectacular view of the shoreline. Fireplaces, private decks, vaulted ceilings and private whirlpools extend an invitation to guests to relax and enjoy the surroundings. For socializing, Bluefin Bay has a volleyball court, indoor pool, sauna, meeting rooms, tennis court, exercise room, The Bayside Gift Shop and an 18-hole championship style golf course nearby. Sumptuous meals are the specialty of the Bluefin Restaurant where seafood is naturally the highlight of the menu. The Bridge offers a more casual atmosphere for dining and is replete with local history and artifacts.

The Bluefin is located in Superior National Forest, which is home to the Superior Hiking Trail. Lutsen Ski Area is just 10 minutes from the resort. Snowmobile and cross-country ski trails permeate the area surrounding Bluefin. There are more than 200 inland lakes within a ten-mile radius of the resort. The Bluefin Bay Resort on Lake Superior possesses excellent accommodations and panoramic surroundings.

RESORT

Cascade Lodge and Restaurant	HC3 Box 445, Lutsen, MN 55612 **Phone: 218-387-1112** **or 800-322-9543 (in MN)** Major credit cards accepted.

Cascade Lodge offers seclusion for honeymooners, natural forest beauty for nature lovers and superior accommodations in a wilderness setting for everyone. Cascade Lodge is a charming 1930's historic North Shore lodge nestled in the midst of the Cascade River State Park and featured in *Country Inns & America's Wonderful Little Hotels and Inns.* Comfortable lodge rooms, two large livingrooms, one with a grand stone fireplace, overlook Lake Superior. For those who prefer a quieter setting, there are log cabins with fireplaces—even the privacy of honeymoon cabins.

There are several mini-vacation packages from which to choose: guest rooms in the main lodge, kitchenette facilities or rustic log cabins. Summer provides endless activities like hiking, fishing from the lodge, tennis, golf, sailing and horseback riding nearby. Wildlife abounds as you take a nature walk through Cascade River State Park which surrounds the lodge.

Enjoy the breathtaking sunsets and sunrises over Lake Superior. During the winter months, there are over 40 miles of groomed cross-country ski trails from the front doors of Cascade Lodge, along the Cascade River and to Deer Yard Lake. Ski and snowshoe rentals are available and an extensive snowmobile trail system is accessible from the lodge.

Just minutes away, you'll find downhill skiing at Lutsen Mountain Ski Area and ice fishing on nearby inland lakes. There are planned activities every day in the summer. In the winter, guests relax in the warmth of the Fireplace Room.

Overlooking the scenic lake, the restaurant provides a superior selection for breakfast, lunch and dinner. The ambiance is warm and wholesome and the menu selections and service are great.

RESORT

The Mountain Inn at Lutsen	P.O. Box 58, Lutsen, MN 55612 **Phone: 800-686-4669** Hrs: Open year-round. Visa, MasterCard and AmEx accepted.

Plenty of recreational activities in a beautiful, natural setting—that's probably what most people look for in a fabulous vacation. If you're one of them, then look no farther than the Mountain Inn at Lutsen.

This four-season inn is located at Lutsen Mountains adjacent to Superior National at Lutsen championship golf course. Just coincidentally, the resort offers stay and play packages. The course offers spectacular views, with Lake Superior as the backdrop for many holes.

Perhaps you're not a golfer. Not a problem. Mountain Inn is located in the heart of one of Minnesota's great outdoor vacation adventures. It's called the North Shore! Try sailing on beautiful Lake Superior. Maybe you'd like to try a canoe adventure in the one million acre Boundary Waters Canoe Area, the largest wilderness retreat east of the Rockies!

Hiking or biking? The Superior Hiking Trail offers a trail system of over 200 miles laid out along the ridge of the ancient glacial worn Sawtooth Mountain Range. Lodge to lodge hiking is a popular activity for many and Mountain Inn is part of the experience. In the fall, the colors are exceptional. Then again, perhaps your tastes run to winter activities. If so, you're in for a pleasant adventure with both downhill and cross-country skiing plus snowmobiling. Lutsen Mountains are nearby and, of course, the many miles of trails make a cross-country ski and snowmobile paradise.

Mountain Inn fits in well with recent trends toward shorter, but more frequent vacations. They offer a variety of accommodations to serve the needs of everyone, from families to singles and seniors. The 30 beautifully appointed guest rooms offer contemporary amenities like remote control color televisions, mini suites with king or queen beds and wet bar, indoor whirlpool and sauna, complimentary Continental breakfasts and private ski lockers. After a full day of activity, they provide a relaxing environment, a good night's rest and a clean, comfortable room. Several fine restaurants are nearby, too. By the way, the staff at Mountain Inn at Lutsen is dedicated to guests with friendly service and welcoming smiles.

RESORT

Village Inn and Resort at Lutsen Mountain

County Road 36, Lutsen, MN 55612
Phone: 218-663-7241 or 800-642-6036
Hrs: Open year-round.
Visa and MasterCard accepted.

The Village Inn and Resort at Lutsen Mountain is true to its slogan, "A few hours north and a million miles away." The Village is approximately four hours drive from the Twin Cities area and only 75 miles from Canada, in the heart of some of the most beautiful country in Minnesota.

This four season resort is in the Sawtooth Mountains, the largest group of mountains in Minnesota, and overlooks both Lake Superior and the Boundary Waters Canoe Area, so you know there are plenty of activities for the outdoors type here. During the summer, there are local art fairs, music festivals and theater. Nearby is the Superior Hiking Trail, fishing, boating and the Superior National Golf Course.

The Village itself offers an outdoor pool, indoor pool, four whirlpools and a sauna, tennis courts, horseback riding, miniature golf, trout fishing, an alpine slide and the North Shore's most complete children's and Naturalist programs. In the fall, the mountains explode with color, the reds and oranges of the North Shore's maple stands. In the winter, guests enjoy Lutsen Mountains, boasting the midwest's highest vertical drop and more than double the skiable terrain of all other mountain ski areas!

For the cross-country skier, there are nearly 200 kilometers of groomed trails to explore and have fun skiing. Once off the slopes, guests enjoy sleigh rides and dogsled races. The spring snow melt brings a riot of color in wild flowers to the shore.

They have many vacation packages available to suit a variety of needs. In fact, what makes this place so special is that everyone can find what they want in a vacation here. They have much to offer—and a lot to give.

ORR

It was 1895 when William Orr set up the first trading post on the beautiful shores of Pelican Lake. The erstwhile captain reigned supreme in this pioneer community for many years until the railway came and brought hundreds of hungry lumberjacks with it.

It was a very different Orr then. The log hoist, King Oscar's Hotel and the tar paper shacks have long since passed into the limbo of oblivion. Captain Orr is gone and only a scattering of the old school lumberjacks remain. But the logging continues.

Today, it is the spectacular beauty of the land and its trees that brings people back to Orr. Located near the 219,000 acres of *Voyageurs National Park,* Orr is home to a number of resorts catering to fisherman and tourists and is located near numerous lakes, including *Crane, Kabetogama, Namakan, Myrtle, Sand Point, Elephant* and *Ash* making it a year-round outdoor paradise.

For further information, contact:
Pelican Lake-Orr Area Resort Association
Orr, MN 55771   Phone: 800-777-8559

SPECIALTY SHOP

The Orr General Store & Mercantile Company	Highway 53 N., P.O. Box 177, Orr, MN 55771 **Phone: 218-757-3534** Hrs: (Summer) 8 a.m.-6 p.m. (Winter) 9 a.m.-5 p.m. Visa and MasterCard are accepted.

Originally built in 1905 and known as Pelican Mercantile Company, this historic building was restored by owners Eleanor and Phil Anshus in 1983. The transition was a family project and the store now offers high quality merchandise.

Old pictures, counter showcases, a barrel stove and other oldtime artifacts adorn the walls and interior of this general store. The general flavor of the store's offerings are antique reproduction toys, household articles, old-fashioned candies, upscale crafts and quality clothing.

Eleanor and Phil pride themselves on obtaining unusual gift items. For example, belts are made by an Amish harness maker. Antiques are displayed on consignment and new sources are continually sought for creative merchandise.

Brand names such as Five Brothers, Filson, Lee, Bemidji Woolen Mills, Red Wing shoes, Sorrel, and LaCrosse line the shelves of the general store.

RESORT

Cabin O' Pines

4378 Pelican Rd., Orr, MN 55771
Phone: 218-757-3122
Open Memorial Day thru Labor Day
Visa, MasterCard and Discover accepted.

Cabin O' Pines Resort and Campground is among those great traditional Minnesota resorts operated by the same family for several generations. It was first homesteaded in 1904 by the great-grandfather of present owners Gary and Lori Coyer. They are fourth generation operators and have been welcoming campers and cabin guests for the past 17 years. The oldest cabin was built in 1910 and was originally an Indian trading post.

Cabin O' Pines is located on beautiful Pelican Lake, nationally known for its bluegills, crappies, large and small mouth bass, walleye and northern pike. But excellent fishing is only one of the many activities offered here. Indeed, the motto of Cabin O' Pines is "Where family fun is No. 1." There's a sauna, nature trails, playground, swings, horseshoes and a sandy beach with tetherball. In the water, there's volleyball, a slide and swimming raft with springboard. There's even a recreation room outfitted with pool table, video games, foosball, jukebox, piano, books, board games and puzzles!

Like nature? Listen to the lonesome call of the loon. Watch spectacular sunsets and sunrises. Hear the water gently lapping at the shore. Smell the scent of pine all around you. You'll leave behind all the noise and crowds of the city at Cabin O' Pines. Here, there's just the richness of nature hidden in the shimmering moonlight or lying quietly beneath the white pine forest. Here is beauty, serenity and fun combined.

Whatever your family likes to do, you'll be glad you came to Cabin O' Pines. And, you'll be back!

PINE CITY

Located only one hour from both Duluth and the Twin Cities, the friendly, small town of Pine City combines the restfulness of a resort with the convenience of a complete, self-supporting community of schools, restaurants, and commercial districts. Set between the serene beauty of Cross and Pokegama lakes, Pine City boasts 50 miles of uninterrupted waterways within city limits. In addition, there's public access to the pastoral *Snake River* at the Pine City boat landing and to the scenic *St. Croix River* at the historic ferry landing.

The fun-filled *Snake River Rendezvous* held at the fur post each September celebrates the annual trade meeting between Indians, voyageurs and fur traders. At the *Knap-In* in July, flint knappers demonstrate their ancient art at the *North West Company Post.*

For further information, contact:
Pine City Area Chamber of Commerce
615 W. Third Ave.
Pine City, MN 55063
Phone: 612-629-3861

HISTORIC SITE

North West Company Fur Post

A Minnesota Historical Society Site. Hwy. 7, 1.5 miles west of I-35, (Pine City) P.O. Box 51, Pine City, MN 55063. **Phone: 612-629-6356.** Hrs: May 1-Labor Day 10 a.m.-5 p.m. Tues.-Sat., Sun. noon-5 p.m. Free.

In the late 1700's, the fur trade was booming in North America and competition between fur trade companies was fierce. The North West Company, one of the biggest in the fur trade, ruled over a network of trappers, voyageurs and fur trading posts that extended from the St. Lawrence River watershed to the Rocky Mountains.

In 1804-05, the company sent John Sayer to establish a new post in the area southwest of Lake Superior. Sayer, his clerk and several French Canadian voyageurs arrived at the Pine City site in September of that year and proceeded to build a wood post.

Sayer kept a journal of his year at the Pine City post and, using his writings as a guide, the Minnesota Historical Society excavated the site and found the charred remains of the main cabin, fireplaces, food caches and stockade. In the 1960's, the Society reconstructed the fur post on top of its old foundations. Today, costumed guides act out the lifestyles of the voyageurs, Indians and fur traders who once roamed the pristine wilderness.

SILVER BAY

First established for the miners of Reserve Mining, Co., Silver Bay got its name from a ship's captain who thought its rocky shores looked like silver.

The North Shore is the center for many attractions and Silver Bay lists several of these among its sights. They include **Gooseberry Falls, Tettegouche State Park, Split Rock Lighthouse** and the **Superior Hiking Trail.**

In addition, fishing, picnicking, camping, skiing and snowmobiling are excellent. There is a 9-hole golf course in the city.

In January, the 400-mile **John Beargrease Sled Dog Races** are held.

For further information, contact:
Silver Bay Area Chamber of Commerce
Box 26
Silver Bay, MN 55614
Phone: 218-226-4870

BED & BREAKFAST

The Inn at Palisade Bed & Breakfast	384 Highway 61 East, Silver Bay, MN 55614 **Phone: 218-226-3505** Hrs.: Open from June through mid-October Visa, MasterCard and Discover accepted.

Nestled among pine and birch and overlooking beautiful Lake Superior, The Inn at Palisade Bed & Breakfast offers a peaceful escape from today's fast-paced life.

All of the five rooms at the Inn are newly renovated and decorated in a casual country style. Four rooms have a bay window giving way to a magnificent view of Lake Superior. Each room has a private entrance, a bath with shower and TV. The Suite has a large sitting area with fireplace and TV, one queen-size bed and sofa bed, kitchen, bath with shower and its own patio with fire pit.

When you awake, drink in the smell of coffee, tea and home-baked breads and muffins. Relish a leisurely breakfast of fresh fruit, juice and entrée in the country style dining room.

While at the Inn, enjoy berry picking, rock hunting, beach combing. Check out nearby antique shops, art galleries and local festivals. Cast for Coho salmon and lake trout in Lake Superior, or try for rainbow trout and steelheads in area rivers and streams.

TOWER/SOUDAN

The oldest mining town in Minnesota, Tower-Soudan has been described as "The Cradle of the Iron Mining Industry." The first shipment of iron ore came from the Soudan underground mine, which was considered the richest in the world. The checkered mining communities of Tower and Soudan were composed of members of many nationalities—Finnish, Swedish, Norwegian, Italian, and Slovenian who often spoke little English and clung to their traditional culture. Nevertheless, the miners and their families eventually forged a close-knit community that through tenacity and determination survived the closing of the Soudan mine in 1962 and went on to create a new future based on cottage industries and tourism.

ATTRACTIONS & EVENTS

The focus for the resort industry is *Lake Vermilion,* one the largest unrestricted motor boating lakes in the area, with 365 islands and more than 1,200 miles of tranquil shoreline.

In celebration of the town's history, the *Tower-Soudan Underground Mine State Park* offers tours of the Soudan mine, the deepest underground mine in Minnesota. The only tour of its kind in the country, it provides a fascinating glimpse into traditional mining operations from 2,300 feet below the earth's surface. Self-guided tours of open pits, the enginehouse, and crusher building also are available. In addition to the mine, history buffs frequent the *Tower Depot and Train Museum,* a restored depot and steam train, and the *McKinley Monument,* reportedly the first monument to be erected to the memory of President William McKinley.

For those who don't care for touring, the *Fortune Bay Casino,* run by the Bois Fort tribe of Ojibwa, offers casino gaming. Other recreational activities are abundant; try fishing, boating, hiking, water skiing, snowmobiling, ice-fishing and cross-country skiing.

Several nicely wooded golf courses are nearby. The *Ely Golf Course* is a public 9-hole, par 34 course. *Vermilion Fairways* at Cook is a beautiful 9-hole, par 36 public course. An 18-hole course is in Virginia, where the public course is par 70. There are other public courses at Eveleth, Hibbing, Hoyt Lakes and Babbitt.

For further information, contact:
Tower-Soudan Chamber of Commerce
P.O. Box 776-B
Tower, MN 55790
Phone: 218-753-2301

RESORT

Bayview Lodge

2001 Bay View Drive, Tower, MN 55790
Phone: 218-753-4825 or 800-628-1607
Hrs: Open year-round.
Major credit cards accepted.

With more than 1,200 miles of shoreline, 365 islands, protected bays and inlets, drop offs and structure, Lake Vermilion provides the perfect backdrop for a relaxing and enjoyable vacation. And there is no resort cozier or more welcoming than Bay View Lodge.

Bay View Lodge is owned by Bob and Barbe Airis, two transplanted suburbanites who know exactly what makes a memorable vacation. They've recently taken over and renovated the cabins and lodge to offer what they hope will soon be a AAA rated establishment. Eight rustic, knotty-pine cabins all come with a beautiful view of the lake and fantastic sunsets.

Also with an outstanding view, the restaurant offers fine dining with that special northwoods ambiance. In the summer, be sure to catch their famous Sunday Champagne brunch.

The bar is a fun gathering place—one of the "hot spots" on the lake. Daily drink specials are offered along with a pool table, darts and jukebox.

Not to forget the kids, they'll want to check out the game room with video games, the safe and sandy beach, swing and play area, plus free use of canoes, kayaks and paddleboats. There is a special activities director for children 12 and under plus a sitter service is available.

Sports fishermen will especially appreciate that Lake Vermilion is stocked with over one million walleye fry annually! For your convenience, they offer a wet boathouse, bait and tackle shop and they even have dock boys to care for your boat and clean your fish.

RESORT

Glenmore Resort

1017 Glenmore Dr., Box 728, Tower, MN 55790
Phone: 800-538-4101
Hrs: Open year-round.
Major credit cards accepted.

Northern Exposure the Minnesota way—that's Glenmore Resort located on spectacular Lake Vermilion. This resort doesn't just have cabins, it has vacation homes ranging from rustic elegance, complete with antiques, to contemporary luxury with all the finest appointments—fireplaces, dishwashers, microwaves, knotty pine interiors and more. In short, top quality lodging in a pristine year-round setting.

Glenmore Resort is situated in a secluded bay of a lake that was deeply etched by glaciers thousands of years ago. Now, hundreds of bays, peninsulas, rocky points and islands make this lake ideal for both fishing and exploring. During the winter season, they offer Arctic Cat snowmobiles for rent to explore the thousands of miles of trails nearby. Winter at Glenmore is indeed magical with snow covered tall pines, the still lake and daily visits of deer and partridge. When most resorts have closed and visitors gone, Glenmore remains open with seven cabins that are warm and snug with indoor baths and fully equipped kitchens.

Cabin 1 is spacious and has a freestanding fireplace, nice after a day in the crisp, fresh air. Cabin 2 is located at the edge of the lake and is charming and rustic with french windows. Cabin 3 has two bedrooms and a beautiful view across the harbor and out onto Pike Bay. Cabin 4 is located high on a hill with a sweeping view of the lake. Cabins 5 and 6 offer contemporary luxury, each with two bedrooms, cathedral ceilings, fireplaces, microwaves, dishwashers and private lake view through a large expanse of glass. Cabin 7, "the Hunter's Lodge," is new and features all knotty-pine and native cedar, open beam ceilings, fireplace, microwave, dishwasher and two bedrooms, all nestled in heavy pines.

Here you'll experience the delightful diversions of Minnesota's famous summers—warm days and cool nights. Splash with the kids on one of the sand beaches. Water ski. Fish, and fry up your catch. Sail into a colorful sunset. And meet new friends around the nightly campfire. You can do it all at Glenmore Resort.

RESORTS

End of the Trail Lodge

4284 End of the Trail Lane
Tower, MN 55790
Phone: 218-753-6971 or 800-353-0123
Open year-round.

End of the Trail Lodge is really the beginning—the start of a memorable vacation in one of the most beautiful and scenic areas of Minnesota. It's located at a private point on spectacular Lake Vermilion. The lake features over 1200 miles of shoreline, 365 islands and is considered one of the most beautiful lakes in the world.

Visitors will find many species of wildlife here. Deer, timber-wolves, beaver, otters, bald eagles, osprey, loons and many songbirds grace these lands. Of course, fishing is fantastic for walleye, musky, northern, small and large mouth bass, plus crappies.

End of the Trail has just 5 cabins, providing an intimate setting consistent with the natural surroundings. The two-bedroom cabins are built right on the lake edge. Other cabins sleep six and are fully equipped for year-round fun.

The Boundary Waters Canoe Area is close enough to make day trips to that unique wilderness area. Guides are available, too.

◆ ◆ ◆ ◆ ◆ ◆ ◆

Gruben's Marina

4296 Arrowhead Point Road, Tower, MN 55790
Phone: 218-753-5000. Hrs.: Summer: Daily 8 a.m. to 7 p.m. Winter: Owner resides on premises. No credit cards accepted. Checks welcome.

When it comes to family fun and access to great fishing and snow sports on Lake Vermilion, Gruben's Marina has been providing it since the 1920s. Gruben's offers two- and three-bedroom cabins, a convenience grocery store, dock space and dry storage, and Mercury outboard motor sales and service.

Gruben's recently completed Phase 1 of its facilities upgrade project. A new gas dock is in place, with new self-service pumps. An attractive, new three-bedroom, two-bath cabin has been built on an old cabin site and it retains the historic 1928 fireplace.

All cabins have a great lake view and are fully equipped for housekeeping and include TV's, VCR's and microwaves. Most cabins have fireplaces. Boat and motor rentals are available for summer fishing. Year-round cabin rentals are now available and snowmobilers are welcome.

Now, more than ever, Gruben's Marina is a great place for complete summer (and winter) vacation accommodations.

TOURS

Soudan Underground Mine State Park

P.O. Box 335
Soudan, MN 55782
Phone: 218-753-2245
Hrs: Seasonally, 9:30 a.m.-4 p.m.

No tour of Minnesota's Iron Range would be complete without a visit to the very birthplace of Minnesota's Iron Industry, the Soudan Mine. Of the many underground shaft mines that once dotted the three major iron ranges of northern Minnesota, the Soudan is the sole survivor.

Today, Soudan Underground Mine State Park offers the rare opportunity to tour one-half mile underground where the miners last worked in 1962. In fact, the Soudan is the only mine of its type in the world open to the general public for tours.

The one hour guided underground tour begins in the visitor center which is housed in the mine's original "dry house," where miners changed and dried their clothes for the next shift. Here are artifacts and photo displays from the mining era, models depicting the mine's design, displays of geological wonder taken from the mine—such as the beautiful Soudan crystal, core samples, pyrite crystals and more.

An orientation film contains actual US Steel footage taken underground during the last days of the mine's operation. Now don hard hats and head 2,341 feet underground via the "cage and shaft" system to the 27th level. Once underground though, the ride is not over. You then board an underground railroad and ride 3/4 mile to the 300' by 200' Montana "stope," the name given by miners for an ore producing cavity. This is the last area where the miners worked before the mine closed. A short climb up a spiral staircase will take you up into the actual working area where you can see and experience how the miners removed the valuable ore.

When you arrive back on the surface, be sure to visit the Engine House and talk to the hoistman. A short walking tour takes you to the Crusher, the Drill Shop and the open pit areas. The Crusher is the building where the extremely hard Soudan ore was crushed and moved into rail cars for shipment to docks on Lake Superior. The next stop on your tour is the Drill Shop where you can see more displays and the actual equipment used by surface workers to keep the drill bits sharp enough to pierce the resistant Soudan ores. The mine is a constant 50 degrees year-round, so wear a jacket and sturdy foot gear.

TWO HARBORS

The first of Minnesota's iron ports, Two Harbors still is a major shipping center for the Iron Range taconite and iron industry. Visitors today can tour the enormous, 1,388-foot long *Duluth and Iron Range Railroad Loading Dock* and watch 1,000-foot ore boats glide into port. *The Lighthouse Point and Harbor Museum* located on Agate Bay feature exhibits of the history of the shipping of iron ore. The restored *Duluth Mesabi and Iron Range Railroad Depot* houses the *Lake County Historical Society Museum,* with its intriguing displays of the area's logging, fishing, and railroad heritage. During the summer, Two Harbors arranges summer band concerts in the city park and serves as the starting point of the nationally known *Grandma's Marathon.*

For further information, contact:
Two Harbors Area Chamber of Commerce
P.O. Box 39
Two Harbors, MN 55616
Phone: 218-834-2600

HISTORIC SITE

Split Rock Lighthouse & History Center	A Minnesota Historical Society Site. Hwy. 61, 20 miles NE of Two Harbors. 2010 Hwy. 61 E., Two Harbors, MN 55616 **Phone: 218-226-4372** Hrs: May 15-Oct. 16 Daily 9 a.m.-5 p.m., Oct. 21-May 4 Fri-Sun. noon-4 p.m. Closed Jan. Admission charge.

Split Rock Lighthouse was completed in 1910 in response to the many shipping disasters along the treacherous North Shore. It operated for some 60 years before closing in 1969 due to the sophistication of new navigational equipment.

The Minnesota Historical Society has restored the lighthouse and its companion building to their pre-1924 appearance. Visitors can tour the brick light tower, a fog-signal building, the keepers' dwellings and several outbuildings. The ruins of a tramway are still visible. The History Center features an award-winning film and exhibit about the lighthouse and the development of the North Shore, as well as a museum shop.

Split Rock Lighthouse's picturesque setting and convenient location just off the North Shore Highway have made it one of the most visited lighthouses in the country. Today, the lonely brick building still perches defiantly atop the cliff above Superior's waters—a stalwart legacy of a bygone era.

RESORT

Superior Shores

10 Superior Shores Dr.
Two Harbors, MN 55616
Phone: 800-242-1988 or 218-834-5671
All major credit cards accepted.

If you're looking for the breathtaking beauty only the North Shore offers, come to Superior Shores for a wonderful vacation. Imagine—the pine and birch forest, the ragged rocks, the famous North Shore waterfalls, majestic Lake Superior and Split Rock Lighthouse. Now put them together with a cozy fireplace in a gorgeous townhouse. Add tennis, swimming and a beautiful lodge and you'll have "The North Shore done right," the motto for Superior Shores resort.

Just twenty miles up the shore from Duluth, Superior Shores is a stunning year-round retreat run by the same family for 60 years! Guests enjoy both indoor and outdoor pools, jacuzzis, tennis courts, snowmobile and cross-country ski trails. The lodge features casual dining and a fireside lounge.

Rustic one- and two-bedroom Lodge Suites have dramatic views of Lake Superior and the surrounding woods. They feature a fireplace, jacuzzi and a king-sized bed with down comforter. Lakehome townhouses are located right on the shore for a spectacular view of the lake. These units sleep from two to eight and have fireplaces, too. Both the Lakehomes and Lodge Suites have large decks with gas BBQ grill, color television, VCR, telephone, linens, gourmet kitchen with dishwasher, stove, oven, microwave, coffeemaker, toaster and cooking utensils.

Superior Shores is tucked away on a marvelous peninsula on Lake Superior with miles of shoreline on each side. It offers guests the peace and solitude that is unique to the North Shore.

SPECIALTY SHOPS

Mimi's Sportswear/ Agate City	731 7th Ave. (Hwy 61), Two Harbors, MN 55616. **Phone: (Mimi's) 218-834-3658 (Agate City) 218-834-2304.** Hrs: 10 a.m.-5 p.m., closed Mon. Visa and MasterCard accepted.

Tired of shopping with the masses? Try the personal and intimate atmosphere at Mimi's, offering a complete collection of clothing and accessories for women. Mimi's and Agate City Rocks & Gifts are located in the historic P.K. Anderson house built in 1896 and now remodeled for retail sales.

Mimi's owner, Cherrol Soiseth, takes great pride in offering the highest quality goods at a reasonable cost. Contemporary, classic and ethnic clothes can be found, including shirts, skirts, sweaters, jeans, jewelry, jackets, shorts, hats, T-shirts, scarves and more.

Shoppers will recognize such names as Basic Threads, Cambridge Dry Goods, Chic Jeans, Debra Lubell, IVY-CHU, Jones New York Sport, Michigan Rag, Renee Hauer, Sangam, We Be Bop, What's In Store? and many others. Mimi's also offers gift wrapping, mailing and gift certificates.

Agate City Rocks and Gifts is just downstairs from Mimi's. Here, owners Robert and Nancy Lynch have created a mecca for 'rock hounds' and they offer a large selection of interesting gifts, as well. They have collector quality Lake Superior Agates, Amethyst, Thomsonite and Green Stone. Among the more interesting gifts are paintings, pottery and prints by local artists plus a large selection of gold and silver jewelry, much of it created right at the shop. In fact, they will custom design jewelry for you using any material you select.

One unusual sidelight is the early North American and American Indian artifact museum on the premises. This shop has been in operation for over 30 years!

VIRGINIA

In the early days, Virginia was both a mining and a logging town, which survived two devastating fires. It was a region of great white and Norway pine, crisscrossed by trails of voyagers, trappers, gold rush prospectors, missionaries and Sioux Indians. Today, it remains a hub of activity, literally at the crossroads of major intersecting roadways.

ATTRACTIONS & EVENTS

Located in the heart of the *Mesabi Range,* this "Queen City of the North" offers visitors a kaleidoscope of experiences that combine the beauty of nature with the spectacular vistas created by the advent of iron ore mining. Area lakes make a perfect setting for boating. Four miles north is the *Laurentian Divide*, a phenomenon of nature where all waters divide, one side flowing north and the other south. Hiking trails offer an excellent view of this unique area.

Golfers can look to the 18-hole municipal golf course for their sport. *Olcott Park* offers picnic areas, playgrounds and a lush, year-round greenhouse. *"The World's Largest Floating Loon,"* on Virginia's *Silver Lake* in the center of town is bordered by duck and goose sanctuary trails that literally stop traffic.

The *Finntown/Kaleva Hall* and the *Virginia Heritage Museum* provide an authentic taste of days gone by when mining and logging ruled the Iron Trail and the lives of its inhabitants. The story of Virginia's rich mining history is visible at *Mineview in the Sky* and the *Oldtown-Finntown Mineview,* providing impressive views of deep open pit mines.

Annual traditions like *Land of the Loon Ethnic Arts and Crafts Festival* celebrate the area's ethnic diversity with over 200 artisans displaying their crafts, along with music, games, milk carton boat races and plenty of food. The annual *Snowmobile Grass Drag Races* held Labor Day weekend are co-sponsored with the city of Eveleth. The races offer both riders and spectators a thrilling preview of winter adventures.

For further information, contact:
Virginia Chamber of Commerce
Box 1072
Virginia, MN 55792
Phone: 800-777-7395

SPECIALTY SHOPS

Canelake's Candy	414 Chestnut Street, Virginia, MN 55792 **Phone: 218-741-1557** Hrs.: Mon.-Sat. 9 a.m.-5 p.m.

Originally started in 1905, the founder of Canelake's Candy Kitchen believed in making his candies with the freshest and best ingredients possible. Grade AA butter, real whipped cream and hand-roasted nuts were used. Chocolates were hand-dipped on marble tables, hand-rolled, hand-decorated and the Canelake boxes were hand-packed. Today this art and tradition are still carried on at Canelake's Candy using the same wonderful recipes the founder created. An original Canelake secret candy recipe is known as "Hot Air." Crisp, fluffy, light and airy, this old-time sensation is an all time best seller! Other selected candies include caramels, dipped nuts, toffee, creams, brittles and bars.

At the 1988 St. Paul Technical Institute candy judging contest, Canelake's Candy was said to be the best assortment of candies in Minnesota. In 1990, the *L.A. Times* name them "best of America by mail." They have a moccasin showroom and have stuffed toy animals, too!

◆ ◆ ◆ ◆ ◆ ◆ ◆

Italian Bakery	205 S. First Street. Virginia, MN 55792. **Phone: 218-741-3464** Hrs.: Mon.-Sat. 5:30 a.m.-5 p.m. Closed Sunday.

The Italian Bakery located in Virginia, the "Queen City" of Minnesota's Iron Range, was founded in 1910. This family-owned business has expanded as its reputation grew.

Using Old World traditional recipes, the Italian Bakery potica and fruitcake gained a national word-of-mouth reputation. In 1965, the Italian Bakery began a mail order business, shipping their delicious potica and fruitcakes all over the world. The potica filling is secret. It requires the finest ingredients: flour, pure creamy butter, whole eggs, honey, lots of walnuts, pure vanilla and no preservatives. It retains freshness by refrigeration or freezing and the same integrity is maintained with the fruitcakes.

Try a tradition that people have been raving about since the turn of the century. Send friends a treat. The walnut and walnut raisin potica, fruitcake and Minnesota wild rice are sent year-round.

Owners/operators are Joe and Bette Prebonich.

TAYLORS FALLS

The logging town of Taylors Falls, with a picturesque setting on the beautiful St. Croix River, is one of the most fascinating historical towns in the state. Incorporated in 1858, the same year Minnesota became the 32nd state of the Union, it was settled mainly by New Englanders; the many examples of Federal and Greek Revival style architecture reflect this heritage. In fact, this quaint town has preserved more than one-third of its original 19th-century buildings.

ATTRACTIONS & EVENTS

Foremost among these is the *Taylors Falls Public Library,* built in 1854 as a tailor shop and residence. In 1861, the city founders erected the *Methodist Church* in the *Angel Hill Historic District* an area of fine homes, a schoolhouse, and a jail recreating an eastern village, and the church has been in continuous use ever since. Angel Hill is also site of the imposing *W.H.C. Folsom House.* Built by city founder and logging baron William Folsom in 1854, costumed guides now offer tours of this five-bedroom pine home.

But Taylors Falls boasts numerous other attractions. Because of its location on the St. Croix River, the town is an ideal starting point for river excursions on historical riverboats with *Taylors Falls Scenic Boat Tours,* as well as for fishing and for canoe and boat rentals. The river provides an excellent view of the many intriguing rock formations and giant potholes left behind by the grinding glaciers that once dominated the area.

Wild Mountain Water Park and Alpine Slides, with its water slides, tube rides, and breathtaking ride down the same hill used for downhill skiing in the winter, features the most refreshing fun in the area. Two major parks, the *Wild River State Park* and the *Interstate Park,* complete the outdoor recreational opportunities in Taylors Falls.

To celebrate the heritage of the city, which before the advent of tourism revolved around the logging industry, the city arranges the *Wannigan Days* during the third weekend of June, and *Log Jam Days* during the last weekend of July.

For further information, contact:
Taylors Falls Chamber of Commerce
Taylors Falls, MN 55084
Phone: 612-465-6661

Bluff Country

They came north by Mississippi riverboat. At first, just a trickle; then, a torrent—settlers drawn to the rugged bluff country of southeastern Minnesota. They came from places like Germany, Norway, Poland, Sweden and they laid claim to the sweeping vistas, the clear rivers, hardwood forests, lakes and fertile soils they found here in abundance.

Where the settlers entered the Mississippi's Hiawatha Valley near Minnesota's southern border, that mighty river narrows its course and gradually there emerges from the flatlands parallel ramparts of steep, wooded bluffs rising hundreds of feet toward the sky. Cliffs stand out above stately oaks, revealing bands of crumbling sandstone and dolomite formed millions of years ago when the region was submerged by a warm and shallow inland sea.

These imposing bluffs, dissected by deep ravines, were left intact while the rest of the state was being razed by ice-age glaciers 20,000 years ago. In the shadows of these magnificent bluffs are clear-flowing streams and rivers that served the settlers as highways for traveling into the dense forests and rolling prairies to the west. These lands were pristine and untamed then—and they remain much the same today largely through the efforts of the people who now inhabit the area. The woods yet teem with deer and wild turkey, the waters still run clear with trout.

Today, the descendants of the early settlers encourage travelers to discover for themselves the rich land and to become acquainted with its history. Quaint river towns display outstanding examples of Victorian architecture and numerous historic sites and museums chronicle a colorful past and bespeak hope for the future.

The Father of Waters offers a wealth of recreational possibilities. Mississippi River houseboats are rented for cruising from town to town in the tradition of steamboat pilots like Mark Twain. Canoeists explore the backwaters with birdbook and binoculars. Anglers attempt to lure Mississippi catfish to join them for dinner. The Mississippi's naturally formed Lake Pepin is perfect for sailing or waterskiing. In fact, it was right here in 1922 that an adventurous fellow named Ralph Samuleson made sports history by strapping eight-foot pine boards onto his feet and allowing himself to be pulled behind a motorboat.

Turn westward from the Mississippi's banks, travel up any wooded draw and the streams and forests of the Bluff Country will envelope you. Beautiful state parks like Whitewater, Beaver Creek Valley and Nerstrand Woods offer the finest camping, picnicking and hiking adventures. Tour the underground caverns at Harmony's Niagara Caves and at the Mystery Caves near Forestville State Park, where horseback riders roam miles of wooded trails. New discoveries await around every bend on the canoe routes and bike paths of the Cannon and Root Rivers.

Fall is a special time in the bluff country. Color overtakes the forests that cover rugged ridges and deep valleys. This backdrop of scarlets and golds frames the historic towns that dot the landscape. In orchards that sit like crowns above the Mississippi, it's time to slow down, enjoy the mellow color and pick wonderful apples that thrive in these ancient soils. Here, too, the settlers left their mark upon the land. Neighbors thought John Harris was crazy when he planted a few spindly apple trees atop the bluff near La Crescent. But when the trees flourished, others followed his lead. Now, more than a century later, hundreds of acres of apple orchards are grown in and around La Crescent, the self-proclaimed apple capitol of Minnesota. During La Crescent's annual Applefest, the aroma of fresh baked apple pie fills the air. More than 50,000 visitors come to enjoy the events. Many apple growers give tours.

Autumn roils from the bluffs to the river's edge, where Steamboat Gothic and Queen Anne homes line the streets of the once-busy river ports. Even the great river seems to linger now, with such beauty at hand. These homes were built in the river traffic's heyday, often by the barons of business who made their fortunes opening the land. Now these homes flourish as bed and breakfasts, antique shops and historic sites open for tours.

In the Root River Valley, old homes, a former furniture factory and even a vintage jailhouse welcome guests as bed and breakfasts. Storefronts house shops offering antiques and crafts, many handcrafted by native Minnesotans. This still valley remains easygoing as well as beautiful.

Visitors who listen well will hear the echoes of long-gone voices in the Polka music spilling forth from entertainment spots. Many buildings that once served the interests of grain, pottery and shoemaking now house a riot of shops, restaurants and lodging.

Bluff country was and remains a land of beauty, history and pride.

AUSTIN

Located just 12 miles north of the Iowa border, Austin sits on the banks of the Cedar River, proving the settlers' first rule of thumb: Always live near a water supply. The river provided power to the sawmills and flour mills, as well as good water to the settlers and the Sioux Indians native to the area. Thus, Austin drew industry to it. The Hormel Company opened in 1887 and has been the primary impetus for growth in the modern era.

Austin provides exquisite beauty in a natural setting while in close proximity to two major metropolitan areas, the Twin Cities and Rochester. 1991 marked the 100th Anniversary of the Hormel Company and of the Austin Daily Herald, two landmarks in Austin's history. One hundred years ago George Hormel wanted to make his company the largest in southern Minnesota; today, it's one of the largest in the world. The Weyerhauser Company is another thriving industry in Austin. It has been manufacturing shipping containers since 1954.

ATTRACTIONS & EVENTS

Austin is the site of the *Miss Minnesota Pageant,* held in early June. This is the official preliminary to the Miss America Pageant. Austin has played host to this event for more than two decades.

Cedar River Days are held midsummer with events including a street dance and a community breakfast.

The National Barrow Show is held in mid-September, attracting people from all over the world to attend the swine exhibition and sale.

In February the *Dobbins Creek Ski Run* is scheduled. It is a 10-kilometer ski race at the Hormel Nature Center which allows men and women in various age groups to participate.

The Jay C. Hormel Nature Center teaches visitors about nature and its creatures. The center is only four years old but has become a very popular attraction.

For more information, contact:
The Austin Area Chamber of Commerce
300 N. Main Street, P.O. Box 864
Austin, MN 55912
Phone: 507-437-4563 or 800-444-5713

LODGING

Holiday Inn *Austin Holidome* *Conference Center*	1701 W. Fourth Street. N.W. Austin, MN 55912 **Phone: 507-433-1000** All major credit cards accepted.

The Holiday Inn Austin is centrally located near Albert Lea and Rochester, and serves northern Iowa as well as southern Minnesota. It offers accommodations and amenities designed to please both business and pleasure travelers, from meeting rooms and shuttle service to swimming pools and a nightclub.

Poolside guest rooms have private verandas; luxury suites offer a whirlpool in every room. The Holidome was created to provide a year-round tropical paradise with three pools, a whirlpool, sauna, billiard and ping-pong tables, arcade games, putting green and an extensive Health Club.

The Conference Center is a sophisticated facility, with state-of-the-art audio/visual equipment and trained sales and catering staff. Four restaurants are available for a variety of dining experiences. Guests may enjoy American/Continental cuisine in the atmosphere of a turn-of-the century library, or the open-air grill and live entertainment in the high-energy nightclub.

RESTAURANT

The Old Mill	Two Miles North of I-90, Exit at Sixth St., NE, Austin, MN 55912. **Phone: 507-437-2076** Hrs: (Lunch) Mon. - Fri. 11:30 a.m. - 2 p.m. (Dinner) Mon. - Sat. 5:30 p.m. - 10 p.m. Closed on Sundays. All major credit cards accepted.

Beautiful antique chairs flank solid wooden tables under hand-hewn beamed ceilings. The scene outside the window is of the historic Ramsey Dam over the Red Cedar River. And inside...classic American food in this delightfully historic setting.

Built in 1872 by Mathew Gregson of Lancashire, England, the Ramsey Mill originally produced flour from the grist brought by farmers in horse-drawn wagons. The three-story wooden building housed a wheelpit and grinding floor and the dam was constructed of logs chinked with dirt and stones, later replaced by concrete. It was a working mill until its renovation into a restaurant in the 1950s, a tradition owner Dave Forland has worked hard to maintain.

Enjoy filet mignon, top sirloin steak, broiled filet of pike or Alaskan king crab, complemented by a wide selection of fine wines. For dessert, choose from a variety of mousse cakes, including Chocolate Truffle Mousse Cake or Almond Amaretto. The Old Mill is perfect for an intimate meal but can accommodate large parties, too.

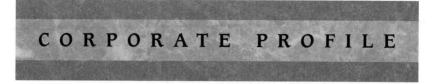

CORPORATE PROFILE

Hormel Foods Corporation　　With little fanfare and a whole lot of hope, George A. Hormel started his meatpacking business in 1891 in an abandoned creamery in Austin, just one-half mile from Main Street.

The location was a beautiful grove of oak trees near the Red Cedar River where, in the winter, George's workers hand-sawed and removed huge cakes of ice to provide needed refrigeration for the plant.

George also opened up a retail store on Mill Street (affectionately called Bourbon Street by the locals because of its impressive lineup of saloons), where he sold a variety of meats but specialized in "nice cuts of pork."

Things have changed. And if George were here today, he'd be bursting his buttons with pride because Hormel is now a world marketer ranked 24th among all food companies in the Fortune 500. Its products are sold on five continents and distributed in more than 36 countries. Of course, it still calls Austin home.

Employing more than 8,000 people, Hormel sales in 1993 approached $3 billion, while net earnings were the highest in company history, up for the tenth consecutive year.

Hormel successes have come about largely because its focus has evolved from that of a commodity producer of meat products to a worldwide marketer of packaged food products. Symbolic of this is the name change from original Geo. A. Hormel & Company to the simpler, more all-encompassing Hormel Foods Corporation.

Proof of this direction change is the fact that over the last 10 years the portion of revenues generated by "value-added" packaged food products has risen sharply to an estimated 65 to 75 percent of the total.

Those who have followed Hormel growth over the years mention two factors as having contributed most to the company's success: integrity and innovation.

While it may sound corny in an age of business sophistication, mega-mergers and gigantic corporations, Hormel's emphasis on integrity stands out. A stickler on fair dealing—"We will never condone 'sharp practices,'" said founder George—the company has developed a reputation for the highest quality products.

Similarly, the drive to innovate stems from George A. himself. "Originate, don't imitate," he declared. Hormel "firsts" include development of the grade-and-yield system of hog buying; introduction of the first canned ham in America; production of such well-known market leaders as SPAM luncheon meat; Hormel chili; Dinty Moore beef stew; Cure 81 ham; Black Label bacon, among others; and, more recently, introduction of hundreds of new products that fit the active lifestyles of today's health-conscious consumer.

The Hormel Museum was established in observance of the 100th anniversary of Geo. A. Hormel & Company and allows visitors a special look back at the history that made this story. The museum is organized into eight areas. These are: George A. Hormel's office; Hormel family; Company chief executive officers; Austin plant operations; other Company branches and plants; Hormel publications; Austin sports and community events; and products/marketing. Items assembled for the exhibit came from the Company's archives or were loaned by current and retired Hormelites.

The museum is located at the OakPark Mall situated along Interstate 90 at the northwest edge of Austin. The exhibit is open each day of the week, Monday through Friday from 10 a.m. to 9 p.m.; Saturday from 10 a.m. to 5 p.m.; and Sunday, noon to 5 p.m. No admission fee is charged.

Visitors are invited to relive the early years of one of America's top meat and food processing firms and get an educational glimpse of the Company's heritage.

CANNON FALLS

The French had named it "Riviere aux Canots" or river of canoes. English speaking settlers took note of the emphasis on "Canots" and took it to mean "cannon." Thus, the river became the Cannon River and the surrounding area Cannon Falls.

Welch Mill offers canoeing and tubing down the Cannon River. *The Cannon Valley Trail* is one of the area's most popular attractions because it is used for hiking, biking and skiing. The trail was judged by *Bicycling Magazine* as one of the dozen most beautiful in the nation.

Annual events include *Cabin Fever Days* held the last weekend in January. *The Cannon Valley Fair* is part of the July Fourth activities, with all of the attractions of a small town fair. The *Cannon Valley Sled Dog Races* are held each January.

For further information, contact:
Cannon Falls Chamber of Commerce
103 North Fourth Street
Cannon Falls, MN 55009   Phone: 507-263-2289

BED & BREAKFAST

Candlewick Country Inn	300 West Mill Street, Cannon Falls, MN 55009 **Phone: 507-263-0879.** Hrs: Open year-round. Visa and MasterCard accepted.

Wanting to relocate in a smaller community, Tom and Dona Morgan chose the friendly town of Cannon Falls to call "home." They have spent enormous effort in renovating this historic home which they opened as a Bed & Breakfast in June 1993. The Morgans enjoy being innkeepers and specialize in catering to their guests' wishes.

The Candlewick Inn, the circa-1880 Benjamin Van Campen residence, is a comfortable country home, furnished in antiques and carefully selected reproductions. It's an inviting, sunwashed place where the cookie jar is always full. Choose from Michelle's Room done in pastel rose wallpaper, with queen-sized brass bed flanked by tall windows with private bath. The quaint Garden View Room is at the top of the grand staircase and features an antique ash double bed, matching Gentlemen's dresser with Early American stenciling and handmade quilt. The latest addition, Henry's Hideaway, features bay windows and twin beds. Breakfast is a memorable occasion. A smoke-free B&B, the Candlewick will warm your stay in Cannon Falls.

BED & BREAKFAST

Country Quiet Inn

Eight miles south of Cannon Falls on County Rd. 9, 37295 112th Ave. Way, Cannon Falls, MN 55009. **Phone: 612-258-4406 or 800-258-1843.** Hrs: Open year-round. Visa, MasterCard, AmEX and Discovery accepted.

When June and Dave Twaites moved to the country more than 20 years ago, they had no idea that someday they'd share their little piece of paradise with you. But that's what's happened. They opened the Country Quiet Inn in 1993, offering country quiet for rest and relaxation, country charm that treats you like family, country elegance in a home built in 1894 but updated extensively and country comfort with cool summer breezes and a serene setting among rolling hills, beautiful flowers and gorgeous trees.

There are just two guest rooms with shared bath. One has a queen size bed, the other a king. The bedrooms and bathroom have their own heating/air-conditioning, each room has a small table and chairs and a 20-inch TV/video player. The whole place is smoke-free and unlike most B&B's, actually encourages you to bring the kids along.

Continental breakfast is included and, if you're not in a hurry, June will make the breakfast of a lifetime for a nominal fee. Come as guests, leave as friends. Let country quiet work for you.

◆ ◆ ◆ ◆ ◆ ◆ ◆

Quill & Quilt

615 West Hoffman St., Cannon Falls, MN 55009 **Phone: 507-263-5507 or 800-488-3849** Hrs: Open year-round. Visa and MasterCard accepted.

With its oak and Italian marble fireplace and its quilt-covered four-poster beds, the Quill & Quilt offers a unique blend of Colonial Revival elegance and country comfort. From each evening's gourmet coffee and desserts, to the dainty chocolates you'll find on your pillow, to the morning's hearty breakfast, this turn-of-the-century bed & breakfast offers exceptional taste in picturesque Cannon Falls. Guests enjoy breakfast in the dining room, on one of the inn's many porches or delivered to their room. Choose from four distinct rooms, each with its own individual atmosphere, including the Colwell Suite with its double whirlpool. Guests also enjoy the spacious common areas.  The finished basement contains a gift shop, cable TV and videotaped movies, a guest refrigerator, books, games and an extensive collection of baseball memorabilia. Rooms are air-conditioned and smoke-free. Ask about Quilter's Getaway Weekends and mid-week specials.

CAMPGROUND

Cannon Falls Campground

Off Highway 19, 30365 Oak Lane, Cannon Falls, MN 55009-4026. **Phone: 507-263-3145 or 800-658-2514.** Hrs: May 1-Oct. 31. Visa and MasterCard accepted.

Loyalty is the true test of a campground. Is it good enough to keep 'em coming back year after year?

At the Cannon Falls Campground, the answer is 'yes'. Maybe it's the amenities. There are 150 sites available, many wooded with water and electricity. There's a large heated swimming pool, volleyball, basketball and horseshoe pits, softball field and bike rentals. Even a recreational building, laundry, store and free hot showers.

Perhaps it's the location, in scenic Cannon Falls, near the Cannon River and the Cannon Valley Bike Trail. Or could it be the people?

Joanne and Ernie Roeber do all of the little things right, including offering free outdoor movies for kids and adults every weekend, arranging cribbage, horseshoe and volleyball games and concocting special events like "Christmas in July." They even offer a small church service for those who want it. They'll do what it takes to make camping in Cannon Falls worth a return trip.

COUNTRY COTTAGE

The Hart House

305 West Cannon Street, Cannon Falls, MN 55009. **Phone: 507-263-3617 or 800-535-6382.** Hrs: Open year-round seven days a week. Visa, MasterCard and Discover accepted.

It seems an odd combination at first, a butcher shop/deli and a Country Inn. But the Lorentz family has brought the same sense of quality and service that has characterized their family business for 25 years to a wonderful new Inn in Cannon Falls.

The Hart House is a newly refurbished, country-decorated two-bedroom cottage just a stone's throw from the Cannon River and the spectacular Cannon Valley Bicycle Trail. The cottage comes completely furnished with linens and towels, food and soft drinks in the fridge, fruit in a basket and cookies in the jar. Cable television and air conditioning add just enough of the modern touch.

The setting is spectacular. There is a front porch with table and chairs, a back deck with patio furniture and grill and a sloping lawn down to the river. And if you get hungry, the deli is right next door. They'll even have a meal ready for your arrival if you like and after a restful night, send you on your way with a box lunch. A great choice.

SPECIALTY SHOPS

| *Auntie Maude's Cracker Barrel* | 333 W. Main, Cannon Falls, MN 55009. **Phone:** 507-263-4410. Hrs: Mon. - Fri. 9:30 a.m. - 5:30 p.m. Open Thursdays until 8 p.m. Saturdays 9 a.m.-5 p.m. Sundays Noon-4 p.m. Visa, MasterCard, Discover and AmEx accepted. |

There's nothing serious about Auntie Maude's Cracker Barrel. It's just for fun.

Located next door to Pine & Prints and the Kitty Applegate Emporium, Auntie Maude's is a one-stop shop for sweets and treats and fun gifts. They carry a complete line of rubber stamps and stickers from a variety of manufacturers and feature in-store video demonstrations.

Decorated in pinks and greens and washed in the smell of candy, Auntie Maude's is the perfect addition to a wonderful collection of shops in Cannon Falls.

◆ ◆ ◆ ◆ ◆ ◆ ◆

| *Hoffmans Doll House* | 212 North 9th Street, Cannon Falls, MN 55009 **Phone: 507-263-2283** Hours: 10 a.m.-8 p.m. Mon.-Sat. Call for Sunday appointments. No credit cards accepted. |

The joy Mary Hoffman experiences each time she creates a new doll is not unlike the joy of a little girl at Christmas discovering her very first. What began as an interest in dolls turned into a fulfilling retirement project for Mary and Carl Hoffman. They produce exquisite porcelain creations, ranging in size from less than an inch to 27 inches, including baby dolls, antique reproductions, fashion, birthday, ethnic, grandpa & grandmas, Mr. & Mrs, Claus, elves, angels and many modern dolls.

After pouring into molds, drying and cleaning, they are kiln fired at 2500 degrees from 9-12 hours, then a 24 hour cooldown before sanding, scrubbing, oiling and finally painting. They are usually fired 3 times before they are finished. Mary offers classes for all and it usually takes 3 to 4 classes to finish a doll.

There is plenty of handmade clothing, shoes, socks and wigs with which to dress up your doll. A supply of furniture is also available. Free group tours are welcome by appointment.

SPECIALTY SHOPS

Pine & Prints	103 S. 4th Street, Cannon Falls, MN 55009 **Phone: 507-263-5360.** Hrs: Mon.-Fri. 9:30 a.m.-5:30 p.m. Open Thursdays until 8 p.m. Saturdays 9 a.m.-5 p.m. Sundays Noon-4 p.m. Visa, MasterCard, Discover and AmEx accepted.

It began with Pine & Prints. But that's just one third of a fine trio of shops run by Larry and Maggie Sibley in Cannon Falls. It specializes in custom framing and gifts for all occasions.

Pine & Prints, located at the corner of 4th and Main in downtown Cannon Falls, features a wide array of country-style decorating accessories and a large selection of prints to add that special touch to any room in your home, including wildlife and art prints, framed or unframed, general and limited edition. Dried and silk floral arrangements are available along with linens and afghans, candles, pottery

and brassware plus dolls and stuffed animals.

You'll love the Mary Engelbreit T-shirts not to mention wooden shore birds and decoys, all attractively displayed in a charming setting.

◆ ◆ ◆ ◆ ◆ ◆

Kitty Applegate's Emporium	333 W. Main, Cannon Falls, MN 55009. **Phone:** 507-263-0189. Hrs: Mon.-Fri. 9:30 a.m.-5:30 P.M. Open Thursdays until 8 p.m. Saturdays 9 a.m.-5 p.m. Sundays Noon-4 p.m. Visa, MasterCard, Discover and AmEx accepted.

Step back in time, back into the Victorian era at Kitty Applegate's Emporium. It's located above Pine & Prints and features imaginative gifts and decorating accessories in the elegant style of the Victorian era.

Kitty Applegate's Emporium features everything from heritage lace curtains to gourmet coffees, a variety of flavored teas and cocoas, gourmet food mixes and specialty kitchen utensils. You'll also discover bath accessories, unique baby gifts, books and cards plus crystal, cut glass and much more. They also carry fabric luggage, linens, doilies and afghans.

Mood-setting music plays continuously as you browse and the gourmet coffee pot is always on.

CHATFIELD

"The Chosen Valley" is how Chatfield is described in Margaret Snyder's book, *Chatfield.* Located minutes from the *Mayo Clinic* in Rochester, it is at the headwaters of the *Root River Canoe Trail* that runs through the *Minnesota Memorial Hardwood Forest.* Gorgeous scenery is found here and around the town, as well as wild game.

The fishing opener is greeted with the *Trout Classic Fishing Contest* sponsored by the Fire Department. The *Chatfield Brass Band Free Music Lending Library* is one of a kind. It has all types of music available for lending. Visit the *Old School House,* where country art depicts scenes from rural Minnesota. *Western Days* is celebrated each August with a parade, street dancing, a horse show, and a twilight trail ride.

For further information, contact:
City of Chatfield-Clerk's Office
Thurber Community Center
21 S.E. Second Street, Chatfield, MN 55923
Phone: 507-867-3810

ART GALLERY

Country Art Gallery	One-fourth mile west of 52 on Highway 30. Chatfield, MN 55923. **Phone: 507-867-4016** Hrs: Mon.-Fri 8 a.m.-5 p.m.; Sun. by appointment. Visa and MasterCard are accepted.

Located in a rural Chatfield schoolhouse originally built in 1892, Country Art Gallery is the rural school once attended by Harvey Bernard, artist and owner. Bernard's goal is to portray the pride and plight of farmers displayed here through his works that tell the story of farm life as it once was.

The original desks and school bell, metal ceiling, hardwood floors and flag pole bring back memories of a heritage now preserved. Artworks depict farm life of yesteryear including threshing time, farmers preparing for the bitter cold winters, country roads and snow and mud, family gatherings, peaceful and rugged nature scenes, barn chores, horse and buggy days, and many more nostalgic farm scenes. These memories come to life at Country Art Gallery, where art and memories mix.

BED & BREAKFAST

Lund's Guest Houses	218 Winona St. SE, Chatfield, MN 55923 **Phone: 507-867-4003** Hrs: Open year-round. No credit cards accepted.

Located at the Northwest entrance to historic Bluff Country, Shelby and Marion Lund's traditional guest houses offer a quiet escape. Lund's takes you back to the era of the 20s, 30s and 40s, complete with period furnishings and graceful accommodations. Decor ranges from Art Deco to Victorian, complete with vintage radio and working Victrola. The two guest houses have been carefully restored with lovely coordinated furnishings, wallcoverings and linens. Each comes fully equipped, including kitchen, dishes, etc. You can rent a room or an entire house, making it a great place for a family getaway or multi-generational gathering.

Privacy is complete and all the comforts of home are available, including living rooms (one with a fireplace), dining rooms, old-fashioned kitchen plus full baths and central air. Each is located on a quiet, shady street where you can sit in the comfort of the wonderful, airy screened porch and let the world slip by. A continental breakfast is included.

MUSIC LIBRARY

Chatfield Brass Band	81 Library Lane, P.O. Box 578 Chatfield, MN 55923 **Phone: 507-867-3275** Hrs: Mon.-Fri. 8 a.m.-4 p.m.

The Chatfield Brass Band Music Lending Library is the only one of its kind in the world. Built by donations from around the world, it has over 75,000 items for lending in all categories of music. Taking pride in preserving music heritage, the lending library accumulates, catalogs, repairs, stores and makes music of all categories available on a loan basis. Tunes are in categories of Dixieland, pop, overtures, waltzes, marches, trombone smears, operettas, serenades and special music for religious and patriotic occasions, holidays and many more. A minimal service charge for staff time, postage and handling is asked to cover the cost of operations. Band and library memberships are also available for a minimal annual fee.

The Chatfield Brass Band was formed in 1969 with 16 players and has since grown to 200 players from 25 states. The lending library supplies all the music for its concerts.

FOUNTAIN

Fountain is a lovely Bluff Country town and western gateway to the *Root River State Bicycle Trail.* It is just a few miles to *Forestville State Park, Mystery Cave, Amish Tours & Niagara Cave. Fillmore County Historical Museum* has everything from arrowheads to airplanes, and extensive geology services and material are available. The latest project focuses on sinkholes which are the mark of the unusual Karst geology in the Fountain area, from which the many area caves have their origin.

The relaxed small town atmosphere is perfect for a pleasant relaxed visit. Restaurant, gift shops, tourist information and related service, B&B's, a furniture store—these are all a part of downtown Fountain. It's a perfect place to start on the Root River State bike trail because it's all downhill from there! A collection of forty antique restored Oliver tractors are housed in their own building. *Trail Days* is an annual celebration held in June. Parades, food and dances are just part of the fun. For more information, contact: *Office of Tourism,* Fountain, MN. Phone: 507-268-4406.

LODGING

Main Street Inn/Cedar Street Inn	205 Main Street/98 Cedar Street Fountain, MN 55935 **Phone: 507-268-4454** Hrs: Open year-round.

Acclaimed as one of the most scenic areas in America, Fountain is located just south of Rochester where you'll find these two lovely cottage-style guest houses. Both emphasize the whole-house rental plan, making them perfect for one family or a group of guests.

The Main Street Inn has three bedrooms, is air-conditioned and furnished in country style. The kitchen is fully equipped but guests bring their own food. The lower level has a living room, dining room, bedroom, cable TV and a full bath. There are two spacious bedrooms and a half bath upstairs. The Cedar Street Inn sleeps six and is a cozy two-bedroom, air-conditioned house with modern traditional furnishings. The living room/dining room has a queen-size hide-a-bed and cable TV. The kitchen, with breakfast nook, is completely equipped. Guests bring their own food. A full bath is on the main floor.

Both inns are ideally situated, close to 35 miles of paved bicycle trails, golf, hiking, cross-country skiing, scenic drives, canoeing, excellent trout streams, fly fishing, festivals and restaurants.

HARMONY

Harmony, one of the better names for a town, earned its title because of bickering over what the name should be. One observer called for harmony to stop the argument and it stuck!

Harmony is yet another river town built by a railroad so it could have access to abundant wood and water for its steam engines. The town still maintains a vital farming community combined with light industry.

Harmony has some of the best trout streams in the state. Endless ski and hiking trails surround the town. An additional attraction is Niagara Cave, which allows visitors to view spectacular rock formations. An Amish community permits tours and an Amish Craft Shop offers unique handcrafted items.

For further information, contact
The Harmony Tourism Center
P.O. Box 141, Dept. K.
Harmony, MN 55939
Phone: 507-886-2469

ART GALLERY

Brokken Arts	121 Main Avenue N., Harmony, MN 55939 **Phone: 507-886-2678.** Hrs: Mon., Wed., Thurs., Sat., 10 a.m.-5 p.m. Fridays 10 a.m.-8 p.m., Sundays Noon-4 p.m. Closed Tuesdays. Visa and MasterCard accepted.

If you're interested in enhancing your personal environment, you should definitely explore Brokken Arts in Harmony. Brokken Arts is Paul and Robbie Brokken's unique gallery. Inside, the 100-year-old former pool hall and Indian trading post has been transformed into a fabulous escape where Robbie displays her incredible face pottery and the work of many other artists from around the country.

For that special piece, Brokken Arts is worth the trip in and of itself. Surrounded by miles and miles of the most beautiful country-side, where else could you find seashells from around the world, first-rate artworks, not to mention gargoyles?

It's an enchanted place, with fountains bubbling, Gregorian chant music playing and mysterious and highly unusual works of art on display, including blown glass, ceramics, stained glass, handmade jewelry, fountains, nature items and toys. When the local Amish park their carriages outside, it's as if you've stepped into another time.

ATTRACTIONS & TOURS

Michel's Amish Tours

45 Main Avenue N., Harmony, MN 55939
Phone: 507-886-5392, Ext. P.
Hrs: Mon.-Sat. Call for reservations.
No Sunday tours.

Like a step back in time, Michel's Amish Tours can transport you to a world so close to home yet so far removed from life as we know it today.

Michel's Amish Tours is the one you've probably read about and heard about in Harmony, in the heart of Minnesota's historic Bluff Country. Visitors to the area can tour the largest Amish colony in the state, a peak into a life led in strong Christian convictions without many of the conveniences now taken for granted by most Americans. The area is rich in culture, history and scenic beauty.

Tours can by taken either by car or by bus and last between two and two-and-a-half hours. A trained guide will ride along in each car to give a show-and-tell tour of the unique and intriguing lifestyle of Minnesota's Amish communities. Guides also help you find traditional Amish wares that visitors may wish to purchase.

The tour views many Amish farms and stops now and then at one of their homes where visitors may purchase baskets, handmade furniture and many other Amish crafts. You'll also have the opportunity to watch the Amish working their fields with horses and machinery reminiscent of the late 1800s.

Tours also pass by a number of historic native limestone houses and barns set in scenic Bluff Country and the first church built in Fillmore County.

Bus tours are available by appointment.

TOURS

Niagara Cave

| Niagara Road, Harmony, MN 55939
| **Phone: 507-886-6606**
| Hrs: Memorial Day-Labor Day 10 a.m.-5 p.m.
| Weekends in May, Sept & Oct, 10 a.m.-4 p.m.

Do you want to be transported out of the ordinary and into the extraordinary? Taken away from the normal and into the unusual? If the answer is 'yes', then Niagara Cave is the place.

Located just two miles south of Harmony, on Highway 139, then two miles west on Niagara Road, Niagara Cave was discovered by three farm boys in 1924. The boys were looking for some lost pigs but what they found instead was a system of underground caverns, some with ceilings more than 100 feet high, and stretching for almost two miles. When they told of their discovery, nobody believed the boys but as more than three million visitors can attest, what they had stumbled upon is something truly spectacular.

Over the eons, subterranean streams carved out Niagara Cave and they are still active today, slowly wearing away the limestone and adding to the cave system. A highlight of the cave is its namesake—a spectacular 60-foot waterfall. Here, visitors can pause on Devil's Bridge built across the chasm and peer some 60 feet down to the foot of the falls or 70 feet up at the vaulted dome of the cavern. All of this is far below the surface in one of the upper Midwest's largest show caves.

Niagara Cave is a type all its own where visitors are introduced to the intricate forces that create awesome stalactites and stalagmites and take a peek at ancient fossils and crystal formations. The Stalactite Room is a fitting climax to the entire underground tour. Hanging from the ceilings are hundreds of vari-hued formations of many lengths, some very delicate, others as strong and sturdy as the walls of the cave itself. You will see some of the largest stalactites found in the upper Midwest's caves. The massive, picturesque rock formations cannot be adequately described. They must be seen to be appreciated.

You'll see the wedding chapel, where hundreds of couples have been married in sacred stillness. Visit the Wishing Well and pause to make a wish of your own. The walking tour takes about an hour. A knowledgeable and courteous guide will escort you through the lighted passages of Niagara Cave and show you the many fascinating features. An all-weather entrance building is located over the cave entrance, with a gift shop and snack area where you may relax or purchase souvenirs, gifts and refreshments. There's a 10-acre picnic area and park surrounding the entrance to the cave, as well.

A visit to Niagara Cave is truly a visit to another world, Mother Nature's underground wonderland millions of years in the making, where the temperature is always a refreshing 48 degrees.

BED & BREAKFAST

The Selvig *Guest House*	140 Center Street, Harmony, MN 55939 **Phone: 507-886-2200** Hrs: Open year-round, seven days a week. Visa and MasterCard accepted.

For 24 years, the former home of Dr. Carlus Selvig, built in the early 1900s, sat empty in Harmony until innkeepers Ken and Karen Kiehne and Jacob Hershberger restored it from the basement up, creating a charming oasis with an Amish touch.

Guests have a choice of four rooms. The extra large Master Bedroom has a sitting area plus its own porch complete with swing. The Amish Touch is done in authentic Amish furniture and style, complete with Amish clothes in the closet. Both rooms share a bath. Eleanor's Room is done in a rose motif with white priscillas and like Doc's Room, formerly Dr. Selvig's main floor study, has a private bath. One of the innkeepers is a former member of the local Amish community, who shares his memories of the Amish lifestyle that has long attracted the curious to Southeastern Minnesota Bluff Country.

The Selvig Guest House prides itself on its warm, comfortable atmosphere, the kind of place where total strangers sit down to a scrumptious breakfast and linger long enough to leave as friends.

SPECIALTY SHOP

Henrytown *Country Store*	Five miles N of Canton, 6 miles NE of Harmony Route 2, Box 58. Harmony, MN 55939. **Phone: 507-886-2610.** Hrs: Mon.-Sat. 9 a.m.-5 p.m. Sundays 12:30 p.m.-5 p.m. Closed December through April. Visa and MasterCard accepted.

Located in the heart of Amish country, the Henrytown Country Store is an old-fashioned, country general store where you can find everything from Grandma's trunk to a 50-pound bag of flour.

Storekeepers Sue Engen and Bonnie Courtney have brought back the charm of a bygone era in this wonderful emporium, located five miles north of Canton and six miles northeast of Harmony. Inside, you'll find everything from antiques to Amish furniture, quilts and crafts to bulk groceries.

Bring back your fondest memories of another time with the smells of everything from fudge to fresh coffee to pot pourri as you browse through the displays, including children's furniture made by the local Amish people. Red Wing Pottery and crocks are also available along with afghans.

Be sure and try the ice cream treats and Spring Grove pop. The Henrytown Country Store is a detour to a bygone era every traveler will be glad to take.

HOUSTON

Houston Bluffs represent an ancient and unique geological area in the north-central United States. Exposed dolomite and Jordan sandstone outcroppings stand as mute testimony to eons past, before even the glaciers once razed the landscape elsewhere in Minnesota.

William G. McSpadden founded Houston, naming it after General Sam Houston under whom he had served in the Mexican War. Here, steamboats made regular stops until the 1870's.

Known as the "Entryway to Bluff Country," Houston is also known for its excellent fishing and hunting. Golfing, swimming and camping facilities are available nearby. State snowmobile trails, cross-country ski trails and the Root River State Trail system are near, as well. The annual *Houston Hoedown* is a major three day festival held in July and attracts thousands. It includes the State Horsepull Championship, Tractor Pull, parade and music jamboree.

For further information, contact:
The Tourist Information Center
Houston, MN 55943   Phone: 507-896-3303

BED & BREAKFAST

Addie's Attic Bed & Breakfast	117 So. Jackson, P.O. Box 677, Houston, MN 55943. **Phone: 507-896-3010** Hrs: Open year-round. No credit cards.

Built in 1903, this lovely old home was restored and opened as a B&B in 1991. The cozy front parlor with its graceful curved glass window always has a good view of the city park, whether it's the serenity of snow in winter or the delightful laugh of children in summer. A beautiful oak stairway greets visitors at the front door and leads to the guest rooms on the second story.

Addie's Attic offers air-conditioned comfort in the summer and is ideal for a cozy winter get-away. Hearty, home-cooked breakfasts are served each morning following your stay in one of the rooms.

The Sewing Room features an antique dress form and treadle sewing machine. The Toy Room has an antique carved wood queen sized bed. The Family Album Room evokes memories of your own ancestors and The Trunk Room has a trunk filled with keepsakes of a bygone era.

KASSON

Kasson is located 13 miles west of Rochester and 70 miles southwest of the Twin Cities. The town was named after Jabez Hyde Kasson, a man of Irish descent who had been one of three to plat the village and secure a railroad depot.

Kasson is primarily a farming community displaying all the charm of small town life. *The Kasson Municipal Building* is on The Prairie School National Register of sites. Built in 1917, this structure served as post office, council chamber, library, fire station, police department and masonic lodge. The major event in Kasson is the *Festival in the Park* held in August.

The city has three parks and an excellent, supervised summer park and recreation program with many activities. Kasson is located just five minutes away from the beautiful *Zumbro Valley Golf Course.*

For further information, contact:
City of Kasson
122 W. Main, Kasson, MN 55944   Phone: 507-634-7071

BED & BREAKFAST

Jacob's Inn	Corner of 2nd St and 2nd Ave NW 108 2nd Ave, NW. Kasson, MN 55944 **Phone: 507-634-4920.** Hrs: Open year-round Visa and MasterCard accepted.

Most of us can only imagine how the wealthy merchant families lived in days past. But you can experience that romantic turn-of-the-century elegance for yourself at Jacob's Inn in Kasson.

This graciously restored 1905 mansion, spacious and uncluttered, now listed on the National Register of Historic Places, features gracious oak pillars and woodwork, stained and leaded glass and vintage lighting. Built for wealthy clothing merchant Jacob Leuthold, Jr., this three-story Queen Anne Victorian has four rooms available, two with private bath. The Inn has wonderful oak furniture throughout, Laura Ashley fabrics and cozy Vermont quilts. A hearty full breakfast is served and fresh baked goods and refreshments are always available. Enjoy your favorites playing on the Victrola, summer breezes in a porch rocker or quiet conversation in a window seat.

Innkeepers Francie and Jerry Petrie take pride in the exceptional care they give their guests. Jacob's Inn is also a lovely setting for showers, luncheons or small gatherings.

KENYON

Kenyon received its name from a British Lord, Lord Kenyon, the second Baron of Gredington—an unusual beginning for a town whose ancestry is over 60% Norwegian!

The first houses were built in 1856, making Kenyon and the surrounding areas an antique hunter's paradise.

The *Martin T. Gunderson House Museum* is a classic example of Queen Anne architecture. Tours are available on summer weekends. *Dancing Winds Farm* produces unique gourmet goat cheeses.

Kenyon's annual *Rose Fest* celebrates the "Boulevard of Roses" each Father's Day weekend. Since 1968, thousands of visitors have come to take part in this spectacular event which includes a parade, rides, games and dances.

Kenyon and the surrounding areas offer year-round recreation and sports activities for young and old alike.

For further information, contact:

Kenyon City Hall, Office of the Administrator
511 Second Street, Kenyon, MN   Phone: 507-789-6415

BED & BREAKFAST

Grandfather's Woods Bed and Breakfast	3640 450th Street Kenyon, MN 55946 **Phone: 507-789-6414**

Five generations of the same family have worked the land around Grandfather's Woods Bed and Breakfast near Kenyon, Minnesota. Now, this working farm offers visitors all the benefits of country living in a romantic setting of rolling woodlands.

This beautiful acreage was homesteaded in 1856, a time still evocative to the visitors of today. Here, you may experience memories of your own youth and visits to a grandparent's home. A hayride in the clean, crystal clear air combines with a peaceful ambiance to make your visit a memorable one. Antique furnishings and hearty breakfasts top off your visit.

If you are attending local events like Kenyon's Rose Festival

Days, Carriage and Cutter Days or the Kenyon Arts Council's old fashioned sleigh ride and dinner, make your stay at Grandfather's. It's a special treat from the past!

LA CRESCENT

La Crescent has been called one of the Minnesota's best kept secrets. Known as the "Apple Capital of Minnesota," this town is located 130 miles southeast of Minneapolis/St. Paul.

The community draws bicycle enthusiasts from all over the Midwest to tour the *Root River State Trail* for a scenic ride along the Bluff Country. The *Apple Blossom Scenic Drive* stretches for eight miles along part of the *Hiawatha Trail* and presents breathtaking scenery at every turn. Miles of cross-country ski and snowmobile trails wind throughout the area. Hunters have come away with enviable game including whitetail deer and wild turkey.

Each September, the *Annual Applefest* is held to celebrate the apple harvest with a weekend of activities, including a street dance, an arts and crafts fair and the King Apple Grand Parade.

For further information, contact:
La Crescent Chamber of Commerce
P.O. Box 132
La Crescent, MN 55947   Phone: 507-895-2800

SPECIALTY SHOP

Apple Valley Antiques and Gifts	23 S. Walnut, La Crescent, MN 55947 **Phone: 507-895-4268**. Hrs.: Mon.-Fri. 11 a.m.-5 p.m., Sat. 10 a.m.-5 p.m., Sun 1 p.m.-5 p.m. Visa and MasterCard accepted.

This delightful antique and gift shop, so named because it is nestled in downtown La Crescent—"The Apple Capital of Minnesota"—attractively displays antiques, country collectibles, and many other gift ideas.

The "I Love Country" atmosphere invites visitors to select from candles, cards, potpourri, apple items, bath products, baskets, afghans, braided rugs, stoneware, dried flower arrangements, Heritage lace, doilies, cookbooks, cookie molds and many Minnesota gift items. There is antique furniture such as refinished cupboards, dressers and tables, along with commodes, rockers, decorating accessories and much more.

The large selection of gift items and bridal registry makes Apple Valley Antiques and Gifts a great place to shop for any occasion.

LAKE CITY

Lake City is the birthplace of waterskiing. The sport was invented there in 1922 by Ralph Samuelson. Lake City is the largest community on Lake Pepin with a population of 4391. Located just 35 miles north of Rochester and 65 miles south of the Twin Cities, Lake City has the largest smallcraft harbor and marina on the Mississippi River.

ATTRACTIONS & EVENTS

Riverwalk is a three mile pedestrian walkway offering a scenic view of Lake Pepin surrounded by bluffs. *Frontenac State Park,* located 7 miles north of Lake City, offers camping, hiking, groomed snowmobile and cross-country ski trails and guided nature hikes. *Mount Frontenac* ski area and golf course spans 280 acres with the steepest vertical drop in Minnesota at 420 feet. Golfers enjoy a challenging 18 holes in spring, summer and fall. *The Wabasha County Historical Museum* provides historical artifacts on Laura Ingalls Wilder as well as a collection of vintage clothing and implements used in daily living in the river valley.

Water Ski Days, held annually on the last full weekend in June, offers a carnival, large arts and crafts fair, musical entertainment, water ski shows, Venetian Boat Parade, classic car show and a grand parade heralded as one of the best in southeastern Minnesota.

Johnny Appleseed Days is held the first full weekend in October, just in time for peak fall colors and the height of the apple season. Lake City's many apple orchards make it a top apple producing area and the nation's largest producer of the Haralson apple.

Winter Fest is celebrated the last full weekend in January with a Golf Classic, horse drawn sleigh and cutter parade, snowmobile drag races and other activities. This fun-filled family event culminates with a fantastic fireworks display over frozen Lake Pepin.

Winter in Lake City presents opportunities for snowmobiling, downhill and cross-country skiing, ice fishing and fabulous eagle watching.

For further information, contact:
Lake City Chamber of Commerce
212 South Washington
Lake City, MN 55041
Phone: 612-345-4123

APPLE ORCHARD

Courtier's Pepin Heights Apples	Hwy. 61 South of Lake City, Lake City, MN 55041. **Phone: 612-345-2305 or 800-652-3779** Hrs: August through December. Mon.-Sun. 9 a.m.-6 p.m. No credit cards accepted.

Nearly half century ago, Gil Courtier had a dream about planting an apple orchard. Back then, there were only a few apple tree varieties that could withstand the winters of Minnesota and Gil was looking for a place that would give his orchard the best chance for success. In 1949, he chose the bluffs along the shores of Lake Pepin with red clay soil similar to Europe's finest wine-growing regions.

Today, his dream lives on at Minnesota's largest orchard. Son Dennis and daughter-in-law Kirsten Lindquist-Courtier, a former Twin Cities television newswoman, carry on the tradition at Courtier's Pepin Heights Apples.

At 400 acres, Pepin Heights is Minnesota's largest apple grower. They produce about three or four apples a year for every person in the state and their products can be found in major grocery retailers like Cub, Byerly's, Lunds and Rainbow Foods. Eighty percent of the Pepin Heights' apples go to the Twin Cities grocery market and during the height of the harvest season, Pepin Heights apples will make up about a third of the stock in most stores. They are probably the world's largest grower of Haralson apples, the most popular Minnesota-grown variety. The company grows about 80 varieties in all, even though only about three dozen of those are sold to consumers.

The apple harvest at Pepin Heights begins in early August and, with luck, continues through October. Trained apple pickers move through the rows of trees with their canvas bags, selecting only those apples that are perfectly ripened and leaving the rest until they're ready. The ripe apples are trucked from the orchard to the packing house where they are washed, sized and hand-graded. Those that are smaller than the minimum size requirements, but just as high quality, go to the cider plant to make wonderful crisp, clean apple cider. And you'll find no better than Pepin Heights cider.

The retail store at Pepin Heights features a wide variety of apples and apple products, from the tasty little Chestnut Crabs (in season) to delectable caramel apples. All of the items represent the highest quality products from regional producers and are taste-tested by the staff. Besides apples, apple cider and apple-related products, they carry a variety of cheeses, jams and jellies, bakery goods, wild rice, popcorn and kitchen accessories.

An apple lover's dream!

ART GALLERY

Wild Wings Gallery

South Highway 61, Lake City, MN 55041-0451.
Phone: 612-345-3663 or 800-248-7312
Hrs.: Mon.-Sat. 9 a.m.-6 p.m.; Sun. 11 a.m.-
5 p.m. All major credit cards accepted.

Nestled among the scenic Mississippi River bluffs, Wild Wings Gallery offers travelers the art of the outdoors in a casual, comfortable gallery setting. This is the national catalog show room of Wild Wings Inc., the nation's leading publisher of fine wildlife and sporting art prints for 25 years.

Founded in 1968 by company CEO Bill Webster, Wild Wings began as a simple cottage industry inspired by Webster's love of wildlife art and deep commitment to conservation. Today, Wild Wings operates 16 galleries nationwide, mails annually over 3 million Wild Wings Collection catalogs and serves a world-wide dealer network of over 2,000 galleries.

Wild Wings Gallery features the works of American's most popular artists including: David Maass, Robert Abbett, Michael Sieve, Nancy Glazier, Terry Redlin, Rosemary Millette, Ron VanGilder, Persis Clayton Weirs, Jim Kasper and Lee Kromschroeder. Also on display is Wild Wings' complementary selection of home furnishings and gift collectibles, including sofas, chairs, tables, porcelain and crystal sculptures and collector plates. In addition to wildlife art, Wild Wings also offers a broad selection of Americana, romance, landscape, floral and fantasy art prints.

To experience the beauty of the outdoors and more, stop by the national headquarters gallery of Wild Wings. Additional Wild Wings Gallery locations include: Centerplace Galleria, Rochester; Burnsville Center, Burnsville; Southdale Center, Edina; and Maplewood Mall, Maplewood.

BED & BREAKFAST

Evergreen Knoll Acres B&B & Country Cottage	R.R. 1, Box 145, Lake City, MN 55041 **Phone: 612-345-2257** Open year-round. No credit cards accepted.

Built in 1919, this charming country home is tastefully decorated with many period antiques. Each of the three guest rooms is furnished with antique iron beds, country furnishings and crafts, for a truly homey feeling. Guests are welcome to share the main level of the home, relaxing by a cozy fireplace or enjoying a movie on the television or VCR.

In addition to the main house, a four bedroom secluded country cottage is also available. Children are always welcome.

Guests are invited to savor the down-home cooking and hearty country breakfast with homemade breads and preserves.

One of the highlights of this bed and breakfast experience is a tour of this modern, working dairy farm, or if you like, enjoy a peaceful stroll through the tranquil countryside. A variety of tourist attractions are nearby for your entertainment.

◆ ◆ ◆ ◆ ◆ ◆

The Pepin House B&B	120 S. Prairie Street Lake City, MN 55041 **Phone: 612-345-4454** Visa, MasterCard and Discover accepted.

This 1905 Victorian home was built by a local brewer, John C. Schmidt. After many years, the house was renovated and restored to its original beauty. Now operated as a bed and breakfast by James and Darlyne Lyons, the inn offers guests the aura of quiet charm and the elegance of a bygone era.

Two common areas are graced with an open-carved staircase, stained glass windows, pocket doors and fireplace. Three bedrooms are beautifully decorated—one with queen-sized canopy bed, private bath and balcony. Two other rooms have queen-sized beds and share two baths. Two porches invite guests who return after a busy day of sightseeing in this scenic area of Minnesota.

A gourmet breakfast is served in a formal dining room. No children, pets or smoking. The inn is air-conditioned for your comfort.

BED & BREAKFAST

Red Gables Inn

403 N. High Street
Lake City, MN 55041
Phone: 612-345-2605
Visa and MasterCard accepted.

Nestled amidst foliage-covered bluffs of the Hiawatha Valley, where the mighty Mississippi widens to become Lake Pepin, is Red Gables Inn, an intimate bed and breakfast. The inn offers a chance to step back into the quiet and unhurried luxury of the Victorian past, without sacrificing the comforts of the present.

Each guest room is individually decorated with period antiques. A generous Victorian breakfast buffet of juices, seasonal fruits, home-baked breads and pastries, special egg dishes and preserves is offered each morning. The inn also offers gourmet picnic baskets, both summer and winter, and many "little extras" are provided to make your stay memorable. An antique shop is on site; bicycles for guests, group murder mysteries and gift certificates are available.

The romantic spirit of the Victorian era is alive at the Red Gables Inn at Lake City.

The Victorian Bed and Breakfast

620 South High
Lake City, MN 55041
Phone: 612-345-2167
No credit cards accepted.

Enjoy the natural beauty of Lake Pepin as you journey back in time in this 1896 Victorian home. The common rooms display carved woodwork, antique furniture, stained glass windows and feature antique music boxes. Juliette's Room features handcrafted furniture, a queen_sized bed, a private bath and a commanding view of Lake Pepin. Teresa's Room is open to the lake on two sides and retains a light airy feel with a country theme and white wicker furnishings. Kari's Room has an off-set window overlooking the marina. Its antique furnishings and Victorian Lace offer true Victorian elegance.

A continental plus breakfast is served either in the formal dining room or in the privacy of your bedroom. It consists of seasonal fruit, home-baked breads, biscuits, muffins and jellies.

FRUIT & VEGETABLES

Bushel & Peck

35878 Highway 61 Blvd, Lake City, MN 55041
Phone: 612-345-4516
Hours: 9 a.m.-6 p.m. March-January
No credit cards accepted.

Lake City is apple country but no place in the area makes fruit and vegetables more fun than Bushel & Peck. Just ask your kids. They'll remember the wonderful maze that's set up out front during the month of October, along with all of the cut out caricatures for your picture taking pleasure. Inside there's different apples, pumpkin, fudge, jellies and more. Make your choices and then picnic outside.

Bushel & Peck offers only the freshest fruits and vegetables in season. Beginning with flowers, bedding plants and strawberries and continuing into the fall with fresh cut gladiolas and locally grown apples. Other crops grown and sold here include peas and beans (pick-your-own or pre-picked), sweet corn, tomatoes, pumpkins, squash and gourds. But there's more.

Bushel & Peck has a wonderful selection of syrups, honey, jams, jellies and other delicacies. You'll also find staples like bread, milk and cheese plus crafts, bird feeders and feed. But the mainstay are Lake City's own apples, fresh cider, caramel apples and apple pie.

GOLF COURSE

**Lake City
Country Club**

Route 2, Central Point, Lake City, MN 55041
Phone: 612-345-3221. Hrs: Mon.-Sun. 7 a.m.-Midnight. Closed January-March. No credit cards accepted.

It's hard to imagine how anything in its seventh decade could still be classed as a "best-kept secret" but that remains the case at beautiful Lake City Country Club.

Built in 1928, this nine-hole course has offered golfers spectacular views of the area bluffs that surround it for nearly 70 years. They take pride in their fully established evergreens and their ongoing commitment to becoming Minnesota's best-groomed golf course.

They can also take pride in their atmosphere. A fun, friendly place, the kind of club where oldtimers sit around the bar and swap tall tales about their round, the club serves supper Wednesdays, Thursdays and Saturdays. The menu can vary from a chicken fry, fish fry or steak fry, and fresh sandwiches and snacks are always available. There is a fully stocked lounge and banquet facilities, pull carts or power carts for rent and a driving range to complement the 3,023-yard, par 36 layout. A family place to be, Lake City Country Club is a great way to spend a relaxing day in historic Bluff Country.

LODGING

Lake City *Country Inn*	1401 N. Lakeshore Drive, Lake City, MN 55041 **Phone: 612-345-5351** Hours: Open year-round Visa, MasterCard and AmEx accepted.

The birthplace of waterskiing, Lake City has everything for the water enthusiast: fishing, canoeing, swimming, windsurfing and, of course, waterskiing. And it has a great place to relax and unwind in comfort and relaxation after a day on Lake Pepin; the newly remodeled Lake City Country Inn.

Lake City rests on the shores of Lake Pepin, a particularly wide swath of the Mississippi River running through the Hiawatha Valley. Originally, the city earned distinction as a grain port, but after the river traffic abated in the late 1800s, Lake City became a haven for leisure travellers as it remains today. Visitors still come to enjoy the lake or to view the spectacular, towering bluffs.

Known for its convenient location and for its modern amenities, the Lake City Country Inn has 26 individually decorated rooms, some with jacuzzi and fireplaces, some furnished with Victorian-style antiques. Choosing a room may be difficult but the view isn't: each room has a wonderful view of spectacular Lake Pepin.

◆ ◆ ◆ ◆ ◆ ◆

Sunset Motel	1515 N. Lakeshore Drive, Lake City, MN 55041 **Phone: 800-945-0192 or 612-345-5331** Open year-round. Visa and MasterCard accepted.

For generations, Lake City has been a year-round destination for family vacations. From the wonderful waterskiing on Lake Pepin (where the sport was invented) in the summer to the blazing colors of the Mississippi River bluffs in fall to the terrific skiing, snowmobiling and ice fishing in winter, this area has it all.

And the Sunset Motel is a great place to experience Lake City. Set amid attractively landscaped grounds, the Sunset offers impeccable kitchenette units, cabins and motel-style rooms, some with waterbeds. Larger groups like the two-bedroom apartment. Owners Phil and Darlene Roland offer excellent service, including complimentary van service to the Marina and local restaurants, free snowmobile guiding, fish cleaning facilities and fish freezing at no charge plus complimentary barbecue grills

Rooms are air conditioned and have cable TV, HBO and direct dial phones. Relax in the outdoor heated pool or indoor whirlpool while the kids have fun in the game room. Babysitting is available.

RESTAURANT

| *Waterman's Restaurant & Lounge* | 1702 N. Lakeshore Drive, Lake City, MN 55041 **Phone: 612-345-5353.** Hrs: Dine Mon.-Sun 11 a.m.-10:30 p.m. Lounge Mon.-Sun 11 a.m. till close. Visa, MasterCard accepted. |

Overlooking Lake Pepin and the Mississippi River in Lake City is Waterman's Restaurant. Here, diners enjoy excellent food and their favorite cocktails amid the beauty that is Lake Pepin.

This fine restaurant offers food and drink in a casual but luxurious atmosphere, with seating both inside or on the deck outside. The restaurant is constructed primarily of cedar and oak throughout, blending in well with its natural surroundings. As you enter, a large brick fireplace provides a warm welcome. Spacious glassed-in dining areas bring in the beauty of Lake Pepin and the nearby bluffs.

Lunchtime fare is ample with fresh garden salads served with any of their homemade house dressings, a variety of soups, sandwiches and chef choices of pasta and seafood, as well as seasonal entreés.

Start dinner with freshly baked bread, warm from the oven. Choose from an extensive menu selection, including walleye pike, rib-eye steak, filet mignon, pasta, chops and fresh seafood. In addition, every day the chef prepares unique offerings using the finest and freshest ingredients and herbs available. When you're finished with dinner, try Waterman's delicious New York cheesecake, fudge-topped peanut butter pie, Mississippi turtle pie, or a warm brownie topped with vanilla ice cream and hot chocolate sauce.

Waterman's is a popular spot for boaters because they have access to deep water docks, but boaters and landlubbers alike thrill to the panoramic view of Lake Pepin. Whether you are in town for boating, fishing, snowmobiling, participating in the local festivals or just taking a scenic drive on the Great River Road, you will find Waterman's memorable.

Banquet and corporate facilities are also available.

RESTAURANT

Chickadee Cottage *Tea Room & Restaurant*	On Hwy 61, 317 N. Lakeshore Drive Lake City, MN 55041. **Phone: 612-345-5155** Hrs: May 1-Oct. 31. Tues. - Sat. 7:30 a.m.-5 p.m. Sundays 8 a.m.-3 p.m. Closed Mondays. No credit cards accepted.

There's something to be said for the traditions of the Old Country and they say it oh-so well at Chickadee Cottage Tea Room & Restaurant in Lake City, a step back to homemade and leisurely.

From the scrumptious coffeecakes and muffins to sausage gravy and biscuits at breakfast to the freshly made scones with strawberry jam and Devonshire Cream at mid-morning to Afternoon Tea served from 3 p.m. to 5 p.m., the traditions of England are upheld here six days a week. The decor is bright and cheerful in this early 1900's home and the staff will do whatever it takes to send you home happy.

Even the gorgeous views of the Wisconsin bluffs and beautiful Lake Pepin are reminiscent of English Lake Country. Owner Donna Hawkins emphasizes food that is heart healthy and light, with lots of seasonal vegetables and fruit. Much of it is locally grown and she believes how food looks and tastes is extremely important. Try the wild rice burgers for lunch and finish with raspberry cream pie. Or sample the homemade breads baked daily and available to go.

ROOT BEER STAND & SPECIALTY SHOP

The Root Beer *Stand & Country* *Craft Mall*	805 N. Lakeshore, Lake City, MN 55041. **Phone:** 612-345-2124. Hrs: Root Beer Stand open April through Labor Day. Mall open April through Christmas. Visa and MasterCard accepted.

Built in 1948, The Root Beer Stand is one of the oldest existing businesses in Lake City, where root beer remains the speciality of the house and that specialty is still pleasantly delivered by tray-carrying car hops to every car window!

The Root Beer Stand drive-in has long been a tradition in Lake City. Visitors to the area's largest marina on the Mississippi and other attractions can enjoy their favorite sandwich along with a malt or root beer, just like it was years ago. For outdoor enjoyment, picnic tables are available overlooking the lake. Dutch elm carvings of an eagle and bear, along with other carvings, surround The Root Beer Stand.

Conveniently located next door you'll find the largest cedar chest in the state of Minnesota. The Country Craft Mall, once a small motel, is now an inviting gift shop with 50 artists.

Stop by for a frosty mug of homemade root beer and a freshly made cheeseburger, like generations of thirsty travellers have, at The Root Beer Stand, a Lake City tradition for more than 45 years.

SPECIALTY SHOP

Home Traditions

106 S. Lakeshore Drive. Lake City, MN 55041
Phone: 612-345-2017. Hrs: Mon.-Fri. 9 a.m.-
6 p.m. Sat. 9 a.m.-5 p.m., Sun. Noon-5 p.m.
Extended summer hours. Closed Sun. in Jan., Feb.,
Mar. Visa, MasterCard and Discover accepted.

Variety, service and traditional themes have become the hallmark of Home Traditions in Lake City, where the selection is wide, the displays creative and the service exceptional.

Their product lines include wood furniture in a variety of styles from small tables and shelves to complete bedrooms and dining rooms including Shaker and Amish in pine, oak and cherry. They also carry Amish quilts and wallhangings, other needlework and patchwork items plus rugs.

A wide selection of pottery is available plus pictures, lamps, books, cards, baskets, decoys, candles, doilies, clocks, bird houses, Yankee candles, spiced teas, compact discs, cassette tapes and much, much more. John and Corrine McGinty's philosophy is to provide quality and variety in the American tradition, all in keeping with the store's motto: "Things to keep for the family."

Special orders, gift wrapping and shipping are available. And if they don't have what you want, they'll find it.

◆ ◆ ◆ ◆ ◆ ◆

"Raccoons in the Barn"

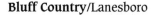

LANESBORO

The scenery around Lanesboro is intoxicating and is accentuated by the Root River, which runs through the center of town. *The Forest Resource Center* can help with selecting a ski or a hiking trail and offers workshops to give insight into the surrounding area. Two of the largest caves in the upper Midwest and a large Amish community are nearby. A great way to spend a summer day is to follow the *Root River Bike Trail,* which stretches over 20 miles along the spectacular Root River.

Summer festivals include *Art in the Park,* which has become one of the largest festivals in southeastern Minnesota, and *Buffalo Bill Days,* with dances, sports events, kid's games, historic tours and more. *Oktoberfest* bids farewell to the warmth of autumn days and offers to those attending a taste of Germany through Polka music, food, beer and dancing.

For further information, contact:
The Lanesboro Community Club
P.O. Box 20, Lanesboro, MN 55949   Phone: 507-467-3722

RESTAURANT

The Victorian House of Lanesboro	709 S. Parkway, Lanesboro, MN 55949 **Phone: 507-467-3457** Hrs.: Wed.,-Sun. 5:30 p.m. By reservation only.

Jean Claude and Sonja Venant bring their international culinary talent to the Midwest by way of the "Song of Norway," a Royal Caribbean Cruise Line where Jean Claude worked as executive chef and Sonja as hair stylist. The Victorian House of Lanesboro is their successful joint venture.

Patrons enjoy authentic French cooking in a Victorian setting, sip wine in the formal parlor and select from several entreés such as Care D'agneau Provencale (lamb breaded with parsley and garlic). Sonja boasts of "the best escargot in Lanesboro" (steaming snails in garlic butter), and of her famous Chocolate Sin dessert.

The Victorian House of Lanesboro was built for Senator Samuel Nelson of Lanesboro around 1870. Antiques from all over the world include an ornate Chinese wedding chest, a cherry wood grandfather clock from Holland, and a square grand piano.

Dinners are served Wednesdays through Sundays starting at 5:30 p.m., and are by reservation only.

BED & BREAKFAST

Carrolton *Country Inn*	R.R. 2, P.O. Box 139, Lanesboro, MN 55949 **Phone: 507-467-2257.** Hrs: 8 a.m.-10 p.m. Visa and MasterCard accepted.

If peace, solitude and an escape from routine for rest and relaxation is what you're after, Carrolton Country Inn, near historic Lanesboro, is the obvious answer.

This 1800s farmhouse, which was formerly in one family for more than 100 years, offers an uncluttered, uncomplicated, uncrowded country getaway. Charles and Gloria Ruen, owners, renovated the home and now provide accommodations for bed and breakfast, whole house rental and family reunions.

This nine-room rural retreat, situated on 389 acres, is nestled among hills in an open valley in the gorgeous historic Bluff Country of southeast Minnesota. There's not a neighbor in sight. Located on the Root River and Root River State Trail, it features hiking, biking, cross-country skiing, fishing and canoeing among your recreational options. The Ox Cart Road Drive takes guests directly to the inn. Once used by the stagecoach lines, it was the first roadway in the area.

The home is completely restored. Victorian overtones run throughout the inn, with antique furnishings, a dumb waiter in the butler's pantry, original milk paint on the woodwork and a beautiful open staircase. Within walking distance, visitors can view the original three-story log home built in 1856. The inn is also located in one of the most heavily populated deer areas in the state. Hunters are offered accommodations on the whole house rental or house-keeping plan. Bed-and-breakfast guests can choose from four private bedrooms. A full country breakfast is provided but prepared by the guest, thus ensuring complete privacy.

Guests will also enjoy the many area attractions of historic Lanesboro. The entire downtown area has been listed on the National Register of Historic Places. The Amish community south of town is the largest in the Midwest. Many fine restaurants, two caves, a winery, museums and much more are available to visit in the area.

Carrolton Country Inn is a hideaway where time has preserved a century-old home for your enjoyment. It's country and comfortable.

BED & BREAKFAST

Historic Scanlan House Bed & Breakfast	708 Parkway Avenue S., Lanesboro, MN 55949. **Phone: 507-467-2158 or 800-944-2158.** Hrs: Open year-round. Visa, MasterCard, AmEx and Discover accepted.

At the Historic Scanlan House Bed & Breakfast, travelers take a trip back into time, a time of quiet and romance. Built in 1889 by the son of Lanesboro's founder and listed on the National Registry of Historic Places, the house epitomizes an elegant but unpretentious Victorian home. Owners and hosts Gene, Mary and daughter Kirsten Mensing, who restored the inn, pride themselves on offering uncommon, yet comfortable lodgings at Lanesboro's oldest operating B & B.

The Queen Anne style Scanlan House, located in a quiet residential section of Lanesboro's main street, is highlighted by a circular tower with a balcony and a sheltered drive where horsedrawn vehicles once stopped so that guests could disembark. The interior is adorned throughout with the elegant woodwork, stained glass and the ornate built-in furnishings typical of a fine and exquisite turn-of-the-century residence.

The solid oak open staircase to the second and third floor, with its decorative spindles, is beautiful. The aroma of fresh coffee and muffins adds that special touch as do the truffles on your pillow and complimentary champagne.

Five bedrooms are available to guests, each furnished with stunning antiques, some with whirlpool and fireplaces. Modern amenities include small colored TV, air conditioning and bike and ski rentals. The communal parlor offers cozy seating in the tower circle and a computer that guests may challenge in a game of chess.

Overnight guests enjoy a famous five-course breakfast in a whimsical dining room with built-in oak china cabinet and rare stamped leatherette paneling. The changing menu features such delectables as homemade muffins and breads, German sausages, Belgian waffles, pumpkin pancakes, quiche, fresh fruit, desert and cinnamon coffee. Champagne is served on special occasions.

During the summer months, walking tours through the historic Lanesboro residential district and points of interest are available.

Located a short distance from antique shops, a winery, live professional theater, Amish Country, canoeing, the bluffs and biking trails, Scanlan House can provide a unique and unforgettable getaway or a lavish package for a honeymoon, birthday or other special occasion. Gift baskets made to order.

MANTORVILLE

Located just 14 miles west of Rochester, Mantorville is an exceptionally well preserved city, a true window into the past. This town is on the National Register of Historic Places, a rare honor for a city.

Mantorville limestone has been the one constant in the economy of this charming town. The stone is soft and easily worked into buildings. Over the years, it becomes harder with weathering, enabling buildings built with it to maintain their original form and beauty while others suffer the ravages of time.

The Grand Old Mansion is a sight visitors should not miss. Built in 1899, this Victorian mansion is now a bed and breakfast with tours available. Additional sights to see are the *Hubbel House,* the 1850's *Original Log Cabin* and the *Mantorville Mercantile Company.*

For further information, contact:
Mantorville Chamber of Commerce
P.O. Box 358, Mantorville, MN 55955
Phone: 507-635-3231 or 507-635-2481

BED & BREAKFAST

The Grand Old Mansion	501 Clay St., Mantorville, MN 55955 **Phone: 507-635-3231.** Open year-round. No credit cards accepted.

A Nationally Registered Historic Site, Mantorville is chock-full of treasures and historic buildings. And the best place to see Mantorville is from the balcony of the Grand Old Mansion.

This Victorian mansion was originally built in 1899 by Teunis Slingerland and authentically restored by owner Irene Stussy Felker. It is a beautiful Victorian home with the original woodwork, prism cut glass, handcarved staircase and a wide assortment of Irene's antiques which she has collected, including a doll collection and a 200-year-old rosewood davenport from Austria.

The Grand Old Mansion has three bedrooms, each air conditioned and complete with private bath, furnished in antiques and having its own period style. A full breakfast is included. Guests can now choose from two guest houses as well, one a real log cabin, the other an old school house. These are great for families. The Grand Old Mansion is a must-see. Tours by individual or bus are available for a nominal fee and Irene is Mantorville's tour guide.

RESTAURANT

Hubbell House Restaurant and Lounge

Main Street, Mantorville, MN 55955
Phone: 507-635-2331. Hrs: Tues-Sat; Lunch, 11:30 a.m.-2 p.m., Dinner 5 p.m.-10 p.m. Sun. 11:30 a.m.-9:30 p.m. Closed Monday. Major credit cards accepted.

Civil War decor, superb food and a rich history have made the Hubbell House Restaurant and Lounge a favorite of connoisseurs from all over the country. Though its guest book reads like a "Who's Who" of the famous of both past and present, this old country inn retains its hospitality, grace and charm.

Casual dining in an atmosphere of 19th century opulence awaits visitors at the Hubbell House Restaurant and Lounge; Civil War antiques, glowing table lamps and historical displays set the tone. The inn's history is reflected in rooms filled with treasures from the past and named for such celebrities as Horace Greeley and Senator Ramsey.

A highlight among the many documents and Civil War mementos on display is a land grant signed by Abraham Lincoln himself. Visited by such notables as W.W. Mayo and U.S. Grant, the restaurant has been serving fine cuisine since the 1850's when John Hubbell built the original log hotel and added the three-story limestone structure that still stands today.

At the Hubbell House Restaurant and Lounge, diners may feast on prime and choice beef selections such as Chateaubriand, properly aged steaks and many chef specialties. Served also are such midwestern favorites as broiled jumbo shrimp, cold-water lobster and Minnesota's own walleye pike. Other items of note include Sunday noon specials, early dinner menu and a complete children's menu.

The Hubbell House Restaurant and Lounge is located 65 miles south of the Mendota Bridge and 20 minutes west of Rochester in Mantorville. Mantorville is on the National Register of Historic places with museums, shops and many historic buildings.

PRESTON

Preston is located at the entrance to the *Forestville State Park.* It is also near the *Root River State Trail System* with biking, hiking, and cross-country skiing all in a beautiful valley surrounded by Minnesota's hardwood forests.

Mystery Cave is the longest cave in Minnesota with more than 12 miles of natural passages. Research conducted in Mystery Cave has yielded insight to the understanding of ground water flow, bat populations, timing of formal glacial advances and retreats, and the deposition of cave sediment. The Old Fillmore County Jail has been transformed into the *Jail House Bed and Breakfast* and is on the National Register of Historic Places. *Preston Trout Days* puts the best of Preston on display.

For further information, contact:
Preston Tourism Commission
109 St. Paul, 2SW, P.O. Box 65
Preston, MN 55965
Phone 507-765-4541

LODGING

Sunnyside Cottage of Forestville	R.R. 2, P.O. Box 119 Preston, MN 55965 **Phone: 507-765-3357**

Sunnyside Farm is a 700-acre farm overlooking the Root River Valley next to Forestville State Park. Built in the 1940's as a summer retreat, the cottage has been refurbished by Darrell and Lois Ray to what it once was—a quiet, peaceful retreat.

Today, it's a delightful little three-bedroom, air-conditioned house, furnished in country-style modern furnishings. The kitchen offers full appliances and utensils for cooking; the dining room and living room with fireplace are combined to offer cozy eating and relaxing. Other amenities include microwave, television, playpen, crib, highchair, gas grill, picnic table, screened patio, sandbox and games for the children, and a rustic swing to relax and enjoy the peaceful retreat in the Forestville woods.

A generous breakfast is provided. A wooden fruit basket is also provided with all the utensils necessary for guests to enjoy a picnic in the woods. Pick berries, fish for trout on the Root River, or just hike through the countryside.

BED & BREAKFAST

The Jail House Inn

109 Houston St., Preston, MN 55965
Phone: 507-765-2181
Visa, MasterCard and Discover accepted.

Located in the Old Fillmore County Jail and listed on the National Register of Historic Places, the Jail House Inn was built in 1869 in Victorian Italianate style architecture. It served as a jail until 1971 before being purchased in 1987 and restored to its original Victorian splendor, now offering bed & breakfast and retreat accommodations.

An open staircase with a curved walnut banister invites guests to the upper bedrooms. Each of the 12 "cells" has been tastefully furnished in a Victorian motif, complete with private bath and queen-sized beds. The inn has seven fireplaces (four in guest rooms) along with jacuzzis and unique bath fixtures. Two large stone fireplaces in the common areas invite guests to relax, make new friends and maybe hear an interesting tale or two of past "cell mates."

A complete breakfast is served weekends. Weekday guests are served a hearty continental breakfast. Group accommodations, mystery weekends, sleigh rides and special packages for winter are also available.

HISTORIC SITE

Historic Forestville

A Minnesota Historical Society Site. Forestville State Park between Preston & Spring Valley. Route 2, Box 126, Preston, MN 55965. **Phone: 507-765-2785** Hrs: May 28-Sept. 2 Tues.-Fri. 10 a.m.-5 p.m. Sat. 11 a.m.-6 p.m. Sun. Noon-5 p.m. State Park Fee.

In the heart of Bluff Country, Historic Forestville offers visitors the chance to step back in time to a village that was a rural trading center where farmers came to trade their farm produce for goods and services.

In 1858, Forestville numbered 100 inhabitants and 20 buildings, including two general stores, a grist mill, a brickyard, two hotels, a school and "mechanics of several trades." By 1890, Thomas J. Meighen, son of one of the town's founders, owned the entire village with 50 employees living and working on his farm.

Visit 1899 Forestville and Meighen's farm village. Chat with costumed interpreters portraying Forestville residents, and pass the time with the gardener or farm laborers as they go about their daily activities. Follow the aromas to meals being prepared in the kitchen of the Meighen residence. Explore the "latest" styles of fabrics, shoes, clothes, and merchandise at the Forestville store. Take home an experience of life in this once-prosperous town.

FRUIT & VEGETABLE FARM

Preston Apple And Berry Farm

Across from highway rest stop. 645 Hwy 52 & 16 E., Preston, MN 55965. **Phone: 507-765-4486.** Hrs: Mon.-Sun. 9 a.m.-7 p.m. Mon.-Sun. 7 a.m.-7 p.m. (strawberry season). Closed in March.

When Joe Gosi fled the Soviet military crackdown of 1956 in his native Hungary, he knew little of the United States and nothing of Minnesota. But when he arrived at an army base in New Jersey and was offered California, he turned down the West Coast because he didn't want warm weather all year long.

"Then they said, 'How about Minnesota?'" Gosi recalls. "I asked, 'Do they have any farms or hills there?' 'Oh yeah,' they replied. 'They have all kinds of them.'"

California's loss was Minnesota's gain, particularly for lovers of apples, strawberries and other fresh fruits and vegetables. Preston Apple and Berry Farm is the culmination of years of hard work and perseverance by Gosi and his family. The first few years he toiled at a variety of jobs, intermittently working at an orchard near the Twin Cities. He knew, even in Hungary, that he enjoyed growing fruits and so in 1964 he began his career in earnest at an orchard, where he was a manager for 21 years.

Then in 1985, Joe launched his own orchard and vegetable business on 17 acres along Highway 52 in Preston. Now, he and his family have 800 apple trees on five acres, four acres of strawberries, a half acre of raspberries and a large garden patch that includes corn, tomatoes, green beans, pumpkins and squash, peppers and gourds.

Along with fresh fruits and vegetables, they have jams and jellies, honey, sorghum, maple syrup, cheese, popcorn and frozen apple pies. There is always an abundance of apples from August through February featuring every variety from McIntosh to Delicious, Spartan to Keepsake, enough choice for any taste or dish. In early spring, their greenhouse offers bedding plants, hanging flowering baskets, potted plants and seeds.

During the fall and holiday season, Christmas trees and poinsettias are available. Other seasonal items include apple turnovers and muffins, doughnuts, apple sauce, caramel apples and fresh apple cider. Fresh fruit baskets and boxes are always on hand and make an excellent choice for gift giving. Stop in for a taste of freshness.

RESORT & CAMPGROUND

The Old Barn Resort	R.R. 3., P.O. Box 57, Preston, MN 55965 **Phone: 507-467-2512.** Visa and MasterCard accepted.

Located in one of the most scenic valleys in historic Bluff Country, the Old Barn Resort is at the top of list when it comes to camp vacations. The Root River meandering through the valley makes the location stunningly beautiful. The historic barn sets the theme.

Built in 1884 by Milwaukee entrepreneur Edward Allis for his playboy son, Jere, as a place to settle down and raise cattle and race horses, it has found new life as the restaurant, hotel, gift shop and camp headquarters for the Old Barn Resort. The careful restoration and unique blend of old and new are exceptional.

The lower level of the Barn contains a 56-bed hostel, which is ideal for individuals and groups. Four dormitories house guests in bunk beds with ample bathroom facilities, director's quarters, kitchenette and game room. Two meeting rooms are available for seminars or other special occasions to accommodate up to 200 people, with complete catering services.

All this and fine dining, too. The Old Barn also offers the best "home cooking" in the area with a complete menu plus a lounge.

In addition to the Barn, The Old Barn Resort has one of the newest, most up-to-date campgrounds in the upper Midwest. There are 80 developed campsites, with water and electrical hook-ups, and more than half with sewer connections. For campers who like to "rough it," wooded tent sites are also available. Complete bath and shower facilities are convenient to all sites.

And for swimmers, a unique solar-heated building with a 900 square-foot heated swimming pool provides swimming from April to November 1. Bikes, canoes, roller blades, and tubes can be rented. You can canoe or tube the Root River or cycle the 35-mile Root River Trail.

The Old Barn Amish Craft Store offers the finest in beautiful Amish quilts, baskets, dolls, furniture and other crafts. Guests can also schedule a fascinating Amish Tour, where a trained guide will take you back in time through Minnesota's largest Amish colony.

If only all camping were this good.

RED WING

Located in the beautiful Hiawatha Valley along the spectacular bluffs and the mighty Mississippi River lies the town of Red Wing, originally the site of a Dakota Sioux farming village. Two missionaries with the Evangelical Missionary Society of Lausanne, Switzerland were the first European settlers in this region. Although French Voyageurs first named the area Barn Bluff, the name permanently chosen was Red Wing, in honor of Chief Red Wing of the Dakota tribe, who first greeted them.

From its origins as a missionary outpost, Red Wing became a busy riverfront trade center. It prospered into the 19th century as an industrial center specializing in leather processing, lime quarries and clay-related industries. The Red Wing boot, manufactured by the Red Wing Shoe Company since 1905, helped make the name well-known. The City Beautiful movement in the early 20th century prompted the building of grand homes and government buildings still majestic today. Red Wing is 50 miles southeast of the Twin Cites on the Mississippi River.

ATTRACTIONS & EVENTS

The *Goodhue County Historical Museum* provides a visual history of the community. The *T.B. Sheldon Auditorium Theatre* presents various events and an ongoing multi-media presentation of Mr. Sheldon's work since opening night in 1904. Among several apple orchards located in the Red Wing area are *Hay Creek Apple Farm* and *Flower Valley Orchards*. For more outdoor activity, the *Welch Village Ski Area* and, for bicyclists, the 18 mile wooded *Cannon Valley Trail* offer exhilarating opportunities. The *Schatze Excursion Boat* offers two- and a half-hour lunch and dinner cruises.

Annual events include *Shiver River Days* in January, which brings mutt races, a figure skating show, and the *Uffda Iceman Triathlon*. *River City Days* in August, the *Red Wing Festival of Arts* in mid-October, and the *Holiday Craft Fair* in November round out each year's festivities.

For further information, contact:
Red Wing Area Chamber of Commerce
P.O. Box 133 P
Red Wing, MN 55066
Phone: 612-388-4719
or 1-800-762-9516, ext. 1

ANTIQUES

| *Hill Street Antiques* | 212 Hill Street, Red Wing, MN 55066
Phone: 612-388-0736
Hours: Open daily 10 a.m.-6 p.m., Sundays
Noon-6 p.m. No credit cards accepted. |

It's only fitting that the setting for an antique shop has just as much fascinating history as have the antiques. And in the instance of the old Victorian home that houses Hill Street Antiques in Red Wing, that is certainly the case.

Built by former Red Wing mayor Jesse M. Hodgman in 1876, the house was actually cut in half and given a quarter turn sideways in 1960. No one knows what became of the other half or the widow's walk that once crowned the building. Inside, you'll find antiques with stories all their own. Proprietors Al Pinkert and Jan Herrly specialize in the more unusual Red Wing dinnerware from the '50s and '60s, including some rare place settings. Their objective is to offer the unusual and only mint condition items.

Located just two blocks west of the antique shops on Old West Main Street, the house has been carefully restored. From furniture to figurines, glassware to collectibles, Hill Street Antiques offers an extensive selection and a wonderful setting for browsing.

BED & BREAKFAST

| *Hungry Point Inn* | #One Olde Deerfield Road, Welch, MN 55089
Phone: 612-437-3660
Hrs.: Check-in 4 p.m. Check-out 11 a.m.
Visa, MasterCard and Discover accepted. |

You'll enjoy the genuine hospitality of early New England at the Hungry Point Inn, set atop the wooded bluffs of southeastern Minnesota. From the moment you step through the door, you are immersed in a colonial atmosphere of hand-woven baskets filled with dried herbs, flowers, nuts and other fruits of the land. A fire crackles in a massive walk-in fireplace where kettles hang, ready for use. The common rooms are delightfully decorated with a kaleidoscope of authentic period antiques and interesting artifacts.

Your bed chamber beckons with period furnishings and a hand-woven coverlet. Unique conversation pieces abound.

A century old log cabin on the property is lovingly restored with antique furnishings, fireplace and double whirlpool; a most romantic hideaway complete with bountiful breakfast delivered in a basket!

BED & BREAKFAST

The	818 West 3rd Street, Red Wing, MN 55066
Candlelight Inn	**Phone: 612-388-8034**
	Hrs: Open every day.
	Visa and MasterCard accepted.

The Candlelight Inn, listed in the Minnesota Historical Register, was built in 1877 by Horace Rich, manager of the Red Wing Stoneware Company. Over the century of its existence, subsequent owners have lovingly maintained the home and, in 1989, The Candlelight Inn was established.

Current owners and innkeepers Mary and Bud Jaeb fell in love with the house because of its warmth and integrity and continue the tradition of preserving this lovely Victorian residence much as it was over one hundred years ago.

The Candlelight Inn has four bedrooms, all with private bath and some with whirlpool and fireplace. Each of the bedrooms is beautifully decorated with antiques of the Victorian period.

The Inn has five unique fireplaces, beautiful hardwood floors, an elegant staircase and original Quesal lighting; cherry, butternut, oak and walnut woods are tastefully blended throughout the house. The superb craftsmanship is apparent in the cabinetry, staircase, parquet floors and trim.

The Candlelight Inn is conveniently located near downtown Red Wing. The T.B. Sheldon Performing Arts Theatre, fine dining and extraordinary shopping are all within walking distance of the Inn. Also nearby are miles of walking, bicycle and ski trails, as well as the various recreational opportunities on the Mississippi River and many fine golf courses. Treasure Island Casino is just minutes away.

Mary and Bud look forward to welcoming you to their home—The Candlelight Inn—where heritage and hospitality dwell under the same roof.

BED & BREAKFAST

Golden Lantern Inn

721 East Avenue, Red Wing, MN 55066
Phone: 612-388-3315
Hrs: Open year-round.
Visa and MasterCard accepted.

If you had to come up with a recipe for a great Bed & Breakfast, you'd put it in a wonderful little town full of wonderful attractions, you'd set up shop in a charming old home, you'd sprinkle an art collection liberally throughout the place and you'd have a little history to tell your guests as they sipped coffee around the fireplace.

Presto! The perfect B & B.

These are precisely the ingredients that went into the creation of the Golden Lantern Inn, launched in 1993. It's in Red Wing, one of America's truly great river towns. It's a wonderful old home, a tudor-style mansion built in the 1930s. The art collection of innkeeper Goldeen Knudtson is to be found everywhere in the house, including the works of Bev Doolittle, Robert Bateman and Robert Olson. And it has history.

The house has been home to three presidents of the Red Wing Shoe Company, the town's best-known enterprise.

Opened in the summer of 1993, the Golden Lantern is quickly developing an impressive reputation. Guests can choose from four wonderful rooms. Shannon's Room is decorated in champagne beige and red, giving it a romantic flair. It has a double bed and private shower. Natasha's Room is done in hues of blue and white, giving it an airy appeal with a queen size bed and private bath.

Hunter green and burgundy dominate in Jennifer's room, a charming enclave with a double bed and double whirlpool. And the creme de la creme is Rebecca's Suite, a perfect honeymoon or anniversary getaway done in dark greens and dusty rose with double jacuzzi and television.

Each of the home's four fireplaces is tastefully sculpted in wood, marble, brass or stone. Walnut, oak, cherry and maple are used throughout the house. A scrumptious full breakfast is served either in the dining room, on the screen porch or in your room. Coffee is

brought to your door each morning at eight. A hot tub is located on the back patio. And the library is the perfect place for smokers.

Gracious and relaxing, the Golden Lantern Inn is located just three blocks from the heart of Red Wing, truly an oasis with a charming past and a promising future.

BED & BREAKFAST

Hearthwood Bed & Breakfast

Between Hastings and Red Wing off Hwy 316.
17650 200th Street E., Hastings, MN 55033.
Phone: 612-437-1133. Hrs: Open year-round.
Visa, MasterCard accepted.

Located halfway between Hastings and Red Wing in the heart of the lower St. Croix and Mississippi River Valleys, this former private home opened in 1986 with a splash on the cover of *St. Paul Homes* magazine. It's making its mark for more than just fine architecture.

Situated on 10 acres, surrounded by woodland trails and the tranquil sounds of the country, Hearthwood blends a quaint timber facade with Cape Cod architectural influences. Hosts Ann and Gary Berg have created a myriad of choices with five distinctly different guest rooms available. They range from the Cuddleton Suite with its cozy country decor, traditional bed and private bath with clawfoot tub, all the way up to the Chancery Suite featuring whirlpool bath, four-poster Rice bed, 18th century decor, fireplace and private entry.

Guests gather for wine, beverages and a snack in the evening in the Great Room with its massive stone fireplace the focal point. Winter, spring, summer or fall, Hearthwood makes for a pampered escape.

◆ ◆ ◆ ◆ ◆ ◆ ◆

Pratt-Taber Inn

706 W. Fourth Street, Red Wing, MN 55066.
Phone: 612-388-5945. Hrs: Open year-round.
Visa and MasterCard accepted.

"When I search for a peaceful moment, I will think of sitting on the porch of the Pratt-Taber Inn." - Garrison Keillor. What better endorsement for an Inn than that of one of its more famous occupants. Keillor stayed here for six weeks in one stretch and is among the hundreds who've left satisfied and refreshed. Listed on the National Register of Historic Places, the Pratt-Taber Inn has been run by Dick and Jane Molander for more than a decade and it has received just about every accolade available.

Maybe it's the setting, a fabulous thirteen-room, Italianate style home originally built in 1876 by A.W. Pratt. Perhaps it's the authentic furnishings, the charming guest rooms, the peaches and cream French toast or the special touches. Or it could be the homemade goodies and apple cider always available to tempt your palate. All that and the prices haven't been raised in years.

Whatever the reason, the Pratt-Taber is among the very best, in Red Wing and beyond. You'll not be disappointed.

CASINO

Treasure Island Casino	5734 Sturgeon Lake Road, Welch, MN 55089 **Phone: 800-222-7077** Hrs: Open 24 hours a day, 7 days a week Visa, MasterCard, Discover and checks accepted.

At Treasure Island, you'll find more ways to play and win. Deal yourself in on some of the most exciting blackjack action around. With 52 tables, you can make bets that range from $3 to $1000. Hit it big with slots of fun. More than 1250 high-return machines to choose from, play your hand at video poker or pick your lucky numbers in a game of video keno. Or, go for the big payouts on any of their exciting progressives.

The excitement happens around the clock with cocktails in Toucan Harry's Lounge, three restaurants and the friendliest bingo hall found anywhere. Check out the Marina and RV park. They're located minutes away from the Twin Cities between Hastings and Red Wing.

Treasure Island is perfect for special events, meetings and conventions, too. The experienced catering staff can arrange everything to perfection when you call. Groups as small as 16 or as large as 500 can work, play and win at Treasure Island!

GOLF COURSE & SKI AREA

Mount Frontenac Ski Area and Golf Course	Highway 61 Frontenac, MN 55026 **Phone: 612-388-5826, 612-345-3504** Visa and MasterCard accepted.

Nine miles down the highway from Red Wing, in the heart of Minnesota's Hiawatha Valley, sits the town of Old Frontenac. It's one of the earliest settlements in Minnesota, established along the Mississippi River bluffs by French fur traders in the 1700s.

The Mount Frontenac Ski Area has been in operation since 1968, and the golf course was opened in 1985. This splendid 330-acre site provides a great recreational opportunity for both skiers and golfers.

The ski area offers a 420-foot vertical drop and a variety of slopes and trails to excite beginner, intermediate or expert skiers. Lessons are available; special rates apply for families on Sundays.

The golf course sits on top of the fabulous Mississippi River bluffs, surrounded by beautiful pine, spruce and oak trees, with a spectacular view of the Hiawatha Valley and scenic Lake Pepin. Group outings are welcome, and arrangements can be made for catered meals or cookouts. A great choice winter or summer.

HISTORIC HOTEL

St. James Hotel

406 Main Street or P.O. Box 71, Red Wing, MN
55066. **Phone: 612-388-2846 or 800-252-1875.**
Hrs: Open year-round.
Major credit cards accepted.

Nestled in the picturesque Hiawatha Valley, the St. James Hotel stands as a tribute to a by-gone era. Built in 1875 when Red Wing was the primary wheat shipping port in the world, this hotel has long been the cornerstone of the community.

After being purchased by the Red Wing Shoe Company in 1977, the hotel was placed on the National Register of Historic Places and restored to its original Victorian elegance and charm.

The 60 individually decorated guest rooms have been decorated with hand-made quilts, antiques and quality reproductions. Each room is named after a river boat which travelled the mighty Mississippi and most offer a breathtaking view of the beautiful Hiawatha Valley carved out eons ago by the meandering river on its long journey to the south.

Upon arrival, guests receive complimentary champagne or cat-awba juice. In the evening, a housekeeper will stop in to remove your quilt and leave a box of chocolates for you. In the morning, awaken to coffee, tea or hot chocolate and, during the week, a paper will be waiting outside your door.

There are a variety of lodging packages to choose from including activities like boating, biking, skiing, eagle watching and photography. And, of course, you may come just for an overnight stay, if you wish.

The hotel boasts two restaurants, two lounges, eleven unique shops, eleven meeting rooms for up to 300 people, complete catering facilities, a full line of audio visual equipment and free covered parking. Whatever else it is to its many visitors, the hotel has become best known for its charming hospitality and warm, friendly staff. At the St. James, you'll be treated like a welcome friend. It's a place where the pace has slowed and guests are graciously received. The St. James truly evokes all that is romantic about those Victorian days of old.

HOUSEBOAT & CRUISE

| *Marine Services, Inc.* | 1628 Greenwood St. Red Wing, MN 55066 **Phone: 612-388-7746** |

Charter "The Shady Lady" for a unique vacation or get-away. Begin your memorable houseboat trip in Red Wing, a lovely, historic riverfront town with factory outlets and an abundance of antique shops. You can take a carefree cruise up river on the majestic Mississippi or the pristine St. Croix, or go downstream to beautiful Lake Pepin with its magnificent bluffs, great fishing and soaring eagles.

Visit other river towns like Pepin, Lake City, Wabasha and spend nights at a marina or anchored in some quiet cove. Cook aboard, select a fine restaurant on shore or take a picnic lunch prepared by Marine Services. Bring your own food, snacks and drinks or have Marine Services stock your houseboat for you.

The "Shady Lady" has a 6.5 KW generator, air-conditioner, microwave, electric stove, stereo, video tape player, color TV, hot water heater, shower and a full-size refrigerator/freezer with ice maker. Storage space is limited so travel light, but don't forget essentials like suntan lotion, paper towels, food staples, shorts, sneakers and warm clothes for cool evenings on moonlit waters.

You can sit back and relax in the sun on the flybridge or in the shade while a U.S. Coast Guard certified Captain operates your boat. Having an experienced Captain operating the boat during your cruise relieves you of all responsibility for the safety of both your family or guests and the boat and its equipment. Of course, you and your guests still have the opportunity to plan the trip and to go wherever you wish.

If you're looking for a really unique vacation or just an interesting weekend or day outing, check out the houseboat cruises at Red Wing by Marine Services, Inc.

LODGING

Sterling Motel *Days Inn-Red* *Wing*	Located at Highway 61 & 63 South, 955 East 7th Street, Red Wing, MN 55066 **Phone: 612-388-3568.** Hrs: Open 24 hours. All major credit cards are accepted.

Location. Location. Location. They say it means everything in business. At the Day's Inn in Red Wing, it means everything and more. Formerly the Sterling Motel, the motel still features unique styling, 50 clean, comfortable rooms and friendly, accommodating service offering a welcome haven for boaters, skiers, golfers and hikers, two parks, within walking distance, on the Mississippi River.

Located just one and a quarter miles from historic downtown Red Wing, the Day's Inn is within easy walking distance of Colvill Park's large outdoor swimming pool and picnic area as well as tennis courts, two marines and boat launches on the Mississippi River. In-room coffee, HBO/cable TV, tubs and showers, direct dial phones and individual heating/cooling controls are among the amenities.

In winter, guests can explore nearby Frontenac State Park on cross-country skis or ski downhill at Welch Village. Golfers will enjoy the breathtaking Mississippi National Golf Course. Or you might even get energetic and bike the spectacular Cannon Valley Trail.

RESTAURANT

Liberty *Restaurant &* *Lounge*	303 W. Third St., Red Wing, MN 55066 **Phone: 612-388-8877** Hrs: Sun.-Thu. 8 a.m.-midnight, Fri.-Sat. 8 a.m.-1 a.m. Major credit cards accepted.

Mouthwatering pizza and a unique antique setting are the hallmarks of Liberty Restaurant & Lounge in downtown Red Wing. Housed in a century-old building, Liberty's decor gives patrons a nostalgic view of yesteryear. However, the restaurant's renowned pizza creations are thoroughly modern and downright tasty!

Pizza isn't all that's to be found here, though. The restaurant also offers American, Mexican and Italian dishes; a popular Sunday brunch; and a chicken, fish and shrimp buffet on Fridays. The diet menu is interesting—it's not often that Canadian walleye pike and broiled shrimp in the shell can be listed under light entreés.

For those staying in nearby motels or visiting the Marina, Liberty offers a complimentary shuttle to and from the restaurant. How's that for service?

Along with the scrumptious dinners, it all adds up to genuine, old-fashioned hospitality, served up with hot and tasty treats any visitor will love.

SHOPPING

Riverfront Centre | Main Street
Red Wing, MN 55066

The historic Riverfront Centre is one of the most relaxing shopping adventures in the state of Minnesota. The shops include:

Main Street Toys offering toys that stimulate and challenge children. They carry such names as Playmobile and Brio along with books, tapes, art supplies and a variety of other items for children of all ages. Phone: 612-388-5900.

Riverfront Gallery offers a wide selection of original and limited edition prints and distributes the works of publishers. Collectors of portraits, Americana, wildlife and Western art will find exactly what they need here. Professional framing offered. Phone: 612-388-3103.

Yours Truly carries unique cards, gifts, T-shirts, candy and stationery. Look for names like Mary Engelbreight, Precious Moments, Dept. 56 Heritage Village. Phone: 612-388-7502.

A-Holiday-A-Fair is a distinctive gift emporium carrying such lines as Heritage Lace, Sno-babies, Dept. 56, Cherished Teddies, Yankee Candles, Kennebunk throws and Armstrong-Haugen prints. It's Christmas all year in the back of the shop. Phone: 612-388-9540.

Riverfront Deli is a most excellent little deli with a European flair. Beautifully decorated inside, the deli is a great place for friendly lunch or a petite coffee break. Enjoy the patio. Phone: 612-388-5366.

Midwest Music Box Company carries a large selection of music boxes from figurines and jewelry boxes, carousels, roses and jeweled eggs. Custom creations are offered. Phone and mail orders accepted. Phone: 612-388-4436.

Good Life Nutrition Centre is a wonderful shop with very personal service and a caring staff to help select vitamins, herbs, sports nutrition and diet products. Phone: 612-388-8517.

Just B Cuz offers country crafts and handcrafted items to please the eye and warm the heart. Check out their store in Stillwater, MN, too. Phone: 612-388-5692.

The Glass Scope is a nationally known kaleidoscope shop that not only carries the work of some 40 American kaleidoscope artists but also carries relaxing CD's and tapes. Phone: 612-388-2048.

Global Express/Carlson Travel Network with 2100 locations worldwide offers more choices including exclusive value added packages. Phone: 612-388-6702.

Red Wing Shoe Store offers a large inventory of sizes and widths, computerized fitting and a 100% satisfaction guarantee. Also offered is a line of clothing. Phone: 612-388-6233.

Irish Macushla's offers unique gifts and specialty items that are the essence of Ireland. Phone: 612-385-0667.

SHOPPING

St. James Hotel Shopping Court	406 Main Street, Red Wing, MN 55066 Hrs: Mon.-Sat. 9:30 a.m.-6 p.m., Thurs. 9:30 a.m.-8 p.m., Sun. noon-5 p.m. Major credit cards accepted.

The St. James Hotel Shopping Court offers affordable merchandise in elegant surroundings and with excellent service.

The staff at **M. Christopher** wants to share their time and talents with shoppers who are looking for women's sportswear, dresses, outerwear and accessories. Phone: 612-385-0550.

Shear Perfection is a contemporary full service salon offering hair cutting, coloring and perming, tanning, manicures and pedicures, facials as well as make up and a full line of skin and body products. Their philosophy? "We consult before we cut." Phone: 612-388-8803.

Steamboat Park is an art gallery showcasing regional and local art and limited edition prints, museum reproduction jewelry, art glass, hand-made porcelain, decorator posters, Victorian prints and more. A wonderfully eclectic gallery where today's treasures are tomorrow's heirlooms. Phone: 612-388-4022.

The **Yankee Peddler** is a complete men's store but also one with some surprises like Red Wing Chocolate, Pendleton Indian blankets and Lady Pendleton. You will enjoy their use of antiques in their store displays. Phone: 612-388-1355.

The **River Peddler Antiques** is where you'll find an excellent selection of antique desks, tables, chests, rockers, cupboards, crystal and china. There are also new accessories to enhance your own antiques. Phone: 612-388-5990.

The Levee offers one-of-a-kind women's clothing along with a friendly, well-trained staff to give you the utmost care and guidance when selecting from the extensive line of updated sportswear and casual coordinates. Phone: 612-388-8792.

Christie's offers the finest in fashion combined with the very best customer service—an outstanding selection of women's apparel, from casual clothing for nearly every activity to professional wear suited for any business occasion. Phone: 612-388-8144.

Red Wing Book Company is a full service book store with the latest best sellers in both paper back and hard cover. Greeting cards, magazines, bookmarks and more. Phone: 612-388-7274.

Maritas offers gifts, furniture, floral and decorating accessories of elegant design at affordable prices. Many of the floral arrangements are one-of-a-kind originals. Phone: 612-388-6631.

Patterson's satisfies both classic and contemporary tastes with fine jewelry and gifts—truly works of art. Phone: 612-388-8140.

Uniquely Yours features a rainbow of accessories—hats, jewelry, belts, hair accessories, specialty tops, sweatshirts and more—grouped by color. Elegance without extravagance. Phone: 612-388-4390.

SPECIALTY SHOP

Red Wing *Mercantile* *Company*	325 Main Street, Red Wing, MN 55066. **Phone: 612-385-0170.** Hrs: Mon., Wed., Fri., Sat. 10 a.m.-6 p.m. Thursdays 10 a.m.-8 p.m. Sundays 10 a.m.-5 p.m. Visa, MasterCard and Discover accepted.

If there's a single Minnesota town known for the quality of its browsing, it would have to be Red Wing. Long a tourist destination, one of the newest additions to its roster of the quaint and the curious is also one of its best.

The Red Wing Mercantile Company opened in 1993 in one of the town's prime locations, one block from the Mississippi River, across from Red Wing Shoes and kitty-corner to perhaps the best-known of Red Wing's many attractions, the historic St. James Hotel. Talk about being at the center of the action!

Located in the former Gambles Store, the Red Wing Mercantile Company specializes in Native American art, unique gifts and antiques. The historic setting is a perfect display case. And the high ceilings and oversized windows give the place a wonderful sense of spaciousness.

Once inside, you'll find everything from museum-quality African fossils to Native American art and artifacts, from authentic beaded Ojibwa creations to Navaho sculptures, from Canadian Inuit art to fabulous jewelry, from Mexican crystal to handcrafted Wabasha loons.

Variety and quality. It's all here. And the atmosphere is as much of an attraction as the wares themselves.

Amid the Native American portraits, the paintings, the rugs and the reproductions of commercial logos and slogans from a bygone era, the coffee is always on and there's an antique dining room set available for those who'd rather sit, sip and listen to the soothing background music while their partner browses. Maybe even buys.

Darlene and Richard Binner have put together an impressive collection of goods in a rather short period of time. From Minnesota-grown food specialties (mixes, honey, jams, wild rice, coffees, sauces, syrups and Shitake mushroom soup mix among them) to the Bob Timberlake throws and quilts to the Amish Bentwood hickory furniture, Southwest furniture and futons, the place oozes quality. There's even a knitting section and an area specializing in health products.

The Red Wing Mercantile Company, a must-see in Bluff Country and a unique attraction where the past and present rendezvous.

SPECIALTY SHOP

| *Red Wing Pottery Salesroom* | 1995 West Main, Red Wing, MN 55066. **Phone:** **612-388-3562 or 800-228-0174.** Hrs: Open 7 days a week. All major credit cards are accepted. |

It's a rare combination indeed.

Not often will you find something of legitimate historical significance offering bargain pricing and tremendous value year-round. But that's exactly what you'll find seven days a week at the Red Wing Pottery Salesroom, the place for pottery in a town known for the same.

The Gillmer family, owners of the Red Wing Pottery Salesroom, have kept the Red Wing Pottery name alive, carrying on a great tradition that could have ended altogether if not for their efforts. When a labor dispute closed the Pottery in 1967, Richard Gillmer took over the inventory and created what is today known as the Salesroom.

The Gillmers now offer the Midwest's largest selection of dinnerware, china, pottery, gifts and collectibles. In fact, some of the original Red Wing dinnerware inventory still remains and is for sale.

They are major discounters of dinnerware, glassware and china. The store is a sprawling place, the kind of mecca a dedicated browser would die for. Name brands like Noritake, Mikasa and Lenox abound. The inventory seems endless with over 500 patterns on display plus gifts and collectibles, too. And the knowledgeable staff, some of whom have been there for more than a decade, is what really makes the difference. Their attitude and extensive background make it a fun place to browse or buy.

The Red Wing Pottery Salesroom is a magnet for tourists from all over the world. On a typical day, a dozen languages and two dozen accents can be heard, all looking for the same thing: high quality and low prices.

Next door is the Candy Store where they make their own fudge, plus the "Loons and Ladyslippers" store featuring Minnesota gifts and gift ideas.

The original factory outlet to the Red Wing Potteries, the Red Wing Pottery Salesroom is located in the big white building, just west of Highway 61 in Red Wing's historic Pottery District.

SPECIALTY SHOPS

Campbell's Curiosity Shoppes	Corner 7th and Bush. 328 West 7th Street, Red Wing, MN 55066. **Phone: 612-388-6659.** Hrs: Mon.-Wed., Sat. 10 a.m.-6 p.m., Thurs.-Fri. 10 a.m.-8 p.m. Sundays Noon-4 p.m. Visa and MasterCard accepted.

Avis Campbell and Cathie Gatz each had a dream. Today, their dreams have been transformed into the reality that is Campbell's Curiosity Shoppes, a unique shopping experience.

The Curiosity Bookstore (Avis) features children's books and interesting educational items. Grandma's Kids (Cathie) sells a fine line of children's clothing, preemie to size 7 in boys and preemie to size 14 in girls, along with stuffed toys, rattles and layette items. In addition, you will find stamps and stencils, gift items for every occasion, the Camille Beckman line of body care products, gourmet coffees and teas, chocolates and many varied craft items by local craftspeople.

Located in a wonderful old "Dolly Madison" Victorian home, it's a perfect setting for "A Shoppe Along the Way." As the ceiling fans gently whir away the afternoon and the scent of fresh ground coffee fills the air, you will want to browse through the sprawling old house with its antique fireplace and varied collection of treasures.

❖ ❖ ❖ ❖ ❖ ❖ ❖

Irish Macushlas' Gifts and Imports	Riverfront Centre, 314 Main St., Red Wing, MN 55066. **Phone: 612-385-0667.** Hrs: Mon-Sat 9:30 a.m.-6 p.m., Thurs. till 8, Sun 12 noon-5 p.m. Visa, MasterCard and Discover accepted.

No Blarney! The Irish have landed at Macushlas' Gifts and Imports in Red Wing. That's because you can find the very essence of Ireland in the unique gifts and specialty items stocked in the store.

Here, you'll find Galway Crystal, Belleek & Donegal Parian China, Royal Tara China, Wicklow Vale Pottery, Dulske Handcut Glass, Irish Heritage Collection of Cottages, Pictures and Banners, Irish Claddagh Jewelry, David Winter Irish Collection and Rynhart Collection. You'll love the 100% cotton afghans.

Yes, it's a veritable Irish paradise. They even have clothing and accessories, fragrances of Ireland, cassettes, CD's, videos and music books.

Stop by their Stillwater store, too, located at Grand Garage. (Macushla means 'sweetheart' in gaelic.)

SPECIALTY SHOP

Mississippi Pearl Jewelry Company

329 Main Street, Red Wing, MN 55066
Phone: 612-385-0082. Hrs: M-W, 10 a.m.-5:30 p.m., Th., 10-8, Fri., Sat. 10-5.
Visa, MasterCard and Amex accepted.

Did you know that some pearls are harvested from Mississippi clams? Occasionally, a natural pearl occurs in these clams.

Natural pearls are among the oldest and most universal gems. Ancient writers called them dew from heaven. They are already beautiful when found and no cutting or polishing is required. Natural pearls are found in many different species of clams and some of the most beautiful gems in the world come from the Mississippi River.

A natural pearl is solid pearl all the way through, but a cultured pearl is mainly a shell bead with a very thin pearl coating. Pearls, like many gems, come in a wide variety of colors and white is the most common. Other colors like pink, cream, purple, red and green are very rare.

At Mississippi River Jewelry Company, you can find all the beauty of these natural pearls taken from the Mississippi River and shaped into lovely jewelry. These fabulous designs are collected by a discriminating clientele and people just like you!

◆ ◆ ◆ ◆ ◆ ◆ ◆

"Canada Geese"

THEATRE

The Sheldon Performing Arts Theatre	Third Street at East Avenue, Red Wing, MN 55066. **Phone: 612-388-2806 or 800-899-5759** Hrs.: Ticket office Mon.-Sat. noon-5 p.m., 2 hours prior to curtain. Visa, MasterCard and Discover.

Celebrating its ninetieth year as the nation's first municipally owned "playhouse," the Sheldon Performing Arts Theatre continues to present a variety of performing and entertaining arts for Red Wing and the surrounding rural region of southeastern Minnesota and western Wisconsin. A $4 million restoration was just completed in the fall of 1988.

Public tours are 1 p.m. Saturdays, November through May and Thursdays, Fridays and Saturdays at 1 p.m. May through October. "In the Shadow of Barn Bluff: The Story of Red Wing" is an 18-minute multi-media presentation shown in the Sheldon's gallery prior to the theatre tour. It introduces visitors to the community's unique history and provides an excellent background for visitors about to explore this wonderful area.

The Sheldon is the nation's first municipal theatre and offers classic and contemporary fare that delights artists and patrons alike. Visual art exhibits, theatre productions, concerts, family programs and classic films all have their place at the Sheldon. Indeed, the theatre's stated mission is to provide the highest quality and variety in the performing arts, as well as to educate students about program production.

Artists such as Leo Kottke and groups such as the Budapest Chamber Orchestra and the Minneapolis Children's Theatre Company have performed here in the past, and the roster of illustrious artists and events at the Sheldon continues to grow.

Not enough time to attend a major show? Then stop by the Sheldon on a Saturday morning and attend the weekly "Echoes of the Sheldon" tour, an introduction to the theatre and restoration of the building. They will point out the many beautiful details within, ranging from the mosaic tile floor in the entryway to the Austrian crystal chandeliers in the intimate auditorium seating 466.

Through its restoration and revitalization, the Sheldon continues to contribute to Red Wing's cultural life, including regional schools which benefit by an arts and educational outreach program.

The Sheldon not only presents local, national and international artists, but it also is a producer and a rental facility for corporate presentations, weddings and private parties.

Be sure to call ahead for performance times and a calendar of events.

CORPORATE PROFILE

***Red
Wing Shoe
Company***
In this place where the surrounding plains open up to form the wide Mississippi Valley, mankind has lived, worked and prospered for a thousand years. Blessed with an abundance of natural resources and strategically located on the banks of the Mississippi, Red Wing was soon to become a booming frontier town. With the nearby materials and ease of transportation, Red Wing became an important center for the production and distribution of flour, linseed oil, lumber, pottery, lime, boats, furniture, wagons, beer, bricks, leather and footwear.

The history of the Red Wing Shoe Company began at the turn of the century when the needs of a growing country compelled a young company to strive for the highest level of quality in a product that would find its way onto the feet of America.

Success was just a dim hope when German immigrant Charles Beckman closed his retail shoe store and, along with 14 other investors, organized the Red Wing Shoe Company. To his benefit, farming, logging, mining, blacksmithing and railroading were booming occupations at the turn of the century, and the workers needed durable shoes and boots. Beckman simply had to figure out a way to serve that waiting market.

On January 26, 1905, the Red Wing daily newspaper announced that a new shoe factory was being built in Red Wing and it would "probably employ 100 people to begin with." The article further reported that it was "generally conceded" the factory would someday employ several times that number. When the doors opened, Red Wing Shoe Company's manufacturing output was 110 pairs of shoes each 10-hour day.

Red Wing's output increased with each new occupational need. To accommodate those needs, the company began offering a wide range of shoe sizes and widths that ensured its customers a comfortable fit. The company discovered a growing market, one that was taking notice of Red Wing's service-minded attitude.

In 1908 Red Wing began manufacturing welt-constructed shoes attaching a leather strip to the shoe upper and sewing it to the sole which offered customers a more comfortable and durable fit. Welt shoes catered to Red Wing's number-one customers: farmers. To accommodate the production needs, the building was expanded to a typical four-story factory. When the new factory was completed, daily production increased to 450 pairs, four times what it was in 1906. Red Wing had another surge of growth in 1912 when it introduced the black and brown "Chief" line.

Commonly known as "The Farmer's Shoe," it featured specially tanned, manure-proof leather and was designed with farmers' needs in mind. The Chief line cemented a public image of Red Wing that the company tailored its footwear specifically to the needs of various occupational and recreational activities.

An example was the army shoe first manufactured in 1918 for World War I and built over the regulation Munson U.S. Army Last, designed to "fit all feet." The Munson last, renowned for its comfort, was used in many other shoe styles for the next 20 years.

After the war, the still-popular army shoe was renamed and manufactured until 1965.

The 1930s were prosperous years for Red Wing. Catering to a booming new market for oil-field workers, Red Wing introduced the "Oil King" boot, which spearheaded new business during a time when work shoes weren't selling. It was another successful attempt to market specialized footwear and service a particular need.

Red Wing also introduced its first elite boot—a men's dress or riding boot dubbed the "Aristo," and it expanded into a women's line of shoes and boots.

But the greatest impact on the company was when then president J.R. Sweasy gambled with a non-leather material for work shoe soles. He introduced the rubber cord sole, which proved to be quite an innovation in the history of shoemaking.

The successful extra-long-wearing soles set a trend in a shoemaking world that would come to rely totally on synthetic materials.

Red Wing took advantage of the availability of rubber products, using Gro Cord soles and Goodyear heels that were still common 20 years later.

During the tumultuous Depression years, Red Wing used innovation and perseverance to keep production moving and weekly paychecks coming out. Dubbed the "living on a shoestring" years, Red Wing offered what was to become the best-remembered shoe of the decade because its price, 99 cents, matched its stock number.

During the 1930s when most people couldn't afford more than $1.50 for a pair of shoes, No. 99 kept the factory going and the community employed. Again, service to customers, employees and the community was the company attitude that kept its doors open.

Business bounced back during World War II when the government contracted for the manufacture of hundreds of combat shoes. Red Wing easily met the U.S. Army's requirements for shoes in 239 different sizes and widths.

In 1949, William D. Sweasy took over as president and immediately increased responsibilities for department heads. Bill's idea was that Red Wing "grew" specialists, and gradually, a management team of specialists evolved from each division. During this time, Red Wing retail stores began opening all over the country.

The new management led the company to 1952, a landmark year

when the No. 877 Irish Setter Sport Boot hit the market like a hurricane and became the new star of Red Wing Shoes. Irish Setters gave Red Wing national prominence and, as many believe, put the company on the map.

The stature of the boot also symbolized decades of hard work and pride invested in the company by its employees, qualities that prevail with today's Red Wing work horse.

The year 1965 was another landmark year, when Bill Sweasy created the Vasque Hiking Boot Division of the Red Wing Shoe Company.

Vasque footwear products grew out of Bill's love of travel and his appreciation for nature. While traveling in Italy, Bill recognized, firsthand, the hand-crafted art form and personal commitment Italian bootmakers built into their products. Bill, together with Sergio Ferlat, Vasque's original partner in Italy, saw an opportunity to bring Vasque products to America so people could experience all the richness and beauty of the outdoors in comfortable, dependable boots. It was the best of both worlds: Old World family hand-crafted shoe making, designed and fit for American feet.

Today, Vasque is globally recognized as a leading brand of outdoor footwear. The Vasque line includes products designed to comfortably take people everywhere—from casual backyard hikes to extreme, heavy duty mountaineering expeditions. They also have a popular line of rugged footwear for children called "Kids Klimbers," plus a line of contoured sandals for men and women.

Red Wing's breakthrough in the 1930s with the rubber cord sole was duplicated in the late 1960s with the introduction of urethane soles.

Red Wing pioneered the concept of molding the urethane to the shoe. Just as sewn welt construction had replaced pegged and nailed soles, urethane was replacing the sewn welt. The advantages were enormous. Lighter weight, more durability, more comfort and less cost. Plus urethane could be molded into any sole pattern, from heavy lug soles for lumberjacks to non-slip soles for auto mechanics.

Special compounds could be formulated for specific performance, such as Red Wing's ESD soles for the computer industry. They bleed off electricity to help protect delicate electronic components from damaging Electro-Static Discharges.

Besides Irish Setters, the urethane SuperSole and ESD shoes, Red Wing's newest product success is its steel-toe line.

It was originally introduced in the late 1930s to give added toe protection in high-risk jobs. OSHA and other employee safety requirements have turned it into a tremendous opportunity for the company, and the steel-toe line has grown each year.

America's work force is more diversified than ever. That's why you'll find Red Wings with 22 different types of leather and a choice of 18 different sole materials.

In fact, at a Red Wing Store, you'll find more than 150 different styles. Red Wing believes that every occupation has certain requirements for comfort, protection and long wear. There's no such thing as one shoe or boot being perfect for every job.

Today, Red Wing Shoe Company supports a payroll of 1,400 employees and manufactures more than 8,000 pairs of shoes and boots each day.

Red Wing products for work, sport and leisure are sold through 400 Red Wing Shoe Stores (including the newly expanded store in Red Wing's Riverfront Centre) and through approximately 5,500 footwear retailers in the United States and Canada. Red Wing Shoes are sold in more than 80 countries.

These numbers are all the more impressive considering the American shoe manufacturing industry is but a fraction of the size it was 25 years ago.

For example, in 1968 the American shoe industry produced 642 million pairs of shoes. By 1985, foreign imports had cut that production to 266 million pairs. During that period, imports of casual, dress and work shoes had risen from 21 percent to 77 percent of the market.

Yet, during those same years, despite the decline in American production, despite the loss of jobs, Red Wing Shoe production grew more than 25 percent and its work force grew 38 percent, vitally important to a small town along the Mississippi River.

Today, with more shoes than ever being imported, Red Wing is one of the few American manufacturers still exporting shoes around the world.

William J. Sweasy, Red Wing's current president, summed up the company's 89-year success in four words: pride, service, fit and quality. "People have come to expect this from Red Wing," he said. "Service is significant to our survival. It has been our number-one priority since the first day Red Wing opened. Service is the new corporate buzzword for the '90s, but we've been doing it all along. We don't just give lip service. We follow through."

In 1905, Red Wing Shoe created its niche by matching products to market needs and establishing customer service as the top priority. Employee pride, knowledge and customer service are hallmarks of the Red Wing Shoe Company today.

ROCHESTER

Rochester is the largest city in southern Minnesota. In 1863, Dr. William Mayo settled here with his sons and began what was to become the world-renowned Mayo Medical Center. The Mayo Complex and IBM are the two largest employers in the surrounding area and together they have a profound economic impact on the community.

Rochester has the world's largest winter concentration of Canadian geese. A former Mayo Clinic patient donated 12 of the geese to the area in 1947 and these attracted others. The flock grew to what it is today and their presence adds greatly to the community.

ATTRACTIONS & EVENTS

The Mayo Clinic is the largest medical complex in the world and treats nearly 300,000 patients annually from around the world. Group tours are available for up to 50.

St. Mary's Hospital is a Mayo Foundation hospital started by the Franciscan Sisters and works in conjunction with the Mayo Clinic. Tours are available. The *Rochester Methodist Hospital* offers tours with advance reservations.

Mayowood is the former home of the Mayo family and is listed on the National Register of Historic Places. *The Plummer House* was home to one of the first Mayo Clinic physicians. *The Rochester Art Center, The Quarry Hill Nature Center* and the *Heritage House* are additional attractions.

Annual events include the *Rochester Festival of the Arts* in June, *The Rochesterfest* in June and the *Threshing Show* in late July. A *Greek Festival* is held near *Silver Lake* in August and offers dancing and authentic Greek food.

There are six golf courses in the area, allowing golfers to enjoy their sport with little or no wait. These include the *Eastwood Golf Course, Maple Valley Golf & Country Club, Northern Hills Golf Course, Rochester Golf & Country Club, Soldier's Memorial Field Golf Course* and *Willow Creek Golf Course.*

For further information, contact:
Rochester Convention and Visitors Bureau
150 S. Broadway, Suite A
Rochester, MN 55904
Phone: 507-288-4331 or 800-634-8277

ART CENTER

Rochester Art Center

320 East Center Street, Rochester, MN 55904
Phone: 507-282-8629
Hrs: Tues.-Sat. 10 a..m.-5 p.m.,
Sun. noon-5 p.m.

For the art lover in all of us, Rochester Art Center offers a cornucopia of events and programs ranging from rotating exhibitions to "hands-on" workshops, classes, lectures and videos. The Art Center brings to the community exciting, innovative programs on the leading edge of contemporary art. Its exhibitions and educational programs provide opportunities for people of all ages to know and enjoy a wide range of art experiences.

Every February, Rochester Art Center sponsors the Whole Earth Auction, an evening of food, fun, and fantastic bidding on an array of donated items. Each June, Rochester Art Center offers the Festival of the Arts, a two day Art Fair. More than 100 craftspeople and visual artists converge to provide a spectacular and unforgettable event.

Rochester Art Center, part of the Mayo Park Cultural Complex since 1953, also provides special educational outreach programs in and around the surrounding community. Admission is free to all gallery exhibitions and videos.

ART GALLERY

Herring Art & Frame

5500 Hwy 63 South, Rochester, MN 55904
Phone: 507-288-4339 or 800-950-2293
Hrs: Mon.-Sat. 9 a.m.-5:30 p.m. Open year-round. Visa and MasterCard accepted.

Herring Art & Frame is located just south of Rochester on Highway 63 between the airport and downtown. The art and framing gallery features the area's largest selection of art work in a wide variety of subjects by local and nationally acclaimed artists. They also feature a number of gift items, including Mt. St. Helen's glass, decoys, accessory boxes, plates, sun catchers and more.

Using the same expertise that has won them numerous awards in national and international framing competitions, the Herrings have used exciting, yet tasteful creative designs to enhance the wide selection of art work on display in their picturesque gallery setting.

The selection includes the widest choice of work by Terry Redlin, Linda Nelson Stocks, Robert Olson, Robert Bateman, Carl Brenders, Bev Doolittle and many other outstanding artists.

The "gallery on the hill," surrounded by beautiful gardens on 21 acres of hilly terrain, has been at this location since 1979. Browsers are welcome so don't drive by—stop in!

LODGING

Kahler Lodging	20 SW Second Avenue Rochester, MN 55902 **Phone: 507-282-2581 or 800-533-1655** Major credit cards accepted.

Kahler Lodging started in Rochester in 1912 when John Kahler built the Zumbro Hotel to provide lodging for Mayo Clinic patients and their families. Today, Kahler Lodging consists of the following: The Kahler Hotel, with 700 guest rooms; Clinic View Inn & Suites, with 266 guest rooms and suites; Holiday Inn Downtown, with 172 rooms owned and operated under the Holiday Inn franchise; and the Kahler Plaza Hotel, with 194 rooms.

All Kahler accommodations have excellent sites in the heart of downtown Rochester. The Kahler Hotel, which covers a full city block, is said to be the second largest hotel in the Midwest. In addition to serving medical guests, this hotel provides a full complement of modern meeting and banquet facilities. Over 60 specialty shops and boutiques grace the lower floor.

Recently renovated, the Clinic View Inn & Suites provides modern amenities and a New England-style restaurant. For convenience, a pedestrian subway connects the inn with the Mayo Medical Complex, Rochester Methodist Hospital and Kahler Hotel.

Holiday Inn Downtown primarily serves business travelers and medical guests.

The AAA 4-diamond rated Kahler Plaza Hotel offers luxury accommodations to medical guests and corporate travelers, as well as excellent downtown service to leisure and business travelers.

Dining opportunities abound within the Kahler Lodging restaurants. The Kahler Hotel's elegant Elizabethan Room offers the finest in Continental cuisine.

American specialties with tasty sauces and accompaniments highlight the Pavilion's menu at the Kahler Plaza Hotel.

Giuseppi's Olive Grove features the finest in Italian and American favorites at Holiday Inn Downtown.

Casual, comfortable dining awaits guests at the Yankee Pedlar in the Clinic View Inn & Suites.

All Kahler Lodging hotels are connected via pedestrian subway and skyway to the Mayo Medical Complex. All are within walking distance of Rochester's Mayo Civic Center and just minutes from Soldiers Field Golf Course, Apache Mall and the well-known Silver Lake, an annual haven for thousands of Canada geese.

LODGING

Best Western *Soldiers Field* *Tower & Suites*	401 Sixth Street S.W., Rochester, MN 55902 **Phone: 507-288-2677** **or 800-366-2067** (reservations only) All major credit cards are accepted.

In a quiet Rochester residential area just four blocks from downtown and two-and-a-half blocks from the Mayo Clinic subway is Best Western Soldiers Field Tower & Suites, a hotel with 128 rooms on eight floors, and 90 popular kitchen suites. The decor in this innovative lodging and entertainment complex is both upbeat and modern. The lobby is designed in a comfortable southwestern style.

Among the most unique offerings is summertime rooftop dining—weather permitting. The hotel's First Class Restaurant's "singing waiters & waitresses" are perhaps the most enjoyable and famous amenity. Music and food all combine to make this dining experience both memorable and a great value.

The complex also offers a lounge, pool with jacuzzi and wading pool, sauna, exercise room, playroom, meeting rooms, laundry, and video game rooms. It offers a free courtesy van service to the Mayo Clinic, hospitals, Civic Center and downtown area. Soldiers Field also features a gift shop, bakery and mini-grocery.

RESTAURANT

Michaels *Restaurant/Pap-* *pageorge Taverna*	15 S. Broadway, Rochester, MN 55904 **Phone: 507-288-2020.** Hrs.: 10 a.m.-11 p.m. Call for information and dinner reservations. Closed Sunday. Major credit cards accepted.

Located in downtown Rochester, Michaels is among the city's premier restaurants. Owned and operated since 1951 by the Pappas family, Michaels has been well-known for its old-country charm along with famous food and service.

Michaels' nearly block long interior is divided into several distinctive dining rooms. From Midwestern favorites to native Greek specialties, customers enjoy traditional American steaks and seafood, Greek foods, roast duck and fresh fish. For special occasions, the beautiful Greek Haraka Dining Rooms are available evenings for private parties or meetings.

A recent addition, Pappageorge Taverna, is a restaurant "inside" Michaels that offers lighter fare, such as pastas, gyros and espressos, in a casual and pleasant atmosphere. Here, just like Michaels, you can expect consistent quality in food and service.

Michaels is connected to the downtown skyway system and has adjacent parking.

RESTAURANT

Wong's Cafe

4 S.W. Third Street, Rochester, MN 55902
Phone: 507-282-7545.
Hours.: Mon.-Sat. 11 a.m.-9:30 p.m. Sun. 11
a.m.-9 p.m. Major credit cards accepted.

Imperial chicken. Steamed cod fillets, Chinese style. Just the words make you hungry, don't they? Wong's Cafe has been serving these and many other sumptuous entreés for more than 40 years in downtown Rochester. Located in a former bank on historic Third Street, Wong's Cafe offers extensive Chinese and American fare at very reasonable prices.

One reason for the success of Wong's Cafe lies in its "made to order" service. Wong's will meet the special dietary needs of customers, upon request. Another reason is the insistence on cooking with the very finest and freshest ingredients. They even grow their own bean sprouts!

Opened by Ben and Neil Wong in 1952, Dennis and Michael carry on the tradition of well-prepared food at reasonable prices with courteous service in pleasant, contemporary surroundings. Very popular are the combination plates, such as Chicken Subgum Chow Mein, complete with cashews, water chestnuts and mild peppers.

SPECIALTY SHOP

The House Of The Crafty Mouse

On Hwy 52, Miracle Mile Mini Mall, Rochester, MN
55901. **Phone: 507-282-7711.** Hrs: Mon. - Fri. 10
a.m.-9 p.m., Saturdays 10 a.m.-5 p.m. Sundays
1 p.m.-5 p.m. Visa and MasterCard accepted.

In every city there is that "one shop," so full of delightful gifts and home decorating treasures that you can't wait to get back there. In Rochester, The House of the Crafty Mouse is it.

Jeanne DeBruin started out making pine cone dolls at home. She's come a long way since and now has a regular newsletter mailing to her 4,000 customers. The reason? Because they treat their customers like they treat their friends.

Jeanne travels the country to bring back pictures, candles, rubber stamps, European lace curtains, cards, figurines, plates, dolls and the special Rochester commemorative afghans and adorable gift baskets from the gourmet pantry. The store is busy with shoppers weaving their way through a mouse maze.

The House of the Crafty Mouse will personalize ornaments and gifts, ship anywhere and wrap gifts free. The store is staffed by dedicated, creative people who love what they do. Stop by and see what they mean by a "unique and personal" gift shop.

SPECIALTY SHOP

| *Historic 3rd Street Shops* | 6 shops located on 3rd street in downtown Rochester, MN 55902 |

During the Victorian era, downtown Rochester was known as "Saloon Alley." As Rochester grew, it was revitalized and many buildings were demolished over the years. However, a number of building facades were saved and these magnificent creations of Terra Cotta and hand-cut limestone were wisely placed on store fronts along 3rd street. Now the street is an inviting blend of period lamps, picnic tables, trees and, of course, the period fronts from Victorian style to Art Deco. Near the famous Mayo Clinic, the area is home to many interesting shops, restaurants, hotels and parks. In particular, there are six shops that visitors will want to see.

John Kruesel's General Merchandise specializes in the unusual. They offer antiques like 19th century lighting, jewelry, military vehicles and more. They also purchase estates. Call 507-289-8049.

The Antique Mall On Third Street has fourteen dealers on location to answer your questions and serve the most discriminating buyers. They feature thousands of collectibles like crocks, pottery, glassware, furniture, jewelry, linens, pictures, advertising and Christmas items. New merchandise is added daily to this varied store. Dealers welcome. Call 507-287-0684.

Plum Tree Primitives offers an interesting blend of folk art, antiques, furniture and Amish collectibles. Some of the featured names include, Byers Choice Carolers, Shadow Dancer, Mary Alice Hadley Pottery, and Bennington Pottery. Also offered are a selection of home decorating items. Call 507-282-8589.

The Horse & Buggy is perfect for the warmth and charm of heritage collecting and old-fashioned country decorating. They offer such items as American folk art, Amish quilts and dolls, stoneware, baskets, tinware, Shaker and colonial boxes, cards and cookbooks, primitives and a sprinkling of antiques and interesting one-of-a-kinds. Call 507-281-1183.

The Iridescent House deals in very high quality art and collectibles. Fine gifts from Boehm, Hummels and Royal Doulton are offered along with art glass, toys, pottery, antiques and sterling. Call 507-288-0320.

Artistic Framers Inc. offers unique framing for fine art and quality giftware displayed in a gallery setting. The owners are certified picture framers and all the work is done by hand. Gifts include hand-crafted glassware, Margaret Furlong fine porcelain, prints and sculptures that delight the heart and warm the home. Call 507-281-4890.

TOURS

Olmsted County History Center and Mayowood Mansion	1195 County Road 22 S.W. Rochester, MN 55902 **Phone: 507-282-9447** Hrs: Call for info and tours.

A must when visiting southeastern Minnesota is a stop at the Olmsted County History Center in Rochester where visitors can learn about the area's history and visit fabulous Mayowood Mansion.

The Olmsted County History Center is more than a museum filled with relics of the past. It is a 17,000 square foot educational facility interpreting the history of the area from geological formation through contemporary times.

The gallery was totally renovated in 1990 and features exhibits dealing with Indian inhabitants, white settlement, immigrants, the Mayo family and the development of the Mayo Clinic, International Business Machines Corporation and area agriculture and industry. The facility also includes an extensive genealogical and research library and a museum shop offering unique gifts and historical reproductions.

Mayowood Mansion,
the 55-room former country home of Mayo Clinic founders Doctors C.H. and C.W. Mayo, is also open to the public for professionally guided tours. The mansion was once the center of a self-contained 3,000 acre estate and is now listed on the National Register of Historic Places. The home is furnished with antiques, artwork, and decorative items collected by the Mayo family.

Two generations of Mayos occupied the house, which has been a cultural and social center for the area for over 70 years. It has also been the temporary home of visiting celebrities and dignitaries, including Franklin D. Roosevelt, Adlai Stevenson and the kings of Nepal and Saudi Arabia.

Tours depart from the History Center on a regular schedule. A nominal admission fee includes bus transportation to the mansion.

CORPORATE PROFILE

**Mayo
Clinic**
Mayo Clinic, a model for medical practice throughout the world, took root and grew in the farm fields near Rochester, Minnesota. It grew from the medical practice of a country doctor, William Worrall Mayo, and his sons, William J. and Charles H. Mayo, affectionately known as Dr. Will and Dr. Charlie.

In 1863, in the pioneer days of medicine, Dr. William W. Mayo opened his medical practice in Rochester. His dedication to serving people became a family tradition when his two sons joined him in medicine.

Dr. Will and Dr. Charlie added innovative ideas to the country practice. Their tireless work in learning new techniques and creating their own attracted international attention and produced an enviable success rate. The Mayo reputation flourished. Physicians and scientists came from across the nation and around the world to watch the Mayo brothers perform surgery. The family practice grew until it outgrew the family. The solution to this problem became the first private group practice of medicine in the world.

As the Mayos expanded their practice, they asked other doctors to join them. Specialists in many fields complemented their medical skills. They formed teams of experts, organized so that they could interact and support each other, yet remain dedicated to patient care.

The rapid growth of their group practice created the need for a new organization. This system would coordinate the activities of physicians and patients, the training of medical specialists and the growth of medical research.

This system would become Mayo Clinic.

Medical excellence and human kindness

The Mayo Clinic story reads like a history of modern medicine. Mayo Clinic has contributed to and shared in the evolution of medicine, learning and growing with one goal in mind: the skilled and compassionate care for its patients. This year, more than 300,000 patients will leave their farms, small towns and cities to seek medical services in Rochester.

They will become patients of a private group practice designed to deliver quality medical care on a large scale. Mayo and its affiliated hospitals, Rochester Methodist Hospital and Saint Marys Hospital, combine to form Mayo Medical Center, a medical community of 16,000 employees who care for more than 4,000 patients every working day.

The Mayo Clinic applies the knowledge and skills of many to the needs of each individual patient.

Mayo Clinic works because it's a special way to practice medicine. It's a medical community focused on patient care, organized so that doctors can spend their time helping patients without worrying about scheduling appointments, locating records or handling administrative details.

The result is a team of medical experts focused on the needs of individual patients and inspired by continuous involvement in education and research.

The result is Mayo's reputation for medical excellence.

Teams of experts

Mayo's system of practicing medicine attracts specialists in every medical and surgical field. These specialists are able to use their skills efficiently and work cooperatively in a team approach to patient care. This team approach is a key to Mayo's success. More than 1,000 physicians and scientists combine their expertise for the benefit of patients.

Mayo is the world's oldest and largest multi-specialty group practice. Its strength lies in the depth of experience and knowledge available, both from the medical staff and from years of compiled medical records that document cases of almost every known disease.

Educating doctors

Mayo's system is designed to offer each patient the highest standard of medical care. This goal is supported by two activities intertwined with patient care: education and research.

Following the example of Mayo's founders, Mayo physicians teach and learn. Their minds are stimulated and their ideas challenged by students in the Mayo Graduate School of Medicine, Mayo Medical School and the Mayo School of Health-Related Sciences. The students work closely with the Mayo consulting staff and learn from the experiences of these specially trained experts.

At Mayo, doctors are both teachers and students. They accept a daily invitation to think, to learn more about how to help their patients. The interaction that education and research create promotes a constant exchange of ideas. And the patients are the prime beneficiaries of this exchange of knowledge.

Progress through research

Research is part of the way Mayo practices medicine. Mayo funds its research through proceeds from its medical practice, through contributions from Mayo friends and patients and through grants from the National Institutes of Health and other organizations. Mayo research inspires new ideas and new methods that help improve patient care. Doctors are aware of the most recent medical developments and of the possible applications of Mayo research to patient care.

More than four million patient records going back almost a century help physicians and researchers learn from the past as they search for answers. Diseases from the most common to the most rare are documented in these Mayo records. This makes Mayo a primary source for medical research and helps the clinic hold its place as a leader in the diagnosis and treatment of disease.

Mayo research has grown from the laboratories of a few physicians to programs that involve more than 250 staff scientists.

Research milestones include: isolation of cortisone and its first use to treat arthritis; development of a high-altitude oxygen mask and anti-blackout suit to protect test pilots from the dangers of high altitudes; contributions to the development of the heart-lung machine, the technology that enables medical teams to perform open heart surgery.

Current research includes the use of computerized lasers to destroy brain tumors, and infusion of chemicals to dissolve gallstones, thus avoiding surgery. Today, more than one-third of the members of the Mayo staff are engaged in research that translates into improved patient care.

SPRING GROVE

Pioneer settlers always looked for wooded land with an abundant water supply for their settlements. At Spring Grove, they found this desirable combination.

Spring Grove has the honor of being the first Norwegian settlement in Minnesota. Located just 155 miles southeast of the Twin Cities, many of its citizens can trace their roots back to Norway. Rosemaling is a Norwegian art form still practiced in Spring Grove. Residents perform this folk painting on wood.

The hamlet possesses an inviting outdoor life, with skiing and snowmobiling in the winter, and fishing and hiking in the summer. During the summer there are outdoor concerts, plays, and musicals. Autumn offers the *Fall Foliage Fest* and provides exceptional tours of "Trolltown, USA."

For further information, contact:
Spring Grove Area
Past, Present and Future
P.O. Box 241, Spring Grove, MN 55974   Phone: 507-498-5221

RESTAURANT

The Bake Shoppe Cafe	131 Main Street, Spring Grove, MN 55974 **Phone: 507-498-5482.** Hrs: Mon.-Thurs. 6 a.m. - 5 p.m., Fri.-Sat. 6 a.m.-9:30 p.m., Sundays 4 a.m.-9 p.m.

There has been thriving commerce conducted on the site of The Bake Shoppe Cafe since 1880. From groceries to general merchandise, books to furniture, even videos have been sold here—but for more than a decade, the fare has been lovingly baked homemade muffins, breads, soups, sauces and much more.

Sharon Danielson's cafe boasts a loyal following. Consistent with the area's Norwegian influence, hungry diners are presented with such specialties as the Ole Burger, the Lena Burger, the Viking Conquest and the Oslo. Sandwiches arrive on baked-daily homemade bread and many are complemented and made unique by the cafe's exquisite sauces. On weekends, the fish dinner is famous, featuring deep-fried, blackened or pan-fried fish served with the chef's special sauces and made-from-scratch pizzas. Sip from the bottomless coffee cups, try a muffin, a generous slice of pie or Norwegian-style lunches.

Daily specials promise something new even to the most regular of customers. Special bakery orders welcome.

SPRING VALLEY

Spring Valley is steeped in the prairie history of the area and people like Laura Ingalls Wilder who once lived here. The *Methodist Church Museum* provides a wealth of exhibits on two floors to delight visitors of every age. *The Pioneer Home Museum* is a delightfully furnished turn-of-the-century home with many exhibits. *The Spring Valley Community Historical Society* is a church/museum built in 1876 when the James Wilder family were members. Under the rolling hills of southeastern Minnesota is a remarkable space—12 miles of mapped passages known as *Mystery Cave*. The Department of Natural Resources operates the cave near Spring Valley as part of *Forestville State Park* located southeast of the city. The annual *Summer Festival* is held the weekend before Labor Day and features family-oriented events with music, dance, fireworks, food, history, theatre, contests and a parade.

For further information, contact:
Chamber of Commerce
Spring Valley, MN 55975

DISPLAY GARDEN & TOUR

The Treehouse	Twelve miles south of Spring Valley on Hwy. 63, Spring Valley, MN 55975. **Phone: 507-561-3785.** Hrs: Open April-October. Mon.-Sat. 9 a.m.-5:30 p.m., Sundays Noon-5:30 p.m. Visa accepted.

The Lamon family didn't plan to create a garden oasis in this unlikely location. It just happened that way. The 80-acre farm has been painstakingly and masterfully built into a successful garden center. The gardens at The Treehouse were originally designed to give retail customers landscaping ideas. Over the years, they've been expanded and enhanced and are an attraction in their own right. Now, two acres of display gardens are open for the public to enjoy a peaceful self-guided walking tour. Visitors can enjoy the vast array of colorful plants featuring perennials, annuals, small shrubs, shade trees, water fountains and statuary. The nursery supplies 250 varieties of perennials, spring annuals, vegetable plants and a wide selection of trees, shrubs, roses and evergreens. Even herbs.

There's a playground and sandbox for the kids and a gift shop, too. All the plant material is well-labeled. Advance arrangements for guided tours for groups are suggested. Take time to be part of the serenity in this relaxing wonderland of flowers and trees.

ST. CHARLES

St. Charles, Minnesota, lays claim to being the Gladiola capitol of the world. *Noweta Gardens* welcomes tours to verify the facts.

Whitewater State Park is five miles from town with a beach, picnic area, hiking and fishing. Two attractive city parks are offered.

There are three golf courses within a 10 mile radius and the city offers lighted tennis courts and a baseball field.

The Flowerfest Celebration is held in August and includes a parade, street dance, flea market, car show and other activities.

The Winona County Fair is held in July with rides, exhibits and fun.

The July Fourth celebration is complete with games, races, parade, lots of food and beverages.

For further information, contact:
Chamber of Commerce Office
1242 Whitewater Ave. Suite #3
St. Charles, MN 55972
Phone: 507-932-3020

BED & BREAKFAST

Victorian Lace Inn	1512 Whitewater Ave., St. Charles, MN 55972 **Phone: 507-932-4496** Hrs: Open year-round.

The ambiance of the Victorian era is yours at the Victorian Lace Inn. Built circa 1868, the home was once owned by the Winona County Historical Society. Many of the original light fixtures remain and the massive doors and windows have had the woodwork restored to its natural beauty.

A curved staircase leads you to four guest rooms and two shared baths. Amanda's Room is a large, sunny room; Rachel's Room is also large and greets the early morning sun; Alexander's Room has a southern exposure; Sarah's Room is small and cozy with a brass bed.

After a good night's rest, you are invited to a full breakfast—cook's choice— served in the dining room or a basket may be delivered to your room.

Owners, Sharon and Curt Vreeman welcome and invite you to relax, unwind and enjoy a quieter time of an age gone by.

RESTAURANT

Amish Market Square

I90 & Hwy. 74 at Exit 233, Rt., 1 Box 12A, St. Charles, MN 55972. **Phone: 507-932-5907** Hours: Convenience Store, 24 hours. Rest. 6-10, Gift 8-8, Shop M-F, 8-8. Major credit cards accepted.

Amish Market Square is a combination gift shop, restaurant and bakery, truck stop with convenience store, and service and towing shop. The "Amish Way" gift shop features Minnesota's largest selection of Amish-made quilts, plus many more handcrafted Amish goods and other unique folk art.

The Amish Auto & Truck Plaza features overnight parking, RV sanitary disposal, hunting and fishing licenses, playground and scenic picnic area, along with all your convenience store needs.

The Amish Ovens Restaurant & Bakery features Pennsylvania Dutch cooking that will feed both body and soul. They use real Amish recipes to make their fresh oven baked pies, bread and muffins. Don't miss their famous cinnamon rolls!

◆ ◆ ◆ ◆ ◆ ◆ ◆

"Black Swallowtail"

© MARTHENA R. RICHTER

WABASHA

Situated on the banks of the Mississippi River, Wabasha was established in the 1830's and lays claim to being Minnesota's oldest community. Lumber and commerce were the main industries before the turn of the century when steamboats plied the mighty Mississippi. Now Wabasha is a frequent port of call for the Delta Queen and Mississippi Queen steamboats out of New Orleans. A newly renovated historic commercial district is being refurbished to the 1890's era. Wabasha's commercial district is listed on the National Historic Register.

ATTRACTIONS & EVENTS

Weekends offer guests festivals, flea markets, unique shopping, and recreation on the bluffs and river—from fishing, water-skiing, power boating to golfing, skiing or hiking. Lodging is available at various motels, B&B's, a country inn, cabins on the Mississippi River or campgrounds in the city or on the backwaters. Dining options include full service cafes, fast food outlets, bar & grills, family dining or carryouts. Wabasha has two marinas, a courtesy dock, fishing float and many city parks for family reunions, picnicking or recreation.

The *EagleWatch Observatory* has gained national and state recognition for being one of the best areas to view the majestic Bald Eagle in its natural habitat throughout the winter months. Self-guided walking tours, carriage rides and fall colors are all part of the experience. A *"Soar with the Eagles"* program is offered each March on the second Sunday with a Raptor Center Program, live Bald Eagles and other raptors.

The Mississippi Queen and Delta Queen dockings occur at various times throughout the summer and fall at Wabasha's Mississippi River front on Lawrence Boulevard. *Wabasha's Annual Riverboat Days* is held on the fourth full weekend in July each year. River events, lighted boat parades, street parades, arts & crafts fair, antiques, food, music and fun abound.

For further information, contact:
Wabasha Area Chamber of Commerce
257 W. Main St., P.O. Box 105PM
Wabasha, MN 55981
Phone: 612-565-4158 ext. 5

BED & BREAKFASTS

Bridgewaters B&B	136 Bridge Ave., Wabasha, MN 55981 **Phone: 612-565-4208** Open year-round Visa and MasterCard accepted.

Awake to the aroma of freshly brewed coffee and a homemade breakfast at this enchanting B&B. Unwind in the parlors or on the wrap-around porch. Their motto is well deserved: "A Country Inn—In Town."

The Inn and each of the five guest rooms are uniquely decorated and furnished with antiques. Rooms range from singles with shared

baths to a large master suite with a private bath.

Innkeepers Bill and Carole Moore have created a place for those who wish to enjoy the pleasures of nature and long lazy walks along the river. It's truly a place that is both tranquil and charming. Visitors linger to enjoy the many attractions of this quaint little valley village, Wabasha, where the peace, serenity and scenery is unsurpassed.

◆ ◆ ◆ ◆ ◆ ◆

Cottonwood Inn Bed and Breakfast	100 Coulee Way Wabasha, MN 55981 **Phone: 612-565-2466** FAX 612-565-2466

Listed on the National Register of Historic Places, the Cottonwood Inn Bed and Breakfast is located along the towering glacial bluffs of the Mississippi River, in the midst of the Hiawatha Valley. Wild flowers, singing birds and an umbrella of Cottonwood trees shroud your stay in idyllic beauty. In the fall, the scenery is spectacular.

Awaken to a hearty country breakfast of eggs, meats, pastries, fruits and juices. Then, take in a variety of activities including

river boating, shopping, fall hunting, hiking, golfing, picnicking, snowmobiling, cross-country and downhill skiing in winter. Or, come to watch one of the largest congregations of the American Eagle in the entire world!

The Cottonwood Inn Bed and Breakfast beckons with the elegance of times past and the luxury of today.

HISTORIC HOTEL

The Anderson House	333 W. Main Street, Wabasha, MN 55981 **Phone: 612-565-4524 or (in MN) 800-862-9702 and (outstate) 800-325-2270** All major credit cards are accepted.

In beautiful Hiawatha Valley, hugging the Mississippi River is Wabasha, one of the original river towns. Tourists and vacationers come year-round for the limitless sights, events, tours, and shops. One most notable of these is The Anderson House, a country inn set in the residential part of town.

The Anderson House opened in 1856, and has been run by four generations of the Anderson family since 1896. The rooms are filled with antiques and furniture dating back to the inn's early days. Present-day innkeepers John, Gayla, and Jean Hall keep Grandma Anderson's popular recipes a part of the daily menus. These recipes are a large part of what made the inn a success over the years and now many may be found in two popular cookbooks. The Anderson House offers "special happenings" coinciding with holidays, and special services including their famous cat rentals. Families with children are welcome, and special package plans are available for individuals traveling alone.

GOLF COURSE

Coffee Mill Golf & Country Club	Skyline Drive, Wabasha, MN 55981 **Phone: 612-565-4332. Hrs: Open April-Oct. 31. Mon.-Sun. 7 a.m.-10 p.m.** No credit cards accepted.

It has been called one of Minnesota's most scenic golf courses. And no wonder! Coffee Mill Golf & Country Club, located on Skyline Drive in Wabasha, is built on top of a bluff overlooking the majestic Mississippi River Valley.

From virtually every hole there is a different panoramic view of this striking valley. On a hot summer day, cooling breezes can make the round more pleasant while autumn brings about a magnificent display of color. The course is a gently rolling nine holes. Always well-groomed, it challenges the experienced player without disheartening the novice. It features two par fives over 500 yards, several lengthy par fours and two solid par-three holes.

The unusual octagonal-shaped clubhouse has bar and snack service and is available for special events and weddings. Sit around the stone fireplace or on the deck. You can rent clubs, pull carts and electric carts and tee times are not required.

HOUSEBOAT CRUISE

Great River House Boats

1009 East Main
Wabasha, MN 55981
Phone: 612-565-3376
Open Spring through October

Great River House Boats offers you the ultimate in comfort and safety to make your house boat vacation both memorable and relaxing. The boats are 48 feet long by 14 feet wide and feature wall-to-wall carpeting, refrigerator, stove and oven, all dishes, flatware and utensils, showers with plenty of hot water and even a BBQ grill on the front deck. House boats are powered by dependable 120 hp inboard/outboard motors.

Fishing is a big part of houseboating in this area, with more species and bigger fish than many northern lakes! But there's plenty of activities for everyone—swimming, water skiing, beachcombing, tennis at nearby river towns, Jon boat exploring, antiquing, bonfires on the beaches, dinner at quaint river town restaurants, canoe trips, hiking, bird watching and more.

When you want to really "get away from it all'" try a house boat adventure. Contact Great River House Boats for an absolutely unique experience.

MUSEUM

Arrowhead Bluffs Museum

Highway 60, R.R. 2, Box 7, Wabasha, MN 55981
Phone: 612-565-3829
Hrs.: Open daily from May to Jan. 1, 10 a.m.- 6 p.m.
Open by appointment only from Jan. 2 to April 30

Located 1 1/2 miles west of Wabasha on Highway 60, Arrowhead Bluffs Museum is the life's work of Les Behrns and his son, John. For 30 years the Behrnses collected objects from around the country for their unique exhibit of old firearms, Indian and pioneer artifacts, and mounted specimens of North American wildlife.

Highlights of the collection include every Winchester gun made from 1866 to 1982, complete with all commemoratives made before 1982 and many other unique firearms from the past made by such famous names as Henry Rifle, Colt, and Smith & Wesson. Visitors can also peruse the collection of early American Indian artifacts and pioneer tools. A main attraction at the museum is a flock of mounted wild sheep posed in a realistic mountain setting.

A gift shop connected with the museum offers a wide assortment of art and handicrafts such as afghans, jewelry, belt buckles, pottery, and furniture. For a fascinating peek at America's wild and wooly heritage, stop by the Arrowhead Bluffs Museum.

LODGING & DINING

Wabasha Boatworks Food & Lodging	10 Church Avenue, Wabasha, MN 55981 **Phone: 612-565-2752** Hrs: Mon.-Thurs. 11 a.m.-2 p.m., 5 p.m.-10 p.m., Fri.-Sun. 11 a.m.-1 a.m.

Who could have imagined back in the 1870s that the site of the Wabasha Boat Yard and Marine Ways would one day be home to fine food, resort condominiums, "grumpy old men" and fun times.

More than a hundred years later, that's what's become of the property which today boasts dining on the banks of the Mississippi River and condominiums for sale and rent.

The Wabasha Boatworks is on the historic site of the Wabasha Boat Yard and Marine Ways (1875-1945) where many of the big Mississippi paddlewheelers were built. Restaurant decor includes an historic display of photographs and artifacts from that era. The 87,000 square-foot year-round recreational complex includes 460 feet of privately owned Mississippi River frontage, three miles south of Lake Pepin. The complex includes a ballroom and conference center, plus Slippery's Bar and Grill, featured in the Warner Brothers movie "Grumpy Old Men."

Slippery's is on the main channel of the Mississippi where there's year-round excitement right out the window. In the spring and fall you can enjoy the spectacular beauty of the Federal Wildlife Preserve across the channel on the Wisconsin shore, with surrounding hardwood forested hills on both sides of the river. In the winter, watch one of the largest concentrations of Bald Eagles in the Midwest from your table. In the summer, relax on the riverside deck as a steady stream of recreational and commercial craft make their way up and down the Mississippi. And there's a 120-foot dock for nautical arrivals.

The menu features everything from burgers to shrimp to intriguing salads and specialty drinks. Treat yourself to a steak or seafood dinner, try the famous "Slippery Burger," the best Bloody Marys on the River, the Friday Fish Fry or Sunday Brunch.

The Marine Ways Resort Condos are on the site, as well, and are being sold to individual investors with prices starting in the upper 50s, including a 20-foot slip in the condo association's own marina. The condos, with jacuzzi, fireplaces and dock, are available for rent by the day or week. To get there, turn off Highway 61 down to the river in Wabasha and turn left. You can't miss it. For the brassiest, classiest place on the river, check out the Wabasha Boatworks.

SPECIALTY SHOP

Bouquet's Gift Outlet

317 Main Street W., Wabasha, MN 55981
Phone: 612-565-3808, 608-781-7208 - La Crosse,
Wisc. Store. Hrs.: Mon.-Sun. 9 a.m.-5 p.m.
Hours may vary. Visa and MasterCard are accepted.

Bouquet's Gift Outlet was born on a Minnesota prairie near Wabasha, by two artisans eager to market their handcrafted folk art pieces. With their commitment to producing a quality product with competitive pricing, they soon discovered they would have to hire additional artisans to meet the demands for orders. Along with this came the necessity of moving from their small backyard shed to larger quarters. They found this new home near Wabasha, but more importantly, it was here they found people who are committed to their artwork. That care shows in the product. The customer in turn recognizes that care as being a distinctive quality of Bouquet's, and so the gift outlet grew. Today their products are found in shops and stores nationwide, but they have not forgotten their humble beginnings, nor their desire to give their customers the best product they can produce.

Visitors to the outlet in Wabasha— and their new store in the La Crosse, Wisconsin location— savor the delight of life as it used to be; peaceful and uncluttered. You, too, can discover the treasures in Bouquet's stores. In these shops you'll find carved Santas and birds, collector dolls, furniture, and miniature villages all made right here near the river, plus gifts from other artisans across the United States.

And if, by the end of the day, they're just too tired to drive home, they spend the night in Wabasha and start all over again the next morning.

SPECIALTY SHOP

Wabasha's Old City Hall	257 West Main, Wabasha, MN 55981 **Phone: 612-565-2585.** Hrs: Sun.-Thurs. 10 a.m. -5 p.m. Fri. & Sat. 10 a.m.-8 p.m. Visa and MasterCard accepted.

"Fine shops under the bridge" is the motto at *Wabasha's Old City Hall,* a collection of interesting shops. Step back 100 years in time when visiting this unique city landmark.

In the former City Hall chambers, with its wonderful pressed tin ceiling and magnificent chandeliers, *Heritage Of Wabasha* combines only the best hand-crafted items, with unique gifts from all over the World—toys to leisure ware, crystal to collectible dolls. Step in and your senses will be delighted.

Step upstairs and explore the many antique and collectible treasures at *Old City Hall Antiques* in the former City Library. Paper goods, stoneware, books, and glassware are handsomely displayed on furniture that could be your next "find." Discover some of the best antique prices anywhere. Downstairs where the Fire Department was housed is now the *Marketplace,* featuring *Adobe Designs,* by Patty Kuhn, uniquely designed and hand painted clothing and accessories with a southwest flair.

European Flavors will tickle your taste buds with specialty coffees, teas and gourmet foods from the Mississippi Valley region. *SE MN. Pottery* features sponge ware and pottery by Pete and Deb Preussner. Check out their hand-painted Indian and wildlife items. *Vintage Corner* offers the finest in vintage clothing and jewelry, along with some victorian scents. *Amelia's Secret Garden* offers herbs and oils to sooth and revitalize, along with dried florals and garden delights. The best in children's toys are where the cow jumped *Over The Moon,* books, toys, arts and crafts kits, furniture, clothing and stuffed animals.

Next door in the former jail is the *Ice Cream Shoppe.* Just try to find a better malt and sub sandwich. Special homemade soups are featured in the winter months or consider their special drink—hot apple cider malt. Give it a try!

Step outside and enjoy Heritage Square Park adjacent to the shops. Visit *Father Time Clocks* for the finest sales and service in clock repair and new clocks. Stop in at the *Wabasha Area Chamber Of Commerce* at the south end of the complex for all your visitor information.

Remember to leave plenty of time to browse the fine shops under the bridge and enjoy a piece of history. Join them for their 100th birthday in 1994!

SPECIALTY SHOP

Southeastern Minnesota Pottery

304 Belvidere, Kellogg, MN 55945
Phone: 507-767-4700
Hours: Mon.-Fri. 9 a.m.-4:30 p.m.
No credit cards accepted.

To the proprietors of Southeastern Minnesota Pottery, small means special and they aim to keep it that way. Deb and Peter Preussner started their business in 1986 and with just one employee, have kept it small to maintain high standards of quality and service. As a result, the Pottery has found its niche in the quiet community of Kellogg, just five miles south of Wabasha.

Within the small factory store, you will find many varieties of ceramics. Everything from useful kitchen items, some decorated in the popular country spongeware design, to Wildlife and Southwest decor, plus many more decorative and gift pieces. Everything is hand-crafted by the potters on the premises and each piece is stamped or hand-signed "Made in Kellogg, MN."

You can watch the potters at work and ask questions, too. A second location at the Old City Hall in Wabasha is open seven days a week and features the work of many other local vendors. Special requests and custom orders are always welcome.

TOURS

L.A.R.K. Toys Inc.

Lark Lane, Kellogg, MN 55945
Phone: 507-767-3387
Hrs: Mon.-Fri. 8:30 a.m.-4:30 p.m., Sat., Sun. 10-5. Visa and MasterCard accepted.

In 1983, Donn Kreofsky, a former art and photography teacher, began making a few toys in his garage and sold them locally. Today, his business, L.A.R.K. Toys Inc., designs and manufactures wooden toys sold across the United States.

Pull toys are crafted by hand of pine with no metal parts. They range in size from six inches to more than three feet! A hippo, giant goldfish, pig and troll, mother ostrich with hatchlings, sea turtle, 900-pound life-size moose and the Four Seasons horses share a large room with other animals and the carver as he works. Toy lovers of all ages are able to view the toy workshops and the carousel carving operation and watch the magical process of turning raw pine and basswood into handmade, all-wood action toys or carved into beautiful carousel animals.

Visitors to the shop also enjoy over 100 different tin windups, hand puppets, shiny marbles from England, hand-painted animals from Germany and nesting eggs from Europe and the USSR.

WINONA

Nestled along the majestic Mississippi River, Winona has its roots deep in the old river that has nurtured it since birth. Winona actually stands on a giant sandbar created by the meandering of the Mississippi. In fact, from 8500 feet up in the air, Winona still looks like an island city.

Winona was settled in 1851 by steamboat Captain Orrin Smith, and quickly grew in population to today's 26,000.

ATTRACTIONS

Many locations in Winona celebrate its long and diverse heritage: The Winona County Historical Society's *Armory Museum,* the historic *Bunnel House, the Arches Museum of Pioneer Life, the Wilkie Steamboat Center, the Polish Museum,* plus many Victorian style buildings and those of unique design like the Merchant's Bank building, a Prairie School masterpiece designed by William Purcell and George Elmslie, and the *Winona National and Savings Bank* building, designed by George W. Maher in the Egyptian Revival style.

Back on the river, the Mississippi provides an abundance of fishing, boating, and just plain watching opportunities from Levee Park. The Julius Wilkie Steamboat Center has an actual replica of a steamboat including an exhibition area on the first deck with artifacts of river history as well as miniatures of several steamboats. The Grande Salon on the second deck captures the splendor of the Victorian era.

Across town at *Lake Winona,* there's a beautiful rose garden, band concerts by the Winona Municipal Band, a multi-use park with softball fields, soccer fields, frisbee, golf, tennis court, and a bike/walking path around the entire lake! There's great swimming at the *Winona Aquatic Center* with a zero depth pool area—just like a beach without sand—lap swimming and diving areas and the super 200 foot waterslide. *Garvin Heights Park* offers a scenic drive and overlook with a magnificent view of Winona and the Mississippi beyond. On a clear day, visitors can see 20, even 30 miles up and down the river valley! *Sugar Loaf Mountain* is a historic site towering 500 feet over what used to be the main channel of the Mississippi River (now Lake Winona). The unusual formation was once a landmark for early river pilots. Indian legend has is that the mountain represented the cap of Chief Wa-pah-sha transformed into stone. Actually, early quarrymen are responsible for Sugar Loaf, which towers more than 85 feet above the remainder of the bluff. It has remained that way for over 95 years. Various civic groups and individual citizens sponsor lighting Sugar Loaf at night.

Bunnell House was built by the first permanent white settler in Winona County, Willard Bunnell. Now listed on the National Register of Historic Sites, it is one of the finest examples of the Gothic Revival architecture in Minnesota. It has a commanding view of the Mississippi River.

Watkins Home was built in the late 1920's in the style of an English Tudor Manor house. The Great Hall houses the large Aeolian organ with nearly 6,000 pipes and the Steinway concert grand piano.

EVENTS

Winter Carnival is a three day event with snowmobile, motorcycle, and 3-wheeler races plus chainsaw contests on frozen Lake Winona. *Mardi Gras* is a New Orleans style buffet with live jazz music. *Eagle Watch* is an evening educational program on bald eagles followed the next day by a coach bus field trip to view migrating bald eagles along the Mississippi. *Polish Heritage Days* celebrates the anniversary of the 1791 Polish Constitution and Commemoration of the Feast of Mary, Queen of Poland.

The Quilt Show is a display of quilts, old and new, at the Armory Museum. *Steamboat Days* is filled with fireworks, carnival, Grande Parade, kiddie parade, beer garden, softball tournament, sport and fun fishing contest, open air art show & food fair.

The Winona County Fair offers grandstand shows, stock car races, 4-H judging, carnival, open-class judging and livestock. *Lake Winona Jazz Festival* offers live jazz music from local and regional jazz groups.

The Sugar Loaf Classic Bike Tour offers bicyclists tours of 63 or 100 miles, to see the best of bluff country. *Goodview Days* is a family-style festival in Goodview. At the *Victorian Fair,* you can watch craftspeople plying the trades of yesteryear. At the Winona Wildlife Weekend, noted wildlife painters and other artists from Minnesota and elsewhere display their works. *Swan Watch* is a 2-day event with evening educational program on tundra swans, followed the next day by a coach bus field trip to view migrating tundra swans along the Mississippi.

A Victorian Christmas is a celebration in the style of the Victorian era with home tours, refreshments, and nostalgic activities.

For further information, contact:
Winona Convention and Visitors Bureau
67 Main Street
P.O. Box 870
Winona, Minnesota 55987-0870
Phone: 507-452-2272 or 1-800-657-4972
24 hour info line, 1-507-457-0021

ANTIQUES

R.D. Cone Antiques Mall	66 E., 2nd Street, Winona, MN 55987 **Phone: 507-453-0445.** Hrs: Weekdays 10:30 a.m.-5:30 p.m. Saturdays 10 a.m.-4 p.m. Sundays Noon-4 p.m. Closed Tuesdays. Visa, MasterCard and Discover accepted.

Located at the corner of Lafayette and historic Second Street in downtown Winona, the R.D. Cone Antiques Mall is a fine new antique shop in a proud old landmark.

For decades, the R.D. Cone Hardware Store was a fixture in Winona. Built in 1855, it was this Mississippi River town's first retailer. Now part of the city's historic district, it houses 10,000 square feet of antiques. Buyers rave about the spacious displays and the excellent selection.

Opened in 1992 as a multi-dealer antiques mall, the commitment to quality antiques and collectibles is obvious. They are particularly proud of their unique selection of furniture and the exceptional quality and variety of the many dealers' pieces. There's always a fine selection of prints, paintings, glassware, rugs, oriental specialties and primitives, too, plus collectibles, books, coins, toys, dolls and more.

Picture frame repair is available as are appraisals. The lower level houses Books Unlimited. There's an adjacent cafe and Boutique Shop.

ART GALLERY

Rivertown Gallery	Choate Building, 160 E. Center, Winona, MN 55987. **Phone: 507-452-8922.** Hrs: Tues.-Fri. 10 a.m.-6 p.m., Saturdays 10 a.m.-4 p.m. and by appointment. Visa and MasterCard accepted.

Located in the magnificent historic Choate Building in the heart of downtown Winona, Rivertown Gallery, owned and operated by Bob Preuss, is renowned for its vast selection of fine art.

Designed in harmony with the beauty of this historic building, established in 1888, this spacious gallery offers a unique shopping experience, with its selection of original paintings by local artists as well as a large inventory of limited edition prints from major U.S. fine art publishers. From portrait and wildlife to Americana and Western art, Rivertown Gallery is an art lover's paradise where you'll find the work of nationally known artists such as Redlin, Bateman, Brenders, Doolittle, Barnes, Olson, Miller, Meger, Cross, Lymon and many more.

Rivertown Gallery specializes in the highest quality and creative custom framing services as well as assisting clients in locating those hard-to-find prints on the secondary market. They've now expanded into office decorating, product leasing and the publishing of fine art by local artists, as well. Nationwide shipping available.

BED & BREAKFAST

*Windom
Park B&B*

369 W., Broadway
Winona, MN 55987
Phone: 507-457-9515
Visa, MasterCard and Discover accepted.

Located just off the Victorian Windom Park, within walking distance of downtown Winona and the Mississippi River, the Windom Park B&B has a rich past and a gracious present.

Built in the Colonial Revival style, the home was constructed in 1900 by banker S. L. Prentiss and his wife Maude and located in a neighborhood of many grand old homes. With its welcoming Greek columned porch, it was a breakaway from Victorian architecture. In the 1940's as Prentiss Lodge, it was a residence for college men.

Inside, the gracious colonial interior has classical details and is tastefully furnished with antiques and family heirlooms, giving it a restful, traditional atmosphere. The guest rooms, located on the second and third floors, offer four choices, each with a charm and style all its own, from the tradition of mahogany and oriental rugs in the Prentiss Room to the airy feel of a perennial garden and wicker in the Perennial Room. Beds are from twin to king-size.

In the morning, enjoy a generous continental breakfast with fruit in season, delicious muffins, cinnamon coffeecake or bagels, cold cereal and juice as you experience the calm graciousness of turn-of-the-century gentry life.

BED & BREAKFAST

Carriage House B&B	420 Main Street, Winona, MN 55987 **Phone: 507-452-8256** Hrs: Open year-round Visa and MasterCard accepted.

It's been more than a century since lumber baron Conrad Bohn built his grand Victorian home in the old river town of Winona. Along with the house, he erected an extravagant three-story carriage house large enough to fit six carriages, several horses, a hay loft and sleeping rooms for the stable boys.

Today, the carriage house has found new purpose as a luxurious and charming bed and breakfast. The current owners of the Bohn mansion, Deb and Don Salyards, have decorated each room with an elegant, unique theme reminiscent of a bygone era. Guests sleep in four-poster canopy beds or sleigh beds and all rooms have private baths. The tariff also includes complimentary beverages and breakfast and the history of one of Minnesota's oldest homes.

Conveniently located in the heart of the city, the Carriage House is within easy walking distance to the Mississippi River and the many sights of historic downtown Winona. For a real treat, guests are welcome to take a tandem bike for a trip around scenic Lake Winona.

COUNTRY COTTAGE

The Winona Farm's Luxurious Country Cabins	Rt. 2, Box 279, Winona, MN 55987 **Phone: 507-454-3126** Hrs: Open year-round. Visa and MasterCard accepted.

The Bluff Country around Winona offers some of the most beautiful scenery in Minnesota. Nestled in East Burns Valley is The Winona Farm and its luxurious Country Cabins. Here, you can find a peaceful, wildlife paradise preserved for all who yearn for the country life.

One cabin is at the junction of two trout streams and overlooks three wildlife ponds. Another cabin offers a panoramic view of the valley. Both are surrounded by heavy woods. Each cabin is equipped with a romantic glass-fronted wood stove.

Guests come year-round to enjoy hiking, bird watching, trout fishing, cross-country skiing, swimming, rollerblading and much more. The farm offers an opportunity to experience a variety of farm animals. All in all, a unique experience amid the magnificent Bluff Country.

HISTORIC SOCIETY

Winona County
Historical Society

160 Johnson Street, Winona, MN 55987
Phone: 507-454-2723
Hrs: Mon.-Fri. 9 a.m.-5 p.m.
Sat.-Sun. Noon-4 p.m.

Founded in 1935 in a Mississippi River county rich with life and history, the Winona County Historical Society boasts the largest county membership of any county historical society in Minnesota.

It was established for the purpose of preserving, documenting and interpreting the human history of Winona County. In addition to operating a national registered historic site and two museums, it maintains a large collection of artifacts that represent daily life from prehistoric times to the present. It also brings history to life, both for Winona County citizens and visitors alike, by sponsoring several wonderful educational programs.

Presenting slices of turn-of-the-century life, the **Armory Museum,** located at 160 Johnson Street, is open year-round, Monday through Friday from 9 a.m. to 5 p.m. and weekends from noon until 4 p.m. The exhibits are laid out like the sections of an old town and a recently completed timeline exhibit interprets county history. Children enjoy a large new exhibit designed just for them, including a cave, tepee and steamboat. A Main Street, blacksmith shop, pharmacy and robbery-proof Security State Bank are some of the exhibits filled with interesting artifacts. There is a nominal admission fee.

Some 11 miles west of Winona is the **Arches Museum of Pioneer Life.** It's located on U.S. Highway 14, midway between Stockton and Lewiston and is open May 1 through October 30, Wednesday through Sunday. Named for the stone railroad arches nearby, the museum houses early agricultural equipment, tools and household items. An authentic one-room schoolhouse, log house and barn harken back to a bygone era. A small admission fee is charged.

Historic Bunnell House is located just off U.S. Highway 14 and 61 in Homer. It's open from Memorial Day through Labor Day, Wednesday through Saturday from 10 a.m. to 5 p.m. and Sundays from 1 p.m. to 5 p.m. The old house overlooks the Mississippi River and a ramble through its hallways transports visitors back in time to the days when the river valley was just being settled.

The society also runs several historical libraries and bookstores. **The Laird Lucas Memorial Library,** located in the Armory Museum, is recognized for having one of the finest local archives in the state. Several special events continuously present the area's rich heritage and fascinating history to visitors. An annual Quilt Show, for example, an exhibit featuring more than 100 different old and new quilts, the Victorian Fair held in the fall, and a holiday tour of homes in December all contribute to Winona's history.

HORSEBACK RIDING

Big Valley Ranch, Inc. Riding Academy	East Burns Valley Road Box 289 (County Road 105) Winona, MN 55987 **Phone: 507-454-3305**

Big Valley Ranch, Inc. Riding Academy strives to make English and Western style riding affordable and safe for all. And with more than 25 years of experience with youngsters and adults riding at all levels, they do it well.

Camps for boys and girls are available from June through August and, in addition, the academy offers a full slate of programs, group lessons and lessons by appointment.

The academy's facilities are excellent. They include: an indoor arena with bleachers; heated lounge with indoor arena view; grooming area with ties; washing area with ties; two large outdoor arenas; four large rotated pastures; heated water tanks; more than 200 acres of bulldozed bridle paths; outside picnic area and campground; plus rabbits, cats, kittens and dogs to pet.

And if riding horses isn't your thing, you still can enjoy the academy's wagon hayrides, which are offered any day at any time by appointment.

LODGING

Sterling Motel	1450 Gilmore Avenue Winona, MN 55987 **Phone: 507-454-1120 or 800-452-1235** All major credit cards accepted.

Located along the gorgeous Mississippi River Valley Bluff, the Sterling Motel has been recognized as a quality value in Winona for more than 35 years.

The Sterling Motel is a full-service motor inn that is ideally situated. It's located just a short walk from shopping, golf, a variety of fine restaurants and five minutes from local colleges. Each of the 32 units has either one or two double beds, telephone, cable television and air conditioning and a king waterbed room is available. Free cribs are also available if you're travelling with children.

The setting is perfect for the overnight traveler and family visiting the Winona area. There are many bike and ski trails to enjoy, along with the sights of Winona, including the Winona Historical Museum, the historic displays at the Wilkie Steamboat Center or a riverboat ride on the Mississippi. Pets are welcome and a 24-hour restaurant is just a few steps from the motel. For clean comfort, the Sterling Motel provides a quality service at very affordable rates.

RESTAURANT

Hot Fish Shop

965 Mankato Ave., Winona, MN 55987
Phone: 507-452-5002
Hrs: Tues.-Sat. 6 a.m.-10 p.m., Sun. 6 a.m.-8 p.m. Closed Mondays.

Founded in 1931, the Hot Fish Shop has earned an international reputation for fine food and outstanding service. Current owners, Joe and Nancy Coshenet, love to tell the history of the Hot Fish Shop and how it all started over 60 years ago with Nancy's grandparents, Henry and Helen Kowalewski.

At that time, they started the Standard Fish Market and soon added a restaurant to serve the batterfried fish Henry enjoyed so much when he was a traveling salesman. The Hot Fish Shop began a few years later when the store was moved to what was deemed by others to be a less desirable location. They were wrong.

Helen and Henry enjoyed a prosperous business in the following years with one small dining room and a seating capacity of 70. In the late 1940's, a second dining room was added, boosting the capacity to over 150. Grandpa and Grandma employed a host of people in these years—some who were very loyal and stayed for over 50 years!

Being a true fisherman himself, Henry included on his menu a great number of different fish and seafoods, especially the "Batterfried Walleyed Pike Dinner" that in 1935 could be ordered for 65¢.

When Henry passed away in 1967, Helen and son, Lambert, and his wife, Helen, managed the restaurant. In 1969, a third dining room and cocktail lounge were added. After Lambert passed away in 1987, Nancy and Joe, who had been co-managers, purchased the entire operation. Since 1988, a new menu idea and some structural changes have been implemented. The lobby is now named the "Aquarium Room" and the dining areas are "The Marine Room and The Heritage Room."

Grandpa and Lambert have passed down this motto to Nancy and Joe: "Good food is not cheap and cheap food is not good!" Thus, the Hot Fish Shop serves only the very best!

RESTAURANTS

Acoustic Cafe	77 Lafayette Street, Winona, MN 55987 **Phone: 507-453-0394** Hrs: Mon.-Thurs. 7:30 a.m.-11 p.m. Fridays 7:30 a.m.-midnight, Saturdays 9 a.m.-midnight, Sundays 10 a.m.-10 p.m.

Perfecting a concept that first came to life in Northfield, MN, the Acoustic Cafe is a relaxing, rustic place where you can get a great sandwich and listen to live music for about the same price as fast food.

Located in the original R.D. Cone Hardware store in Winona's historic district, the Acoustic Cafe features live music two or three nights a week, including folk, bluegrass and string instruments.

Sit and relax in one of the high-back wood booths with an espresso, a cafe latte or a cappuccino or sample one of their many terrific hoagies.

"Let no one hunger for lack of a better sandwich," is their slogan. And they live up to it. With soup and sandwich combos for as little as $2.99, the value is outstanding. Try the ice cream or cookies for dessert.

Beer and wine available. Second location in Menominee, WI.

◆ ◆ ◆ ◆ ◆ ◆ ◆

Jefferson Pub & Grill	58 Center Street, Winona, MN 55987 **Phone: 507-452-2718** Hrs: Mon.-Sun. 11 a.m.-1 p.m. Visa and MasterCard accepted.

Sizzle and Suds, Shakes and Spuds. That's what the Jefferson Pub & Grill in Winona is all about. That and a whole bunch of fun!

The "sizzle" refers to Jefferson's specially seasoned quarter-pound hamburger served on a homemade bun baked daily right at the restaurant. For "suds," choose from an ample offering of domestic, imported and draft beers available in half-yards or by the glass. If you like ice cream, you'll love the "shakes," sundaes or try it by the scoop. It, too, is made right on the premises with only the best ingredients. And the "spuds" are Jefferson's french fries, made from fresh, jumbo Idaho potatoes, hand-cut with the skins still on.

Located in an historically significant building, this is the only establishment in Winona with NTN, the live, interactive television network that lets you play along with patrons in bars and restaurants throughout North America. Or you can check out the upstairs game room complete with billiards, darts and video games. Good for large groups, parties and bus tours.

SPECIALTY SHOP

Winona Knits

1200 Storr's Pond Road
P.O. Box 5400
Winona, MN 55987
Phone: 507-454-3240 or 800-888-2007

Among the industrial founders of Winona is Winona Knitting Mills. Since 1943, three generations of the Woodworth family have owned and operated the mill. In the mid-1970's, Pat Woodworth became president of the newly incorporated sweater retail company now known as Winona Knits.

The first store was originally located adjacent to the knitting mill. Today, Winona Knits stores can be found throughout the Midwest with new specialty and outlet stores opening in eastern and western states. In 1989, Winona Knits moved to a new location on the shore of Lake Winona.

Having started as a sweater store, Winona Knits now offers a wide variety of beautiful and comfortable sportswear for today's lifestyles. The specialty stores carry a unique line of quality goods for everyone in the family, including sportswear, outerwear and accessories.

Outlet stores provide a mixture of in-season apparel and special values. In addition, they offer overstocked and last season's items at greatly reduced prices.

Winona Knits offers a unique guarantee—if you are ever dissatisfied with a product, you can return it for a full refund or exchange.

The company is dedicated to being a good citizen by supporting the community through corporate sponsorship. Community sporting events and local charities throughout the Midwest are supported. Some of their products are produced by ORC, a sheltered workshop for the disabled. Of course, Winona Knits donates clothing, as well.

The company is also committed to wildlife and habitat preservation. Winona Knits works to support LoonWatch, a preservation and education program of the Sigurd Olson Environmental Institute. The Common Loon appears as a part of the corporate logo.

CORPORATE PROFILE

The Winona Knitting Mills, Inc.   Today, Winona, Minnesota, is the home of one of our nation's foremost sweater manufacturing corporations. The Winona Knitting Mills, which celebrated its 50th anniversary in 1993, was an offshoot of the Stone Knitting Mills in Cleveland, Ohio.

Walker R. Woodworth (1883-1948), grandfather of the Winona Knitting Mills' current president, Pete Woodworth, was one of a breed of the nation's 20th-century entrepreneurs who worked their way up to the top through hard work, honest dedication and practical experience.

In 1918, Walker Woodworth was a cutting-room supervisor at Bemis Burlap Bag Company in Indianapolis, Indiana, when he accepted a mid-level production supervision position with the Rich Sampline Knitting Mills in Cleveland, Ohio; four years later he was the plant manufacturing supervisor.

During the 1920s, Cleveland was the heart of the knitting industry in the United States and home to 25 large mills. The economic depression of the 1930s took its toll on many of the firms, while poor business practices and union troubles added to the decline of others. As a result, only one knitting mill remains in Cleveland today. These woes forced the closing of the Rich Sampliner mill in 1925.

It was at this point that Walker Woodworth joined forces with Harry J. Stone (who had been the principal salesperson at the Sampliner enterprise) to forge a new knitting company in Cleveland. The Stone Knitting Mill was to maintain production in the Ohio location from 1926 to the present. Walker Woodworth's son, Leslie R. Woodworth, present Winona Knitting Mills board chairman, began working in the Cleveland operation as a teenager and later earned a bachelor of science degree in textile engineering from the Georgia School of Technology in 1939.

Les Woodworth then became production manager at the Stone Knitting Mill before accepting a commission with the U.S. Navy as World War II drew near. Upon reporting for duty in 1941, little did Les Woodworth realize that he would never work with the Cleveland mill. Winona, Minnesota, was beckoning.

Minnesota, hats off to thee

Walker Woodworth had been familiar with the name Winona, Minnesota, for many years because a major yarn supplier had been located in the city. He and Stone made the decision to expand their manufacturing capability away from the heavily industrialized

Cleveland area; an expansion necessary because of war-related garment orders from the government.

The southeastern Minnesota area had many charms: the looming limestone bluffs that follow the curves of the Mississippi River along the fertile soil in the Hiawatha Valley attracted many hundreds of strong-willed and strong-backed immigrants from Germany, Ireland and Poland in the 19th century. Descendants of these hearty pioneers would provide the nucleus for the Winona Knitting Mills work force.

The Winona Knitting Mills opened its doors and knit its first garment on August 14, 1943. Three years later Les Woodworth returned from war service as a lieutenant commander and joined the Winona Knitting Mills as general manager.

Changes in consumer demand affected the entire knitting industry in the years which followed World War II. Winona Knitting Mills' major wartime production of wool sweaters was shifted over to mens' cotton shirts. In 1948, Walker Woodworth died suddenly and Les Woodworth, along with his sister Marge and brothers John and Walker Woodworth, Jr., continued to manage the business.

The year 1952 was a milestone in Winona Knitting Mills' history: after five years of declining profits, plant operations were conducted at a loss. Harry Stone, still the majority stockholder, decided to either sell his interest or to liquidate the company entirely.

There was even talk of moving the mill to Buffalo, New York. The now Winona-based Woodworth family wanted to keep the mill intact and maintain operations at the Minnesota location. After extensive negotiations, controlling interest was transferred to the Woodworth family and the Cleveland connection was finally severed.

Time marches on

Through hard work, creative financing and sincere dedication to the company by management and employees alike, the Winona Knitting Mills was able to overcome the uncertain and sometimes unstable economic times of the 1950s.

The 1960s brought increased sales to the company. Yet, new challenges loomed as cheaper, lower-quality imported garments were just beginning to capture a small share of the U.S. market.

Sears and Roebuck became Winona Knitting Mills' major account—a relationship that continued throughout the 1960s and well into the 1970s. In 1961, "Style #1911" established a record for the number of orders for a sweater through a Sears and Roebuck Christmas catalog.

In 1966, Winona Knitting Mills became the first company to win the Sears Award for Excellence, an honor of international consequence. During the ensuing 10 years this prestigious award was bestowed on Winona Knitting Mills three more times, a real and lasting tribute to the quality consciousness and work ethic of the Winona work force. Other major accounts were added: Manhattan, Van Heusen, Munsingwear, J.C. Penney and the Donaldson Company.

As the 1970s dawned, Sears and Roebuck began making an increasing number of large foreign purchases of apparel products. Cheaper goods were grabbing a larger chunk of the domestic garment industry's market, rising from a 15 percent market share in the mid-1960s to more than 70 percent 10 years later. By 1978, Sears and Roebuck had moved out of the lead, dropping to Winona Knitting Mills' fourth-largest account. Surpassing them in sales volume were: Pendleton Woolen Mills, Izod, and The Winona Factory Outlet Company (Winona Knitting Mills' retail branch then totalling three stores).

Let's hang on

As the 1980s were ushered in, the Winona Knitting Mills had grown to more than 500 employees and was one of Winona's leading employers.

At a time when many U.S. knitting mills were buckling under the fierce competition and squeeze put on by cheap imports, Winona Knitting Mills persevered to become one of the 25 largest of the 550 remaining knitting organizations.

While imports continued to swallow up a greater share of the market, Winona Knitting Mills was able to capture and hold more than 1.2 percent of the entire sweater market by 1987.

Sales increased from $9 million in 1980 to more than $20 million by the end of the decade in large part due to outperforming domestic competitors.

Another reason for Winona Knitting Mills' success in a consolidating industry was its foresight. The 1980s brought a restructuring of management procedures, an increased awareness of the importance of employee involvement and a branching out to broaden market presence.

By the end of the 1980s, Winona Knitting Mills was developing programs with more than 75 customers in wholesale, retail, mail order and career apparel markets. The largest of these were: L.L. Bean, Izod, Pendleton, Lands' End, Dayton's, Hartmarx and Eddie Bauer.

A new management style

In 1983, Les Woodworth stepped down as president and handed control over to his son Pete, a Cornell University graduate and U.S. Naval Officer. Pete Woodworth had been with the company for 11 years and was one of the moving forces behind the company's astounding 60 percent growth in productivity from 1978 through 1983.

Part of this growth was the result of the physical changes made in the plant through additions and renovations. But, perhaps more importantly, was a change in management style which allowed each production department to set its own goals and granted them the necessary authority and freedom to achieve these goals. Employee involvement was also greatly encouraged and promoted at all levels.

Employees were regularly informed about the company's performance and benefited directly when it did well through a profit-sharing plan which pays out one-third of all after-tax income in annual cash bonuses.

Whereas workers could produce only one complete sweater per hour before 1978, by the early 1990s the workers were capable of producing two complete sweaters per man hour.

Today

Physical changes to the Winona Knitting Mills plant in Winona completed in the late 1980s have become important. After decades of sweltering heat in the summer months, employees now work in air-conditioned comfort.

The newest electronic, state-of-the-art model knitting machines have been added to the manufacturing line to maintain competitiveness in a world market. New computer-driven information systems keep them in control of all facets of the production, inventory, supplies and customer activities. TQM, total quality management, has taken Winona Knitting Mills by storm. Employee involvement in decision-making and their empowerment to do so by management has become even more widespread. Team-building training and other specialized instruction has been provided to production employees. Teams are formed to address all sorts of problems, some of a short-term nature to solve immediate concerns, while others speak to wider issues which may take years to grapple with.

The Winona Knitting Mills looks forward to the years and opportunities ahead. Blessed with an experienced, aggressive workforce, a rich heritage, a nationwide reputation for quality, a tradition of value, two productive plants and some of the best equipment, the company has positioned itself for sustained growth as the 21st century approaches.

THE WINONA KNITTING MILLS, INC.

CORPORATE PROFILE

Watkins   It is truly a vacation wonderland, from northern
                     Minnesota's sparkling lakes and deep pine woods to
                     the rippling streams that meander south feeding the
mighty Mississippi River. To experience the delights that southern
Minnesota offers, take time to travel the old river road. In addition to
a beautiful nature drive, this winding road, also known as Highway
61, leads travelers to the Watkins Administration Building in downtown Winona, revered as one of the most beautiful private office
buildings in the United States.

To get a better understanding of the Watkins story, let's turn
back the pages of time to 1868.

J.R. Watkins was making his first product, liniment, and selling it
to his neighbors and friends in the Plainview area. The proximity of
Winona's budding railroad and river traffic prompted J.R. to move his
liniment business to Winona in 1885.

It was a move that would lead to the advent of numerous
Watkins salesmen across the frontier and Watkins as the producer of
the world's best Imitation Vanilla Extract and award-winning spices,
over 100 food products, plus a large offering of health aids, personal
care and household products. It would inevitably lead to worldwide
expansion of the J.R. Watkins Medical Company.

J.R.'s keen business philosophy, quality products at a fair price
and satisfaction guaranteed or money back, made Watkins products
household words.

To reinforce his philosophy, J.R. molded a "trial mark" part way
down the side of his liniment bottles. Customers could use the liniment down to the "trial mark" and if not satisfied could return the
bottle and get their money back on J.R.'s return trip. Very few bottles
were ever returned. Today, that same "trial mark" is used on the bottle of Imitation Vanilla Extract, as well as on the Red and White
Liniments.

By 1911, the now-famous Administration Building was built and
even though J.R. never lived to see its completion, it stands as a tribute to the man who invented direct selling and implemented the concept of satisfaction guaranteed.

The interior of the block-long granite building is adorned with
four different varieties of Italian marble and uniquely designed
mahogany woodwork. The curved roof encloses Tiffany stained-glass
skylights; three Tiffany half-moon windows, depicting Winona's ver-

sion of Sugar Loaf Mountain, grace the front of the building. Elegant tinted-glass mosaic lines the walls as well as the rotunda area, which is accented with 24-karat gold.

Mini tours of this magnificent piece of architecture, also known as the Home Office, can be arranged by calling 507-457-3300.

Five of the six buildings connected to the Home Office, built between 1889 and 1914, house the production and packaging areas, while the other buildings provide warehouse space for raw materials, packaging material and finished product storage.

For those who enjoy antiques and historical memorabilia, visit the J.R. Watkins Heritage Museum and Store, which is truly a trip down memory lane. Located on Third Street between Chestnut and Liberty, museum hours are 10 a.m. to 3:45 p.m., Monday through Friday.

In addition to this main complex, Watkins has a 65,400-square foot East End facility that houses the Agri Manufacturing and Warehouse, as well as its Research and Development areas. The 53,400-square foot West End facility, the Distribution Center, handles the pick/pack and shipping operations.

In 1978, Watkins was purchased by Minnesota's highly successful business entrepreneur, Irwin Jacobs, and by 1990, sales revenues had increased 250 percent.

In addition to increased sales revenues, Watkins has experienced phenomenal growth in its number of directors—from 200 in 1978 to more than 600 in the United States and nearly 300 in Canada. Independent Representatives number more than 50,000 across North America.

Many are enjoying unprecedented success in their home-based businesses.

Under the experienced eye of growth-oriented leadership, Watkins is developing into the business of the 1990s.

Great strides have been made in enhancing Watkins' sales and marketing strategies and in developing industry-leading sales tools.

Because of the power of Watkins' integrated marketing strategy as a viable solution to the uncertainties of today's economic environment, Watkins hopes to triple its size by 1995 and regain its place as the most successful and admired direct-selling company in the world.

This common goal, based on the founding principles of quality service at a fair price, has been shared throughout Watkins' history, with its Independent Representatives, with Jacobs, and originally, with none other than J.R. himself.

WYKOFF

Wykoff, Gateway to Forestville State Park and Mystery Cave, is located just southwest of Rochester. This small town was first settled by wealthy men from New York who brought the railroad to Wykoff.

Cyrus Wykoff was president of the Southern Minnesota Company that surveyed and plotted villages at regular intervals along the railroad right of way. Thus the village of Wykoff came into being when the railroad came in 1871.

Three disastrous fires in the late 1800's burned nearly all the buildings in the town, including the school. The buildings were promptly replaced with brick structures that are still standing as historic buildings today.

ATTRACTIONS & EVENTS

Wykoff's *Historic Jail Haus, Ed's Museum, The Bank Gift Haus, The Bartlett-Doh's House* are a few of these historic buildings. Ed's Museum is named after Edwin Krueger. In 1901, the Krueger family moved to Wykoff where Edwin's father became Postmaster. In 1933, Edwin acquired a building built back in 1876 and put in a store which he eventually turned into a museum in the 1940's. Edwin also ran the local theatre during the silent film era and enjoyed grand opera on the radio. Ed was the city's historian, treasurer, part-time maintenance person, volunteer fireman and self-appointed collector of Wykoff memorabilia.

He kept the memorabilia in his museum and eventually willed the store and its contents to the city so that all that he had worked for over his many years of life would be preserved for posterity.

The Wykoff Area Historical Society now oversees the preservation and operation of this interesting museum, a testimony to one man's determination to preserve the history of Wykoff.

The annual *Wykoff German Fall Fest* is held the last weekend in September with German bands, dancers, German food. A large parade, craft show and a play are part of the festivities. Obviously, Wykoff is a little German town with a lot of German pride!

For further information, contact:
c/o Lila Eickhoff
101 Centennial Street E.
R.R. 1, P.O. Box 6
Wykoff, MN 55990
Phone: 507-352-4011

BED & BREAKFAST

The Historic Wykoff Jail Haus

219 N. Main Street
Wykoff, MN 55990
Phone: 507-352-4205
Visa and MasterCard accepted.

Probably the smallest bed and breakfast visitors will ever find, The Historic Wykoff Jail Haus is certainly the most unique. It's the old Wykoff city jail originally built in 1913, laboriously restored by area residents and now open to the public as a B&B.

It's been restored to retain the unique characteristics of an old jail but with modern comforts. The outside still has the original screens and bars. The interior has been repainted and carpeted, and water and electricity installed. The three rooms inside include two bedrooms and the bathroom. The interior is furnished with period decor and antiques. One of the bedrooms retains the original jail cell with two bunks. Breakfast vouchers for the local restaurant are included.

The Historic Wykoff Jail Haus is handicapped accessible. All proceeds go toward area historical preservation projects.

SPECIALTY SHOP

The Bank Gift Haus

105 Gold Street, Wykoff, MN 55990. **Phone:** 507-352-4205. Hrs: Mon.-Sat. 10 a.m.-5:30 p.m., Sundays 1 p.m. -5 p.m. Memorial Day through Christmas. Visa and MasterCard accepted.

Chock-full of history and reflecting the distinctly German heritage of the area, The Bank Gift Haus in Wykoff is a truly unique place to do your gift shopping.

While the entire block on the west side of Gold Street burned in 1895, the new bank withstood the fire thanks to brick construction. Over the years, the building housed a variety of businesses before being completely remodeled in 1991. Parts of the bank interior were purchased in Illinois. The mahogany wood and ornate grill work are believed to date back to the 1860s.

The interior of The Bank Gift Haus has a contemporary design, using cut-outs to show the fire damage and the original vault. But you'll also find wonderful gifts, from hand-blown glass to beer steins, Russian china, crystal, lace and linens. They carry a wide variety of Christmas gifts and ornaments as well as dolls, toys, cards, books, limited edition prints and much, much more. And don't leave without trying the fabulous homemade fudge.

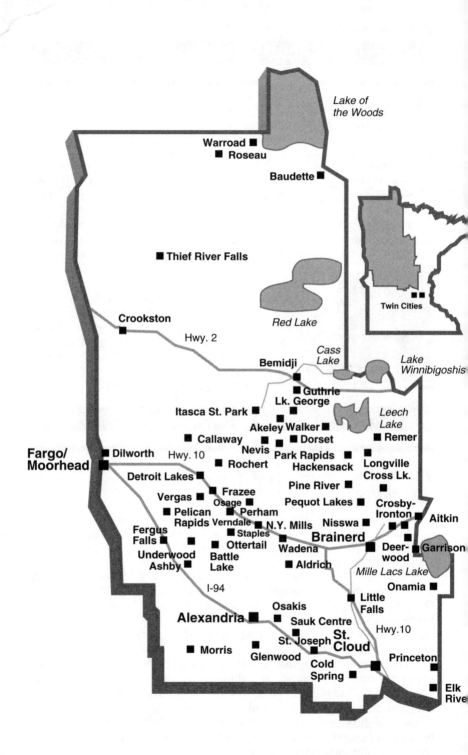

Heartland

Northward, the vast prairies gradually give way to a mosaic of verdant forests and sky-blue lakes. Here, the fish are big, the golfing is great (more than 100 courses) and the people are friendly.

This is the Heartland.

Extending from Alexandria in the west, on to St. Cloud, through Brainerd and north to the Canadian border, the Heartland is where millions come each year to drop the facade of modern life and redis-cover themselves in a natural setting.

Perhaps the spirit of self-renewal is best symbolized by the well-head of the nation's greatest river—the Mississippi. It is here, in Itasca State Park, that the river's source has been sheltered from encroaching civilization and now provides a backdrop for the wilder-ness experience. The epic journey of the river begins humbly, amid dense stands of virgin pine that have stood guard over these lands for the last 20,000 years.

Of course, there is much more to discover in the Heartland besides our natural connections. It is intriguing to the Scandinavian descendants who settled much of the land that even earlier family members—the Vikings—may have visited here long before Columbus sailed from Spain. In Alexandria, ethnic pride has given rise to the prominent display of a mysterious stone chiselled with an archaic runic script that has been embroiled in controversy since it was brought to public attention in 1898. It was in that year that a Swedish farmer claimed to have discovered the Kensington Runestone entwined in the roots of a tree on his land. A Viking historian trans-lated the script as being an account of a group of Viking adventurers traveling through the region in 1362. You can decide for yourself whether or not this story is plausible and whether Alexandria deserves the self-proclaimed title, "Birthplace of America," by examining the Runestone firsthand at the Alexandria Chamber of Commerce's historical museum.

Travelers of a literary bent will be delighted to discover the birthplace of America's first Nobel laureate for literature, Sinclair Lewis. Sauk Centre was the site of what biographers have called an "unhappy boyhood" for Lewis. The town was also the fictionalized setting for several of the author's best-known novels in which he offered a lively critique of America's small town, middle-class values.

Landmarks that occupy the pages of *Main Street* and other Lewis books can be seen much as they were described by Lewis early in this century. Other things in Sauk Centre have changed, however. Today, signs on Interstate-94 point the way to the Sinclair Lewis Interpretive Center, and what was once the intersection of Third Avenue and Main Street is now the junction of The Original Main Street and Sinclair Lewis Avenue. Lewis's boyhood home is also open for tours.

Aviation fans will want to visit the birthplace of one of this country's greatest aviators and most intriguing citizens, Charles A. Lindbergh Jr. This reserved Minnesota Swede was an explorer, inventor and a champion of the technology that carried him solo across the Atlantic to world fame in 1927. At the same time, he worked as a devoted humanitarian and prophetic advocate of the natural environment. His restored family home and an excellent museum are located along the banks of the Mississippi in the town of Little Falls.

Visitors to the Heartland enjoy a variety of other interesting attractions, as well. The legend of the lumberjack is ubiquitous and is broadly displayed in Bemidji with its statues of Paul Bunyan and Babe the Blue Ox. Connected to Bemidji by the Paul Bunyan Trail is the Brainerd Lakes Area, where visitors find endless opportunities to enjoy the classic Minnesota vacation. The call of the loon, the rippling waters, splendid sunsets and the ancient seduction of a golden campfire—these await the traveler in search of respite.

This vacation area extends to Lake of the Woods on the Canadian border and west to the Detroit Lakes area with its hundreds of lakes and resorts. The Moorhead area is home to three universities. For gaming enthusiasts, seven casinos can be found in the Heartland. State parks, museums, wildlife areas and interpretive centers add interesting accents to the region.

Lake of the Woods is arguably one of the most interesting and beautiful lakes in Minnesota. This natural wonder is over 90 miles long, with 65,000 miles of shoreline and 14,000 islands. Fishing and natural beauty attract many thousands of visitors to the area each year. An amazing number of resorts and year-round lodges offer a large variety of accommodations and services. The winter season provides a myriad of activities like snowmobiling, cross-country skiing, fishing and the many seasonal events offered by the communities of the area.

As its name suggests, the Heartland is central to the Minnesota experience and offers great adventure to all who come to enjoy it.

AITKIN

The city of Aitkin was named after William Aitkin, a fur trader who established a permanent settlement on the Mississippi River in 1831. In 1871 the Northern Pacific Railroad built a line through Aitkin in order to connect the great pine forest areas to Lake Superior and Minneapolis. For half a century, Aitkin was the gateway to the northwestern Minnesota frontier.

Although logging and timber-related industries are still very important, the economy of Aitkin has broadened to include agriculture, tourism, retail trade, service industries and small manufacturing.

ATTRACTIONS & EVENTS

The production of *Mille Lacs Wild Rice* is a natural in a city surrounded by 365 lakes, which are also the main attractions for vacationers and travelers, who flock to the town to enjoy the many fine resorts in the area. *Lake Mille Lacs* and the *Mississippi River* are two of the world's best walleye fisheries.

The *Wackiest Fishing Hat Competition* kicks off the fishing season opener in May, with prizes awarded to the person wearing the strangest and most creatively decorated fishing hat. Bass season opens a few weeks later with the *Bass Super Angling Saturday*—an event which features celebrities and, of course, a fishing contest.

The Aitkin area is also host to a number of festivals and special events throughout the year. *Riverboat Days,* held in late July, celebrate Aitkin's riverboat heritage with three days of family fun, blackpowder shoots, riverboat captain's parades, stock car races, chainsaw demonstrations, dances and much more.

The *Aitkin County Fair* is held in mid-August and on the Fourth of July there are fireworks.

The Minnesota Northwoods Classic, held the first weekend of February, is a unique triathlon which involves skating, snowshoeing and cross-country skiing. Aitkin also takes part in the *Mid-Minnesota 150* sled dog race on this same weekend.

Interesting shopping experiences include the art deco-style *Rialto Theater,* the *Green Bough* gift shop, *Booktowne*—a new and used bookseller—and *Northern Images Gallery,* a country art shop.

For further information, contact:

Aitkin Area Chamber of Commerce
P. O. Box 127
Aitkin, MN 56431
Phone: 218-927-2316

SPECIALTY SHOP

The Green Bough

20 2nd Street N.E., Aitkin, MN 56431
Phone: 218-927-3419. Hrs: Mon.-
Sat. 8:30 a.m.-5:30 p.m., Sun. 11 a.m.-3 p.m.
Major credit cards accepted.

The Green Bough in Aitkin started out in a garage when owner Trudy Gross decided to expand on what she had learned in a night class, manufacturing up to 3,000 wreaths a year and shipping throughout the country. This store caters to corporate customers as well as tourists that stop to shop. Most items in the store are discounted, allowing shoppers to leave with an armful of merchandise for what a bag full would normally cost.

The Green Bough built its reputation on the beautiful wreaths created in the store, but there are many other items available as well. A complete line of dolls from all over the world can be found on the shelves. Dolls ranging from basic to collector's items, and priced all the way up to $10,000, offer a broad selection. Custom flower arrangements are designed daily and customers are able to contribute their ideas to the design. A year-round Christmas display features ornaments and original holiday arrangements.

Hunting season is an especially busy time for the store, followed by the bustle of Christmas shoppers. The Green Bough has expanded Aitkin-made articles to an international level, with orders shipped overseas, as well as having showrooms in Dallas and Atlanta. In Dallas, The Green Bough emphasizes freeze-dried flowers and arrangements shipped to other stores throughout the country.

AKELEY

The world's largest statue of Paul Bunyan and his cradle are at home in Paul's birthplace, Akeley, Minnesota. On the shores of the 11th Crow Wing Lake, The Headwaters to the famous Crow Wing Chain, Akeley's history goes back to the late 1800's when logging was its main industry. Approximately eight million logs were cut between 1898 and 1917 when the pine forests were depleted and the mill burned. Tales of Paul's exploits were told and retold in the logging camps that surrounded the town.

ATTRACTIONS & EVENTS

Memorabilia and artifacts from this era are on display in the *Paul Bunyan Historical Society Museum,* open during the summer months. The area around Akeley has many signs of these bygone logging days. Many of the forest roads in the *Paul Bunyan State Forest* and the *Chippewa National Forest* were once railroad spurs that fed the mill. These same trails provide snowmobiling and cross-country skiing in the winter months. An abandoned railroad track has been turned into *The Heartland Trail,* a multi-use recreational trail that stretches for 27 miles. The paved surface is used for hiking and biking in the summer and for snowmobiling in the winter.

Today, recreation plays a big part in the climate of the Akeley region. During the summer months, the clear, clean lakes are a big attraction. Akeley has a large city park and campground on the shores of *11th Crow Wing.* Fishing in area lakes will provide the angler with walleye, northern, bass and panfish. Summer also finds the *Woodtick Theatre* in full swing and a foot stomping-hand clapping musical jamboree takes place in the theatre in downtown Akeley.

The last Saturday in June, the *Woodtick Jubilee* fills the streets with music, arts and crafts and food. *Paul Bunyan Days* are celebrated the first weekend after the Fourth of July with parades, a fish fry, treasure hunt and a pie social. Paul's Patio is the location of the annual *pig roast* the Sunday of Labor Day weekend.

For further information, contact:
Akeley Civic & Commerce
P.O. Box 222
Akeley, MN 56433
Phone: 800-356-3915

LODGING & RESTAURANT

Headwaters Restaurant and Motel

Jct. Hwy. 34 & 64, Akeley, MN 56433
Phone: 218-652-2525
Hrs: Open every day.
Visa and MasterCard accepted.

Blessed with a terrific year-round location, the Headwaters Restaurant and Motel has now been revived into a wonderful family place to stay and to eat. Located in downtown Akeley, just a half block from the Woodtick Theater and one block from the Heartland Trail, the Headwaters Motel has been refurbished in '90s pastels and complementary decor. Each room has two double beds, cable TV, air conditioning and rates are very reasonable.

The restaurant, which has grown from its original dozen or so seats to a capacity of 70, is decorated with knick-knacks and old tools. It specializes in small-town home cooking. Daily specials are a mainstay and they use only fresh lean ground beef in their burgers. Try the broasted chicken, the best around!

The Paul Bunyan State Forest is a few minutes away, as is the Northern Lights Casino. Snowmobiling is a local favorite in the winter months while cycling and hiking are great summer choices. For fishing and water sports, 11th Crow Wing Lake is within walking distance.

RESORT

Crow Wing Crest Lodge

11th Crow Wing Lake
R.R. 2, Box 33, Akeley, MN 56433
Phone: 218-652-3111 or 800-279-2754
Visa and MasterCard accepted.

The Crow Wing Chain of lakes extends some 80 miles through the pines and birch of northern Minnesota. At the crest of this famous and beautiful chain lies the 11th Crow Wing Lake and Crow Wing Crest Lodge. Nature has provided a beautiful setting and Crow Wing Crest provides the rest.

Specializing in family vacations, facilities include a sandy swimming beach, playground and log playhouse, sand volleyball court, basketball, horseshoes and more. Activities include fishing, canoeing, hiking, biking and a variety of family events. Eighteen modern country furnished cabins are scattered throughout the 15 acres of wooded grounds. The lodge has a library, a game room, TV area, snack bar and sun deck.

The 27-mile Heartland Trail and the Paul Bunyan State Forest are at the lodge's doorstep for some of the best hiking and biking in Minnesota. Golf and tennis are available nearby. Crow Wing Crest offers northwoods family vacation fun in a friendly atmosphere.

RESTAURANT

Brauhaus German Restaurant & Lounge	Between Walker and Park Rapids. A mile and a half west of Akeley on Hwy 34. Akeley, MN 56433. **Phone: 218-652-2478**. Hrs: Tues.-Sun. Lounge opens at 4 p.m. Dinner served from 5 p.m. No credit cards accepted.

If traditional German cooking is what you're looking for, then the Brauhaus German Restaurant and Lounge just outside of Akeley is the place for you. Even European travelers proclaim the 'Old Country' homestyle cooking to be equal or a notch above the original.

The Brauhaus features German and American entrées. A few German selections include Sauerbraten (marinated beef), Wienerschnitzel, Schweinehaxen (pork hocks) and Rouladen (beef rolls). American selections are no less delicious. A few American entrées include traditional steaks or pan-fried walleye. However, one should taste before seasoning due to the original style of cooking.

In summer, try the Brauhaus Plate featuring Cold Vesper variety with beef, pork and Kassler garnished with cheese, tomatoes, pickles and olives. Or sample some Goulash, perhaps Jager Schnitzel. It's all authentic food.

The meaning of 'Brauhaus' is 'brewing house' or brewery so, of course, the Brauhaus offers an adequate selection of German beer and wine in addition to a full bar. Almost every small town in Germany used to have a brewery where they brewed their own special beer. These breweries still have their "Schanke" or Gasthaus," where they serve their own beer and homemade food. The beer and food were different for each brewery and Brauhaus follows in that tradition with its own unique ambiance.

For a taste of the 'Old Country', it's the Brauhaus German Restaurant and Lounge where children are always welcome and travellers find delectable respite!

ALEXANDRIA

Is Alexandria the birthplace of America? The controversy has not yet been settled. In 1898 an amazing discovery was made by an Alexandria farmer. Olaf Ohman found a black stone tablet caught in the roots of a tree stump as he cleared his land.

Scholars translated markings carved on the tablet, which told the story of a Viking expedition through Hudson Bay and down the Red River in 1362. This would make the Vikings, and not the Columbus expedition, the earliest known European discoverers of America.

Debated for years, the stone, now called the "Kensington Runestone," is an interesting historical curiosity.

ATTRACTIONS & EVENTS

"Big Ole," the world's largest Viking statue at 28 feet tall, stands guard over the *Kensington Runestone Museum* which houses the runestone along with displays of Indian artifacts and other historical displays of the area.

The Runestone Farm is open to visitors, who can see the exact spot where Olaf Ohman found the *Kensington Runestone.*

The *Fort Alexandria Agriculture museum* features log cabins, antique cars and farm machinery, an 1885 school house and a general store. Alexandria is a popular year-round vacation destination. Boating, canoeing, windsurfing, waterskiing, swimming and fishing are just some of the recreational choices available.

There are five golf courses within minutes of the city limits. The 18-hole *Alexandria Golf Club* is the site of the *Minnesota Resorters Tournament* in early August of each year. It is one of the largest golf tournaments in the country and has been held every year since 1912 and is open to everyone.

The lakes are the city's top attraction during the winter when visitors can enjoy ice fishing, ice skiing, snowmobiling and cross-country skiing. Several of the lakes are connected by the more than 500 miles of groomed snowmobile trails. *Andes Tower Hills* is a great ski area with 11 downhill runs and 20 kilometers of groomed cross-country trails.

For more information contact:
Alexandria Area Chamber of Commerce
206 Broadway
Alexandria, MN 56308
Phone: 612-763-3161 or 800-245-2539

BED & BREAKFAST

The Robards House Bed & Breakfast	518 Sixth Avenue West, Alexandria, MN 56308 **Phone:** 612-763-4073 Hrs: Open all year. Visa and MasterCard accepted.

The Robards House on Lake Winona is an elegant Victorian bed and breakfast located near downtown Alexandria. Constructed of brick, the house was built in 1889 by a prominent hardware merchant, Oscar Robards and his new bride, Cecile Bernard. The Robards were at the center of an elite social circle and entertained frequently in their handsome brick house, hosting parties, teas, formal dinners and civic functions. Cecile loved to decorate the house with fresh flowers for these occasions, ordering them from Minneapolis to be delivered to Alexandria by train.

Each of the four rooms in The Robards House is named after families of historical significance to Alexandria. The LeRoy Room has a private bath, dressing room and small porch with a view of Lake Winona. Pederson's Room is the bridal chamber, offering an exquisite view of the grounds as well as the lake. This room also has a hand-crafted king-size bed and private bath. The Cowing Room has a view of the grounds, private bath and full-size bed. The Kinkead Room has twin beds and is furnished with antiques. The Penthouse Suite on the third floor is truly fashioned for romance. It has a private patio with a view of the surrounding scenery, a sunken living room, dining area, mini-library and a private bathroom.

Fresh ground coffee, home-baked breads and muffins, fresh fruit and juice are served for breakfast each morning. A cookbook from the early 1900's was found in the house and some of the original recipes are still used. Visitors enjoy summertime activities with a game of

Croquet on the lawn overlooking the lake, or drive to one of several nearby golf courses and, of course, fish on the famous lakes of the Alexandria area. In winter, cross-country skiing and snowmobiling on nearby trails are popular sports.

Comfort, timeless elegance, delicious treats and smiling faces await those who enter The Robards House—an experience fondly remembered.

BED & BREAKFAST

Carrington House On The Lake

4974 Interlachen Drive NE, Alexandria, MN 56308. **Phone: 612-846-7400**
Hrs.: Open year-round
Visa and MasterCard accepted.

The Carrington House Bed and Breakfast Inn is a New Orleans style mansion with an abundance of Old South elegance. There are four guest rooms in the main house, all with private bathrooms, 12 foot ceilings, original hardwood floors and brass beds. A seasonal honeymoon cottage featuring a double whirlpool is open May through October.

Antiques and family heirlooms adorn the interior of this mansion. A four-season porch overlooking Lake Carlos features a spectacular view of the area. Right outside is a private lakeshore with a sand bottom for swimming and fishing.

Lake Carlos is a clean, clear spring-fed lake in the Alexandria Chain of Lakes. The surrounding bluffs around Lake Carlos offer hiking and cross-country ski and snowmobile trails. A full breakfast is served each morning with juice, fresh fruit, coffee or tea, various egg dishes, fresh rolls or muffins, and cereal. Breakfasts are served in the dining room or can be served on the lakeside porch.

SPECIALTY SHOP

The Farmhouse

609 N. Nokomis, Alexandria, MN 56308
Phone: 612-762-2243. Hrs: Mon.-Sat. 10 a.m.-5 p.m., Sun. 1 p.m.-4 p.m.
All major credit cards accepted.

Located in the heart of the city of Alexandria, this combination gift shop and home decorating store provides shoppers with an opportunity to browse through this wonderfully decorated nine-room house. Shoppers can get a real perspective of how things fit into a home.

Holiday seasons, especially Christmas and Easter themes, reflect the spirit and beauty of these special times of the year. In addition to the seasonal themes, The Farmhouse also carries a large assortment of dolls, quilts, wall shelves, and pictures. Each room is filled with decorating ideas including authentic hand-crafted Amish furniture and unique floral arrangements for both tabletops and walls.

The Farmhouse also has a wide selection of brass and pewter accessories along with baskets in every shape and size imaginable.

Gifts for children include an array of books, toys, and ornaments.

On-site interior designers are ready to help and offer creative suggestions to help you through any decorating dilemma.

SPECIALTY SHOP

My Favorite Things

515 Broadway, Alexandria, MN 56308. **Phone: 612-762-8750.** Hrs.: Mon.-Fri. 9 a.m.-7 p.m., Thurs. 9 a.m.-9 p.m., Sat. 9 a.m.-5:30 p.m. (Memorial Day-Christ-mas), Sun. 11 a.m.-4 p.m. Visa, MasterCard accepted.

Imagine finding a shop where visitors felt they could take a step back in time just by entering the store, a place that carried a wide assortment of gift items in a blend of Victorian and country tradition. There they would find My Favorite Things.

Two artistic women opened the shop in October of 1989 and developed the inventory around their own talents. Vicki Johnston created hand-sculpted, poured and painted porcelain collector dolls. Ginny Kluver does folk art painting and makes Santa Clauses in every style, shape and size imaginable. The artists combined their skills in making a 3' wide x 5' tall Victorian carousel. Sharing residence in the largest collector doll house in central Minnesota are a variety of collector Teddy Bears, including Ginny's own "Fuzzies and Scuzzies."

The lower level of the shop, "My Favorite Dungeon," features artistic crafts and antiques.

Each person employed at My Favorite Things is involved in craft making of some sort, from quilting and folk art to paper-maché, and can help assemble custom-designed gift baskets, offer free gift wrapping and shipping services.

Other delights to be found include gourmet foods and vintage candy cases displaying a variety of truffles, assorted chocolates, hard candies, gourmet jelly beans, sugar free candies and homemade butter creme fudge.

Visitors to this charming shop will surely find it to be a place "where Valentine romance lingers all year long and the comfort of country makes you feel right at home."

RESORT

Arrowwood-A ***Radisson Resort***	P.O. Box 639, 2100 Arrowwood Lane, Alexandria, MN 56308. **Phone: 800-333-3333 or** 612-762-1124. Hrs: Open year-round. Major credit cards accepted.

About two hours northwest of the Twin Cities, Arrowwood is comfortably situated on 540 acres of spectacular lakeshore and gentle, rolling grasslands.

Once you get there, you'll understand why this AAA vacation resort was rated one of the top 20 family resorts by *Better Homes & Gardens* and *Ladies Home Journal.*

The resort offers 200 rooms, including 18 new suites, many of which come with fireplace and jacuzzi. Most offer a lake view and private balcony, as well. Many packages and weekend specials are offered that include outdoor recreation like golf, horseback riding, outdoor tennis, sailing, canoeing, bicycling and more.

Camp Arrowwood provides organized activities for children ages 4-12. Other activities for kids include the pools, swimming beach, playground, sledding hill and skating pond—all safe and guaranteed fun.

In fact, there's fun here for the entire family. Take, for example, the beautiful 18-hole golf course. Or try the private marina with ski boats, pontoons, fishing boats and jet skis. In winter, rent a snowmobile and cruise the DATA Trail system. Cross-country ski on miles of groomed trails. Naturally, equipment and lessons are available to enhance your experience. Also, try the new indoor tennis, basketball and volleyball courts.

Want more?

OK. Indulge your epicurean fantasies at either of two exceptional restaurants. Lake Cafe features authentic Swedish and tasty North American cuisine in a romantic setting overlooking the lake. Give Luigis a try, too. It will please any family with its build-your-own homemade pizza and ice cream sundaes. Luigis is also the place to sharpen your skills on the latest video games. Be sure to check out the Deck Bar & Grill in the summer, serving light snacks and poolside beverages.

No wonder Arrowwood is one of Minnesota's highest-rated resorts. For atmosphere, service and amenities, Arrowwood is truly superior.

For business meetings and group events, they offer 28,000 square feet of meeting space for groups up to 1000. They will plan every detail for you, then guarantee its success. That's just a part of the service at Arrowwood—and it's what keeps visitors coming back season after season, whether for company business or for family pleasure.

BEMIDJI

For over half a century, logging was the lifeblood of the economy of the Bemidji Headwaters area. Local legend tells of a giant lumberjack Paul Bunyan and his faithful helper Babe The Blue Ox, who together carved out the lake areas of the state.

It was just natural as the legend goes, that Paul, the world's greatest lumberjack, was born here because only the Bemidji outdoors was big enough to accommodate him.

ATTRACTIONS & EVENTS

The many lakes in the Bemidji area form the center of a beautifully scenic park system. One-hundred-year-old *Itasca State Park*, site of the headwaters of the Mississippi, is perhaps the most notable of the eleven parks which make up this system. *Chippewa National Forest* is known as the "parent" of the Mississippi, and is believed to be the first and oldest national park in the U.S.

Three diverse 18-hole courses, *Bemidji Town & Country Club*, *Castle Highlands Golf Course* and *Greenwood Golf Course* are in the area. Two popular state tournaments are held in Bemidji every year, the *Birchmont* and the *Vandersluis.*

A Bemidji winter is jam-packed with sports, activities, festivals and special events.

The impact of the Bunyan legend is readily evident. The *Paul Bunyan Theater* is Minnesota's oldest professional summer theater. The famous statues of *Paul and Babe* greet visitors on the shores of *Lake Bemidji,* near the *Paul Bunyan Amusement Park.*

Pioneer Park is a working museum of pioneer life, complete with homesteads, trading post and general store.

The Bemidji area also offers opportunities to explore Native American culture. Traditional Indian culture, dance and friendship are renewed several times each year at the *Leech Lake* and *Red Lake Reservations'* pow wows.

A variety of gaming entertainment is featured in the area. There are two Las Vegas-style casinos, *Leech Lake Bingo Palace & Casino* and the *Northern Lights Emporium.* Red Lake offers high-stakes bingo on weekends.

For further information, contact:
Bemidji Visitors & Convention Bureau
P. O. Box 66
Bemidji, MN 56601
Phone: 800-458-2223

ANTIQUES

AnnTiques

301 NW Third Street, Bemidji, MN 56601
Phone: 218-751-2144. Hrs: Mon.-Sat. 10 a.m.-
5:30 p.m. Sundays by chance.
Visa and MasterCard accepted.

It's only fitting that you'll find one of the best selections of antiques and collectibles around in a building that's been home to commerce for nearly a hundred years.

AnnTiques, located in the 19th Century Troppman Building in Bemidji, continues that time-honored tradition of business and has for the better part of a decade by buying, selling and trading in all manner of antiques. Founded by Ann B. Moran in a small back room, AnnTiques has prospered and expanded to occupy the entire building now. Inside, you'll find antiques, collectibles, housewares, furniture and a vast selection of unusual items, too.

The store also features a bargain area where the displays are always changing and where you're sure to find a great selection of specially priced items. If you fancy figurines or like to garner glassware, if you're looking for stoneware or jewelry, AnnTiques offers you a wide array of choices, from unique to unusual. Be sure to stop when you're near Bemidji.

LODGING

Americinn Motel of Bemidji

1200 Paul Bunyan Drive NW, Bemidji, MN 56601
Phone: 218-751-3000 or 800-634-3444
Major credit cards accepted.

"Your home away from home" is the motto of the Americinn Motel of Bemidji. From the cozy fireplace and lobby that greet you to the complimentary continental breakfast served each day, the motel and its staff stand ready to make your stay a memorable one. They treat you just like family!

The motel is just three years old and has 62 rooms, some with their own whirlpool tubs. The swimming pool, sauna and whirlpool area combine to present an inviting and relaxing experience.

Bemidji, in the "true northwoods," offers great skiing and wonderful fishing, and Americinn Motel is an ideal host for these and other activities like Mardi Gras, Sled Dog races and Water Carnival.

Free HBO is provided, along with wheelchair accessible rooms and hearing-impaired apparatus.

The motel is ideally located next to the Perkins Family Restaurant, near the hockey arena and the Paul Bunyan Mall.

RESORT

Ruttger's Birchmont Lodge

530 Birchmont Beach Road, N.E.
Bemidji, MN 56601
Phone: 218-751-1630 or 800-726-3866
Hrs: Open year-round.

There's something for just about everyone at Ruttger's Birchmont Lodge, whether you want a quiet getaway or an activity-filled vacation for the family. With 1700 feet of sandy beach, it is perfectly suited for sunning, swimming, fishing or boating.

If you don't like the water, try tennis, golf, biking or hiking. Winter fun? You bet. Hundreds of miles of groomed snowmobile trails start at Ruttger's door. How about sled dog races, Logging Days, the wonderful new Mississippi connection of the Mardi Gras Celebration, downhill and cross-country skiing or even snowshoeing! And Ruttger's provides all the warmth!

In the May 1993 issue of *Better Homes & Gardens*, Ruttger's was named one of the best family resorts. With an outstanding restaurant, an acclaimed children's program and the classic northwoods atmosphere, Ruttger's is just the place to fulfill that lakeside vacation fantasy. Whether you choose to stay in the beautiful Main Lodge, the deluxe Cedar Lodge or in one of the many lakeside cabins, your stay will be both gracious and memorable.

In addition, Ruttger's staff takes pride in arranging unforgettable family reunions, weddings and celebrations of all sorts. Try them for important business conferences, too.

RESORT

| *Brucki's "Break On The Lake" Resort* | On County Rd. 33 off County Rd. 75, Route 2, Box 254, Cass Lake, MN 56633. **Phone: 218-335-2422 or 800-443-5101.** Hrs: Open Year-Round. Visa, MasterCard and Discover accepted. |

The Great Escape.

Traditionally, that is what city folks sought when it came time to vacation. And that's what many of the old-time resorts offered. Today, when space is limited, what a treat it is to come across a place where you can still vacation in complete solitude, where the only place you'll run across other travellers is on the lake.

That's Brucki's "Break on the Lake" Resort, located on the north shore of Allen's Bay on Cass Lake. Because most of the land surrounding Cass Lake is either state- or forestry-owned (the resort is located in the Chippewa National Forest), Jerry and Virginia Brucki can offer a secluded vacation.

When they bought the resort back in 1979, it was a simple six-cabin fishing spot. Today, "Break on the Lake" features a dozen cabins, five of which are three-bedroom A-frames. There is a handicapped-accessible four-bedroom cabin with fireplace. Plus the original six are still in use, consistently upgraded and enlarged over the years.

In the summer months, this is a family place.

The swimming pool and sand beach are popular gathering spots for young and old. So is the lodge where you'll find a complete game room for the kids and the Broken Bow Lounge for kids at heart. Mondays are Spaghetti Nights, when guests get together to share in a local tradition. Wednesday is steak night, a tradition that's catching on quickly, too.

Cabins come well-equipped. Most have microwaves. They are fully insulated for year-round comfort and have electric heat. Each has a full bath/shower combination, color TV, carpeting throughout, a large picture window with a view of the lake and a 24-foot cantilevered deck. Recreational options include volleyball, badminton, horseshoes and croquet or you might enjoy hiking nearby trails. And the resort is just minutes from a myriad of recreational pursuits.

From the docks at Brucki's, you have easy access to eight lakes, including Lake Windigo (a 100-acre freshwater lake within a lake on Star Island). Guide service and fish cleaning are available. Or you can cruise up the Mississippi or Turtle rivers. Plus tens of thousands of acres of prime deer habitat are accessible for your hunt.

Spring and fall are available at reduced rates.

RESORT

Finn 'n Feather Resort

Route 3, Box 870, Bemidji, MN 56601
Phone: 218-335-6598
Hrs: Open May through October.
Visa and MasterCard accepted.

Pictures might be a good substitute for words but even that wouldn't do enough to convey the essence of a week spent at Finn 'n Feather Resort with its prime location on Lake Andrusia and the Upper Mississippi Chain of Lakes.

How do you describe a perfect day spent on a lake that offers fine fishing for walleyes, northerns, bass, muskies and panfish? Or the simple pleasure of a Minnesota sunset? It's the kind of place people go when their sole objective is a great family vacation.

Heated pool, hot tub and an array of recreational facilities are included. Vacation homes are modern and spacious and come fully equipped for some serious relaxation. Many have fireplaces, decks or screen porches and feature wonderful views of the lake.

Located ten miles east of Bemidji and six miles northwest of Cass Lake, there are golf, bike trails and plenty of regional attractions nearby including Itasca State Park, the Chippewa National Forest, casino-style gambling and Professional Summer Stock Theatre.

RESTAURANT

Griffy's

319 Minnesota Ave., Bemidji, MN 56601
Phone: 218-751-3609
Hrs: Mon.-Fri. 6-5:30; Sat. 6-3.

Located just two blocks from the Paul Bunyan & Babe statues in Bemidji is Griffy's, an interesting little deli and eatery with many regulars. That's because the food is so good at Griffy's, you will want to come back anytime you're in the area.

JoAnn Staker, Griffy's owner, has a flair for delicious breakfast and lunch delights, proven now by Griffy's success with over ten years in business. Breakfasts consist of various egg dishes, fresh bakery items and fruit. But lunch is where the real deli items are. Try the Washington D.C. Special with ham, turkey breast and Swiss. The Baltimore Express is made with Irish roast beef and cream cheese on a croissant. Or, make it a Sunny Californian with avocado, green pepper, cucumber, lettuce, sprouts, and blue cheese.

The most popular sandwich is The Griffy Deluxe, an Irish roast beef and turkey breast sandwich with Swiss and served on wild rice bread. But whichever sandwich you choose, you'll find at Griffy's "the object is excellence."

SPECIALTY SHOP

Lady Slipper Designs Retail Outlet	315 Irvine Ave. NW, Bemidji, MN 56601 **Phone: 218-751-7501.** Hrs: Open Memorial Day weekend through Dec. 31. Visa, MasterCard and Discover accepted.

More than just another cottage industry, Lady Slipper Designs is truly a success story in Bemidji. As a private, not-for-profit corporation, it's dedicated to improving the economic quality of life of low-income, rural northern Minnesota residents. Lady Slipper Designs is a national model demonstrating how work-at-home alternatives can create economic opportunities for persons with limited experience living in remote areas that have consistently high unemployment.

The products are made locally by about 300 area craftspeople and have come to be appreciated by discriminating gift buyers from all over the world. The designs are now carried by more than 5000 retail accounts worldwide.

The Lady Slipper Designs Retail Outlet, the only one of its kind anywhere, offers buyers an opportunity to purchase first quality, seconds, show samples and discontinued lines. The savings are substantial. In some cases, you'll spend as little as just 25 percent of the retail price for these cherished designs. In most cases, the prices average about 35 percent below the regular retail price on first quality merchandise. Close-out lines, seconds, show samples and prototypes offer even more savings, up to 75 percent in some cases.

Located next to Bemidji Woolen Mills in downtown Bemidji, the Lady Slipper Designs Retail Outlet is a soothing place to spend some time. With nature's music playing in the background, you can browse through the incredible selection. They have birchbark and rustic decorating accessories plus birdhouses and birdfeeders that are often featured in national decorating magazines.

You'll also find leaf-impression duck and goose eggs, dream catchers and authentic Ojibwa beadwork. There's even black velvet cats. Or check out the whimsical wearables, including aprons, oven mitts and bibs.

Of course, there's more than just Lady Slipper Designs here, too. Other gift lines are also available including the works of independent craftspeople from the Bemidji area, crafters who specialize in wreaths, pillows, hand-blown and stained glass, ladyslipper flowers and hand-painted ornaments.

Shipping is available, too, and the store remains open through Christmas so you can get Santa's shopping done, too. Nationally known and Minnesota-made, Lady Slipper Designs make great gifts for that special someone.

SPECIALTY SHOP

The Old Schoolhouse

2335 Monroe Ave. S.W.
Bemidji, MN 56601
Phone: 218-751-4723

As you drive up to The Old Schoolhouse you may be reminded of the school you attended as a youngster. There is the small hill where you might have slid down on waxed pieces of cardboard and the ball diamond with dugout and bleachers where you had games with rival schools.

Upon entering the 10-room, three-story brick schoolhouse, you will be aware that it still looks like it did in 1917 when it was built. The radiators and blackboards are still there and the floors still squeak. The radiators no longer are in operation with wet winter-time mittens drying on them, but some of the rooms still have metal ceilings.

The school closed in 1972 and since 1973 has been privately owned by Lois and Herb Dale of Bemidji. Daughter, Diane Halverson, teaches dance in a larger portion of the third floor. Diane's Dance Studio has been in operation since 1965.

The remainder of the building (six rooms, two cloak halls and hallways) is filled with a wide variety of locally handcrafted gifts. Approximately 500 consignors have items on display for sale. A Christmas room offers decorations and ornaments. Art work covers the walls of the second floor—quilts, pillows, stuffed toys, rosemaling, toleworks, Indian birchbark and beadwork, birdhouses, shelves and handcrafted wood ornaments of Paul Bunyan and Babe are just some of many things you will find.

The Art Studio-Gallery has for sale an extensive supply of fine art and technical illustration supplies. You will find hundreds of frames, brushes, paints, matboard and papers. Picture framing is a special service.

Relive childhood memories while you shop at The Old Schoolhouse. It's worth the drive from anywhere. The location: 1 mile south of Bemidji on #197 and 1 mile west on Carr Lake and Old Schoolhouse Road.

The Old Schoolhouse, Bemidji, Minnesota

SPECIALTY SHOP

Busby's Country Charm	1726 Jefferson Ave. S.W., (Two and a half miles west of Bemidji) Bemidji, MN 56601. **Phone: 218-751-6163** Hrs: Mon.-Fri. 10 a.m.-5 p.m., Sat. 10 a.m.-4 p.m., Sun. noon-4 p.m. after May 15. Visa and MasterCard accepted.

Busby's Country Charm is "Real country charm nestled in the pines," featuring affordable quality jewelry and gifts with a country flavor.

They offer fine jewelry including diamonds and precious gems, gold and sterling silver rings, necklaces, bracelets, earrings, as well as unique household items and gifts like stained glass, copper, brass, lace, crystal, china and hand-thrown pottery.

Country items include cast iron toys, pots and pans, trivets, door stops, braided rugs, recipe boxes, Amish hand-carved oak hay forks, and wall plaques.

Stop out and browse. There's always a smile and a friendly word at Busby's Country Charm.

Take 5th Street West out of Bemidji for a half a mile and turn left (south) on Jefferson Avenue. Go straight south one and a half miles. Busby's is the fourth drive on the left after the Mississippi River bridge. Look for the big sign and have fun!

◆ ◆ ◆ ◆ ◆ ◆ ◆

Morell's Chippewa Trading Post	301 Bemidji Avenue, Bemidji, MN 56601 **Phone: 218-751-4321** Hrs: Open 7 days a week year-round Visa, MasterCard, Discover and AmEx accepted.

For a piece of America's past and a taste of American Indian heritage, Morell's Chippewa Trading Post offers a wide selection of Native American artifacts from the region.

It's a unique store, well-stocked with quality artifacts, gifts and souvenirs including birch bark baskets, mini-canoes, birdhouses, teepees and utility holders. They also carry cradle boards, quivers and arrows, peace pipes, wallhangings and pottery. The beadwork is beautiful, all of it locally made, including pins, bracelets, medallions, belt buckles and earrings.

Morell's Chippewa Trading Post also has porcupine quill items, tom tom drums, medicine bags, key chains, a large variety of moccasins, souvenir sweatshirts, caps and T-shirts. The Black Hills silver is worth a look and if you like wild rice, you can find it here, too, along with recipe books and pamphlets containing all the secrets to great wild rice dishes. Located across from the giant Paul Bunyan, Morell's is open seven days a week, year-round.

SPECIALTY SHOP

Netzer Floral Gift and Greenhouse	1632 Bemidji Ave., Bemidji, MN 56601 **Phone:** 218-751-1485. Hrs: Mon.-Fri. 9 a.m.- 5;30 p.m. Sat. 9 a.m.-5 p.m. Discover, Visa and MasterCard accepted.

Netzer Floral Gift and Greenhouse is one of those gentle places where fresh flowers, green plants, classical music and potpourri all combine to relax the spirit and delight the heart. Established in 1952, it's been owned and operated by Linda and Wayne Ward since 1975.

Besides flowers and greenery, the store offers dried and artificial flowers, silk plants, wicker baskets, pottery and brass, crystal, Department 56 villages, porcelain dolls, decorator blankets, music, antiques, a fragrance collection for the body and the home, a large variety of ribbon, gourmet foods, candles and much more.

There's an annual Christmas open house in November that is very festive. Shipping for gifts is available.

✦ ✦ ✦ ✦ ✦ ✦ ✦

Nordic Gifts	Paul Bunyan Mall, Bemidji, MN 56601 **Phone:** 218-751-8254. Hours: Mon.-Fri. 10 a.m.- 9 p.m.; Sat. till 6 p.m.; Sun. noon-5 p.m. Visa, MasterCard and Discover accepted.

Elaine Larson's Scandinavian heritage gives Nordic Gifts its name and charm, but satisfied customers have given the store its well-deserved reputation.

Conveniently located in the Paul Bunyan Mall, Nordic Gifts has expanded to include not only treasured collectibles but other gifts as well. Its merchandise includes Dept. 56 Villages, snowbabies, David Winter Cottages, Tom Clark gnomes, Cherished Teddies, collector Santas and porcelain dolls.

Visitors enjoy the rustic wood decor and rosemaled cabinets while they discover imported goods from Scandinavia and other European countries.

Warm, friendly sales clerks make it fun to find the Portmeirion dinnerware, crystal, linens and afghans, books and cassettes, napkins, candles, and Minnesota and north-country items. Specialty clothing includes sweatshirts and T-shirts with artistic and North Country designs. Gift wrapping and shipping is available.

BRAINERD

In the heart of Minnesota, Brainerd is situated on the historic Mississippi River. Brainerd was established in 1870, when the Northern Pacific Railroad crossed the river at this site to create the first transcontinental railroad. The railway headquarters and general offices located here. Along with the railway, lumber brought hundreds of settlers to the "City of the Pines." At this time, the legend of Paul Bunyan, the giant lumberjack, began.

The Paul Bunyan legend encompasses the entire Midwest, but its home is the Brainerd Lakes Area. Today, Brainerd calls itself "the hometown of Paul Bunyan" in defiance of neighboring Bemidji's same claim to this local legend.

ATTRACTIONS

Paul Bunyan is big enough for both cities. In fact, his legend is popular enough to sustain a number of attractions in both Bemidji and Brainerd. *Paul Bunyan Recreational Corridor Trail* ties together a vast system of trails enjoyed in summer by bikers, wheelchair athletes, roller bladers, walkers, and hikers. Winter use includes snowmobiling and cross-country skiing. This trail is one of the most popular and beautiful in the state.

Overall, there are some 1600 miles of snowmobile trails to be enjoyed in the area. *The Paul Bunyan Arboretum* offers lighted cross-country ski and snowshoe trails. *Gull Lake Downhill Ski Area* offers some downhill fun, as well. In total, there are 13 cross-country ski and snowshoe areas ranging from 7 to 50 kilometers.

There are 450 clear, sand-bottom lakes within a 15-mile radius of the area, offering almost limitless opportunities for family vacation fun. Snowmobile and boat rentals can be had at every turn in the road. The *Nisswa Guide League* is home to 20 professional fishing guides for the ultimate in fishing pleasure. Even the Mississippi River, which runs through the area, offers some of the best fishing around.

Crow Wing County Historical Museum, perfect for those who desire more lumber-lore, is an authentically restored home decorated with primitive paintings of the early logging and railroading days. *Lumbertown USA* depicts a typical lumber town of the 1870's.

Today, Brainerd is a resort center with fabulous fishing opportunities in the nearby 464 freshwater lakes and miles of rivers. *Crow Wing State Park* is known for its fishing, excellent camping and hiking facilities. *Pillsbury Forest* is just west of Brainerd offering over 90 lakes and ponds with 26 miles of cross-country ski, snowmobile, horse and hiking trails. In addition, the whole area offers excellent birdwatching and nature observation.

Other sporting attractions include the well-known **Brainerd International Raceway** which annually hosts major competitions in drag, Classic and Formula One racing; the **Granny's Softball on Ice;** and **Annual Snow Golf tournaments**.

Golf courses in the Brainerd Lakes Area have been nationally recognized as some of the top courses in the midwest. Lush green fairways winding through beautifully wooded areas and waters create courses that are not only enjoyable for golfers of all skill levels, but are beautiful to play on. No matter where you stay in the area, you'll be within minutes of 19 distinctive courses featuring 245 holes of golf. These courses come in all varieties, from the challenging to courses designed for novices.

Here is a sampling:

Breezy Point Resort on Pelican Lake offers two 18-hole courses, one championship and one recreational. Birch Bay boasts some of the finest greens in the Lakes Area. Ruttger's offers 27 of northern Minnesota's most scenic holes. The Whitefish Golf Club is a Par 72, 6172-yard course open to the public. Mille Lacs Lake Golf Resort is a Par 71, 6400-yard course complete with all the amenities. Izaty's offers Minnesota's only "Dye Design" 18-hole championship course. Madden's boasts 45 holes of golf. Crosslake Executive Golf Course is a 9-hole, Par 29 course. Grand View Lodge's **The Pines** was named "Best new resort course" by **Golf Digest** and is ranked one of Minneosta's top public courses.

EVENTS

There are a variety of events scheduled every year in the area. A few of these include: **Winterfest,** a celebration of winter, held in Brainerd during January. The **Arts and Crafts Festival** is held in Brainerd during May and features arts and crafts made by local craftspeople. In June, the **Tour of the Lakes Bike Ride** is offered, along with the **Champion Auto Drag Races.**

July sees the **Fourth of July Celebration, Art in the Park,** the **Minnesota Loon Festival, Bean Hole Days** and the **Merrifield Fun Fest.**

August features the **Gull Lake Yacht Club Regatta,** the **Annual Corn Feed,** and **Chili Cook-off.**

September is the time for **Fall Color Touring** and the **Minnesota Street Rod Campout.**

October brings **Oktoberfest** and the **Heartland Symphony.**

For further information, contact:

Brainerd Lakes Area Chamber of Commerce
Sixth and Washington Streets, Brainerd, MN 56401
Phone: 218-829-2838   Outstate and Canada: 800-950-1162
MN: 800-450-2838

MUSEUM

This Old Farm

7344 Highway 18 E, Brainerd, MN 56401
Phone: 218-764-2915
Hrs: Sat.-Sun 9 a.m.-5 p.m.
Memorial Day-Labor Day

If you've seen the Disney film "Iron Will," you may recognize a thing or two about This Old Farm just east of Brainerd. That's because Dick and Marian Rademacher have on display the store and depot (shown below) featured in the adventure film about a 1917 sled dog marathon. In exchange for use of their Model T's and other old equipment in the movie, the Rademachers got to keep the sets.

Even if you haven't seen "Iron Will," you'll be fascinated by the more than 10,000 items at this unusual museum, where a lifetime hobby has been transformed into an old-time village. Here you'll find life just as it was years ago.

There's an original log house from a nearby homestead standing equipped just as it might have been in its prime, complete with kitchen, parlor and bedroom and filled with irreplaceable antiques from toys to glassware. The collection of gas engines and farm machinery is endless.

Stop at the Long Horn Saloon, fully decorated with an authentic player piano, Texas Long Horns, one arm bandit, nickelodeon and the brass rail bar.

Visit an old, one-room schoolhouse, fully equipped with books and ink wells. The school bell still rings just like it did in the early 1900's.

Pull up to the filling station where the gas pump rings up only pennies per gallon. Check out the barber shop, dentist's office, post office and more. See the line of antique cars, horse buggies and tractors. A fascinating journey for young and old.

HISTORIC VILLAGE & MUSEUM

Lumbertown U.S.A.	8001 Pine Beach Peninsula, Brainerd, MN 56401 **Phone: 218-829-8872** Hrs: May-mid-Sept. 9:30 a.m.-5:30 p.m. Visa and MasterCard accepted.

Lumbertown U.S.A. is an authentic 1870's logging village established within the Madden Resorts. Jack Madden originally built the town as an historic museum to preserve the bustling lumbertown lifestyle of those early days. However, many of the structures are originals that have been moved to the site.

This is a place where visitors experience history for themselves. They visit the "Last Turn" Saloon, Town Hall and the Old Red School. They come face-to-face with Buffalo Bill Cody, Annie Oakley and other turn-of-the-century celebrities in the Lumbertown Wax Museum.

Children enjoy going to the levee on the Blueberry River to take a ride on the riverboat or take a scenic ride on a replica of the first Northern Pacific locomotive to the area.

Lumbertown U.S.A. is a fun and educational experience for groups and school tours, also. A picnic area, nine-hole miniature golf course and gift shop offer something for just about everyone.

RESORT

Kavanaugh's on Sylvan Lake	2300 Kavanaugh Drive SW, Brainerd, MN 56401 **Phone: 218-829-5226 or 800-562-7061** Hrs: Open four seasons. Visa, MasterCard and Discover accepted.

Acclaimed by *Better Homes and Gardens* magazine as one of America's Favorite Family Resorts, Kavanaugh's has provided the finest accommodations, dining and hospitality for three decades.

Located on beautiful Upper Sylvan Lake, Kavanaugh's has deluxe lake villas and cottages with decks and fireplaces. Recreational options include two sand beaches and marinas featuring boating, sailing, swimming, fishing and skiing. Boat rentals are available and 99 holes of golf are nearby. Enjoy the indoor heated pool, sauna and whirlpool as well as tennis, croquet, hiking and mountain biking. Spring, fall and winter promise unique opportunities for nature lovers with secluded hardwood forest trails for hiking, skiing and snowmobiling.

Kavanaugh's lakeside restaurant is comfortably elegant and serves award winning seafood, prime steaks and vintage veal, all prepared from scratch by members of the Kavanaugh family. The Pine Bough Gift Shop offers specialty art and handcrafted gifts.

RESOURT

Cragun's Lodge, Resort, Spa & Restaurant	2001 Pine Beach Road, East Gull Lake, Brainerd, MN 56401. **Phone: 800-CRAGUNS (272-4867) or 218-829-3591.** Hrs: Open year-round. Major credit cards accepted.

For over 50 years, Cragun's has set the standard for quality, service and hospitality in the Minnesota resort industry. Whether you are looking for a romantic weekend get-away, a fun-filled family vacation or a top-notch business meeting center, you'll find Cragun's at Gull Lake able to meet all of your needs and expectations.

First off, Cragun's offers a host of activities—something for everyone in any season. For example, golf is definitely above par here. Six distinctive golf courses nearby offer 90 holes total with four true championship courses! As a Cragun's guest, you're entitled to a discount and Cragun's will even arrange tee times for you.

Beach activities include over half a mile of clean, sandy beach, fire rings, picnic tables, volleyball, shuffleboard and playground. In fact, Cragun's has a children's program, too, one of the best around.

Cragun's has boats, motors, gas, live bait, a full-service marina and will arrange guided fishing trips if you desire. In the winter, enjoy cross-country and downhill skiing, dog sled rides and ice fishing in heated houses. There's 1200 miles of snowmobile trails and Cragun's new SnowMo Center has 45 new Arctic Cat snowmobiles and clothing for rent. A horse drawn hayride offers another winter activity.

Cragun's is the largest connected resort and conference center in Minnesota. Two hundred rooms and cottages are connected by heated and enclosed hallways. Guests may walk to meeting rooms, dining rooms, indoor pool, sports dome, lobby and lounge. Luxury rooms offer private balconies, fireplaces, wet bars and more. Other accommodations include cottages, suites, townhouse units, deluxe and premium rooms.

Cragun's is known for their delicious homemade breads, rolls, pastries and desserts prepared from scratch on site. You can sample these treats and more during the summer months at the Hungry Gull Restaurant or in the Lodge Dining Room year-round.

The resort boasts a new Sports Center, a breathtaking 21,000-square-foot facility with tennis, volleyball and basketball courts, running track, exercise equipment, golf simulator and teen center.

Of course, Cragun's is a premier meeting and convention center with many meeting rooms and the largest planning team of any hotel or resort conference center in Minnesota. Despite all of this, Cragun's is still a family-owned and operated business with unquestionable quality and luxury in a spectacular northwoods setting.

RESORT

Madden's On Gull Lake

8001 Pine Beach Peninsula, Brainerd, MN 56401
Phone: 218-829-2811 or 800-247-1040
Hrs: Mid-April-late Oct.
Visa and MasterCard are accepted.

This expansive resort was built on land that was owned by the Northern Pacific Railroad in the 1860's and was developed from the modest beginnings of a small golf course with a single clubhouse. Today, Madden's on Gull Lake offers three separate resort facilities, each with its own style and conference facilities, excellent dining and endless recreational possibilities for vacationers.

On scenic Pine Beach Peninsula of Gull Lake, 130 miles northwest of Minneapolis/St. Paul, the three resorts include the colonial-style Madden Lodge, the rustic Madden's Pine Portage and the Madden Inn and Golf Club. These combine to provide 285 air-conditioned cottages and luxury units as well as modern lodge and hotel rooms. The three resort centers have individual dining facilities, a banquet facility and an informal coffee shop. Groups may plan special indoor or outdoor meal functions, from elaborate banquets to casual cookouts. Theme buffets and table service are available for traditional meals.

Madden's also provides versatility in planning meetings. All details, from room set-up to scheduling and catering, can be coordinated by Madden's staff. Thirty meeting rooms of varying size and seating capacity, including the Town Hall Conference Center, allow personalized meeting support services.

Visitors may enjoy 45 holes of golf on three courses, the Croquet & Tennis Center, volleyball, shuffleboard, game rooms, cycling, jogging, and trapshooting. Two fully equipped marinas, three sandy beaches, five heated pools—three indoor with spa and sauna—provide facilities for water sports activities. In the evening, relax with friends at the 19th Hole Lounge, or enjoy live entertainment in the O'Madden Pub.

Madden's offers many special services, from business to party planning. Holiday and special value package plans are also available.

RESORT

Quarterdeck Resort and Restaurant

1588 Quarterdeck R. W., County Road 77, Brainerd, MN 56401. **Phone: 218-963-2482** Hrs.: Open Daily. Sun.-Thurs. 11 a.m.-10 p.m., Fri.-Sat. 9 a.m.-11 p.m., Sun. 9 a.m.-3 p.m. Major credit cards accepted.

In the heartland of Minnesota and along beautiful Gull Lake's shorelines is an incredible family resort and restaurant with vacation pleasures for adults and children—the Quarterdeck Resort and Restaurant. Two-, three- and four-bedroom lakeside vacation homes are complete with living and dining room areas, fully equipped kitchens and some have fireplaces. Luxury villas all have fireplaces and are attractively furnished for couples. All homes have breathtaking views of Gull Lake.

The sandy beaches are excellent for swimming. There is a planned and supervised recreational program for children and other outdoor activities include tennis, basketball, shuffleboard, badminton, horseshoes and volleyball. A short walk from the resort lies Birch Bay Golf Club, with several other golf courses nearby. The fishing is excellent and special packages for boat and motor rentals are available. Children enjoy panfishing right off the docks. For leisure tours, pontoon boats are also available.

The renowned Quarterdeck Restaurant and Supper Club overlooks Gull Lake, offering over 100 menu items, with nightly entertainment in the lounge. The Quarterdeck offers outstanding facilities for groups, conventions and family reunions. The staff will design packages to accommodate the menu and lodging required for individual groups. Winter enthusiasts enjoy the 1,000+ miles of groomed snowmobile and cross-country ski trails. The Quarterdeck is situated on the trail between the Pillsbury State Forest and Minnesota's only lighted lake trail on Gull Lake. Downhill skiing is less than a mile away and ice houses are available for ice fishing.

RESTAURANT

Iven's on the Bay	5195 N. Highway 371, Brainerd, MN 56401 **Phone: 218-829-9872.** Hrs.: Open daily (dinner) 5 p.m. until close. Sunday brunch 10 a.m.-1 p.m. All major credit cards accepted.

If you've been searching for good food that's good for you, then there's good news—Iven's on the Bay in Brainerd is your kind of place. Throw in a wonderful view, fabulous service and a commitment to quality and you have a recipe for the ages. You also have Iven's on the Bay.

Iven's on the Bay is a quality seafood house established in 1984 overlooking the west bay of North Long Lake. An exceptional dining experience in a pleasant and relaxed atmosphere awaits all guests.

Owned by Marlene and Iven Hudalla, Iven's on the Bay is the realization of a dream. The Hudallas had an idea a decade and a half ago to establish a quality seafood house on North Highway 371. It became a reality when the ideal property was offered for sale and purchased by the Hudallas. The rest, as they say, is history.

From its start, only the highest quality, nutritionally prepared food has been served here. Most entrées are broiled, charbroiled or steamed, and many menu items meet "heart healthy" serving standards. Special attention is given to details, cleanliness and professionalism. This reflects the entire staff's commitment to excellence in hospitality and service.

Wonderful choices pervade Iven's prize-winning menu.

The house specialty is golden, pan-fried walleye and it is the most popular menu item. Leading seafood specialties are garlic broiled jumbo shrimp, broiled fresh sea scallops and grilled fresh salmon. A host of other seafood delicacies await you on the menu.

Though seafood is the emphasis, meat, meat/seafood combinations and vegetarian items are offered. For example, you can sate your appetite with a New York strip, try a lamb or red deer tenderloin, sup on mouth-watering chicken selections, or make a vegetarian choice like wild mushroom rissotto.

Fresh fish flown in is always available as the chef's feature of the day. Most popular are Halibut, Mahi Mahi, Grouper, Tuna and Monkfish. Oysters on the half-shell are always available.

The most often-asked question at Iven's on the Bay?

"Can we have a window table?"

And why not. The view, like the food, is terrific.

For an evening of fine dining or an indulgence in a great Sunday brunch, a visit to Iven's is a memorable choice. Iven's is also a great choice for a small group function or private party.

CROSSLAKE

Crosslake, a quiet northwoods village of 1,118 people, is about as different from the urban scene as possible. It's situated on Crosslake, which is one of 14 lakes in the Whitefish and Ossawinnamakee Chain of lakes, making it an ideal vacation spot.

Points of historic interest include the *Old Town Hall Museum* and an authentic *1895 Log Home.* Crosslake is known in antique circles for its many antique and gift stores.

Always a popular event, the *July Fourth* fireworks display from *Sand Island* is a summer favorite. August features two special events —the annual *Art Show* and a delicious *Chili Cook-off.*

The entire Crosslake area boasts of numerous resorts, inns, motels and campgrounds whose prime purpose is to help guests to relax and enjoy the beautiful country, all year-round.

For further information, contact:

Crosslake Chamber of Commerce
P.O. Box 315
Crosslake, MN 56422   Phone: 218-692-4027

RESORT

Beacon Shores Resort

HC 83, Box 745, Crosslake, MN 56442
Phone: 218-543-4166 or 800-950-5907
Hrs: Open year-round
Visa and MasterCard accepted.

The perfect place in the woods for a nice quiet getaway, Beacon Shores Resort on Whitefish Lake is open all four seasons.

This is a family resort, specializing in warm, friendly hospitality, the right kind of place for a relaxing, old-fashioned northwoods vacation complete with all of the modern conveniences. All cabins are knotty pine paneled and have country furnishings and many of them have fireplaces and screened porches, as well. Kitchens come complete with microwaves and you can choose from cabins or townhomes.

In the winter months, there is terrific cross-country skiing nearby as well as snowmobile trails. In the warmer months, hike the beautiful marked nature trails nearby, try out the pickle ball court, swim off the sandy beach, go fishing or play golf at Whitefish Golf Course (discounts for guests). Plus there are plenty of children's activities, too, along with nearby attractions, dining and shopping. Or soak up the unrivaled beauty of a northwoods sunset.

HOUSEBOAT RENTALS

Chain O'Lakes Houseboats	East Shore Road, P.O. Box 154 Crosslake, MN 56442. **Phone: 218-692-4677** **or 800-247-1932** Hrs: May-Oct. Visa, MasterCard & Discover accepted.

How would you like a vacation in the northwoods that allows you to move to another location whenever the mood strikes? That's exactly what you can have with Chain O'Lakes Houseboats on the beautiful Whitefish Chain of Lakes in Crosslake, MN. They're located a little north of Brainerd or approximately three hours from the Twin Cities.

Houseboating offers a unique form of family vacationing. Perhaps the fish aren't biting. Maybe you desire a change of scenery or need a little more privacy. If so, just pull up anchor and move your cabin to another location. Cruise as you explore the 14 lakes of the Whitefish Chain. Enjoy the beautiful sunrises and sunsets from a vantage point that you decide.

Rent for the weekend, midweek or weekly. Your home away from home comes complete with hot and cold running water, toilet facilities, room heater, kitchen with a cook top, refrigerator, dishes and a gas BBQ.

Take a swim or sit in the sun on the decks. Stop at a bait or convenience store to pick up some supplies. Or just boat up to a restaurant and eat out. It's all up to the captain and his crew.

Lest you think you're completely isolated, remember, this is the Brainerd area, known for its many activities like hiking, golfing, shopping, horseback riding, amusement centers, water slides, restaurants and much more.

DEERWOOD/CROSBY/IRONTON

The discovery of a rich deposit of iron ore by Cuyler Adams in 1890 gave birth to the mining cities of Crosby, Deerwood, and Ironton. Known collectively as the Cuyuna Range, formed by combining "Cuy" for Cuyler with "Una," the name of his St. Bernard dog and faithful companion during those early days.

Mining this precious resource fed the nation's industrial giants, producing 100 million tons of ore before the resource was depleted.

ATTRACTIONS & EVENTS

Today, 14 of the vast open iron pits have been turned into gem-like lakes, some over 500 feet deep. These lakes have miles of undeveloped shoreline perfect for every kind of water and outdoor sport. Stocked with more than 40,000 rainbow and brook trout, along with other native fishes that thrive in this water, these lakes provide some of the hottest fishing around. Visitors are invited here to scuba dive in the cleanest and deepest lakes in the midwest, unequaled for clarity anywhere in Minnesota.

This mining heritage is everywhere and is the subject of most of the historic attractions in the area. Visitors will literally step into history at the *Croft Mine and Historical Park.* The highlight of this experience is a trip into the simulated underground mine.

The Cuyuna Range Historical Museum, also in Crosby, presents mining memorabilia including tools and artifacts. The museum is a restored railroad depot from the same era, an 1880's general store, and stocked dining kitchen. Displays of logging days tell of the diverse ethnic groups who settled here.

Deerwood, the oldest city of the three, greets visitors with a leaping deer and the landmark *Deerwood Auditorium,* constructed in 1936. Also located in Deerwood is *Ruttger's Bay Lake Lodge,* one of the oldest resorts in Minnesota established in 1898. Summerfest is an annual event, held in August which offers guests a unique opportunity to experience a small-town celebration.

Ironton, the most restful of the three, is proud to proclaim that they are a small town with old-fashioned friendliness and progressive ideas. *Ironton City Park,* tucked in the heart of town, is the perfect place for picnic lunches, tennis and playground fun.

For further information contact:
Crosby Area Chamber of Commerce
P.O. Box 23
Crosby, MN 56441
Phone: 218-546-6990 or 800-545-2841

BED & BREAKFAST

| *Walden Woods Bed & Breakfast* | 16070 Highway 18 S.E., Deerwood, MN 56444
Phone: 612-692-4379
Hrs: Open year-round.
Visa, MasterCard and AmEx accepted. |

Because it's located just 15 miles from Brainerd, you might think Walden Woods B&B is part of the fabric of traditional tourism—golf, tennis, fishing, biking, boating and more. But it's really very different from those things, starting with the half-mile long driveway.

Not that you can't join in those activities, if you're so inclined. It's just that Walden Woods marches to a different drummer, one that is quieter, slower and surrounded by the tonic of natural splendor.

Here, owners Richard and Anne Manly have carved out of the deep woods a most delightful B&B to relax the mind and ease the spirit.

It's a log home, as you might guess, and offers solitude willingly. There's a choice of four bedrooms and two shared baths. Each room is lovingly furnished with family antiques and treasured collectibles gathered by the Manlys during travels to various parts of the world. The Lakeview Room offers a queen-size bed and tranquil view of the lake. The Jenny Lind Room contains an heirloom antique high bed. Grandma's Attic finds an eclectic collection of treasures you might expect in such a room. The Trapper's Cabin is a rustic retreat filled with an intriguing array of typical trapper's gear.

Wander the trails down by the lake or simply sit on the screened porch to enjoy it. Watch for the loons, beaver and other wildlife that also call these woods and water home.

So, leave the humdrum world behind and visit this special place. You'll be glad you came to Walden Woods.

RESORT

| *Ruttger's Bay Lake Lodge* | Rt. 2, Box 400, Deerwood, MN 56444. **Phone: 218-678-2885 or 800-950-7244 or 800-450-4545 (MN).** Open May through Oct. MasterCard, Visa and Discover accepted. |

Ruttger's Bay Lake Lodge is one of those Minnesota traditions everyone loves to experience. It's been in continuous operation since the Ruttger family established the family resort in 1898. Now, the fourth generation is working in the business that so many guests have made a part of their lives, too. In fact, Ruttger's was featured among favorite family resorts in the May 1993 issue of *Better Homes and Gardens,* a tribute to Ruttger's standards for impeccable cleanliness, comfort and service.

Visitors have a variety of lodging alternatives at Ruttger's, including cozy log cottages, scenic golf course condominiums and elegant villas. Guests may choose from several package plans for meals and lodging to suit their individual needs. Group packages are available, too.

Next to fine service, it's Ruttger's food that draws the most compliments. It's another tradition created from the famous Ruttger recipe for delicious entrées, garden fresh vegetables, homemade pastries and breads—all served up with old-fashioned hospitality in a wonderful lodge of hand-hewn native logs.

In the true tradition of family resorts, Ruttger's offers a wide variety of activities for everyone. With 2000 feet of sandy beach and acres of pine-scented forest, visitors relax by swimming in both indoor and outdoor pools, playing tennis, boating, canoeing, shopping, hiking, and, of course, golfing at Ruttger's championship Lakes Course, designed by noted golf course designer Joel Goldstrand. Each hole is unique and memorable.

There are many day activity programs, as well, including an exceptional children's program. Oktoberfest is held annually in mid-October and features authentic German food, music and dancing, with a craft show featuring 75 exhibitors.

If you're looking to start your own family tradition, there is no place more special than Ruttger's!

MILLE LACS LAKE

Mille Lacs Lake is as close to a fisherman's paradise as they come. Every summer, 175,000 anglers try their luck on Minnesota's second largest lake with 200 square miles of water. During the winter, diehards congregate in a veritable city of more than a thousand ice fishing shacks hauled out on the ice so they can fish in the frigid waters. The lake's most popular species is the walleye, of course, and has an estimated population of more than one million! Each year, 500,000 lbs. are harvested.

ATTRACTIONS & EVENTS

Visitors to the area can choose among hundreds of lake resorts located in small communities from Isle in the south to Garrison in the northwest.

Though fishing is perhaps the number one activity, there are many alternatives for the non-fisherman and family, as well. Mille Lacs Lake is graced by three recreational areas offering activities like hiking, swimming, camping and cross-country skiing. These are: *Father Hennepin State Park* near Isle, *Mille Lacs Kathio State Park* near Vineland and *Wealthwood State Forest* on the north side of the lake.

Golfers will find the *Mille Lacs Lake Golf Resort* in Garrison offers a par-71, 18-hole course along with a challenging nine-hole course in Garrison. *Izaty's Golf and Yacht Club* offers championship play while *Mille Lacs Lake Golf Resort* is a forested dream.

On the west shore of the lake is the *Grand Casino Mille Lacs.* The casino features slots, poker, blackjack and other games for the indoor enthusiast. Each summer the tribe holds a *pow wow* with traditional dances, songs, food and games.

Those searching for something special can venture north of Garrison to the *Stone House* and its selection of various gift items as well as wild rice, honey and other Minnesota products.

February brings the *Governor's Snowmobile Ride.* May offers *Cabela's North American Walleye Anglers Tournament.* August offers the *Minnesota PGA Championship.*

For further information, contact:
Mille Lacs Area Tourism Association
P.O. Box 692
Isle, MN 56342
Phone: 612-532-3636

BED & BREAKFAST

Cour du Lac

RR1, Box 269A, Onamia, MN 56359
Phone: 612-532-4627
Hrs.: Open year-round.
MasterCard and Visa accepted.

Most known for its outstanding fishing, Mille Lacs Lake provides a spectacular natural setting for Cour du Lac Bed and Breakfast, the only B&B on the big lake. It's a perfect hideaway from which to launch a host of activities in the area around Onamia and southern Mille Lacs.

There are three guest rooms upstairs, each with their own bathroom, and an upstairs sitting room for all guests to enjoy. The guest rooms offer an excellent view of the lake and surrounding woods.

Visitors wake to the aroma of a country breakfast and hot coffee served in a beautiful china cup. Your hostess may be cooking up one of her specialties: pumpkin pancakes with hot apple sauce, maple syrup, sausage, homemade bread and fresh fruit.

One interesting aspect of Cour du Lac is that the owners have built much of the furniture using wood harvested right from the land surrounding it. This country setting perfectly complements its secluded location.

With a country/French elegance and charm, Cour du Lac greets the visitor with sensory delights that will not be soon forgotten!

RESORT

Izatys Golf & *Yacht Club*	40005 85th Avenue, Route 1, Box 460 Onamia, MN 56359. **Phone:** 800-533-1728 Hrs: Open year-round. Major credit cards accepted.

For decades, the name Izatys has been synonymous with Mille Lacs family vacations. Today, it has been transformed into an outstanding playground with all of the amenities you'd expect from the very best.

Named after the historic Sioux Indian Village on Mille Lacs Lake which was discovered by Duluth on July 2, 1679, Izatys was founded on the present site in 1922 and named "Camp Izatys." From 1922 until 1988, Izatys operated as a seasonal family resort. The name changed to Izatys Lodge during the 1940's. In 1988, the resort was purchased by Chip Glaser and transformed into Izatys Golf & Yacht Club. It is located just 90 miles north of the Twin Cities.

Today, it features Minnesota's only Dye Designs championship 18-hole golf course, an outstanding test of golf unlike any other in the state. Home of the Minnesota PGA Championship, the 6481-yard layout offers 40 acres of natural water and marsh hazards, 40 acres of native, deciduous trees, four acres of wildflowers plus Dye's signature use of railroad ties, pot bunkers and undulating grass greens. In a survey of golf professionals throughout Minnesota, *Minneapolis-St.Paul* Magazine found Izatys' 11th hole, a 612-yard monster, as the toughest par five in the state. Izatys' signature 16th hole, a 217-yard test over water, was ranked as the third most difficult par three in Minnesota. Besides championship golf, Izatys also offers a driving range, putting green and three-hole Leisure Links course perfect for twilight "Glo-Ball" golf.

Majestic Mille Lacs Lake is renowned for its walleye fishing. Izatys' "Lady of the Lake" is a 25-passenger launch that will take you to the hot spots for hours of fishing pleasure. Pontoons and professional fishing guides are available, too. Or cruise the lake aboard the "Harbor Girl," perfect for dinner cruises, sunset cocktail or sunrise breakfast cruises. Rent a Jet Ski, swim in the pool or play tennis on one of four courts. Sandpit volleyball, shuffleboard, platform tennis, croquet or horseshoes are among your options.

Of course, there are other diversions nearby. Grand Casino Mille Lacs, for example, offers Las Vegas-style gaming just 12 miles from Izatys. Complimentary shuttle service to the casino is available for Izatys' guests. Hunting, trap shooting and horseback riding are available nearby and there are plenty of fine antique and craft shops in the area. In winter there is cross-country skiing, snowmobiling and ice fishing. Izatys can host up to 30 people in the 500 sq. ft., twenty-hole ice fishing party "Igloo," highlighted by its 12 ft. high rotunda.

As they like to say at Izatys, "Resort to the best."

RESTAURANT

Headquarters Lodge	(One mile south of Garrison on Hwy. 169) Garrison, MN 56450. **Phone: 612-692-4346** Hrs: Open 11 a.m. daily, year-round for lunch and dinner. Visa, MasterCard and Discover accepted.

After a day of sightseeing or fishing, Headquarters Lodge is a great place to go for a great dinner. A fishing resort since 1925, it has become a landmark restaurant in the area. Owner/chef-operated for more than ten years, the restaurant is located on scenic St. Alban's Bay of Lake Mille Lacs and is near Grand Casino Mille Lacs.

Loyal patrons and newcomers alike appreciate the casual lakeside atmosphere of Headquarters Lodge. It has evolved into a favorite Mille Lacs dining spot by adapting to the changing tastes of its customers. John and Mary Stenback and Bill Malone have all brought their own cooking expertise to the partnership that produced this restaurant. John, Mary, and Bill's extensive restaurant experience is seen in some of the famous ethnic buffets. Entrées on the extensive menu are made using only the freshest ingredients. Even the meat is cut to order on the premises. Exotic spices and unusual sauces flavor shrimp, walleye, fresh seafood and locally produced rainbow trout. A nightly dinner special is offered in addition to the regular menu, all of which include the popular soup and salad bar. Parents will appreciate the special "Minnow Menu" for children, designed to make the evening an enjoyable experience for the whole family. A lovely outdoor screened porch has a fabulous view of the lake, where food and cocktails may be savored in the sunshine or by moonlight.

The reputation for excellent food at Headquarters Lodge is accompanied by its additional menus and services. Look for the daily happy hour, late night menu and senior citizens discounts. Catering for banquets and private parties is an irresistible way to entertain friends. Individuals and charters may take advantage of the 55-foot pontoon launch for walleye fishing, or stay closer to shore on the

lighted dock, convenient for boating, fishing, skiing, or a quiet stroll after dining. Gaming packages are available for Grand Casino Mille Lacs with dinner purchase.

Headquarters Lodge offers the only authentic, fresh-brewed espresso and cappuccino on Hwy. 169 between Minneapolis and the Canadian border!

RESTAURANT

Sodbusters *Supper Shed*	12468 380th St., Onamia, MN 56359 **Phone:** 612-532-3941 Hrs: 11 a.m.-10 p.m., Fri, Sat, Sun.; 4 p.m.- 10 p.m. weekdays.

Yes, it is. A shed. A farm. And it's more.

It's a restaurant; art, craft and gift shop; a place to play softball; a dance hall; RV or primitive camping available. It's a place where you can, if you wish, cook your own steak or even catch your own chicken! It's Sodbusters Supper Shed, where no neckties are allowed and violators are cut off!

As you enter the relaxed atmosphere of this delightful restaurant, you'll see pictures on display of past generations of sodbusters, those hearty folk who took life from the earth and then gave it back again. Note the old tools and artifacts as you enter the "Water Hole." Shake a leg in the "Corral Area" if you wish, but be careful of the barbed wire and don't bang the buckets.

Step up to the 100-year-old bar and soak up the hospitality by ordering one or two "Hot Toddies for your cold bodies." Then head off to the "Feed Room" where you can order a steak cooked on an open fire or the local seafood, walleye. They're famous for their country style Sunday chicken dinner and tender, juicy steaks. They've got the only charcoal pit in the area.

Relax in an atmosphere unique to the Sodbusters of long ago.

After dinner, stroll around to the driving range and drive a few balls. Note the eagles and deer on the grounds.

The motto? "There ain't no place like this place—so, this must be the place." And where can you find it? Eight miles south of Grand Casino on Highway 169, then 1 mile west on Sodbusters road. (Or, go 2 miles north of Onamia on Hwy 169.) Sodbusters—it's out of the way and a little hard to find, but it's worth looking for!

NISSWA/LAKESHORE

Situated in north-central Minnesota, the Nisswa area is heavily forested with more than 50 freshwater lakes within a 20-mile radius. Founded in 1886 by fur traders, the town now features quaint Bavarian-style specialty shops. In addition to handcrafted treasures, an excellent selection of antiques has made the town a popular vacation destination.

The Nisswa area features more than 20 beautiful golf courses to choose from including the 18-hole *Pines at Grand View,* named by *Golf Digest Magazine* as one of the top ten new resort courses in the U.S. Numerous resorts offer excellent facilities and comfort.

Annual events include the *Minnesota Loon Festival* in July, which brings out the best in those competing to make the best loon call.

For more information contact:
Nisswa Chamber of Commerce
Box 185, 549 Main St.
Nisswa, MN 56468   Phone: 218-963-2620 or 800-950-9610

RESORT

Eagles Nest	1516 Poplar Ave. Nisswa, MN 56468 **Phone: 218-963-2336**

Visitors to Eagles Nest resort will find quiet, safe surroundings in a family-oriented resort. Peacefully located among the pines and birches of northern Minnesota, the resort offers daily children's activities along with water sports and, of course, excellent fishing for game and panfish alike. Kids catch sunnies right off the docks!

The beach front is clear, shallow and sandy. There's also a two-acre playground. Or, guests can grab a bike and ride along the Paul Bunyan Trail to Nisswa's unique shops. Accommodations include a housekeeping cabin (most with screened porches), 14-foot boat, use of paddlebike and canoes, plus weekly campfires.

The lakes area is host to many fine restaurants and challenging golf courses along with tennis, hiking, horseback riding and much more.

Eagles Nest is genially hosted by the Masimores—Steve, Audrey, Alli, Erin and Drew. Eagles Nest—it's Nisswa's natural choice for a family vacation.

RESORTS

Lost Lake Lodge

6415 Lost Lake Road, Nisswa, MN 56468
Phone: 218-963-2681 or MN 800-450-2681
Hrs: Open May 15-Oct. 15

Lost Lake Lodge is not the average resort. It's a small, intimate lodge with an emphasis on the surrounding natural setting—80 acres of undisturbed northwoods on a 14-acre private lake.

Accommodations include full breakfast and evening meal, daily maid service, special activity programs, fishing boat, canoes and water bikes. Each unique meal is prepared by the owners and features breads and baked goods using flour and grains stone-ground right at the resort. A variety of activities are offered for children and adults including nightly nature programs and campfires. Of course, fishing is excellent on Gull Lake, where the resort has more than 2000 feet of shoreline.

◆ ◆ ◆ ◆ ◆ ◆ ◆

Lykins Pinehurst Resort

7872 P Interlachen Rd., Nisswa, MN 56468
Phone: 218-963-2485 or 800-963-2485
Hrs: Open May 1 - Oct. 15.

Located on the west shore of beautiful Gull Lake, Lykins Pinehurst Resort is just the kind of place where you might expect your youngster to catch that first sunfish, bass or maybe even a walleye, the kind of place to build that perfect sand castle or get up early to catch a wonderful sunrise. In short, a great family resort.

Honored by the Congress of Minnesota Resorts, Lykins has nine units ranging from one to three bedrooms. Located amid whispering pines, away from the hustle and bustle of urban life, it's a quiet 10-acre property with 350 feet of shoreline. Cabins have been upgraded extensively and come fully-equipped, including a 14-foot aluminum fishing boat. Of course, the fishing on Gull Lake is exceptional.

The beach is the center of activity. You can fish, swim, play basketball, volleyball, or try the pickle ball court. There's a game room and a store for groceries and supplies. Golf and tennis are nearby plus dining and other recreational opportunities.

Start your own family tradition at Lykins Pinehurst Resort.

RESORT

Grand View Lodge

South 134 Nokomis, Nisswa, MN 56468. **Phone: 218-963-2234 or 800-432-3788 (in Minnesota) or 800-345-9625 (outside Minnesota).** Hrs: Open May-Sept.

Listed on the National Register of Historic Places, the Grand View Lodge in Nisswa offers a wealth of options for vacationers. Whether it's for the opportunity to stay in the original 1919 lodge or the lake view across the beach, three generations of guests have returned year after year.

First of all, there is golf, and lots of it. The original Gardens Course, a nine-hole, par 35 layout well-known for its spectacular scenery, has been followed by, The Pines, a championship 27-hole course, one of the state's most challenging. The Pines was rated by *Golf Digest's* 1994 "Places to Play" as one of the top 35 public resort courses in the U.S. The Pines was designed by renowned Minnesota golf course architect Joel Golstrand. Both courses are situated to maximize views of the natural environment and provide outstanding golf. Related to the two are professional golf instruction and school, a large driving range, putting greens, and clubhouse. Tennis enthusiasts take advantage of seven LayKold tennis courts, with tennis pro and lessons. There is an incredible 1,500-foot sandy beach, which provides enough space to launch a variety of rental boats and all kinds of water sports. Indoor workouts can take place in the heated swimming pool, sauna, and exercise room. Families will enjoy learning and adventure programs for youngsters, organized activities for teenagers, shopping, biking and hiking tours. Accommodations for approximately 220 vacationers are provided by 14 rooms in the Grand View Lodge, and over 60 luxurious lake townhomes and cottages. There is a wide range of plans available at individual and family rates. Choose from two dining atmospheres. A lounge with live music and regular dances offers evening entertainment.

Over 15,000 flowers and shrubs influenced *House and Garden Magazine* to call the resort "a floral masterpiece of the northland." Mesaba-Northwest Airlink offers daily flights to Brainerd. Private planes may also use the airport and will be met by lodge staff.

RESTAURANT

Bar Harbor

6512 Interlachen Road, Lakeshore, Nisswa, MN 56468. **Phone: 218-963-2568**
Hrs.: Daily noon-1 a.m. Visa, AmEx, Diners and Bar Harbor accepted.

For over 30 years, Bar Harbor was known as the "fun spot of northern Minnesota." People came from miles around to hear all the famous big bands and to take in the action of legalized gambling. It was a great loss when Big Bar Harbor Pavilion burned to the ground in 1968. Constructed on the same location are the new Bar Harbor Townhouses. Across the street is the Bar Harbor Supper Club on beautiful Gull Lake, open year-round for fine dining in a lovely natural setting.

Much of the success of Bar Harbor can be attributed to the long-time staff of Bar Harbor with the new chef, Jeff Smith. Jeff brings his own special flare to Bar Harbor, with 17 years' experience in some of the finest restaurants around. Jeff says, "I love to be creative with food and I find the restaurant business provides a constant learning experience. My kitchen staff and I enjoy pleasing people with all types of food, from the giant lobster tail to the fruitwood smoked walleye."

In the summer, guests may choose to dine at the outdoor patio and barefoot bar. The 24 boat slips allow access to the restaurant by water and, when the lake freezes over in the winter, snowmobiles are welcome. Special events at Bar Harbor keep the restaurant jumping year-round. One such celebrated event in the winter is the weekend nine-hole golf course on the ice, followed by a fantastic cocktail party and dinner. Live entertainment, excellent dining and proud service are the hallmarks of the Bar Harbor experience. The club is considered a local landmark and attracts a following from residents as well as vacationers.

SPECIALTY SHOP

The Swedish Timber House	7678 Interlachen Road, Lakeshore, Nisswa, MN 56468. **Phone: 218-963-7897.** Hrs.: Open daily 10 a.m.-5 p.m. from early May to late Oct. (Fri., Sat., Sun. in Dec.)

The Swedish Timber House was hewn of spruce, constructed and erected in Leksand, Sweden, Brainerd's sister city in Dalarna. The building was dismantled, numbered and shipped to Minnesota where it was reconstructed on the western shore of Gull Lake in 1970. It is a Scandinavian store filled with merchandise from Sweden, Norway, Denmark and Finland. The store is located 12 miles north of Brainerd on Highway 371 and left five miles on County Road 77 (Interlachen Road).

The scenery surrounding the store is worth a visit in itself, where wildflowers cover the five acres on which the store is built. Maple and oak trees surround a trail from the store down to the lake. In the fall the trees are beautiful.

The Swedish Timber House carries clothing from Swedish weavers and clogs and woolen sweaters from Norwegian knitters. Jewelry of silver amber and lapis and the famous Solje designs of Norway are featured, as well. Home accessories of wrought iron forged in Sweden and Denmark display the traditional patterns of these countries. The crystal selection includes pieces from all the Scandinavian countries.

Collector's treasures and gifts line the shelves. There are 20 different sizes of Swedish Dala horses from Nusnas in Dalarna as well as Dala roosters and pigs. Unique Christmas decorations are extra special items of Old World charm. Each year owners Lloyd and Ingrid Anderson go to Sweden to personally choose the best items the Scandinavian countries have to offer and bring them back to the store for their customers.

SPECIALTY SHOPS

The Melting Pot

531 Main Street, Nisswa, MN 56468
Phone: 218-963-4738
Hrs: Open 7 days a week.
MasterCard, Visa and Discover accepted.

If you're looking for a variety of gifts, The Melting Pot in Nisswa is a spot you'll want to visit. Owner Sharon Baker started the store in May of '93 and she offers items from as far as Guatemala and everywhere in between. She's done a good job of stocking the store with gifts and accessories to meet a variety of home decors.

Hand-blown and fused glassware is offered, along with unique handmade stained glass for large window insets and one-of-a-kind kaleidoscopes. Then there's a nice selection of men's gifts, Christmas items, jewelry boxes, cards, stationary and books.

One of the best reasons to stop in is that virtually all budgets are accommodated. The Melting Pot does special orders, direct mail and offers complimentary gift wrapping.

◆ ◆ ◆ ◆ ◆ ◆ ◆

Zaiser's Souvenir & Gift Shop

529 Main Street, Nisswa, MN 56468
Phone: 218-963-2404
Hrs: Open every day summers. Call for hours.
Major credit cards accepted.

It's long been a tradition in many Minnesota families. Each year, while "up north," they pay a visit to Zaiser's Souvenir & Gift Shop in Nisswa for a new pair of moccasins for the whole family.

And there's no better place. Located in the heart of the Brainerd Lakes region, Zaiser's carries Minnesota's largest selection of traditional moccasins (six brands in all) and all the latest styles, too.

Zaiser's has been in business for half a century but the present owners, Mark and Kay Ulm, are only the second proprietors there. Many of the moccasin styles have stayed the same over the years but plenty of new styles are added every year, as well. Check out the map on the wall that tracks the destination of the many moccasins they sell. So far they're in every state and 29 foreign countries!

Of course, there's much more to Zaiser's than just moccasins. You'll also find a large variety of T-shirts, unique jewelry and toys for kids of all ages. Plus a terrific reputation for small-town service.

PEQUOT LAKES

Located in the heart of the lake country, Pequot Lakes is a true fisherman's paradise—a fact that is proudly proclaimed by its water-tower landmark, a huge replica of Paul Bunyan's fishing bobber!

The small town atmosphere of Pequot Lakes offers plenty of recreational opportunities for everyone.

Breezy Point Resort, one of four golf courses in the area, offers 36 holes and private lessons. There's live theater and music, gift shops and art galleries, tennis courts and riding stables, convention center and marinas, airport for the private pilot and the **Paul Bunyan Trail** open for year-round use.

The annual **Bean Hole Days** in July is where 150 gallons of beans are cooked in the ground, and the unique **Fourth of July Celebration** features a liars contest, bed race, pie eating contests and other antics.

For further information, contact:
Pequot Lakes Area Chamber of Commerce
P.O. Box 208, Pequot Lakes, MN 56472   Phone: 218-568-8911

BED & BREAKFAST

Stonehouse Bed & Breakfast	HCR 2, P.O. Box 9, Pequot Lakes, MN 56472 **Phone: 218-568-4255** Hrs: Open year-round. Visa and MasterCard accepted.

Stonehouse Bed and Breakfast is a cozy, private, stone cottage in the woods near Pequot Lakes. Designed and built by host Craig and Claire Nagel, Stonehouse offers a scenic and peaceful retreat for its guests. Constructed of local materials and situated several hundred feet from the main residence, Stonehouse provides uncommon beauty and privacy.

Stonehouse has comfortable beds, a split-stone fireplace, private bath, electric heat, a kitchen, a screened porch and a beautiful terrace complete with a barbeque and a fountain. Two stained glass windows, designed by Claire, enhance the beauty of the sunrises and sunsets at Stonehouse. The cut stones in the fireplace were chosen by Craig to show the variety of the rock in the area. The wood used to make up the interior was cut from the local woods.

Breakfast is served each morning in the friendly kitchen. Pleasant conversation combines with the hearty country fare. After breakfast, try the nature trails winding through the nearby woods.

RESORT

Breezy Point Resort

HCR-2, P.O. Box 70, Breezy Point, MN 56472
**Phone: 218-562-7811 or 800-432-3777 (MN)
or 800-328-2284 (Outstate)** Hrs: Open year-
round. All major credit cards accepted.

Breezy Point Resort sparkles on the edge of magnificent Big Pelican Lake, offering an unparalleled choice of vacation options. Three thousand acres of glorious woods and water in central Minnesota are home to Breezy Point, a complete four-season resort.

More than 200 luxurious accommodation choices include town-homes, complete with indoor spas overlooking the lake, to apartments, chalets and tastefully decorated individual resort rooms. The "gemstone" of the resort is the original home of Captain Billy Fawcett, founder of Breezy Point. This ten-bedroom mansion is available for rent and continues to provide a very special haven as it did once for the likes of Carol Lombard and Clark Gable.

Breezy Point's indoor recreation complex, Breezy Center, hosts a heated pool, children's pool, sauna, whirlpool, tanning booths, game room, poolside eatery and lounge. Popular dance bands fill the Marina Lounge and fine dining is offered in the Marina Restaurant where a delightful view complements the excellent menu. Plus, Charlie's Restaurant features smoked barbecued ribs and chicken as well as interesting pasta selections and special "Just for the Health of It" entrées.

Walleye, bass, pike and panfish abound in the clear lake, making Breezy Point a superb choice for fishing enthusiasts. Fishing boats are available for rent as well as ski boats, pontoons and paddleboats. A 57-foot cruiser—"The Paddlin' Pelican"—makes daily tours around the lake while guests soak up the sun and view lush scenery.

Two 18-hole golf courses offer amateurs and professionals alike a challenging as well as beautiful golf experience. Yet all this is but a start to the many recreational activities available at Breezy Point Resort. Four Laykold tennis courts, indoor and outdoor pools, biking, hiking, trail rides as well as scheduled recreation programs are just a sampling of what's offered.

So, if you're looking for a place of beauty designed for relaxation and contemplation in a northwoods paradise, if you love the song of the loon and the silent wonder of sunsets amid the pines, Breezy Point Resort has it—and more!

PINE RIVER

A ghostly wisp of early morning mist is rising off a northern Minnesota stream, the Pine River. A white birchbark canoe rounds a slight curve in the gently rolling, clear, gravel bottomed stream. "Hail the shore," rings the call from one of the hardy paddlers. The crew of trappers pull up to the shore to meet with the fur traders assembled there to do business under the lofty White and Norway pines. The date is the early 1800's. Pine River is the name of the stream and the name of the city where this scene was enacted many times during its colorful history.

The Pine River has for centuries been a route for travelers, both Indian and Caucasian, through the north-central region of Minnesota. The Indian people used it for transport and for access to their hunting and harvest grounds. The white men that came after used it to transport millions of board feet of huge White Pine timber to sawmills farther to the south.

Along the river bank gradually grew the community of Pine River. Its residents came as early pioneers and lumbermen to settle on the shores of this little-known tributary of the Mississippi River. They were hardy souls and worked in the lumber trade or endeavored to make a living from farming the sandy and rocky soil in the Pine River area. Many of their relatives still live in the area today.

Today the city of Pine River and the area around it bustle with a new energy. Although lumbering and farming are still a mainstay of the area economy, the area has also become a major destination for those in search of clean air, clean water and pine-scented woods. They find them all in the Pine River area.

ATTRACTIONS

Pine River boasts a number of amenities unknown and probably unthought of by earlier settlers. *The Pine River Country Club* is a beautiful nine-hole golf course on the western edge of the city. The new hardsurfaced *Pine River Regional Airport—Garrett Field* is located just on the east edge of town and its new pilot's building is ready and able to accommodate the many fliers that frequent the Pine River area year-round. You'll also find a public fishing pier and picnic grounds along the river.

Pine River offers many opportunities for outdoor pursuits. Snowmobiling, cross country-skiing, horseback riding, swimming, water skiing, bird watching, hiking, fishing and hunting are just some of the activities to be found.

Pine River is the "Birthplace of the Paul Bunyan Trail," a one hundred mile long recreational trail which starts at Brainerd and winds its scenic way through Pine River and on to Bemidji. The trail is currently open for snowmobiling and future plans include hard surfacing the entire trail for bicyclists and hikers.

Deep Portage Conservation Reserve is a 6,000-acre natural reserve just north of Pine River that has been established to teach conservation to young and old alike. There is always some activity going on at Deep Portage and it is open to the public.

EVENTS

Pine River is a year-round town and you'll find activities taking place just about any time you venture there. The highlight of the summer season is the *SUMMERFEST* celebration. It is a three-day celebration that includes a parade, street dance, fly-in breakfast, gospel sing-along and more. It happens the last weekend of June each year.

In July, Pine River hosts both the *Cass County Fair* and the *Pine River Art Club Show.*

There are lots of resorts and motels in and around the Pine River area. With over 400 lakes within 40 miles, there is no lack of water-related activities. The Pine River itself has been designated an *Official Canoe Route* by the Minnesota Dept. of Natural Resources. You'll find two scenic parks in Pine River with shelter houses built from the huge pines that grow in this area. There is also a public swimming area available.

Those early travelers found Pine River to be a beautiful stop along their trail and modern day travelers are finding the same to be true, as well. Discover it for yourself!

For further information, contact:
Chamber of Commerce
P.O. Box 131
Pine River, MN 56474
Phone: 218-587-4000

Photo courtesy of The Pine River Journal.

RESTAURANT

Marlene's Cottage Cafe, Inc.

Barclay and 2nd St., Pine River, MN 56474
Phone: 218-587-2588
Hrs: Mon.-Thurs. 5 a.m.-4 p.m., Fri. 5 a.m.-
7 p.m., Sat-Sun 5 a.m.-3 p.m.

Many travelers will tell you the small town cafes and restaurants have some of the best, tastiest and most reasonably priced food to be found. Such a place is Marlene's Cottage Cafe, Inc. in Pine River. Here you'll find home cooking that will send you down the road with a smile on your face and warmth in your heart.

A varied menu includes hot sandwiches—pork, turkey, roast beef or hamburger with two scoops of mashed potatoes and gravy. Or try the "famous" Cottage Burger, with two slices of cheese, two strips of bacon, lettuce, tomato, and mayo on a grilled bun.

Breakfast specials are both bountiful and numerous. The sausage gravy on baking powder biscuits is melt-in-your-mouth goodness!

Marlene and Cecil Kottschade welcome you to this country motif cafe. You can't miss it in downtown Pine River. The attractive exterior is done in country cottage design and colors.

SPECIALTY SHOP

Wilson Junction

Hwy. 371, Pine River, MN 56474
Phone: 218-587-2522
Hrs.: (Winter) Mon. - Sat. 6:30 a.m. - 8 p.m., Sun. 7 a.m.-7 p.m. (Summer) Mon.-Sat. 6:30 a.m.-9 p.m., Sun. 7 a.m. 7 p.m. Major credit cards accepted.

Tom and Carol Hedberg are fulfilling a dream—a dream of ownership, a dream of family togetherness and a dream of living the northwoods lifestyle. In 1992, they purchased Wilson Junction, a convenience store/gas station located in the heart of vacation country just two miles south of Pine River.

Tom, Carol and their kids run the store as a family stop for locals and those traveling through. You can buy gas, propane, bait and tackle, gifts, groceries, sandwiches, fishing and hunting licenses and toys at the log building.

There's an RV camp right across the highway and the Paul

Bunyon Trail runs right by the store. If you are heading to the Brainerd/Walker area, be sure to stop with the family for your vacation needs.

COLD SPRING

The city of Cold Spring, a community situated in the beautiful Minnesota lakes area, was first settled in 1856 by John Batice Arcenea and Samuel Wakefield. Located at the gateway to the Horseshoe Chain of Lakes on the Sauk River, the site was ideally suited for industry.

In 1874, the Cold Spring Brewing Company was started by Michael Sargl, a German immigrant brewer. The city, named after its pure "cold spring" water, was an ideal site for one of Cold Spring's oldest businesses in continuous operation. The brewery still uses "cold spring" water to produce its nationally-known beer and mineral water—North Star Sparkling Water, said to be more pure than Perrier. It is one of only three major breweries operating in Minnesota.

ATTRACTIONS & EVENTS

For the sightseer, the *Cold Spring Granite Company,* the famous *Cold Spring Bakery* and the interesting *Grasshopper Chapel* should not be missed. *Rich Spring Golf Course* offers 18-holes of challenging play on the scenic *Sauk River.*

Lions Park, located within city limits and one of three public boat landings on the Horseshoe Chain of Lakes, is the start of hundreds of miles of outstanding fishing, boating and waterskiing, as well as a variety of wintertime activities, including snowmobiling, cross-country skiing and ice fishing. *The Kegle Brau Trail* is one of many beautiful snowmobile trails in the area.

Blue Heron Rookery provides non-disturbing observation of the great blue heron colony. This is the first Minnesota Nature Conservancy area to be preserved for its breeding birds.

St. Benedict's College in St. Joseph, *St. John's Prep School and University* in Collegeville, and *St. Cloud State University* and their multi-cultured campuses, are all located within a few minutes drive.

Cold Spring Funtastics Days are held the last week of July. This celebration includes a style show, community breakfast, street dances, sport car show, cribbage tourney, boccie ball tourney, turtle races, softball games and more.

For further information, contact:
Cold Spring Area Chamber of Commerce
P.O. Box 328
Cold Spring, MN 56320   Phone: 612-685-4186

CORPORATE PROFILE

Cold Spring Granite Company   In the past 100 years, the towns of Central Minnesota have grown, prospered, modernized and developed an identity of their own. So has the Cold Spring Granite Company. The company that today is a world-leading quarrier and fabricator of granite products began in Rockville, Minnesota, in 1898 with one quarry and a small fabricating plant.

In reality, however, the history of Cold Spring Granite begins thousands of years ago with the formation of the stone. The hard, beautiful rock substance called granite was once molten liquid magma.

It boiled through cracks in the earth's crust and was deposited in pockets below the land surface. The cooling rate of the magma determined the strength and crystal structure of the granite; the materials and metals evident in the stone determined the distinctive colors and textures.

Glacial action scraped off the covering crust over the granite, exposing the stone outcroppings that would one day be quarried.

It was the presence of this ancient resource that brought Henry Nair Alexander from Inverary, Scotland, to central Minnesota in 1886.

He arrived in Waite Park with his bride, Maggie Milne, and went to work for a granite firm that already employed a number of Scotsmen. In 1889, Henry Alexander and seven partners formed the Rockville Granite Company.

One of their first major contracts was eight large columns for the Minnesota State Capitol.

In 1898, Henry purchased the interests of his partners. He and Maggie settled on a farm in Rockville and raised their six children, three sons and three daughters.

The Alexander sons worked in the quarry and plant with their father. Pat, the first-born, was an accomplished stone cutter by age 16, with good mechanical ability that he would later use masterfully in the Cold Spring plant. William (Bill) found the blacksmith shop of interest and made his contribution there and as manager of the family farm. John, the youngest of the six children, worked all jobs during his early years.

Although all the children had an elementary education, John was the only son to attend high school and later one year of college. The girls all went to school. Nellie went to business college and then did the company's bookkeeping. Isabelle and Marian both went on to college, becoming a teacher and a librarian, respectively.

With the deaths of Henry Alexander in 1912 and Maggie in 1916, John and Pat, in settlement with the family, became owners of the company. Pat was called into the Army in World War I and John postponed college to run the plant. On Pat's return, John completed one year on scholarship at Denison University in Ohio. He returned home with plans for a second year at Denison. However, a major business decision awaited on the Rockville Granite Company.

The Clark and McCormack Company had arrived in Rockville in 1907, and with greater resources had eventually purchased the available quarry land. This left no room for expansion by anyone. In 1919, for the Alexanders to continue in the stone business they were forced to seek a new location for the Rockville Granite Company and make a fresh start.

The new location was Cold Spring in 1920. Although the company had the financial backing and advice of local businessmen, the first years in Cold Spring were those of hard work and growth, including building a new plant and working a new quarry. In order to preserve their hard-won reputation, the "new" company continued to be known as Rockville Granite until 1924. At that time the company had proven itself and the name was changed to Cold Spring Granite. (In 1940 Cold Spring Granite Company purchased the assets of The John Clark Company of Rockville, including a quarry and fabrication plant.)

Over the years the machinery and methods that contributed to Cold Spring's long-term competitiveness were most often developed in the Cold Spring plant and quarries. Employees from the president on down contributed to improve and create necessary mechanical technique. Gang saws, special lathes for column construction, wire saws, semi-automatic polishing equipment, material handling methods and vertical finishing machinery all had their beginning or perfection in the Cold Spring quarry or plant. On-site maintenance was done by the machine shop and foundry.

Some of the more unusual mechanical engineering challenges were met during World War II. With building stone production coming to a virtual standstill, the main plant was retooled to manufacture ship hulls and anchors. To the Cold Spring employees, being part of the war effort made the mechanical engineering challenges that arose all the more important. While government inspectors appreciated the high-quality product emerging from the "stone sheds," they were amazed at the unique adaptations of the machinery. Citations for work of unequaled quality and effort followed as the war progressed and ended.

Since 1983 the company has gone to outside sources for state-of-the-art equipment and quarrying techniques. Today much of the equipment comes from foreign manufacturers, although it is often adapted to the needs of the company.

A strength of Cold Spring Granite is the virtual rainbow of granites available from quarries owned and operated solely by the company. Beginning in the late 1920s, Cold Spring has pursued a program of planned acquisition. Building from one quarry in 1919, this has enabled the company to offer the colors of 28 quarries strategically located across North America.

Cold Spring Granite has gone through a great deal of growth and change in its 96-year history. Moving to Cold Spring from Rockville was only the beginning in more than one way, as adapting to change has become a way of life for the company. Increased competition from around the world, and the economic and building recessions over the years all have contributed to the shaping of Cold Spring Granite as it exists today. In the 1980's plans were laid to diversify product lines and expand markets. These plans are being carried out as the company expands product lines and services, and markets to customers around the world.

With the growth, modernization, success and development over the years, one constant that has remained is the caliber of the employees. In the 1890's Henry Alexander employed roving stone-men who traveled the country looking for work. While these men were good craftsmen, the realization emerged that the best employee was the craftsman with a home life, with roots.

Cold Spring Granite has its roots in family ownership and operation, from Henry Alexander's to his sons Pat and John, and his grandsons Tom and Pat. The company also has its roots in the people of central Minnesota. Of the 1,250 people employed by Cold Spring Granite today, more than 800 live in central Minnesota, many second- and third-generation employees.

Building on these strengths, 1,250 employees, five production plants, 28 quarries and 96 years of history, Cold Spring looks to the future. The company's projects now extend throughout North America and around the world. These include Peachtree Center in Atlanta, the Texas and Pennsylvania State Capitols, the Bank of America and the Crocker Center in San Francisco, and the horizons of the future, stone set at the Collins Exchange in Melbourne, Australia, B.V.I. Bank in Frankfurt, Germany, Makuhari Convention Center, Tokyo, and the Doug Ah Insurance Building, Seoul, Korea.

In Minnesota, the Zapp Bank in St. Cloud, the Carlson Center in

Minnetonka, St. Paul Companies Buildings, Minnesota Judicial and Historical Society Buildings, Hamm Plaza, and the Minnesota Vietnam Veterans Memorial in St. Paul are state projects that showcase both product and craftsmanship.

The Alexander ancestors would be proud of their company of today.

DETROIT LAKES

The Detroit Lakes area is one the most important vacation areas in Minnesota. A variety of quaint, interesting towns dot the area, along with hundreds of excellent walleye lakes.

An experienced and friendly travel industry provides the bulk of the area's income, although Detroit Lakes itself boasts a few major manufacturing industries. Detroit Lakes is also where most of the area's major attractions are located, except for the fishing lakes and resorts which crop up around every bend and are host to a myriad of families seeking relaxation in the sun.

ATTRACTIONS & EVENTS

Vacation fun is virtually guaranteed at the bustling, one-mile long public sand beach within the city limits. The beach offers a full-service marina, lifeguards, a fishing pier, walkways, benches and playground facilities. There's a variety of other diversions like *The Human Maze*—a large scale labyrinth, the *Go, Putt 'N' Bump* amusement park with Go-Karts and bumper boats, and *Wet 'N' Wild Minnesota,* the state's longest waterslide.

The *Shooting Star Casino* is located 35 miles north of Detroit Lakes on Highway 59.

A romantic dinner cruise can be had on the *Island Girl,* cruising the shoreline. The *Detroit Country Club* is the site of the nationally known men's amateur *Pine to Palm Golf Tournament.*

History buffs will enjoy the *Becker County Historical Museum* and the *Buggy Wheel Antiques* with an excellent antique selection.

In winter, *Detroit Mountain* provides downhill skiers and cross-country skiers some of the best skiing in the area. *Maplelag* is a cross-country ski resort offering some 53 kilometers of groomed trails

Eight miles northeast of Detroit Lakes is the outstanding *Tamarac National Wildlife Refuge,* with miles of trails and nesting eagles.

The *We Fest* country music festival in August attracts more than 80,000 fans and stars like Johnny Cash and Alabama. *The Northwest Water Carnival* has ten days of fun family events. *Dairy Days* features a 600-foot long banana split!

For further information, contact:
Detroit Lakes Regional Chamber of Commerce
P.O. Box 348
Detroit Lakes, MN 56501   Phone: 800-542-3992

BED & BREAKFAST

The Log House & *Homestead On* *Spirit Lake*	East Spirit Lake, 13 miles east of Pelican Rapids on County Rd. 4, Vergas, MN 56587 **Phone: 218-342-2318.** Hrs: Open year-round. Visa and MasterCard accepted.

The Log House & Homestead On Spirit Lake is a delightful bed & breakfast retreat, a romantic, secluded getaway situated on 4,000 feet of private lakeshore amidst 60 acres of maple woods. Located between Detroit Lakes and Fergus Falls, this fully restored, beautifullyfurnished log house was built in 1889. Across the meadow is the Homestead, where Augusta's room has a double whirlpool and fireplace and both rooms have lake views.

This B&B offers one of the best breakfasts around, served at a beautifully set table on the screen porch overlooking the lake. Freshly-squeezed orange juice and fresh ground coffee are "de rigueur." Local berries and sausage and a main dish such as puff pancakes with strawberry-almond butter and orange pecan waffles will start your day off right. From terry robes to goosedown comforters, no detail is too small at this wonderful escape.

CAMPING

Wold's R.V. Sales *& Campground*	Hwy 10 West, Detroit Lakes, MN 56501 **Phone: 218-847-6333** Hrs: Campground open May 1-Oct. 1. R.V. Sales open year-round.

Located two and a half miles west of Detroit Lakes just off Hwy. 10 on Long Lake, Wold's "Good Sam" Campground is a wonderful place to relax and vacation, whether you prefer an R.V., camper, trailer or tent. The beautiful, clear, spring-fed lake is perfect for fishing, canoeing, paddleboats or pontoon boats, all of which can be rented on-site. Most camp sites are heavily wooded and there's water and electric service, full hook-ups, fire rings and some primitive sites if you prefer. Free hot showers, flush toilets and a convenience store for all your provisions are available not to mention a recreation building complete with pool table, TV, video games and more. There's also a boat launch plus a sand beach and a spacious playground for the kids.

If you're shopping for an R.V. or need some accessories or service, then Wold's R.V. Sales is only two miles west of Detroit Lakes on Highway 10. They have travel trailers, fifth wheels, motorhomes and tent trailers plus sales, service, rentals, parts and accessories.

GARDEN CENTER

Swanson Floral and Greenhouse

1008 Washington Avenue, Detroit Lakes, MN 56501
Phone: 218-847-2627 or 800-572-9667
Hrs: Mon. - Fri. 9 a.m.-5:30 p.m. Saturdays 9 a.m.-
4:30 p.m. Extended holiday and summer hours.
Visa, MasterCard, AmEx and Discover accepted.

Don't be fooled when you drive up in front of Swanson Floral and Greenhouse in Detroit Lakes. The building is much, much larger than it looks and most people are surprised to find out just how much it has to offer. And once inside, you'll be amazed by the huge selection of wonderful plants, gifts and collectibles.

The setting is very Minnesota with the large birch trees enhancing the shop. Soft music plays in the background as you browse among the fragrant flowers, Yankee candles, pot pourri and bath notions creating a heavenly environment to look for that perfect gift. The carefully-created displays and ambience of the store make it a fun place for browsing.

Swanson's newly remodeled gift shop overflows with unique and exciting home decorating ideas, wedding gifts and gift ideas for any occasion. They offer smart values and variety, making the shop an experience you'll enjoy. And the friendly and knowledgeable staff is available for consultation, should you need it.

Swanson's offers top quality green and blooming plants in large greenhouses. They boast award-winning designers who work wonders with fresh, dried and silk floral arrangements that can be customized to suit your individual tastes. The gift shop really does have something for everyone. Swanson's carries the Dept 56 collectibles, including Dickens, Snow Village, Xmas in the City, North Pole Series, New England and Alpine. They also have All Throughout The House, Snow Babies, and Merry Makers, each proudly and carefully displayed in its own little world.

But there's more.

Keep browsing and you'll discover unique lines of gift cards, bath oils, home decorator items, silk plants, candles and much more. And best of all, they have a sister store in Fergus Falls, too.

As an added extra, Swanson's also offers free wedding consultation, delivery, custom silk and dried floral arrangements, plant rental, a garden center and free gift wrapping. See why they like to say, "Nature makes it beautiful, Swanson's makes it number one."

GOLF COURSE & SKI AREA

Maple Hills Golf &
Ski Club

Highway 10 East, four miles east of Detroit
Lakes. **Phone: 218-847-9532**
Hrs: Daylight to dark
No credit cards accepted.

For years, Les Kertscher had a dream of having his own golf course. So the high school teacher and wrestling coach built one, using volunteer labor and plenty of sweat equity. Today, that dream has been a reality for more than 15 years and the Maple Hills Golf & Ski Club remains one of Minnesota's best-kept golfing secrets.

Located four miles east of Detroit Lakes on Highway 10, Maple Hills is a scenic nine-hole course. It's perfect for family golf, something that's highly encouraged. It plays to just over 3,000 yards and is challenging enough to keep the good players coming back but forgiving enough to make it a pleasant place for beginners to play, too. The rolling hills and maple and oak trees that surround the course are particularly beautiful in the fall.

Maple Hills features a practice putting green and a full-line pro shop with custom clubs, reasonably priced pro line clubs, club repair, lessons, motorized carts and rental clubs. Snacks are available.

LODGING

Holiday Inn -
Detroit Lakes

Highway 10 E., Detroit Lakes, MN 56501
Phone: 218-847-2121 or 800-HOLIDAY
Hrs: Open year-round.
All major credit cards accepted.

The Detroit Lakes area is one of the northwoods' most popular fun and vacation spots and the Holiday Inn-Detroit Lakes is ideally located on 500 feet of sandy shoreline on the north shore of Big Detroit Lake, at the heart of this great resort community.

Sun and fun is the name of the game, here. Besides the obvious attraction of the beach during the summer months, there is the added bonus of the year-round Holidome Fun Center. That's where you'll find an indoor heated pool, sauna, hot tub, video games and ping-pong.

Free cable television is provided for your viewing enjoyment in every room. Docking facilities are available as well as the services of the Island Girl Cruise Liner for charters and sight-seeing tours.

You can dine with a view of the lake at the Ice House restaurant before kicking up your heels at the Harbor Lights Lounge. A beautiful site for meetings or conventions from five to five hundred, the Holiday Inn has it all in Detroit Lakes.

RESORTS

Fair Hills Resort

R.R. 1, P.O. Box 128, Detroit Lakes, MN 56501
Phone: 218-847-7638 or 800-323-2849
Hrs: May 1 to Oct. 1, 6 a.m.-11 p.m.
Major credit cards accepted.

It was way back in 1906 when the Ashelman brothers began to take in boarders at their farm house on the eastern shores of Pelican Lake. Fair Hills has come a long way since then but it carries a proud tradition, including seven decades of being run by the Kaldahl Family. Today's Fair Hills has something for everyone. It's a family resort (no lounge or liquor on the premises) that offers either the American Plan (meals included) or the Housekeeping plan (kitchen provided). The menu changes daily at the full-service restaurant.

Fair Hills includes 93 units, both cabins and motel-style lodging, that can serve more than 250 guests. It's a full-service resort featuring windsurfing, sailing, speedboats, fishing, paddleboats, canoes and kayaks on one of the cleanest and safest lakes in the area. A new 18-hole golf course (Wildflower) opened in 1993 on the property and the 36-hole Detroit Country Club is only five miles down the road. Six tennis courts, a swimming pool, wading pool and whirlpool offer more outdoor fun.

◆ ◆ ◆ ◆ ◆ ◆ ◆

Lakecrest Resort

Highway 10 West on Long Lake, Route 1, Box EP
Detroit Lakes, MN 56501. **Phone: 218-847-5459
or 800-435-5459.** Hrs: Open May 1-Oct. 1. Visa,
MasterCard and AmEx accepted.

Ron Paskey began this resort with one cottage back in 1958. Today, he and wife Ruth have one of the nicest resorts in the Detroit Lakes area, situated on the north end of beautiful Long Lake. With seven cedar-sided cottages on the lake front, a two-story house and seven deluxe three-bedroom mobile homes available, Lakecrest Resort has created a unique family atmosphere that continues to attract people from all over, most lured by word-of-mouth. There are trikes and bikes, sand toys, a beautiful sand beach, enclosed swimming area, fishing boats, motors, a speedboat, canoe, sailboat, paddleboats, waterski equipment and more. Tennis, volleyball, badminton, shuffleboard, horseshoes and an indoor recreation area are also offered, plus gas, bait, laundry, some groceries and snacks.

The cottages, which are well-spaced for privacy, come with grill, picnic table and an aluminum fishing boat. Dining, entertainment, golf and shopping are nearby. Special packages and transportation to airport, train or bus depot are available.

RESORTS

| *Melissa Beach Resort* | Five miles south of Detroit Lakes on Lake Melissa
Rt. 5, Box 234A, Detroit Lakes, MN 56501
Phone: 218-847-1742
Visa, MasterCard and Discover accepted. |

Whether you're looking for a place in the sun or a cozy winter hideaway for snowmobiling, skiing or ice fishing, you'll find Melissa Beach Resort just the place for a quiet, relaxing getaway. Spotlessly clean housekeeping units feature all the amenities; stove, refrigerator, microwave, toaster, cooking utensils, dishes, bedding and cable TV. Charcoal grills and picnic tables are also provided. Fishing is excellent at the resort and everything you need for water sports can be rented at the marina—boats, motors, pontoon, paddle boat, sailboat and canoe. With 365 feet of lakeshore on the east side of Lake Melissa, the large sandy beach swimming area is completely enclosed by the docking facility. The lodge features a game room, snacks and beverages. Many outdoor games are available, as well. Located just five miles south of Detroit Lakes, Melissa Beach Resort offers easy access to a host of activities like horseback riding, supper clubs, shopping and amusement parks. Two 18 hole golf courses are within walking distance of the resort. Reservations are a must for July and August.

◆ ◆ ◆ ◆ ◆ ◆ ◆

| *Wakanda Resort* | Between Detroit Lakes and Park Rapids on Island
Lake, Box 119, Rochert, MN 56578
Phone: 218-847-4943 or 800-279-6930 Ext. 8 |

Wakanda Resort on beautiful Island Lake is the perfect spot for a carefree family vacation in the northwoods. Fishermen give Island Lake high marks as one of the most consistent walleye producers in the area, but northern pike, smallmouth bass, perch, bluegill and crappie are all plentiful. The kids will enjoy Wakanda Resort, too. For the tots, a swing set and sandbox fill the bill. For the older crowd, volleyball and badminton games are known to last for hours. Of course, everyone enjoys the clean and clear sand beach, safe for all to swim. If you like wildlife and hiking, check out the nearby Tamarac Wildlife Refuge. Located just one mile from Wakanda Resort, Tamarac plays host to ducks, a large deer population and the elusive bald eagle.

In the fall, Wakanda Resort is your hunting headquarters. Enjoy the fall colors along with superb deer, duck and grouse hunting. Most of all, don't miss the Wakanda Resort Lodge, where every Friday night serves up an "all you can eat" ribs and chicken dinner!

RESTAURANT

The Fireside *Restaurant & Bar*	East Shore Drive, P.O. Box 346, Detroit Lakes, MN 56502. **Phone: 218-847-8192** Hours: Open seasonally at 5:30 p.m.

For more than 50 years, The Fireside has been one of Detroit Lakes' most popular restaurants, earning a reputation for great food and great service. If you're looking for that special place, The Fireside is nestled along the east shore of Big Detroit Lake where you can take in the beautiful sunsets, romantic views enjoyed not only from an outside patio but also from the entire dining room.

The Fireside offers the best in food and beverages including its nationally-famous barbecue ribs, steaks and other entrées cooked over a real charcoal fire in full view of dining room patrons. There's also a fine selection of fresh and salt water seafood plus nightly specials. Your meal will be served by the most experienced waitstaff in the area.

Owners Tom and Jennifer Graham will greet you as you arrive to share The Fireside tradition. On Saturday nights during the summer, take advantage of the expected wait to relax with your favorite cocktail by the lake. The wait will be well worth it.

SHOPPING

Washington *Square Mall*	808 Washington Avenue, Detroit Lakes, MN 56501. **Phone: 218-847-1679.** Hrs: Mon.-Fri. 10 a.m.-8 p.m., Sat. 9:30 a.m.-5:30 p.m., Sun. Noon-5 p.m.

If you're looking for a unique shopping experience while vacationing, discover the Washington Square Mall located in downtown Detroit Lakes on Washington Avenue.

A portion of the original "Main Street" of Detroit Lakes was recreated into an enclosed 100,000-square-foot shopping mall with a wide variety of shopping and attractions. It offers 30 stores, three family restaurants, candy and snacks, a video arcade and the Cinema V movie theaters. Included are several national ladies fashion stores, a limited edition wildlife art gallery, two hairstyling salons, sporting goods, fine gifts and country crafts and several variety and specialty stores. In other words, virtually everything you want under a single roof.

The Washington Square Mall hosts many events and shows throughout the year. The Mall provides easy and convenient access and parking. The hometown atmosphere is pleasant and inviting. More than just another mall in downtown Detroit Lakes.

WILDLIFE REFUGE

Tamarac National Wildlife Refuge

HC 10, P.O. Box 145. Rochert, MN 56578
Phone: 218-847-2641
Hrs: Mon.-Fri. 7:30 a.m. to 4 p.m. (Memorial Day
-Labor Day) Sat.-Sun. noon to 5.

Tamarac National Wildlife Refuge was created by executive order in 1939 by Franklin Roosevelt to provide a breeding ground for migratory birds and other wildlife. This refuge also provides a safe haven for endangered species such as the bald eagle.

Currently Tamarac has one of the highest nesting densities of bald eagles on a national wildlife refuge with 16 active bald eagle nests. This refuge is also home to timber wolves, bear, moose, deer, and beaver.

Run by the U.S. Fish and Wildlife Service, total acreage of Tamarac is 42,724 acres consisting of half wetlands and half timberland. In the fall the White Earth Indians harvest the wild rice while the fall colors surround the refuge in earthy beauty. There is an interpretive center open to the public with regularly scheduled presentations.

There are over 200 species of birds found in Tamarac, making it the perfect bird-watchers' retreat in addition to being a hospitable environment in which to study nature. Hunting and fishing are permitted in designated areas. Tamarac Lake is one of the spots that is open to fishing during all state fishing seasons. A wildlife film series and interpretive program are scheduled each weekend during the summer months.

For cross-country skiing, the Pine Lake-Tamarac Lake area has nearly eight miles of trails. Average snowfall for the area is around four feet so there is always a good snow base. Leaflets available at the visitor center provide direction for a ten-mile self-guided auto tour May through October. Group presentations are available by calling in advance. Tamarac National Wildlife Refuge provides access to view wildlife in a natural environment.

© MARTTENA K. KICHTER

ELK RIVER

Early Indians knew this place well and often camped by the green-tinted waters of the Elk River where it joined the great Mississippi. Although the elks that inspired the name are no longer part of the scenery, the city has become the metropolitan gateway to the scenic northwoods.

The *Sherburne National Wildlife Refuge* offers miles of trails and excellent wildlife observation opportunities.

Culturally, Elk River is able to offer a *Community Theater, Community Band & Chorus, Land of Lakes Choirboys* and an annual *Fine Arts Festival.*

Summer festivals include the *Sherburne County Fair, Antique Engine Show* and *Pioneer Threshing Weekend* at the living history *Oliver H. Kelley Farm.*

For further information, contact:
Elk River Area Chamber of Commerce
729 Main Street
Elk River, MN 55330   Phone: 612-441-3110

HISTORIC SITE

Oliver H. Kelley Farm

A Minnesota Historical Society Site. 2.5 miles SE of Elk River on Hwy. 10. 15788 Kelley Farm Rd., Elk River, MN 55330 **Phone: 612-441-6896.** Hrs: (May 1-Oct. 31) Mon.-Sat. 10 a.m.-5 p.m., Sun. noon-4 p.m. (Nov. 2-April 30) Sat. 10 a.m.-4 p.m., Sun. noon-4 p.m. Admission charge.

From the very beginning, Oliver H. Kelley was clearly a progressive thinker and an ambitious farmer. He and his wife, Lucy, purchased their farm in 1849 and soon Kelley mortgaged it to purchase implements, turning his farm from a labor-intensive operation into a mechanized business. In 1867, he founded the Patrons of Husbandry—better known as the Grange—a farmer's organization that demanded reduced railroad rates and better social and economic conditions for farmers.

The fascinating lives of Kelley, his family and other Minnesota farm families are depicted at the Oliver H. Kelley Farm, a "living-history" farm where interpreters in period clothing perform the tasks and chores of a typical mid-19th century farm family. Visitors can participate and learn about the many changes occurring in agriculture at that time.

An Interpretive Center has exhibits and a bookstore featuring books about agricultural history, women's history and gardening.

FERGUS FALLS

Located 177 miles northwest of Minneapolis/St. Paul on I-94, Fergus Falls is in the heart of beautiful lake country. With a population of over 12,000, it's well-suited to play host to the thousands of vacationers and visitors it sees each year. At the same time, Fergus Falls offers a strong industrial base, providing an environment suited to larger businesses, as well.

There is an abundance of wildlife in the Fergus Falls area, one of the benefits enjoyed by both residents and visitors. Ruffed grouse, ring-necked pheasant, Canada geese, white-tailed deer and many other species inhabit these lands. Sportsmen and naturalists alike can experience for themselves the awesome scenes that only nature can provide.

ATTRACTIONS

The Otter Tail County Historical Society is recognized by the Minnesota Historical Society as one of the top county historical societies in the state. The Society offers tours and tourist information, exhibits, a large interpretive museum, gift shop and other rich cultural programs.

Approximately 500 acres of park land are located within the city. Skating, skiing, sledding, snowmobiling, walking, hiking, biking, camping, picnicking, swimming, boating, fishing, horseshoes, golfing, tennis, and playground facilities can be found in one or more city parks.

DeLagoon Park and Campgrounds is located on *Pebble Lake* and has beautiful level sites with facility hook-ups. Located just south of Fergus Falls on Highway 59, DeLagoon and its associated facilities offer a fantastic all-purpose recreational area, including:

- Sandy beach and swimming area.
- Fishing for bass, northern, walleye, rainbow trout and crappies.
- Scenic picnic area for both large and small groups.
- Softball diamonds complex.
- Perfectly groomed 18-hole, par 72 golf course.
- Campground complete with toilet facilities, water and electricity hook-ups.

Inspiration Peak is the second highest peak in northern Minnesota and offers a panoramic view of many lakes and parts of three counties. It makes an unusually beautiful picnic area. In the fall, it is a beautiful spot for the photographer.

Maplewood State Park is the perfect place to picnic, ride horseback, snowmobile, cross-country ski, camp, swim, fish and hike.

Maplewood is located in the transition area between the state's eastern forests and western prairies. The park is known for its large hardwood trees and includes the largest ironwood tree in the state. The highest hill in the park approaches 1,600 feet and provides a dramatic vista of its 9,000 acres. Cross-country ski trails are maintained in Maplewood State Park and at *Spidahl's Ski Gard.*

Phelps Mill, built in 1889 to harness power from the Otter Tail River grinding wheat into flour, now uses its New England-style charm to attract thousands of visitors each year. Originally known as the Main Roller Mill, the building hugs a picturesque curve in the river immediately below the frothy white waters of the dam which once powered machines in the four-story structure. Visitors are welcome to tour the complicated jungle of wheels, cogs, belts and levers all just as they were on their last day of operation in 1931.

EVENTS

Fergus Falls Summerfest takes place the third weekend of June. Watch a good old-fashioned parade and dance in the streets. Eat Scandinavian foods. Shop at one of the largest arts and craft shows.

Fergus Falls is the home to the action-packed *Minnesota State High School Rodeo Finals* at the Otter Tail County Fairgrounds. Dozens of high school students from all over the state compete in a variety of rodeo events. Winners at the state level qualify for the national finals. The students compete hard for a chance at the national finals, but they also put on a colorful show, with the thrills that a rodeo always brings.

One of the region's favorite events, the *Phelps Mill Festival* is held annually in mid-July at Phelps Mill County Park. This arts and crafts sale, show and entertainment is where you can shop over 80 arts and crafts exhibits and sample delicious foods.

The *West Otter Tail County Fair* is eagerly awaited by over 30,000 fairgoers every August. Located on the southern edge of Fergus Falls, the fairgrounds burst with the fun and excitement of daring rides, challenging games, foot-long hot dogs, cotton candy, rainbow sno-cones and mini-donuts.

A real highlight of the county fair is the 4-H and area residents' ribbon-winning exhibits of sewing, canning, gardening, carpentry, livestock—the list goes on and on. Don't miss fair time in Fergus Falls held in August.

For further information, contact:
Fergus Falls CVB
112 W. Washington, Box 868
Fergus Falls, MN 56538
Phone: 218-736-6979 or 800-726-8959

MUSEUM

Otter Tail County *Historical* *Museum*	1110 W. Lincoln, Fergus Falls, MN 56537 **Phone: 218-736-6038** Hrs.: Mon.-Fri. 9 a.m.-5 p.m., Sat.-Sun./Holidays 1 p.m.-4 p.m.

The Otter Tail County Historical Society was established to preserve and display the history of Otter Tail County throughout the years. As history was compiled, the need for expansion grew, with the most recent addition in 1983 giving the museum over 15,000 square feet of exhibit space.

There are 107 different displays viewed by nearly 15,000 visitors annually. The E.T. Barnard Library gives easy access to maps, census records, platbooks, newspapers, photographs and various history records. The Otter Tail Historical Society is supported by 1,152 members and 125 active volunteers. Always concerned with the enrichment of the younger citizens, there is constant development of educational programs. In the Educational Center are museum tours, slide/tape shows, traveling kits, programs, traveling exhibits, and a historical sites tour. Currently the Historical Society publishes a booklet entitled "Educational Programs for Teachers and Groups" for the benefit of area educators.

RESORT

Woodlawn Resort	Blanche Creek Road Rt. 2, Box 365, Battle Lake, MN 56515 **Phone: 218-864-5389 (Winter: 402-435-5858)** Hrs.: June 1-Sept. 1

Owned and operated by one family since 1948, Woodlawn Resort offers a lot for vacationers to do, which probably accounts for the many guest families returning every year. Owners Bud and Phyllis Narveson provide enough activities to keep even the busiest person occupied. Windsurfing and sailing lessons are available, as are a tennis court, canoes and fishing boats, and a shallow water volleyball net. Woodlawn has an excellent library full of books and games. New in 1994 is a recreation building for rainy day pastimes. Golf courses, riding stables and a variety of restaurants are nearby.

Nine fully equipped cottages are located right on the lakeshore. The comfortably furnished cabins have from two to four bedrooms and completely outfitted kitchens. All the cottages have spectacular views from large, lakefront decks. One cottage is barrier free.

The resort is situated in a secluded wilderness perfect for watching wildlife. A written guide is provided for those who want to wander off and explore the territory.

RESORT

Ashby Resort & Campground

P.O. Box 57, Ashby, MN 56309
Phone: 800-332-9209 or 218-747-2959
Hrs: Open year-round
Visa and MasterCard accepted.

When Ann Margaret, Jack Lemmon and Walter Mathau needed a good Minnesota walleye for their film "Grumpy Old Men," they came to Pelican Lake in Ashby for all eight and a half pounds of it.

Of course, they're not the first to have success in Pelican Lake nor the last. Just ask anyone who's spent vacation time at Ashby Resort & Campground. They'll tell you the fishing's always good and the hospitality, too.

Located two miles east of Ashby on County Road 82 and just five miles off Interstate 94 between Fergus Falls and Alexandria, the Ashby Resort & Campground is a year-round vacation spot. In the summertime, people come for the fishing on Pelican Lake, a 3,600-acre lake surrounded by acres of untouched land. There are many bays and coves for some of Minnesota's finest fishing including sunfish, crappie, bass, northern pike and, of course, walleye. While on the lake, explore Bird Island, where thousands of birds of many different species are found, including egrets, blue herons and double-crested cormorants who migrate here to raise their young.

In the fall, vacationers come for the hunting, including pheasant, duck, geese and deer. And in winter, ice house rentals are available and there is easy access to excellent snowmobile trails in the area.

Year-round, Ashby Resort & Campground offers quality accommodations including air-conditioned lakeside cabins, kitchenettes, sleeping rooms and mobile homes. Linens, cooking utensils, a boat and color TV are included with each unit. There are even cribs and highchairs for your convenience. There are also 33 shaded seasonal campsites with full hook-ups, dump station and storm shelter plus a clean bathhouse and showers.

In the summertime, check out the sandy swimming beach with slide in the water plus a playground, volleyball court and horseshoe pits. A recreation and game room is available as are paddle boats and pontoon boats, boat and motor rentals plus licenses, bait, tackle, groceries, freezer service and boat launching.

If you're up for a day away from the water, there are three golf courses nearby. Visit Donna Jean's coffee shop (a great place to meet people) serving breakfast, sandwiches, pizza, ice cream, candy, homemade goodies, plus groceries and T-shirts. Be sure and try one of the old-fashioned malts.

And if it's your first time to the Ashby Resort & Campground, be sure and ask Charlie for a free boat ride to tour the lake. You'll be glad you did.

SPECIALTY SHOPS

Victor Lundeen Company

126-128 W. Lincoln, Fergus Falls, MN 56537
Phone: 218-736-5433
Hrs.: Mon.-Sat. 9 a.m.-5:30 p.m.
Visa, Discover and MasterCard accepted.

Visitors experience a piece of history when they step into Victor Lundeen Company, the oldest family-operated business in Fergus Falls. Still doing business from the original storefront, Victor Lundeen Company specializes in printing services, as it has for 80 years, and is a bookseller and stationer. The store displays unique gifts, stationery, office products, artist supplies, drafting tools and a wide variety of books—bestsellers and classics, regional books, children's, cookbooks, how-to books and publisher's remainders.

Generations of shoppers have found their way to Victor Lundeen Company. The store is large and can take several hours to browse through. The printshop offers a complete spectrum of printing services, including an in-house design and layout department. Such specialty advertising items as name-imprinted pens are typical orders for the Victor Lundeen Company. So, whether you have printing or advertising needs, or you just want a good book or gift item, Victor Lundeen Company is there to meet your needs effectively.

◆ ◆ ◆ ◆ ◆ ◆

The Phelps Mill Store

Rt. 2, Box 218, Underwood, MN 56586
Phone: 218-826-6158. Hrs: (Memorial Day-Labor Day) Mon.-Sat. 10 a.m.-6 p.m., Sun. noon-6 p.m. (May, Sept., Oct.) Sat.-Sun. noon-5 p.m.

For a hundred years, The Phelps Mill Store has stood guard over County Road 45 across from the old Phelps Mill. Now on the National Register of Historic Places, the store harkens back to a time gone by and is kept well-stocked with old-fashioned treasures.

For example, visitors especially like the shop's ice cream counter and its abundance of stick candies. The two main rooms in the store are filled with handmade country gift items, country decorating accessories, sweatshirts, T-shirts, baskets, cookbooks, candles, hand-loomed rugs and a variety of souvenir items of Minnesota.

Sweet delights can be enjoyed outside on a park bench stationed on the sweeping front porch. The solitude is punctuated by bird songs and the water which still cascades down the falls at the old mill across the street.

The Phelps Mill Store has put history to good use by offering gifts, warmth and education for more than two decades. Stop by and enjoy the ambiance of another era.

GLENWOOD

Long before the first Europeans explored the Minnesota Territory, the Glenwood area was inhabited by the Dakota and Ojibwa Indians.

In 1849, Captain John Pope led an expedition through an area later named after him, Pope County. Captain Pope took special note of a "grand" lake located in the center of the Minnesota territory. The large lake was known as Lake Minnewaska, possibly named after Minnewaska, a Dakota Indian princess.

ATTRACTIONS & EVENTS

Glenwood calls itself "the best-kept secret in Minnesota." Its excellent resorts offer a full range of year-round recreational activities including sailing, tennis, waterskiing, hiking, camping, fishing, ice fishing and snowmobiling.

Peters' Sunset Beach and Golf Club is a resort listed on the National Register of Historic Places. Peters' golf course and ***Minnewaska Golf Club*** are 18-hole courses which allow challenging play in spacious and scenic surroundings.

Glacial Lakes State Park is located at the crossroads of the original prairie land to the west and central hardwood forests to the east.

Ann Bickle Heritage House, a turn of the century craftsman-style home, is known as the finest home in Glenwood in its day.

The Pope County Historical Museum houses the ***Hebling Gallery of Indian Arts and Crafts,*** a collection sought after by the Smithsonian Institute. Other displays include a country store and a pioneer kitchen.

Morning Glory Gardens, an old chapel surrounded by more than 30 varieties of flowers, the ***Indian Burial Grounds*** and the ***Terrace Mill*** are all points of interest that should not be missed.

Waterama, an annual three-day celebration is held the last full weekend in July. Highlights of this extravaganza include a lighted pontoon parade, waterskiing shows, sailboat regattas, theater productions, dances, fireworks, bike races and parades.

For further information, contact:
Glenwood Chamber of Commerce
137 E. Minnesota Ave.
Glenwood, MN 56344
Phone: 612-634-3636

HACKENSACK

Located along the shores of beautiful Birch Lake, Hackensack offers year-round fun for everyone. Summer, by far, has got to be the favorite season for vacationers coming to the area. With 127 lakes in a ten-mile radius, it's no wonder why visitors return time and again to enjoy the ultimate in fishing, water skiing, canoeing, or to have just plain fun.

ATTRACTIONS & EVENTS

From June through August, you can experience a real *Native American Pow-wow* every Thursday at 2 p.m. The one-day summer *Flea Market* at Sacred Heart Church in June, July and August is one of the biggest and most popular flea markets in the North Country.

In July, St. Paul's Lutheran Church sponsors an old-fashioned *Country Fair* complete with a variety of homemade items, booths, attic treasures and a silent auction.

Crystal clear lakes, natural trails, golf courses, shopping, dining, dancing and a beautiful sunset; it's all here in "God's Country" waiting for you. The most beautiful season is fall. The combination of clean, brisk air, along with green leaves turning to yellow, orange and crimson offer an awesome array of colors to enjoy and photograph. Thousands of acres of public land, alive with a variety of game, provide ample opportunities for hunting, while area lakes offer excellent fall fishing.

For those who enjoy winter activities, Hackensack has something for you, too! You can snowmobile over hundreds of miles of trails, ice fish any of the area lakes, experience cross-country skiing through acres of forests, or just enjoy the beauty of winter. Afterwards, you can relax by a blazing fire savoring the memories of the day.

Spring offers yet another season to enjoy the beauty of the area. As the sun gets warmer and the ice starts to melt, the lakes, forests, and all of nature come to life. Walk a trail at *Deep Portage Reserve* or blaze your own in the *Chippewa National Forest* or the *Foothills State Forest.* The countryside is fresh, vibrant, alive and you will be, too.

For further information, contact:
Hackensack Chamber of Commerce
P.O. Box 373
Hackensack, MN 56452
Phone: 218-675-6135

BAKERY

Pastries Plus, Inc.

Highway 371, Hackensack, MN 56452
Phone: 218-675-5211
Hrs: Open at 6 a.m. weekdays, 8 a.m. Sundays
Closed Mondays. Closing times vary.

Who can resist the wonderful aroma that fills a bakery with the unmistakable scent of bread, pastries and muffins made fresh each morning?

That's what you'll discover at Pastries Plus, on Highway 371 in Hackensack. New in 1993, Pastries Plus opens at the crack of dawn each morning; you should arrive early for the best selection of quality baking.

You'll find a large variety of doughnuts, filled and unfilled rolls, pastries, muffins, cookies and bars available; all are attractively displayed to entice your taste buds. Of course, they offer fresh-baked bread, buns and hard rolls. However, it's best to pre-order pies, cakes and special requests.

The coffee shop seats 20 with your choice of booths or tables and chairs. In-store specials are offered frequently. Plenty of off-street parking is available.

RESORT

Woman Lake Lodge

50 miles north of Brainerd on Woman Lake, H.C.R. 74, Box 2000, Hackensack, MN 56452. **Phone: 218-682-2426 or 800-950-0032.** Visa, MasterCard and Discover accepted.

Even in the Land of 10,000 Lakes, who could forget the names "Girl Lake," "Child Lake" and "Woman Lake." And who could forget a stay on one of Minnesota's most breathtaking at Woman Lake Lodge. Located 50 miles north of Brainerd, Woman Lake Lodge is 18 quiet, comfortable cabins nestled along a wonderful sand beach. Just minutes from Deep Portage Conservation Reserve and the Chippewa National Forest, the Lodge features extraordinary fishing for walleye, northern and muskie plus panfish and bass.

Cabins are equipped with kitchen, shower, utensils, microwaves and bed linens. Outside, you'll find a fire ring for nightly sing-alongs or quiet contemplation. A full range of activities (paddleboats, volleyball, basketball, video games room, etc.) are available with horseback riding, golf, tennis, fine dining, water slides and casino gambling nearby. A convenience store provides those last-minute provisions.

Mentioned in the September 1992 edition of *National Geographic*, Woman Lake Lodge is a place where families become friends.

SPECIALTY SHOPS

Greentree

Hwy. 371 & Whipple Ave., Hackensack, MN
56452. **Phone: 218-675-6006 or 800-950-7440**
Hrs: Open 7 days a week Memorial Day-Labor
Day. Visa, MasterCard and Discover accepted.

Nothing says "Minnesota" more than the call of the loon.

That's what you'll find here at Greentree in Hackensack—the sounds of northern Minnesota, the call of the loon and pleasant music to go with it. Of course, there's another enticement, too. Fresh fudge. Taste a sample on the house and you'll definitely be back for more.

Established in 1973, Greentree features upscale gifts at reasonable prices. They carry Minnetonka moccasins, "Critter Sox" and many exclusive T-shirt designs for adults and kids alike, all printed right here. They also feature maple furniture, a large selection of cotton throws, stationery, note cards, glassware and unique souvenirs. Or check out their selection of windsocks.

And of course loons, loons and more loons.

The friendly staff will make you feel important from the moment you walk in the door. Conveniently located on Highway 371, look for the big flag pole and bright flowers. Shipping is available.

◆ ◆ ◆ ◆ ◆ ◆ ◆

John's Sawdust Shop

Half mile north of Hackensack on Hwy. 371,
Woodland Drive, Hackensack, MN 56452
Phone: 218-675-6130

Quality and craftsmanship. Those are two things that are becoming increasingly difficult to find these days but you'll see them in abundance at John's Sawdust Shop in Hackensack, specializing in patio furniture you can be proud of.

The quality is outstanding, displaying true, old-fashioned craftsmanship. The Double Glider Swing, for instance, is most innovative, featuring contoured seats for your comfort, a roof for those drizzly days or as a shield from the hot sun. Nothing's more relaxing after a hard day's work. They also produce the traditional Adirondack Chair, the Glider Chair and Glider Bench, Stationary Chair, Stationary Bench and 18-inch Table plus 60-inch or 48-inch round picnic tables. John's Sawdust Shop uses only the best Western Red Cedar with all exposed edges rounded and smoothed. And the finish is outstanding.

Drive a half mile north of Hackensack on Hwy. 371 to Woodland Drive. Follow Woodland Drive for a mile and a half to Fire # H1721.

SPECIALTY SHOPS

Northern Trails Saddle Shop	Hwy. 371, P.O. Box 308 Hackensack, MN 56452 **Phone: 218-675-5131** Hrs.: Mon.-Sat. 9 a.m.-5 p.m.

Visitors to Northern Trails Saddle Shop are welcome to watch the saddle maker at work on custom saddles and tack made in the the old tradition. Bill Engren, the owner of Northern Trails Saddle Shop, works on the leather in a fenced-in corral area of the shop.

It's an interesting little shop replete with the smell of leather and a variety of western wear to browse through. Boots, hats, shirts, dresses and a good selection of new and used saddles and bridles are available to choose from. There's a nice selection of line-dancing dresses. Hats range from straw-type to Stetsons.

The store buys, sells, trades and repairs all types of saddles and tack, so you'll have no problem finding just what you need. When you're in the area, be sure to amble on in to Northern Trails Saddle Shop.

❖ ❖ ❖ ❖ ❖ ❖ ❖

Swanson's Bait Shop	Highway 371, Hackensack, MN 56452 **Phone: 218-675-6176.** Hrs: (Summer) 7 days 6 a.m.-10 p.m. (Winter) 7 days 7 a.m.-6 p.m. Visa, MasterCard, Discover and Amoco accepted.

Minnesota's fishing may be famous but you won't get very far if you've forgotten the essentials. That's where Swanson's Bait Shop comes in.

Located in a unique log structure on Highway 371 in Hackensack, Swanson's has everything you need for Minnesota's best fishing, from bait to tackle, gas to groceries, whether you're spending your summer in a boat or your winter on the ice.

They sell all types of live bait, including minnows, night crawlers, leeches, frogs and waxworms and have a large selection of tackle for summer and winter fishing, including decoys. Other essentials they have that you might need include LP Gas, outboard gas, oil products, diesel fuel and kerosene plus ice augers, fish shelters and fish house stoves not to mention boots, gloves, T-shirts, souvenirs, gifts, ammo, targets, hunting supplies and convenience foods. Nicely situated on the main highway in the heart of fishin' country.

SPECIALTY SHOPS

Wild Rose
Trading Post

Highway 371
Hackensack, MN 56452
Phone: 218-675-6154
Hrs: Open May-September

Far more than just another gift shop, the Wild Rose Trading Post on Highway 371 in Hackensack offers an unusual collection of wares, from rare soapstone carving to a wide array of sterling silver items.

Best of all, you can not only buy soapstone and silver but you can watch the carvers at work right on the spot and take classes in how to create your own art in both mediums.

Rock is another speciality. The Wild Rose Trading Post carries a variety of polished and rough rock specimens plus rock tumblers. They have semi-precious gemstones like jade, hematite, turquoise, sea opal, mozarkite and agate. Their selection of Rada cutlery from Iowa is another highlight.

And you can choose from a variety of souvenir items including handpainted magnets, wonderful Minnesota loons and unusual stamp dispensers. Or select your favorite pieces from among the many wooden crafts and petrified wood on display.

◆ ◆ ◆ ◆ ◆ ◆ ◆

The Woodshed

One mile east on County Road 5, Hackensack,
MN 56452. **Phone: 218-675-6599**
Hrs: Mon.-Fri 8 a.m.-4:30 p.m.
Hours can vary

Specializing in custom-designed wood products, Butch and Cheryl Moore's Woodshed in Hackensack features excellent handcrafted items made to your specifications. Located one mile east of town on County Road 5, The Woodshed features a large variety of custom-designed cabinets, furniture and antique reproductions. They make very nice round oak tables, hutches, gun cabinets and bar stools among many other things but spend the majority of their time doing custom kitchen cabinetry. Individual attention is the key. That's what they give every single piece, no matter how large or small, no matter what kind of item they're crafting. Oak is a popular choice but they've worked in pine, cedar, hickory and ash, too. This unique business has been satisfying customers who seek quality for better than a decade and Butch and Cheryl would be more than happy to design and manufacture your special request. Or if you're just curious, you can stop by any time and watch the work in progress at The Woodshed in Hackensack.

LAKE GEORGE

Lake George doesn't just offer excellent fishing—especially crappies, northerns, walleyes, bass and panfish—it offers so much more. This tiny community is a restful haven, a rejuvenating vacation spot complete with small family-run industries, restaurants, bait shops and resorts. Lake George is considered to be the eastern gateway to *Itasca State Park.* The second-largest state park in Minnesota, Itasca forms a protective shield of lakes, marshes and dense woods around the famed headwaters of the *Mississippi.*

Vacationers can enjoy swimming, canoeing and water skiing. Hikers and campers will find the birch and pine forests a nature lover's paradise, filled with all varieties of birds, animals and wild flowers. In July, people come from all over to pick the wild blueberries and enjoy the *Blueberry Festival.*

For more information contact:
Lake George Area Association
P.O. Box 1635 B
Lake George, MN 56458   Phone: 218-266-3468

SPECIALTY SHOP

Itasca
Moccasin

Hwy. 71, 7 miles east of Lake Itasca
P.O. Box 228
Lake George, MN 56458
Phone: 218-266-3978

After you tramp the northwoods, pamper your feet at Itasca Moccasin where they've been making beautiful handmade moccasins since 1986 for both the retail and wholesale trades. When you stop in, moccasins are custom fit and sewn especially for you, so any unusual-shaped foot can be accommodated.

Choose from many leathers including elk, moose, buffalo, deer, sheepskin and steer-hide. Many styles are available. Try Dancers, Canoes, Lightfeathers or Papoose. Knee-hi's and 6" boots are popular, too. Moccasins can be made with either soft or hard soles. Itasca Moccasin is truly a one-of-a-kind place. Don't miss it when near Lake George.

SPECIALTY SHOPS

Schoolcraft Gallery Collection Of Shops

Highway 71 & 200, 7 miles east of Itasca State Park.
Lake George, MN 56458. **Phone: 218-266-3977.**
Hrs: Summer, Mon.-Sat. 10 a.m.-6 p.m., Sundays
Noon-6 p.m. Other hours vary, call ahead.
Visa, MasterCard and Discover accepted.

This unique log schoolhouse was built in 1905. In 1981 the school was restored by Gregory and Paulette Giese and opened as the Schoolcraft Gallery, offering the finest in northwoods gifts.

This rustic log building features original art in many forms, including a collection of Ojibwa crafts, decorative handmade quilts, stoneware pottery by the Hamiltons and decorative art pottery by Pat Shannon.

Old-fashioned candies and fine chocolates are available along with many northwoods gourmet items like wild rice, preserves and maple syrup. Traditional Post items include genuine pelts, Ojibwa jewelry and basket-work, handcrafted buckles, knives and coonskin caps. The Teddy Bear House is a child's delight and the Books 'n Print Shop has a wide choice of nature books, works of regional authors and nature prints plus a carefully chosen collection of children's books, greeting cards and custom-designed stationary.

Phone and mail orders can be made year-round.

* * * * * * *

Wigwam

Hwy. 71, 7 miles east of Lake Itasca
P.O. Box 1621
Lake George, MN 56458
Phone: 218-266-3968

For over 40 years, the Wigwam has been delighting tourists and travelers with handmade lawn ornaments, cement figurines, beautiful flower pots, trinkets, toys and souvenirs of all kinds. The Wigwam is always filled with thousands of exciting items and each year more are added.

Kids have a ball in the "circle," an area filled with hundreds of toys and trinkets. Visitors can spend hours going through the buildings and backyard discovering the new items each season. Check out the unique birdhouses, windmills and birdbaths, too.

Your family won't want to miss The Wigwam, which still has the original paints on the outside.

LITTLE FALLS

Little Falls was named, it is said, for a rapids in the Mississippi that thwarted the efforts of explorer Zebulon Pike to find its source. Its most famous native son, Charles Lindbergh Jr., was also cast in the mold of explorer and pioneer.

Visitors enjoy touring the *Charles A. Lindbergh Home and Interpretive Center*. The *clock tower* at the courthouse in Little Falls is just one of a number of historical buildings and homes in the area which includes the *Rosenmeier home,* the *Dewey Radke house, the train depot* and the *Weyerhauser and Musser homes.*

Popular events include the *Rock and Mineral Show* in June, the *Antique Auto Show and Swap Meet* in June, the *Morrison County Fair* in July, and the *Celebrity Golf Tournament* also in July.

For further information, contact:
Little Falls Chamber of Commerce
202 S. E. First Ave.
Little Falls, MN 56345
Phone: 612-632-5115 or 800-325-5916

HISTORIC SITE

Lindbergh House

A Minnesota Historical Society Site., 1200 Lindbergh Dr. S., Little Falls, MN 56345. **Phone: 612-632-3154**
Hrs: (May 1-Labor Day) Mon.-Sat. 10 a.m.-5 p.m., Sun. noon-5 p.m. (Sept. 10-Oct. 23) Sat. 10 a.m.-4 p.m., Sun. noon-4 p.m. Admission charge.

Charles A. Lindbergh Jr., famous for his solo, non-stop airplane flight from New York to Paris in 1927, spent a happy childhood on his parent's farm in Little Falls. His father, Charles Sr., was elected to Congress in 1906 and the family moved to Washington, D.C. However, each summer, Charles and his mother returned to the farm and, here, the young Lindbergh spent hours gazing up at the drifting clouds, dreaming of flying.

After Charles Jr. became famous, souvenir hunters converged on the house, which was standing empty, and stripped it of everything they could find. Eventually, the conservation-minded Lindberghs gave the house and farm to the state of Minnesota as a memorial to Charles Sr. The former farm is now a state park.

The Minnesota Historical Society has restored the house to its original turn-of-the-century appearance and added a visitors center nearby. The center details the life and times of three generations of Lindberghs.

LONGVILLE

A unique little town in north central Minnesota noted for its beautiful scenery and friendly people, Longville is surrounded by about a hundred lakes. Abundant pine and birch add to its year-round beauty. Resorts are plentiful and the tiny city has some of northern Minnesota's finest gift shops, gallerys, sporting goods stores, marinas, golf courses, restaurants and supper clubs.

The city has a public access on Girl Lake which is part of the beautiful Woman Lake Chain, offering recreation and fishing for wall-eye, northern, panfish, bass and even the elusive muskie. The many area lakes give visitors easy access to great fishing wherever they try their luck. There's also a 3,800-foot paved, lighted and beaconed airstrip.

ATTRACTIONS

Longville enjoys four seasons of entertainment and attractions. Spring brings the beauty of the state flower, the showy *Ladyslipper,* along with thousands of *Trilliums* exploding in the forests and along the roadsides. As the ice breaks up on area lakes, resort and cabin owners scurry to prepare for spring fishing.

In summer, of course, all recreation opens and tourists and natives alike enjoy all the activities the chamber and residents have planned. Many folks return year after year and enjoy renewing old acquaintances.

The fall offers the beautiful, scenic *Chippewa National Forest* to spend some time taking in the wonderful colored leaves enhanced by green pines and white birch. It would be difficult to find a more beautiful combination. Often, visitors see deer, bear, coyote, fox and even the elusive timberwolf. The area also has one of the nation's largest eagle populations. The lakes are rather noisy with duck hunters in the fall and the area soon turns to the redcoats as they come to see if they can "bag" a deer.

Deep Portage Conservation Reserve with a modern interpretive center lies at the edge of the area. It's 6,100 acres of public land dedicated to recreation and conservation by Cass County. Nowhere, it seems, is there such a diversity of scenery, activities and recreational opportunity as in the natural setting that is the Longville Lakes area.

Winter has become one of the most beautiful and fun seasons in Longville. There is access to hundreds of miles of beautiful snowmobile trails, as well as cross-country skiing, and, of course, lots of lakes to ice fish on. Snowmobile trails are truly a lovely outing with the snow covered pines, a deer often crossing, a fun cookout over an open fire, and then back to a cozy cabin or motel room. Surely, visitors go home feeling nature and friendly folks are some of God's greatest gifts. The folks in Longville know when you come here once, they'll see you again—and again—and again.

The *Ridgewood Golf Course* with 18 holes is a great place to play golf when in the Longville area.

EVENTS

Via legislation in 1989, Longville is noted as the *Turtle Race Capitol of the World!* Every Wednesday afternoon between Memorial Day and Labor Day they entertain the area with their famous downtown main street turtle races. With only about 200 population, the city has had as many as 400 turtles registered in an afternoon! Each turtle has a racer and each racer usually has family and friends who come to town to watch.

Flea Markets, Bake Sales, Bazaars, Specialty Dinners and an elaborate 4th of July celebration with fireworks are a few of the other exciting and fun things to do in Longville. Winter offers an *Old-Fashioned Christmas Celebration* including a tree lighting ceremony and hayrides with Santa.

For further information, contact:
Longville Lakes Area Chamber of Commerce
P.O. Box 33-GM, Longville, MN 56655
Phone: 218-363-2630 or 800-756-7583

ART GALLERY

King Gallery

Main Street, Longville, MN 56655. **Phone: 218-363-2646.** Hrs: (April 1-Dec. 31) Mon.-Sat. 9 a.m.-5 p.m. (Beginning Memorial Day) Sun. 9 a.m.-3 p.m. Visa, MasterCard and Discover accepted.

The King Gallery features a wide assortment of quality artwork, much of it by Minnesota artists and craftspeople. The friendly staff caters to their customers and will go out of their way to please you.

King Gallery offers a large custom framing department, specializing in needlework, limited edition and decorator prints. They're noted for the wide assortment of handmade porcelain and stoneware they carry, both whimsical and functional. They represent local potters as well as quite a few others from around the country.

The Gallery always has delicious gourmet food items to tempt your taste buds or to make that perfect special gift. You'll find an assortment of dried arrangements, jewelry, handpainted pillows and shirts, cotton throws, T-shirts and sweatshirts, holiday items, cards, locally-made Native American items and their always popular handpainted decorative accessories.

For that perfect gift or special something for yourself, check out friendly Longville and The King Gallery, a special combination.

RESTAURANT & GOLF COURSE

Patrick's Fine Dining and Ridgewood Golf Course

P.O. Box 295, Longville, MN 56655. **Phone: 218-363-2995.** Hrs: (Summer) Mon.-Sun. 8:30 a.m.-10 p.m. (Winter) Mon.-Fri. 11:30-2 p.m., 4:30 p.m.-9 p.m., Sat-Sun 11:30 a.m.-9 p.m. Major credit cards accepted.

Set on an island in beautiful Girl Lake, Patrick's Fine Dining features delectable cuisine and quality local entertainment in a tranquil, remote location. A year-round porch overlooks the lake and the bright, country-style dining room makes guests feel at home. Patrons can even twirl and spin around the lounge's dance floor to the lively strains of local musical acts.

Customers who dine at Patrick's choose from a menu that includes walleye fillets, barbequed loin-back ribs, roast duck a l'orange and Chateaubriand made with Patrick's own Chateau sauce. For those who want to work off the results of their indulgence, the Ridgewood par 72 golf course offers 6,535 yards and 18 holes of challenging golf, as well as a practice driving range, putting green, pitching area and sand bunker. And they now have a par 29 Executive course.

Both fine dinning and recreation make Patrick's an attractive stopover for rest and relaxation.

RESORTS

Broadwater Lodge	Seven miles west of Longville on Cty Rd. 5. Hackensack, MN 56452. **Phone: 218-682-2552** Hrs: Open May 2nd to Mid-November No credit cards accepted.

Broadwater Lodge is located on Woman Lake, one of Minnesota's most beautiful bodies of water, about seven miles west of Longville.

Situated on more than 40 acres, adjacent to the Chippewa National Forest and featuring over 1,200 feet of shoreline, Broadwater Lodge is a wonderful family vacation spot. Cottages are nestled among the tall Norway pines and come complete with fire-places, decks, full baths and gas grills and a 14-foot Crestliner boat. Kitchens have microwaves and every cooking utensil.

There are nature trails, a game room and a terrific swimming beach with new sun decks. That, and the scheduled children's activities, make this a great place to bring the kids. Kayaks, canoes and fun bugs are available along with boats, motors and guide service. The Finnish Sauna is a wonderful place to unwind at day's end.

Open to mid-November for deer season. Excellent fishing on the Woman Lake Chain, including sheltered Broadwater Bay.

◆ ◆ ◆ ◆ ◆ ◆ ◆

Hunter's Bay Lodge	Hwy 84 South of Longville, Longville, MN 56655 **Phone: 218-363-2437** Hrs: Open May 14 - Oct. 2 No credit cards accepted.

"The nicest and cleanest resort we have stayed at in 20 years."

That's how one guest, no doubt speaking for many, summed up a stay at Hunter's Bay Lodge, a family housekeeping resort on beautiful Woman Lake. It has that relaxing and restful atmosphere Minnesota's northern lake country is so famous for.

They offer clean, pleasant accommodations. Cabins are well-spaced and have spectacular views of the lake and Horseshoe Island. Each is comfortably decorated and has a complete kitchen and bathroom. Guests bring their own towels. Several have fireplaces. There's more than 1,000 feet of sandy beach with a great swimming area and a swimming pool, too. There's also a game room for the kids plus golf, tennis, restaurants and shopping nearby.

Each cabin comes with a fishing boat so you can sample the crystal clear water of Woman Lake, noted for walleye, northern, bass, panfish and muskie. Extra boats and motors are available. Senior citizens, ask about mid-week discounts spring and fall.

SPECIALTY SHOPS

Gallery 3

Main Street, Longville, MN 56655
Phone: 218-363-2324. Hrs: (Summer) 9 a.m. - 5 p.m. 7 days. (Winter) Thurs.-Sat. 10 a.m.-5 p.m. Visa, MasterCard and Discover accepted.

If elegance in all price ranges appeals to you, then Gallery 3 in Longville is the perfect place. From humble beginnings in just 20 square feet, Gallery 3 has grown in 15 years to 6,000 square feet of pure visual entertainment. With the soothing sounds of piano music playing in the background and the smell of cappuccino and fresh treats filling the air, Gallery 3 offers a wide selection of one-of-a-kind gifts, boutique clothing, jewelry and accessories, art supplies and rubber stamps. Their picture framing is truly creative. And in the spring they offer a greenhouse with hanging and bedding plants, fountains, birdbaths and statuary. Gallery 3 also has fresh flowers for all occasions. The atmosphere is great, the staff is particularly friendly and they'll ship anywhere. You can be part of the art, too, with classes available in watercolor and rubber stamp art.

They have original watercolors for sale, some painted right at the gallery, as well as sculptures, porcelain and clay art masks. Pamper yourself in the tanning bed or paint a day away.

◆ ◆ ◆ ◆ ◆ ◆ ◆

Lori's Luvs

Main Street, Longville, MN 56655
Phone: 218-363-2333. Hrs: Mon. - Sat. 9 a.m. - 5 p.m., Sun. 10 a.m.-2 p.m. (summer only) Visa, MasterCard and Discover accepted.

If you're driving north or south on Highway 84 through the turtle racing capital of the world, Longville, look toward the main street and you will spot the Turtle Mall. Located in the mall is a Hallmark shop that really lives up to Hallmark's motto: "Care enough to give your very best." Inside, you'll find one of the finest gift selections anywhere featuring an excellent variety in selections as well as price range. The crafter will find a full range of craft supplies plus there are collectibles, handmade treasures and a wonderful choice of books for sale. Yes, you'll also find a full array of Hallmark gifts, gift wrapping and cards. Maybe best of all, you'll find an atmosphere to your liking.

In business for 15 years, the store is arranged in a neat, attractive manner, the kind of place where the clerks have smiles that say "We care about you. We're here to answer your questions and help you with your selection. We're glad you came to shop at this store. Please come again." And you probably will.

SPECIALTY SHOPS

May B's Videos & Trolls Etc.

Main Street
Longville, MN 56655
Phone: 218-363-2199

When you walk through the front door of May B's Videos & Trolls Etc., in Longville, beware! You'll be greeted by dozens and dozens of trolls, ranging in height from a mere five inches to a rather imposing five feet! Legend has it that some of these trolls are actually 600 years old.

But not to worry.

Trolls Etc. only carries "good luck" trolls, in all different shapes and sizes and varieties. Trolls live in the deep, mystical region between your imagination and reality. Their magical powers have never been equalled. Very few have ever seen them. They move with lightning speed and do their work with loving care. They expect the same of you.

And while you're exploring the world of trolls, you might want to rent a VCR or a movie at May B's. They have the largest selection in the area. So, if you're looking for entertainment, this store will provide it from the moment you step inside!

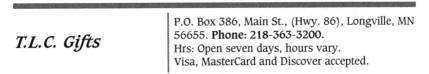

T.L.C. Gifts

P.O. Box 386, Main St., (Hwy. 86), Longville, MN 56655. **Phone: 218-363-3200.**
Hrs: Open seven days, hours vary.
Visa, MasterCard and Discover accepted.

Gifts, gifts, gifts and more gifts! That's what you'll find at T.L.C. Gifts in Longville. Any occasion gifts and, of course, free gift wrapping are hallmarks of the store.

Many theme areas are sectioned off so you can go right to the area you want. There's a Christmas corner, country gifts section, picture frames area, candles, coffee, mugs, loons, ducks, over-the-hill fun books, stationery, playing cards and paper products sections.

They also carry diverse T-shirts and sweat shirts for men, women and children. Check out the wide selection of afghans, too.

The Christmas corner has collector plates featuring artists like Terry Redlin, Dirk Hansen and many others. Right next door is "The One Stop," for all your traveling needs. They've got food, bait, tackle and even fast food if you're in a hurry.

Traci Carpenter is your genial salesperson, so just walk right in and get a warm greeting from her and a great gift for someone special on your list.

MOORHEAD/FARGO

Moorhead along with its sister city, Fargo, are the cultural capitols of the Heartland region. Together, they offer educational facilities, shopping centers, restaurants and hotels unmatched in the area. Lively entertainment is also a major attraction to the area.

Like many other communities in the region, Moorhead had an inauspicious beginning as a riverbank settlement. In 1871, the Northern Pacific Railroad came to the area and secured Moorhead's future as the leading farm processing center for the booming agriculture of the Red River Valley.

ATTRACTIONS & EVENTS

The area has many historical attractions like *Clay County Museum* with its frontier exhibits. *Comstock Historic House* is the home of Ada Comstock, first president of Radcliffe College. *Heritage Hjemkomst Interpretive Center* offers historic and science exhibits and a fascinating 76-foot Viking ship replica that sailed from Duluth to Bergen, Norway.

The *Concordia Language Village* is a nationally recognized program for 7-18 year-olds sponsored by *Concordia College of Moorhead.* Cultural attractions include the *Fargo-Moorhead Symphony Orchestra,* the *Fargo-Moorhead Civic Opera,* and *Red River Dance & Performing Company. The Plains Art Museum* features Native American and West African art.

The *Children's Museum at Yunker Farm* is a wonderful and magical place that offers children a way to make sense out of the world, and to stimulate their imaginations while doing it! It's a strictly hands-on educational experience.

Bonanzaville is a reconstructed prairie village and a living history museum of pioneer life. *The Fargo Farm Show* offers farm and ranch-related services and products with close to 700 booths.

The *Scandinavian Hjemkomst Festival* in June offers ethnic dancing, food and entertainment for all. *Valley Fest/VolksTanz* is a German heritage celebration with—among other things—excellent food. A *Merry Prairie Christmas* is a three-week extravaganza starting after Thanksgiving, offering parades, a costume ball and many other special events.

For further information, contact:
Moorhead-Fargo Convention and Visitors Bureau
P.O. Box 2164, Fargo, ND 58107
Phone: 701-237-6134 or 800-362-3145 ext. 155

ART GALLERY

Archie's West Art Gallery & Gift Shop

On Highway 10, Dilworth, MN 56529
Phone: 218-236-0775. Hrs: Mon.-Sat. 10 a.m.-
5 p.m., Sun. Noon-5 p.m.
Visa, MasterCard and Discover accepted.

Legend has it that the American West begins in the Badlands of South Dakota or even farther west of there. Truth is it starts here, one mile east of Moorhead, in Dilworth. That's where Archie Miller has created one of the finest collections of Western Art found anywhere and displayed it free of charge.

Miller's extraordinary collection of original bronze sculptures and wonderful Western paintings is housed in a huge cedar structure, complete with high beamed ceilings, a giant fireplace and trophy animals. A gift shop offers gifts of affordable elegance from around the world and in December is transformed into The

Old Fashioned Christmas Store. Teachers are encouraged to bring their classes for field trips to view the works of internationally known artists like Bob Scriver, Ace Powell, Frederic Remington and C.M. Russell.

ART GALLERY & MUSEUM

Rourke Art Gallery Museum

523 S. 4th Street, Moorhead, MN 56560
Phone: 218-236-8861. Hrs: Fri., Sat, Sun. 1 p.m.
-5 p.m. Also by appointment. Open year-round.
Visa and MasterCard accepted.

For more than 30 years, the Rourke Art Gallery Museum has promoted the knowledge and love of art in the community. Here, art is displayed in 13 rooms on three floors.

Each June, the Midwestern opens, the region's oldest, largest and most important exhibition. It includes the works of 125 living artists. The Permanent Museum Collection includes work from 20th Century America, 19th and 20th Century Native America, Pre-Columbian and 19th Century Mexico and also from West Africa. Temporary exhibi-

tions of regional art include the paintings of Charles Beck, Catherine Mulligan sculptures, Gordon Mortensen woodcuts, George Pfeifer watercolors and John Scott Postovit's pastel drawings. Art by national artists Fritz Scholder, James Rosenquist and Leonard Baskin is exhibited. The gift shop has pottery, jewelry, baskets, blown glass, books, notecards and T-shirts, all by local artists.

ART GALLERY & MUSEUM

The Plains Art Museum

521 Main Avenue, Moorhead, MN. **Phone: 218-236-7383.** Hrs: Tues. - Sat. 10 a.m. - 5 p.m., Thurs. 10 a.m. - 9 p.m., Sun. Noon - 5 p.m. Closed Mondays. Free admission.

The Plains Art Museum's focus is contained in its mission: to foster and promote a knowledge of art by providing facilities for exhibitions, to maintain a repository for art collections which form an artistic legacy of the region and to provide programs to improve education in the arts. It is a regional museum with a national reputation.

The permanent collection of the Museum includes art objects selected on the basis of artistic merit and preserved so that significant information about our heritage and culture may be passed on to present and future generations. The Museum develops special exhibitions and features art from the region, including American Indian Art of the Northern Plains, Contemporary American Art with a regional focus and African Art. Public tours are offered Thursdays at 7 p.m., Saturdays at 11:30 a.m and 2:30 p.m. and Sundays at 2:30 p.m. Children's activities and reception facilities are available and the Museum is fully accessible. For souvenirs of your visit, the Museum Shop offers items from the outrageous to the elegant.

HISTORIC SITE

Comstock House

A Minnesota Historical Society Site. Fifth Ave. S. and Eighth St. S. (Highway 75) 506 Eighth St. S. Moorhead, MN 56560. **Phone: 218-233-0848.** Hrs: May 28-Sept. 30. Sat.-Sun, 1 p.m.-5 p.m. Admission charge.

In 1871, Soloman Comstock arrived in "wild and lawless" Moorhead, a frontier town in western Minnesota. He shaped the development of Moorhead and much of the Red River Valley. For more than 60 years, Comstock served as Clay County attorney and served in the state legislature. In 1888, he was elected to Congress. He also served on the board of regents for the University of Minnesota and became one of the founders of Moorhead State College, built on land he donated. His family was active in education. Daughter Ada became the University of Minnesota's first dean of women and was president of Radcliffe College from 1923 to 1943.

Today, visitors can relive the era of the young immigrant family from Maine at the Comstock home, open to visitors in the summer. Built in 1881 and maintained by the Minnesota Historical Society, the 11-room, two-story woodframe structure is resplendent with Queen Anne and Eastlake designs popular in Victorian architecture, now faithfully renovated to its original appearance.

MUSEUM

Heritage Hjemkomst Interpretive Center	202 First Ave. N., Moorhead, MN 56560 **Phone: 218-233-5604.** Hrs: Mon.-Sat. 9 a.m.-5 p.m.; Thur. 9 a.m.-9 p.m.; Sun. noon-5 p.m. Visa and MasterCard accepted.

It's all here...in photographs, recordings, and an award-winning film chronicling the construction of the Viking ship "Hjemkomst" and its incredible voyage across the Atlantic.

At the Hjemkomst Center, you can see how Robert Asp of Moorhead made his magnificent dream come true. Fulfilling Asp's dream, the ship sailed 6,000 miles from Duluth, Minnesota, to Bergen, Norway, the home of his ancestors.

The ship was modeled after Viking vessels that roamed the seas a thousand years ago. See how the 76-foot ship was hand-built in a small nearby "shipyard" in Hawley and learn about the story of the dedicated crew, including the children of Robert Asp, who carried out his dream.

You can feel the massive ship; touch the water-worn wood. You'll see why it symbolizes the Center's theme, "Dare to Dream."

Heritage Hall has 7,000 square feet devoted to traveling exhibits. Every four months, a new program is offered. Major exhibits from regional, national, and international museums are featured, including those of the Smithsonian Institution.

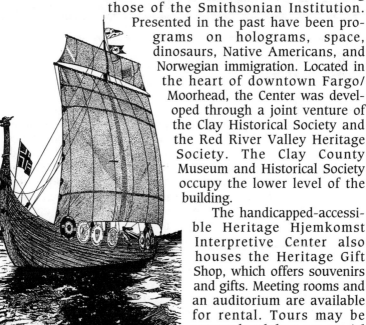

Presented in the past have been programs on holograms, space, dinosaurs, Native Americans, and Norwegian immigration. Located in the heart of downtown Fargo/ Moorhead, the Center was developed through a joint venture of the Clay Historical Society and the Red River Valley Heritage Society. The Clay County Museum and Historical Society occupy the lower level of the building.

The handicapped-accessible Heritage Hjemkomst Interpretive Center also houses the Heritage Gift Shop, which offers souvenirs and gifts. Meeting rooms and an auditorium are available for rental. Tours may be arranged and there are special group rates.

LODGING

Radisson Hotel Fargo

201 5th St. N., Fargo, ND 58102
Phone: 701-232-7363 or 800-333-3333
Hrs: Open year-round.
Major credit cards accepted.

The Radisson Hotel Fargo, located in the heart of downtown, offers 151 well-appointed rooms in a luxurious 18-story high-rise. Each room is decorated and furnished to create a warm, welcoming atmosphere with such amenities as mini refreshment centers, pay per view movies and remote-controlled T.V. Nonsmoking and handicapped accessible rooms are available as well as complimentary parking.

For a romantic adventure, reserve one of four specialty suites including the French or Oriental honeymoon suites with private jacuzzi. The hotel is just 15 minutes from the airport and offers easy access to the Heritage Hjemkomst Center, FARGODOME and three universities.

Passages Cafe offers casual fine dining in a relaxed atmosphere. Fresh seafood, chef specials and sinfully delicious desserts are signature items. Perspectives lounge offers blackjack and pull-tab gaming. So experience for yourself first hand the Radisson style of hospitality and service.

RESTAURANT

The Historic Conservatory Restaurant

613 1st Ave. N., Fargo, ND 58102
Phone: 701-241-7080. Hrs: Dinner,
5 p.m.-9 p.m., Lunch, 11 a.m.-2 p.m.
Major credit cards accepted.

The Historic Conservatory building, which was built in 1910, originally housed the Stone Piano Company and is now listed on the National Register of Historic Places. In late 1991, the building was refurbished and the Conservatory Restaurant was opened there.

This AAA restaurant offers guests the most unique atmosphere in the area, featuring Fargo's premier espresso/cappuccino bar. Its casual elegance captures the attention immediately upon entering. Soaring 25-foot ceilings, antique pilasters, gilded dome, and original woodwork highlight the main dining room.

Of course, the food is excellent—from the Havarti en Croute, Wild Mushroom Ragout and Caesar Salad to the Filet Mignon. This upscale, upbeat restaurant offers new American cuisine—a collection of the finest foods from across the country. Classic steaks in the midwest tradition, light pastas from the West Coast, spicy seafood and shellfish from the East; The Historic Conservatory has something special every day!

RESTAURANT

Tree Top Restaurant & Skol Room Lounge

7th Floor, 403 Center Avenue Moorhead, MN 56560.
Phone: 218-233-1393. Hrs: (Lunch) Mon. - Fri. 11 a.m.-
2 p.m. (Dinner) Mon.-Sat. 5 p.m.-10 p.m. Open Sundays
from Labor Day to Memorial Day 5 p.m.-9 p.m.
Major credit cards accepted.

First class. If that's what you're after in a dining experience, then Tree Top is the place in Fargo-Moorhead. And, that's been the case for more than 40 years since the restaurant opened on the seventh floor of what was then the luxurious Frederick-Martin Hotel.

The hotel took its name from the infant son of one of the original investors, a local group that was determined to bring luxury lodging to the area. Knutson Construction Co. of Minneapolis was hired and construction began in the spring of 1948. Knutson took over the project from the original investors, opening in 1950. It boasted the Tree Top Restaurant, located as today on the west side of the seventh floor, and a grand ballroom called the Top Of The Mart, which occupied the space of the present day Skol Room Lounge and banquet facilities. Originally the first floor of the hotel was occupied by The Barn (restaurant/coffee shop) and the Skol Room (bar).

The hotel has long since closed (it became the Metropolitan Federal Bank Building and an office complex in the 1970s), but the Tree Top Restaurant and Skol Room Lounge continue to flourish. They host the finest view in town, where you can watch the seasons change through the glass walls and nothing can match the magnificent sight of Fargo-Moorhead changing into a galaxy wonderland as the sun disappears below the horizon and the city lights emerge.

From the outstanding prime rib, shrimp fettuccini and homemade soups, to the chef carved turkey buffet and homemade ice creams, this is the best lunch in town. Every Wednesday a different area merchant has a fashion show during the lunch hour.

Executive chef Colleen Kraft uses only the finest of ingredients when creating quality cuisine to match the epicurean excellence of the Tree Top's memorable past. Start with oysters in the half shell, escargot or steak tartar. Dine on your favorite steak or seafood, or the chef's nightly feature. Experience a meal prepared especially for you, at tableside (try Bananas Foster for dessert) and finish by sipping espresso, cappuccino or cognac. Fresh cut flowers, white linens, chandeliers and candlelight only add to the elegant, relaxing atmosphere in the evening as you listen to the grand piano.

Meeting rooms, banquet and party facilities available. Attention to every detail.

NEVIS

The city of Nevis is located between the Mantrap and Crow Wing Chain of Lakes that once formed a natural waterway through the northern wilderness for explorers, hunters and trappers travelling by canoe. Today, modern-day explorers can canoe this same route and revisit the place on the Eighth Crow Wing Lake where a Hudson Bay Company trading post once stood.

The natural beauty of these lakes is preserved by the permanent dams which control their water levels, providing ample opportunities for fishermen to catch eating and trophy-sized walleyes, crappies, northern pike, bluegills and bass.

ATTRACTIONS & EVENTS

Nevis offers four seasons of fun. Pine and hardwood covered hills surrounding the lakes provide beauty for hikers and a variety of upland game for hunters.

The Heartland Trail, along the former Burlington Northern Railroad bed, is a major pathway to the trails of the *Paul Bunyan State Forest.* With a paved center for bikers and gravel sides for those desiring a more rugged surface, the trail provides bikers and hikers in summer, and snowmobilers and skiers in winter, a pleasant scenic route.

Winter in the Nevis area invites snowmobilers, cross-country skiers, and ice-fishermen to enjoy the clean fresh air. Former logging trails and railroad beds provide the longest FREE snowmobile trails in the world.

North Beach and the *Pines Supper Club* on *Potato Lake* feature two tennis courts, an indoor heated pool, and conference facilities, as well as fine dining. *Papoose Bay Lodge,* on the same lake, offers free waterskiing and lakeside jacuzzi and sauna. *Big H Resort* on the *Eighth Crow Wing Lake* has handicapped accessible cabins and sandlot volleyball.

If you have a secret chili recipe or if your friends go wild over your chili, you might want to enter the *State Chili Cook-Off* in early July. July also brings out fishermen for *Nevis Muskie Days* and the *C & C Fishing tournament.*

For further information, contact:
Nevis Chamber of Commerce
Box Fish
Nevis, MN 56467
Phone: 218-652-FISH or 800-332-FISH (3474)

RESORTS

Camp Liberty Resort	On 8th Crow Wing Lake, Rt. 3, Box 469 Nevis, MN 56467. **Phone: 218-652-3533 or 800-472-0506.** Hrs: Open May-September Visa and MasterCard accepted.

Spread along the west shore of the 8th Crow Wing Lake, Camp Liberty Resort is an excellent choice for family vacationers. The beautiful natural setting, clean and comfortable rooms, plus excellent swimming and fishing, combine to make this a great place for families to unwind and relax.

One of eleven lakes on the famed Crow Wing Chain of Lakes, 8th Crow Wing Lake is abundant with northern pike, walleye, bass, crappie and panfish. The lake is more than two miles long and a mile wide and covers 492 acres. Guests can fish the 9th and 10th Crow Wing Lakes, as well, and the canoeing is excellent.

You can choose from a variety of cabins, all fully equipped. Each comes with a 14-foot fishing boat and docking space is available. Guests have free use of canoe, paddleboat and funbugs. There is a play area for the kids, a sandy beach, hiking trails and more. Fishing supplies, groceries and gas are available. Located near Itasca State Park, the Heartland Trail and a variety of other attractions.

◆ ◆ ◆ ◆ ◆ ◆ ◆

Pine Beach Resort	Off Hwy 34, 10 miles east of Park Rapids, 1 mile west of Nevis. R.R. 1, Box 250 Nevis, MN 56467. **Phone: 218-652-3985** No credit cards accepted.

If cycling is your thing, then the Pine Beach Resort is the perfect vacation destination. It's located near the 40-mile Heartland Trail running from Walker to Park Rapids and named the best trail in Minnesota in 1991. Even if you don't cycle, Pine Beach Resort is a great destination for singles, couples and families.

Located on about 40 acres along Lake Belle Taine, a six-mile long lake with 25 miles of irregular shoreline, many islands and excellent fish habitat, the resort is bordered by a state forest extending along the lake. The well-equipped cottages (some with fireplaces) are spaced out over 2,000 feet of sugar-sand lakefront beach.

It's just as easy to find a quiet walk in the woods as it is to pick a spot on the beach to join in all the activities. They include speedboat rides, kids' aerobics, waterskiing, sailing, volleyball, a 250-yard golf driving range, recreation room, canoes, waterbikes, skiboards and playaks. A 14-foot aluminum boat comes with each cabin. And after a day of play, relax and unwind in the sauna.

SPECIALTY SHOPS

Danny's Ice Cream & Antiques	Downtown, Nevis, MN 56467 **Phone: 218-652-3919** Hrs: Mon. - Sat. 10 a.m. - 10 p.m. Sundays 6 p.m. - 10 p.m.

You haven't been in Nevis unless you've been to Danny's for ice cream, antiques, pizza, games and more. Midway between Walker and Park Rapids on Highway 34, Nevis is the gateway to the Paul Bunyan State Forest, on Lake Belle Taine and the Heartland Trail.

There's fun for everyone 12 hours a day, except Sundays. The Fishers reserve that day for church and family fun at home or in the water or on the trails. But Danny's is open from 6 p.m. to 10 p.m. on Sunday evenings, just in case you have an ice cream craving.

Danny's parents built and operated the Gambles Store in downtown Nevis from 1958 to 1981. Danny grew up in the business and spent his summers running the arcade and soda fountain. In 1993, the owners of Someone's Attic and other dealers combined with Danny's, providing a greater variety of antiques, collectibles, furniture and gift items. Danny's is a must-see in Nevis, with good browsing and fun for young and old. Most of all, it's a place to gather for good fellowship and, of course, Bridgeman's ice cream and snacks.

◆ ◆ ◆ ◆ ◆ ◆ ◆

Log Cabin Bait & Tackle & Cafe	Seven miles east of Park Rapids. Highway 34. Park Rapids, MN 56470. **Phone: 218-652-2100.** Hrs: May-August. Bait Shop open Mon.-Sun. 7 a.m.-9 p.m. Cafe open Tues.-Sun. 7 a.m.-3 p.m. Visa and MasterCard accepted.

Tony Dean and Darlene Rasmusson have turned back the clock at the Log Cabin Bait & Tackle & Cafe, offering home cooking, personal service and a great selection of tackle and live bait.

If you've forgotten your minnow bucket, not to worry because they'll provide oxygen bags to keep the minnows healthy. The bait is always fresh. Break a ferrule or crush a guide on your favorite rod? Log Cabin Bait & Tackle has what you need to get you back on the lake in no time. There's plenty of new tackle and a number of bulk items for every angler's needs. Guide service is available as well as the latest fishing reports and information on area lakes and resorts.

The cafe is open for breakfast and lunch, 7 a.m. to 3 p.m., six days a week. The cafe serves breakfast all day. Try the blueberry pancakes or the biscuits and gravy. A gift shop is located in the bait shop, with an emphasis on Native American crafts. The shop has a North Country flair with items reflecting the area and the log building is a unique setting.

NEW YORK MILLS

Founded in 1884, New York Mills got its name from the lumber barons who first settled here in the 1870's, hoping to take advantage of the vast stretches of valuable trees that typified the as yet unpopulated region. With that start, New York Mills grew into a thriving community based largely on agriculture. Other important and productive businesses developed as well—businesses like the Lund Boat Company, which was founded locally in 1950.

Today, New York Mills remains strong, benefiting from quality medical and educational facilities, an active business community and a warm, friendly populous. Such a climate has drawn many to New York Mills in the past, and—as the city of 1,000 continues to expand—many more look to this small, central-Minnesota community for the same benefits.

ATTRACTIONS & EVENTS

Located in the heart of Minnesota lake country, New York Mills offers year-round entertainment for those with a love of the outdoors. Fishing, boating, vacationing, snowmobiling and more are enjoyed by both visitors and residents alike.

Indoors, however, New York Mills offers just as much. *The New York Mills Regional Cultural Center,* in bringing the arts to rural Minnesota, has garnered national headlines with such annual events as *The Great Midwestern Think-Off* and the *Continental Divide Music and Film Festival.* The Center also features continuous exhibits throughout the year.

In celebration of the local Finnish heritage, *The Finn Creek Open Air Museum* offers a realistic look at the life of the immigrant farmers who came here in the late 1800's. With these attractions and other annual celebrations, there is always something going on in the city of New York Mills.

Stop and see the *Continental Divide Monument* and other local points of interest.

For further information, contact:
New York Mills Civic & Commerce
P.O. Box 158
New York Mills, MN 56567
Phone: 218-385-2275

OSAKIS

The Lake Osakis area was home to the Dakota Indians who named the Lake, O-Za-Tee which means fork in the road or river. The Ojibwa called the Lake Oh-za-kees, meaning "place of the Sauk" after the Sauk Indians who roamed the area for a short while.

Lake Osakis is also called the *Mother Walleye Lake* because it is the source of walleye eggs for a five-county stocking program by the DNR. This is why Lake Osakis rates among the top ten fishing lakes in Minnesota.

Besides fishing, the *Osakis Festival* is held every June. It's a ten-day extravaganza: carnivals, bingo games, beauty pageants, float plane rides, contests, music, dancing and much more awaits visitors.

For more information contact:
Lake Osakis Resort Association
Dept. Q
Osakis, MN 56360
Phone: 612-859-4794 or 800-422-0785 ext. 17

RESORT

Idlewilde Resort And Lodge

811 Lake Street, P.O. Box 299, Osakis, MN 56360. **Phone: 612-859-2135 or 800-648-1713**
Hrs: Open year-round.
Major credit cards accepted.

Best known for sunfish and crappie fishing, Lake Osakis boasts an excellent population of walleye, northern and bass, as well. But Lake Osakis is not just a fisherman's paradise, it offers a variety of water sport activities, too.

Idlewilde Resort provides the perfect resort on which to enjoy those activities anytime of the year. Ten cabins with two to four bedrooms are available as well as five housekeeping units and motel units in the lodge. A store, laundry facilities, and sporting equipment provide for visitors' vacation needs.

An indoor pool and sauna provide a haven in the event of temperamental weather. A sand volleyball court offers a great opportunity for a friendly game with the neighbors. Or shop, dine and golf in nearby Alexandria.

Relax in the family atmosphere of Idlewilde Resort. Watch the golden sunset across Lake Osakis. Fish the clear blue water. You're on vacation!

BED & BREAKFAST

Just Like Grandma's

113 W. Main, Osakis, MN 56360. **Phone: 612-859-4504.** Hrs.: (Memorial Day - Labor Day) 10 a.m. - 5 p.m. Weekends in Sept.
Visa, MasterCard, Discover and AmEx accepted.

Just Like Grandma's offers as many things to do as a real trip to Grandma's. The house was originally built in 1903 and had been privately owned until 1984. Never having any intention of buying a house in Osakis, Carol Mihalchick took a look at the home with a friend and two weeks later she and her husband Steve were property owners in Osakis.

With a great deal of help, Carol and Steve worked frantically to open Memorial Day weekend 1985. Just Like Grandma's is currently a bed and breakfast, tea room and gift shop. The abundance of antiques and gifts led to the expansion of Osakis Antiques on Main Street. In 1989 the School House, Summer Kitchen and Tea Room were incorporated into the business. 1991 saw expansion into the Annex across the street, specializing in seasonal gift items.

Just like Grandma's also sponsors a 5K Race toward the end of June and Grammafest, which is a two-day summer celebration in mid-August.

A gazebo for outdoor meals from the Summer Kitchen is also available. The barn area offers more gifts and an ice cream counter to enjoy sweet treats.

In mid-October the Twelve Days of Christmas Boutique invites patrons to get a jump on the holiday season by offering unique gift items. Just Like Grandma's provides a variety of activities with a cozy atmosphere.

OTTERTAIL

Ottertail is a wonderful blend of scenic beauty, historical attractions and recreational facilities making it an exciting vacationland for the entire family. Over 1,000 lakes mean year-round fun for visitors to Ottertail. The entire family can fish, swim, play or just relax in a beautiful, quiet and peaceful place and still be close enough to one of the areas' towns to enjoy a day of unhurried shopping and touring.

Golfers have a choice of playing any of the area golf courses including three, 18-hole courses and two 9-hole courses, all featuring lush greens and fairways.

Other recreation opportunities include many campgrounds, fine dining establishments, and a variety of specialty shops.

At the annual *Art of the Lakes Festival* at *Phelps Mill,* many local fine artisans display their work.

For further information, contact:
Otter Tail County Tourism Association
Box 1000, Ottertail, MN 56571

RESORT

Hook-Line & Suchers	Six and a half miles south of Perham on Highway 78. Perham, MN 56571 **Phone: 218-346-6007** No credit cards accepted.

Located six and a half miles south of Perham on Rush Lake, Hook-Line & Suchers gets its unusual name from owner Tim Sucher who offers both cabins and camping at this family resort.

There are nine cabins, one-, two- or three-bedrooms each, complete with showers, hide-a-bed, carpet, color cable TV, complete bedding and a 14-foot deep bottom Lund boat with a boat lift, all included. Motors, paddle boats and pontoon boats are also available plus a store for your convenience and a game room with pool table and video games. You'll need your own towels.

For camping, there are 32 concrete sites for trailers, with complete hookups, cable TV and telephone. A central showerhouse is available plus fire pits and grills throughout the property. There are also volleyball, basketball and tent sites, too. The safe, sandy beach is great for swimming and Rush Lake has great fishing with an abundance of sunken islands.

RESORT

Shady Grove Resort	Route 1, Box 436, Ottertail, MN 56571 **Phone: 800-356-7644** Hrs.: Open from May through September Visa, MasterCard and Discover accepted.

Shady Grove Resort works on the philosophy that this is "your vacation," not "our resort." It's an important difference, a difference that means they have a customer-friendly approach designed to make you feel welcome.

Located on 5,400-acre Rush Lake, Shady Grove is one of Ottertail County's largest resorts. It features 16 modern cabins and three new luxury condominiums providing a good mix of accommodations and price ranges. Full-hookup RV sites are spacious and well-shaded. The mini convenience store is always well-stocked and includes an ice cream shop, live bait, tackle and licenses.

The family atmosphere offers something for everyone, with 18-hole miniature golf, cable TV, guide service, heated pool and a 24-foot pontoon. Rush Lake holds all Minnesota game fish and is regarded as a premier fishing lake. You can dock your own boat or use one of the new Deep-V Lund boats.

RESTAURANT

The Pier	Hwy. 78, P.O. Box 128, Ottertail, MN 56571 **Phone: 218-367-2260. Fax: 218-367-2306** Hrs: (May-Aug.) 7 days a week. (Sept.-April) Thurs. - Sun. dinner 5 p.m.-10 p.m., Sun. brunch 10 a.m.-2 p.m. Major credit cards accepted.

The Pier is one of those classic restaurants that everyone will enjoy. Its combination of casual elegance, superb food and a panoramic view of beautiful Otter Tail Lake make it a "must stop" for anyone passing through. The restaurant features a three-level deck, beach bar, live entertainment and dancing, and those spectacular northwoods enthusiasts!

Water access is made easy with a floating dock system on the lake. Of course, the food is wonderful at the Pier. From four to six different fresh fish are offered nightly, along with succulent prime rib, beef Wellington or any one of the other 50 entrées!

The Pier boasts one of the finest Sunday brunches in Minnesota with beautiful desserts, omelets made to order, fresh baked breads, seasonal fruits, carved beef, all with a fantastic view.

PARK RAPIDS

Few other towns in Minnesota have a longer history of catering to travelers than Park Rapids, a community of 3,000 surrounded by 400 lakes and more than 200 resorts. Early in the 20th century, vacationers arrived by train at the Park Rapids station where they were met by resort owners with teams and wagons. Other tourists rented launches to venture up the rivers to camps located on one of the numerous lakes. The Park Rapids area has had ample opportunity to develop fascinating attractions and events for visitors while at the same time maintaining its small-town atmosphere.

ATTRACTIONS & EVENTS

Summerhill Farm features the work of artisans and crafts people from all across the country. *Silver Star City* is a wild west family entertainment theme park. *The Aqua Park* is a wildlife museum, aquarium and park with wild animals. There are three 18-hole courses and two 9-hole courses, all open to the public. *The Heartland Bike Trail* begins in Park Rapids and extends 27 miles to Walker. It's a beautiful ride through the lake country. It's also wonderful for hiking and horseback riding and, in the winter, snowmobiling and cross-country skiing can be a special experience along this trail. The *World of Christmas* is year-round outdoor fun with bumper boats, train rides, batting cages and more! Then there's *Smokey Hills Artisan Community,* a village of crafters like glassblowers, jewelry makers and pottery makers.

A visit to the area wouldn't be complete without a stop at *Itasca State Park* just north of Park Rapids. Everyone should be able to say they walked across the mighty Mississippi at its source! It's a lovely park to explore with 32,000 acres of natural beauty.

The Headwaters Hundred Bike Ride is held in September each year. There are three major *Arts & Craft Shows* throughout the year. The *Park Rapids Rodeo* is followed by the annual *Taste of Dorset*—a fun-filled day hosted by the tiny village of Dorset east of Park Rapids, where visitors can sample the local cooking.

For further information, contact:
Park Rapids Chamber of Commerce
P.O. Box 249 G
Park Rapids, MN 56470
Phone: 218-732-4111 or 800-247-0054

ANTIQUES

House Of Jensen

Hwy 71 North, 16 miles north of Park Rapids
H.C.O. 5 Box 117. Park Rapids, MN 56470
Phone: 218-732-7333
Hrs: Seasonal.

Stepping inside the House of Jensen is like stepping straight into another time. Even the name is from the old world of Denmark.

Betty Lou and Dr. Warren Jensen's slogan, "We're in the Pink," will make perfect sense once you're inside this unique emporium, where Victorian pink and grey trim stands in sharp contrast to the nearby north woods of Itasca State Park. The mood is set by soothing music and good coffee and the place is done in Americana.

"My mother taught me to always serve coffee to my guests," Betty Lou says. And they do treat their customers like guests.

Betty Lou's been collecting and dealing in antiques for a quarter century. Her specialty is "The Basket," each filled with a place setting for two of china, crystal, linen and flatware, all in a wonderful mix and match in color, design and period. The House of Jensen features art glass, furniture, period clothing and toys, and primitives. Take time in the present to get in touch with the past at the House of Jensen.

◆ ◆ ◆ ◆ ◆ ◆ ◆

Rich's Antiques

409 S. Park Avenue, Park Rapids, MN 56470
Phone: 218-732-3949. Hrs: Mon.-Sat. 9 a.m.-5 p.m., Sun. 10 a.m.-4 p.m.
No credit cards accepted.

From the rather humble beginnings of a 1985 garage sale, Rich's Antiques has blossomed into a wonderful collection of furniture, glassware and collectibles. And it's been go-go ever since. "But this is no museum," owner Rich Anderson is quick to remind. "This stuff's for sale. You snooze, you lose!"

Located in an older home with a big addition and painted a vivid blue, you can't miss Rich's Antiques on Highway 71 in Park Rapids, four blocks south of Highway 34. This is the third—and best—location Rich and Linda Anderson have had since they began. Customers come from all over the country and they're not only attracted by antiques and the Andersons' excellent reputation. Most items are acquired from estate sales and they buy everything so there is substantial appeal for everyone, not just antique collectors. Name it, they've likely got it.

From furniture to old cupboards to books, Rich's has it all. Plus they're open seven days a week year-round and they deliver!

BED & BREAKFAST

Carolyn's Bed and Breakfast

7 miles north of Park Rapids off Hwy. 71
HC 05 Box 350 AC
Park Rapids, MN 56470
Phone: 218-732-1101

Carolyn's Bed and Breakfast is one of the more unique of the B&B genre. It's located about seven miles north of Park Rapids at the end of a private road on a private lake. In fact, it may be the perfect getaway. While thousands of vacationers enjoy the area's summer activities, Carolyn's is open year-round and offers a quiet, secluded hideaway.

Their guest rooms welcome visitors with dried flowers, comfortable furniture and a cozy atmosphere. A honeymoon suite is perched atop the lodge and provides a spectacular view of the lake and surrounding deep woods. This suite is complete with canopy bed, fireplace and deck.

Families with children will enjoy the warmth of Carolyn's kitchen, where she prepares breakfast for the guests. A wine cellar adds to the ambiance and a large, lakeside deck provides a grill and seating for outdoor meals. The large kitchen table is perfect for family-style dinners and, later, a family game or two.

Breakfasts at Carolyn's are wonderful and hot, served where and when you want them. Coffee and conversation abound in the kitchen where Carolyn may be baking a birthday cake for a special guest.

Golf, fishing, hunting, biking, cross-country skiing and a variety of restaurants and supper clubs are near. If you're in the area, stop in. Carolyn's offers the ideal retreat for those who want the experience of northwoods solitude and beauty.

BED & BREAKFAST

LadySlipper Inn

Rt. 2, Box 75, Osage, MN 56570
Phone: 218-573-3353 or 800-531-2787
Hrs: Open year-round.
Visa and MasterCard accepted.

As Minnesota's State Flower, the Showy Lady Slipper symbolizes the best of Minnesota's natural environment. And, like the flower, the LadySlipper Inn is well loved for its uniqueness and rare beauty in a natural setting.

Here, you'll find twin spring-fed ponds for swimming, fishing and canoeing. Horseback riding is available in the nearby Smokey Hills Forest, or bike on country roads and forest trails.

In winter, you can be as active as you wish. Snowshoe the woodland trails, ride a horse-drawn sleigh, or cross-country ski through the pristine wilderness of Tamarac National Wildlife Refuge. Many miles of groomed snowmobile trails are a short distance away.

From the ponds, Straight Lake Creek flows through a cedar bog where the Lady Slipper in all its glory may be found. With this wondrous beauty as a backdrop, the LadySlipper Inn provides a perfect setting for a romantic getaway, be it honeymoon or anniversary. Or maybe you just need a restful escape from the stress of everyday life. No matter, this is the place.

There are five rooms offered, each with its own double whirlpool tub, private bath, deck and private entrance. Four of the rooms also have a wet bar and fireplace.

After exploring the natural scene, you'll enjoy a quiet soak in the tub. Then watch classic movies on the in-room VCR and T.V. A full breakfast is served in the dining room, sunroom or request breakfast in your room! Whatever cares you have before you come to the LadySlipper Inn will quickly disappear amid the scenic beauty of this modern B&B.

BOOKSTORE

Sister Wolf Books

Route 3, Box 29, Dorset, MN 56470
Phone: 218-732-7565
Hrs: 11 a.m.-9 p.m. Mid-May-mid Oct.
Visa and MasterCard accepted.

Sister Wolf Books is a unique bookstore with a name that reflects a northern ambiance and our human kinship to animals and nature. Their slogan? "When it comes to books, we're ahead of the pack."

Located on the Heartland Trail, Sister Wolf Books provides a relaxed, accessible atmosphere combined with a commitment to solve customer needs. A diverse selection of books and publications for

adults and children includes fiction, non-fiction, nature guides and regional books.

Here, you'll find a diversity of perspectives along with historical, natural and recreational material focusing on the region.

They also carry a selection of greeting cards, books on tape, games, puzzles and crafts.

RESTAURANT

The Red Lantern

600 N. Park, Park Rapids, MN 56470. **Phone: 218-732-9377.** Hrs: (Summer) Daily 11 a.m.-10 p.m. (Winter) Sun. 11 a.m.-8 p.m., Tues.-Thurs. 11 a.m.-9 p.m., Fri.-Sat. 11 a.m.-10 p.m. Major credit cards accepted.

Located on the outskirts of Park Rapids is The Red Lantern offering a large variety of food and drink. Everything from Mexican and Chinese to down-home hearty cooking is offered. They even have a tantalizing array of low-fat, low-sodium and low-cholesterol dishes like teriyaki chicken breast and broiled walleye.

Favorites include prime rib, slow-cooked pork ribs, New Zealand lobster, and chimichangas deep fried and stuffed with roast beef, cheese and taco sauce. At The Red Lantern, steaks are hand-cut and beef is ground on the premises. Their daily specials will satisfy even the most discriminating palate. You can always count on great drink specialties to cap your meal.

Along with the great food, guests enjoy the stained-glass lights and the rustic decor. Intimate booths allow for quiet conversation, while tables are widely scattered and not too close. With both good food and interesting atmosphere, The Red Lantern is able to offer a quality dining experience at a reasonable price.

LODGING

Spirit Lake Motel, Gift Shop & Cafe	Hwy. 71 South (11 miles south of Park Rapids) Menahga, MN 56464. **Phone: 218-564-4151** Visa, MasterCard, AmEx and Discover accepted.

Specializing in that personal touch, Dave and Dorothy Haataja's Spirit Lake Motel & Gift Shop in Menahga is the epitome of old-fashioned small-town hospitality.

The area first attracted settlers because of the logging industry. Today, visitors come primarily for recreation. Open year-round, the Spirit Lake Motel & Gift Shop is located right on a sugar sand beach with swimming and lifeguard. Of course, the fishing is great or, if you're a little more adventurous, try windsurfing.

The motel has 10 units plus two housekeeping units, your choice of smoking and non-smoking rooms, each with direct dial phones, color cable television, individual heating and air conditioning controls. The gift shop specializes in American/Finnish articles, with Iitalla crystal, Aarikka jewelry and fine hunting knives from Finland.

It's located near terrific cross-country skiing and groomed snowmobile trails plus golf, tennis and a variety of tourist attractions. Canoe trips and horseback trails are available through local outfitters.

RESORT

Bambi Resort On Toad Lake	Off Hwy. 34 between Detroit Lakes & Park Rapids. Rt. 1, Box 342 Osage, MN 56570 **Phone: 218-573-3416**

Looking for world class walleye fishing at a family resort? Look no further than Bambi Resort on Toad Lake. Toad Lake is ranked as one of the top 100 walleye lakes in Minnesota. Department of Natural Resources surveys show 4-5 times the state average in size and quantity of walleye, northern pike and bluegill. Walleye fishing in the fall is especially good.

When fishing is over, check out Bambi Resort's complement of activities for everyone: campfires, supervised children's activities, weekly fishing contest, bingo, volleyball, basketball, horseshoes, playground equipment, pontoon and, in the lodge, the latest video games and pinball machines. Want more? Try the safe, sandy beach. There's no charge for canoe, playak or paddle boat usage. Or visit one of the many local attractions like Itasca State Park where the mighty Mississippi begins its journey to the Gulf of Mexico.

To have a great time, bring family, bring friends, but don't bring Fido because no pets are allowed at Bambi Resort.

RESORTS

The Timberlane Lodge

RR. 3, Park Rapids, MN 56470
Phone: 218-732-8489
Hrs: Open year-round.
Visa and MasterCard accepted.

Four miles east of Park Rapids on Long Lake is The Timberlane Lodge. It's a northwoods paradise that's easy to get to, but hard to leave.

Built in 1948, The Timberlane Lodge boasts knotty pine interiors throughout. Grand fireplaces of stone grace the lounges and cabanas. Cabanas sleep up to ten. Both cottages and cabanas have full housekeeping and come with microwaves, coffee makers, pullman or full kitchens, carpeting and full baths.

Guests have complete access to lodge facilities, including an enclosed three-season pool, sauna, whirlpool, outdoor ice-skating rink, cross-country skiing, walking trails and snowmobiling trails.

Fishermen will enjoy Long Lake because it is one of the top walleye producing lakes. There's ample beach frontage for all activities and a special children's program will keep the kids busy.

The lodge offers fine dining and, in summer, outside dining overlooking the lake is especially popular.

◆ ◆ ◆ ◆ ◆ ◆ ◆

Vacationaire

Island Lake Drive, HC05, Box 181, Park Rapids, MN 56470. **Phone: 218-732-5270**
Hrs: Open year-round.
Major credit cards accepted.

Vacationaire combines the beauty of the northwoods with all the amenities of a Minnesota resort. Your hosts are May and Jim Grewe, both dedicated to making your stay memorable.

Located on Island Lake, Vacationaire offers so many activities it may be difficult to decide just what to do! Spring and summer provides the conditions for excellent fishing, waterskiing, horse shoes, tennis or shuffleboard. Fall and winter options include hunting, snowmobiling, cross-country skiing, ice fishing, indoor swimming or sauna.

A variety of accommodations are offered from lodge rooms and suites to cabins and condominiums. Knotty-pine cabins come with a fireplace and kitchen.

If you don't feel like cooking, their full-service restaurant offers breakfast, lunch and dinner meals every day. House specialties include prime rib and barbecued ribs plus there is a cocktail lounge in the lodge.

RESORTS

Brookside Resort

On Two Inlets Lake, H.C. 05, Box 240,
Park Rapids, MN 56470
Phone: 218-732-4093 or 800-247-1615
Visa and MasterCard accepted.

To be enjoyable, a family resort must offer activities and services for all ages. At Brookside Resort, the activities include free waterskiing, bingo, miniature golf and sand sculpture contests. Teens and adults will enjoy golf and tennis tournaments, softball and volleyball. Children's activities include field games, hayride, pool party and a supervised child care program (ages 2 to 8) each morning.

Included in the cabin rates is a 14-foot aluminum fishing boat as well as free use of beach front equipment, canoes, kayaks, paddleboats, fun bugs and life jackets. The facilities include a snack bar and game room in the lodge, laundry, tennis courts, par-three golf course and an indoor-outdoor swimming pool with sunning deck. The sandy beach, low elevation and tall pines add to the charm of the Northwoods.

This unique family place, named by *Family Circle Magazine* as one of America's best five cabin resorts, gets rave reviews and is included in Jordan & Cohen's "Great Vacations With Your Kids."

◆ ◆ ◆ ◆ ◆ ◆ ◆

Jolly Fisherman Resort

18 miles west of Itasca State Park, Highway 113,
Waubun, MN 56589. **Phone: 218-734-2262 or 800-927-2262.** Hrs: Open May 15 - Oct. 30.
Visa and MasterCard accepted.

Secluded comfort in a northwoods style. That's what the Jolly Fisherman Resort offers on Big Elbow Lake. The lake is one of Minnesota's top 100 for walleye with 13 miles of shoreline and minimal development. There are many quiet fishing spots and an abundance of wildlife. The resort itself is a great place for families, where you can fish for sunfish and crappies right from the dock. The lakeside cabins, most with knotty-pine interiors, come fully equipped except towels. A 14-foot fishing boat, canoe and paddleboats are included. There are a sandy swimming beach, a children's program and free loon wake-up calls!

The smoke-free lodge is a gathering place with an extensive library, board games, puzzles, pool table and video games. They stock basic groceries and bottled water plus beer, sandwiches, pizza and soda fountain treats. There's a playground and sports equipment for the kids and a Finnish sauna and spa for adults. Ask about their special "Lovers Only" and "Honeymoon/Anniversary" packages.

RESORTS

Little Norway Resort

Hwy. 71 N., 16 miles north of Park Rapids
HC 05, Box 145
Park Rapids, MN 56470
Phone: 218-732-5480

Nestled on the north shore of Little Mantrap Lake on a quiet peninsula is a gem—Little Norway Resort. From the moment you arrive, the crystal clear waters, the call of the loon, the restful sunsets captivate both mind and spirit.

Little Norway Resort is a full-service family resort offering the classic Minnesota family vacation. All cabins are paneled in pine, have hardwood floors and a deck facing the lake. Each cabin has a Weber grill for your convenience. These ultra-modern housekeeping units are fully equipped for your family's restful stay.

A well-equipped playground with swings, slides, climbers and a large sandbox keeps the tots busy. In addition, scheduled activities are offered throughout the week.

Fishing? Excellent, for you and the eagles who soar overhead! After all, Little Mantrap is one of Minnesota's most pristine lakes. If you want vacationing at its Minnesota best, bring your family to Little Norway Resort. You'll be back year after year!

◆ ◆ ◆ ◆ ◆ ◆ ◆

New Frontier Resort

County Rd. 6, 3 miles SE of Park Rapids, Route 4. Park Rapids, MN 56470. **Phone: 218-732-3643 or 800-932-3643.** Open May through October. Visa and MasterCard accepted.

Quaint. Quiet. Quality. Those three words best describe the New Frontier Resort on the west shore of Long Lake, where every cabin is like a secluded hideaway and 24 acres of mature Norway pine and birch forest surround you.

Cabins come with virtually everything you could ask for, including a barbecue grill and microwave oven. A variety of accommodations is available including the "Chateau," a spectacular cottage retreat that can comfortably sleep a family of eight.

A 14-foot fishing boat is included with most cabins or dock space for your own boat. Kayaks, paddleboats, canoes, a sauna, whirlpool, waterskiing and a wonderful sand beach are among the amenities that come as part of the package. Sailboats and windsurfers are available.

And Long Lake features exceptional fishing. According to the Department of Natural Resources, it yields two to five times the state average so you'll go home with more than just fish stories.

RESORT

**Northern
Pine Lodge**

On Northern Pine Road, Hwy 71 North
H.C.R. 06, Box 129
Park Rapids, MN 56470
Phone: 218-732-5103

Chances are if you let the kids choose a vacation spot this year, they'd probably pick a place like Northern Pine Lodge on Potato Lake.

That's because it's a mecca of children's activities. From arts and crafts and outdoor games to sand castle building and nature hikes, both parents and children alike rave about the kid's activities at Northern Pine Lodge. Children meet at the lodge most days for scheduled, supervised fun.

But there's plenty for big kids here, too.

From clay court tennis to terrific fishing on Potato Lake, from waterskiing, canoeing and sailing to hiking the surrounding trails, the choice is yours. Each lakeshore cottage is completely furnished with full kitchen facilities. Bedrooms have one double and one single bed. And all linen (towels excepted) is supplied. A few log cabins with stone fireplaces are particularly beautiful. But the best part just might be the log sauna, the perfect end to a great day.

SPECIALTY SHOP

**The 3rd Street
Market**

120 W. Third Street, Park Rapids, MN 56470
Phone: 218-732-9063. Hrs: Mon.-Fri. 9 a.m.-5
p.m. Saturdays 9 a.m.-3 p.m.
No credit cards accepted.

The 3rd Street Market is a unique blend of shopping and dining. Specializing in natural, gourmet and specialty foods, things like natural and organic cereals, flours, herbs, spices, pasta, nuts, dried fruit and beans, they have a good selection of coffee beans and teas available, either pre-packaged or in bulk. They also supply basic foods, snacks, cheeses and milk replacements for people needing staples that are lactose-free, sugar-free, salt-free or glucose-free.

The luncheon area seats 34 in a homey, smoke-free setting. Homemade soups and made-to-order sandwiches are served at your table from 11 a.m. to 3 p.m. daily with coffee, herbal teas, espresso and natural colas plus muffins, bars, cookies and pies. Takeout is also available. The pies are decadent from the real whipped cream through layers of fillings and fruit to a rich, nutty crust!

The floral table covers and fresh flowers lend a European charm. The smell of fresh baking in the air makes the 3rd Street Market an inviting place for lunch, shopping or meeting friends.

SPECIALTY SHOP

Summerhill Farm

Highway 71 N., Park Rapids, MN 56470
Phone: 218-732-3865
Hrs: (mid-May - mid-Sept.) Mon. - Sat. 10 a.m. - 6 p.m.,
Sun. 12 noon - 4 p.m.
Visa and MasterCard accepted.

Located just seven miles north of Park Rapids and on the way to Itasca State Park, the Summerhill Farm shops are built into the hillside overlooking Summerhill Pond. The farm was built in 1937 and the original exteriors are painted in slate blue with white trim and railings to exhibit a warm country charm. The brick walkways are bordered with beautiful flower beds and baskets, adding to the area's enchantment. Each of the five gift shops provides a unique display of the finest gifts and decorative accessories from around the country.

"The Stable" features pottery by Mary Melancon and calligraphy by Mary Mittlestadt, both Minnesota artists. Children will be delighted with "The Carriage House" displaying toys and miniatures, Minnesota jams and jellies, and candy. Women's apparel, jewelry, afghans, decorator pillows, books, and many other unique handcrafted American gifts can be found at "The Cottage."

Visitors looking for a perfect gift in "The Second Story" will find a nice selection of quality designer T-shirts to choose from. The "Sun Porch Restaurant" offers a restful setting in which to savor a light lunch or homemade dessert. Specializing in strawberry-rhubarb pie and wild rice soup, other popular menu items include "The Sun Porch," a light lunch including soup, french bread, cheese, and fresh fruit; or enjoy "The Summerhill Sub," served on a french roll with a cup of homemade soup.

Summerhill Farm is highly recommended by area resorts for its incredible selection of quality and unique gifts. The beautiful surroundings and pleasant staff make for enjoyable browsing and a memorable shopping experience.

SPECIALTY SHOPS

*Monika's Art &
Craft Supplies*

210 South Main Street, Park Rapids, MN 56470
Phone: 218-732-3896. Hrs: (Summer) Mon.-Fri. 9 a.m.-
6 p.m., Sat. 10 a.m.-5 p.m., Sun. 11 a.m.-3 p.m.
(Winter) Mon.-Fri. 9 a.m.-5:30 p.m., Sat. 10 a.m.-
5 p.m., Sun. Closed

Monika Wilkins' store was truly born as a labor of love in 1984. Starting as a hobby, it has become one of the largest, most diverse art and craft supply stores in northern Minnesota. Located in Park Rapids, the heart of resort country, Monika's Art & Craft Supplies store offers some quite interesting shopping for the arts and crafts enthusiast. Monika's is well known for its custom framing with a large selection of mats and frame mouldings. The store also offers wedding accessories, hobby supplies and even antiques! A few years ago, Monika added a gift shop and gallery to the store, offering many unusual and wonderful gift and home decor items. In the future, Monika plans to add more items and more space, including a craft studio for teaching classes to meet the increasing demand for arts and crafts.

So, if you're more interested in the finer arts than you are in hot fishing tips, give Monika's Art and Craft Supplies a try. You may come home from vacation with some trophies of a different kind!

◆ ◆ ◆ ◆ ◆ ◆

*Sarah's Country
House*

Seven blocks south of Hwy. 71 and 34 stoplight. 708
South Park Avenue, Park Rapids, MN 56470.
Phone: 218-732-4740. Hrs: Mon. - Sat. 10 a.m. - 5
p.m., Sundays 11 a.m. - 4 p.m.
Visa, MasterCard and Discover accepted.

Looking for that perfect addition to your home? Perhaps a special gift you'd be proud to give anyone? Then Sarah's Country House in Park Rapids is the place. Located seven blocks south of the Highway 71 and 34 stoplight, Sarah's is a beautiful country store filled with gifts and collections you'd love to have or give.

This charming two-story, white stucco house, complete with red shutters and window boxes, is beautifully decorated. It has a living room, dining room, kitchen and doll room, all filled with wonderful treasures. There's also a Christmas room and a den you'll want to browse through. Soft piano music, combined with the scent of pot pourri, creates a place that's unique and a pleasure to shop.

From baskets to lamps, wood ducks and solid wood furniture to cards and signs, the choices are endless. There are country lace curtains, rugs, dishes and more. Sarah's offers free gift wrapping, a bridal registry and gift certificates. Ask about special orders. Closed from Christmas to April 1.

SPECIALTY SHOPS & GIFTS

The Smoky Hills Artisan Community	1.5 miles West of Osage on Hwy. 34. Between Park Rapids and Detroit Lakes. R.R. 1, Box 625. Osage, MN 56570. **Phone: 218-573-3300.** Open Memorial Day-Labor Day, Seven days a week, 10 a.m.-5:30 p.m. September and October weekends, 10 a.m. -5:30 p.m.

A day of adventure. That's how the folks at Smoky Hills Artisan Community like to describe a visit to their unusual and intriguing collection of art and artisans.

Set among the 67 acres of cool towering trees in the Smoky Hills State Forest, located in Minnesota's Heartland, the Smoky Hills Artisan Community is a beautiful complex of 18 buildings, all laid out in a circular fashion. It's home to artists and craftsmen making and displaying their wares. It's live entertainment. And a huge playground to test every last one of your senses.

Among the things you'll see are Native American and Early American crafts, porcelain, jewelry, clothing, furniture and wooden treasures, dried flowers and potpourri, interlocking wood art, ironwork, gallery art, an entire consignment shop plus Anderson's Fabrics. In addition, you'll find pottery, painting, glassblowing, beadwork, candledipping and weaving. There's also metalworking, doll making, tie-dying, woodburning, olde-tyme photos, jewelry making, tole painting, caricatures and willow furniture making.

As if that's not enough, the Smoky Hills are also a nature-lover's paradise.

That's because they're located in the biological center of North America. Here the Great Plains meet the Northern Coniferous (pine) Forests and the Eastern Deciduous (hardwood) Forests. The hills touch prairie, lakes and bogs. This unique biodiversity creates the environment for more species of living things than anywhere within North America. And if you're up for it, you can trek through it all on nature trails designed with the adventurous in mind.

Visitors can eat in the full-service restaurant with their famous wild rice soup ready and waiting. There's seating for more than a hundred. Try the homemade pie, too. Or satisfy your sweet tooth at the ice cream soda parlor or the candy store. There's also a horse trolley ride, sled dog demonstrations, a black powder shoot, the lookout tower and more.

It's all located between Park Rapids and Detroit Lakes on Highway 34 in the Smoky Hills.

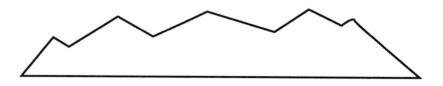

PARK

Itasca State Park

28 miles north of Park Rapids on Hwy 71
Lake Itasca, MN 56460
Phone: 612-296-6157 or 800-652-9747

More than 2,500 miles of river stand between Itasca State Park and the Gulf of Mexico, for the mighty Mississippi—Father of Waters—begins its long journey here, amidst 250-year-old forests of red pine and white wine. As the source of the river, Itasca State Park is one of the most famous state parks in the nation. Here, a little brook emerges from Lake Itasca, so small and so shallow that visitors can wade across it. More that a million visitors come to Itasca each year just to see the humble beginnings of that legendary river, to experience the remnant of soaring forests that once covered northern Minnesota, and to experience the many outdoor activities and attractions to be found here.

The many activities for visitors include 33 miles of hiking trails set amid the splendid northwoods scenery. There is a seven-mile bike trail, scenic ten-mile wilderness drive, an historic log lodge and an excursion boat trip that follows the route explorer Henry Rowe Schoolcraft took across Lake Itasca when he "discovered" the Mississippi headwaters. (Actually, Schoolcraft's Ojibwa guide knew that Lake Itasca was the river's source and led the explorer there.)

Within the park's 50 square miles, visitors will see an abundance of Minnesota flora and fauna, including the endangered trumpeter swan, bald eagles, deer, 27 different species of orchids and rare carnivorous peatland plants. Also, there are two prehistoric sites: the Nicollet Creek area where 8,000-year-old Indian artifacts have been found preserved in lake sediment; and Itasca Indian Mounds that are 500 to 900 year-old burial mounds. Itasca's natural and geographical history spans millions of years.

As you discover the Mississippi's headwaters, it is easy to reflect upon a rich and colorful history of this land. Imagine, for example, the flashing paddles of Ojibwa birch bark canoes. Listen to the rollicking songs of the voyageurs. Then envision the wilderness exploits of the lumberjacks. At Itasca, you can camp, hike and canoe in the footsteps of Indians, fur traders and explorers. You can also climb a fire tower or enjoy a meal of walleye.

Itasca State Park is quite large and offers so much to see that it is a good idea to stop first at the Forest Inn Visitor Center located in the South Itasca Center to get information. During the summer, a park naturalist is on hand to answer questions seven days a week. Interpretive programs are conducted all year, with additional outings offered during the summer months.

The park also has a variety of lodging from rustic to plain-but-modern. Call ahead for reservations.

PERHAM

Perham is located in the heart of the lakes regions, on the former Red River Trail, an ox cart path, that was used to cross the prairie to the mountainous western frontier. Easy accessibility to most anything a visitor could desire—antiques, crafts, pottery, dining, golfing, to name just a few—makes Perham a wonderful place to vacation. There are over 76 resorts and more than 1,000 lakes in the region.

Year-round there's something going on to please just about everyone, from the opening of fishing season in May, the June *Turtle Fest,* the *Otter Tail County Fair* at the end of July and *Pioneer Days* in August, featuring the pioneer village just north of the city limits. Perham has become a mecca for those seeking stress-free, down-home fun in an environment that will beckon back all who have experienced the clean lake air.

For further information, contact:

Perham Area Chamber of Commerce
P.O. Box 234, 155 East Main Street, Perham, Minnesota 56573
Phone: 218-346-7710 or 800-634-6112

ANTIQUES

Antiques And Compatibles	147 E. Main Street, Perham, MN 56573. **Phone: 218-346-4050** Hrs: Hours vary seasonally. Call ahead. Visa and MasterCard accepted.

Looking for a piece of goofus glass? A 19th century hair-weaving set? Then Antiques And Compatibles is the place. They carry a constantly changing selection of antiques and increasingly valuable treasures from the past. Antique cabinetware, glassware, stoneware, lamps and primitives fill two floors of this well-organized and attractively displayed shop, which also happens to boast the area's largest collection of cookie jars.

Opened in 1990, it has expanded to meet the growing demand for fine quality antiques and collectibles. In addition to everyday objects like Red Wing crocks and Fiesta Dinnerware, don't be surprised to find rare art glass or an unusual hand-carved piece of furniture. The inventory is gathered from sources everywhere and sold on commission, offering the best price for both the current owner and the potential collector. Owners, Lina Belar and Jerome Boedigheimer, stress the importance of attractive displays and affordable prices. "It's not a museum," they say. Even though it looks like one.

RESTAURANT

Strom's Cafe

136 W. Main, Perham, MN 56573. **Phone: 218-346-5920 (cafe) or 218-346-2555 (steak house)** Hrs: Mon.-Sat. 5:30 a.m.-9 p.m., Sun. 5:30 a.m.-2 p.m. No credit cards at cafe. Visa and MasterCard accepted at steak house.

When it comes to food and fun in Perham, Strom's is the place to be. Not only Strom's Cafe and Strom's Pizza, located next to each other on West Main, but Strom's Steak House on Fort Thunder Road, where they also happen to have a bowling alley and charitable gaming.

The cafe specializes in homemade food, from soups and specials to pies and cookies. The menu features several great breakfast specials and coffee is only 20 cents with breakfast. They have a special section on the menu just for students and their dinners include the likes of buffalo steak, a 15-ounce T-bone steak and a shrimp dinner. Ask about homemade pies and pastries. Strom's Pizza features lunch specials with carry out and home delivery available.

At the Steak House, check out the dinner specials from BBQ ribs to steak and shrimp or prime rib to all-you-can-eat walleye. In Perham, it's Strom's.

SPECIALTY SHOP

Country Tailored Designs

130 E. Main St., Perham, MN 56573 **Phone: 218-346-4499.** Hrs: Mon.-Sat. 10 a.m.-5 p.m., Sun. (summer only) 12:30 p.m.-4 p.m. Visa and MasterCard accepted.

If you like a "beautiful home" look, it can be created with the help of Country Tailored Designs in Perham. They strive for a uniqueness that is created especially for individual customers and their homes and they do it in a fun, friendly atmosphere.

They can light up your lamps with lamp shades that are handcrafted by Marie. You can take one home or bring your own lamp and have a shade custom-designed to complement any decor, whether it's Country, Victorian, Traditional, French Country or whatever you may have. Country Tailored Designs can warm your windows, as well, with elegant Heritage Lace Curtains from Europe. Then add the perfect finishing touch to your room with coordinating lace doilies, runners and table cloths, all requiring minimal care. They have the area's largest selection of lace.

Unique handcrafted dolls are available in the Doll Room plus a wide array of collectible porcelain dolls. Prices are good and picking special holiday gifts can be fun with four great rooms to browse in.

SPECIALTY SHOPS

Ma's Little Red Barn

126 W. Main, Perham, MN 56573
Phone: 218-346-6812
Hrs: Mon.-Sat. 9 a.m.-5:30 p.m.
Visa and MasterCard accepted.

What better way to send a unique and fun message to someone you know than sending it with balloons. And Ma's Little Red Barn in Perham will do it for you.

With a professional balloonist on staff, they are the balloon and party professionals in the area. They'll do first-class balloon decorating for weddings, schools, class reunions, etcetera. From balloon arches to hearts to sculptures, from logos to balloon bouquets.

Ma's Little Red Barn party and gift shop has a complete collection of cute and whimsical rubber stamps, unique gifts and gift ideas. They offer fresh flowers and plants and do singing telegrams. Plus their famous "Laughter Zone" is worth a visit.

Rental equipment available includes helium tanks, a gazebo, arch, bench, bookstand, screens, center pieces and air inflators. Plus they have paperware, party supplies, wedding accessories and they do imprinting. And if that special someone lives a fair distance, not to worry. Ma's Little Red Barn has mailing service available.

◆ ◆ ◆ ◆ ◆ ◆

Main Street Place

235 W. Main, Perham, MN 56573. **Phone: Main Frames Art Gallery** 218-346-3003. **Down Home Foods** 218-346-5767. **Classic Closet/Tan'fastic** 218-346-2770. **Bev's Book Nook** 218-346-2556. Hrs: Varies by store.

In a former life, the building housing Main Street Place was a Chevrolet dealership. Now, it's a multi-tenant shopping mall with several stores well worth a look. **Main Frames Art Gallery** carries everything from posters to wildlife and floral limited edition prints. Minnesota artist works and quality custom framing available.

Down Home Foods is a cheese shop/health food store that features whole foods, bulk spices, coffee, tea, snacks, books, herbs and vitamin supplements.

At the **Classic Closet,** there's a large variety of womens, childrens, infants and mens clothing. Clean your closet out and earn $$$.

Tan'Fastic has the fast tanning 20-minute bulbs in a Wolff system tanning bed.

Bev's Book Nook has more than 10,000 new and used books in stock, greeting cards, unique stationery, notecards and related paper products. Great browsing, good food and fine works of art, all at Main Street Place in Perham.

SPECIALTY SHOPS

Photo Magic Of Perham

115 1st Avenue N, Perham, MN 56573
Phone: 218-346-2141
Hrs: Mon.-Sat. 9 a.m.-5:30 p.m.
Visa and MasterCard accepted.

Everybody loves to take photos of their vacation. But nobody likes waiting until they get home to have those precious pictures developed. It's just not the same as instant recollection.

Enter Photo Magic of Perham.

This full-service developer stresses getting your pictures developed before you've even left for home. They offer one-hour service for fastest turn-around and, in addition, sell film and batteries. They also do minor camera repair, so you won't miss out on great vacation shots when the camera gives up on you.

Photo Magic offers new, modern technology enabling them to process 35mm film in one hour. They process the film and analyze the negatives, taking the necessary steps to ensure only the highest quality prints are returned to you.

Additional services include a portrait studio, fax service and convenient film drops. And every Tuesday, the second set of prints are just five cents apiece.

◆ ◆ ◆ ◆ ◆ ◆ ◆

Place In The Country

132 E. Main, Perham, MN 56573. **Phone: 218-346-7969.** Hrs: Mon.-Sat. 10 a.m.-5:30 p.m.
Sundays (summer only) 1 p.m.-4 p.m.
Visa and MasterCard accepted.

A Place In The Country isn't actually in the country anymore. After five years there, it moved to East Main in Perham in 1992 and it truly is a complete country store. They offer unique handcrafted creations, collectibles and reproductions for every room in your home. Many of the items are made right there, including pine shelves and cupboards and decorative birdhouses. If they don't have it, they'll either get it for you or make it themselves.

Set in a wonderful rustic atmosphere, with pine plank flooring, a multitude of dried flowers and baskets hang from the beamed ceilings. It really is a charming oasis. They use primitive antiques to display the pieces and you can purchase the antiques as well. Background music is always playing and it's for sale, too!

For everything from primitive antiques and collectibles to wonderful gift ideas, from bears and folk dolls to candles, pillows, gourmet coffee, soups, muffin mixes, calendars, linens and quilts, A Place In The Country is the right place in Perham.

SPECIALTY SHOPS

The Cellar Pottery And Gallery

124 E. Main Street, Perham, MN. 56573. **Phone: 218-346-2105.** Hrs: (May 1 - Sept. 1) Mon.-Sat. 9 a.m.-5:30 p.m. (Sept. 1-Jan. 15) Mon.-Sat. 10 a.m.-5 p.m. Visa, MasterCard, AmEx and Discover accepted.

As you step inside, you'll be struck by the wonderful aroma of gourmet tea and coffee that permeates the air at The Cellar Pottery and Gallery. Gourmet tea is one of their specialities and you're more than welcome to a free cup. The coffee selection is excellent.

Originally a pottery studio and gallery, they've now added T-shirts, sweatshirts and gifts, all of the highest quality. There is original pottery and paintings by Lorene Schumacher, jewelry by Lula Brown and Pam Riepe, paintings by Bob Neegard and more.

The Cellar has a year-round Christmas corner with tins, ornaments, limited edition figurines, music boxes and A Cup Of Christmas Tea. They carry glass by Fenton and others plus mugs, napkins, books, afghans.

Be sure and explore their many Minnesota-made items, including a fine selection of loons and wildlife artifacts.

◆ ◆ ◆ ◆ ◆ ◆

The Pines Gifts & Apparel

101 W. Main, Perham, MN 56573. **Phone: 218-346-5435.** Hrs: (Summer) Mon.-Fri. 8:30 a.m.-8 p.m., Sat. 9 a.m.-5:30 p.m., Sun. 10 a.m.-4 p.m. (Winter) Mon.-Fri. 9 a.m.-5:30 p.m., Sat. 9 a.m.-5:30 p.m. Visa and MasterCard accepted.

Located on the corner by the stoplights, The Pines Gifts & Apparel in Perham has a little bit of everything for just about everyone.

In business for more than 30 years (five years under the current ownership), The Pines is a quaint old-fashioned store, the kind you remember from when you were a kid. It's like an old-style candy store or a mini-department store, with the wonderful scent of potpourri in the air, the continuous playing of nature sounds in the background, a relaxing atmosphere throughout.

The Pines is a Kenny's Candy factory outlet. They have souvenirs, women's apparel, collectibles and gifts. And it's Christmas there year-round. They'll do gift wrapping, deliver your gifts, they offer a bridal registry plus there's always something new happening.

Owners Kurt, Jeana, Bill and Lois Nelson offer friendly, personalized service that keeps people coming back again and again.

PRINCETON

The community of Princeton was founded in 1856 and named in honor of John S. Prince who platted the village. It began as a lumbering town, but by 1900, agriculture became its economic mainstay. The manufacturing of bricks using a special clay in the area was also important.

Princeton has four designated state historical sites including the *Depot Center,* the *Robert Dunn House,* the *Stanley House* and the *Rum River Citizens League building.* Just south of Princeton, the *Sherburne National Wildlife Refuge* is also an area of interest.

The Rum River Golf Club is a beautiful nine-hole, par 37 course.

Visitors also enjoy the *Rum River Festival* in June and the *Mille Lacs County Fair* in August. *The World's Largest Invitational Cross-Country Race* is held in September.

For further information, contact:
Princeton Chamber of Commerce
909 East LaGrande, P.O. Box 381
Princeton, MN 55371   Phone: 612-389-1764

BED & BREAKFAST

Oakhurst Inn B&B	212 8th Ave. S., Princeton, MN 55371 **Phone: 612-389-3553** Open year-round Visa and MasterCard accepted.

Located in the gentle community of Princeton is a most romantic B&B, the Oakhurst Inn. A Victorian home built at the turn of the century for a local banker, Oakhurst is now the perfect place to escape the hectic pace of everyday life and return to the serenity and charm of a bygone era. The quaint neighborhood and small town ambiance lull you to that simpler time, a time when folks enjoyed gentle rocking on an expansive wrap-around porch, a time when people attended teas and indulged in sweet delicacies.

Three large and beautiful guest rooms come with queen-sized

beds and private baths. Your hosts try very hard to anticipate guests' every need and they add many romantic touches that make a memorable stay.

Rooms come with a full breakfast, complimentary beverages, afternoon appetizers and special treats.

REMER

The tree-lined streets of Remer highlight the beauty and serenity of this small neighborhood of friendly folk. The quiet town of 342 is located on the southwest corner of the Chippewa National Forest at the junction of Minnesota Highways 200 & 6. Cozy resorts and campgrounds are nestled on the secluded shores of area lakes, offering a variety of fishing from the famous Minnesota Walleye to pan fishing for the whole family. Other activities include swimming, boating, dining, shopping, nature watching (including bald eagles and hummingbirds), golfing, hunting, snowmobiling and cross-country skiing.

ATTRACTIONS & EVENTS

It is possible to go to New York or North Dakota via the *North Country Hiking Trail,* but if you are interested in a shorter trip, try the trail that circles north of Remer for a spectacular nature experience. Ample parking and access points are available. Visitors may choose to stop and picnic at the quaint *Main Street City Park* which includes a gazebo and picnic tables. The local Yard & Garden Club has cared for and decorated the park for 35 years.

From May through September, visitors can shop at *Remer Arts and Crafts.* All of the products are quality handmade items from local residents and you will certainly find an original to bring home.

Step into old San Francisco when you step into *Masters on Main,* a one-of-a-kind gift shop, where the visit is as much fun as the purchase.

Other points of interest include the Northland Remer Elementary and High School, a restored Depot, and the Old Potato Warehouse, currently under renovation.

The Mid-Minnesota 150 Sled Dog Race goes through Remer on the SooLine Trail each February. A *St. Patrick's Day* celebration in March includes a parade down Main Street and an Irish Stew dinner. *Fireman's Day* is the third Saturday in June. Remer's *Harvest Festival* is the second weekend in August.

For further information, contact:
Remer Area Civic & Commerce Association, Inc.
Visitor's Center
P.O. Box 134
Remer, MN 56672
Phone: 218-566-1680 or 800-831-5262

ST. CLOUD

Growing faster than any other city in the state, St. Cloud holds a unique position as the gateway to northern Minnesota's major outdoor recreation areas. It serves as the commercial and business hub for a three-county region with a population expected to grow some 25% by the year 2000. Yet it continues to offer the best of both worlds: life near a major metropolitan center, yet just minutes away from some of Minnesota's most scenic and secluded woods, lakes and rivers.

While the area's economy is diverse, there are three main industries that have a long history in the St. Cloud area: granite, printing and lens manufacturing. The discovery of colored granite deposits in 1868 launched an important phase of industrial growth and earned St. Cloud the nickname, "The Granite City." Today, area granite companies continue to ship building stone and monuments throughout the country. In 1905 Watab Paper (now known as Champion Paper) began producing paper along the banks of the Mississippi in Sartell. The printing industry is very strong, and several major paper suppliers and printers thrive in the area. The U.S. optics lens industry has its beginnings in Stearns County and many of the country's major optical and eye wear manufacturers and laboratories are based in the region.

A catalog direct mail firm, Fingerhut Corporation is the city's largest employer.

ATTRACTIONS

For a small glimpse of the industries that have helped make St. Cloud a 1990's boomtown, stop by *Champion International* for the summer tours of its paper mill. Other tours of interest include *Golden Shoe Tours,* covering the greater St. Cloud area by horsedrawn carriages, trolleys or motorcoach; and *Pirates Cove Paddle Boat Tours,* which follow the Mississippi River as it winds its way slowly through St. Cloud's historic downtown district. Walking, not sailing, provides the best view of the historic buildings in the downtown area, however. The landmark *Stearn's County Courthouse* with its six, 36-foot-high granite pillars earns the highest accolades from most visitors, but history buffs also find their way to some of the many other historic buildings (most of which are listed on the National Register of Historic Places): the *Fifth Avenue Commercial Buildings* which are designated an historic district; *St. Mary's Cathedral;* the *Paramount Building;* and the *County Stearns Theatrical Building* built with pillared grandeur. The latter serves as the venue for the performances of the *County Stearns Theatrical Company,* but St. Cloud is also home to a number of other performing arts companies, including the *St. Cloud Symphony, The New Tradition Theater* and *St. Cloud Chamber Music Society.* For shopping, the *Mall Germain* is the spot to be.

Visitors discover the history of St. Cloud at the *Stearns County Heritage Center.* Exhibits are on natural history, granite, brewing and automobile legend Samuel Pendolfo.

Munsinger Gardens on the corner of Riverside Drive and Michigan Avenue provides a glorious kaleidoscope of color with more than 70,000 annual plants to view. This beautiful park features picnic tables, bench swings, horseshoe courts, fountains, a wishing well, lily pond and a gazebo. It is a very popular spot for wedding ceremonies and picture taking.

The *Virginia Clemens Rose Garden and Clemens Garden* are two adjacent gardens situated across from the Munsinger Gardens. One is devoted to a beautiful array of hundreds of colorful rose bushes while the other is filled with sun-loving annuals and perennials.

EVENTS

A city of St. Cloud's size comes alive with events virtually every week. Some of the largest, however, include the lively *Mississippi River Music Fest* offering different musical themes each year in May with strolling artisans, musicians and craftspeople, with a special musical performance in the evening.

The colorful *Upper Mississippi Hot Air Balloon Rally* in June is where balloonists from the upper midwest converge for their annual rally.

The community-oriented *Wheel, Wings and Water Festival* is held in July and features a parade, variety shows and more. It's the biggest festival in Minnesota outside of the Twin Cities.

The *Swayed Pines Folk Festival* on the campus of *St. John's University* offers craftspeople showing woodworking, pottery, quilt-making and violin making. An evening music program culminates the festivities.

The Millstream Arts Festival held in September on the campus of the *College of St. Benedict* offers arts, crafts and delicious food.

For further information, contact:
St. Cloud Area Convention and Visitors Bureau
P.O. Box 487
St. Cloud, MN 56302
Phone: 612-251-2940 or 800-264-2940

LODGING

Radisson
Suite Hotel

404 St. Germain, St. Cloud, MN 56301
Phone: 612-654-1661 or 800-333-3333

The Radisson Suite Hotel is the only Four Diamond Hotel in St. Cloud. An impressive addition to the skyline, this hotel offers the finest of everything.

From the beautiful glassed-in elevator complete with a spectacular view of the city to the tastefully decorated guest rooms with wet bar, these accommodations are the very best. Rooms even have a refrigerator and microwave and some offer a jacuzzi and a VCR. Other amenities include an indoor pool, whirlpool and sauna.

The award-winning Chanticleer Restaurant serves enticing meals using only the freshest ingredients. An impressive array of champagnes and wines are at your service, too.

A complimentary, hot breakfast buffet is served each morning and two complimentary cocktails are provided each evening in the Fox Lounge.

The hotel is connected by skyway to the St. Cloud Civic Center, gateway to the downtown business district.

MUSEUM

Stearns County
Historical
Museum

235 S. 33rd Ave., St. Cloud, MN 56302
Phone: 612-253-8424. Hrs: June 1-Aug. 31
Mon.-Sat. 10 a.m.-4 p.m., Sun. noon-4 p.m.
Spring, fall, winter closed Mon.

The Stearns County Historical Society is dedicated to preserving the history of Stearns County for generations to come. The museum is one of the largest history museums in Minnesota.

The museum is located in the Heritage Center, a new historical and cultural center in central Minnesota. It has over 9,000 historical items and some 200,000 photographs and images, along with 10,000 biographies and over 500 lineal feet of historical documents in its archival collection.

The Heritage Center allows visitors to discover and experience life in Stearns County in the 1850's. There is a recreation of Indian dwellings of the Dakota and Ojibwa tribes. A granite quarry replica depicts the industry from prehistoric times to the present. One exhibit features one of the largest collections of dairy farming artifacts in the Midwest.

The Stearns County Heritage Center is "A lifetime of experience under one roof."

RESTAURANTS

Bo Diddley's Deli	129 25th Ave S. and 1501 Northway Dr., St. Cloud, MN 56301 **Phone: 612-252-9475 and 612-255-1500** Hrs.: Mon.-Sun., 10 a.m.-10 p.m.

Opened in 1992 and 1994, Bo Diddley's Deli has two locations in St. Cloud. The St. Cloud establishments have all the charm of the original Bo Diddley's in St. Joseph, just down Interstate 94, offering the same unique fast-food dining in a relaxing coffeehouse atmosphere. The deli menu features such delectables as Pita Pocket sandwiches, Submarines and the popular Greek Gyros made with spiced beef, lamb, shredded vegetables and tzatziki sauce. Bo Diddley's is well-known for their signature homemade soups such as Portuguese Sausage, Kentucky Gumbo, Hearty Italian or Crab and Shrimp Chowder.

Enhancing the ambiance at Bo Diddley's is a unique assortment of taped folk, ethnic, classical and traditional jazz background music. Both locations have outdoor seating in the summertime—one on a deck overlooking 25th Avenue, the other in a quiet courtyard. Beer and wine are served. Or, if you're in a hurry, take it to go. Either way, you're assured of a memorable meal at Bo Diddley's Deli.

◆ ◆ ◆ ◆ ◆ ◆

D.B. Searle's	18 S. Fifth Ave., St. Cloud, MN 56301 **Phone: 612-253-0655.** Hrs: (Restaurant) Sun.-Thurs. 11 a.m.-10 p.m.; Fri, Sat. 11 a.m.-11 p.m.; (Bar) 11 a.m.-1 a.m.

D.B. Searle's is a most innovative restaurant with an exceptional selection of entrées along with luncheon and dinner specials. Top sirloin, teriyaki, filet mignon and rib eye steaks grilled over mesquite wood—these are just a few of the mouthwatering adventures that await the hungry traveler. A fine selection of seafood, barbeque ribs and chicken is also available.

House specialties include sliced breast of turkey with asparagus spears, chunks of seafood with broccoli, or diced ham with fresh mushrooms and broccoli, all crowned with Hollandaise sauce over a popover shell.

Before or after dinner there is a full bar offering nightly bar drink specials to enjoy in the lounge or to complement the meal. Banquet facilities are available, as well, for meeting needs for any occasion.

D.B. Searle's is the perfect place for an intimate atmosphere enjoyed in the "lover's booth," and as their saying goes, "Hang your hat on Searle's hospitality."

SPECIALTY SHOP

A Little Bit Country

North of I-94, East of Hwy 15. Midtown Square. Shopping Center, 3333 West Division, St. Cloud, MN 56301. **Phone:** 612-259-7923. Hrs: Mon.-Fri. 10 a.m.-9 p.m. Saturdays 10 a.m.-5 p.m. Sundays Noon-5 p.m. Extended holiday hours. Visa, MasterCard and Discover accepted.

If shopping is your idea of fun, and the prospect of a shopping adventure makes you "tingle," then A Little Bit Country in St. Cloud should be part of your "must do" list.

Don't let the name fool you...this country shop has the unusual for all interests. It's 6,500 square feet of individual rooms—each represents a shop in a village—that will capture your attention (if not your pocketbook) for at least a few hours, if not an entire afternoon!

Here's just a sampling of what you'll find:

The Country Cottage—Handmade pieces, folk art and braided area rugs displayed amid pine primitives and upholstered furnishings.

The Lodge—A wide assortment of fine Ojibwa handcrafts, each item created from natural materials, working in harmony with nature.

Northern Lights—This is the place to locate country lamp shades, offering you hundreds to choose from. You'll find reproduction floor and table lamps, along with those hard-to-find accessories.

The Pantry—An amazing collection of culinary delights from where else? The U.S. of A.

Mosquito Bite Inn—A great spot for tourists and Minnesota lovers to visit, offering unique Minnesota specialities, in addition to custom gift baskets.

Kathryn's Korner—An endless variety of discriminate cards for all occasions.

ST. CLOUD
EST. 1856

Full service is their motto. A Little Bit Country offers lay-away and mail order. Returns are due back in 30 days. You can get on their catalog mailing list simply by writing or calling the store. That way, you'll be informed about those special events customers have come to love.

Plan to stop by frequently. This is the kind of place where you never know from one day to the next what may appear.

ST. JOSEPH

The city of St. Joseph, Minnesota, is a healthy and thriving community of 3,300 residents whose homes and businesses are just beyond the western borders of the economically strong metro area of St. Cloud. The roots of the city reach back to 1854 when the first settlers arrived in the area.

Located close to an abundance of wildlife, lakes, beautiful parks and trails, residents have endless opportunities for outdoor recreation during all seasons of the year—including walking, running, biking, cross-country skiing, swimming and golfing.

The *Millstream Art Festival* has been a successful annual event ever since it began in 1982. It features performances by a wide variety of individuals and groups of entertainers as well as arts and crafts of all kinds

For further information, contact:
City Clerk
P.O. Box 668
St. Joseph, MN 56374

RESTAURANT

Bo Diddley's Deli

19 College Ave N., St. Joseph, MN 56374
Phone: 612-363-7200
Hrs.: Mon.-Sun., 10 a.m.-12 p.m.

"A meal in minutes... but you'll want to stay longer." That's the motto at Bo Diddley's Deli located 1/2 mile off Interstate 94 in downtown St. Joseph. If you're looking for a unique fast-food experience in a relaxing coffeehouse atmosphere, Bo Diddley's is a treat you won't want to miss. Like its sister establishment in St. Cloud, the deli menu features such delectables as Pita Pocket sandwiches, Submarines and the popular Greek Gyros made with spiced beef, lamb, shredded vegetables and tzatziki sauce. And don't even think of leaving without trying one of their signature homemade soups, be it Portuguese Sausage, Kentucky Gumbo, Hearty Italian or Crab and Shrimp Chowder.

Music is a large part of the ambiance at Bo Diddley's with live concerts and taped ethnic, folk, classical and traditional jazz background music. Beer and wine are served and you can eat in or take out. The college crowd loves Bo's and so will you.

STAPLES

The area around Staples was settled in the 1870's by the lumbering companies that saw the area as a good place to establish temporary mills. The white pine trees were five and six feet in diameter and some Norways were as much as seven feet through and 150 feet tall.

In the early 1880's, the Northern Pacific Railroad built a cut-off from its route to the west. This connecting point for the railroad officially established Staples as a community that would survive into the next century and beyond.

Most of the remaining history of the community revolved around the railroad as Staples became known as "the rail hub of the northwest." The train depot, built in 1910, is still an active part of the community. Visitors will see trains arriving and departing regularly, with new crews boarding for the run to Minneapolis or Dilworth.

ATTRACTIONS

Parks, playgrounds, tennis courts, ball fields and picnic facilities of all sorts are in plentiful supply, both in the city and surrounding the community. *The Dower Lake Recreation Area* is two miles west of the city and features great fishing, camping, life-guarded swimming and two fenced softball fields. Beautiful *Terrace Golf Course* is nestled in the woods along the scenic *Crow Wing River,* popular for swimming, fishing and canoeing. Canoe rental (with transportation) is available for large groups or for a couple who just want to get away for a quiet float down the river. Dozens of large and small lakes are within a half hour drive of Staples.

Winter is another great reason to visit the community. Snowmobiling, ice fishing and cross-country skiing are favorite activities for locals and visitors alike. The *Community Center* offers year-round swimming in an Olympic-size pool and an exercise/fitness center and gym.

The new 400+ seat *Centennial Auditorium* is home for the Lamplighter Community Theatre and many high school music and theatre productions. Other special events occur on a regular basis and include the Minnesota Orchestra, Minnesota Opera Company and other professional entertainers.

History is alive in the *Old Wadena Settlement,* located just four miles north of Staples on the Crow Wing River. From the hills overlooking the river, a visitor can imagine the Indians and Fur Traders gathering to exchange stories and goods.

The historic *Rondorf Building* is the headquarters for the Staples Historical Society's Museum and area information center. This beautiful, century-old three story brick house stands proudly on the major intersection of the community and welcomes all visitors.

Historically, Staples has been a railroad town. However, recent years have seen a shift to a very diversified industrial economy. Staples is home to many companies, large and small, in a variety of fields—manufacturing, engineering, processing, research and development, to name a few. The availability of a capable, ambitious and contented work force has been a hallmark of the area, inspiring numerous firms to locate there.

The *Irrigation Center/University of Minnesota Research Farm* has been a helpful asset for the agricultural community. The Staples business community offers a variety of merchandise and services from printing and plumbing to cowboy boots and computers—all with that hometown hospitality.

The churches of Staples also play a major role in shaping the quality of life there, as do the many civic and service organizations. Staples' motto, *"a lifestyle you can live with,"* is more than just a slogan, it is a fact of life for the citizens who live there. Many traditions bring people together in a spirit of unity and cooperation. The result is a community wherein is found solid family values, a good work ethic and a desire to build upon the dreams of those who came before.

EVENTS

Gatherings in Staples are many. The Staples Area Chamber of Commerce Special Events Committee creates memories for everyone who wants to just "kick back" and enjoy one or all of their events. *Mud Doggin' Days* (4-wheel drive competition), *Miss Staples Pageant, Chili Cook-off* (teams creating good food and fun), *Dower Lake Beach Party* and *Volleyball Tournament, Lefty's Softball Tournament* and the *Grass Roots Festival and Parade* are some of the summer celebrations well worth attending in Staples.

Located in the very center of Minnesota (approximately two hours from Minneapolis-St. Paul, Fargo-Moorhead, and Duluth-Superior), Staples is an inviting drive all seasons of the year.

For further information, contact:
The Staples Area Chamber of Commerce
P.O. Box 133
Staples, MN 56479
Phone: 218-894-2479

SPECIALTY SHOP

Aldrich Cheese Mart | Between Staples and Wadena, on Highway 10. Aldrich, MN 56434. **Phone: 218-445-5503.** Hrs: Mon.-Sun. 8 a.m.-6 p.m. (Jan. - Feb.) Hrs. 9 a.m.-5 p.m. No credit cards accepted. Checks welcome.

Little has changed at the Aldrich Cheese Mart since the doors opened in 1957. And in this case, that's good news because the quality and the service have always been great. The cheese? The best!

There's still neon out front. And inside, it's like stepping back into the Fifties, with natural wood paneling and ceilings and the original cooler cases you remember from the Forties and Fifties.

But if you didn't know better, you'd think this was just another cheese store from the outside. Once inside the front door, however, you'll soon discover it's hardly ordinary.

It came by its quality honestly. John and Martha Friedli came from a long line of fine cheesemakers in their native Switzerland and in 1946, they brought the skills of generations to Aldrich, opening a cheese factory here. Later, in 1957, John and Martha opened the Cheese Mart and Coffee Shop. The Coffee Shop is long gone but the Cheese Mart remains and the current owners were carefully trained by Burton and Doris Friedli-Peterson, the daughter and son-in-law of the original owners. They are committed, as were John and Martha Friedli, to quality natural cheese at reasonable prices.

There are many different varieties of cheese available. Aldrich Cheese Mart ages its own cheddars and there are several different types of unusual cheese to choose from that will fill most every ethnic taste in the area. They also have honey cremes and jellies, too.

The Aldrich Cheese Mart offers old-fashioned charm, high quality cheese plus gifts featuring Minnesota artists. And they have a few select antiques available as well.

Many travelers along lazy Highway 10 wouldn't complete their trip without stopping in Aldrich for a taste of the old-fashioned cheese they have remembered through the years. Aldrich Cheese has been sent to 15 of the 16 NATO countries so the little community of Aldrich has taste in common with a vast global family.

Generations of customers return year after year after year. That's why the two-and-a-half inch jawbreakers are stocked for future generations to try. Stop in and join the chorus of "oohs" and "ahs." You'll be glad you did.

SPECIALTY SHOP

CeCe Craft Boutique	123 5th Street N. Staples, MN 56479 **Phone: 218-894-1862** Hrs: Mon. - Sat. 9 a.m. - 5 p.m.

Located in what many people remember as Batchers back room in the old Batchers department store, just off Highway 10, CeCe Craft Boutique carries a wide selection of craft items for all occasions.

Founded by Cathy and Colleen (thus the name CeCe), and joined by a second location in Little Falls, the CeCe Craft Boutique has such things as jewelry, crocheted items, clothing, baby blankets, wooden toys, lawn ornaments and home decor. They also specialize in dolls and have doll furniture and toys plus cows, bunnies, bears and puppies for your cuddling pleasure.

If you'd like to make your own crafts, you can buy craft supplies and kits plus take classes, too. And there's a bridal registry, as well. The decor is always interesting and they try to display items in a fitting setting, like placing lawn ornaments on grass, for instance. It's an inviting store, with the lovely smell of potpourri and floral arrangements punctuated by the oohs and ahs of browsers and buyers alike.

◆ ◆ ◆ ◆ ◆ ◆ ◆

©MARTIENA R. RICHTER

THIEF RIVER FALLS

Located at the junction of the Red Lake and Thief Rivers, the Sioux and Chippewa Indians first named this area "Robbers River." Legend has it that a Sioux warrior living nearby robbed those passing by.

Incorporated in 1896, the city of Thief River Falls developed with the growing lumber industry of the Northwest. The name was changed to Thief River by Major S.H. Long during an Army survey of the Red River. The "Falls" was added when a series of steep rapids were converted to waterfalls by the construction of a dam.

ATTRACTIONS & EVENTS

Thief River Falls is relaxing, exciting and scenic. Recreational activities for young and old, sportsman and vacationer abound beginning with the remarkable *Agazzis National Wildlife Refuge.* This 61,000-acre haven of wilderness and wildlife diversity is unequaled in Minnesota. The *Thief Lake Wildlife Management Area, Beltrami Island State Forest, Roseau Bog Owl Management Unit,* and the *Pembina Wildlife Management Area* all offer excellent birding and wildlife-viewing opportunities and are within a short driving distance.

The *Thief* and *Red Lake Rivers* offer many opportunities for summertime recreation including fishing, boating, canoeing, swimming, and tubing.

The *Thief River Golf Club* offers golfers a scenic view of the area as they play this challenging nine-hole course.

The Audubon Society's native plant management area, *Wetland, Pines and Prairie Sanctuary,* is one of the few places where one can see the junction of three natural ecosystems (tall grass prairie, boreal forest, and aspen parklands).

The fascinating *Pennington County Pioneer Village* is a living history museum complete with buildings filled with historical artifacts.

The main event of the summer is the *Pennington County Fair* which celebrates the agricultural heritage of this community with farm-related exhibits, rides, demolition derbies, concerts and great food.

For further information, contact:
Thief River Falls Chamber of Commerce
2017 Highway 59 S.E.
Thief River Falls, MN 56701   Phone: 218-681-3720

WADENA

Located in central Minnesota, Wadena, like many cities in the state, was once a small trading post on the Red River Trail, a path built in the 1840's for ox carts carrying goods between St. Paul and Winnipeg, Manitoba.

The city was named after an Indian word which means "little round hill," by the Northern Pacific Railroad Company in 1874.

Although largely agricultural, Wadena is also well-known to outdoor enthusiasts and vacationers as the gateway to some of Minnesota's most famous lakes, and as an area abundant in whitetail deer and upland game.

ATTRACTIONS & EVENTS

An all season recreation area, Wadena offers something for everyone from hunting, fishing, canoeing, and horseback riding, to snowmobiling and cross-country skiing.

Tennis courts, swimming pools, softball diamonds, an archery range and numerous playgrounds, some with horseshoe pits, can be found throughout the city, not to mention ice rinks and cross-country ski trails.

Golfers can enjoy a challenging nine holes at the *Wadena Country Club and Golf Course.* The modern, 35,000-square-foot *Wadena Community Center* features racquetball, a well-equipped weight lifting room, sauna, and whirlpool.

The historical marker at *Sunnybrook Park,* a cozy community park with picnic grounds, duck pond, campgrounds, and mini-animal zoo with deer, buffalo, and peacocks, tells of the hardships experienced by the early settlers back in the Red River Trail days.

Art lovers will enjoy the June *Art In The Park* show during the *Wadena's June Jubilee* celebration, an annual event that spotlights area artists and crafts people. Theater goers can look forward to regular productions of plays and musicals staged by the *Madhatters Community Theater Group.*

The *Wadena Area Christmas Festival* is also a very popular yearly event that attracts many visitors each year.

For further information, contact:
Wadena Area Chamber of Commerce
222 Second St., S.E.
Wadena, MN 56482
Phone: 218-631-1345

ART GALLERY & FRAMING

Hanson's Art Gallery

1413 Jefferson St. N., Wadena, MN 56482
Phone: 218-631-3615. Hrs: Mon. - Fri. 10 a.m.-5 p.m., Saturdays 9 a.m.-1 p.m. By appointment at other hours. No credit cards accepted.

A genuine interest and care. That's what led to the establishment of a fine arts supply business many years ago that has today grown into a full-service gallery. Hanson's Art Gallery offers not only art supplies but picture framing and matting services as well as fine art prints. From Terry Redlin to Les Kouba, Julie Kramer Cole to Charles Peterson and many, many more, Hanson's Art Gallery has a wide array of prints on display. The building is specially designed to display signed and numbered prints with plenty of space to lay out your picture samples and make the right decision. And the building is handicapped-accessible.

Hanson's also offers more than 500 frame styles, hundreds of mat choices, they do conservation framing and offer fine art supplies, oil paints, watercolors and acrylics, canvases and a variety of brushes. Framing of memorabilia, special awards or keepsakes and correct framing of needlework are available and the Hansons take the time to offer friendly advice and information about all of their products.

SPECIALTY SHOP

The Bookpeople/ Midland Music

213 S. Jefferson, Wadena, MN 56482
Phone: 218-631-1739. Hrs: Mon.-Sat. 9 a.m.-5 p.m., Thursdays 9 a.m.-9 p.m. Visa, MasterCard and Discover accepted.

Question: Where in Minnesota's Heartland can you find children's books written in Spanish? Answer: At the Bookpeople/ Midland Music on the main street of Wadena.

Duane Schmidt is well into his second decade of providing quality reading material and music with a wide range of choices in both. The store stocks an excellent variety of fiction and non-fiction with a large selection in the childrens and young readers sections. They also have children's Sesame Street and Dr. Seuss videos available. And the fine choice of bargain books is always worth a look as are the used books.

Some of the sections include cooking, health, counselling, nature, history, Minnesota authors and topics, business, humanities, crafts, hobbies, travel and humor. Plus there's an excellent selection of magazines. Don't forget the music, either. From music accessories to sheet music, from cassettes of classical greats to tapes of nature sounds, the selection is terrific at The Bookpeople/Midland Music.

SPECIALTY SHOP

The Peddler

Between Staples and Wadena on Highway 10.
Verndale, MN 56481. **Phone: 218-445-5798**
Hrs: Mon.-Sun. 9 a.m.-6 p.m.
No credit cards accepted.

At The Peddler, they like to say they have "something for everyone" and it's hard to argue with that contention.

From antiques to collectibles to flea markets to consignment items, The Peddler sells it all. Housed in a former turkey barn, a gigantic emporium measuring 400 feet by 60 feet for a grand total of 24,000 square feet of floor space, The Peddler is located on Highway 10, some six miles east of Wadena, a quarter mile west of Verndale. They offer row after row after row of antiques and collectibles for browsing and buying.

Every weekend, a flea market is held and there's a weekly auction of consignment items and specialty items, too. They'll sell everything from crafts to furniture, tools to boats, guns to coins. And of course, antiques and collectibles.

Open seven days a week. Truly a bargain hunter's paradise.

TOURS

Verndale Custom Homes

Hwy. 10 East, Verndale, MN 56481
Phone: 218-445-5128 or 800-247-1482
Hrs: Mon.-Fri. 7:30 a.m.-4:30 p.m.,
Saturdays 8 a.m.-Noon

Kids are fascinated by construction. Of course, most parents are, too. So what better way to learn all about the house you live in than with a tour of Verndale Custom Homes, a unique opportunity located between Staples and Wadena on Highway 10 East.

Tours are available six days a week and there's usually a variety of homes to see in various stages of construction. Verndale Custom Homes builds a quality product, utilizing one-piece construction to avoid settling problems that can cause cracks in walls and ceilings.

Verndale Custom Homes designs homes to your specifications, not someone else's floor plan that doesn't quite fit your lifestyle. You can bring in your own design or a handful of ideas and watch them turn those dreams into reality. And because they build in all-weather facilities and buy in bulk, costs are kept down.

Think how much fun it would be to come back and see your dream house being built! It's a unique opportunity to get an insider's look at new home construction.

WALKER

Originally a trading post for fur trappers, Walker later grew to become a lumber production town as the demand for wood increased. Now, like many northern cities, it has changed again to become a beautiful resort community. Located on the southwest corner of Leech Lake, this four-season vacationland offers 109,415 acres of clean, pure water and thousands of acres of forest for visitors to enjoy.

ATTRACTIONS & EVENTS

The Deep Portage Conservation Reserve, featuring 6,000 acres of pristine woods and marshes, offers a breathtaking view of nature.

And, if you are still looking for more natural beauty, then the *Lake Itasca State Park,* site of the headwaters of the Mississippi, provides excellent nature trails, picnic areas, excursion boat rides and a wildlife museum.

Golfers can enjoy playing among towering pines at the 18-hole *Tianna Country Club* championship course.

For those who like to hunt, the Walker area offers an abundance of migratory waterfowl, grouse and white-tail deer.

Winter recreational activities include miles of snowmobiling and cross-country ski trails all waiting to be explored and enjoyed.

Those interested in history can learn more about Minnesota and the Walker area at the *Walker Wildlife and Indian Artifacts Museum,* the *Museum of Natural History* and the *Cass County Historical Museum* with its adjacent Rock Garden and Fountain.

During the year, Walker hosts numerous fishing and golf tournaments and popular festivals including the famous *International Eelpout Festival* in February, and the *Mariner Walleye Open Classic Tournament* in June.

The Leech Lake Regatta and the *Federal Dam Muskie Tournament* in August, numerous *Crazy Day Sales* and celebrations including a *Fourth of July Parade and Fireworks* display and an *Ethnic Fest* held each September offer visitors a wide variety of events and activities to choose from.

For more information contact:
Leech Lake Area Chamber of Commerce
P.O. Box 1089
Walker, MN 56484
Phone: 218-547-1313 or 800-833-1118

ANTIQUES

Old Stuff/ Antiques	Village Square, Walker, MN 56484. **Phone:** 218-547-2303. Hrs: (May - Oct.) Mon.-Sat. 10 a.m.-5 p.m. (July -Sept.) Sundays 11 a.m.-4 p.m. (November-April) open Saturdays and by chance.

Eating an ice cream cone on the patio at Village Square is one of summer's great delights for visitors to Walker. Just two doors away is another Walker delight—the Old Stuff/Antique shop, aptly described as 1,500 square feet of quality antiques and neat old stuff.

They feature fine American Indian antiques, including local Ojibwa moccasins, beadwork and ricing baskets, as well as Navajo rugs. Items with northwoods appeal include duck decoys, old skis and snowshoes, spearing decoys plus fishing, hunting and boating collectibles. The front room offers a variety of pottery, including Watt, Shawnee, Rosemeade, Roseville and art pottery. There are many old toys, some in original boxes, and several shelves display Fiesta and Blue Ridge dinnerware, depression glass, cut and pattern glass, LuRay, Blue Willow and a bargain room offers treasure hunting.

There's a room full of primitives, an area of books, advertising calendars, railroad china, antique furniture, lamps, paintings and a vast choice of Christmas items. Something for every collector, indeed!

BED & BREAKFAST

PeaceCliff B&B	HCR 73, Box 998D, Walker, MN 56484 **Phone:** 218-547-2832 Hrs: 8 a.m. - 10 p.m. every day. Major credit cards accepted.

PeaceCliff B&B sits atop an 85-foot bluff overlooking Walker Bay on beautiful Leech Lake. Spectacular views of summer storms or soaring eagles make memories not soon forgotten about this interesting inn.

Lovingly cared for by hosts Dave and Kathy Laursen, this B&B is filled with antiques, old books and all the peace and quiet anyone would want. Five different rooms are offered, each with its own distinctive features, but all have a magnificent view of the lake.

Nearby is The Heartland Trail—45 miles of paved trail leading to Park Rapids and Itasca State Park. The North Country Trail is 68 miles of scenic wonderland through the Chippewa National Forest. A hearty breakfast starts you on your way.

BOOKSTORE

Imagination Station

Main Street, Walker, MN 56484, **Phone: 218-547-2111,** 218-547-3118 (Evenings fall and winter) Hrs.: (Memorial Day - Labor Day), Mon. - Sat. 10 a.m. - 5 p.m.(Mid-May - Memorial Day and Sept - Dec.) Sat. only Visa and MasterCard are accepted.

Stepping through the doorway of Imagination Station Bookstore will take you into a different time and space—one with softer edges, a slower pace. Weathered barnboards provide a mellow background for a hand-crafted toy train and railway baggage cart, a cast iron pot-bellied stove, and displays of some of the best and brightest books in print. Selection·is a top priority at this bookstore, which offers quality books for all ages, specializing in children's picture books and young adult literature. Other strong areas are the nature, Native American, and regional literature collections. Reader-friendly places invite readers to browse, reflect, and relax.

Though rustic in its atmosphere, fast, efficient, individualized service is provided through connections with the largest book warehouses in the country. Returning customers from across the country who love books, offer their suggestions, and are listened to, have contributed to the unique blend of old and new, small and large, fast and slow that is Imagination Station Bookstore.

RESORT

Big Rock Resort

Ten miles east of Walker on Leech Lake H.C.R. 84, Box 751. Walker, MN 56484 **Phone: 218-547-1066 or 800-827-7106** Open year-round.

Are you after a little rip-roarin' action on the volleyball court? A little basketball? Maybe some tennis? Perhaps a quiet stroll in the woods or a perfect morning on the lake is more your thing.

Whatever your style, Big Rock Resort on Leech Lake has it all.

From a lodge well-supplied with everything from good conversation to groceries, snacks and supplies, a big screen TV and a recreation room for the kids to a perfect inland harbor with full-service marina, this is Leech Lake's finest. Not to mention the brand new pool, whirlpool and gigantic sun deck. The spacious cottages, featuring cable TV and microwave ovens, come completely furnished, including fully equipped kitchens. Your hosts Karl and Karen Kelnhofer will also supply Weber grills and have boats and motors available for rent, too.

Mentioned in the September 1992 edition of *National Geographic,* Big Rock Resort is located just east of Walker, with casino, restaurants, golf, a water slide park and wild game farm nearby.

RESORT

Ivanhoe Resort of Leech Lake

H.C.R. 73, Box 1018. Walker, MN 56484
Phone: 800-962-2842
Hrs: May 15 to Oct. 2
Visa, MasterCard and AmEx accepted.

Can't decide if you want bright lights or quiet contemplation, fine fishing or fine food on your next vacation? Pick both! It's no decision at the Ivanhoe Resort of Leech Lake.

That's because the Ivanhoe is located within the serenity of the Chippewa National Forest on the shores of a beautiful protected bay on Leech Lake. Yet it's just minutes from Walker where recreational pursuits can include golf, gambling, nightlife and good food.

Sixteen spacious, well-equipped cabins make up the resort and come in a variety of styles and price ranges. Every cabin offers a wonderful lake view plus an AM/FM clock radio, toaster, electric coffeemaker, dishes and cookware. Everything except towels.

Boats and motors are available to pursue the renowned muskies of Leech Lake and recreational choices include volleyball, badminton, canoes, paddleboats, horseshoes and more. With a history dating back to the 20's, the Ivanhoe has been a great choice for generations.

Three miles south of Walker on Highway 371.

SPECIALTY SHOP

Antoinettes

Village Square, Walker, MN 56484
Phone: 218-547-3747
Hrs: Mon.-Sat. 9 a.m.-5:30 p.m. Sundays Memorial Day-Labor Day. Closed January-March
Visa and MasterCard accepted.

Casual. Sophisticated. Charming. Those are some of the words customers have used to describe Antoinettes in the Village Square, located in the heart of downtown Walker.

Antoinettes offers fine gifts and collectibles, from Austrian crystal to brass and glassware, from dolls to sculptures and Indian artifacts.

If you have a doll collector to buy for, Antoinettes carries exclusive brand names like Precious Moments, Bradleys, Brinns, Carlson and more. For a little different taste, they carry a wide selection of Indian artifacts, including dreamcatchers, handcrafted jewelry, beadwork and other unusual articles. Minnetonka moccasins are always on sale.

Sculptures by Austin and Western looks by Daniel Monfort are available along with handcrafted decoys, plates by Derek Hansen and Sandra Kuck, porcelain figurines, globes and music boxes. Plus there's Black Hills gold, sterling silver, fine jewelry and inspirational gifts. Or just browse. You'll find something for that special someone.

SPECIALTY SHOPS

Heritage Arts & Gifts

Hwy 371 S., P.O. Box 224, Walker, MN 56484
Phone: 218-547-3501
Hrs: Open year-round.

As you drive into Walker on Highway 371, coming from the south, you'll find Heritage Arts & Gifts where you'll be greeted by a unique blend of specialty items, all high quality and well worth a look. Step inside and you'll be greeted by the subtle fragrance of fine potpourri and a collection of unusual gift items, many quality hand-made items, decorator pieces and accessories to enhance any home. There are lovely silk flowers, greenery and arrangements plus baskets, both imported and domestic. The store features a beautiful selection of imported lace curtains and table linens, accessory oak furniture and choice antique furniture, framed prints and a custom framing gallery specializing in creative matcutting. They are an authorized Marty Bell art dealer.

For the artistic, there is a full line of artists' supplies, paints, canvas and brushes plus drawing supplies, cross-stitch, embroidery and quilting books, kits and supplies. Jewelry-making supplies are also stocked and you can choose from a multitude of beads. Worth a trip.

❖ ❖ ❖ ❖ ❖ ❖ ❖

Liten Hus

Fifth Street, Walker, MN 56484
Phone: 218-547-3919
Hrs.: (Mid-May-mid-Oct.) open daily.
(Summer) open evenings.
Visa, MasterCard, and Discover are accepted.

Liten Hus was created as a result of the owner's personal interest in Scandinavian heritage, an interest shared by many Minnesotans with the same lineage. Much of the merchandise displayed throughout the store is shipped directly from northern Europe. Included among the selections are Norwegian cotton and wool sweaters; distinctive sterling jewelry; Iittala crystal; George Jensen of Denmark silver; porcelain by Royal Copenhagen and Porsgrund; books that draw  on Scandinavian heritage; cassette tapes; Tom Clark gnomes collection series; Scandinavian food items; a unique card selection and much more. Each visit to Liten Hus yields a new discovery, a piece of crystal, a new sweater, or a wonderful card that may have escaped the shopper's eye on previous visits.

Stop by Liten Hus, where the flags fly in downtown Walker and see why it's one of the busiest corners in northern Minnesota.

SPECIALTY SHOPS

Tiger Lily's - A French Country Boutique

P.O. Box 178. Walker, MN 56484. **Phone: 218-547-3727.** Hrs: (Summer) Mon.-Sat. 10 a.m.-6 p.m., Sun 11 a.m.-4 p.m. (Winter: Jan.-Apr.) Fri.-Sat. 10 a.m.-6 p.m. Visa, MasterCard and Discover accepted.

Originally built in the 1940's by local artist Austin Sarff, Tiger Lily's is a delightful and quaint three-level French Country boutique that served as a private home for over 40 years.

Out front, large sloping lawns accented by plantings of tiger lillies, and a delicate fragrance of potpourri permeating throughout the interior, create an ambiance attractive to shoppers and browsers alike. The front entry and living room feature artistic greeting cards, rugs, limited edition prints and collectibles. The remaining rooms are filled with hand-crafted Victorian goods, luxurious bed and bath linens, kitchen accessories, designer fragrances and jewelry, Christian gifts, exceptional toys and accessories for babies and children plus a choice selection of Crabtree and Evelyn toiletries.

Select gourmet foods and candies including chocolate truffles, homemade fudge, caramels and "Jelly Belly" jelly beans satisfy the most discriminating sweet tooth. Tiger Lily's is located on North Highway 371 across from Jimmy's Restaurant in Walker.

◆ ◆ ◆ ◆ ◆ ◆ ◆

Village Square Pizza and Ice Cream

Village Square, In the Heart of Downtown Walker Walker, MN 56484. **Phone: 218-547-1456** Hrs: Open seven days a week. Ice Cream Parlor is seasonal.

Located in the heart of downtown Walker, the Village Square Pizza and Ice Cream is part of the Village Square shops, a collection of businesses including Antoinettes fine gifts and Old Stuff/Antiques.

The Village Square Cafe offers a combination of American, Mexican and Italian food, with portions and a price you're sure to agree with. They specialize in homemade pizza, with crust and sauce made from scratch with only the freshest ingredients right there in the kitchen. Try the Calzone pocket pizza. They also boast humongous half-pound burgers that have claimed the reputation as the biggest in Walker.

After dining in the cafe, step across the the patio to the old-fashioned Ice Cream Parlor serving the finest in Kemps ice cream. There are 16 flavors of ice cream and eight flavors of frozen yogurt and sherbet, enough to satisfy even the pickiest lickers. Before and after dining, you'll want to browse the shops of Village Square, offering the finest in gifts, jewelry, antiques and clothing. Good food. Good fun.

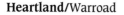

WARROAD

In 1820, the American Fur Trading Post was founded on Lake of the Woods. This site happened to be at the end of a natural trail formed by a ridge which extends northeast from the Red River to Lake of the Woods. Chippewa and Dakota Indians often used this route in their battles against one another.

The Chippewa named the trading post "Ka-Beck-A-Nung" or "dark and bloody end of the trail." French traders called it "chemin de guerre" or "road of war." Thus, the logging and farming community that grew around the trading post site a century later was named "War Road."

ATTRACTIONS & EVENTS

The entire Lake of the Woods area is a sportsman's paradise. Year-round opportunities for such recreational activities like hunting, fishing, sailing, boating, hiking, camping, cross-country skiing, ice fishing and wildlife watching abound.

The *Northwest Angle Area* or the northernmost point of the Lower 48 is a short 50 miles. Flight service is available for sightseeing tours or transportation.

The *Ka-beck-a-mung Trail,* established by the *Warroad Historical Society,* will delight history lovers. This "road of war" trail makes its way through the community and its historical highlights.

Marvin Windows, a leading international custom window manufacturer and *Christian Brothers,* the only American hockey stick manufacturer, both offer interesting tours of their facilities.

During the first weekend after July Fourth, the town hosts the *ESCAPE (Exciting Scenic Canadian American Powerboat Excursion),* where up to 100 powerboats participate in the four-day cruise around the lake.

An informal sailboat cruise is sponsored by LOWISA (Lake of the Woods International Sailing Association) in the last week of July.

Warroad Estates has a public, 18-hole championship golf course rated as one of the 10 toughest in Minnesota by the Minnesota Golf Association in 1983. Each July, the golf course hosts the *Hockey Celebrity Golf Tournament.* There is always a Class A PGA member on hand.

For further information contact:
Warroad Area Chamber of Commerce
P.O. Box 7
Warroad, MN 56763   Phone: 218-386-3543 or 800-328-4455

LODGING

The Patch Motel and Restaurant	Hwy. 11 W., Warroad, MN 56763 **Phone: 218-386-2723.** Hrs: Motel open 24 hrs. Restaurant 6 a.m.-11 p.m. (Winter, til 9:30 p.m.) Visa, MasterCard and AmEx accepted.

The Patch Motel and Restaurant is located on Highway 11, the "Fisherman's Freeway" leading to the famous walleye waters of Lake of the Woods. It was built on what was once a strawberry patch, hence the name. In fact, the registration desk is handcarved oak with strawberries etched into the glass.

The Patch Restaurant offers three dining areas with combined seating of 156, a complete menu along with excellent food and service. Its famous pan-fried walleye and homemade apple, rhubarb and berry pies make it a real favorite with traveling groups such as athletic teams and bus tours.

The Patch Motel offers single, double, quad and waterbed rooms. Amenities include indoor pool, jacuzzi, exercise room, color TV, air conditioning, VCR and movie rental, babysitting service, gift shop and conference facilities.

Outside, the kids will find a playground. A picnic area is available and a path leads you to the "The Patch."

TOURS

Christian Brothers, Inc.	Warroad, MN 56763 **Phone: 218-386-1111.** Hrs.: (20-minute tours Monday-Friday) 8-10 a.m., 10:30 a.m.-noon 12:30 p.m.-2:30 p.m., 3-4 p.m.

The name "Christian" has been associated with the game of hockey since 1960. Roger Christian and brother Billy were key players in winning the first Olympic gold medal for the United States in hockey while Dave Christian led the next generation to gold at Lake Placid in 1980. The brothers returned to Warroad and formed a partnership with Hal Bakke, Roger Christian's brother-in-law, and built Christian Brothers, Inc.

The Christian brothers combined their knowledge of hockey with that of carpentry to develop a line of hockey sticks. The company now offers stick models with more than 250 styles and patterns. This impressive selection includes shafts made with combinations of unidirectional glass and solid or laminated wood core of poplar, aspen, white ash or birch. The blades are rock elm reinforced with graphite or fiberglass mesh wrap. In the 1980s Christian Brothers introduced its aluminum shaft to the American and Canadian markets and continues to be a market leader.

CORPORATE PROFILE

Marvin Windows & Doors

Through craftsmanship, innovation and dedication to service, Marvin Windows & Doors has become the third-largest manufacturer of fine wood windows and doors in the United States, with international markets in Canada, Japan and Mexico. The firm remains the only major manufacturer of made-to-order windows in America and, today, offers more than 11,000 standard shapes and sizes.

But a company this size does not spring up overnight.

Marvin Windows & Doors and its guiding force, William Marvin, find their modest roots in the small Canadian border town of Warroad. In 1904, George Marvin arrived in Warroad to establish and operate a grain elevator for his employers in Canada. A few years later, Marvin's company tore down the elevator and moved it to Saskatchewan; but George Marvin stayed in town, purchased a lumberyard and founded the Marvin Lumber & Cedar Company.

Years later he built his own elevator and started a pulpwood and railroad tie brokerage business. Time brought continued diversification as the company entered the hardware, feed and seed cleaning markets. With his eldest son, William, at his side working summers at the company, George Marvin prospered.

Marvin Windows & Doors begins

In June 1939, William graduated from the University of Minnesota with degrees in agronomy and agricultural economics, and a minor in plant pathology. He spent that summer in General Mills' training program but was called home to replace his ailing uncle in the family business. William became the company's eighth employee.

That winter, lumberyard manager Harry York became bored. He convinced George and Bill to buy him a saw, so he could fill the slack time by making cellar and barn sash and screens. The foundation of Marvin Windows was laid.

During World War II, the company used the window and door manufacturing equipment to produce ammunition boxes for the military. It was also during this time that George and William discussed potential opportunities for relatives and friends returning from the war. "We didn't want to see all the kids we grew up with leave the area if they didn't want to," says William Marvin. "We knew they wouldn't all choose to go into farming, so we tried to find something that would divorce us from the local economy." They decided to follow the path they had already begun: window manufacturing.

The windows were a success and the company began to grow. By 1950, William felt ready to pursue wood windows in a big way. He and his brothers steered the company in that direction, and business continued to blossom as the Marvins learned the market.

Success through innovation

Success continued to bless Marvin Windows & Doors, thanks in part to William's penchant for innovation which he inherited from his father. But that innovation resulted in more than company prosperity; Marvin Windows & Doors became a leader in the building industry. In fact, many of the products and services Marvin Windows & Doors has introduced over the years have become industry standards.

For instance, Marvin Windows & Doors was the first manufacturer in America to assemble window units that dealers received completely set up and ready to install; Marvin was the first to deliver windows with its own fleet of trucks (it still does); it was one of the first in the industry to introduce wood-bead glazing, which is now standard in the industry; and, because of its location in frigid northern Minnesota, Marvin has consistently been among the first to offer high-tech energy features, including Low E with Argon gas, on its entire product line.

Today, after some 50 years of exceptional growth, William Marvin is chairman of the board and innovation is still his watchword. His company continues to introduce new products, such as switchable privacy glass and power drive windows. Previous innovations include the EZ-Tilt (sash tilts in or comes out for easy cleaning) and trapezoid windows; exterior aluminum cladding; factory applied jamb extensions; factory applied aluminum brick mould casing; exterior prefinishing; and the nation's first standard-sized curved and bent glass windows. Marvin Windows & Doors was also one of the first companies to offer authentic divided lites; and in 1981 it reintroduced the Round Top window, which had almost disappeared from the market.

Unimagined growth

Marvin Windows & Doors has probably reached further than founder George Marvin ever imagined, in both sales and impact on the area. In 1970, Marvin Windows & Doors employed nearly 200 people, almost all of them from Warroad. In 1981, the ranks had swelled to about 875. Presently, the company employs more than 2,700 people (the population of Warroad is slightly more than 1,800) and 300 high school, vo-tech and college students take advantage of the company's summer "Earn and Learn" program.

As Marvin Windows & Doors' workforce grows, so grows the

company's hometown. In the last few years well over 20 new businesses began in Warroad, including a retail store, car dealership and a second drug store; five new churches have been established; a new, larger high school was erected out of necessity; housing is up considerably; the main hotel in town has been expanded twice, and a new motel has gone up down the street; and a national food chain has begun operating in Warroad.

But Marvin Windows & Doors is responsible for more than the citizens of Warroad. A number of employees commute from surrounding towns, such as Baudette, 35 miles away; Greenbush, 40 miles away; and Grygla, 65 miles away. In an area where high unemployment inevitably leads to population reduction, these towns are able to maintain their present populace largely because of Marvin Windows & Doors.

How secure is employment at Marvin? The company has not laid off any of its workforce since 1975. Even when housing hit bottom in the late 1970s, early 1980s and again in 1990 and 1991, the company kept its employees on the job by switching to four-day work weeks and building inventory for future growth.

That growth eventually came and employees are enjoying the fruits, as Marvin's profit-sharing program (begun in the late 1950s) approaches $1,705 per employee in 1993.

Solid future

George Marvin probably never envisioned the current size and scope of Marvin Windows & Doors, either. The company reaches into all 50 states, Canada, Japan and Mexico. In 1986 it completed expansion of its state-of-the-art facilities to two million square feet of floor space in preparation for the future.

Marvin's future happens now, according to Jake Marvin, President and one of William's sons. "There are many niches in the industry that have yet to be filled," he says. "We are responding to those voids by expanding our facilities, and gearing production capability for the future. We are very optimistic about our opportunities in many areas of the marketplace."

There is evidence that Marvin is pursuing those opportunities with vitality and foresight. In 1981, the company's new door plant began operations in Ripley, Tennessee, with 92,000 square feet of floor space. The Ripley plant now has expanded to nearly 600,000 square feet of floor space.

As for William Marvin, he continues to direct and oversee the five of his six children involved in the company's management. Nephews, a daughter-in-law, a son-in-law, and grandchildren are also involved in the business.

And, though his company's business is largely responsible for the prosperous times in Warroad, Marvin extends his concerns to civic affairs as well. He served as chairman of a successful fund drive for a new community hospital, as chairman of the city's Chamber of Commerce and contributes to local programs such as a chemical dependency support group. In 1991, William donated a new swimming pool to Warroad's middle school. And in 1990 his wife, Margaret, donated a new library/museum to the city of Warroad.

In 1980, William's life achievements were rewarded with an induction into the Minnesota Business Hall of Fame. He and his company were also honored with the 1986 Greater Minnesota Economic Development Award, bestowed by the Minnesota Association of Commerce and Industry (MACI). In 1987, the students of Minnesota's Moorhead State University entered him into the MSU Business Hall of Fame. And in April of 1990, he was awarded the Distinguished Minnesotan Award as an outstanding entrepreneur, family man and community service volunteer.

From George Marvin to William Marvin to the third and fourth Marvin generation, Marvin Windows & Doors has progressed from a tiny lumber yard in 1904 to a thriving, future-oriented leader in the manufacture of fine wood windows and doors.

Marvin Windows & Doors will continue to operate and grow toward the future by learning from its past, which is reminiscent of classic American success: use a strong back and visionary desire to give customers quality goods at a fair price. That is, and always has been, William Marvin's and Marvin Windows & Doors' trademark.

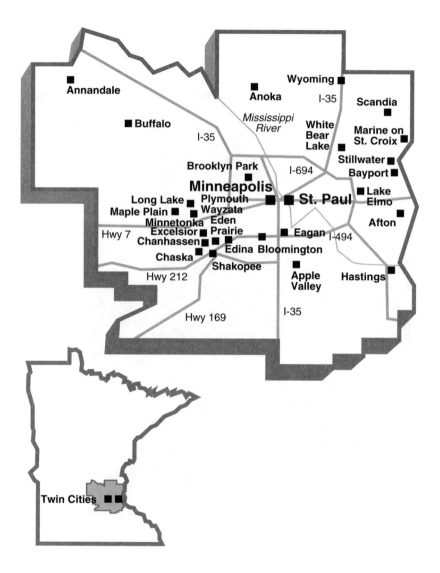

Metroland

These are the nineties and people are making different choices than they used to.

Take, for example, the way people pick where it is they will live and work and raise their families. In the past, we often went where the jobs were or stayed close to home, close to family. Those in search of a specific lifestyle or the more adventurous among us had to seek out the right locations to live the way we wanted.

Today, it is different. People make their choices for a variety of reasons. They're after lifestyle as much as a paycheck. And one of the most popular choices of the nineties, for reasons ranging from employment opportunities to quality of life, from health care to education and the great bounty of nature, are the Twin Cities of Minneapolis and St. Paul. Consistently rated among America's most liveable cities in poll after poll, one need not look far for reasons why.

Take that lifestyle issue, for example.

In fact, you can live just about any way you want in the Twin Cities, so varied is its landscape.

The young and trendy might choose a loft in the warehouse district of Minneapolis or an apartment at Galtier Plaza in downtown St. Paul. Those whose tastes run toward the eclectic might be found near the University of Minnesota in downtown Minneapolis. If an upscale urban dwelling with an historic twist is what you're after, Kenwood is an outstanding choice as are the magnificent tree-lined Victorians along St. Paul's Summit Avenue.

Perhaps country living is more your thing. You can be driving along freeways one minute in the Twin Cities and the next finds you in some rural enclave in Stillwater or Afton or Minnetonka. Cruise down Lake Street in Wayzata and you'll feel as if you've been transported to some trendy lakeside resort town.

Or if suburbia is your scene, there's plenty of that, from Eden Prairie to Brooklyn Park, Plymouth to Eagan. And all of it, you can be sure, is within walking distance of a lake.

Is there any other metropolitan area in all of these United States that can make such a claim? We think not. These are the Twin Cities, after all, with history and culture oozing from every corner, with charm and exuberance written all over, with so much to offer that it's difficult to know where to begin.

Of course, you do need to make a living.

It's not that difficult in Minneapolis, St. Paul and the many surrounding suburbs, a metropolitan area with well over two million inhabitants and home to more than two dozen of the Fortune 500. Known as an area of highly educated, highly civilized citizens, the Twin Cities has always spawned and continues to grow great corporate enterprises, outfits you know well with names like 3M, Honeywell, Carlson and Cargill. Then there's the new hotshots like Nordic Track and Rollerblade and so many more.

The two cities have come a long way, indeed, from the days of Father Hennepin and Pierre "Pig's Eye" Parrant. Yet they have not forgotten their roots. The influence of those early French explorers is still around. So, too, the significant impact of the Swedes and Norwegians whose footprints can be found on much of modern Minnesota life.

All of these attributes have combined to make Minneapolis-St. Paul and the surrounding cities a tourist mecca. Thanks to a string of major sporting events which brought untold publicity to the area, the Twin Cities has made it onto many travellers wish lists. Arthur Frommer, noted travel authority, continues to rave about Minneapolis and St. Paul. But it is perhaps the Mall of America that has done the most to bring folks in from far and wide.

Fitting, too, that the nation's largest shopping and entertainment complex ("Mall" hardly seems a fitting description) should be built just minutes away from the nation's first enclosed shopping center, Southdale. Built in Edina in the 1950's and since renovated many times over, it remains a wonderful place to shop. But it is the Mall of America that draws people here by the busload to sample all of the splendor the Twin Cities has to offer.

Still, in spite of the notoriety, in spite of the growth, in spite of all of the changes that have shaped Minneapolis and St. Paul, they've managed to hang onto their small-town attributes in so many ways, hang on to their reputations as friendly places for residents and visitors alike.

After all, this is still Minnesota and the fish are still biting.

AFTON

A town has to be pretty special to attract those who would make the trek only for an ice cream cone. Such is the charm of Afton, where generations have flocked from the city on a hot summer's day to sample the delicious waffle cones at Selma's.

Afton, population 2,645, had a rather inauspicious debut as a three-acre field of corn and potatoes in 1893 but not long after became a progressive agricultural community. Residents built Minnesota's first flour mill and later tested the first steam-powered threshing machine here. Settlers brought with them the architectural charm of New England. Many of the clapboard houses and historical buildings still stand today in the ten-block by four-block area known as "The Village," a wonderful collection of shops, eating establishments, services and marinas. While Afton still has its share of farmers, most of today's residents are former city dwellers who've constructed modern homes on country acreage. Although the city covers some 25 square miles, it maintains the rural charm that is its heritage.

ATTRACTIONS & EVENTS

Afton Alps, with 18 chair lifts, 36 groomed runs and miles of cross-country ski trails, is one of Minnesota's largest ski areas. It now features a rather hilly 18-hole golf course for the so-called "off-season."

The scenic, protected *St. Croix River* lures thousands of boaters each year with *Afton Cruise Lines* offering tours on the water. *Afton State Park* has hiking and cross-country trails, swimming, camping and picnic spots. *The Afton House Inn* has traditional New England-style dining and accommodations. It is the centerpiece of the village where you'll also find the *Afton Toy Shop, The Little Red House, Selma's Ice Cream Parlour* and *Lerk's Bar,* home of the famous Lerk Burger. For a taste of history, explore the *Afton Historical Museum* or the *Carpenter St. Croix Nature Center.*

Afton's *Fourth of July Parade* goes down the main street and back again. The *June Strawberry Festival* is a major summer attraction while *Art in the Park* attracts locals and visitors alike each October.

For further information, contact:

The City of Afton
P.O. Box 386
Afton, MN 55001
Phone: 612-436-5090

BED & BREAKFAST

Afton's Mulberry Pond on River Road	3786 River Road Afton, MN 55001 **Phone: 612-436-8086** Visa and MasterCard accepted.

In less than a half hour, you can be transported from the noise and bustle of the city to the quiet and serenity of the countryside. Nearly two acres of woods and lawn surround Mulberry Pond, ending on 200 feet of private beach on the beautiful and scenic St. Croix River. This wonderful B&B even offers free overnight docking for guests.

On the grounds in the shade of a mulberry tree is a small, water lily-filled pond. Decks surround the entire front of the house. Two rooms are offered. The Tammarind Room is furnished in a delightful blend of antiques and contemporary furniture. The feeling of the room is open, light, and airy. The east facing room is a wonderful place to watch the sun rise over the beautiful St. Croix River. On warm summer mornings, you can enjoy your breakfast on your own private deck. Other amenities include a private entrance and private bath with a mirrored whirlpool and glass shower, a king size bed, a gas fireplace and a colored TV with built-in VCR. Furnishings include English and Italian antiques. A continental breakfast is served in your room.

The Mulberry Room has the-old fashioned warmth of an earlier time in history. Roses adorn everything from the curtains and bed-spread to the teddy bear, providing a bright counterpoint to the Victorian, walnut bedroom set. The ceiling-high headboard and mar-ble-topped dresser dominate the room. Amenities include the exclu-sive use of a contemporary loft library, a queen size bed, a gas fire-place, a private bath with a mirrored whirlpool and hand-held show-er, and a colored TV with a built-in VCR. Again, a continental break-fast is served in your room.

Ski in winter, swim in summer, relax all year round. Mulberry Pond is the perfect place to get away from it all. Your hosts, Nick and Elaine Mucciacciaro.

HISTORIC INN

The Historic Afton House Inn & Afton Cruise Lines

3291 South St. Croix Trail, Afton, MN 55001
Phone: 612-436-8883
Hrs: Open 7 days a week year-round.
Major credit cards accepted.

Since 1867, the Historic Afton House Inn has offered fine dining and traditional lodging to travellers and tourists alike, a legacy that continues today in this peaceful New England-style village. Located just east of the Twin Cities on the St. Croix River, the Historic Afton House Inn is a charming place to spend a weekend relaxing and a great place to hold corporate meetings and gatherings of all kinds.

Enjoy the elegant setting of the Wheel Room, where intimate dinners by candlelight are always a highlight. Weekend entertainment, tableside cooking and excellent service are the norm. Appetizers such as Escargots or Tortellini Genovese will tempt you as will special entrées such as Pork Tenderloin "Black Forest," Scallops Creole or Tournados "Bernaise." Be sure and try Bananas Foster or Cherries Jubilee for dessert and a fine display of tableside flambé cooking.

The Pennington Room offers a more private setting for weddings, rehearsal dinners or corporate entertaining. The Inn's high standards carry over to their famous Sunday Gourmet Brunch and the Catfish Saloon and Deli is always available for casual meals and great hamburgers.

Staying overnight is an experience all to itself. With all the charm of an historic inn, the Afton House has decorated each of its rooms with antique and reproduction furnishings plus the modern convenience of telephones, private baths and televisions in every room. Deluxe rooms feature whirlpool tubs, some with outdoor balconies overlooking the magnificent St. Croix River. There are cozy rooms, too, with double beds and spacious rooms with king size beds.

Afton Cruise Lines can make your visit that much more special. Tour the St. Croix aboard the "Afton Princess," a luxury cruiser with capacity for groups from 49 to 149 that's perfect for a fun-filled day in the sun or a formal cocktail cruise and dinner buffet. The "Sweet Afton" is a luxury vessel that can accommodate groups from 10 to 49. Theme parties on board are very popular, including Jungle Fever, Tropical Vacation or Casino Cruises with lady luck.

And if you really want to make a weekend of it, opt for limousine service. The Historic Afton House Inn offers deluxe packages that include travel to and from the Inn by limousine,  complete with TV, VCR, sunroof and a beautiful wood bar, just one of many special touches you'll find along the way.

SPECIALTY SHOPS

Afton Merchant

3321 St. Croix Trail, South, Afton, MN 55001
Phone: 612-436-6753. Hrs: Wed.-Sat. 10 a.m.-
5 p.m., Sun. Noon-5 p.m.
Visa and MasterCard accepted.

With all the touches of a time gone by and a charming, historic location to match, the Afton Merchant is a gift shop to remember on the eastern edge of the Twin Cities metro area. Located in the Old Bank Building, which dates to 1913 and has been home to everything from a grocery store to an art gallery, the Afton Merchant occupies the upstairs space and features unique gifts from around the country. You'll find everything from a newly developed scented liquid hand soap to baskets by an artist whose works have been in the Smithsonian. Owners Carol and Hayne Sudheimer have painstakingly renovated this historic site and the result is drawing people from Afton and parts elsewhere.

Downstairs you'll find Our Shop, featuring the finest of consignment clothing gathered from all over the country. Our Shop, named for the many people who make a consignment store possible, also has new clothing and accessories that are unique and particularly well-made, including factory samples.

❖ ❖ ❖ ❖ ❖ ❖ ❖

The Little
Red House

3192 St. Croix Trail S., Afton, MN 55001
Phone: 612-436-7102
Hrs: Mon.-Sat. 11 a.m.-5 p.m.,
Sun. 1:30 p.m.-5 p.m.

An excellent example of how the early settlers added on room after room after room when more space was needed, The Little Red House in Afton is today a quaint place to find unusual gifts and wonderful Christmas accessories year-round.

Housed in a building originally constructed as a two-room log cabin in the early 1850's, The Little Red House is located on the main street of this quaint, New England-style village. Reverend Putnam, a Baptist minister, lived in the house and served as chaplain in the Civil War. Today, owner Charlotte Rotzel offers unusual beeswax candles, decorative accessories and more.

Explore the Gourmet Room and all its gadgets and implements to whet your appetite or browse the Christmas Room, with its year-round displays of 14 different theme trees. The Little Red House is an exceptionally quaint shop in an exceptionally quaint town. Located on the St. Croix River on the eastern edge of the Twin Cities, just south of I-94.

ANNANDALE

If you want a leisurely fishing excursion but don't have time to waste on travel, then Annandale is the perfect alternative. Located less than an hour northwest of Minneapolis, Annandale is surrounded by a host of lakes and rivers teeming with big fish. Numerous resorts cater to visitors, including those not interested in fishing.

The city's historical landmark is the 1895 *Thayer Hotel,* a national historic site with 14 rooms and period furnishings. A different, but no-less-attractive, lodging alternative is *Maple Hill Resort,* which offers luxury condominium accommodations.

The *Maple Syrup Festival* in April features pancake meals in *Pioneer Park.* The *Fourth of July Celebration* boasts the state's oldest continuous running parade. Old-time music fills the air on the third Sunday of August during the *Fiddler's Contest.*

For further information, contact:
Annandale Chamber of Commerce
R.R. 3, P.O. Box 233
Annandale, MN 55302   Phone: 612-274-5365

HISTORIC INN

The Thayer Inn—A Turn of the Century B&B Hotel	60 West Elm Street, P.O. Box 246, Annandale, MN 55302. **Phone: 800-944-6595 or 612-274-8222.** Hrs.: Open year-round. Visa, MasterCard, Discover and AmEx accepted.

Experience the romance of a bygone era in this charming Victorian inn. Built in 1895 and listed on the National Register of Historic Places, The Thayer Inn offers guests the graciousness of yesterday with all of the conveniences of today.

Each of the 13 themed, air-conditioned rooms is lovingly furnished with authentic antiques and handmade quilts, plus a private bath with claw-footed tub. A sumptuous petite De'jeuner is served bedside or breakfast in the depot lounge.

The Thayer Inn is minutes from the Twin Cities in the heart of the lakes region and no matter what the season, activity abounds. Enjoy skiing, snowmobiling, fishing, swimming, boating, horseback riding, walking paths, Pioneer Park, a petting zoo and antiquing.

After a busy day, relax in the cozy lounge with a specialty beer, one of their famous Margaritas or Irish coffee, then off to the hot tub or sauna. Mystery and Psychic weekends, packages, group and corporate rates are available.

ANOKA

If things had gone differently 100 years ago, Anoka might be known today as Minnesota's largest metropolitan community. Anoka was a booming city then; today it is comedian and storyteller Garrison Keillor's hometown and the inspiration for his fictional Lake Wobegon.

Known as the "Halloween Capital of the World," Anoka stages a giant **Halloween Celebration** each year. **The Anoka County Historical Museum** contains local artifacts dating back to before the Civil War. History buffs also enjoy the **Father Hennepin Stone** near the mouth of the Rum River. The stone carries the inscription "Father Louis Hennepin," which may have been carved by the Franciscan explorer. For summer entertainment, weekly free **Concerts in the Park** are held in **George Green Park.**

For further information, contact:
Anoka Area Chamber of Commerce
222 E. Main St., Suite 108
Anoka, MN 55303   Phone: 612-421-7130

SPECIALTY SHOP

All Sea Sun Engraving

222 E. Main Street, Anoka, MN 55303
Phone: 612-421-0508
Hrs: 9 a.m.-5 p.m., Mon.-Sat.

Specializing in attention to service and detail, All Sea Sun Engraving creates quality custom engraving for all seasons and all occasions.

As you enter the pleasant atmosphere of this establishment, you are greeted with warm smiles and cheerful greetings by owners Jim and Donna Rivers. Located in the heart of historic downtown Anoka, All Sea Sun Engraving is more than just another engraving store.

Since 1988, All Sea Sun Engraving has provided visitors and residents alike with a remarkable array of goods and services. Their shop features handcrafted merchandise as well as a variety of award and gift ideas for many occasions.

Plaques produced here can be found in airports around the world, but their product line is not limited to plaque engraving. Trophies, jewelry, glassware, in fact, anything "engravable" can be customized at this store. They also offer rubber stamps, provide packing and shipping services and can FAX a money-gram for you.

BAYPORT

The first permanent settlement in the area now known as Bayport was built in 1840. At that time, this area was comprised of three little towns on the shores of the St. Croix River; Bangor, Baytown and Middletown. In 1922, these combined towns became the Village of Bayport.

Early settlers to the area were involved with the fur trade, river boat piloting, and had built a saw mill and a grist mill in town.

The *Andersen Corporation* was established in Bayport in 1912 as the Andersen Lumber Company. Today, this company employs nearly 4,000 people at its window making facilities.

Attractions include the beautiful *St. Croix River,* and the surrounding area parks continue the tradition with a variety of recreational facilities.

For further information, contact:

City of Bayport
294 North 3rd Street
Bayport, MN 55003   Phone: 612-439-2530

ANTIQUES

Bayport House Antiques	210 N. 3rd (Hwy 95), Bayport, MN 55003 **Phone: 612-439-0330.** Hrs: 11 a.m.-5 p.m., every day except Thursday. Visa, MasterCard and AmEx accepted.

The Bayport House Antiques just opened in 1993 in a restored, 1880's house. It's chock full of beautiful antiques and collectibles—fine items for the discriminating collector.

There's a real variety here, from fine furniture to country, art, china, jewelry, pottery, lamps, stained glass, quilts, baskets, Red Wing crocks, old toys, sheet music, post cards and advertising memorabilia.

They even have a garage with furniture in the rough. This fine

establishment is located in the beautiful St. Croix River valley, just five minutes south of Stillwater on Highway 95. Bayport is the home of Andersen Windows.

If you are in the area, be sure to stop. With such an interesting variety of merchandise, there's bound to be something for everyone.

RESTAURANT

Clyde's On The St. Croix

101 S. Fifth Ave., Bayport, MN 55003
Phone: 612-439-6554
Hrs: Open daily at 11 a.m.
Major credit cards accepted.

When in Bayport, you'll want to visit Clyde's On The St. Croix. Just a short drive south of Stillwater, this fine restaurant is located on the grounds of the former Pavilion—a 1920's dance hall hotspot that attracted such star performers as Benny Goodman and the Memphis Five. With style and class, Clyde's recalls those long ago days of glamorous entertainment.

As befits the history of the area, Clyde's is devoted to exquisite dining by offering a tantalizing array of entrées to tempt the most discriminating tastebuds. Besides traditional fare like chicken, ribs, pasta dishes, burgers and seafood, they offer more exotic items like broiled walleye with asparagus and crab with Hollandaise sauce. Or try a tri-pepper filet broiled the way you like it—to perfection!

Lunch and dinner menus are the same all day, so sandwiches are available anytime. Try their walleye club, a truly unique and delicious sandwich!

Friday and Saturday, prime rib is the specialty of the day. On Sundays, Clyde's serves a brunch with more than 40 different items.

For those summer visitors, Clyde's offers outdoor dining on a beautiful patio complete with outstanding view of the St. Croix River. Did you know that the St. Croix River is one of the cleanest and most scenic rivers in the world?

When boaters feel the hunger pangs setting in, they simply land at Clyde's dock and let the chef handle the rest. Clyde's On The St. Croix is a dining experience you won't want to miss.

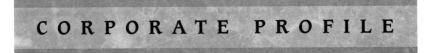

CORPORATE PROFILE

Andersen Corporation Welcome to Bayport, and the beautiful St. Croix Valley, where Andersen Corporation has made its home for 90 years. Since 1903, they've been part of a Bayport community fondly referred to as "the friendly valley."

In 1993, Andersen Corporation celebrated its 90th anniversary. The first 90 years are marked with a rich history of innovation, tradition and heritage. This history continues 90 years after the founder Hans Andersen and his two young sons started a business founded upon the sound principles they are still practicing.

Today, nearly 3,700 employees work side-by-side as "working partners." The best way to begin their story is to introduce you to a young man from Denmark who came to America to seek his fortune.

Hans Jacob Andersen, 1854-1914

In 1870, a 16-year-old Hans Andersen arrived in Portland, Maine, to start a new life. Bringing with him his only possessions—a set of drafting tools and a diploma from night school in Copenhagen—his goal was to get to the midwest.

Heading west, he purposely sought work from employers who did not speak his native language so he would have to learn English. Hans learned his first three English words while helping a team of field hands clear tree stumps: "All together boys." The phrase has come to represent his outlook on life and the business he founded.

He ended up in Spring Valley, Minnesota, and by his early 20's, he began operating a lumber yard. Shortly thereafter, he was hired by the largest sawmill in LaCrosse, Wisconsin, to dispose of a huge surplus of lumber that was the result of low demand and the depression of the 1880's. Hans possessed retail experience that served him well in this position. He was so successful that when the project was complete, he was able to buy a sawmill of his own in St. Cloud.

In 1886, he learned of another major lumber surplus of about one-million board feet just south of a town called Hudson, Wisconsin. Later, when he began managing the sawmill in town, he brought in some of the best men who had worked for him in St. Cloud. But when fall came, the mill's owners insisted these laborers be laid off during the slow winter months. Hans refused to be disloyal to these men and resigned on the spot. He then launched his own retail lumber yard and hired the men to work for him.

This loyalty to employees and "working partners" was a cornerstone for what was later to become Andersen Corporation. In addition, Hans set down three rigid principles:

1. Make a product that is different and better.

2. Hire the best people and pay top wages.

3. Provide steady employment insofar as humanly possible.

These time-honored principles have guided the company ever since.

Starting a business

Not long after Hans and his sons went into business together, they embarked on a venture that not only revolutionized the window-frame business, it impacted the manufacture of windows as well.

At the time there existed no accurate window frame on the market. So, the Andersen Lumber Company began to manufacture standardized window-frame units made of durable white pine. At the time, other firms were making frames in carload lots but did not follow any standard designs. By standardizing a few basic dimensions, the company gained the advantage of mass production. (Henry Ford came up with a similar assembly line idea of automobile production nine years later). These window frame units were made with such precision they surpassed the quality of any frame available to home builders at the time of their introduction.

By mastering what, by all accounts, was fairly logical at the time, Hans and his sons opened the door for many more innovations in the manufacture of window and door frames as well as business innovations.

The actual manufacture of windows and door frames began in earnest in 1904. By 1912, frame production reached 132,455 frames. With growth came expansion and in 1913 the Andersen Lumber Company moved to Stillwater, which later became Bayport, the company's current home. The new plant was a 66,362-square foot facility that today covers more than 2.7 million square feet.

Hans developed the "two-bundle" method of packaging knocked down window frame units in 1905. Eleven sets of both horizontal and vertical members, packaged separately, could be assembled in a variety of combinations that fit together perfectly without cutting or treating.

Just before Christmas of 1914, Hans originated another business practice that has been maintained throughout the company's history: a profit-sharing plan. That year the company paid out $1,420, which was 5 percent of the $28,400 annual payroll. 1914 also saw the death of Hans.

His son Fred, fondly known to everyone as "F.C.," was elected president. His son Herbert was elected vice-president and secretary-treasurer, a position he held until his untimely death in 1921 at the age of 36.

More industry 'firsts'

The next landmark for Andersen, and the entire window industry, was the introduction of the Andersen Master Casement in 1932. The Master Casement was a complete window unit sash, frame and hardware. With this new unit, Andersen continued to grow, despite the country's economic turmoil.

In 1940, big news was shaping up for the world and Andersen. The 40's brought the beginning of the Second World War. At Andersen the introduction of the Gliding Window revolutionized home design.

In 1952, history was made again with the introduction of the Flexivent Awning window. In the two years following that introduction, Andersen's share of the national window market doubled. More than 1 million Flexivent units were sold, equaling 50 percent of Andersen sales.

Adding to the list of Andersen firsts, the welded glass unit was introduced in 1952, dramatically increasing energy performance.

The 1960's also brought innovations. The ten-millionth Flexivent was sold. The gliding door was introduced. And, perhaps the most monumental innovation by Andersen was the introduction of the Perma-Shield system in 1966.

The low-maintenance vinyl cladding quickly made its way through the Andersen product line and became the standard of the industry.

Andersen today

Throughout the 1970's and 80's, growth was fueled by more product innovations and growing awareness of quality American products.

Terratone color sparked sales in the mid-1970's. In the early 80's, Andersen High-Performance glass was introduced. This low-e glass dramatically increased the energy efficiency of the product line and led to further sales.

The company's first entry into network television linked with an ever-growing product line and an expanding housing boom in the early 80's launched Andersen into the position of preeminent manufacturer in the nation.

Today, Andersen products are constructed of clear treated pine. Exteriors feature long-lasting Perma-Shield, while interiors feature the warmth and beauty of clear, unfinished wood, giving homeowners the choice of painting or staining them to match any decor.

A complete standard-sized product line is offered, including awning, gliding, utility, circle top, elliptical, arch, roof windows, skylights, circle and oval windows. Specialty windows, called Flexiframes, can be manufactured in sizes up to 60 feet and include trapezoids, triangles, hexagons and other shapes. Optional hardware, interior and exterior grilles, casing, extension jambs, screens, window blinds, electric operators and other accessories are available.

Andersen windows can also be brought together to create Feature Windows, exciting combinations of standard-size windows found in-stock at retail locations.

In just about every new home there is a large window combination with every shape imaginable incorporated into a large area of glass. A new generation of homeowners, builders, remodelers and designers are "designing with light" by using windows as focal points in their homes.

Today, new products are developed to meet the changing lifestyles of the 90's. In 1993, the Andersen DC Tilt-Wash Window, a window with a sash that pivots, was introduced to offer consumers an energy-efficient window designed for easy cleaning. Another new product is the Art Glass Collection, seven original stained-glass art designs to add a creative accent to Andersen windows.

From what might be called a "humble" beginning, the Andersen Corporation has grown into what it is today: the most recognized brand name in the window and patio door industry. The Andersen brand is preferred 2-to-1 by builders and remodelers and outsells the next three largest competitors combined.

No longer just a locally distributed product line as it was back at the turn of the century, Andersen markets products throughout the United States, Canada, the United Kingdom and Japan.

The three principles set down in 1903 by Hans Andersen are as alive today as when they were first penned. They are carried on by a new generation of Andersen officers, board members, family members and working partners.

Tours

Visitors to the St. Croix Valley area are welcome to visit Andersen Corporation. Daily plant tours are available but must be prearranged. For more information about reservations, call 612-439-5150.

BLOOMINGTON

Bloomington has always been a fun destination. From the past glory of the Minnesota Vikings and Twins at Met Stadium to the hard-charging North Stars at Met Center, people have long come here to have a good time. The sports teams may have gone elsewhere but the fun lives on.

Today, it is the Mall of America that brings them in, from all corners of the globe. Ever since the Mall opened in the summer of 1992, tourists have made Bloomington a prime destination for shopping and entertainment fun. And many have discovered that Bloomington has a lot to offer. Located just minutes from the Minneapolis-St. Paul International Airport, it is the home to leading corporations, such as Ellerbe, Inc., Thermo King and Donaldson Company. Companies are attracted to Bloomington's convenient location and excellent communications and infrastructure. The city is dissected by Interstates 35 and 494, which has made it a favorite location for visitors to the Twin Cities through the years.

ATTRACTIONS & EVENTS

Bloomington's attractions begin with the *Mall of America,* the nation's largest shopping and entertainment complex. This 4.2 million square-foot megamall features some of the country's top retailers and entertainment facilities. But not everything in Bloomington is as obvious as the mall. One-third of the city has been set aside for recreation and conservation, including 8,000 acres of beautifully landscaped parks. Two of them are the *Hyland Park Reserve* and the *Minnesota Valley National Wildlife Refuge,* a magnificent area embracing the river, swamps and woods and offering miles of trails for biking, hiking and skiing.

Bloomington hosts a number of arts-related events throughout the year. The most notable of these is the *Minnesota Midsummer Music Festival,* a bi-annual extravaganza featuring top-name performers and a different international theme each year. *Arts in the Park* is a citywide program held during the summer months, featuring band concerts, festivals, puppet shows, dance and theater performances. During the winter, *Winterrific* heats up the town with sporting events, an ice-fishing contest, skiing competitions and more.

For further information, contact:
Bloomington Convention and Visitors Bureau
9801 Dupont Ave. S.
Suite 120
Bloomington, MN 55431   Phone: 800-346-4289

LODGING

Hilton— *Minneapolis/* *St. Paul Airport*	3800 East 80th Street Minneapolis, MN 55425 **Phone:** 612-854-2100 **FAX:** 612-854-8002

The Hilton is just minutes away from the Mall of America and Knott's Camp Snoopy. Complimentary transportation is provided for those who wish to "Shop 'til you Drop!"

With easy access to all major freeways, the Hilton is the closest full-service hotel to the Minneapolis/St. Paul International Airport. Yet despite its three-minute distance from this traveler's gateway, it still enjoys relative tranquility from air traffic due to restrictive flight patterns over the nearby wildlife preserve. Tranquility indeed! From the moment you enter the Hotel's atrium and tree-filled lobby, you are struck by the quiet flow of a two-story waterfall and colors displayed in the rays of sunshine passing through 30-foot windows.

With 300 deluxe guest rooms and suites, the Hilton is truly in a class by itself. Each room features either a king or two double beds, remote control cable television with feature movies, two computer modem compatible telephones and all of the bathroom amenities that go with the Hilton name. Non-smoking and fully accessible rooms are also available.

There is a large, glass atrium indoor pool area, with two whirlpool spas, a redwood sauna and a complete exercise area with state-of-the-art equipment.

If quiet conversation over food and drink are your style, enjoy the relaxing Lobby Lounge or try Cafe Carabella for breakfast, lunch or dinner. If high energy is more to your liking, the Flamingos night club should fit the bill; happy hour and hors d' oeuvres will give you the strength to dance the night away. And if you prefer the finer things in life, then Biscayne Bay is the place for you. This AAA Four Diamond Award Winning restaurant features the finest in seafood, flown in daily from all three coasts and Canada to please the most discriminating of palates. Bon Appetit!

An interesting note about the Hilton is its commitment to the environment as one of the most environmentally conscious hotels in the country. Situated as they are near the wildlife refuge, it is only a natural extension for them to institute a comprehensive recycling program. From paper, glass, cardboard and cans, they go so far as to recycle food waste as animal feed.

Just minutes away and easily accessible are downtown Minneapolis and St, Paul, the Minnesota Zoo, Mystic Lake Casino, Valley Fair Amusement Park and the Metrodome.

LODGING

The Thunderbird Hotel

2201 East 78th Street, Bloomington, MN 55425
Phone: 612-854-3411
Hrs: Open year-round.
All major credit cards accepted.

There are many hotels in Minnesota, and there are many landmarks. But there are few hotels that are also landmarks. One of them is The Thunderbird Hotel. Convenient to both Minneapolis and St. Paul, The Thunderbird is centrally located along the popular Interstate 494 entertainment strip in Bloomington, only minutes away from the Minneapolis/St. Paul International Airport and directly adjacent to the new Mall of America.

You enter The Thunderbird to one of the finest and most spacious lobbies of any hotel in the upper midwest. A striking focal point is the reflecting pool and suspended stairway leading to the dramatic Hall of Tribes.

The Totem Pole Dining Room offers a relaxed atmosphere for dining and dancing, with superb cuisine at popular prices. The decor highlights the rich and beautiful atmosphere of Native American culture.

The "Pow-Wow" Cocktail Lounge features a warm and intimate atmosphere and is adorned with fascinating authentic Native American curios and relics.

The Bow & Arrow Coffee Shop is also available seven days a week and features homemade soups and daily specials.

The accommodations at The Thunderbird offer the ultimate in comfort and service. All 263 rooms and suites are tastefully decorated and equipped with the latest in RCA remote controlled tv/clock/radio sets with HBO, ESPN and CNN channels. There are also handicapped equipped and non-smoking rooms available.

With 31,154 square feet of facilities, The Thunderbird Hotel has the third largest amount of banquet, convention and meeting room space in the entire Twin Cities area. The spectacular Hall of Tribes seats up to 800. In addition, Olympic-sized indoor and outdoor pools and an exceptional exercise room, a gift shop and a game room are all conveniently available on the premises.

LODGING

| *Hotel Sofitel* | 5601 W. 78th Street
Bloomington, MN 55439
Phone: 612-835-1900 or 800-876-6303
All major credit cards accepted. |

Hospitalite. The French originated the word and Hotel Sofitel Minneapolis continues the tradition...nothing gets lost in the translation. You feel it from the first "Bonjour" of the staff and concierge. There is no welcome like that of the Hotel Sofitel.

A sense of European style can be felt throughout the hotel. All 282 luxurious guest rooms maintain that feeling from huge fluffy towels and French bath products to the nightly turndown service with a fresh-cut rose. At Hotel Sofitel, three fabulous French-inspired and award-winning restaurants are available to choose from. Enjoy hearty provincial dining at Chez Colette's brasserie, or the finest haute cuisine at Le Cafe Royal. And, for casual dining, La Terrasse is a long-standing favorite. Take a taste of France home with you from the celebrated French bakery, Le Petit Marché. Hotel Sofitel provides the style of France with the Spirit of America. It is hospitality you will savor, like the fresh baguette given to each guest at check out with a parting "Merci et à Bientôt."

❖ ❖ ❖ ❖ ❖ ❖ ❖

| *Mall of America*
Grand Hotel | 7901 24th Avenue S., Bloomington, MN 55425
Phone: 612-854-2244 or 1-800-222-8733
Across from Mall of America |

Mall of America Grand Hotel provides the ultimate in elegant accommodations. Guests' every wish is attended to by the gracious staff whose attention to detail is remarkable. 321 luxurious guest rooms and suites feature individual temperature controls, color remote television with HBO, ESPN, and in-room movies. On the concierge floor, complimentary continental breakfasts and evening cocktails with hors d'oeuvres are available to guests, as are extra amenities like terry bath robes, mineral water and fresh flowers.

Dine at Nine Mile Grill overlooking the pool atrium or enjoy 24 hour room service. Cocktails and dancing are enjoyed in Ravels lounge, which has a complimentary buffet during happy hour. People-watching beside the fireplace in The Bar is a favorite pastime. Sunday Brunch in the Grand Salon is a well-known weekly tradition.

An Executive Business Center offers computer, fax, copy machine and conference table. The athletic and health facilities are a great way to relieve stress after a busy day in meetings or at the Mall!

RESTAURANTS

Billabong Aussie Grill & Pub

5001 W. 80th Street, Bloomington, MN 55437
Phone: 612-844-0655
Hrs: Mon.-Sat. 11 a.m.-1 p.m., Sun. 10 a.m.-
11p.m. Major credit cards accepted.

Here's a pub and grill with great ambiance! The Australian theme is both contemporary and fun in a casual setting. Try their 100% Australian wines—they're very good! Or have a "Dingo Red" beer, specially brewed for the Billabong.

Step out on the beautiful patio for something to eat. They have a full menu. Favorites include Artichoke Crab Dip, Jackeroo ribs, Shepard's Camp Pie, Billabong Steak or Boomerang Chook (chicken) Sandwich.

In a hurry? All menu items can be ordered "to go."

Billabong means watering hole in Australia and this one is unique in Minnesota.

◆ ◆ ◆ ◆ ◆ ◆ ◆

Kincaid's

8400 Normandale Lake Blvd., Bloomington, MN 55437. **Phone: 612-921-2255**
Hrs: Hours vary, call ahead.
All major credit cards are accepted.

If this isn't the hottest spot in the suburbs, no one has told the crowd that pounds the doors down day and night. A sheet of window walls capture the drama of Hyland Park Nature Preserve that borders this restaurant, which anchors an ultra-modern office tower. Inside, a wall of plants continues the nature theme, borne out by clubby, masculine trappings of hunting and fishing pursuits. Kincaid's routinely captures top honors in area popularity polls, not only for its agreeable, informed service, stand-out lineup of international beers, and generous portions, but for what counts even more: skillfully prepared food.

Kincaid's chophouse menu goes beyond great steaks and prime rib. Equally quick to disappear are imaginative pastas and seafood from the fresh catch sheet. Entrées include the now-legendary herbed pan bread, and salads topped with Maytag blue cheese. Those who can still dream of dessert won't be disappointed with the smooth-as-satin creme brulee.

WILDLIFE REFUGE

Minnesota Valley National Wildlife Refuge	At the 34th Ave. exit off I-494. 3815 E. 80th St. Bloomington, MN 55425. **Phone: 612-335-2323** Hrs: Visitor Center: 9-9 Tues.-Sun. (April-Dec) Call for other hours. Refuge: Daily, daylight hours only.

Stretching for 34 miles along the Minnesota River from Fort Snelling to Jordan is the unique Minnesota Valley National Wildlife Refuge. Here are beautiful blufflands comprised of oak savannas and prairie grasses; valley woodlands dominated by giant cottonwoods, basswoods and silver maples; and extensive wetlands where cattails and bulrush flourish.

Within the metropolitan area, the refuge is a perfect home for over 300 species of wildlife that live alongside their human neighbors. The refuge Visitor Center and Headquarters, located in Bloomington, is a leading center for the U.S. Fish and Wildlife Service. Here, visitors can browse through exhibits about wildlife management.

A 12-minute, 12-projector slide program provides an orientation to the area. The exhibits are interactive and feature photos, computers and other displays that are of interest to the whole family.

A bookshop and a resource library are also located in the Visitor Center offering brochures and information including maps of the extensive hiking trails. Visitor guides to four management units that offer facilities are also available. These units are: Louisville Swamp, Wilkie, Black Dog and Long Meadow Lake.

The wildlife refuge exists to preserve and protect wildlife habitat and to encourage visitors to take advantage of this unparalleled urban preserve by participating in some of its many activities. Hiking is very popular and is permitted anywhere in the refuge except in biologically sensitive or "closed areas." Along with biking trails and horseback riding, fishing and cross-country skiing are permitted in designated areas.

SHOPPING MALL

Mall of America

60 East Broadway
Bloomington, MN 55425
Phone: 612-883-8810
Hrs: Varies by attraction

When it comes to shopping and entertainment, everybody's tastes are a little different. Chances are, only one shopping and entertainment complex can satisfy them all. Of course, it would be the biggest and the best. It would be the Mall of America.

"Minnesota's Mall of America has it all—from a $170,000 pewter village at the refined Michael Rickter Pewter Gallery to a pair of pink pig earrings for a buck at Everything's A $1," wrote *Home & Away Magazine.* How true.

Even the shear enormity of it is worth a second look. It is 4.2 million square feet of fun with approximately 2.5 million square feet of retail space, enough room to fit Rome's St. Peter's Basilica inside 20 times. It features nearly 400 specialty stores, from Oshman's Supersports, where they take "try it before you buy it" to a new level, to Everyday Hero, Marshall's, Kids' R Us and Filene's Basement. The four anchor stores, Nordstrom, Macy's, Bloomingdales and Sears, offer the best in American retail.

Then there's Knott's Camp Snoopy, an indoor amusement park for kids of all ages. It's seven acres of fun with more than 50 rides, attractions and venues. The LEGO Imagination Center is sure to impress the kids as will Golf Mountain, the ultimate in indoor miniature golf. On the Upper East Side, you'll find the entertainment district with its restaurants, night clubs, sports bars, comedy clubs and live music. And there's a 14-screen theater.

In all, more than 30 restaurants make their home at the Mall of America along with approximately 30 fast-food outlets. From upscale sophistication to downhome cookin' to the wide array of fast food selections, you'll find something to tempt your tastebuds.

Parking is not a problem, either, with 12,750 free spaces on two seven-level parking decks and four surface lots, none more than 300 feet from the closest entrance to the Mall of America. Although hours vary by store and attraction, the Mall of America itself is open Monday through Friday from 10 a.m. to 9:30 p.m., Saturdays from 9:30 a.m. to 9:30 p.m., and Sundays from 11 a.m. to 7 p.m. Knott's Camp Snoopy and the Upper East Side are open beyond Mall hours. Call for details.

Guest services available at the Mall of America include message services, foreign language translation, strollers, wheelchairs, Electronic Convenience Vehicles, lockers, a lost and found, directories and shopping bags. In short, everything you'd require for a great day of shopping and entertainment, which is exactly what millions have had at the Mall of America.

BOOKSTORE

Readwell's	Mall of America, North Garden, Bloomington, MN **Phone: 612-853-0230** Hrs: Mon.-Sat. 10 a.m.-9:30 p.m., Sun. 11 a.m.- 7 p.m. Major credit cards accepted.

When you visit Mall of America, don't miss Readwell's, a unique and interesting bookstore. Here, you'll be entertained in a theatrical setting while you browse for your favorite reading material.

An abundance of lightboxes, 3D art and video monitors display material in an active environment. There's even a listening station that allows you to preview selected books on tape!

With over 25,000 titles in stock, Readwell's offers a complete assortment of hardbacks and paperback books. Naturally, both fiction and non-fiction are represented, plus there are special extended selections in cooking, travel and children's books. Hundreds of travel videos, pens, bookends, paperweights and busts of historical figures make excellent gifts for your favorite reader or for yourself!

Author signings are frequent and they offer a monthly flyer featuring specially priced titles. Free gift wrapping and special orders are also offered.

Readwell's pricing policy is unique, too. *New York Times* bestsellers in all formats are on sale every day at up to 25% off, a real buy for the avid reader. Many additional titles are offered at up to 15% off and these selections are constantly changing.

Readwell's represents a new concept in mall book selling, more upbeat and much more stimulating than traditional stores.

ENTERTAINMENT

| *America Live* | E402 East Broadway
Mall of America
Bloomington, MN 55425
Phone: 612-854-5483 |

The Mall of America is the country's largest, most talked about shopping and entertainment complex. It's only fitting then that it should have America's finest collection of entertainment hotspots. That would be America Live.

Located on the fourth floor in the area known as the Upper East Side, America Live is a collection of eight different entertainment showcases, each offering something a little different, all guaranteeing a heavy-duty dose of fun. *America's Original Sports Bar* is the ideal setting for meeting or mingling, playing, competing or just taking in the action. With a capacity of 1,150, it features 34 televisions plus big-screen TVs and giant-screen TVs and a state-of-the-art sound and video system. Patrons can take in a plethora of sporting events via a multi-satellite and cable feed system that allows nine different events to be shown simultaneously. Plus there's a Sports Hall of Fame, a combination boxing ring/dance floor, basketball free-throw court, electronic golf games and a putting green. Check out the Owner's Box, designed to make everyone feel like a VIP with seating for up to 13.

Dueling pianos highlight *Ltl Ditty's,* a classic nightclub with two corner bars and a warm atmosphere. The Theater in the round with center stage, giant screen, VCR and sound system provides an ideal setting for continuous, live, sing-along entertainment.

Players Bar & Grill is home to great food and fun. The menu ranges from a delicious selection of fresh salads, soups and vegetables to entrées of fine continental cuisine and international flavor.

If you're looking for a wild 'n crazy Karaoke club with dance floor, stage and private bar, look to *Puzzles.* Music ranges from rock to the latest dance music and a 10-foot monitor brings all the action to you. Puzzles also features live music.

Gatlin Brothers Music City is America Live's home for country, featuring family dining and Southern hospitality. The Grille offers Southern food and fun. Gatlin's showroom is the midwest's premier country nightspot—first class country and nothin' but fun!

America's best stand-up comics pay regular visits to *Knuckleheads Comedy Club.* Nightly dinner packages are available and tiered seating ensures you'll never miss a laugh. Groups and parties are more than welcome. Voted best comedy club for two years!

At *Gator's,* you'll find Minnesota's year-round beach party club with great food, a huge dance floor and rockin' music from the DJ booth. Take the sound of the Caribbean, add the flavor of the West Indies, throw in a dash of Cajun seasoning and you've got Gator's.

Whatever your choice, you'll find it all at America Live.

ENTERTAINMENT

StarBase Omega:
The Ultimate
Laser Game

| 318 South Ave., Mall of America, Bloomington, MN 55425. **Phone: 612-858-8001** Hrs: Mon.-Thurs. 10 a.m.-10 p.m., Fri.-Sat. 10-11., Sun. 11-8. Visa and MasterCard accepted.

Message from StarBase Omega: *StarBase Omega and the planet Previa are under siege. Mutant alien lifeforms are attempting to take over this quadrant of the galaxy. This includes the planet Earth, formerly thought to be too war-like for contact by the Galactic Council. Now, that very quality is the purpose for recruiting Earthers for the battle against the aliens.*

Always wanted to be an intergalactic traveler? You won't find a more realistic simulation than at StarBase Omega, a family entertainment center with gameroom, gift shop and snack bar. Get recruited into the 21st century. Suit up and disappear right before the eyes of onlookers as a 30 foot-wide, hovering saucer beams you to Previa or StarBase Omega. Battle the aliens in a spectacular laser beam fantasy. The sounds, the sights, the movement, the whole atmosphere creates the reality in this fascinating game play. After you rid the galaxy of the aliens, stop by the StarBase Omega Snack Bar and Retail shop for unique gifts, space toys or souvenirs.

RESTAURANT

Ruby Tuesday

| Mall of America, 234 N. Garden Street, Bloomington, MN 55425. **Phone: 612-854-8282.** Hrs: Fri.-Sat. 11 a.m.-12 p.m.; Mon.-Thu 11 a.m.-11 p.m.; Sun. 11 a.m.-10 p.m. Major credit cards accepted.

When you've been shopping all day and you're ready to relax, you'll thank your lucky stars for Ruby Tuesday restaurant. Ruby Tuesday is a casual restaurant that combines service, food and atmosphere in just the right proportions.

Authentic memorabilia decorate the walls—guitars, horns, baseball gloves, bats and tennis racquets. A beautiful blue tile ceiling, classic wall hangings and wooden ceiling fans provide the backdrop. Then there are the colorful stained-glass hanging lights adorning each booth and the bar.

The complete menu features everything from soups, salads and quiche to burgers, chicken, ribs, fajitas and steaks. The full-service bar is well attended and offers a wide selection of import, premium and domestic beers along with wine and cocktails. Specialty drinks are featured daily.

Ruby Tuesday offers good tunes, good food and drink and even TVs for your relaxing enjoyment—every day of the week.

RESTAURANTS

California Cafe Bar & Grill	Mall of America, 368 South Boulevard (adjacent to Macy's) Bloomington, MN 55429 **Phone:** 612-854-2233. Hrs: Open every day for lunch and dinner. Major credit cards accepted.

Voted 'Best New Restaurant' in the *Minneapolis/St. Paul* magazine diners' poll when it opened in 1992, the California Cafe in the Mall of America continues to be one of the most popular restaurants in the Twin Cities. Dine in casual yet elegant surroundings while you savor sensational appetizers, seasonal salads, gourmet pastas, wood-fired pizzas, fresh seafood and flavorful entrées from the grill. Sample the famous sourdough bread flown in daily from San Francisco and wines from California's leading viticulture areas. Other amenities include a full bar and an exhibition kitchen where you can watch a whirl of activity while talented chefs prepare your order.

Although the California Cafe's all-fresh menu has a distinct Mediterranean accent, it travels the culinary globe with dishes influenced by Southwest, Pacific Rim and American cuisines. Homemade soups are followed by numerous first courses, salads, light entrées, pastas, pizzas and main courses, plus a special dessert menu.

◆ ◆ ◆ ◆ ◆ ◆

Napa Valley Grille	2nd level Mall of America, between Macy's and Nordstrom, Bloomington, MN 55425. **Phone: 612-858-9934.** Open Mon.-Sat. lunch and dinner; Sunday brunch and dinner. Major credit cards accepted.

The Napa Valley Grille has won accolades from the Twin Cities press for its inviting ambiance and innovative Wine Country cuisine. Light to robust seasonal entrées include fresh fish, top quality meats and game from the rotisserie and grill, elegant pastas and housemade desserts. The extensive collection of premium California varietals — many seldom available in restaurants—is on display in The Wine Cellar which doubles as a stylish and intimate banquet room.

One Sunday evening a month, they offer a Winemaker Dinner hosted by a representative from a selected California winery. The executive chef prepares a special meal for this event specifically to highlight the featured wines. It has proven quite popular to locals who love great wine and fine food.

Reflecting the name of the restaurant, the decor includes displays of Napa Valley photos and art, large wine bottles and antique wine-making equipment. Signage is patterned after old-fashioned winery signs and labels.

RESTAURANT

Tucci Benucch

Mall of America, W-114 West Market Bloomington, MN 55425. **Phone:** 612-853-0200. Hrs: Mon.-Thurs. 11:15 a.m. -10 p.m., Fri.-Sat. 11 a.m.-11 p.m., Sundays Noon-9 p.m. Major credit cards accepted.

Some restaurants have a great location, some serve wonderful food. Some restaurants have atmosphere and some have character. But very few have it all.

Welcome to Tucci Benucch.

You want location? How about smack dab in the middle of America's greatest shopping and entertainment complex, the spectacular Mall of America in Bloomington. You'll find Tucci Benucch conveniently located just inside the West Market Entrance of the Mall of America on the main level.

Of course, what's a restaurant without wonderful food. That, too, you'll find at Tucci Benucch. The restaurant, like its sister establishments in the Chicago area, has gained a reputation for serving old-world favorites at reasonable prices. The baked spaghetti is the house specialty. The restaurant offers Italian cuisine featuring thin crusted pizzas, pastas, fresh tossed salads and traditional favorites. Try the Baked Minestrone Soup with Mozzarella cheese or the Roasted Garlic Chicken or take home a bottle of their private label olive oil. Tucci Benucch even has its own private label wines to complement any meal, a Chardonnay and a Cabernet Sauvignon.

You say atmosphere is important to your dining experience? Of course it is. And at Tucci Benucch, you'll find the charming ambience of a countryside Italian home, featuring a variety of rooms each decorated in its own unique country style. From the Wine Room to the Barn to the eclectic Kitchen to the Turn-of-the-Century dining room, each has a charm and atmosphere all its own.

Perhaps you'd like a little character with your meal? You'll find that at Tucci Benucch, too. Each of the different rooms has a character all its own, each offering guests a unique dining experience. In the Barn, for example, you'll find harnesses hanging from the walls along with bridles and other riding accessories. In the Kitchen, you can watch the chefs at work. And then there's the Patio, for 'outdoor' dining, just like in Italy.

And for the little ones in your life, a kids menu is available, including beverage and ice cream in the price. There's also several family style party menus to choose from for groups from 12 to 50.

And if all that isn't enough to lure you in, the enticing aromas surely will. Reservations are accepted.

SPECIALTY SHOPS

Pueblo Spirit/ Americana

S-124 South Avenue & N-288, North Garden
Mall of America, Bloomington, MN 55425
Phone: 612-858-8801
Visa, MasterCard and AmEx accepted.

Americana and Pueblo Spirit have a lot in common with each other, not the least of which is that they both are located in the famous Mall of America.

Pueblo Spirit is an enchanting adobe style specialty store located just inside the south entrance of the mall. It features Native American gifts and jewelry from over 300 Indian artisans. Special items include turquoise and silver jewelry, pottery, sandpaintings, ceremonial pipes, buffalo skulls, war and dance shields, masks, drums, head dresses, traditional dolls, weavings, baskets, rugs, mandelas and dreamcatchers, as well as cards, books, magnets, tiles, specialty foods and Native American flute tapes. Pueblo Spirit's gift line comes in a wide range of prices and styles.

Americana presents gifts of the American Spirit, from Native American specialties to Western art, home furnishings, clothing and jewelry. Pottery and Pendleton blankets as well as exquisite spirit fetish carvings by Zuni artist Rhonda Quam and award winning contemporary jewelry by Navajo Ray Tracey are found in this wonderful, truly American gift store.

Customers also find Stetson hats, Black Hills Gold and reproduction Frederic Remington bronzes.

SPECIALTY SHOPS

Al's Farm Toys

Mall of America, 370 W. Market, Bloomington,
MN 55425. **Phone: 612-858-9139**
Hrs: Mon-Sat., 10 a.m.-9:30 p.m., Sun. 11-7
Visa and MasterCard accepted.

We've always valued farming in this country. Perhaps it's because the farm represents many of the values we hold dear—values like honest hard work, self-determination, the family, and wholesome food on the table.

It should not surprise us then, that Al's Farm Toys is so popular. They offer the complete line of ERTL farm toys that includes a wide variety of farm animals, tractors, equipment, buildings and accessories. They also offer a wide variety of other items like T-shirts, sweatshirts, metal signs, socks, plaques, figurines, games, books, puzzles, pillows—everything related to the farm. Complete farm sets are available and are perfect for collectors who want to combine their love of farm life with a unique hobby.

Their slogan is, "We'll keep ya' toy farming," and indeed they do! They offer mail order. Just send $1 for a price sheet and $7 for a full-color catalog. They also have a store at the Apache Mall in Rochester. Phone: 507-288-1616.

◆ ◆ ◆ ◆ ◆ ◆

Love From
Minnesota

W-380 West Market, Mall of America,
Bloomington, MN 55425. **Phone: 612-854-7319**
Hrs: Mon.-Fri. 10 a.m.-9:30 p.m.; Sat. 9:30-9:30;
Sun. 11-7. Major credit cards accepted.

Visitors and souvenir lovers won't want to miss this interesting store at the Mall of America. Love From Minnesota offers unique items, most of which are manufactured right in Minnesota, that reflect the state in hundreds of ways.

For example, take the gourmet fudge sauce, offered in a variety of flavors and conveniently named "Mississippi Mud." Of course, what would a Minnesota winter be without hearty wild rice soup; Love From Minnesota offers a variety of recipes for this hearty potage.

Their Minnetonka moccasins have become very popular because of comfort and durability. Handcrafted items represent many Minnesota memories, thanks to the Minnesota artisans represented here. A huge selection of T-shirts, sweatshirts and Minnesota artist prints—including James Meager—offer the Land of 10,000 Lakes in a unique medium. You can even design your own custom gift basket!

Love From Minnesota can easily handle special orders and will ship anywhere in the continental U.S.

SPECIALTY SHOPS

Chuckles

390 North Garden, Mall of America.
Bloomington, MN 55425. **Phone: 612-854-5979**
Hrs: Mon.-Fri. 10 a.m.-9:30 p.m.; Sat. 9:30-9:30;
Sun. 11-7. Major credit cards accepted.

Chuckles is a unique store in the Mall of America that will make you...well, chuckle!

Practical jokes and gag gifts abound, along with cards and gifts for every occasion and every person on your shopping list. They always carry the hottest items! For example, Mary Englebrite T-shirts and accessories plus 3-D cards and prints. There are many popular items here that will surprise and delight those who think they already have "everything."

They have posters and, count 'em, over 75 styles of balloons to choose from. Try a balloon bouquet; it's a unique gift for your special someone. They also carry a wide variety of Minnesota specialty souvenirs and seasonal items like Easter lighted houses and beautiful windchimes.

Chuckles is happy to accommodate special orders and they will ship products anywhere in the continental U.S. Be sure to stop for a smile and a chuckle when you visit the Mall of America.

◆ ◆ ◆ ◆ ◆ ◆ ◆

Minnesot-Ah!

157 East Broadway, Mall of America,
Bloomington, MN 55425. **Phone: 612-858-8531**
Hrs: Mon.-Fri. 10-9:30; Sat. 9:30-9:30;
Sun. 11-7. Major credit cards accepted.

Take a piece of Minnesota home with you!

You can find it at Minnesot-Ah, in the Mall of America. Ninety-five percent of their inventory consists of items handcrafted by Minnesota artisans and most are one-of-a-kind. Pick one of their chainsaw carvings, for example. Each piece is carved individually by a highly talented artisan in northern Minnesota and each is unique in its shape and beauty. Or choose a handpainted decoy or birdhouse, lovingly created by a native Minnesotan.

Their jewelry is made in east-central Minnesota and exemplifies the Native American influence. The biggest selection of Minnesota T-shirts, sweatshirts and color prints all bear witness to the natural beauty that is Minnesota. Keep an eye out for their pottery, also made by Minnesota artisans. It's another specialty of the store.

Whether you're a visitor or native, you'll love the variety, novelty and affordable merchandise at Minnesot-ah! They'll special order and ship in the continental U.S., too.

SPECIALTY SHOP

Hologram Fantastic

Mall of America, W368 West Market, Bloomington, MN 55425. **Phone: 612-858-9416.** Hrs: Mon.-Fri. 10 a.m.- 9:30 p.m., Sat. 9:30 a.m.-8 p.m., Sun. 11 a.m.- 7 p.m. Visa, MasterCard, AmEx and Discover accepted.

We live in a world filled with amazing discoveries, new and wonderful technology, computers, electronics and constant change. But is there anything more fascinating among all of this than the hologram?

One step inside Hologram Fantastic and you'll know what we mean.

Located in the West Market at the Mall of America, just across from Oshman's Supersports, Hologram Fantastic lets you step into the mystical world of 21st century art created with the latest in laser technology.

Holograms are true three-dimensional photographs recorded on film by a reflected laser beam. The result, on first glance, may not look all that special. But take a second look! You'll be amazed by what your eye and mind can comprehend, a stunning world full of color, light, reflection and wonder. And there is no better place to explore this unique art form than Hologram Fantastic.

The store features the cutting edge of art and science. Laser generated and embellished gifts, toys and greeting cards are all designed to dazzle the eye. These creations make wonderful conversation pieces and exotic gifts.

Something so seemingly simple as a sticker will amaze you. On first glance, it looks like a silver square. Nothing more. But look again. Inside you'll find a three-dimensional view of the earth. First it's orange, then purple, then blue, then green. No two people interpret it in quite the same way. It's truly something that must be experienced to be appreciated.

Inside the store, take in a demonstration of new scientific principles. Explore the subject yourself through the wide variety of books available on the subject and related topics, as well. Hologram Fantastic also carries other products in related fields, things like unique and unusual optical illusions, three-dimensional objects and items demonstrating other strange and fascinating qualities of light.

If all of this sounds a little bit mysterious, it is. That's why a visit is a must. The friendly staff will be all too happy to enlighten you on the technical aspects of holograms. You can even play with the toys and try things out for yourself. And they offer complete holographic services as well as framing of holographic art.

Are you looking to see things in a new light? You'll see plenty at Hologram Fantastic. And plenty you never imagined.

SPECIALTY SHOPS

Lotta Hotta
Hot & Spicy

174 E. Broadway, Mall of America, Bloomington, MN 55425. **Phone: 612-854-7250.** Hrs: Mon.-Sat. 10 a.m.-9:30 p.m., Sun. 11 a.m.-7 p.m. Visa, MasterCard, AmEx and Discover accepted.

Some like it hot. And if you count yourself among them, there's no better place to find hot, hot, hot than Lotta Hotta Hot & Spicy, the store for spice in the Mall of America. Lotta Hotta Hot & Spicy is an award-winning retailer where you'll find everything from the world's hottest pepper (the Habanero) to chili mixes, barbecue sauces, hot ketchup, hot mustard, hot oils, hot vinegar, cooking spices and Cajun seasonings and, most of all, mild to hot salsas and hot sauces.

Lotta Hotta Hot & Spicy took first place at the Fiery Foods Challenge in Albuquerque for Best Overall Product in 1993. They also won first prize at the Atlanta Gourmet Food Show for their Bloody Mary Mix and first place Best Salsa at the Salsa Bizarro in Minneapolis. Best of all, there's one of almost everything open for you to sample so you'll find out for yourself just how hot is hot.

Mail order, shipping and gift boxes are available. Call 1-800-LOT-THOT for a free catalog and heat gauge to help you decide if you want wimpy, snappy, fiery or meltdown. FAX them at 612-854-7719.

◆ ◆ ◆ ◆ ◆ ◆

Wicks N' Sticks

252 East Broadway, Bloomington, MN 55441
Phone: 612-858-9726
Hrs: Mon.-Fri. 10 a.m.-9:30 p.m.; Sat. 9:30-9:30
Major credit cards accepted.

Wicks N' Sticks is a small, quaint store that lures visitors with the sweet aroma of candles. The store has many glass windows that provide any passer-by with an interesting stop to enjoy the wide variety of shapes, sizes and colors of candles.

Speaking of sights, you can see camp Snoopy's log flume pass by the store which is located next to the escalators for easy access to the first and third floors.

Wicks N' Sticks is very affordable and offers even the most discriminating shopper a wide variety of candles and gifts, CD's and tapes. They also carry wedding merchandise like unity candles, cake-tops, guest books and much more. Check out the other home decor items, as well.

Shipping and gift boxes are also available.

SPECIALTY SHOP

The Victorian Photographer

Mall of America, E148 East Broadway,
Bloomington, MN 55425. **Phone:** 612-854-1853
Hrs: Hours vary, call ahead.
Major credit cards accepted.

If your taste runs to the romantic Victorian Era and the tintype photos of the past, you'll want to stop at The Victorian Photographer in the Mall of America for a custom photo. But don't smile in the photo because Victorian Era portraits were somber and distinguished in an attempt to portray the 'regal' qualities of the subject!

Owner and photographer Ralph Berlovitz says that "many people like the idea of looking at themselves as what they might have looked like 100 years ago. By dressing up as a Civil War soldier, gun-toting cowboy or a winsome saloon girl...they can explore roles they don't normally get to play in their regular lives." Clearly, this portraiture fulfills some romantic longing we all have for a different time and place. And, fortunately, these photos make wonderful gift items, too!

Mr. Berlovitz has gone to great lengths to provide authentic 19th century portraiture. The costumes are all from that era and even the photographic equipment is specialized for this process. The photos come out brown-toned just like they did 100 years ago. Mr. Berlovitz has even gone so far as to reproduce backgrounds like those in early photos.

This desire to be unique is reflected in his studio and the many unusual costumes he has assembled there. "I've done a lot of studying of old photos and I've tried to recreate the look as well as the 'feel' of them," he says, "and it's very important for me to make my studio different from any others."

In one hour and for less than $20, you can dress up in an authentic costume and be photographed like your great-grandparents were. You may even want to have The Victorian Photographers at your next party, dance or business event! They'll come to you and provide memorable entertainment for your guests.

SPECIALTY SHOPS

Painted Tipi	387 W. Market, Bloomington, MN 55425 **Phone: 612-854-9193.** Hrs: Mon.-Sat. 10 a.m.-9:30 p.m., Sun. 11 a.m.-7 p.m. Visa, MasterCard and Discover accepted.

Painted Tipi specializes in authentic Native American art and crafts. The items available are purchased from artists throughout the United States and focus on local Minnesota artists and artists of the Southwest U.S. Items range from limited edition prints to Zuni fetishes, from Pueblo pottery to Southwestern sterling silver jewelry and from contemporary Navajo weavings to Lakota Sioux quillwork.

Weaponry replicas, collector sandpaintings and a large selection of dreamcatchers and mandellas adorn the walls of this restful store. Native American music plays from the stereo, with tapes available for purchase. Beadwork and unique jewelry items produced by local Native American craftspeople are featured as well.

The Painted Tipi is located in the Mall of America, on the third floor West near Macy's. Many items available through the Tipi are made according to your own specifications. The staff is quite knowledgeable and all items can be shipped to you. Phone orders are accepted with credit card payment.

◆ ◆ ◆ ◆ ◆ ◆ ◆

Ralph Marlin & Company, Inc.	Mall of America-E 139, Bloomington, MN 55425 **Phone: 612-858-8106** Hrs: Mon.-Fri. 10 a.m.-9:30 p.m., Sat. 9:30 a.m.-9:30 p.m., Sun. 11 a.m.-7 p.m.

A success story is hard to come by, yet Ralph Marlin and Company, Inc., a novelty neckwear manufacturer, evolved from an idea for a single product into a successful and diversified enterprise. Recognized by *INC.* magazine as the 142nd fastest growing company in America, the company was propelled into the fashion spotlight by the infamous "fish tie."

Since its introduction in 1986, the fish tie has paved the way for fun in fashion and business and fostered a new category of "conversational" neckwear that has proven essential for fashionable expression. Now, these icons of popular culture have set new standards in fashion and menswear.

Currently, Ralph Marlin retains over 45 licensing agreements including the Three Stooges, Sierra Club, Star Trek, Paramount Studios, Columbia Pictures and Hanna-Barbera. The company also sports graphically designed neckwear from the NFL, NBA, NHL, Major League Baseball, World Cup Soccer and the 1996 Olympics.

SPECIALTY SHOP

The Wooden Bird | Mall of America, 140 E. Broadway, #E-140
Bloomington, MN 55425. **Phone: 612-851-9374**
Hrs: Mon.-Sat. 10 a.m.-9:30 p.m., Sun.
11 a.m.-7 p.m. Visa and MasterCard accepted.

From its humble beginnings in 1975 as a manufacturer of hand-crafted wooden decoys, The Wooden Bird has developed a fine reputation as an art gallery specializing in quality representations of North American wildlife, Americana, Western, figure and landscape art. In addition to the over 50 finished wood-carved products, the store offers premium limited edition art prints and collector plates of artists such as Terry Redlin, Jerry Raedeke, Clark Hulings, Steve Hanks, Ozz Franca, Ted Blaylock, Les Didier, Mike Capser, Olaf Wieghorst and Bryan Moon.

The Wooden Bird has 27 galleries in the midwest and California specializing in custom framing and representational art from Hadley House and other leading publishers. Original designs using only acid-free materials have established The Wooden Bird as trusted, conservation-quality framers. Outdoor and western theme gifts, some exclusive to The Wooden Bird, have made the galleries prime sources for gift buyers seeking the beautiful and unique.

The Wooden Bird brand, hand-carved and finished wooden decoys are loyally collected by people who value their fine quality, often passing them on as heirlooms for generations to come. The brand itself stands for the quality and tradition The Wooden Bird is known for.

Additional locations: Northtown Center, Rosedale Center, Brookdale Center, Eden Prairie Center, Southdale Center, Burnhaven Mall, Knollwood Mall and Ridgedale.

SPECIALTY SHOP

The Zoo Store™ | Mall of America, W372, Bloomington, MN 55425
Phone: 612-854-5660
Hrs: Mon.-Sat. 10 a.m.-9:30 p.m., Sun. 11-7
Major credit cards accepted.

The Zoo Store is the only store where animals profit from every sale. You see, each purchase made at The Zoo Store results in a cash contribution to the Minnesota Zoo.

Safari The Zoo Store in the Mall of America and you'll experience a truly *wild* shopping experience. You begin by entering a mythical, wild-animal kingdom through two large rock formations. Next, you encounter a revolving "animal tree" where anyone can make a new animal species by matching the head, body and legs of different animals.

On your safari at The Zoo Store, you'll also see a broad selection of animal and sealife products. There's mechanical lions, giraffe, hippos and penguins roaming freely throughout the store. You'll see one of the world's largest selections of endangered and exotic plush animals at The Zoo Store. With help from the "people handlers," you can "adopt" (buy) any one these marvelous creatures including polar bears, tigers, elephants, snow monkeys, platypuses, kangaroos or timberwolves to name but a few.

Large rock formations along the animal foot print trail reveal life-like sand-filled snakes, geckos, turtles, frogs and other critters.

The Zoo Wear garment section features unique sweatshirts, T-shirts, tote bags, hats and belts, all with dramatic animal graphic designs on them.

Continue on your safari and you will come to the African Continent Exhibit. Here you see hand-crafted wood and "soap stone" animal figures, pottery and decorative plates imported from Africa. If you get hungry on your safari, just head to the nearby quonset hut and pick up a box of Rain Forest Crunch™ or Zookies™, the cookie where animals profit from every bite.

Toward the end of your safari, or beginning depending on your route, you will happen upon a waterfall featuring Splash Art™, poster art of animal and nature scenes made for the shower. Jewelry, games, books and videos are also found on your safari. In fact, your safari may even lead you past a live 'possum, boa snake, owl, hissing cockroach, eagle or other wild animal on loan from the Minnesota Zoo.

So, if you love animals and you love collecting unique products that feature animal designs, shop where every purchase is for a good cause. Safari The Zoo Store! It's the only store where animals profit from all sales.

BROOKLYN PARK

The city of Brooklyn Park is located 10 miles northwest of downtown Minneapolis. In a little more than 20 years, Brooklyn Park has grown from a farm community to the fourth largest city in the Twin Cities Metropolitan Area and the sixth largest in the State.

Edinburgh USA is an outstanding municipal 18-hole golf course, designed by Robert Trent Jones II in the Scottish tradition.

Residents enjoy some of the finest facilities of any metropolitan suburb for recreation and education, with many parks and trail systems, an activity/ice arena/armory complex, a vocational/technical school, a community college and an historical farm to preserve its past. Brooklyn Park boasts as one of its famous residents ex-wrestler *Jesse "The Body" Ventura* who served a term as the city's mayor.

For further information, contact:
North Hennepin Chamber of Commerce
8525 Edinbrook Crossing, Suite 1
Brooklyn Park, MN 55118

SPECIALTY SHOP

Bob Evans Gifts	8501 Wyoming Ave. N., Brooklyn Park, MN 55445. **Phone: 612-425-2214** Hrs: Mon-Fri 9-9, Sat 9-5, Sun 12-5 Major credit cards accepted.

Bob Evans Gifts is one of the largest gift and collectible stores in the metro area. Three generations of customers have come from far and wide to maintain a family tradition for wedding, birthday and special occasion gifts, home accessories and collectibles.

One alcove is devoted entirely to country items, one to fragrance and potpourri, one for European lace, another for collectibles such as Lladro, Precious Moments and Heritage Houses from Department 56. Floral arrangements make up twenty percent of the shop's business and a floral design studio on the main floor gives customers a view of fantastic designs and custom work.

Bob Evans Poker Chip Sales, held twice a year in November and in April, are much anticipated events and well worth a visit for the excellent discounts available.

The store prides itself on good customer service, offers free gift wrapping and over 8,000 square feet of shopping space!

GOLF COURSE

Edinburgh USA

8700 Edinbrook Crossing, Brooklyn Park, MN
55443. **Phone: 612-424-9444**
Hrs: Open daily 6 a.m.-1 p.m.
Visa, MasterCard and AmEx accepted.

It isn't often than mere mortals get to tread on the same turf as the finest golfers in the world. They can at Edinburgh USA, however, a Robert Trent Jones design that is home to the Minnesota LPGA Classic, an annual event featuring the world's finest women golfers. You can also sample a little piece of Scotland here, too, the birthplace of golf, not to mention excellent food and outstanding facilities, all for a reasonable price.

Owned and operated by the City of Brooklyn Park, Edinburgh USA is recognized nationwide as an outstanding public golf facility. It opened in 1987 and was immediately given runner-up honors by *Golf Digest* magazine as the Best New Public Golf Course in the United States. In 1990, *Golf Digest* rated Edinburgh USA in the Top 50 Public Courses in the USA and it was also named one of the Top 100 Golf Shop Operations in the country four times in the last few years. It was host site for the 1992 National Public Links Championship.

High praise, indeed. It's no wonder. With nearly 70 bunkers and 12 acres of water, you'll be challenged on every shot. Golfers come face-to-face with features like an island fairway, a peninsula green and one of the world's largest putting surfaces, the enormous green that serves as both the 9th green and the 18th green plus the practice putting green.

The course is always in outstanding condition and, considering the level of difficulty, the pace of play is consistent. Although residents of Brooklyn Park do get preference, the course is open to everyone and green fees, at less than $30, are one of the country's truly outstanding bargains. Tee times (call after 1 p.m.) may be booked up to four days in advance. Golf carts and caddies are available.

And if the course proves too much for you, get some instruction from an excellent staff of qualified PGA professionals. The Clubhouse at Edinburgh USA is a public facility with a First Class Membership Club called the St. Andrews Club. The St. Andrews Club offers five different memberships: individual social, individual golf, joint golf (for couples), corporate social or corporate golf. The elegant dining and locker areas are the finest around and are part of 40,000 total square feet that make up the Clubhouse.

There's much more than just golf at Edinburgh USA. The Clubhouse hosts events such as wedding receptions, golf outings, holiday parties and business and social gatherings. An extensive catering brochure lists choices for the menu of preference. Fashioned after a classic Scottish manor, the Clubhouse can provide a unique touch to any gathering. A wonderful facility all around.

LODGING

The Northland Inn

7025 Northland Drive, Brooklyn Park, MN 55428
Phone: 800-441-6422 or 612-536-8300
Hrs: Open year-round
Most major credit cards accepted.

From the stunning atrium featuring two world class restaurants to its spacious whirlpool suites, The Northland Inn offers Four-Diamond luxury at affordable rates.

Opened in 1989, The Northland Inn has quickly become the place to stay in the northern region of the Twin Cities. Conveniently located at I-94 and Boone Avenue in Brooklyn Park, the hotel offers ample free parking and a staff known for courtesy and service.

Whether for business travel or a weekend getaway, this luxury hotel has it all. Each of its 231 guest rooms is actually a suite offering a separate living room, large work area, two telephones, two cable-ready televisions and an oversized whirlpool bath. Corner suites with separate meeting rooms for private meetings or entertaining are also available.

For relaxation, The Northland Inn offers a heated indoor pool and exercise room, special privileges at the nearby Northland Fitness Center, and a wide selection of golf courses, including the nationally known Edinburgh USA golf course. And with the hotel's proximity to I-94, you have easy access to the best of the Twin Cities, including the renowned Guthrie Theater, Orchestra Hall, the Metrodome and Target Center. And the Mall of America is less than half an hour away, with Dayton's and other local favorites nearby at Brookdale.

Best of all, perhaps, is the sensational dining The Northland Inn has to offer. For an intimate dinner, discover Wadsworth's. Prime rib, chops, steaks, seafood and pasta entrées are served in an elegant ambiance by an attentive wait staff. The Chef especially recommends the Baby Back Ribs and Caesar Salad, prepared at your table to your specifications. Wadsworth's is open Tuesday through Saturday nights and reservations are highly recommended.

For a less formal meal, enjoy a bountiful Regional American Cuisine at America's Harvest, open seven days a week. You'll love the fresh air setting of the atrium as you visit the breakfast and lunch kiosks, which offer a wide selection of hot entrées, lean meats, fresh fruits and vegetables. Or order a hamburger or other barbecued sandwich cooked to order at the Hearth. Later, choose from thirteen fabulous entrées on the dinner menu. Both lunch and dinner offer an absolutely sumptuous dessert buffet featuring homemade cakes, pies, cookies, and tarts—as well as frozen yogurt sundaes. And The Northland Inn offers one of the most scrumptious Sunday brunches in the Twin Cities!

BURNSVILLE

Burnsville is located in the rolling hills of Dakota County at the intersection of Interstate 35W and 35E, just south of Minneapolis and St. Paul and across the Minnesota River.

Burnsville is the southern gateway to Minneapolis and St. Paul and in close proximity to the Minneapolis/St. Paul Airport. It is centrally located near many quality attractions such as *Mall of America, Minnesota Zoo, Valleyfair, Mystic Lake Entertainment Complex,* the *Guthrie Theater, Murphy's Landing* and the *Renaissance Festival.*

Visitors to this community of over 51,000 are important to Burnsville and they take pride in providing a safe, friendly atmosphere in which to enjoy the many activities this area has to offer.

For further information, contact:
Burnsville Chamber of Commerce
14577 Grand Avenue South
Burnsville, MN 55337
Phone: 612-435-6000

LODGING

Burnsville FantaSuite Hotel	250 North River Ridge Circle, Burnsville, MN 55337. **Phone: 612-890-9550, outside metro** 800-666-7829. Major credit cards accepted.

From the ancient land of Caesar's Court to the futuristic Space Odyssey, FantaSuites suites transport you to the world of your dreams. Each suite is a unique experience, an adventure, a romantic retreat designed to completely immerse you in the getaway of your choice. Choose from any one of the 30 theme suites to capture that special mood, including Arabian Nights, Jungle Safari, Le Cave, Casino Royale, The Castle, Pharoah's Chambers, Sherwood Forest, Eastern Winds, Cinderella, Northern Lights, Lover's Leap and the ever popular Wild, Wild West family suite.

Every FantaSuite Suite includes a spacious whirlpool spa, one or more color televisions, customized furnishings and other amenities.

No matter which you choose, you will be delighted with these extraordinary accommodations. FantaSuite suites offer the ultimate in escapes and are perfect for special occasions of all kinds. Snack and whirlpool baskets, cheese trays, flowers, champagne, and robes are available. Minotti's Ristarante is located on the property.

RESTAURANT

Minnesota Steakhouse

13050 Aldrich Ave. S., Burnsville, MN 55337
Phone: 612-890-4350
Hrs: Sun.-Thurs. 4 p.m.-10 p.m., Fri.-Sat. 4 p.m.-midnight. Major credit cards accepted.

Minnesota Steakhouse is a down-home, family restaurant and proud of it. From the rustic exterior and the crackling fire that greets visitors to the knotty pine interior, visitors will feel like a part of the northwoods experience. It's just like going up north to your frontier cabin lodge!

This "Land of 10,000 Steaks" specializes in USDA choice and aged beef. The steaks are uniquely seasoned and grilled to create a delicious taste experience. The beef comes in a dozen shapes and sizes at Minnesota Steakhouse, from top sirloin to prime rib or a 20-ounce porterhouse, with plenty of choices in between. These fabulous dinners are served with a huge baked-potato, a generous salad and fast service.

Let's just say it has big portions at a mid-range price. Even the utensils are big here, sized for lumberjacks and other big eaters.

The restaurant also serves fresh seafood, baby back ribs, chicken and pasta. You can begin your dinner with a Paul Bunyan onion, a great big onion that's slivered, fried and served with an out-of-this-world sauce. Or, try the potato canoes, loaded with cheese and other good stuff.

The entrées are served with a large order of wonderfully soft Bob's bread, seasoned with Parmesan, butter and chervil. It arrives at your table too hot to touch for a minute or two, but it's worth the wait.

There's a full-service bar overlooking the fireplace from which you can order your favorite beverage or fine wine.

CHANHASSEN

Nature used its finest brushes when painting Chanhassen's landscape. The city's founders named the community Chanhassen ("sugar maple" in the Dakota language), and the name notes the most important features of the area—the woods, lakes and rolling hills of the *Minnesota River Valley.* Today a growing community only a short drive west from Minneapolis, Chanhassen has retained much of its natural beauty. In all, there are 11 lakes in the city limits, protected from excessive development by a foresighted city administration.

The *University of Minnesota Landscape Arboretum* displays the wealth of nature in Chanhassen. The arboretum houses more than 4,000 species in a 900-acre area. For spectacular indoor entertainment, there's the incomparable *Chanhassen Dinner Theatres,* a 600-seat, four-stage theatre that's one-of-a-kind in the nation.

For further information, contact:
Chanhassen Chamber of Commerce
80 W. 78th St.
Chanhassen, MN 55317   Phone: 612-934-3903

RESTAURANT

The Riviera Restaurant	560 W. 78th Street, Chanhassen, MN 56317 **Phone: 612-934-9340** Visa, MasterCard, AmEx, Diners Club and Discover are accepted.

There is something special about a family-run restaurant. Maybe it's the atmosphere of quiet elegance, run by those who know exactly what families want on a special night out. Or, perhaps it's the special camaraderie among staff, some of whom have been part of the team for 20 years. Better yet, maybe it's the wonderful food, expertly prepared by a skilled chef. The Riviera Restaurant is a combination of all of these. Tom and Lou Krueger, with son Steve and a dedicated staff, together operate one of Chanhassen's top notch family restaurants. One can't beat this combination of impeccable service and great food.

The Riviera opened to the public in 1972 and has not lost the feel of the private restaurant it once was. Homemade soups, steak and seafood entrées, succulent seafood (shrimp, walleyed pike, lobster), Beef Stroganoff, Chicken Kiev and a well-stocked salad bar make dinner at the Riviera worth a special trip. Reservations are not required for small groups, but recommended for weekend evenings.

ARBORETUM

Minnesota *Landscape* *Arboretum*	3675 Arboretum Drive, Chanhassen, MN 55317. **Phone: 612-443-2460.** Hrs.: Grounds: Mon.-Sun. 8:00 a.m.-sunset. Building & Library: Mon.-Fri. 8 a.m.-4:30 p.m., Sat. -Sun.11 a.m.-4:30 p.m. Open 361 days a year.

The Arboretum calls itself "a resource for northern gardeners," but it's also an exquisite setting for any visitor who enjoys beauty and the outdoors. Lavish gardens, extensive natural areas, and plant collections grace its 905 acres of rolling hills and woods.

Visitors may walk paths through rose gardens, herb gardens, a Japanese garden, and many others. Hikers will discover trails through woods, restored prairie, and marshes. The Three-Mile Drive—which visitors may follow by hiking, driving, or taking a narrated tram tour—winds through lovely collections of shrubs, pines, firs, balsams, miniature trees for smaller yards, flowering and fruit trees, and the hardy Northern Lights azaleas developed especially for northern climates. In the Leon Snyder Building, visitors can stroll through the Meyer-Deats Conservatory; shop in the gift shop for books, jewelry, gardening items, or stop for lunch at the Tea Room. The Anderson Horticultural Library is a nationally recognized resource for professional and home gardeners, featuring over 9,500 volumes on gardening, horticulture and natural history.

The Arboretum itself was established in 1958 by the University of Minnesota's Department of Horticultural Science, while the adjacent Horticultural Research Center was founded at the turn of the century. Since then, the Center has introduced more than 70 cold-hardy fruit varieties, and the Arboretum's Research Department has developed special cold-climate landscape varieties of azaleas, dogwood, honeysuckle, and red maple.

The Arboretum is open year-round so that visitors can enjoy the beauty and promise of all the seasons. The delights of summer gardens, gorgeous fall colors, cross-country skiing in the winter, and maple syruping in the spring—plus the seasonal special events—make the Minnesota Landscape Arboretum a treasure for all its visitors.

BED & BREAKFAST

Bluff Creek Inn

1161 Bluff Creek Drive, Chaska, MN 55318
Phone: 612-445-2735
Hrs: Open year-round.
Visa and MasterCard accepted.

If you're interested in B&B's, don't miss this one in Chanhassen, a suburb of the Twin Cities. Anne and Gary Delaney are your gracious hosts at this historic spot. (The land deed began in 1812 and the buildings were constructed in 1854!)

Naturally, the buildings were professionally restored and all the rooms are now beautifully decorated with expensive quilts, linens and antiques. Four suites at the main house have full private baths, some with whirlpools. The river bluff country setting is enhanced by the many porches and decks of the main house.

There is absolutely no lack of service or ambiance here. That includes a three course gourmet breakfast along with hors d'oeuvres with refreshments in the evening.

A most romantic and popular private suite is the Hollyhock Cottage, a dormered suite built over the barn. The suite has a private entrance, up a stairway and across a deck that looks over surrounding fields. Inside is a king-size bed tucked into an alcove. Another recess holds a double whirlpool. A cozy sitting area is arranged in front of the green and black Italian marble fireplace. The centerpiece is a table for two, set with linens, crystal and china. In the morning, the innkeeper arrives and discreetly leaves a breakfast basket.

Adjacent to the Inn are wonderful nature trails for walking. A twenty mile bicycle/skiing path runs nearby along the enchanting river bluffs. Wildlife abounds amid the seasonal Minnesota landscape.

Within minutes of the Inn are many of the Twin Cities top attractions: Minnesota Landscape Arboretum, Chanhassen Dinner Theatre,

Rennaisance Festival, ValleyFair Amusement Park, Mystic Lake Casino and the Mall of America.

Bluff Creek Inn has won many awards and raves from publications far and wide. We join the list—and so will you!

DINNER THEATRE

Chanhassen Dinner Theatres

501 W. 78th Street, Chanhassen, MN 55317
Phone: 612-934-1525 or 800-362-3515
Hrs: Open Wednesday-Sun.
All major credit cards accepted.

For 25 years, the Chanhassen Dinner Theatres have entertained local theatergoers as well as visitors from around the globe. Chanhassen Dinner Theatres present Broadway quality plays along with delicious dinners to 5,000 patrons weekly.

The *L.A. Times* calls Chanhassen Dinner Theatres "...the best dinner theatre in the country." and *Gourmet Magazine* calls it "...one of the very best." As the largest professional dinner theatre complex in the nation, Chanhassen presents such top Broadway productions as "Fiddler on the Roof" and "Phantom."

The sprawling attraction encompasses four separate theatres, two cocktail lounges, meeting and banquet rooms and a ballroom.

Full service dining rooms offer meals ranging from seafood to pasta. Group rates are available and pre-theatre cocktail parties are one way to add a special touch to an evening at the theatre. The exclusive Director's Room overlooks the main dinner theatre and can accommodate up to 32 guests in an exclusive dining area.

Tickets for productions are available with and without dinner. Another very popular ticket option is the "Show Dessert" ticket. One special price includes the show, a luscious Chanhassen specialty dessert and coffee, tea or milk.

Chanhassen Dinner Theatres is a wonderful way to introduce anyone to live theatre. Gift certificates are available. They also handle wedding receptions, cocktail parties, luncheons, private parties, business meetings, banquets or any event dinners. It's a short drive from downtown Minneapolis or St. Paul, just 5 minutes west of I-494 at State Highways 5 and 101.

A visit to Chanhassen Dinner Theatres fits the bill!

LODGING

Chanhassen *Country Suites* *by Carlson*	591 W. 78th Street Chanhassen, MN 56317 **Phone:** 612-937-2424 All major credit cards accepted.

Located just west of I-494 near the intersections of Highway 5 and 101, Chanhassen Country Suites is adjacent to the Chanhassen Dinner Theatres, and only a short jaunt from such attractions as the Old Log Theatre, Valley Fair Amusement Park, Mystic Lake Casino and the Mall of America. Although it's an ideal location for those looking for a day—or night—full of fun and entertainment, Chanhassen Country Suites is also a quiet retreat of lovely country furnishings and subdued luxury.

As the name suggests, Chanhassen Country Suites offers suites, rather than rooms, for the discriminating traveler. All suites feature king- or queen-size beds, and a full, built-in wet bar. Every suite features a large, well-lit work area and two telephones equipped with computer hook-ups. Some suites are equipped with a private whirlpool.

Visitors will especially enjoy the historic decorations in the lobby and other common areas. The centerpiece of the vaulted, two-story lobby is a unique fireplace with a hood from "Charlie's Cafe Exceptionale," a renowned Minneapolis restaurant. The old desk in another corner was once a school master's desk. Today it's still riddled with carvings of dates and initials. An antique cupboard, reconditioned sleigh seats, rugs and other antiques complete the sense of grace and warmth from an era gone by. Those who are looking for a home away from home in the Chanhassen area, coupled with the added comforts of continental "plus" breakfast, exercise room, free coffee and newspapers, and indoor pool, have been quick to find their way here.

EAGAN

The city of Eagan, Minnesota, is a Twin City suburb well suited to both citizen and business alike. It was officially designated a city in 1974 and named a "Star City" in 1984, meaning that it has prepared well for economic and industrial development. Eagan covers some 35 square miles, has 47 parks, and has over 53,000 residents.

Eagan's planned growth has attracted major multi-national, regional and local businesses. These include West Publishing, Unisys, Blue Cross/Blue Shield, Northwest Airlines, United Parcel Service, Coca-Cola and Cray Research.

ATTRACTIONS & EVENTS

In addition to abundant parks and recreational fields, Eagan offers six main attractions: *Diamond T Ranch* for horseback riding, hay and sleigh rides; *Grand Slam Entertainment Center* with miniature golf, video arcade, batting cages, krazy kars, basketball and a children's entertainment area; *Dakota Civic Theatre* offering musicals to drama throughout the year; *Caponi Art Park* lets you experience the harmony of nature and sculpture; *Scherer Flower Garden* is a fragrant, picturesque garden open to the public; and *Indoor Splatball,* a challenging sport as teams wage battles in space-age and badlands settings.

Equidistant to both Minneapolis and St. Paul, Eagan's wonderful countryside is only minutes away from cultural excitement and attractions in the metro area. Eagan is close to the Mall of America, the Minnesota Zoo, Valleyfair, casinos, professional sports and the airport.

Eagan's hospitality industry welcomes all visitors with fine accommodations *(Holiday Inn, Best Western Yankee Square Inn, Holiday Inn Express and Residence Inn by Marriott)* at reasonable prices. There are excellent restaurants and shopping centers nearby.

There is a special excitement in Eagan for such events as the *Fourth of July* celebration, *Evening in the Park Entertainment* series, *Halloween Spook Trail, Summer in the Park and Winter Weekends.*

For further information, contact:
Eagan Convention and Visitors Bureau
1380 Corporate Center Curve, Suite 116
Eagan, MN 55121
Phone: 800-324-2620

ENTERTAINMENT

Diamond T Ranch & Riding Stables	4889 Pilot Knob Road, Eagan, MN 55122 **Phone: 612-454-1464** Hrs: 7 days 10-10. Winter 10-8. Visa, MasterCard and Discover accepted.

Like to 'horse around'?

Try Diamond T Ranch & Stables in Eagan, horseback riding at its best. This is a large operation, offering more than 100 horses daily, a snack bar and miles and miles of beautiful, wooded trails in Lebanon Hills Regional Park. Owners, Jerry and Carol Thomas, offer a warm welcome to guests who enjoy the natural scene with a Western flair. In fact, Jerry is a John Wayne look-alike and has appeared often as the "Duke."

Diamond T Ranch offers its guests a variety of services including trail rides, riding lessons, horse sales, horse rentals, boarding, a Western shop, hay rides, sleigh rides, dance lessons and cross-country skiing.

If you are in need of large group entertainment, this is a unique way to satisfy your group. Diamond T has party rooms and caters food as well. Menu items include such delicacies as roast pork, top round beef, steaks, chicken and ribs combo, roast pork and turkey combo, roast turkey or chicken breast. (Custom menus are available.) Beverages, entertainment and even campfires can be arranged.

Country and Western dance lessons are held on selected weekday evenings in one of the party rooms. There are classes for both the beginner and the advanced dancer. Call for information and bring a partner!

Of course, riding lessons are offered for adults and they have a day camp for children. Diamond T is fortunate to be located next to Lebanon Hills Regional Park with over 5,000 acres of heavily wooded trails for riding, hiking, biking and skiing. This makes the Diamond T experience special for the whole family.

So, how 'bout it, pilgrim. Why not get back in the saddle at Diamond T Ranch & Riding Stables?

LODGING

Best Western Yankee Square Inn

3450 Washington Drive, Eagan, MN 55122
Phone: 612-452-0100 or 800-624-2888
Hours: Open 24 hours.
All major credit cards accepted.

This sophisticated hotel has been recently remodeled and updated to offer first class accommodations for business or pleasure. Located at Yankee Doodle and Pilot Knob Roads on Interstate 35E, the Minneapolis/St. Paul International Airport is just 10 minutes away.

This location offers a panoramic view of both downtown Minneapolis and St. Paul.

Visitors can eat at the Liberty Cafe or enjoy a continental breakfast with room service. There is also free, unlimited use of whirlpool, sauna, exercise facilities and HBO.

The hotel is only a five-minute drive from the Mall of America, Minnesota Zoo and just twenty minutes from Canterbury Downs, Mystic Lake Casino and ValleyFair Amusement Park.

Shoppers will enjoy nearby Yankee Square Shopping Center. Free shuttle service is available seven days a week to the Mall of America. The service is also available for Mystic Lake Casino and the Airport.

RESTAURANT

Al Baker's

3434 Washington Drive, Eagan, MN 55122
Phone: 612-454-9000. Hrs: Mon.-Sat. 11 a.m.-1 a.m., Sun. 9 a.m.-midnight, Sunday buffet breakfast 9 a.m.-1 p.m. Major credit cards accepted.

Good food and drink in a casual atmosphere that includes antiques and memorabilia describes this charming family owned and operated restaurant in Eagan. The Baker's menu offers a variety of delicious, mouth-watering selections for diners to choose from, all carefully prepared and served in very generous portions. For starters, Al Baker's Rib Appetizer or Bread Sticks "New York Style," are just two of the many tasty treats that await you.

Served until 3 p.m. daily, Al Baker's lunch menu features a variety of soup and sandwich combinations along with a fine selection of pasta dishes. Baker's famous thick and juicy burgers are all made from a half pound of extra lean ground beef, flame broiled and served on a fresh grilled bun with lettuce, tomato, pickle spear and french fries.

Sandwich lovers should try Baker's 6 oz. Tenderloin Steak Sandwich on a toasted French roll. Diners can also choose from superb pasta dishes and a selection of south of the border meals.

RESTAURANTS

Dougherty's Restaurant

1312 Town Centre Drive, Eagan, MN 55123
Phone: 612-681-1570
Hrs: M-F 11 a.m.-1 a.m., Sat. 4 p.m.-1 a.m., Sun.
4 p.m.-10 p.m. Major credit cards accepted.

Say you've finished power shopping at the Mall of America. Your energy is low and your nerves are jangled. Would a big, juicy prime rib in a relaxed setting help?

You bet it would!

Located just a few minutes from the Mall is Dougherty's Restaurant with an abundance of excellent food. A house speciality is the top sirloin with choice of potato, veggies and a super salad. Or try the pasta specialties like Chicken Cacciatore or Bacon and Broccoli Alfredo. Fresh seafoods and regional specialities abound, as well.

Gorgeous patio facilities include blooming flowers and tasteful umbrellas to shade the sun. A bar serves all your favorite beverages. Stained glass windows adorn the restaurant. Three TV's and separate banquet facilities round out the services.

Dougherty's Restaurant also caters for all your special activities. The staff is friendly and helpful—the mood unhurried.

◆ ◆ ◆ ◆ ◆ ◆

La Fonda de Los Lobo's

3665 Sibley Memorial Highway (Hwy 13)
Eagan, MN 55122. **Phone: 612-452-0334**
Hours: Mon.-Sat. 11 a.m.-12 midnight, Sun. 11 a.m.-
10:30 p.m., Sports Cantina open to 1 a.m.
All major credit cards accepted.

Bienvenidos, amigos and welcome to Otis Trujillo's humble abode, "the affordable family place" to dine. Guests are invited to enjoy authentic Mexican music in a relaxed and festive atmosphere as they select from a variety of Mexican and American dishes that fill the dining room with wonderful aromas. La Fonda's ambiance is enhanced by numerous examples of new Mexican artwork, pottery, and coyote (the restaurant mascot) statues.

All dishes are freshly prepared daily by La Fonda chefs who follow Mama Feloniz's great recipes. Menu selections include "sizzling" Fajitas and the house specialty LoboRito, which is a combination taco and burrito.

The Sports Cantina on the lower level features a variety of games including five pool tables and dart boards. Sports fans can watch their favorite team on any of the two big screen televisions and several smaller sets located throughout the bar area. Look for excellent, frothy Margaritas and food specials.

RESTAURANT

Caspers' Cherokee Sirloin Room	4625 Nicols Road South, Eagan, MN 55122 **Phone: 612-454-6744.** Hrs: Mon.-Sun. 11 a.m.-10 p.m., Sunday Brunch 10 a.m.-2 p.m. Major credit cards accepted.

It's no secret that Caspers' Cherokee Sirloin Room serves great steaks. In fact, this family owned restaurant is known by the locals as the "best steak place in town."

A 1993 recipient of the Beef Backer Award for beef presentation, the Cherokee continues the fine family tradition of guest satisfaction and restauranteuring established by founders Bob and Dorothy Casper 22 years ago.

Now owned and operated by the Casper's sons Tom, Rick and Jim, the original Cherokee Sirloin Room located in West St. Paul and their Eagan restaurant offer the most enjoyable menu selection of foods and beverages that are sure to please everyone young and old. Meal choices include a wide variety of hearty meat and potato dishes including ribs, chops and choice cut steaks grilled to perfection.

On the lighter side, the Cherokee offers guests a choice of chicken dishes, pasta, seafood, and a variety of Healthy Heart Program selections. Parents will find the children's menu to be reasonably priced and geared for the hungriest of little appetites.

The Casper brothers have taken great care to preserve and build on the family values that were the foundation of the original Cherokee Sirloin Room. The design of their new menu was inspired by the prayers and menus handwritten by their mother over the past 22 years.

A 100-year-old tractor in front of the restaurant gives guests a tantalizing taste of the nostalgia that awaits within. Memorabilia of simpler times decorate the walls along with many antiques, and lend charm and interest to this fine family eatery.

Casper's Sports Barn with daily specials on food and drink also boasts of having "the largest sports viewing screen in captivity." Besides the 20-foot "big screen," other TV screens are located throughout, providing ample viewing opportunities.

The Sports Barn offers Saturday night laser karaoke, darts, video games, pinball, a large bar, good rock & roll music, sports uniforms of Minnesota teams and a collection of Saloon antiques.

The Cherokee offers excellent private party facilities for everything from receptions to business meetings and banquets. Cherokee gift certificates are available in any dollar amount and make a great tasteful gift to give and receive.

RESTAURANT

Doolittles
Air Cafe

2140 Cliff Road, Eagan, MN 55122
Phone: 612-452-6627
Hrs: Mon.-Sat. 11 a.m.-1 a.m., Sun. 10 a.m.-12
p.m. Major credit cards accepted.

"Just Plane Good Food" is Doolittles' claim to fame with large portions of great food. Enjoy excellent dining in the hangar-like atmosphere of this uniquely decorated Eagan restaurant.

As you let your eyes taxi down the long list of reasonably priced menu items, you may find yourself in a holding pattern for the Buffalo Wings or the Chicken Caesar in the Aviation Salads section, both house specialties.

If your appetite clears you for take-off, then you'll want to try one of Doolittles' large assortment of Squadron Specialties including Sizzlini or the famous Doolittle Burger topped with Swiss cheese, fried onions, bacon, lettuce, and tomato served on seven-grain bread delicately grilled with Parmesan cheese. Or try the chimichangas, spaghetti or fish 'n' chips. There's a huge cargo of sandwiches, burgers and other tasty delights to send you wafting high above the usual fare found elsewhere.

Before landing, you may want to soar through the selection of heavenly delights that awaits you including a Mud Slide Pie guaranteed to satisfy any sweet tooth. First time visitors get a free sample of this famous dessert!

Aviation enthusiasts young and old will find Doolittles' large collection of WW I and WW II pictures and other memorabilia including propellers, parachutes and uniforms adorning the walls both fascinating and interesting. Looking up from your table you can see, suspended overhead, model planes that help create an atmosphere of planes in flight.

Owner Barbara Olson invites guests to visit at the large rectangular bar specializing in friendly service or to socialize during the daily happy hour that features "Happetizers" weekdays from 4 p.m.-7 p.m. and Sundays from 8 p.m.-10 p.m.

Sports fans can enjoy watching their favorite teams on Doolittles' large screen TV or at any of the eight additional viewing areas. There's plenty of seating for everyone including a great patio area for outdoor dining.

Throughout the year, Doolittles hosts numerous promotions, tournaments, and parties including prize drawings for a $100 bar tab and other valuable gifts. Good food, friendly patrons, and a wonderful atmosphere can all be found at Doolittles, the place to have high-flying fun in Eagan.

With so much passenger service and good food, too, Doolittle's Air Cafe is sure to make you a frequent flyer.

EDEN PRAIRIE

City meets country in Eden Prairie, a community of 39,000 located in the wooded hill country along the bluffs of the Mississippi River southwest of Minneapolis.

Although Eden Prairie has all the modern infrastructure and conveniences including large shopping malls typical for a city its size, it still maintains a rural flair with a substantial number of protected forest and wetland acres. The city earned its idyllic name in 1853. An eastern journalist, Elizabeth Eliot, arrived in the area and promptly called it "Garden of Eden," and the name Eden Prairie has stuck ever since.

Apparently the natural beauty of the place is still a strong lure because it is one of the Minneapolis-St. Paul metro area's most popular choices for newcomers. From an outstanding parks and recreation system to excellent schools, from natural beauty to the attention paid to preserving it during growth and development, Eden Prairie has so much to offer.

ATTRACTIONS & EVENTS

Eden Prairie residents often turn to the city's extensive park system for recreation. At the 20 developed neighborhood parks, such as those surrounding *Round Lake, Staring Lake* and *Riley Lake*, residents and visitors can enjoy swimming beaches, tennis courts and playgrounds. The two regional parks in Eden Prairie, *Anderson Lakes Regional Park* and *Bryant Lake Regional Park,* encompass several hundred acres of marsh and woodlands with excellent opportunities for fishing, boating and hiking—all within a 45-minute drive of downtown Minneapolis.

Another intriguing attraction in Eden Prairie is the *Air Museum Planes of Fame,* with its collection of World War II aircraft lovingly restored to flying condition. The major events in town include outdoor concerts every Wednesday, Friday and Sunday at 7 p.m. at *Staring Lake Amphitheater;* the *Fourth of July Celebration* at Round Lake Park and the *Schooner Days Celebration,* an old-fashioned ice-cream social in the first week of June where residents mingle and visitors can get a sense of the strong community feeling in Eden Prairie.

For further information, contact:
Eden Prairie Chamber of Commerce
250 Prairie Center Drive
Suite 130
Prairie, MN 55344   Phone: 612-944-2830

AIR MUSEUM

Planes of Fame *Air Museum*	14771 Pioneer Trail, Eden Prairie, MN 55344 **Phone: 612-941-2633** Hrs.: Tues.-Sun. 11 a.m.-5 p.m. Memorial Day weekend Warbird Airshow

Designated a "World War II Commemorative Community" in 1993, the Planes of Fame Air Museum is dedicated to the preservation of America's World War II aviation history. The air museum is committed to preserving the memory of these majestic warbirds, the gallant men who flew them and their courageous crews. Past visitors have included Medal of Honor winners and American, German and Japanese fighter Aces. The museum's 50,000 square feet of exhibit hangar space is home for one of North America's largest collections of "airworthy" WW II vintage aircraft. Each plane in the collection is flown on a regular basis and many have been featured in numerous aviation publications and television and motion picture productions.

Visitors can see informative military aviation exhibits, Stan Stokes murals and paintings, authentically reproduced ship and plane models, aerial combat films and over two dozen of the most famous aircraft of WW II. This outstanding flying collection features Army Air Corps, Navy and Marine aircraft including the area's only B-17 Flying Fortress. Other legendary aircraft in the exhibit include a B-25 Mitchell, P-38 Lightning, P-40 Warhawk, P-47 Thunderbolt, F4U Corsair, TBM Avenger and all of the Gruman "Cats." Foreign aircraft in the exhibit include a British Mk XIV Spitfire, Russian Yak-11 and the rare German-designed and Swiss-built Schlepp target tug.

The Planes of Fame Air Museum is located near the northwest gate of Flying Cloud Airport off of Pioneer Trail (Cty. Rd. #1) in Eden Prairie. Museum admission is $5.00 for adults and $2.00 for children 7-17. Big Band Hangar Dances and other special events occur throughout the year. Gift certificates, group rates, tours by appointment and WW II aviation speakers are available. Handicapped accessible.

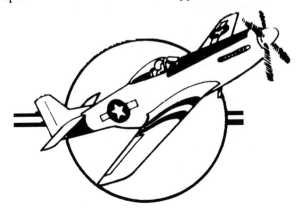

RESTAURANT

Lion's Tap Family Restaurant

16180 Flying Cloud Drive, Eden Prairie, MN 55347.
Phone: 612-934-5299. Hrs.: Mon.-Thurs. 11 a.m.-
11 p.m., Fri. and Sat. 11 a.m.-midnight., Sun. 11:30
a.m.-11 p.m. Handicapped accessibility.

Originally a roadside vegetable stand, this Eden Prairie landmark became Lion's Tap Family Restaurant in 1977. It has been cited in local and national surveys for its famous hamburgers and is included in the Top 500 Restaurants in the United States. Lion's Tap combines a comfortable atmosphere with reasonable prices making it popular with travelers, families with children, locals, business people and students.

Owners Bert and Bonnie Notermann create their famous 1/4 pound burgers using the freshest lean ground beef and a sprinkle of their own secret seasoning. Your choice of toppings are cheese, lettuce, tomatoes, bacon and great onions. Add to your order their tasty french fries and you have the Lion's Tap speciality at a great price.

Two large dining rooms and a friendly bar provide comfortable seating for small and large groups in a warm, casual atmosphere. Value, service and quality make Lion's Tap Family Restaurant an experience in dining you won't want to miss!

SPECIALTY SHOP

Crafters' Market of Minnesota, Inc.

896 County Road 42 West, Burnsville, MN 55337
Phone: 612-898-4664 and 12500 Plaza Drive
Eden Prairie, MN 55344. Hrs.: M-F, 10-9; Sat.,
10-5; Sun., 12-5. Visa and MasterCard accepted.

It's called the "year-around craft show" and "the crafters' showcase." If you're a crafts enthusiast, just call Crafters' Market paradise. Crafters' Market is a store that's laid out like a craft show, with individual displays.

Home to the work of more than 150 crafters in each store, Crafters' Market offers shoppers the opportunity to find items ranging from the whimsical and seasonal to the truly artistic. Crafters' Market also offers crafters a secure and convenient way to have their work always on display and available for sale in two great locations.

The bright, cheery, upscale appearance provides a fitting home for crafts of exceptional quality. The creations on display vary from florals to pine furniture, ceramics to oil paintings, and jewelry and clothing to wood painting. Real variety.

Crafters' Market features two locations: in Burnsville near Target and across from the Burnsville Center; and in Eden Prairie, near Menard's at I-494 and Highway 5.

EDINA

The Irish and Scot families who settled Edina in the mid nineteenth century would not recognize it today. An eclectic and active citizenry of 46,000 inhabit the city now and it is a thriving urban city.

The *Sylvan Learning Centers* provide individualized help for students in a variety of subjects.

The *Braemar Golf Course* is a regulation 18-hole course with driving range and banquet facilities. The *Edina Art Center* provides a facility and staff for area residents to enjoy the visual arts, particularly the fine arts. *The Edina Historical Society* supports a museum on the area's history. *Centennial Lakes Park* is a twenty-four acre park area with outdoor amphitheater, trademark landscaping, a paved pedestrian pathway system and many recreational opportunities.

For further information, contact:
Edina Chamber of Commerce
5701 Normandale Road
Edina, MN 55424   Phone: 612-922-0676

SHOPPING MALL

Southdale Shopping Center	66th & France Avenue, Edina, MN 55435 **Phone: 612-925-7885.** Hrs: Mon.-Fri. 10 a.m. - 9 p.m., Saturdays 10 a.m.-8 p.m., Sundays 11 a.m.-6 p.m. Most major credit cards accepted.

Who could have imagined when the doors first opened back in 1956 that Southdale Shopping Center, the nation's first fully enclosed regional shopping center, would spawn more than 1,800 imitators and still be going strong nearly 40 years later?

With 1.6 million square feet, 23 eateries and 180 of the country's top retailers, Southdale remains a leader in the shopping center industry. It offers virtually anything a shopper could want, including such well-known names as Dayton's, The Disney Store, Crate & Barrel, The Rand McNally Store, The Museum Company and The Bombay Company plus JC Penney and Carson Pirie Scott.

Not one to rest on its laurels, Southdale continues to upgrade and innovate. It offers such amenities as a computerized gift locator, free stroller and wheelchair usage, a gift-wrapping service and express tellers. And it was one of the first malls to offer family restrooms for the comfort and safety of parents and children alike. See how easy shopping can be...at Southdale.

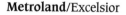

EXCELSIOR

For a glorious 40 years, from the late 1800's to the 1920's, Excelsior was one of the nation's premier resort towns. Arriving by steam railway, visitors were whisked off to the many grand hotels, or ferried across the lake by steamboats. Today, Excelsior retains much of the flavor of this romantic history in the many small and intriguing antique and specialty shops—Antiquity Rose, D.B. & Company, and The Sign of the Eagle—housed in the century-old buildings.

ATTRACTIONS & EVENTS

There are more than 50 historical buildings and sites in the Excelsior area. *The Christopher Inn,* a large Victorian summer house listed on the National Register of Historic Sites, has been restored and is open for guests. As in the early days of Excelsior, several excursion boats are waiting to take visitors on a scenic excursion of Lake Minnetonka. Restoration of the *"Minnehaha,"* a streetcar boat sunk in the 1930's and rescued from Lake Minnetonka in 1979, will be rebuilt by a group of volunteers and completed in 1995. It will then be able to ferry passengers around the lake.

Today, citizens and visitors to Excelsior still enjoy the picnic grounds, swimming beaches, and softball fields in *Excelsior Commons,* an area set aside in 1853 to be used by the "common" public. Another favorite meeting ground is *Old Log Theatre,* a dinner theatre offering farce and drama for half a century.

The second Saturday of June features an *Art On The Lake Festival* on Excelsior's Commons beside the shores of Lake Minnetonka. Excelsior celebrates fall with an antique market, parade, and good food during *Apple Days* on the first Saturday after Labor Day. There is a homecoming parade every fall and, for the last 50 years, a Halloween parade for the Excelsior children.

On the first weekend in December, there is an old-fashioned *Main Street Christmas* with tree lighting and a community concert.

For further information, contact:
Excelsior Chamber of Commerce
P.O. Box 32
Excelsior, MN 55331
Phone: 612-474-6461

ANTIQUES & DINING ROOM

| *Antiquity Rose Antiques and Dining Room* | 429 Second Street. Excelsior, MN 55331. **Phone: 612-474-2661.** Hrs.: (Antiques) Mon.-Sat. 10:30 a.m.-4:30 p.m. (Lunch) Mon.-Sat. 11 a.m.-2:30 p.m. Visa and MasterCard accepted. |

This two-story turn-of-the-century house holds an antique shop where visitors can browse through treasures and collectibles with the aroma of fresh-baked muffins and bread wafting from room to room. Antiquity Rose holds many delights waiting to be discovered, including Rose's Dining Room, a popular spot for lunch. Hooks provided for gentlemen's Derbies!

Owner Bernadine welcomes visitors to spend hours perusing the jewelry, pictures, clothing, china, glassware, and furniture that can be found throughout the house, then to relax in the dining room and enjoy creations cooked by Rona and Martha. Homemade soups, breadsticks, sandwiches, casseroles and desserts from Grandma's treasured old recipes, as well as flavorful teas are only some of the offerings on the menu. Cookbooks with favorite recipes are available.

Quality consignments are welcome.

ANTIQUES

| *The Country Look in Antiques* | 240 Water Street, Excelsior, MN 55331 **Phone: 612-474-0050.** Hrs.: Mon.-Sat. 10 a.m.-5 p.m., Thurs. 10 a.m.-8 p.m., Sun. 1 p.m.-4 p.m. Visa and MasterCard accepted. |

If you like antiques, take time to visit this charming country store with all the warmth of colonial New England featuring country antiques from the 18th, 19th and 20th centuries. You'll find some of the finest antiques available in the metro area. Chests, armoires, trunks, cupboards and all manner of treasures await to be discovered.

Thirteen years in the same location, The Country Look In Antiques prides itself on the quality and authenticity of the items attractively displayed and on the knowledge of its staff. In fact, several of the dealers and the owner have been featured in national magazines on antiques.

The store specializes in hard-to-get handmade furniture. It also features a selection of hand-loomed rugs, folk art, original painted furniture and accessories including paintings, pewter, stoneware, mirrors and a fine display of sports memorabilia. In addition, the store offers a decorating service for homeowners.

BED & BREAKFAST

Christopher Inn

201 Mill Street, Excelsior, MN 55331
Phone: 612-474-6816
Hours: Check-in 4 p.m., checkout 12 noon
Visa, MasterCard and AmEx accepted.

The Christopher Inn B&B prides itself on the warmth and hospitality of a bygone era. Designed and built in 1887, the Inn is listed on the National Register of Historic Places. It's located in Excelsior on scenic Lake Minnetonka.

The Inn offers eight rooms furnished with Victorian antiques, Persian rugs and color coordinated appointments. Six of the rooms have private baths. The Inn has been meticulously restored to provide guests with modern conveniences without detracting from the original elegance of the house.

Guests enjoy a complimentary full breakfast of fresh fruit, home-baked breads and a varied entrée. The Christopher Inn also makes an elegant setting for weddings, receptions and rehearsals.

BOOKSTORE

Frog Island Bookstore

50 Water Street, Excelsior, MN 55331
Phone: 612-474-7612
Hrs.: Open 7 days, Mon. & Fri. evenings until
9 p.m. Major credit cards accepted.

A visit to Frog Island Bookstore in Excelsior is a rare experience. Named after an island in Gideon's Bay in Lake Minnetonka, Frog Island was home to many frogs and many children taking refuge from daily household chores. The shelves are overflowing to the ceiling with books and other eclectic treats for the mind. Frog Island Bookstore specializes in children's books and limited press releases along with a collection of rare books that many other bookstores don't normally carry.

A complete collection of mystery, biography, fiction, reference, sports, regional and international travel, crafts and cooking books fill the shelves along with books dealing with current events and social issues. Maps, posters, games, hand puppets and puzzles can be found in Frog Island. Out-of-print searches and special order services are available. There is always someone available to help with selection and history on local publications.

BOAT EXCURSIONS

Paradise Charter Cruises

P.O. Box 563
Excelsior, MN 55331
Phone: 612-559-8058
Hours: Seasonal

Step aboard the "Paradise Princess," or one of her sister ships, and explore the beautiful waters of scenic Lake Minnetonka. Enjoy cruising the picturesque shoreline, while entertaining friends or business associates on one of Minnesota's most historic lakes.

Only minutes away from the city, your cruise will make you feel like you've escaped to paradise. Choose from two-, three- or four-hour weekday and weekend cruises complete with an experienced uniformed crew and complimentary dry snacks. A variety of charter packages are available that include hors d'oeuvres, luncheon and dinner buffets, and a special selection of Captain's Choice menu selections.

Paradise Charter Cruises' yachts feature teak wood decks, contemporary decor, stereo sound systems, serving areas and ample seating with spacious sun decks.

If you are looking for a unique and refreshing new way to entertain your friends or business associates, then why not try a relaxing charter cruise on beautiful Lake Minnetonka.

◆ ◆ ◆ ◆ ◆ ◆ ◆

QE Queen of Excelsior II

10 Water St., Excelsior, MN 55331
Phone: 612-474-2502
Hrs: Seasonal
All major credit cards accepted.

If you're looking for fun and relaxation under the sun or the stars, then step aboard the Queen of Excelsior or her sister ship, the 63-foot luxury yacht QE II. A magical experience awaits, as you cruise on historic Lake Minnetonka. Enjoy the enchantment of soft disco lights, glowing sunsets, intimate dancing, starlight reflections, and glimmering lights. A professional crew and galley staff including a Swiss chef, are eager to meet your every need, serving the finest in cuisine as you dine, cruise, and entertain in luxury.

These luxury cruises are ideal for celebrating business or personal occasions, weddings, anniversaries, birthdays, graduations, reunions, meetings or any occasion you want to make special.

Excursion packages include two-, three-, and four hour daytime, evening and Sunday cruises. A complete selection of menu options and drink selections is available and can be arranged to fit any budget. The ever popular Sunday Brunch cruise combines an exquisite meal with a relaxing sail on scenic Lake Minnetonka.

SHOPPING

The Excelsior Mill   310-320 Water Street
Excelsior, Minnesota 55331

The Excelsior Mill was originally a historic lumber mill. Much of the early 1900's architecture has been retained in the transformation into a mini-mall, which is now home for four exceptional specialty shops. The interior mall, which provides access to the shops, takes you back to the main street of a turn-of-the-century country village, with its brick paving, park benches, plantings and authentically detailed storefronts. The windows of the four complementary shops are packed with a variety of wonderful items which invite customers to "come on in and look around."

During the holidays, the Mill brings a touch of old-fashioned cheer to the modern world with entertaining craft demonstrations and Christmas decorations reminiscent of that earlier, slower-paced time. Shopping at the Mill is always a relaxing, pleasurable experience. Here are the shops of the Excelsior Mill:

SPECIALTY SHOPS

D.B. and Company

310 Water Street, Excelsior, MN 55331
Phone: 612-474-7428. Hrs.: Open 7 days
a week and until 7 p.m. weekdays
Visa and MasterCard accepted.

At D.B. and Company visitors will find "gatherings for heart and home," a wide collection of fine handcrafts, gifts, and decorative accessories gleaned from Minnesota to Europe. Many local artists' and artisans' works are featured at the store.

Step inside and be charmed immediately by the delights displayed everywhere. The shelves are full of nostalgic accessories, wall decor, pillows, holiday and collectible ornaments and dolls of all kinds. In one corner find baskets brimming with flowers, treasures and treats, while on the wall nearby hang dried and natural arrangements, wreaths of pine cones or grape vines and framed prints.

Visitors can also indulge their creativity by purchasing ribbons and bows, wreath or wall hanging components, and many other gatherings. D.B. and Company offers a wide range of ideas for making the heart a little happier and the home a little cozier.

❖ ❖ ❖ ❖ ❖ ❖ ❖

The Sampler

314 Water Street, Excelsior, MN 55331
Phone: 612-474-4794. Hrs.: Mon.-Fri. 9:30 a.m.-
6:30 p.m. Thurs. 9:30-8:30 p.m., Sat. 9 a.m.-
5:30 p.m., Sun. noon-4:30 p.m.
Visa, Discover and MasterCard accepted.

Specializing in quilting and needlework, The Sampler calls to mind the wonders of Grandma's attic stuffed with stitchery, pillows, lace doilies and loads of other beautiful creations. Along with finished products, visitors will also find here the basic supplies for quilting, needlework, lace making, rug braiding and related crafts.

In addition to a wide variety of inventory, The Sampler offers classes for children and adults in quilting, quilted clothing, needlework, battenburg lace, basic stenciling, braided rugs, smocking and lampshades. The Sampler can give advice on how to make crafts of all kinds. The shop also specializes in handmade gifts, custom orders, quilt finishing, framing, pillow making, doll making and most other decorative services such as lampshade making. Now everyone can enjoy the beauty of homemade wares, just like Grandma.

SPECIALTY SHOPS

Provisions

320 Water Street, Excelsior, MN 55331. **Phone: 612-474-6953.** Hrs.: Mon.-Wed., Fri.-Sat. 9:30 a.m.-5:30 a.m., Thurs. 9:30 a.m.-8:30 p.m., Sun. noon-4:30 p.m. Visa, AmEx and MasterCard accepted.

Provisions makes dinner parties and entertaining fun again. Offering a myriad of interesting and useful items for the kitchen and table, this shop has everything to make meals truly memorable.

Provisions carries tableware, porcelain dinnerware and exquisite serving pieces. The shop also carries the little touches that add so much—serving bowls, teapots, canisters, aprons, towels, placemats, even candles and an extremely varied collection of greeting cards and paper products. Hundreds of satisfied and loyal customers attest to the popularity of Provisions' merchandise. Many out-of-state customers even call in to order special gifts or just stock up on their favorite kitchenware.

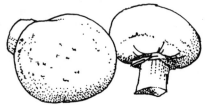

The Sign Of The Eagle

312 Water Street, Excelsior, Minnesota 55331 **Phone: 612-474-2315.** Hrs.: Mon.-Sat. 9:30 a.m.-5:30 p.m., Thurs. 9:30 a.m.-8:30 p.m., Sun. noon-4:30 p.m.

If you love decorating in early Americana, Shaker, or country decor, you'll love The Sign of the Eagle. This exceptional shop specializes in early Americana and country reproduction furniture and accessories. You'll find lovely tables, chairs, hutches, beds and all manner of country cupboards in pine, birch and cherry.

The shop has a large selection of accessories and they specialize in hard-to-find quality authentic items in lighting, rugs, linens, framed prints and other necessaries for the colonial or country home. They have an unusually large selection of authentic lighting fixtures and lamps.

The friendly staff will be happy to help you with your decorating or gift selections and you can always special order exactly what you want at The Sign of the Eagle.

The Eagle is always worth the visit whether for serious decorating or just for the pleasure of browsing.

SPECIALTY SHOPS

The Doll Buggy

234 Water Street, Excelsior, MN 55331
Phone: 612-474-1861. Hrs.: Summer, Mon. -
Sat. 10 a.m.-5:30 p.m. Seasonally, evenings and
Sundays. Visa and MasterCard accepted.

You're greeted by many friendly and familiar faces as you step into this charming store. The Doll Buggy offers dolls and bears, bears and dolls—hundreds of them line the shelves in every style and size imaginable!

The dolls and bears range from playable to highly collectible. Some are handmade locally or are imported. All are delightful and a treat to look at.

Prices range from a few dollars to hundreds of dollars. There are lots of unique dolls and items for seasonal or other themes, too. Baby dolls, amusing dolls, elegant dolls, tiny dolls, Christmas dolls, huge dolls, one-of-a-kind dolls and antique dolls—all abound.

So many lovely treasures! And the knowledgeable sales people provide excellent service and a detailed background on each item.

Need a gift for someone special? Or do you collect these wonderful friends? The Doll Buggy has just what you need!

◆ ◆ ◆ ◆ ◆ ◆

Mary O'Neal & Company

221 Water Street, Excelsior, MN 55331. **Phone:**
612-470-0205. Hrs.: Mon.-Sat. 10 a.m.-5 p.m.
Sunday-12 noon to 4 p.m. Closed Sundays
January-March. Visa and MasterCard accepted.

"Home of gently used furniture" is the motto at Mary O'Neal & Company located in Excelsior, Minnesota. The store is filled with consignment household furnishings of all kinds, from the usual to the unusual, including art and antiques of exceptional quality from all over the U.S. Art works and furnishings may include paintings, prints, tapestries, linens, lamps, chandeliers, mirrors, silver, china, crystal, old books and rugs. At the store you can find a variety, ranging from a fine antique hand-carved walnut rocker to a wonderful contemporary glass-topped dining table and chairs that sells for much less than retail!

There are times when a complete estate will be consigned to Mary O'Neal & Company. Mary O'Neal & Company will also conduct your estate or moving sale for you in your own location.

Consignment stores are a popular trend and this one provides an exceptional alternative to traditional furniture shopping. Be sure to stop. You'll be surprised at the store's uniqueness, charm and variety.

SPECIALTY SHOP

Area Wide Cycle

229 Water Street. Excelsior, MN 55331. **Phone:** 612-474-3229. Hrs.: Mon., Tues., Wed., Fri. 10 a.m.-6 p.m., Thurs. 10 a.m.-8 p.m., Sat. 9 a.m.- 6 p.m.Visa, AmEx and MasterCard accepted.

Are you the outdoors type? If you are, you'll want to make a special trip to Area Wide Cycle for a variety of equipment needs. In business since 1972, Area Wide Cycle offers bicycles, in-line skates, cross-country skis, ice skates, hiking boots, outdoor clothing and more.

Personal service and reasonable prices are a hallmark of the store, which is located in a building built in the 1880's. Rental equipment is offered for those who want to "test the waters" and they have a skate exchange program.

The store features a super collection and selection of all items for hiking, skiing, skating and biking in the great Minnesota outdoors. So whether you want to sell, rent or buy, Area Wide Cycle is where the trail begins!

RESTAURANT

Lord Fletcher's On Lake Minntonka

3746 Sunset Drive, Spring Park, MN 55384 **Phone: 612-471-8513** Hrs: Lunch and Dinner hours vary, call ahead. Visa, MasterCard and AmEx accepted.

Located on beautiful Lake Minnetonka, Lord Fletcher's is one of the most popular gathering spots for food and beverage in the Twin Cities area. What makes this a favorite of visitors and residents alike? Outstanding food, lakeview dining, seasonal activities and relaxed, elegant surroundings have a lot to do with it.

Summertime provides guests with three volleyball courts, boat docking and superior outdoor dining. Boaters of all types—interesting to watch—frequent Lord Fletcher's. Lake Minnetonka is the largest lake in the metro area with over 100 miles of shoreline. It's excellent for fishing, swimming, waterskiing and all activities associated with beautiful water in a natural setting.

In winter, snowmobiling, broomball and cross-country skiing are the favorites. And what better place to warm up than Fletcher's? Their menu is eclectic: walleye pike, prime rib, roast lamb, and pasta dishes. Lord Fletcher's is also excellent for private parties and for people-watching in general.

THEATRE

Old Log Theatre	P.O. Box 250 Excelsior, MN 55331 **Phone: 612-474-5951** Hrs: Box office 9 a.m.-9:30 p.m. daily.

Near the shores of Lake Minnetonka, on ten acres of wooded grounds, is the Old Log Theatre. It became the Northwest's first professional theatre company when it opened in 1940. It is known as the "oldest continuously running professional theatre in the United States."

The Old Log Theatre began as a summer stock company, performing 13 shows in 13 weeks in a converted log stable. In 1960, a new theatre was built and operation became year-round. The wooden benches and earthen floor were exchanged for comfortable, widely spaced opera seats and sloping, carpeted aisles. Seating capacity is now 655.

Dining facilities for a luncheon or dinner before the show accommodate up to 400 people. It is possible to provide chuck wagon dinners on the lawn by special arrangement.

The resident company of actors and actresses are members of Actors Equity and come from all over the country. There is also a resident staff of designers and technicians who provide the quality work seen in each production.

Productions include classic American drama, Broadway comedy, English farce and children's shows. Alumni of the Old Log Theater include such well-known actors and actresses as Lois Nettleton, Loni Anderson, Nick Nolte, and Julia Duffy.

Don Stolz was hired as the director in 1941 and in 1946 he purchased the Old Log Theatre. Since then, the Stolz family has been intimately involved in every aspect of the theatre. Don and his wife, Joan, and their five sons have done everything from working the box office and parking cars to acting, directing, and leading in the active management of this successful theatre. Each of their five sons shows outstanding talent in various aspects of the theatre and are actively involved at the Old Log Theatre.

HASTINGS

A scenic rivertown steeped in tradition, Hastings features rugged and colorful scenery along the Mississippi River, over 60 buildings on the National Register of Historic Places, a downtown area studded with historic buildings, and the shopping facilities, restaurants, industry and other features of a modern city. The city's beginning is a story worth telling. Supply boats headed to Fort Snelling in St. Paul were stopped here by low water in 1819. One Lt. W.G. Oliver was sent down with a detachment of soldiers to guard the provisions for the winter. They built a log cabin in a grove of trees, giving the place a name which stuck for 34 years, Oliver's Grove.

By the 1850's Oliver's Grove was a growing settlement. The founding fathers, land speculators, decided that each of them should suggest a name for the settlement and throw his choice into a hat. Hastings, the middle name of Henry Sibley, was the lucky draw. With its natural harbor on the "Great Mississippi River Highway," proximity to the St. Croix River, and the forests and fertile land surrounding the site, Hastings soon became a gateway for explorers, traders, businessmen and settlers searching for their American dream. By the time the city was officially incorporated in 1857, Hastings already had a population of 1,918, two hundred more than nearby St. Paul had at the same time. Hastings eventually attracted major companies such as Smead Manufacturing (a leading national manufacturer of filing systems), Con Agra Mill (the longest continually operating mill in the state), Tom Thumb, and Koch Refinery.

ATTRACTIONS

History is the focus for many visitors to Hastings and an excellent starting point is the historic downtown area on Second Street. Another stop is the Hudson River Gothic revival *LeDuc-Simmons Mansion.* Erected by General William Le-Duc, once secretary of agriculture for President Hayes, the mansion is now being restored by the Minnesota Historical Society to its former grandeur, complete with nine fireplaces, servant's quarters and a chapel. For more historic sites, visitors may choose to take the walking/driving tour of 44 buildings. This tour includes such landmarks as the Greek Revival *Olson House,* the Italianate *Pringle House,* and the unique *Norrish "Octagon" House.* Not to be missed is the beautiful *Vermillion Falls,* called "Hastings' best-kept secret." The falls are the site of one of the state's oldest flour mills. A final must see is *Lock and Dam No. 2,* completed in 1931 to provide sufficient depth for river traffic. Located just north of the city, the lock and dam includes an observation platform for visitors to view the great barges passing on their way from St. Paul to St. Louis.

But all is not history in Hastings. Just south of the city is *The Alexis Bailly Vineyard,* where they bury their French-adapted grapevines during the winter to help them survive Minnesota's frigid winter temperatures. The Hastings area also features a variety of parks and nature areas. The *Carpenter Nature Center* offers daily access to self-guided trails, featuring a diverse landscape of wooded ravines, oak savanna, orchards and a scenic view of the lower St. Croix River. *The Spring Lake Park Reserve* just northwest of the city features hiking and cross-country ski trails and the spectacular *Schaar's Bluff Picnic Area.* For other types of recreation, *Welch Village Ski Area* and *Afton Alps* offer winter fun, while eight area golf courses and driving ranges prove popular in the summer months. *Treasure Island Casino and Bingo,* located on the Prairie Island Reservation, is another popular attraction.

EVENTS

The city holds several annual events to celebrate its heritage and ties to the mighty Mississippi. *Rivertown Days* in July is the premier festival, featuring three days of music, water-ski shows and other events. *The Front Porch Festival* in mid-May focuses on the historic heritage of the city and includes entertainment such as theatre performances, maypole dancing and rocking chair marathons. Finally, the *Main Street Festival* in late September features events with an old-fashioned theme in the historic downtown area.

For more information, contact:
Hastings Area Chamber of Commerce
119 West Second Street, Suite 201
Hastings, MN 55033.
Phone: 612-437-6775
FAX: 612-437-2697

BAKERY & DELI

Emily's Bakery and Deli	1212 Vermillion Street, Hastings, MN 55033 **Phone: 612-437-3338** (bakery) or **612-437-2491** (deli). Hrs: Mon.-Fri. 5 a.m. - 7 p.m., Sat. 5 a.m.-5 p.m., Sun. 7 a.m.-2 p.m.

Located in the Midtown Shopping Center is Emily's Bakery and Deli, still owned and operated by the same family for over 40 years. The owners have proudly maintained the family tradition of top quality, made-from-scratch bakery items.

In the bakery section, visitors are presented with a tempting array of breads, buns, rolls, doughnuts and muffins. Homemade pies and a variety of cakes decorated to order are also offered.

In the deli, which includes tables for dine-in customers, patrons can choose from an astonishing array of more than 30 different types of salads, ranging from fresh fruit salad to Szechwan pasta and old-fashioned potato salad. Sandwiches are also available, made from top-quality deli meats and the bakery's own bread.

Emily's box lunch is a tasty and wholesome alternative to a fast-food meal. How about a smoked ham sandwich with homemade cheese bread, potato salad and a bakery treat to cure those highway blues?

BED & BREAKFAST

Thorwood	315 Pine Street Hastings, MN 55033 **Phone: 612-437-3297** Visa, MasterCard and AmEx accepted.

Romance, luxury, privacy, and resounding Victorian elegance—Thorwood is one of three Victorian bed-and-breakfast inns located in Hastings and is on the National Register of Historic Sites. In 1880, Thorwood was built by William and Sarah Thompson who at that time had a lumber business on the Mississippi River.

Dick and Pam Thorson purchased the building in 1979 and with extensive renovation and redecorating opened the first Bed and Breakfast in Hastings.

The seven impeccably designed rooms are complete with feather-filled comforters, old-time working radios, fireplaces viewable from double pearl whirlpools; and warmly decorated with Victorian antiques.

There are musical wedding dolls for honeymooners. Victorian picnics are also available. Each room is a perfect setting for an intimate breakfast of oven omelets, hot pastries, sausage, muffins, fresh fruit, and fruit-filled croissants—a true Thorson trademark.

SPECIALTY SHOPS

Fancy That!

110 Second St. East, Hastings, MN 55033
Phone: 612-437-6851. Hrs.: Mon., Tues., Wed., Fri. 10
a.m.-6 p.m.; Thur., 10 a.m.- 8 p.m.; Sat. 10 a.m.- 5 p.m.;
Sunday, noon-4 p.m. (Holiday) 10 a.m.-8 p.m.
All major credit cards accepted.

Fancy That!, a specialty shop with more than 20 years of expertise, uses antiques to display its wonderful variety of gifts.

Fancy That! boasts gifts and novelties for all seasons, ages and interests and is known for its fabulous assortment of cards. There are 46 different card lines to choose from, including some handmade cards. The shop also uses separate display areas for different gift categories. A Kid's Korner, Kitchen Nook, Bath Shop and permanent Christmas Room are stocked with gifts of fine art, pottery, books, listening/feeling tapes, note cards, Hastings souvenirs and guide books, handpainted T-shirts, tennis shoes and baby things.

Stepping off the streets of century-old Hastings, visitors feel the 1890's charm carried on within the walls of the shop. The antique display units, checkout counter and cash register date back to the 1890's. A tin ceiling and pot-belly stove, old trunks and quaint tables each add the kind of warmth and charm that make this a special store you'll want to come back to time and time again.

◆ ◆ ◆ ◆ ◆ ◆ ◆

The Gift Tree

1266 W. Highway 55, Hastings, MN 55033
Phone: 612-437-5090. Hrs: Mon.-Fri. 9:30 a.m.-8:30
p.m., Sat. 9:30 a.m.-5:00 p.m., Sun. noon-4:30 p.m.
Major credit cards accepted.

Known for it gifts and collectibles for all occasions, no store could be more appropriately named than The Gift Tree.

Located in the southeast corner of the Twin Cities metro area on Highway 55 in Hastings, The Gift Tree is a unique and wonderful shop, a place with those extra special touches where you'll find the perfect gift for every occasion.

But Christmas is particularly special. From the first weekend in November you'll discover an outstanding array of keepsake ornaments on nine different decorated trees. Browse through Old World Santas, Nutcrackers, Angels, dolls and other wonderful collectibles and keepsakes.

The Gift Tree continues to believe that nothing is more important than their customers and the service you'll get from Ellen and Bob Mattila and their employees reflects that idea. Take advantage of UPS shipping and free gift wrapping.

RESTAURANT

Mississippi Belle

101 Second Street, Hastings, MN 55033
Phone: 612-437-5694. Hrs: (lunch) Tues.-Sat. 11 a.m.-
1:30 p.m. (dinner) Tues.-Thur. 5-9 p.m.
Fri.-Sat. 5 p.m.-10 p.m. Sun. noon-6 p.m.
Major credit cards accepted.

Diners can have the fun of eating aboard a riverboat that is as stable as the earth itself at Mississippi Belle, the well-known restaurant in a boat-shaped building. A local architect designed the building to look like a riverboat with a paddle wheel, instantly making the place famous.

Mississippi Belle seats 70 in a dining room highlighted by red and white Victorian furnishings; the upper deck seats 40 for private meetings, parties and other special occasions. Lovely gold leaf mirrors and steel engravings of an 1883 riverboat adorn the walls. The interior also boasts stained glass windows and crystal chandeliers; an intimate bar lies tucked to one side.

The only thing that tops the decor is the food; the luscious Canadian Walleye Pike has become quite popular and the Seafood Au Gratin is excellent. Homemade soup makes for a tasty appetizer and the orange rolls served with dinner are a treat. Diners should save room for a piece of one of the heavenly dessert pies.

Mississippi Belle earned its superlative reputation by serving great food in a warm, friendly atmosphere. Excellent service adds the perfect touch to this rare dining experience.

MINNEAPOLIS

For far too long, it was known only as the backdrop for television's Mary Tyler Moore Show, another flyover city in the Midwest. But gradually, word got out that there was much more to Minnesota's largest city than snow and cold and Mary and Lou. Then came the success of the Minnesota Twins and a host of major sporting events and a reputation as one of America's most liveable big cities and there was no turning back.

Today, Minneapolis is known across the country as one of the nation's finest urban centers, a vibrant, thriving kind of place where high-tech industries co-exist nicely with 22 lakes, where growth has not meant grime, and where family life still counts as something special. And it's known as a great place to vacation.

Why not?

Besides all those great sporting events, things like the U.S. Open golf championships, the World Series, college basketball's Final Four and the Olympic Sports Festival, Minneapolis has long been known as a cultural mecca. Throw in fabulous shopping, terrific educational and health facilities, an excellent business climate and nature's bounty and you have a recipe for greatness.

Of course, Mary and Lou knew it all along. And now the rest of the country—you included—knows it, too.

ATTRACTIONS

Mention theater and Minneapolis in the same breath and those in the know will immediately mention the *Guthrie.* It is, after all, the place that put Minneapolis theater on the map. Ironically, it was because a committed theater-going public already existed here that the famous Irish/English director Sir Tyrone Guthrie selected Minneapolis to establish his theater in 1963. It was a marriage made in heaven because Minneapolis was and is generous with its dollars for the arts and its support of the end product and Sir Tyrone made certain the product was worthwhile.

Those in the know will also tell you there is much, much more to the Minneapolis theater scene than just the Guthrie. Visitors will want to explore all manner of playhouses offering everything from the tradition of Shakespeare to the latest in avant-garde farce. The nationally renowned *Children's Theatre Company,* for example, offers professional adaptations of classical children's literature, with an occasional new production tossed into the mix to keep things fresh. *The Mixed Blood Theatre* specializes in multi-cultural productions. *Cricket Theatre* offers audiences the work of local, contemporary playwrights. *Theatre de la Jeune Lune* is a French and American company whose roots are in mime and farce. And then there's the *West Bank Theater,* located near the *University of Minnesota* campus, and *Dudley Riggs' Brave New Workshop* where you'll laugh until your guts hurt.

However, culture in Minneapolis doesn't stop on the stage. Oh, no.

Music has long been a part of the city's heritage, as well, and continues to prosper. *The Minnesota Orchestra,* for example, features the best in classical concerts with some of the world's finest musicians and conductors. Likewise, the *Minnesota Opera* brings the best in its genre to Minneapolis. Of course, the city is home to *Prince* and his peculiar brand of music, too. In fact, you'll find just about every taste represented on the local scene, scattered as it is throughout the clubs and cafes of the city. From blues to jazz to folk to rock and classical, it's all here.

Need yet more culture?

When it comes to museums, Minneapolis can hold its own thank you very much. *The Minneapolis Institute of Art,* for example, has a fine collection of European and American art. *The Walker Art Center* is nationally acclaimed and specializes in modern art and sculpture. Adjacent to the Walker is the *Minneapolis Sculpture Garden,* hailed by critics as one of America's best outdoor sculpture gardens. For history buffs, there is the *Bell Museum of Natural History.* For a taste of Minnesota's heritage, the *American Swedish Institute* features hundreds of Swedish artifacts displayed in the lovely surroundings of a turn-of-the-century mansion once owned by a prominent Swedish-American. Or if the stars are more to your liking, visit the *Minneapolis Planetarium* where you can be part of the latest in space exploration and knowledge.

"Enough already," you say? Give me shopping or give me death!

Shopping it is. If Minneapolis doesn't have it, chances are you can't get it. *Downtown Minneapolis* rivals America's best when it comes to selection. The place to begin is *Gaviidae Common,* an upscale retail paradise anchored by Neiman Marcus and Saks Fifth Avenue, and featuring some 60 high-class specialty stores surrounded by a wonderful glass atrium. Gaviidae Common (don't refer to it as a mall, please) is located on *Nicollet Mall* which isn't a mall at all. In fact, it is a street long closed to vehicles, a pedestrian walkway that connects the best in Minneapolis retail and anchors the downtown business district. Just a few blocks from the *IDS Tower's Crystal Court,* it also boasts *The Conservatory,* another upscale dining and shopping emporium. The recently remodelled *City Center* is worth a visit while *Dayton's,* a Minneapolis mainstay, is the downtown anchor department store.

For more eclectic shopping and exploration, travel south on Hennepin Avenue to *Uptown* where you'll find folks of all descriptions and retail opportunities to match.

When the day is done, you may want to rest your weary feet

awhile. What better place to do it than at the *Hubert H. Humphrey Metrodome,* Minneapolis's 65,000-seat indoor stadium. It is home to baseball's *Minnesota Twins,* the *NFL Minnesota Vikings* and the *University of Minnesota Golden Gophers* football team. On the other side of downtown is *Target Center,* home of professional basketball and major concerts and entertainment events. Both are outstanding facilities, as good as any in the United States.

By morning, you might truly be in need of relaxation. That being the case, stroll *Lake of the Isles, Lake Harriet* or *Lake Calhoun* or visit *Minnehaha Falls,* a lovely waterfall hidden in its own path. Man-made or natural, Minneapolis has the best of both worlds.

EVENTS

Winters can be long in Minnesota so Minneapolitans like to spend as much of the year outdoors as is humanly possible. As a result, that's where you'll find most of their festivals and events.

And why not? With so many fabulous lakes and terrific parkland and incredible summer weather, it's the perfect combination for events like the *Minneapolis Aquatennial.* It makes its annual appearance in mid-July and is a time for high spirits and light-hearted competition. A salute to the lakes, Aquatennial features some 250 events including two of the best parades anywhere.

In August, the *Uptown Art Fair* is a major event, a weekend filled with art of all descriptions being sold on the streets of the city. *Concerts in the Parks* is a series of outdoor music concerts held in various parks throughout the city all summer long. *The Minnesota Orchestra* offers a special summer concert series called *Viennese Sommerfest* where guest conductors and soloists join the orchestra for special appearances. A festive *Marketplatz* is part of the fun offering food and drink and entertainment outside *Orchestra Hall.*

Or if sweat equity is more your thing, the *Twin Cities Marathon* runs in October and attracts thousands of runners from around the world. Perhaps you'd like to join them.

For further information, contact:
Minneapolis Convention & Visitors Association
405 S. Eighth Street
Minneapolis, MN 55404
Phone: 612-348-4313 or 800-445-7412

ANTIQUES

Antiques Minnesota	1516 E. Lake Street, Minneapolis, MN 55407 **Phone: 612-722-6000.** Hrs: Mon, Wed.-Sat. 10 a.m.-5 p.m., Sun. noon-5 p.m. Closed Tues. Major credit cards accepted.

First opened in 1979, Antiques Minnesota has clearly become the leader in multi-dealer antique shops with 225 dealers represented in the showrooms. The showrooms are arranged as a mini-mall of four levels, offering the most diverse collection of vintage merchandise in the five-state area. Browse through 35,000 square feet of antiques and 5,000 square feet of collectibles, including furniture, textiles, pictures, glassware, linens, paper goods, china, jewelry, silver, toys, dolls, primitives and much more. Dealers are very helpful and can answer most questions. Antiques Minnesota offers some unique advantages—they offer three repair shops includ-

ing an antique clock shop, furniture restoration and lampmender. Free parking, no admission fees and educational displays round out your visit.

At Antiques Minnesota, you'll find something special in every price range. Another store is located at 1197 University Ave. W.

ART CENTER & GARDEN

Walker Art Center and Minneapolis Sculpture Garden	Vineland Place, Minneapolis, MN 55403 **Phone: 612-375-7622.** Hrs: Tue.-Sat. 10 a.m.-8 p.m., Sun. 11 a.m.-5 p.m., closed Mon. Sculpture Garden, 6 a.m.-midnight.

The Walker Art Center is internationally recognized for its exhibitions of 20th-century art, and for its innovative presentations of music, theatre, dance and film. Adjacent to the Walker is The Minneapolis Sculpture Garden, eleven-plus acres of gardens, walkways and plazas containing more than 40 sculptures ranging from human-scale pieces to large structures. The focal point is the Spoonbridge and Cherry.

The Walker Art Center, founded in 1879 by Thomas Barlow Walker, opened at its present location in 1927. The award-winning building, designed by Edward Larrabee Barnes, opened in 1971 and expanded in 1984.

Exhibitions at the Walker Art Center have included Picasso: From the Musee Picasso, Tokyo: Form and Spirit, and the first large-scale exhibition of Russian Constructivist art. A remarkable showcase of contemporary artistic expression, The Walker Art Center has an extensive schedule of performances and film/video.

ART GALLERY

Minneapolis Institute of Arts	2400 Third Ave., S., Minneapolis, MN 55404 **Phone: 612-870-3131.** Hrs: Tues.-Wed., Fri.-Sat. 10 a.m.-5 p.m., Thurs. 10 a.m.-9 p.m., Sun. Noon-5 p.m.

Home to more than 80,000 works of art, the Minneapolis Institute of Arts spans all cultures and time periods and includes painting, sculpture, decorative arts, prints and drawings, photographs, period rooms and textiles from around the world and the Minnesota Artist's Exhibition Program for the best of local art.

There is no general admission charge, except small entry fees to some special exhibits and all are free Thursday evenings. The permanent collection includes works by Rembrandt, Monet, Picasso and Van Gogh. Popular annual events include "Art in Bloom" and "Rose Fete" and feature food, entertainment, stunning floral arrangements and a sale of hand-crafted items.

The Institute offers a number of public programs, including films, lectures and family days. Tours are offered for adults and school groups. Special tours for the visually- or hearing-impaired. Visit the Studio Restaurant or Coffee Shop for lunch or a snack, the Museum Shop for posters, prints, jewelry, gifts and toys.

BOOKSTORE

Borders Book Shop	Calhoun Square, 3001 Hennepin Ave., S. Minneapolis, MN 55408. **Phone: 612-825-0336.** Hrs: Mon.-Thurs. 10 a.m.-10 p.m., Fri. - Sat. 10 a.m.-11 p.m., Sun. noon-6 p.m. Major credit cards accepted.

There are book stores and there are book stores. And as any truly dedicated reader in Minneapolis can tell you, Borders Book Shop in Calhoun Square is one of the best anywhere.

Located in the cutting-edge Uptown area, Borders Book Shop offers a huge selection, a diverse collection of titles, a wonderful atmosphere for comfortable browsing and discounts, too. Author readings and signings are frequent and there is a weekly children's story time.

Borders offers a 30 percent discount on current New York Times hardcover bestsellers, a 10 percent discount on most other hardcovers and a 30 percent discount on monthly staff selections. There is an impressive magazine and literary journal section as well as great choice in literature, history, computer books and cookbooks, more than 90,000 titles in all. Staff members have diverse interests and can provide a wide range of information. Domestic and international newspapers are also available.

BOOKSTORE

Baxter's Books

608 Second Avenue South, Minneapolis, MN 555402.
Phone: 612-339-4922. Fax: 612-339-6134.
Hrs: Mon.-Thurs. 7:30 a.m.-5:30 p.m., Fri. 7:30 a.m.-
6:30 p.m., Sat. 10 a.m.-4 p.m.
All major credit cards accepted.

Baxter's Books is a booklover's dream come true. Booklover and owner Brian Baxter has created an elegant space in which customers can browse and read at their leisure. With its handsome wood interior, comfortable tables and chairs, and many walls of books, Baxter's provides a quiet and welcome retreat from the hectic rhythm of downtown Minneapolis.

In addition, Baxter's friendly, knowledgeable staff offers personal service and professional guidance to help its customers in choosing a book that is just right for their needs.

Located in the heart of downtown Minneapolis' business district, Baxter's Books specializes in business-related publications. To satisfy the demands of its professional clientele, Baxter's boasts the widest selection of business books in the Twin Cities and serves numerous local companies on an exclusive basis.

Baxter's maintains an efficient book ordering service for its busy downtown readers and is able to locate any book in print. Baxter's also provides a delivery service that can have books on any Twin Cities doorstep within 24 hours of ordering or ship books anywhere in the world.

But Baxter's is not only for business readers. Featuring a large and varied fiction collection, many hardcover classics and the downtown's best children's section, Baxter's is a complete bookstore offering variety, eclecticism, and a huge selection of books to satisfy the discriminating literary tastes of its customers.

With its focus on personal customer service, Baxter's is attracting more and more lovers of good literature from an ever-wider area. To keep in touch with its readers, the store distributes a newsletter and facilitates several book discussion groups. Brian Baxter and fellow book expert, Ruth Heer, both make frequent presentations to Twin Cities businesses and philanthropic organizations on how to further expand the role of books in business and life.

In business now for more than five years, Baxter's Books is celebrating its success as one of the area's few thriving independent bookstores by becoming increasingly involved in local charities and events that promote literacy and a love of good books.

COMEDY CLUBS

Acme Comedy Co. & Sticks Restaurant	708 North 1st St., Minneapolis, MN 55401 **Phone: 612-338-6393.** Hrs.: Dining, Mon.-Thur., 11 a.m.-10:30 p.m.; Fri., 11 a.m.-midnight; Sat. 5 p.m.-midnight. Showtimes, Tues.-Thurs. 8 p.m.; Fri. and Sat. 8 p.m., 10:30 p.m. All major credit cards accepted.

When you go out for an evening of comedy, you want to enjoy the best available. The Acme Comedy Co. was voted "Best Comedy Club in the Twin Cities" by the *Twin Cities Reader* poll. But that's no surprise. Acme features the talents of top national and regional comedians, names and faces you'll recognize form HBO, A&E, Showtime and more.

Conveniently located in the popular warehouse district, Acme Comedy Co. is the only Twin Cities comedy nightclub with a full-service restaurant on site. In warm, friendly surroundings, Sticks Restaurant's award-winning chef presents innovative American cuisine at reasonable prices with the great service you expect. Dinner and show packages are available.

Perfect for corporate and client entertainment, Acme Comedy Co. and Sticks Restaurant offer the flexibility to cater to any group and its needs. The facility can graciously host groups from 10 to 250, as well as smaller parties.

◆ ◆ ◆ ◆ ◆ ◆ ◆

Scott Hansen's Comedy Gallery	219 Main Street SE, St. Anthony Main, Minnespolis, MN 55414 **Phone: 612-331-JOKE (5653)** Major credit cards accepted.

THIS PLACE IS A JOKE! Yes, the Comedy Gallery is a joke! A gut-busting, laugh 'til-your-face-hurts joke that has made over a million Minnesotans laugh.

From a humble beginning on top of a bar in Minneapolis, the Comedy Gallery has  developed into two award winning comedy clubs that have been chosen as Minnesota's favorite eleven times by local media polls! The two convenient locations—the Comedy Gallery in Historic St. Anthony Main in Minneapolis and the Comedy Gallery in Galtier Plaza in St. Paul—are both state-of-the-art comedy theaters with full bar service.

The Comedy Gallery has become a notorious national hot-spot for the comedy industry and a showcase for virtually every rising national comedy star. Roseanne Arnold, Jay Leno, Larry Miller, George Wallace, Jerry Seinfeld, Yakov Smirnoff, Judy Tenuta and dozens more have made their regional debuts at the club!

COMEDY THEATRE

Dudley Riggs' Theatres

Brave New Workshop, 2605 Hennepin Ave. S. Minneapolis, MN 55408. **Phone: 612-332-6620.** Hrs: Wed., Thurs., 7 p.m. Fri. 8 p.m., Sat. 8 p.m. and 10:30 p.m., Sun. 2 p.m. and 7 p.m. Major credit cards accepted.

Dudley Rigg's Brave New Workshop is a veritable institution in the Twin Cities. It is the oldest, continuing, satirical comedy revue theater in the country.

For more than 35 years, the workshop actor/writers have combined their flair for improvisation with an unflinching eye for social commentary, serving up show after show of razor-sharp, cutting-edge satire. These folks, the resident satire company on National Public Radio's "All Things Considered," are truly funny!

Alumni from the show have gone on to write for such shows as "Saturday Night Live," "Night Court" and "Murphy Brown." Louie Anderson, Susan Vass, Franken and Davis and the Flying Karamozov Brothers all started here, where the goal is to produce comedy theater for thinking people. The audience is key. "Involving audiences keeps us energized, informed and honest," says Riggs. The Workshop is handicapped-accessible, is on a bus line and has parking available. Group rates and catering offered.

GALLERY

Minneapolis Photographers' Gallery

2117 Lyndale Ave. S., Minneapolis, MN 55405. **Phone: 612-872-4020** Hrs: Tues.-Fri. 11 a.m.-7 p.m., Sat. noon-6 p.m. Major credit cards accepted.

The Minneapolis Photographer's Gallery specializes in contemporary fine art photography. The gallery exhibits emerging, mid-career and established artists from the local, regional and national scene. Photographers are welcome to submit portfolios for exhibition or consignment.

The gallery specializes in custom archival photography matting and framing. Frames are available in a variety of woods and aluminum, styles and colors for prints, posters, paintings and photography. The gallery offers six to eight shows a year including one juried show of Minnesota photographers. Each show lasts five or six weeks. To find out about upcoming shows, call for information.

Photographers represented include internationally known artists like Thomas Arndt and Ramon Muxter, Massachusetts photographer Alan W. Beam, New York-based Gretta Pratt and Minneapolis photographers Robert Anderson, Chris Faust, Deb Grossfield and David Korte.

ENTERTAINMENT

St. Anthony Main *Entertainment* *Center*	On the Mississippi across from downtown Minneapolis, 125 Historic Main St. S.E. Minneapolis, MN **Phone: 612-378-1226** **Pracna on Main: 612-379-3200**

St. Anthony Main is truly the birthplace of Minneapolis, for it was here that Father Hennepin came with the French LaSalle expedition in 1680. Father Hennepin dubbed the only cataract on the Mississippi, the "Falls of St. Anthony" in honor of his patron saint, Saint Anthony of Padua. It was the "Falls of St. Anthony" that built the city of St. Anthony and, later, Minneapolis that now sit proudly on the banks of the Mississippi River.

In the 1850's, along the Mississippi on the Main Street of the City of St. Anthony, there was the constant buzz of sawmills mingled with French, Irish brogues and Italian voices which made up the area's population. As Minneapolis grew, the importance of the structures lining Main Street became increasingly more historically significant and valuable. Today, St. Anthony Main is a renovated warehouse of the era and site of a five screen cinema, historic restaurants and saloons with outdoor cafes, outdoor concerts, historic tours and 4th of July fireworks. Or take a horsedrawn carriage ride along the cobblestone historic Main Street and view St. Anthony Falls which has attracted tourists for over 100 years.

Be sure to stop at Pracna on Main, an historic dining saloon and the oldest restaurant in Minneapolis. It is also the river's largest full-service sidewalk cafe and offers 20 distinct draft beers on tap.

"Pracna Saloon" was born in 1890 with construction of the present brick building which bears the Pracna name on the crest. The business was originally owned by Frank Pracna in partnership with the Minneapolis Brewing Company, brewers of Golden Grain Belt Beers. It served the needs of the local work force until 1919 when Prohibition stalled the business. After extensive restoration in 1973, the old Pracna re-emerged, happily opening its doors as **"Pracna on Main—A Civilized Bar and Cafe."**

Be sure to try their excellent specialty sandwiches, pastas and steaks. They are open seven days a week from 11:30 a.m. to 1 a.m. Catch the River City trolley to Pracna on Main!

HISTORIC SITE

St. Anthony Falls Interpretive Center

125 South East Main Street
Minneapolis, MN 55414
Phone: 612-627-5433

The Falls of Saint Anthony was once Minnesota's premier tourist attraction. In the nineteenth century, the only true waterfall on the Mississippi was tamed to provide the power that transformed Minneapolis from a frontier resort town into the milling capitol of the world. Visitors are once again coming to the falls to explore the area's rich history on walking tours conducted by the Minnesota Historical Society.

Many historians consider the Saint Anthony Falls historic district to be one of the most important in the country. It includes many historic buildings, some dating to the 1850's, ruins of the old mills and power canals, areas of surprising natural beauty, several islands and a wealth of colorful stories.

The stretch of the Mississippi River that runs through downtown Minneapolis between Plymouth Avenue and the I-35W bridge is called the Mississippi Mile. Today the area has reclaimed its place at the heart of the city, not as a milling center but as a vibrant entertainment district. It is now a magnet for Twin Citians and out-of-town visitors who come to play on the banks of the Father of Waters.

Abandoned mills and warehouses have found new life as nightclubs, restaurants, theaters, artist's studios and specialty stores. Shaded paths offer glimpses into the past as well as spectacular vistas of the river and downtown skyline. And open-air concerts and street performances fill summer nights with music and laughter.

The crowds can usually be found in and around Saint Anthony Main and Riverplace, twin entertainment complexes occupying massive brick warehouses dating back to the 1850's. Saint Anthony Main is the artsier and more family-oriented of the pair.

The Saint Anthony Falls Interpretive Program Office, run by the Minnesota Historical Society, offers a nice free stop for visitors who want to know more about this historic area. It occupies the main floor of the 1855 Upton Block, the oldest remaining masonry building in all of Minneapolis.

A large-scale model of the Pillsbury A Mill—once the largest flour mill in the world—is on display, along with historic photographs and illustrations of early Saint Anthony and Minneapolis.

A variety of tourist information and Minnesota history publications are also available. Call for hours and tour schedules.

James J. Hill's 1883 Stone Arch Bridge will be opened in 1994 to complete the St. Anthony Falls Heritage Trail. The sweeping curve of the bridge crosses directly in front of the falls and has been declared a National Engineering Landmark.

HISTORIC INN

Nicollet Island Inn

95 Merriam Street, Minneapolis, MN 55401
Phone: 612-331-1800
Hrs: Restaurant hours vary, call ahead.
Major credit cards accepted.

The Nicollet Island Inn is certainly a Minneapolis landmark. It's fascinating history began in 1893 when the building was erected on Nicollet Island in the middle of the Mississippi River. The granite building housed the Island Door and Sash Company for many years, was a warehouse and was used by the Salvation Army. It was refurbished and became an inn in the early 1970's. A restaurant was added in the 1980's.

Now the Inn offers the relaxed and cozy atmosphere of a charming country inn amidst the metropolitan Twin Cities. Twenty four charming and uniquely decorated guest rooms come with views of the Minneapolis skyline, the Mississippi River, Nicollet Island Park and St. Anthony Falls. The rooms have a king or queen size bed, a sitting area, cable TV and VCR and full size bath. Two jacuzzi suites feature down comforters, antique furnishings and views of the downtown area or the river.

The award-winning restaurant features a beautiful view of the Mississippi as a backdrop to exquisite local and regional cuisine. At the fireside lounge, adjacent to Nic's Bar, one can enjoy a quiet moment relaxing by the fire with the housecat, Misha. In fact, there are plenty of places to sit quietly and enjoy the cozy atmosphere.

The Inn also offers banquet facilities for groups of 10-200 people and recently implemented an offsite catering service due to high demand for their excellent food and service. Tours can be arranged, as well as special requests for group meetings, gift certificates, weekend packages or restaurant specials.

The Inn is near The Walker Art Museum, Guthrie Theatre and, of course, great shopping on Nicollet Mall or the Mall of America. Or, guests can also take the "Mississippi Mile" walking tour.

The Nicollet Island Inn is a quiet spot where one can find a relaxed home-style atmosphere. A genuinely friendly staff strives to make guests feel comfortable and at home.

LODGING

Minneapolis *Hilton and Towers*	1001 Marquette Avenue, Minneapolis, MN 55403. **Phone: 612-397-4817** Hours: Open 24 hours. All major credit cards accepted.

Conveniently located in the heart of downtown Minneapolis, the Minneapolis Hilton and Towers is connected by skyway to the vibrant downtown shopping and entertainment districts, with easy access to the Convention Center, Orchestra Hall, Metrodome, Guthrie Theatre and Walker Art Center.

The hotel has 814 luxurious rooms, including 52 suites and an upgraded Towers Level, and the largest concierge lounge in the city.

Meeting and conference facilities provide a total of 40,000 square feet including Minneapolis's largest hotel ballroom of 25,000 square feet. Carver's offers fine dining with extraordinary service, featuring American cuisine with a continental flair. Harmony's is a casual restaurant serving traditional American favorites for breakfast, lunch and dinner. The Crystal Terrace, a gracious lounge area, is the perfect place to meet for business or pleasure.

Hotel facilities include indoor pool, health club and spa featuring top of the line exercise equipment and sauna.

◆ ◆ ◆ ◆ ◆ ◆ ◆

Hyatt Regency *Minneapolis*	1300 Nicollet Mall, Minneapolis, MN 55403. **Phone: 612-370-1234 or 800-233-1234** Hours: Open 24 hours All major credit cards accepted.

The Hyatt Regency Minneapolis is located in the heart of the downtown business and financial district with a direct connection to the Minneapolis Convention Center via the enclosed skyway system.

This newly renovated hotel is designed to accommodate any size event, featuring 60,000 square feet of total function space, including a 30,000 square foot exhibit hall and two elegant ballrooms that divide into 18 distinctive meeting areas.

A dramatic and sophisticated two-story atrium is the introduction to 533 guest rooms, including 21 suites. Guests can enjoy the fully equipped health club and fitness center including indoor racquetball and tennis, heated pool, whirlpool and sauna.

Located only 20 minutes from the Minneapolis/St. Paul International Airport and less than one mile from the Metrodome, Walker Art Center and Guthrie Theatre, the Hyatt Regency Minneapolis is right in the center of it all, downtown.

LODGING

Best Western Kelly Inn

2705 North Annapolis Lane, Plymouth, MN 56441. **Phone: 612-553-1600** **FAX 612-553-9108.** Visa, Discover, AmEx and MasterCard accepted.

For a great weekend getaway, try the Best Western Kelly Inn in Plymouth. This charming hotel greets the visitor with a light, bright comfortable entrance decorated with palms and a tile floor. The pool area beckons with comfortable tables and umbrellas for year-round comfort and an airy, outdoor feel. Or try the sauna and exercise room to relieve the stresses of a busy day.

The Kelly Inn features 137 comfortable guest rooms. All rooms are tastefully decorated in pastels to give a cheery, modern look and a restful stay. Five new whirlpool suites add a touch of luxury.

Also combined with the Kelly Inn are the legendary Green Mill restaurant and the Plymouth Playhouse—that's three hotspots under one roof! The Plymouth Playhouse is an intimate 200-seat theatre best known for its toe-tapping, fast-paced musical comedies. It's hosted a myriad of professional productions. For a complete night—or weekend—of fun, stay at the Kelly Inn, dine at the award winning Green Mill restaurant and take in an exciting show at the Plymouth Playhouse.

The Kelly Inn was remodeled recently and now features seven meeting, conference and banquet rooms. The friendly, efficient staff will welcome and serve your conference needs.

The Kelly Inn is conveniently located in west Minneapolis at the intersection of Interstate 494 and Highway 55. Just minutes from downtown Minneapolis and just 25 minutes from the Mall of America, it's a perfect choice for your meeting and your lodging needs.

LODGING

Holiday Inn Metrodome	1500 Washington Ave. S. Minneapolis, MN 55454. **Phone: 612-333-4646 or 800-448-3663.** Hrs: Open year-round. Major credit cards accepted.

The Holiday Inn Metrodome is situated "right in the middle of everywhere!" The "everywhere" is a lot of famous landmarks like the Metrodome, the University of Minnesota, playhouses, comedy cabarets, excellent restaurants, fun-filled night clubs and sporting events.

But whether or not you need such a prime location, the Holiday Inn Metrodome is an excellent lodging choice. Choose from traditional double-bed guest rooms, two-room suites with king-size bed or opt for one of the cozy and romantic spa suites. All rooms are attractively designed, tastefully decorated and immaculately maintained. The Inn also offers many special packages combining deluxe accommodations with sporting events or live theatre including tickets and other perks.

The popular Grill Room and Balcony Lounge make an ideal setting for relaxed dining in a gracious atmosphere. A 14th floor health club with heated pool, sauna, whirlpool and workout room overlooks the Minneapolis skyline and the Mississippi River.

◆ ◆ ◆ ◆ ◆ ◆ ◆

Hotel Luxeford Suites	1101 LaSalle Avenue Minneapolis, MN 55403 **Phone: 612-332-6800** All major credit cards accepted.

The location is central, the setting is choice and the suites are spacious and comfortable. That's what makes the Hotel Luxeford Suites an excellent choice when you visit the Twin Cities of Minneapolis/St. Paul. Located just one block from the famous Nicollet Mall, the hotel offers the opportunity for fashionable shopping, world class entertainment and dining experiences.

The suites, with wet bars, refrigerators, microwaves, coffee makers, dual television and telephone, lend themselves well for business or for pleasure.

Cafe Luxeford serves food with a flair in an unpretentious bistro atmosphere. The lobby and adjoining clubroom are a quiet mix of interesting architecture, warm floral carpet and tapestried sofas, a good spot for a pause to reflect on the day or plan for the next.

The Luxeford offers a gentle atmosphere in an urbane setting and the superb service that only the finest hotels provide.

MUSEUMS

Bell Museum of Natural History	College of Biological Sciences University of Minnesota 10 Church St. S.E., Minneapolis, MN 55455 **Phone: 612-624-0225 or 612-624-4112**

The Bell Museum of Natural History on the campus of the University of Minnesota allows visitors to learn from nature through exciting exhibits, film, art displays, field trips and a wide variety of other educational programs.

Have you ever wondered what it's like to touch a snake or stroke a turtle? You can experience these and more at the Bell Museum. Here, you can peek inside skins, skulls and other wonderful natural things. Watch a bobcat stalk a grouse just inches in front of you. Or watch sandhill cranes leap in their spectacular courting dance.

From bears to bass, wild things abound in the museum. More than six new exhibits are added each year, offering enjoyment for the whole family. And the friendly staff will help you to discover answers to your questions about the wonderful world of nature.

Memberships are available for the museum. There is a wildlife bookstore on site that will take phone orders, special orders and mail orders.

◆ ◆ ◆ ◆ ◆ ◆ ◆

Frederick R. Weisman Art Museum	At the University of Minnesota. 333 East River Road, Minneapolis, MN 55455. **Phone: 612-625-9444**. Hrs: Mon.-Fri. 10 a.m.-6 p.m.; Weekends noon-5 p.m.

Businessman, art collector, and philanthropist Frederick Rand Weisman, after whom the museum is named, was born in Minneapolis in 1912 to Russian immigrant parents. He developed a love of art that grew into the Frederick R. Weisman Art Foundation and one of the nation's foremost private collections of contemporary art.

The striking facility, designed by internationally acclaimed architect Frank O. Gehry, serves a university community of more than 60,000 students, faculty and staff and fills an important role in the thriving arts community of the Twin Cities and greater Minnesota.

The primary mission of the Weisman Art Museum is to educate students about art and to make the visual arts an important part of their everyday experience. The museum presents and interprets works of art, offering exhibitions that place art within relevant cultural, social, and historical contexts. Several major exhibitions are offered each year.

MUSEUM

Bear-Hawk Indian Store & Museum	1207 East Franklin, Minneapolis, MN 55404 **Phone: 612-872-9166** Hrs: Mon.-Fri. 10 a.m.-6 p.m. Visa and MasterCard accepted.

It was a dream for a long time. Now it's happened. Dresses of buckskin and beaded trade cloth. Leather leggings, grainy photographs. Winchester and Springfield rifles. A war club, lance and flint knife. A quilled pouch. A child's gourd rattle.

These and many more items make up the dream-come-true of Myron Rosebear, an Ojibwa Indian who has opened the Bear-Hawk Indian Store & Museum in Minneapolis.

Many of the items have been in his family for years, but all the items and displays represent his hopes for the future—and his life savings.

The museum has things that children can touch—the gourd rattle, a musical instrument, a buffalo hide, badger fur. There is a traditional tepee big enough to hold a fifth-grade class of 39.

Another display depicts a scene from the 1890 tragedy at Wounded Knee, S.D., which the Army called a battle but Indians know as a massacre. In the scene, four Sioux women and a child lie dead in a snowy ravine, shot by soldiers as they tried to flee.

"I understand why this happens," Rosebear said, looking at the mannequin bodies in the snow, "It is what hate can do. Those young soldiers—all they had heard was these Indians were savages. Even when they had them disarmed, they were afraid because of what they had heard."

"Those young soldiers were shaking, and most of them fired in fear. That's why 31 of their own were killed in the cross-fire."

Other pieces in the museum have a special effect on him, including one of the old photographs that line the walls. It shows two white women looking condescendingly at an Indian woman.

The museum is dedicated to "all the American Indians of the past 500 years who have struggled to maintain their life," Rosebear says. But it's also for every body, he says—especially children.

And, what a great dream it is!

NIGHTCLUBS

Fine Line Music Cafe	318 First Ave. N., Minneapolis, MN 55401 **Phone: 612-338-8100.** Hrs: Mon.-Fri. 5 p.m. Music starts 8:30 p.m.; Sun. 12:30 p.m. for brunch. Visa, MasterCard, AmEx are accepted.

The Fine Line Music Cafe features some of the nation's finest live entertainment combined with sumptuous cuisine. "Come for the food, stay for the music" is truly a slogan that best describes the mission of the Fine Line. The Fine Line features entertainers running the entire musical spectrum. Blues, jazz, reggae, folk, and rock music provide the ambience in an intimate cafe setting.

Since 1988, an assortment of rising national acts perform throughout the year in addition to several top local bands that perform on a weekly basis. Sundays bring a Gospel Brunch to the cafe. This unique event has become a favorite in the area; various gospel choirs offer their chorus for an inspirational Sunday afternoon.

The food at the Fine Line has been praised on its own accord. Appetizers of spicy chicken wings and calamari are among the best. Antipasto, spinach and pasta salads, and entrées of blackened fish and beef tenderloin medallions are particularly good choices from the menu. Desserts are as varied as the entrées.

＊ ◆ ◆ ◆ ◆ ◆ ◆

Glam Slam	110 Fifth Street N. Minneapolis, MN 55401 **Phone: 612-338-3383** Hrs: Tues.-Sat. 8 p.m.-1 p.m.

Glam Slam is a completely new concept in nightclub entertainment featuring elaborate, live performances by internationally known artists on a theater-size stage, while guests dance the night away on a sweeping 1,300-square-foot dance floor below.

To the delight of his many local fans, the nightclub—which can accommodate as many as 1,200 guests—features Prince himself and other Paisley Park groups at regular intervals.

But top-named performers are not the only attractions at Glam Slam. The sound and light system is state-of-the-art, and the interior skillfully incorporates the original look of the renovated textile building to produce a bold, airy effect. The balcony seating is intimately arranged in lounge-type fashion with tables, chairs, and couches. Here, patrons enjoy an unrestricted view of the dance floor.

The 26-foot ceiling, meanwhile, makes the Glam Slam dance floor one of the most attractive in the city.

RESTAURANT & BREWERY

The
Rock Bottom
Brewery

LaSalle Plaza, Lobby Level, 825 Hennepin Ave.,
Minneapolis, MN 55402. **Phone:** 612-332-2739
Hrs: Sun.-Thurs. 11 a.m.-11 p.m., Fri., Sat. 11 a.m.-
midnight. Bar open till 1 a.m. nightly.
Major credit cards accepted.

A surprising experience, the Twin Cities finally hits Rock Bottom—Rock Bottom Brewery, that is! This unique restaurant opened its doors first in Denver, Colorado, to an enthusiastic reception. And its showing in Minneapolis is equally grand.

The Micro-brewery concept is alive and well at the Rock Bottom Brewery. Crisp, clear and brewed to a lively art right on the premises, these ales are among the very best you'll find. Those who love fine beers will appreciate the care and know-how that goes into them.

A fine complement to the exquisite ales is the menu of quality foods freshly prepared. You'll find the delightfully different here. Like alder smoked salmon fish and chips, or vegie lasagna, or buffalo fajitas. Then there's Brown Ale Chicken or BBQ ribs, both mouth-watering treats anyone will love.

Try it and you'll know that you've Hit Rock Bottom! Weekend entertainment, except summer, and a first-rate billiards area are accompaniments.

CAFE & BAKERY

French Meadow
Bakery & Cafe

2610 Lyndale Avenue South, Minneapolis, MN
55408. **Phone:** 612-870-7855
Hours: Sun-Wed 6:30 a.m.-10:00 p.m., Thurs.,
Sat. until 11. Visa, MasterCard accepted.

When *Bon Appetit* Magazine recently name America's finest bread bakeries, they were right to include French Meadow Bakery. But the Bakery's Cafe is more that just a place where Minnesotans and tourists may purchase 20 varieties of hearth-baked breads fresh from the oven. This unconventional, European-style cafe serves an eclectic, largely vegetarian menu of wholesome breakfasts, home-made soups, sandwiches, salads and entrées. Enjoy a cinnamon-current scone and an almond cappuccino amidst the Cafe's charming decor, or better yet have a seat outside in the abundant shade of their emerald-green awning. Lest you think that French Meadow Bakery has nothing for the chocolate lover, think again. Their truly decadent Chocolate Killer Cake and Cappuccino Torte satisfy even the most discriminating chocolate connoisseur.

Whether you go to French Meadow Bakery for their celebrated bread or for their seemingly endless variety of wholesome foods, it's for certain you'll be back again and again!

RESTAURANT

Shelly's Woodroast

6501 Wayzata Blvd., St. Louis Park, MN 55426
Phone: 612-593-5050. Hrs: Mon.-Thurs.
11 a.m.-10 p.m.; Fri., Sat. 11-11; Sun. 10 a.m.-
10 p.m. Major credit cards accepted.

If you like signature cuisine, you'll love Shelly's Woodroast in suburban Minneapolis. What is truly unique about Shelly's is the Woodroast cooking done in special patented ovens that are one-of-a-kind and can't be found anywhere else. These Woodroast ovens burn five types of aromatic hardwoods. Slow roasting and frequent basting results in food that is lean, tender and succulent beyond belief! Shelly likes to say that the foods at the lodge are as fresh and natural as the great northwoods that inspired them.

And indeed they are! Most Woodroast items are marinated in a special blend of herbs and spices. Some items are marinated for up to five days! Shelly's menu offers a variety of simple, yet tasty foods that you might expect to find anywhere across the U.S. For starters, you might try the Crispy Walleye Fingers, or the incredible tender Woodroasted Chicken Fingers. One of the most popular items before dinner is Shelly's unique Corn Cob Chowder. Everybody raves about it. Hearty homemade soups and stews, grilled and sealed sandwiches and garden-fresh salads complete with dressing made right in the lodge can be enjoyed at Shelly's.

Regular guests rave about the Woodroasted chicken breasts, the large and tender beef short ribs, the Walleye shore lunches, and the mouthwatering double-cut pork chops. Each meal is served with piping hot and fresh-baked popovers accompanied by plenty of delicious honey butter.

Shelly's also offers a terrific, hearty Sunday brunch. Try the fabulous stuffed French toast, hearty campfire breakfast or Shelly's own beef brisket, potato and sweet pepper hash.

The restaurant is comfortable, warm and is a meticulously hand crafted lodge, complete with two stone fireplaces, vaulted beam ceilings, a dining porch and cozy Birch Bar. It's a place for a truly elegant yet casual dining experience.

Shelly's has been the subject of many flattering reviews in virtually all of the Twin Cities media and is widely noted elsewhere.

RESTAURANTS & EATERIES

Azur

Gaviidae Common, Fifth Floor, 651 Nicollet Mall, Minneapolis, MN 55402. **Phone: 612-342-2500** Hrs: Hours vary, call ahead.

Azur draws a hip and classy crowd to sup on southern fare—south, as in the sunny shores of France, Spain and Italy. This fashion-forward dining room is dressed with faux wood, real marble, concrete floors streaked with neon and a fireplace stolen from some Olympic festival. The ad crowd loves the place and so do others who dote on Mediterranean fare such as snapper with artichokes and scampi.

Black Forest

1 E. 26th St., Minneapolis, MN 55404 **Phone: 612-872-0812** Hrs: Hours vary, call ahead.

The Student Prince is alive and well and living in Minneapolis. His present-day cronies wander over from the nearby College of Art and Design to lift frosty steins of beer aside older Bohemians who appreciate a good strudel when they see one. In summer diners mingle in the outdoor arbor for burgers and brats, augmented by schnitzels and such from the owner's family recipes.

Bryant-Lake Bowl

10 W. Lake St., Minneapolis, MN 55404 **Phone: 612-825-3737** Hrs: Hours vary, call ahead.

What, dine in a bowling alley? You bet, and we're not talking packets of peanuts and potato chips. Since two young ladies assumed ownership of the classic 40's beer-and-bowl establishment, things have changed: beer, yes—from micro-breweries these days. A wine list. Cappuccino. And, at the beat-up tables, tuna with atoll, great chili, fabled soups and—of course—tiramisu for dessert.

Coco's

5410 Wayzata Blvd., Minneapolis, MN 55416 **Phone: 612-544-4014** Hrs: Hours vary, call ahead.

Milan, eat your heart out: this is where the action is. Marble-lined walls divide the high ceiling from the polished floor. And just as true to the Old Country are the rows of closely packed tables packed with jubilating diners.

Chef Rosanna's Roman recipes include designer pizzas, gourmet pastas and a dessert cart to die for.

RESTAURANTS & EATERIES

D'Amico Cucina | Butler Square, 100 N. 6th St., Minneapolis, MN 55403. **Phone: 612-338-2401** Hrs: Hours vary, call ahead.

The landmark Butler Building has been historically preserved—but there's nothing dated about the first-class restaurant it harbors. The design could be a centerfold for *Architectural Digest,* while the food would feel at home in *Bon Appetit.* The menu is a hybrid of Californian and Italian inventions, featuring deluxe pastas followed by fish, game or fowl with cutting-edge sauces and pleasant service.

Figlio | Calhoun Square, 3001 Hennepin Ave., Minneapolis, MN 55408. **Phone: 612-822-1688** Hrs: Hours vary, call ahead.

When it's hot, it's hot—and that's Figlio, the hit of trendy Uptown. Singles make it their mecca for spicy chicken wings and calamari. Neighborhood folk wander by for pizzas from the exhibition kitchen or a plate of well-sauced linguine. For dessert the morte nel cioccolato—death by chocolate—is as good a way to go as any. The adjoining bar attracts jocks and wanna-bes of all ages.

510 Restaurant | 510 Groveland, Minneapolis, MN 55403 **Phone: 612-874-6440** Hrs: Hours vary, call ahead.

The former grande dame of fine dining recently shed its patrician air in favor of a little joie de vivre, and the menu's gone through a little lightening, too. The pretty gray walls and crystal chandeliers remain, however, and so does the kitchen's attention to quality. Sweetbreads, herb-crusted lamb and salmon vie with wild-mushroom pasta as fine choices.

Goodfellow's | The Conservatory, Fourth Floor, 800 Nicollet Mall Minneapolis, MN 55402. **Phone: 612-332-4800** Hrs: Hours vary, call ahead.

Yes, the Warhols on the walls are real, and so are the celebs at the tables. The elegantly understated room with its well-spaced tables and savvy staff turn any night into a special occasion, with a look at the menu as proof you've arrived in heaven. It celebrates Wisconsin veal, Minnesota wild rice, local trout and northwoods berries, paired with chipotle peppers, tropical papayas or whatever else is trendy.

RESTAURANTS & EATERIES

Jax Cafe

> 1928 University Ave. NE, Minneapolis, MN
> **Phone: 612-789-7297**
> Hrs: Hours vary, call ahead.

Jax has been a landmark of northeast Minneapolis's Polish populace for four generations and 75 years. Little by little it's grown to include a now-famous Old World Garden, where diners can net their own trout in a mini-millstream. Long the site of birthday and anniversary celebrations, its veteran waitresses call customers by name as they deliver the T-bones.

Loring Cafe

> 1624 Harmon Place, Minneapolis, MN 55403
> **Phone: 612-332-1617**
> Hrs: Hours vary, call ahead.

This could be Soho. This could be San Francisco. But it's Minneapolis, where a bit of Bohemia blooms. Poets, artists and corporate bankers rub shoulders in a series of theatrical rooms that include an artsy bar with stage for local talent and an inner courtyard where a lone sax player sits atop the roof and tweedles mournful magic into the night. The food's every bit as eclectic.

Lucia's

> 1432 W. 31st St., Minneapolis, MN 55408
> **Phone: 612-825-1572**
> Hrs: Hours vary, call ahead.

The welcome sign "ouvert" is the first clue that chef/owner Lucia Watson learned her love of food in France. The second is her menu, crafted with the finesse of a food fanatic. Her small and cheery Uptown restaurant and adjoining wine bar provide respite from the fast lane. So does the relaxed cuisine. Soups are supreme here, as are the country salads and home-baked breads.

Manny's
Steakhouse

> Hyatt Regency Hotel, 1300 Nicollet Mall,
> Minneapolis, MN 55402. **Phone: 612-339-9900**
> Hrs: Hours vary, call ahead.

This is a gentlemen's steakhouse, no two ways about it—bare wood floors, well-spaced tables, magnums of wine and steak cuts best described as Jurassic, which waiters of the old school wheel out to display for your selection. Everything is a la carte, from football-sized baked potatoes to forests of broccoli. Ladies leave here with designer doggie bags—or choose the salmon.

RESTAURANTS & EATERIES

Market Bar-B-Que | 1414 Nicollet Ave., Minneapolis, MN 55403
Phone: 612-872-1111
Hrs: Hours vary, call ahead.

The Market has been smoking the best ribs in town since the 30's. Urban renewal took that original site, but the owners' sons made a successful move, and business is booming. The original wooden booths made the junket, too, complete with the brass plaques that honor their famous occupants—jazz greats to stage stars to sports heroes. The classic jukebox still stands, too.

Monte Carlo
Bar & Grill | 219 3rd Ave. N., Minneapolis, MN 55401
Phone: 612-333-5900
Hrs: Hours vary, call ahead.

The Monte, as folks around here know it, began life as a workingman's bar and grill. Today the setup's a bit more polished, as is its trendy clientele gathering at the showcase mirrored back bar. But the waitresses still wear little black uniforms and deliver the town's best burger. The meatloaf and caesar salad have won their share of allies, too.

Murray's | 26 S. 6th St., Minneapolis, MN 55402
Phone: 612-339-0909
Hrs: Hours vary, call ahead.

Murray's invented steak—at least, as far as Minneapolis is concerned. Pat Murray follows his father, who opened the landmark restaurant in the 40's. He's proudest of his Silver Butterknife Steak, named for the delicate tool he claims is all you'll need to carve it. Pat's list of diners include showbiz and sports celebrities, who know enough to ask for Murray's famous bread basket and icebox pie, too.

New French Cafe | 128 N. 4th St., Minneapolis, MN 55401
Phone: 612-338-3790
Hrs: Hours vary, call ahead.

Some of the best cooking in the Twin Cities happens here. Although almost as spare as a monk's cell in decor, it's a temple of fine dining, where TLC and the best of ingredients combine to create state-of-the-art French food, from patés to creme caramel. You'll find everyone from Baryshnikov to bus drivers supping here, or stopping in for an early-morning croissant and cafe au lait.

RESTAURANTS & EATERIES

Palomino

825 Hennepin Ave., Minneapolis, MN 55402
Phone: 612-339-3800
Hrs: Hours vary, call ahead.

They call it a Euro-metro bistro. We call it a hoot. The deliciously fake, L.A.-type decor makes a good conversation-opener while you're narrowing down the menu choices: pizzas from the brick oven or wood-grilled meats, fowl and fish plus the basic pastas. The hip servers are prone to coddle their customers, too. Especially popular when a hit show is playing at the nearby State or Orpheum theaters.

Sebastian Joe's
Ice Cream Cafe

1007 W. Franklin Ave., Minneapolis, MN 55402
Phone: 612-870-0065
Hrs: Hours vary, call ahead.

An ice cream parlor and a whole lot more—snazzy marble counters, newspapers on sticks, and over a dozen flavors of the city's best homemade scoops, from best-selling Oreo chunk and raspberry chocolate chip to oddball winners like chocolate coyote (with cayenne). Ice cream's the mainstay, but the fresh-baked scones, muffins and cookies also make a hit with a devoted designer-coffee crowd.

Sri Lanka
Curry House

2821 Hennepin Ave., Minneapolis, MN 55408
Phone: 612-871-2400
Hrs: Hours vary, call ahead.

There's only one Ceylonese restaurant in all the country, and it's right here in Minneapolis, serving aficionados from afar with what is reputed to be the spiciest food in town. Sri Lanka—once Ceylon—is the source of family recipes for curries of vegetables, seafood, chicken, lamb or beef, served as mild or hot as you fancy, with sides of homemade chutney and warm, crusty naan.

Tejas

3910 W. 50th St., Edina, MN 55435
Phone: 612-375-0800
Hrs: Hours vary, call ahead.

Deep in the heart of The Conservatory shopping complex lies Tejas. Named for the home state of its founders, it boasts a menu as hip as its decor, where coyotes howl at life-size cactus and strings of chili pepper lights loop over walls of adobe white. The flavors blend the best of northwoods and southwest cooking: try venison chili, rabbit tostadas, a cayenne caesar salad or chocolate cake fired up with chilies.

SPECIALTY SHOPS

Coffee & Tea, Ltd., Inc.	Linden Hills, 2728 W. 43rd Street Minneapolis, MN 55410. **Phone:** 612-926-1216 **Mail orders:** 1-800-2-Finest Hrs: Vary at each location.

There is nothing like the smell of freshly roasted coffee. Heady, aromatic and pungent, this tantalizing aroma fills the air at Coffee & Tea, Ltd. Inc. Customers drop in for their regular supply of bulk coffee and stay to sample a new blend and to chat with owner Jim Cone.

Coffee & Tea, Ltd., Inc. is among just a handful of shops in the Midwest to offer such a wide variety—142 kinds of coffee and 160 kinds of tea. Consumption of gourmet coffee continues to increase and Jim ships ever-greater amounts of mail order coffee to each state every month. They roast all their own coffee and import their teas.

Jim has other shops in Aurora Village Mall, Burnsville; Victoria Crossing Mall, St. Paul; Sears-Mall of America; Dinkytown; and Minnehaven Square in Wayzata. The Coffee & Tea, Ltd., Inc. shops also sell accessories. Shiny plunge pots and top-rated Espresso and Cappuccino machines promise delicious home-brewed treats.

In warm weather, tables and chairs are set up outside for sampling and socializing. Now, how about that cup of coffee?

◆ ◆ ◆ ◆ ◆ ◆ ◆

The Reindeer House	3409 W. 44th Street, Minneapolis, MN 55410 **Phone:** 612-920-6950 Hrs.: Mon.-Sat 10 a.m.-6 p.m.; Thur., 10 a.m.-8 p.m. Visa, MasterCard and AmEx are accepted.

Two decades after it first opened, The Reindeer House gift and card shop has become a Minneapolis institution. Located in a cheerful, renovated home near Lake Harriet in the southern part of the city, the gift shop is brimming with wreaths, teddy bears, cut design shades, figurines, potpourri and other handcrafted items, all artistically displayed in a friendly, aromatic atmosphere.

The Reindeer House was founded by the late, renowned greeting-card designer anita beck (cq.) to display her work, and the shop remains the home store for cards designed in her name. The Reindeer House always has been a center for local craftspeople to display their creations, and today, many artists participate in this cooperative venture. One of the best known is Mary Thiele, a highly imaginative teddy bear creator.

Aside from teddy bears, cards and crafts, people keep coming back to The Reindeer House for the personal service of one of Minneapolis's oldest and most authentic gift shops.

SHOPPING

Gaviidae Common	60 South Sixth Street, Minneapolis, MN 55402 **Phone: 612-372-1673** Hrs: Mon.-Fri. 10 a.m.-8 p.m., Sat. 10 a.m.- 6 p.m., Sun. noon-5 p.m.

Shopping with style.

If that sounds like something appealing to you, then you've come to just the right place. Located in the heart of downtown Minneapolis on Nicollet Mall, Gaviidae Common is a stunning multi-level retail development anchored by Saks Fifth Avenue and Neiman Marcus, two of America's finest department stores.

Spanning a two-block stretch of Nicollet Mall between 5th and 7th Streets, Gaviidae Common features two wings of specialty stores offering wonderful variety in many styles and price ranges. The Neiman Marcus wing houses the only upward flowing water fountain in the world, which moves nearly 800 gallons of water every minute into a dance and light show lit by fibre optics. The Saks Fifth Avenue wing features a unique barrel-vaulted ceiling handpainted to represent a northern Minnesota night sky, complete with pinpoints of light.

The food court features a variety of fare and there is fine dining at Morton's of Chicago and Azur. An outstanding retail experience.

TOURS

MetroConnections	1219 Marquette Ave., #110 Minneapolis, MN 55403 **Phone: 612-333-8687** Hrs: 8 a.m.-10 p.m. Winter, 8 a.m.-5 p.m.

A unique and fascinating way to see the Twin Cities is via deluxe motorcoach by MetroConnections. They offer the only ongoing tour in the cities with a standing tour guide providing the commentary.

Tour highlights include the famous Nicollet Mall and skyway network of downtown Minneapolis; the Hubert H. Humphrey Metrodome; St. Anthony Falls area, the birthplace of Minneapolis; the Tyrone Guthrie Theatre; the Minneapolis Sculpture Gardens: the Kenwood residential area, television home of Mary Tyler Moore; many lakes and lagoons; Mall of America; University of Minnesota; a stop at the legendary Minnehaha Falls; following the Mississippi River past Fort Snelling and into St. Paul's stately Summit Avenue area to see the magnificent Cathedral of Saint Paul; the State Capitol; the home and haunts of F. Scott Fitzgerald; and the revitalized downtown St. Paul area including Rice Park, Ordway Music Hall, Landmark Center and the World Trade Center.

THEATER

*The Guthrie
Theater*

725 Vineland Place, Minneapolis, MN 55403.
Phone: 612-377-2224 or 800-848-4912, ext. 2712.
Hrs: When performing: Mon.-Sat. 9 a.m.-8 p.m., Sun.
11 a.m.-7 p.m. When not performing: Mon.-Sat. 9 a.m.-
6 p.m. Major credit cards accepted.

It began with a dream.

Sir Tyrone Guthrie wanted to found a new kind of American theater, where serious artists could work together to provide the community with quality theater and the nation with a standard of excellence
for theatrical production and performance. His search for the perfect
location led him to Minneapolis, where he found civic and arts communities that embraced the concept of a repertory theater. In its very
first season, 1963, it set new standards of excellence and continues in
that pursuit today.

The theater was planned by architect Ralph Rapson and built next
to the distinguished Walker Art Center. It was designed with a 1,441-
seat auditorium sweeping 200 degrees around an asymmetrical thrust
stage. In 1993, just prior to 30th Anniversary celebrations, it under-
went an extensive renovation and facelift and today seats 1,309 in a
180-degree arc. The expanded inner lobby is now fronted with a glass
curtain wall that gives a spectacular view of downtown Minneapolis,
the new outdoor terrace and the Walker Art Center's sculpture garden.

Once inside, you'll find only the absolute best in live theater.

Under the current artistic leadership of Garland Wright, it is one
of the few theaters in America that features a resident acting
company, a rotating repertory schedule and a commitment to plays
from world literature whose themes transcend the specifics of their
time and place. Central to the work is the principle that theater is the
"shared act of imagining between actors and audience."

The Guthrie Theater presents the world's classics and is internationally recognized for its high professional standards and innovative
interpretations. The resident company and guest performers are
joined by world renowned playwrights, directors, designers and
artists on a regular basis.

The Guthrie schedules special performances interpreted in
American Sign Language for deaf and hard-of-hearing patrons, performances that are Audio Described for blind and low-vision patrons
and Infrared Listening Systems to enhance audibility. Brochures and
programs are available in Braille and on cassette tape.

Public Backstage Tours of The Guthrie Theater are scheduled for
every Saturday morning and selected weekday mornings at 10 a.m.
(except on national holidays) and last about an hour. An American
icon well worth a visit.

ZOO

Minnesota Zoo

13000 Zoo Blvd., Apple Valley, MN 55124
Phone: 612-432-9000
Hrs: 9 a.m.-4 p.m. Summers til 6 p.m. (8 p.m.
Sundays) Visa, MasterCard and AmEx accepted.

As sensitivity toward and appreciation for the earth's non-human inhabitants grows, so does the Minnesota Zoo. Situated just ten minutes south of Mall of America in Apple Valley on 500 acres, the zoo has been dubbed one of the country's ten best by wildlife experts.

Committed to strengthening the bond between people and the living earth, the zoo, its exhibits and its animals and habitats provide a fascinating window into the natural world. Families who explore this sanctuary will come away rich in the knowledge of the inhabitants of oceans, jungles, lakes, forests and plains. And they learn about increasingly important conservation issues, too.

Entertainment abounds as well in the form of shows, special exhibits, animal feedings and animal antics. The zoo, like nature itself, continuously alters and fluctuates. Six trails amble around nationally acclaimed habitats that more than 2,800 mammals, birds, fish, reptiles and amphibians call home. The habitats, many of which are staged in beautiful outdoor spaces, are carefully composed to ensure that animals reside in a place similar to their environment in the wild.

Reflective of the changing seasons, visits at various times of the year reveal different wonders. In winter, the trails open to cross-country skiers who glide by camels, caribou, Japanese snow monkeys and native wildlife.

During the summer, special shows are frequent; visitors marvel at the choreography of dolphin shows, see wildlife close up during live animal demonstrations and float over the zoo's Northern Trail aboard the Skytrail monorail.

A children's zoo offers demonstrations on llamas and reindeer. Summer camel rides also are offered at the Children's Zoo and puppet shows entertain youngsters, too. Also, the Zoo features a program called Zoomobile, a traveling mini-zoo that can be scheduled to present wildlife programs at schools, community events and meetings. Different programs are targeted to interest grades K-12.

Any time of year, the Minnesota Zoo has something exciting happening. See the colorful Tropical Coral Reef, sun bears and gibbons in the Southeast Asian Tropics. There's never a routine day at the Minnesota Zoo—surprises pop up around every corner!

MINNETONKA

Minnetonka is an attractive community, ranked the twelfth largest in Minnesota with a population nearing 50,000. Many lakes, creeks and wetlands motivate the city to maintain a balance of development and preservation of natural amenities unique to the city.

Minnehaha Creek is a favorite of canoeists and flows through several communities before reaching Minnehaha Falls and the Mississippi River. *Purgatory Creek* in the southwest, and *Nine Mile Creek* in the southeast provide additional natural areas.

Numerous retail shopping centers are located within the community, including *Ridgedale,* a major regional shopping center serving the western suburbs of the Twin Cities. Five major highways traverse Minnetonka, making it readily accessible to everyone within the metropolitan area.

For further information, contact:
City of Minnetonka
14600 Minnetonka Blvd.
Minnetonka, MN 55345   Phone: 612-939-8200

RESTAURANT

Sherlock's Home	11000 Red Circle Drive Minnetonka, MN 55343 **Phone:** 612-931-0203 Hrs: Hours vary, call ahead

Sherlock's Home is a restaurant, pub and brewery complex based on a typical 19th-century Victorian English establishment and influenced by the stories about the beloved detective of fiction, Sherlock Holmes.

The Dining Room (Simpson's, after Sherlock's favorite restaurant) and Pub (Watson's, after the cohort who documented Sherlock's adventures) both serve the same full English and American luncheon and dinner menus. Daily specials include appetizers, soups and salads, fish 'n chips, roast beef and Yorkshire pudding, steaks, Scottish salmon, hot and cold sandwiches (pub-burgers), meat pies, Ploughman's lunch, pasta, lamb, veal, pork, seafood and a fine selection of special desserts made on the premises.

Sherlock's Home brewery is the first full-stage brewery in a Minnesota restaurant, though common in Victorian period public houses or pubs. Sherlock's full bar stocks most wines and liquors to service the dining room and pub.

SPECIALTY SHOP

The General Store Of Minnetonka

One-quarter mile west of I-494 on Hwy 7. 14401 Hwy 7, Minnetonka, MN 55345. **Phone: 612-935-2215.** Hrs: Mon.-Fri. 9:30 a.m.-6 p.m., Mon. and Thurs. evenings until 9 p.m., Sat. 9:30 a.m.-6 p.m., Sun. noon-5 p.m. Extended hours during the Holiday Season. Visa, MasterCard and Discover accepted.

The gifts of yesteryear were almost always handmade, just as they are today at the General Store of Minnetonka.

Nestled among 9,000 square feet of space, including a fieldstone fireplace, vaulted ceilings and rustic timbers, you will find the quality works of over 250 artists and craftspeople.

You'll be greeted by the scent of simmering potpourri in the Kitchen area, where the cupboards are overflowing with lots of hand-made collectibles, cookbooks, personalized country crocks, bright and cheery Mary Engelbreit accessories and lots of specialty foods for creating your own gift baskets.

The center courtyard is brimming with Victorian accessories, including handpainted procelain pottery, baskets of silk and dried flowers, watercolor prints and handmade jewelry.

The Country Folk Art area features woven coverlets, checkerboards, hand-dipped candles, many styles of salt glaze pottery and a large collection of handmade dolls, bears and rabbits.

There's plenty for the kids on your list, too. The General Store has a wonderful selection of items that can be personalized plus lots of "fun stuff" for kids of all ages.

The Minnesota Wildlife Area is the perfect place to shop for that unique Minnesota souvenier. Choose from loons and ladyslippers to handcarved duck decoys and original watercolors.

Visit the General Store soon and enjoy a cup of hot spiced tea while you browse through the area's largest collection of quality handcrafted goods.

So bring a friend and spend the day at the General Store!

SHOPPING MALL

Ridgedale Center

Minnetonka, MN 55305. **Phone: 612-541-4864**
Hrs.: Mon.-Fri. 10 a.m.-9 p.m., Sat. 10 a.m.-8 p.m., Sun.
11 a.m.-6 p.m. Department stores and holiday hours may
vary. All major credit cards accepted (varies by store).

Ridgedale Center consists of 1.1 million square feet of pure shopping pleasure. The mall is anchored by such names as Dayton's, Carson Pirie Scott, JC Penney and Sears, but also offers a wide variety of other stores (140-plus) including kiosks and carts featuring everything from antiques, imports, gifts, jewelry, clothing, local arts and crafts to pottery, fitness equipment, framed prints, restaurants, home accessories and much more—a veritable feast of merchandise and services.

The center is bright and clean, with large skylights and lots of greenery and water. It's comfortable and easy to shop for everyone. At Your Service customer assistance center offers services like shopping and merchandise information, gift certificates, bus schedules, complimentary stroller and wheelchair checkout, lost and found and event information. The center also offers a women's lounge, changing tables, Express Tellers, Federal Express drop box, Notary Public service and a walking program. They'll even jump start your car, if needed!

Serving the western and northwestern suburbs of Minneapolis, there is a broad merchandise mix at the center including unique offerings and gifts for visitors. There are two auto service stores and even a shoe repair. Don't forget to check out the art gallery, either. There's always something new.

It's a friendly mall that is community oriented with a personal touch. Near I-494 and I-394, Ridgedale offers easy access no matter what your location.

CORPORATE PROFILE

Carlson Companies, Inc. Curtis LeRoy Carlson, who emerged from his humble background as the son of Swedish-American immigrants to build one of America's largest corporations, is a classic Horatio Alger success story in the American free enterprise system. He has become "The Ultra Entrepreneur" in the free world.

As board chairman and sole owner of the $11 billion-a-year Carlson Companies, Curt Carlson today heads an international business conglomerate which includes more than 75 different companies providing employment for more than 112,000 people in 36 countries. These businesses include operations in hotels, resorts, travel and travel tour agencies, restaurants, marketing, and property ownership/management. His Carlson Companies is one of the nation's largest privately held companies.

Carlson Companies is an international leader today in the areas of travel, hospitality and marketing its three main operating groups. During the next few years, Carlson Companies plans to continue to increase its presence globally and its penetration of world markets in hospitality, travel and marketing.

Carlson Travel Group (Carlson Travel Network) is one of the largest travel management companies in the world, with more than 2,300 travel agencies spanning the globe, serving corporations and the individual traveler. Carlson Travel Network (formerly Ask Mr. Foster) travel agencies in North America, Europe and the Pacific Rim combined with P. Lawson Travel in Canada, Voyages Bel-Air and Harvey's Travel, and A.T. Mays in the United Kingdom do in excess of $7 billion annually in systemwide revenues.

Carlson's surge into the hospitality business in the 1980's and 90's has produced one of the fastest-growing upscale hotel operations in the world—the Radisson Hotels International which features plaza hotels, suite hotels, hotels, inns and resorts throughout the world. This rapid growth has pushed Radisson to the forefront in the hospitality industry with more than 315 properties stretching coast-to-coast in the United States and around the world.

Besides Radisson Hotels International, the Carlson Hospitality Group also includes Colony Hotels & Resorts, which manages condominium resorts in the Hawaiian Islands and at selected destinations on the U.S. mainland, Mexico, the Caribbean, the Pacific Rim and the Far East. Carlson Hospitality Group expects to have 450 properties, one opening an average of every 5.5 days.

Also included in the Carlson Hospitality Group is the Country Hospitality Corporation, which includes Country Kitchen restaurants and Country Lodging by Carlson with locations throughout North

America and at selected destinations in the Far East, and TGI Friday's with restaurants throughout the United States, Europe and the Far East.

Colony Hotels & Resorts, which expects to be a major resort operator in the world, currently includes more than 40 properties with expansion continuing in 1994.

Country Hospitality operates more than 240 Country Kitchen restaurants across North America.

Besides Country Kitchen, Country Hospitality includes Country Lodging by Carlson. This growing operation includes both suites and inns.

TGI Friday's is a premier restaurant chain in the United States with average annual sales per unit of $3.45 million, highest of any national chain in the industry.

Carlson Marketing Group is the largest marketing services organization in the world. It helps clients achieve their sales, marketing and communications objectives by creating programs that stimulate sales, increase profits, capture customer loyalty, build customer-focused organizations, motivate and recognize employee productivity and enhance organizational esprit de corps.

Carlson Marketing Group moved into worldwide leadership in sales and marketing services with its acquisition of FKB, London, England, Great Britain's largest marketing and incentive company. Carlson Marketing Group has recently increased its presence in Canada and Australia/New Zealand with the acquisition of motivation and marketing companies in those two nations. It has offices throughout Europe and in Japan. This group also includes Gold Bond trading stamps, which were the founding and beginning of the Carlson Companies.

It was the world of incentives, which includes trading stamps, that launched Carlson on his business career in the late 1930's to become one of the world's top businessmen and entrepreneurs of the century.

Carlson's rise in the business world came with a simple idea—his own trading stamp called "Gold Bond." He originally sold them to small grocery stores in the 1930's and 40's. This idea would rocket Carlson to national prominence in the 1950's and 60's and his Gold Bond trading stamp idea would become a household word across North America. Eventually, his trading stamps made their way to Europe and Japan. It also would mark him as one of the world's top salesmen.

Curt Carlson was born in Minneapolis in 1914, the son of Charles and Letha Carlson. His father was born in Sweden and emigrated, with his parents, to Minnesota. His maternal grandmother was born in Sweden and grandfather in Denmark. They emigrated to Wisconsin, where Letha was born on a farm near Downing, Wisconsin.

Carlson grew up in south Minneapolis. He attended elementary school and high school in Minneapolis. Ironically, it was the same south Minneapolis area where he would begin selling his Gold Bond trading stamps.

Following graduation from the University of Minnesota in 1937 where he majored in economics, Carlson went to work for Procter & Gamble as a soap salesman for $110 per month. During that time he noticed that the Leader retail department store in downtown Minneapolis was giving away red coupons for so many dollars in purchases. These coupons could be redeemed for cash or merchandise at the department store. He reasoned that if these coupons stimulated business in department stores with their exclusive lines of merchandise, why wouldn't they be as effective for grocery stores, too. After all, Carlson figured, grocery stores needed a point of difference since they all sold identical products.

This was, and still is, the objective of the Gold Bond Stamp Company that, by saving many of these stamp incentives, you can obtain worthwhile and valuable gifts (premiums) from the Gold Bond Stamp Company as a reward for your loyalty to the merchant who carries the trading stamps. Today's frequent flyer and other frequency programs, many of them managed by Carlson Marketing Group, are an extension of the trading stamp objective to spur sales and command customer loyalty.

Carlson continued his regular job with Procter & Gamble for 16 months. However, during the evenings and on weekends he continued to perfect and sell his trading stamp idea to local merchants, particularly the small "mom and pop" food stores in the Minneapolis area.

Carlson worked the neighborhoods throughout Minneapolis and, in the fall of 1938, quit his job with Procter & Gamble to devote full time to his new trading stamp concept. The year 1938 proved to be another important time for Curt Carlson. He married his college sweetheart, Arleen Martin, whom he met in class when they attended the University of Minnesota. They eventually had two daughters, Marilyn and Barbara.

In the late 1930's and very early 1940's, merchants, particularly food stores, began giving Gold Bond stamps in ever-increasing numbers throughout the city. His trading-stamp concept was beginning to catch on first locally, then regionally and eventually it would spread nationally and finally internationally.

During the 1960's the trading stamp business had grown to such phenomenal extent that further growth projections were impossible. Nineteen of the top 20 food chains issued trading stamps and 50 percent of all gasoline stations were giving stamps on purchases.

As a result, Carlson began to diversify his capital into other businesses, including real estate in the western suburbs of Minneapolis, part of which would be the future home of his Carlson Companies World Headquarters which opened in 1989.

The diversification into other businesses prompted the changing of the name of his company from the Gold Bond Stamp Company to

Carlson Companies, Inc. in 1973.

In 1988, Curt Carlson celebrated 50 years in business. To commemorate the occasion, Carlson brought thousands of employees from all over the world to Minneapolis and St. Paul to attend business meetings and see a massive exhibit depicting each of the company's businesses.

The event, held in July 1988, at the Civic Center in downtown St. Paul, was climaxed with a two-hour show, featuring Bob Hope as master of ceremonies.

In step with the expansion of his businesses over these past 55 years, Carlson took on leadership responsibilities in civic and community organizations.

His company was a pioneer and charter member of the "Five Percent Club" (now called the Minnesota Keystone Club) which is made up of top Minneapolis-St. Paul area corporations which give 5 percent of their earnings to non-profit organizations. This innovative giving program has been duplicated by other U.S. companies.

In 1980 Carlson gave a million dollars to the University of Minnesota to help reorganize its Political Science School into the new Hubert H. Humphrey Institute of Public Affairs. He chaired the committee that raised $12 million to fund the new school. One of the functions of the prestigious institute is to bring distinguished and influential world leaders to the university's campus to address the student body and the general public.

In April of 1986, Carlson gave a personal gift of $25 million to his alma mater, the University of Minnesota. This was the largest single gift ever given to a public university. At the same time, Carlson agreed to spearhead a three-year drive that raised $365-plus million with the specific objective of moving the University of Minnesota's ranking into the top five of public universities in America. In 1993, Carlson gave another $10 million to the University to help launch a new building for the Carlson School of Management.

Carlson's philanthropic efforts earned him *Town & Country* Magazine's prestigious "Generous American Award" for 1987-88, plus a major story on his philanthropy in the publication's December 1987, issue. *Town & Country* called Carlson "a visionary with a different tactic...the man who has inspired the new philosophy of corporate giving."

Carlson Companies Inc.

ST. PAUL

Collectively, they are known as the Twin Cities. They share some geography, their sports teams, an image and an identity. At least in the minds of outsiders, Minneapolis and St. Paul may as well be one.

But if these two cities are indeed twins, they are certainly not identical. Far from it. In fact, to those who call St. Paul home, the two towns are as different as oil and water.

Minneapolis is glass towers and upscale, St. Paul is historic buildings and downhome. Minneapolis loves to focus on its business community and its economic drive. St. Paul prefers architecture and history and charm. It's true that modern economies have been much kinder to Minneapolis. But history has been very good to St. Paul, the state capitol and home to so much more than meets the eye.

St. Paul's done all right for a settlement that began its existence under the name Pig's Eye, named for Pierre "Pig's Eye" Parrant, an infamous fur trader saloon owner. Thankfully, Father Lucien Galtier came along in 1841 and built a log-cabin chapel he dedicated to St. Paul. He petitioned to have the name of the Mississippi River settlement changed and thus, St. Paul came to be.

Built on the banks of the mighty Mississippi, St. Paul has 29 miles of shoreline. Its waterfront is still hard at work, servicing industry and commerce. But it also takes time out to play. And if it's play you're after, St. Paul has plenty to offer.

ATTRACTIONS

In the summer of 1993, something happened that perhaps says as much about St. Paul as anything. A new minor league baseball team was founded here, reviving the name *St. Paul Saints* and resurrecting the old *Northern League.*

This was professional baseball but barely. Still, the atmosphere was fun, the promotions wacky and most importantly, the name on the players' jerseys said "St. Paul." Not Minnesota. Not Minneapolis. But rather St. Paul. Fiercely loyal to anything that is theirs, the people of this great city packed the ballpark night after night after night.

If you can get a ticket, a Saints game is well worth the minimal price of admission, for watching people if nothing else. The baseball team is now joined by a minor professional hockey club known as *The Moose* and playing its home games at the 16,000-seat *St. Paul Civic Centre,* long the anchor of downtown entertainment, conventions and events in St. Paul.

The elegant *Ordway Music Theatre* is at the heart of the cultural city. This fabulous facility, with its gorgeous wood panelled walls and magnificent glass-encased lobby, is home to visiting theatre productions, musicals and concerts. It is also the home of the world-renowned *St. Paul Chamber Orchestra* which has thrilled audiences from one end of the globe to the other. There are also several theatre companies that call St. Paul home, including the *Penumbra Theatre,* an all-black company, and the classical *Park Square Theatre.* Then there's the *Great North American History Theatre,* an unusual company which focuses its efforts on plays that relate to a specific event or individual in history. Of course, we can't omit the restored turn-of-the-century *World Theatre* which put St. Paul on the map during its stint as home to Garrison Keillor's *"A Prairie Home Companion"* on National Public Radio.

St. Paul boasts the *Science Museum of Minnesota,* long a Twin Cities attraction, and the *William McKnight Omnitheater* with which it shares space. Both are terrific for kids. While downtown, shop *Galtier Plaza* and the *World Trade Center* or steal a moment in one of the many European squares. Grab a bite at the splendid *St. Paul Hotel* or visit *Landmark Center* just across the street, once a federal courthouse and home to gangster trials and today a center for performing and visual arts. Or stop by the *Town Square Park* where you'll find *Cafesjian's Carousel,* built in 1914 and saved from destruction in recent years by concerned citizens.

Kids will also love a visit to *Harriet Island,* across the Mississippi from St. Paul, or the *Como Zoo and Conservatory* in *Como Park.* The Park has undergone a massive restoration and renovation project in recent years and boasts a golf course and amusement park, as well. *The St. Paul Farmer's Market* is a wonderful place to browse through fresh fruits and vegetables or if historic farming is of interest to you, explore the *Gibbs Farm Museum,* where costumed guides take you back in time.

The *Minnesota Air Guard Museum* depicts the fascinating history of Minnesota's Air National Guard. In 1915, a grand scheme called for a mammoth two-mile concrete racetrack near Fort Snelling. But the opening races on Labor Day, 1915, were less than promoters had hoped and the grandstand was sold for scrap lumber in 1917 when it became apparent the concrete track would not hold up under Minnesota winters. Happily, while the track foundered, barnstorming aviators looking for a place to land and tie-down found the infield ideal and it also provided a perfect spot for the first Minnesota Air Guard squadron. The Minnesota Air Guard Museum exhibits depict how that single squadron with fewer than 100 members has grown to 25 distinct operational units and elements at Twin Cities and Duluth bases. It is a distinguished history.

Bandana Square, a restored railway operation and now a retail center on the city's north side, features the hands-on *Children's Museum.* Parents can kill a little time at the *Twin City Model Railroad Club* which is located there, as well. And what would a visit to a genuine Mississippi River city be without a ride on a paddleboat. Sample the city from the water aboard the *Jonathan Padelford* and the *Josiah Snelling*, two riverboats offering narrated cruises between downtown *St. Paul* and *Fort Snelling.*

All of that is well and good but if there is an architecture buff among you, be warned. That particular member of your entourage is unlikely to want to leave *Summit Avenue.*

One of those glorious tree-lined avenues from a bygone era, Summit Avenue boasts the country's longest stretch of residential Victorian architecture. In the heart of St. Paul, this endearing stretch, which is a now a haven for cyclists and joggers, was home to *F. Scott Fitzgerald, Sinclair Lewis* and *Amelia Earhart,* among others. At the top of Summit stands the magnificent *St. Paul Cathedral,* modeled after St. Peter's Basilica in Rome. *The James J. Hill House* is less than a block away. Built in 1887 at a cost of $280,000, it was home to the railway baron James J. Hill. Now owned by the *Minnesota Historical Society,* it is open to the public for tours and is a must-see.

Just a few streets away is the *Alexander Ramsey House* which was home to the territory's first governor. Of course, the *Minnesota State Capitol Building* is equally charming, especially when illuminated at night. Even the freeway bridges in St. Paul have been reconstructed with architecture and history in mind.

And then there's *Grand Avenue,* a quaint district of shops and restaurants and boutiques and cafes, a multi-block run of 300 retailers that is a must-see in charming St. Paul.

EVENTS

In spite of fabulous summer weather and a host of year-round attractions, St. Paul is still a winter city and proud of it. *The St. Paul Winter Carnival* is its crown jewel, the largest winter celebration in the nation and a tribute to the voyageurs who founded the city. With its ice castles and contest and games, it is a fun-filled week that draws visitors from all parts.

Each May, St. Paul comes alive again during the *Festival of Nations,* celebrating the city's rich cultural and ethnic heritage. In June, *Grand Old Day* is a one-day celebration on Grand Avenue. In June, it's the gigantic food fest, *Taste of Minnesota,* held on the doorstep of the state capitol. On July 4th, the *Minnesota Orchestra* performs accompanied by fireworks. *Riverfest,* held on *Harriet Island,* takes place in late July, featuring 10 musical days.

Come August, the state's biggest and perhaps best celebration is held in St. Paul, the *Minnesota State Fair.* One of the nation's largest, the State Fair offers a midway, top-notch entertainment, agricultural displays and more.

For further information, contact:
St. Paul Convention Bureau
600 NCL Tower
445 Minnesota Street
St. Paul, MN 55101-2108
Phone: 612-297-6985 or 800-627-6101

HISTORY THEATRE

Great American History Theatre

30 East Tenth Street, St. Paul, MN 55101
Phone: 612-292-4323
Hrs: Call for current scheduled performances and dates.

The Great American History Theatre was founded in 1978 as a project of COMPAS. For 16 years, the Theatre has been turning the stories of Americana, specifically, of Minnesota and the Midwest into great drama.

No other metropolitan area in the country has an Equity theatre which celebrates the ghosts, heros and villains which make up our country's rich heritage.

The Theatre invites its audiences to step through the looking glass and take an entertaining trip to other times. The types of plays and musicals which have become the Theatre's trademark are like its subject, America—rich and diverse.

From the sophistication of "Gatsby" to the herring and meatball humor of "Olle From Laughtersville," to the violent, searing tale of Iron Range miners in "Mesabi Red" or the rodeo arena, where the hearts and bones of "Cowgirls" are broken—these plays entertain all types of audiences.

The Great American History Theatre won the highest award possible from the American Association for State and Local History and more Kudos Awards in two years from the Twin Cities Drama Critics Circle than any other theater its size.

Also known for its strong educational programs, the Great American History Theatre's staff guides students to write and produce their own stories.

"Another Minnesota Onstage" was written by a company of African American, Native American, Hmong, Korean and Puerto Rican actors. The play wove their own personal stories into Minnesota's history.

The innovative and entertaining style of the Great American History Theatre is what makes it special.

As our cities become covered in concrete, Americans hunger for roots and continuity. There's a feeling that a lot of the American spirit and its ghosts are lost. They're not. They've found a friendly stage at the Great American History Theatre.

HISTORY CENTER

Minnesota *Historical Society* *History Center*	345 Kellogg Blvd. W., St. Paul, MN 55102 **Phone: 612-296-6126 or 800-657-3773.** Hours vary. Free.

What Minnesota has that other states do not is a huge new History Center, home to the 145 year old Minnesota Historical Society. Roughly equivalent in size to the State Capitol, this architectural masterpiece encompasses 420,000 square feet; the first level of the east-west leg is approximately the length of two football fields!

The History Center houses an innovative museum with lively exhibits. Hear vintage Betty Crocker radio broadcasts, see Prince's costume from "Purple Rain," or watch a movie about Vietnam veterans returning home. The History Center's comprehensive research center allows you to research your house history and family genealogy, and to access artifacts, books, maps, newspapers and photographs from the Society's extensive collection. The education wing includes lecture spaces, classrooms and hands-on activities for children and families every Sunday. Two museum stores offer gifts, jewelry and other Minnesota-made specialties and Café Minnesota, the History Center's acclaimed restaurant offers luncheons and Sunday brunch.

HISTORIC SITE

Minnesota State *Capitol*	A Minnesota Historical Society Site north of downtown St. Paul, off I-94 and 35E. Aurora and Constitution avenues. St. Paul, MN 55155. **Phone: 612-296-2881** Hrs: Mon.-Fri 8:30 a.m.-5 p.m., Sat. 10 a.m.-4 p.m., Sun. 1-4 p.m. Free.

The Minnesota State Capitol, more than anything else, symbolized the start of a new age for the great Northwest. When construction of the massive granite and marble edifice began in 1896, Minnesota was no longer a frontier, but a growing, ambitious state eager to make its mark in the nation. It went without saying the new Capitol should be grander than any other of its kind.

Incorporating classical elements with Minnesota symbols and materials, St. Paul architect Cass Gilbert based the capitol structure on the Italian Renaissance style, complete with terraces, balustrades, and steps made with grey granite from St. Cloud, and a 223-foot marble dome. Inside the Capitol, the rotunda, the governor's reception room, the senate, and house and state supreme court chambers are decorated by commissioned paintings, sculptures, historic flags, gold leaf and chandeliers.

Today, the Capitol is open for visitors to marvel at both the art and at the political processes underway in its chambers.

HISTORIC SITES

Alexander Ramsey House

A Minnesota Historical Society Site. Exchange and Walnut streets. (two blocks south of the St. Paul Civic Center) 265 S. Exchange Street, St. Paul, MN 55102. **Phone: 612-296-8760.** Hrs: (April 5-Nov. 23); Tues.-Sat. 10 a.m.-4 p.m. Expanded hours Nov 25.-Dec. 31. Admission charge.

Alexander Ramsey was Minnesota's first territorial governor. Built in 1872, his home was an extravagant, 15-room architectural gem set in the fashionable Irvine Park district west of St. Paul. Ramsey purchased only the finest decorations and materials for his mansion, including black walnut woodwork, marble fireplaces, crystal chandeliers, ornate brass door fittings, fashionable rugs, furniture, and china. Even his carriage house was ornately decorated, befitting a man who entertained such eminent visitors as President Hayes.

Today, the carriage house is the starting point of guided tours of Ramsey's mansion, which was willed to the Minnesota Historical Society by Ramsey's last descendants in 1964.

A costumed guide takes visitors on tours of the house, even allowing them to peek into the kitchen where Annie, the cook, is busy baking Victorian-era goodies. The house is still furnished with the original family pieces—silent witnesses to the success of Minnesota's first statesman.

◆ ◆ ◆ ◆ ◆ ◆

Historic Fort Snelling

A Minnesota Historic Society Site. At Highway 5 and 55, St. Paul, near the Twin Cities Airport. Fort Snelling History Center, St. Paul, MN 55111. **Phone: 612-726-1171.** Hrs: May 1-Oct. 31 (fort and visitors center), Mon.-Sat. 10 a.m.-5 p.m., Sun. noon-5 p.m. Call ahead. Admission charge.

As the most remote U. S. fort in the northwest, Fort Snelling was a bustling center of law and commerce when it was built in 1820 upon the bluffs overlooking the Mississippi and Minnesota rivers. The 5th Regiment of Infantry guarded U.S. interests, kept the peace, and protected the valuable fur trade. At the same time, representatives of the United States administered government policy to the Dakota and Ojibwa Indian tribes.

Now Fort Snelling has been restored and invites visitors to view history enacted within its walls. Historically dressed interpreters go about everyday life. Officers put the soldiers through drills while the blacksmith fashions and repairs tools in his nearby shop and the post surgeon mixes medicines in the hospital. Visitors, too, can participate in fort duties and chores such as shouldering muskets, patching clothes, or scraping hides. And after a tour of the fort, they can stop in the sutler's store to stock up on any frontier supplies they may be needing. Fort Snelling truly is a gateway to the past.

HISTORIC SITE

James J. Hill House

A Minnesota Historic Society Site. On Summit Avenue, one-half block west of the St. Paul Cathedral. 240 Summit Ave., St. Paul, MN 55102. **Phone: 612-297-2555.** Hrs: Wed.-Sat. 10 a.m.-3:30 p.m. Admission charge.

The Great Northern Railway was one of the keys to the early expansion of the United States and the settlement of the west. And the man behind the success of the Great Northern was James J. Hill, the great "Empire Builder."

Hill saw to it that his railroad had the flattest grades, the straightest track, the most powerful locomotives and the longest trains. He was a man of superlatives, and when it came to building his mansion in St. Paul, he demanded the same degree of perfection.

The James J. Hill House has 36,000 square feet, including 32 rooms, 13 bathrooms, 22 fireplaces, and a 100-foot reception hall. With its carved woodwork, stained glass, and skylit art gallery, the house is a testimony to Hill's success, as well as being one of the most impressive residences ever constructed in the Midwest.

MUSEUM

Minnesota Children's Museum

1217 Bandana Blvd., St. Paul, MN 55108 **Phone: 612-644-3818** Hrs: (Summer) Mon., Tues. 9 a.m.-5 p.m., Wed.-Sat. 9-8, Sun. noon-5 p.m.

"Learning was never this fun!" is the slogan at Minnesota Children's Museum. It's a hands-on, interactive Museum offering fun learning adventures for children six months to eight years old. All exhibits are scaled to the physical and intellectual abilities of young children.

For example, kids explore TV special effects and the effect TV has on them at an exhibit called TV•FX. In the Shadow Catcher, shadows are frozen on phosphorescent walls. There's a high-action maze, electromagnetic crane, outdoor garden and much more for all to explore and have fun!

Every weekend, the Museum features workshops and classes free with admission. The current facility will add eight new exhibits in 1994-95 and, in the fall of 1995, a new building will open in downtown St. Paul that will be 3 times bigger than the current facility.

Try Minnesota Children's Museum at either location—it's a perfect kid-sized fit!

MUSEUMS

Science Museum of Minnesota and William L. McKnight-3M Omnitheater	30 East Tenth Street, St. Paul, MN 55101 **Phone: 612-221-9444.** Hrs.: Mon.-Fri. 9:30 a.m.-9 p.m.; Sat. 9 a.m.-9 p.m.; Sun. 10 a.m.-9 p.m. Visa and MasterCard accepted.

At the Science Museum of Minnesota, visitors can get their hands on science through fun, exciting exhibits that will forever debunk the "science is boring" myth. Visitors can walk around and under the museum's 82-foot-long, two-story-tall dinosaur and marvel at the 12-foot fossil fish that didn't get away.

In the Experiment Gallery, you can even touch a tornado and have fun with physics. In Anthropology Hall, you'll discover the food and cultures of the world. In Green Street, you'll learn which of your appliances are energy hogs. And in the Our Minnesota hall, you'll learn all you need to know to help keep Minnesota's lakes and lands healthy for generations to come.

Special exhibits open every four months. In the Omnitheater, visitors are surrounded by beautiful, larger-than-life images and sound on the 76-foot-diameter dome screen. The museum also offers live science theater and demonstrations that bring science to life in ways you and your kids might never have imagined.

◆ ◆ ◆ ◆ ◆ ◆ ◆

Minnesota Museum of Art	Landmark Center, Fifth at Market, Saint Paul, MN 55102-1486 **Phone: 612-292-4355. Tours: 612-292-4369** Hrs: Hours vary, call ahead.

Minnesota Museum of Art (MMA) occupies two historic buildings in downtown St. Paul. The Art Deco-period Jemne Building, an example of fine American Art, is home to the museum's collections. The Museum School, MMA administrative offices, and additional galleries occupy the largest part of the Landmark Center, a Romanesque structure which used to be the old Federal Courts Building.

The museum's primary focus is its commitment to American art, particularly artists of this region. Artwork of all media and all regions of the United States is featured in the permanent collection as well as special exhibitions, interpretive and educational programs. Featured in the Jemne Building are exhibitions of American art and that of selected non-Western cultures. Films and theater productions are held in the Jemne Building auditorium.

Admission to all MMA galleries is free, as are tours of galleries and special exhibitions. MMA visitors may also enjoy the Deco Restaurant in the Jemne Building.

MUSIC THEATRE

| *Ordway Music Theatre* | 345 Washington Street, St. Paul, Minnesota, 55102. **Phone:** 612-224-4222
Hours: Call for show times and ticket information. AmEx, Visa and MasterCard accepted. |

Founder of the Ordway, Sally Ordway Irvine, envisioned a theater which would truly "serve all the arts." Today, the Ordway Music Theatre is one of the leading performing art centers in America.

This recently renovated facility is a treat for sight, sound and comfort. Structural changes to accommodate the 12-week run of The Phantom of the Opera enables the Ordway to present large-scale Broadway theater productions.

The Ordway is home to three prestigious performing arts organizations—The Saint Paul Chamber Orchestra, The Minnesota Opera, and the Schubert Club. In addition, the Ordway is the St. Paul venue for the Minnesota Orchestra.

Broadway musicals, drama, comedy, jazz, diverse ethnic music and dance, ballet, modern, classical, contemporary, solo concert, and chorus, the Ordway truly serves all the performing arts.

The Ordway also brings the world of the arts to young people, as well as to the educators through their Performing Arts Classroom.

LODGING

| *The Saint Paul Hotel* | 350 Market Street, St. Paul, MN 55102
Phone: 612-292-9292
Major credit cards accepted. |

When The Saint Paul Hotel opened in 1910, it was the ultimate in hotels of its day. Built at a cost of $1 million, the Italian Renaissance style edifice boasted a roof garden, a grand ballroom, a fine dining room and no less than 284 porcelain bathtubs!

Seventy years later, The Saint Paul was renovated and has now regained its place as the city's grandest and finest hotel. Today, its 254 guest rooms and suites overlooking the fashionable Rice Park area and the Ordway Theater once again attract the discriminating visitor.

Guests arrive via the circular driveway, and are treated to a unique lobby dominated by a huge fireplace and ten-foot columns. The rooms feature plush carpeting, new furnishings, remote control TVs and computer modem phone lines.

Four-star dining, easy access to downtown via the skyway system and incomparable service make The Saint Paul Hotel a favorite destination for an increasing number of travelers from all over.

LODGING

Radisson Hotel St. Paul

11 East Kellogg Boulevard
St. Paul, MN 55101
Phone: 612-292-1900
All major credit cards accepted.

Welcome to the Radisson Hotel St. Paul. Centrally located in downtown St. Paul, overlooking the Mississippi River, the hotel is convenient to business, shopping and entertainment, and connected by skyway to major downtown stores and buildings.

The newly redecorated lobby of Radisson Hotel St. Paul reflects the warmth and comfort of a fine hotel. A concierge in the lobby is eager to assist with any needs you may have while traveling. You'll find the intimate lobby bar a perfect place to meet friends, with soothing music providing a quiet background for cocktails and conversation.

Whether you travel for business or pleasure, you'll discover that the Radisson Hotel Saint Paul combines modern convenience and traditional hospitality.

Radisson Hotel St. Paul offers a variety of exceptional accommodations, with 475 beautifully appointed guest rooms, including elegant suites and cabana rooms adjacent to the indoor garden court and pool. Guests of the hotel enjoy complimentary use of the indoor swimming pool, whirlpool and fitness center.

There are 80 plush, new executive rooms for the busy corporate traveler. These rooms are located on privately keyed access floors. They are appointed with upgraded amenities including complimentary carbonated water, modem hookup, in-room iron and ironing boards and in-room hairdryers. Newspapers are delivered to the door on weekdays. Executive floors provide a quiet, secluded location for the corporate travelers who appreciate fine comfort and service.

Dining is a memorable experience at Radisson Hotel St. Paul. The Carousel Restaurant, located on the hotel's top floor, is the Twin Cities' only revolving restaurant. The panoramic view of the Mississippi River and city skyline is the finest view in town. Carousel is open for breakfast, lunch and dinner featuring an American cuisine with an Italian accent. A private dining room is available for special events and business meetings.

The banquet areas are exceptional, including three ballrooms and an outdoor reception terrace overlooking the Mississippi River. Radisson Hotel St. Paul also offers flexible space for any type of business meeting or social gathering.

RESTAURANTS

W.A. Frost and Company	374 Selby Ave., St. Paul, MN 55102 **Phone: 612-224-5715** Hrs: 11 a.m.-1 a.m. Major credit cards accepted.

W.A. Frost and Company was built in 1887 and was extensively renovated by the current owners in 1974. Now, it takes its place proudly on historic Cathedral Hill.

The restaurant features tin ceilings, original artwork, antique furniture and woodburning fireplaces. In the summer, the restaurant is noted for its large outdoor dining area.

Ambiance is not the only quality here. The food is exquisite, adding to the romantic atmosphere and charm. On the lunch menu, try the Focaccia Club with the classic ingredients enhanced by chive mayonnaise on a focaccia roll. Or, try any one of their delicious salads like Szechuan Chicken, Greek salad or smoked Turkey and Wild Rice!

The dinner menu is equally exciting. You'll enjoy such delights as Grilled Spicy Catfish, Grilled Dry Aged Ribeye, Nantucket Chicken or Grilled Yellowfin Tuna.

But, whether you go for the food or because of the romance of the place, your visit will be a memorable one.

◆ ◆ ◆ ◆ ◆ ◆

Cafe Latte	850 Grand Ave., St. Paul, MN 55105 **Phone: 612-224-5687** Hrs: Hours vary, call ahead.

Peter and Linda Quinn were furniture restorers whose fascination with things Victorian led them to undertake home renovations in this historic Crocus Hill neighborhood of St. Paul. Soon they found themselves in a mid-life career change and proud owners of Grand Avenue's most popular cafe. Cafe Latte is a San Francisco-style coffeehouse-cum-cafeteria whose tables are perpetually packed with everyone from couples courting on a budget to socialites straining to see and be seen, to would-be poets composing their next sonnet over a caffe latte. That specialty coffee drink is their best seller followed closely by the espresso and flavored cappuccinos.

But the cafe's fame has been won with its line of delicious homemade desserts that range from a mile-high chocolate turtle cake to cheesecakes rich with fruit and berries. Rustic breads from the Quinn's bakery form the basis of Cafe Latte's sandwiches, augmented by pan-ethnic soups and salads. Scones fresh from the oven are another signature attraction.

RESTAURANTS & EATERIES

Boca Chica

11 S. Concord St., St. Paul, MN 55107
Phone: 612-222-8499
Hrs: Hours vary, call ahead.

For over a quarter of a century Boca Chica has been the dining pillar of St. Paul's Mexican community, centered on colorful Concord Street. Amidst the sounds of mariachi music and adobe-style decor, the casual neighborhood cafe serves the tacos and enchiladas that are the mainstay of border cooking. But the forte is the authentic specialties like green chile and nopales (cactus), made from family recipes.

Buca St. Paul

2728 Gannon Rd., St. Paul, MN 55116
Phone: 612-722-4388
Hrs: Hours vary, call ahead.

It's movie-set Italian, from Perry Como's crooning to half-draped Roman statues to the sea of knicknacks from Granny's attic in the old country—and the food's just what she would have served for supper, too. Bring lots of hungry diners. Portions of everything—be it spaghetti or chicken cacciatore— are huge and meant for sharing. The original Minneapolis Buca is equally lively and outrageous.

Cafe Minnesota

Minnesota History Center, 345 Kellogg Blvd., St. Paul, MN 55102. **Phone: 612-297-4097**
Hrs: Hours vary, call ahead.

Located in the stunning new Minnesota History Center, this cafe is making history, too, from its crisp, cutting-edge design to museum-quality food at affordable prices. Open for breakfast, lunch and brunch, the Minnesota-forward menu of this cafeteria offers the gamut from elegant salads like smoked trout with blueberries and wild rice to farm kitchen fare with a gourmet spin.

Cherokee Sirloin Room

886 S. Smith Ave., St. Paul, MN 55118
Phone: 612-457-2729
Hrs: Hours vary, call ahead.

Here's where taxi drivers deliver customers when they beg for a great steak. Three generations of Caspers oversee this casual supper-club, which has grown over the years from the original dark and cozy bar to a series of sprawling dining rooms featuring photos of old St. Paul. Rick Casper recommends his unique 16-oz. sirloin, but the filet and prime rib find plenty of takers, too.

RESTAURANTS & EATERIES

Cossetta's

211 W. Seventh St., St. Paul, MN 55102
Phone: 612-222-3476
Hrs: Hours vary, call ahead.

This homey mecca of Italian cooking lures diners to its door with striped awnings, a broadcast of Neapolitan ballads and heroic aromas. It's a cafeteria set-up, showcasing everything from homemade lasagne to meatballs in Cosetta's lusty homemade sauce. But pizza's their real claim to fame, and when the place is busy, crusts fly like frisbees before the fiery ovens. Check out the attached deli-grocery, too.

Dakota Bar & Grill

Bandana Square, 1021 E. Bandana Blvd., St. Paul, MN 55102. **Phone: 612-642-1442**
Hrs: Hours vary, call ahead.

The turn-of-the-century bricks and beams of Bandana Square once framed a railroad roundhouse. Today people make tracks for the nifty new flip on farmhouse cooking that's the specialty here. Dine at the courtyard's umbrella tables, or at the candlelit dining room for creations like Minnesota brie and apple soup, trout with dill and crayfish or walleye with wild rice salad. Best live jazz in town.

Dixie's Bar & Smokehouse Grill

695 Grand Ave., St. Paul, MN 55105
Phone: 612-222-7345
Hrs: Hours vary, call ahead.

The tropics are the theme, from palms to flamingoes, and the food segues all over the map from Florida key lime pie to Texas chili—but it's the deep-south barbecue on which they stake their reputation, bones long-smoked and ready for your choice of sauces. And the list of brews with which to quench the heat numbers in the hundreds.

Forepaugh's

276 S. Exchange St., St. Paul, MN 55102
Phone: 612-224-5606
Hrs: Hours vary, call ahead.

When Minnesota was a brand-new state, this elegant Victorian mansion was the belle of the neighborhood. Today the clapboard queen flaunts lacy curtains, gingerbread trimming and period furnishings, from its cozy, firelit lounge to a series of dining rooms. This destination restaurant, complete with French chef and staff in period costumes, prides itself on its buttery escargot, fish and veal.

RESTAURANTS & EATERIES

Leeann Chin Restaurants

Union Depot Place, 214 E. Fourth St., St. Paul, MN 55101. **Phone: 612-224-8814**
Hrs: Hours vary, call ahead.

In 1980 Leeann Chin, the town's doyenne of Chinese cooking, opened her first restaurant. This restaurant, and the ones she's added to St. Paul and at the Minneapolis International Centre, offer elegant dining in a museum-like setting, chosen to highlight her collection of Chinese artwork. It also calls attention to the array of Cantonese and Szechuan specialties on the daily-changing buffet table.

Muffuletta Cafe

2260 Como Ave., St. Paul, MN 55108
Phone: 612-644-9116
Hrs: Hours vary, call ahead.

Muffuletta is the kind of dining find every neighborhood deserves. A dowager house in the St. Anthony Park neighborhood has been converted into a series of bright dining nooks that boast an equally fresh and sunny menu. Homemade pasta is the specialty here, along with a signature spinach salad and its namesake muffuletta sandwich. Summertime the umbrella-clad deck is the popular spot.

St. Paul Grill

Saint Paul Hotel, 350 Market St., St. Paul, MN 55102. **Phone: 612-224-7455**
Hrs: Hours vary, call ahead.

Prime people-watching, St. Paul style: This bustling, clubby place is a favorite of everyone from CEOs to their filing clerks to local politicos and the throngs of theater-goers on their way to the Ordway. The menu salutes tried-and-true winners such as beefsteak to liver steak, along with creative pastas and fish dishes for the avant-garde. You can't resist their caesar, either!

Table of Contents

1648 Grand Ave., St. Paul, MN 55105
Phone: 612-699-6595
Hrs: Hours vary, call ahead.

Table of Contents adjoins The Hungry Mind, a popular bookstore on the Macalester College campus, and the hankie-size cafe boasts a menu as sophisticated as its modern setting. The chef's trick is to keep the list short and sweet—pork, chicken and seafood that gain their verve from inspired sauces. The exotic pizzas are always in demand, as are the irresistible homemade desserts.

SPECIALTY SHOPS

| *The Bibelot Shop* | 1082 Grand Ave.
St. Paul, MN 55105-3001
Phone: 612-222-0321 |

If you're looking for a perfect gift for that special someone, then The Bibelot Shop (pronounced "bee-be-lo"), French for "a small precious gift," is the place to go. This unique store offers shoppers an amazing collection of gifts, clothing and jewelry collected by owner Roxana Freese and her staff, who travel throughout the country to locate these wonderful items.

Some of the special gifts you will find as you browse through this eclectic shop include jewelry made by local and national artisans and contemporary clothing made of all natural fibers. Shoppers looking for youthful gift items can choose from a wide selection of toys including stuffed animals, numerous handmade games, and challenging puzzles for young and old alike. A one stop place to shop for all your gift needs, The Bibelot Shop also features a wide selection of artistic gift wrapping materials and greeting cards for all occasions.

Gift shoppers can visit either the Grand Avenue store or the original shop, which is located at 2276 Como Avenue also in St. Paul.

◆ ◆ ◆ ◆ ◆ ◆ ◆

| *Maud Borup Candies* | 20 W. Fifth Street, St. Paul, MN 55102
Phone: 612-293-0530. Hours: Mon.-Fri. 9:30 a.m.-5 p.m., Sat. 10 a.m.-3 p.m., Closed Sun.
Visa and MasterCard accepted. |

Famous for its delectable handmade chocolates since 1907, Maud Borup Candies is a bit of heaven for all chocolate lovers. The secret of these masterpieces in chocolate is a combination of careful preparation of small batches and the use of only the best ingredients.

Made the "old-fashioned way," using original recipes and formulas along with copper kettle cooking methods, assures that every Maud Borup candy box is perfectly filled with delicious chocolates, smooth creams and chewy caramels. Customers, drawn inside by the mouth watering aromas, must decide from over 100 varieties of hand dipped chocolates.

A Maud Borup specialty are the fondant-dipped nuts. Other delicious selections include eggshell glazed fruits, a variety of caramels made with dairy fresh cream, and decorated hand-dipped bon-bons, each with their own special chocolate curlicue filling codes.

Maud Borup candies have delighted kings and queens and discriminating chocolate lovers all over the world.

SPECIALTY SHOP

Stormcloud *Trading Company*	725 Snelling Ave. N., St. Paul MN 55104 **Phone: 612-645-0343** Hrs: Mon-Sat 10 a.m.-6 p.m. Closed Sun. Visa, MasterCard and Discover accepted.

When you walk through the nondescript entrance, you enter a world of endless possibilities. Stormcloud Trading specializes in a wide array of craft supplies, finished craft products and fine artwork for the discriminating buyer. Finished craft and art items are produced by local and nationally recognized Native American artists. Craft supplies are available for those who want to create their own Native American-inspired works.

Stormcloud has one of the largest bead selections in the Twin Cities area. Among the beads carried are seed beads for loom and free-hand beading—available in a rainbow of colors—bone beads for chokers and breastplates, and old African trade beads, some dating back to the 1700's. There are also Balinese silver beads, enameled beads and glass beads in a wide variety of sizes. The bead stock is constantly added to, plus special orders are not a problem.

In addition to beads, they carry a wide variety of findings including clasps, earring wires and hoops, various stringing supplies and metal beads of all sizes. Sculpey, for the do-it-yourselfer is available in a wide range of colors.

Aside from beads, Stormcloud also carries buckskin and elk hide, rawhide, furs of various kinds, horsehair and feathers for craft applications. The staff is well trained and knowledgeable, plus they give pointers to help design your project and pick the best products to achieve the result you want. A wide selection of sterling silver jewelry from Navajo, Hopi and Zuni craftspeople can be seen at this store. Artwork ranging from posters to original art is featured and custom framing is available, too.

Stormcloud Trading has been a retail outlet for Native American art and crafts since 1987 and in the industry since the late 1970's. The owners of Stormcloud Trading travel the country to offer the collector the best in Native American art and crafts. They have developed an excellent reputation among collectors for their selections of Hopi kachinas, Pueblo pottery and Navajo weavings. They believe in featuring authentic Native American items and purchase directly from the artists to assure their authenticity. To assist the customers in their understanding of Native American history and culture, a large selection of books for both adults and children are available for sale at the store.

If you are looking for a special item not in stock, custom orders are accepted. There is a vast world of Native American art and crafts at the Stormcloud Trading Company. They are a member of the Indian Art and Crafts Association.

RAPTOR CENTER

The Raptor Center | 1920 Fitch Ave.
St. Paul, MN 55108
Phone: 612-624-4745

The Raptor Center at the University of Minnesota is the largest medical facility in the world for the care and treatment of birds of prey (raptors) and other species of rare or endangered birds. The Raptor Center has recently moved into its new building which features exhibits of live birds, educational displays, indoor flight pens and medical facilities in which to treat the raptors. The treatment techniques used at the center have spread throughout the world to veterinarians. The objectives of the center are scientific investigation, rehabilitation, veterinary education and public education.

Many of the raptors are brought to the center for treatment after injuries from migration and hunting seasons. Many others are injured by cars or by ingesting poisonous chemicals in their environment. Many of the trumpeter swans that developed lead poisoning were treated at the center. The center is part of the veterinary hospital at the University of Minnesota but has been able to incorporate exhibits, public events and education into its mission. One of the more popular events is the release of raptors that have recovered. This event takes place each spring at the Minnesota Landscape Arboretum and each fall at Fort Snelling State Park.

The Raptor Center is funded almost entirely by private contributions and grants from foundations. Donations combined with volunteers help in accomplishing the commitment of this center.

Tours for large groups may be scheduled ahead of time or visitors may stop during the week and view the exhibits at their own pace. Donations of $1.50 per child or $3.00 per adult are requested and a gift shop is available to purchase souvenirs.

ZOO

Como Zoological Society

P.O. Box 131192
St. Paul, Minnesota 55113
Phone: 612-487-1485
Fax: 612-487-0388

For nearly a century, Como Zoo has remained one of St. Paul's best kept secrets. Tucked in the middle of a major metropolitan area, this zoo is home to over 350 animals, many of which are threatened or endangered species. Adding to the popularity of the zoo are the surrounding Como Park facilities which include the Como Conservatory and gardens. Como Zoo is also one of the few zoos that does not charge an admission or parking fee.

Major exhibits of Como Zoo include the Large Cat Facility which is home to lions, tigers, snow leopards and cougars. Both indoor and outdoor viewing is available year-round for many of these large cats.

The Primate building is home to gorillas, orangutans and various other primates, while the African Hoofed Stock Exhibit houses giraffes, zebras, sable and greater kudu antelope. The Aquatic Animal Building consists of polar bears, harbor seals, penguins, sea lions, sea birds and freshwater fish.

Sparky, the resident sea lion, entertains visitors with performances throughout the summer. Sparky's show has been a tradition for more than 30 years.

Seal Island and the Land and Water Bird Exhibit are also major attractions to the zoo. Bison, mountain goats and miniature horses can be found in the hoofed stock barn and Eastern Timber Wolves are at home in the Wolf Woods Exhibit. The Main Zoological Building contains the educational center, Zooroom, as well as the zoo's gift shop, Zoodale.

Como Zoo is open every day of the year and is dedicated to recreation, education, conservation and scientific study and is certain to hold fun and entertainment for all who visit.

SHAKOPEE

Located in the scenic Minnesota River Valley and on the southwest Metro Area border, Shakopee plays host to entertainment that will delight every member of the family. From Valleyfair Amusement Park to Mystic Lake Gambling Casino to the Renaissance Festival, millions of visitors come to Shakopee each year. Without a doubt, Shakopee is the Midwest entertainment showcase. And, whether it's a hotel, motel, quiet bed and breakfast or campground, Shakopee has the type of lodging to fit any need.

Despite its notoriety, Shakopee is still a small town at heart. Once the site of a Dakota Indian village, the city was named after the chief of that tribe. Its heritage as a Minnesota River Frontier Town was strong in those days, and is still played out in attractions such as Murphy's Landing, a living history museum of the 1800's. Shakopee has the distinction of building the first bridge across the Minnesota River.

Shakopee has experienced steady growth in the last few years and expects the trend to continue in the future. Its location on or near major arteries, like I-35W, Hwy 169, and Cty Rd. 18, make it ideal for access and development. A new downtown bypass has eased traffic through Shakopee and that trend should continue as highway construction is completed on a new bridge across the river at Cty. Rd. 18 and on a Hwy. 169 bypass to the south of the city.

ATTRACTIONS

In a word, abundant! Let's start with one of the most popular attractions in the state, the ***Minnesota Renaissance Festival.*** Here bards and scops, kings and queens, dance, songs and incredible gift and food shops delight visitors in a medieval setting. Or try ***Valleyfair Amusement Park,*** 68 acres of rides, entertainment, food and attractions. There are 50 exhilarating rides for the thrill seeker in all of us! The park's offerings range from strolling musicians and live stage shows to the magnificent six-story IMAX Theater where an entertaining and educational film is shown each summer.

Mystic Lake Casino is your next stop, with all the excitement of Vegas without the desert! The new 135,000 square foot casino features more than 128 blackjack tables and more than 2,100 video slot machines. It's the most technologically advanced bingo palace in the country. With five themed restaurants and nightly entertainment in Wild Bill's Saloon, everyone will be able find their way to this gaming mecca.

Raceway Park offers the best figure eight racing in America. It's

Minnesota's finest one-quarter mile asphalt race track. Racing occurs every Sunday evening when a field of more than 20 cars will take to the one-quarter mile figure-eight course. The beautifully maintained, modern facility seats more than 5,000 and boasts special events on holidays.

Historic *Murphy's Landing* is a re-creation of an 1890's village, complete with interpreters costumed for the period. Donning pioneer dress and mannerisms, they bring to life colorful characters from this inspiring time in history for nearly 50,000 visitors each year.

Creative River Tours operates a river excursion boat from Murphy's landing. The Emma Lee, a custom-built excursion vessel piloted by a licensed captain, is specially designed to provide comfortable travel and a full view in all weather for as many as 49 passengers.

Minnesota Harvest Apple Orchard invites you to join the celebration for harvest-time fun and the best apples in the country. When the leaves begin turning colors and apples ripen, when the flocks fly south and apples tumble along the packing line, you'll want to join the thousands of folks who drive up Apple Lover's Lane to become part of the apple action!

Shakopee is also within a few minutes of some other famous Minnesota attractions: these include the *Mall of America,* the *Minnesota Zoo* and the *Chanhassen Dinner Theatres.*

EVENTS

A variety of events are available to visitors each year. Raceway Park hosts the *NASCAR Winston Racing Series.*

Murphy's Landing is the site of the *Annual Eagle Creek Rendezvous,* which is a reenactment of the annual meeting between fur traders and Indians. Historic Murphy's Landing hosts several other events during its season including *Laura Ingalls Wilder Day, Fiddlers Contest* and *Folk Music Festival, Halloween* and *Christmas* events.

The Renaissance Festival is held from late August through the end of September including Labor Day. Valleyfair Amusement Park is open from May to September.

For further information, contact:
Shakopee Convention and Visitors Bureau
1801 East Highway 101
Shakopee, MN 55379
Phone: 612-445-1660

GOLF COURSE

Stonebrooke

2693 County Road 79, Shakopee, MN 55379
Phone: 612-496-3171
Hrs: 7 a.m. to dark.
Visa and MasterCard accepted.

"Before there was golf, nature was creating Stonebrooke." Stonebrooke was literally built around the existing landscape. The layout of the land was preserved when designing and building this course. The trees that line the course are very old and majestic and Lake O'Dowd was incorporated right into the golf course on the seventh and eighth holes. A ferry boat carries golfing parties across the lake to their second shot on the eighth hole.

Another interesting feature of the course is the cattail marsh that creates both an interesting enhancement to the course as well as a test of the golfer's ingenuity. The course itself is in immaculate condition; the "bent grass" greens are large and very undulated. The staff is proud of the surroundings and genuinely enjoys working with visitors.

All of these factors work together to make Stonebrooke one of the finest courses in the state. Challenging and breathtakingly beautiful, Stonebrooke must be played to be fully appreciated.

LIVING HISTORY MUSEUM

Living History Museum Murphy's Landing

2187 East Hwy. 101, Shakopee, MN 55379
Phone: 612-445-6901. Hrs.: Vary according to seasons and events. Call ahead for information. Visa and MasterCard accepted.

Once a stepping stone to the great, uncharted frontier, Murphy's Landing is again alive with the sights and sounds of the 19th century. Come and travel back in time from 1840 to 1890. As you walk down the sandy road, you will meet people from the 1800's who will tell you about their lives and times.

Marvel at the authentic animals and crops at the Berger Farm. Visit the Shopkeeper and Blacksmith in the village and hobnob with the wealthiest woman in town.

During December, return to a "Currier and Ives" Christmas while you visit a re-creation of the 19th century holidays in the Minnesota River Valley.

Add to this the ambiance of an 1890's Ice-cream Parlor Restaurant and a beautiful gift shop. Now you will have an idea of the wonderful day you can spend at Murphy's Landing!

STILLWATER

Stillwater is one of those rare places where the powers that be aren't required to go to great lengths to entice visitors to their town. People just come, as they always have, drawn by the awesome splendor of the St. Croix River and the historic charm.

After all, this is the quintessential river town. Where once the river meant commerce and transportation, today it just means fun. And plenty of it!

ATTRACTIONS & EVENTS

Those who first settled Stillwater could scarcely have imagined the *St. Croix River* today. A haven for boaters of all descriptions, the St. Croix can be a busy place on summer weekends, which only adds to the atmosphere.

If you are without a vessel or would rather let someone else do the navigating, the *Andiamo Showboat* is the ticket, offering dinner cruises accompanied by music and entertainment. Landlubbers might prefer the fascinating *Joseph Wolf Brewery Caves,* beer storage caves hand-dug in the 1840's, and the *Minnesota Zephyr,* an elegant dining train from the 1940's that makes a romantic three-hour journey north along the *St. Croix River Valley.*

If stationary dining is more your thing, Stillwater is one of Minnesota's prime locations. *The Freighthouse* is a popular gathering spot with its railway motif and gigantic outdoor patio. *Brine's* is a family-operated meat market, deli, bakery, restaurant and bar. *The Dock Cafe* is an excellent choice for riverside dining.

Walking off all those calories is a snap. After all, you will have to explore the many boutiques and galleries and shops that line Stillwater's historic streets. *The Brick Alley* building or the *Grand Garage* would make a great place to begin. *Northern Vineyard Winery* offers a brief respite where you can sample the end results of local vineyards. *Warden's House Museum* and the *Washington County Historic Courthouse* are worth a stop or try an historic walking tour.

Lumberjack Days, held in July, is the area's heritage celebration. *The Rivertown Art Fair,* the *Fall Colors Art Fair* and *Taste of the St. Croix Valley* are all held at *Lowell Park* as is the popular *Music on the Waterfront* series.

For further information, contact:
Stillwater Area Chamber of Commerce
423 S. Main Street
Stillwater, MN 55082   Phone: 612-439-7700

ANTIQUES

Mulberry Point *Antiques*	270 N. Main, Stillwater, MN 55082 **Phone: 612-430-3630.** Hrs: Mon.-Sat. 10 a.m.- 6 p.m., Sun. 11 a.m.-6 p.m. Extended summer hours. All major credit cards accepted.

Authentic quality antiques. More than 16,000 square feet worth on four levels. That's what you'll find at Mulberry Point Antiques, the oldest group antique shop in Stillwater. Housed in a 1929 warehouse, it features the treasures of some 60 dealers, all committed to an atypical antique shop. They specialize in high quality furniture in room-like settings.

Take your time. You'll need it to browse the unique and attractive displays, all well-lit and all tastefully done with quality accent pieces. There are no reproductions displayed here. Mulberry Point Antiques does not accept them. The knowledgeable staff do a great job of answering customers' questions in a professional manner and the coffee pot is always on. If you've got a knack for restoration or are in search of a bargain, then the "Rough Room" is a must-see. It features as-is furniture for the do-it-yourselfer. Located in a three-story red brick building at the corner of North Main and Mulberry. Shipping and delivery available.

BED & BREAKFAST

The Elephant *Walk B&B*	801 W. Pine St., Stillwater, MN 55082 **Phone: 612-430-0359** Hrs: Open every day. Visa and MasterCard accepted.

Built in 1883 for Stillwater's first jeweler, the Elephant Walk B&B is today a jewel box of antiquities and collectibles from all over the world. The stick style Victorian has been lovingly restored by Rita and Jon Graybill following their return from over twenty years of diplomatic service. They collected many antiques from Europe, the Far East and America, and these are displayed throughout the Elephant Walk.

A wrap-around front porch provides casual dining and a quiet place to relax on the porch swing and accompanying peacock chairs. The home is graced by two parlors on the first floor where new and interesting friend-ships are sure to be made.

The Elephant Walk is truly a unique bed and breakfast full of fascinating objects and surrounded by beautiful flower gardens.

BED & BREAKFAST

Asa Parker House	17500 St. Croix Trail N. Marine on St. Criox, MN 55047 **Phone: 612-433-5248** Visa and MasterCard accepted.

Just on the outskirts of William O'Brien State Park is the Asa Parker House, a restored lumber baron's home and now a four-star bed and breakfast. Built in 1856, the house overlooks the spectacular St. Croix River Valley and offers guests a choice of five individually decorated rooms.

Each room has its own, charming ambiance and is named after an historic person who actually lived in Marine on St. Croix. The three-room Alice O'Brien suite has a whirlpool bath and a large, private flower-filled deck. Innkeeper Marjorie Bush brightens the room with her own arrangements of fresh and dried flowers and offers her guests a three-course breakfast served on antique china and Bavarian crystal. Her outstanding breakfasts earned Marjorie an entry representing Minnesota in *Better Homes and Gardens*. The Chicago *Tribune* travel section has recognized her culinary talents, rating her hospitality and cooking the best in the Midwest.

After breakfast, explore the paved bike and walking paths, and cross-country ski trails at the nearby William O'Brien State Park or join other guests in a game of croquet or tennis on the Parker grounds. Guests also can stroll through the historic village of Marine on St. Croix, admire the vintage homes and shops or take a ten-minute drive to Stillwater.

A stay at the Asa Parker House is definitely a one-of-a-kind vacation. When guests step inside this stately, romantic bed and breakfast, they have entered a quieter, gentler era.

There is no smoking and no pets allowed at the Asa Parker House.

BED & BREAKFAST

James Mulvey *Residence Inn*	622 W. Churchill St., Stillwater, MN 55082 **Phone: 612-430-8008** Hrs.: Open all year. Visa and MasterCard accepted.

Visitors to the James Mulvey Residence Inn feel like they've stepped back to a slower and quieter time, a bygone era when warm, gracious welcomes and lingering visits were commonplace.

Those qualities still are treasured at the James Mulvey Residence Inn, a bed and breakfast that features a four-course breakfast, with irresistible chocolate-covered strawberries served every day for dessert on the Victorian sunporch.

The Mulvey residence, built in 1878 by a Civil War veteran, treats its guests in the spring and summer to a colorful array of gardens and flowers. Inside, the home is filled with a veritable gallery of art and antiques. The center of the parlor, for example, contains a magnificent and rare Grueby tile fireplace, one of two known fireplaces of such kind in Minnesota. Three of the five rooms have fireplaces, double whirlpools and private baths. Anniversary and birthday specials are available, and guests also can use the Inn's mountain bikes. A non-smoking inn.

WINERY

Northern *Vineyards Winery*	402 N. Main Street, Stillwater, MN 55082 **Phone: 612-430-2012.** Hrs: Mon.-Sat. 10 a.m.-5 p.m., Sun. Noon-5 p.m. (January through April) Wed.-Sat. 10 a.m.-5 p.m., Sun. Noon - 5 p.m. Visa and MasterCard accepted.

"Wine is constant proof that God loves us and wants to see us happy."—Benjamin Franklin. Words to live by if you're a winegrower. And words to remember during a visit to the Northern Vineyards Winery in downtown Stillwater. Located in the historic Staples Mill, the Winery is operated by the Minnesota Winegrowers Cooperative, a collection of winegrowers from Minnesota and western Wisconsin, wherever site and soil, sun and rain are found in combinations pleasing to the vine. Their products are pleasing, too, particularly the St. Croix dry red and the Seyval Blanc, a flinty, dry white wine made from Seyval, Minnesota's premium wine grape. Inside the winery, you can participate in free tasting sessions daily as well as soak in the unique aroma found only at a winery. Don't let Minnesota's severe weather fool you into thinking this isn't wine country. Step inside Northern Vineyards Winery and find out for yourself.

HISTORIC INN

| *Lowell Inn* | 102 N. Second Street, Stillwater, MN 55082
Phone: 612-439-1100
MasterCard and Visa accepted. |

A Williamsburg-style country inn located in historic Stillwater opened its doors in 1927 and was managed by Arthur S. and Nelle Palmer since 1930. They purchased the Inn in 1945 and were joined by Arthur Jr. and Maureen Palmer in 1951. Their goal was to create an atmosphere that would make their guests feel that they were in a real home, with fine art pieces, antiques, linens, tableware and glassware. This collection may be seen throughout the Lowell Inn today.

The Lowell Inn is a striking three-story, red brick, colonial mansion. The broad veranda is supported by 13 columns, each flying the historic flag of the original colonies. There are 16 guest rooms plus five suites, all with private bath. Each room features an eating/sitting area and complimentary wine and liquor, a service originated by the Lowell Inn. The George Washington Room was the original dinning room. It has Williamsburg Colonial furnishings. Sheffield silver services and a Dresden china collection are displayed on buffets around the room.

The Garden Room was the first addition to the Lowell Inn in 1939. It features an indoor trout pool formed by natural springs from the adjoining hillside. The earthy atmosphere of the room is accentuated by huge, round, polished-agate tables.

The Cocktail Lounge was added in 1957. In 1959, Arthur and Maureen added the Matterhorn Room to reflect their Swiss ancestry. They decided the beauty of Swiss woodcarving would be the basis of the decor for the new dining room. Also featured are imported table settings and stained glass windows.

Stillwater has many other historic buildings, too. A tour of the many antique shops, the Minnesota Historical Museum or a Paddlewheel Boat ride at St. Croix Falls can make an ideal weekend at the romantic Lowell Inn. Gift certificates are available, as is a conference room for meetings.

DINING EXCURSION

Minnesota Zephyr

601 North Main, P.O. Box 573, Stillwater, MN 55082. **Phone: 612-430-3000, outstate 800-992-6100.** Hours: Call for information. MasterCard, Visa, and Discover accepted.

The Minnesota Zephyr (Zephyr meaning "Breeze from the West") is an elegant dining train offering a chance to experience for the first time, a journey back in time; and for some an opportunity to relive and reminisce the era of the late 1940's.

The Minnesota Zephyr features five dining cars all carefully restored. Each car is different in design and color, recreating prestigious railroad dining of decades gone by.

The Lounges in the Vista Dome Club Cars located at the front and rear of the train, are designed for the gathering of guests before and after dinner for beverages, cocktails and relaxation. Each car offers a magnificent view of the scenic area while traveling the leisurely course.

This exciting adventure and romantic three-hour journey boards in the historic city of Stillwater and travels along the river, streams and woodland bluffs of the beautiful St. Croix River Valley.

Identical afternoon and dinner excursions feature a superb five-course, white linen dinner exquisitely prepared. Zephyr chefs take great pride in preparing each of the delicious courses to ensure only praises from guests who can choose from one of three delectable entrées.

Main entrées include The Zephyr, a choice cut of prime rib and featuring a sharp Zephyr sauce served with buttered and chived potatoes, green vegetables and French bread rolls; The St Croix, a delicious North Atlantic flounder combined with lobster and crab meat with white wine filling served with drawn butter, lemon, white rice, green vegetables and French bread rolls; and, The Stillwater, a tender, moist rock game hen roasted to perfection and covered with an orange glaze served with Minnesota long-grain wild rice, green vegetables and French bread rolls.

Guests board at the historic Stillwater Depot, which is also a marvelous logging and railroad museum. Historical relics, displays, and numerous photographs vividly dramatize what logging and railroad life was like in the Stillwater area. A variety of gifts, souvenirs, and refreshments are available to meet your every need.

A special, two-hour group afternoon excursion trip and charter is also available featuring a variety of menu choices to suit any occasion and to fit any budget. Gift certificates and group rates are available.

HORSE FACILITY

Horseshoe Lake Arabians

13600 Hudson Blvd., Stillwater, MN 55082
Phone: 612-436-7551
Hrs: Mon.-Sat. 10 a.m.-4 p.m., Sun.
by appointment.

Near the St Croix River Valley and southeast of historic Stillwater, Paul and Ann Emerson have been raising and breeding Arabian horses for more than 25 years. They began with Shetland and Welsh ponies purchased for their three young children in 1955. After ten years of raising quarterhorses and Palominos in addition to ponies, the Emersons decided to make a commitment to breeding Arabians.

Horseshoe Lake Arabians has been in operation for about ten years on a beautiful 350-acre farm just off of I-94 between the Twin Cities and Stillwater. It is a nationally known Arabian horse breeding, training and sales facility where visitors are welcome to drop in for a tour. The sizable establishment includes a 57-stall barn, one 12-stall barn, six pastures, five runs, an outdoor arena, a large indoor arena and an outdoor work ring. Expansion plans include additional paddocks and possibly a racetrack. Approximately 55 horses are on hand at any given time at the farm. Visitors may view horse training sessions and a video presentation. The Emersons are happy to share the experience they have gained through breeding and showing quality horses. Riding lessons and seminars with topics ranging from basic horse care to specific riding techniques have not only served to educate new clients, but have also brought new people into the Arabian horse business. The Horseshoe Lake Arabians have outstanding success in competitions. From spring through fall, horses are shown two and three times a month.

Through a combination of hard work, good stock and commitment to the Arabian horse, the Emersons have made Horseshoe Lake Arabians the successful breeding and marketing venture it is today, with sales around the country as well as overseas. In spite of their busy schedule, they also find time to operate a land development business and to collect antique cars.

RESTAURANTS

Dock Cafe

425 E. Nelson, Stillwater, MN 55082
Phone: 612-430-3770
Hours: Hours vary, call ahead.
Major credit cards accepted.

There's just something special about waterfront dining, particularly on the scenic St. Croix River in Stillwater. And when the service is excellent and the food's outstanding, the whole package can be irresistible.

For example, the Dock Cafe. Featuring everything from the usual (a Grilled Tuna Melt and Turkey Club, for example) to the unusual (try Gravlax or Spinach Ramekin from the list of appetizers), and everything in between (Chicken Ziti, Salmon Pasta or River Valley Pasta, perhaps), the Dock Cafe is a wonderful choice for lunch or dinner. Although the setting and atmosphere and cuisine are all superb, the Dock Cafe is also known for its excellent value. All lunches can be prepared for take out, too—nice to know if you're boating.

A great place to have dinner for two, the Dock is equally capable for large groups, with private rooms accommodating groups from 20 to 70.

◆ ◆ ◆ ◆ ◆ ◆ ◆

Freight House

305 S. Water Street, Stillwater, MN 55082
Phone: 612-439-5718. Hours: 11 a.m.-
8 p.m., Fri.-Sat. 11-9. Closed Mondays.
Major credit cards accepted.

There's nothing like a sunny weekend afternoon on the St. Croix River in Stillwater, a Minnesota pastime that's been drawing crowds for decades. And there's nothing like a couple of cool ones and a casual dinner on the deck at the Freight House.

Located just off Stillwater's main drag with its galleries and boutiques and historic charm, between downtown and the river, the Freight House is a Stillwater institution that always draws a crowd. Besides great food, it offers plenty of fun. Nightly entertainment includes a disc jockey or live bands on the weekend.

From chicken wings to burgers and steaks or just a cool drink, the Freight House offers consistent quality and good value. Of course, you don't have to sit outside to enjoy the food and drink and you don't have to wait until a summer weekend to sample some of the fun and hospitality Stillwater is famous for. It's on the menu year-round at the Freight House.

RESTAURANT

Lake Elmo Inn

3442 Lake Elmo Ave., Lake Elmo, MN 55042
Phone: 612-777-8495. Hrs: Lunch Mon.-Sat.
11a.m.-2 p.m.; Dinner Mon.-Sat. 5 p.m.-10 p.m.;
Sun. Champagne brunch 10-2. Dinner 4:30-8:30.

The Lake Elmo Inn was originally built in 1881 to serve as an inn and stagecoach stop. Current owners, John and Kathy Schiltz, are dedicated to offering customers the same country, yet sophisticated atmosphere with elegant dining that the inn is known for. You will be welcomed and well taken care of here. Come in a suit or in jeans, either way you'll fit right in.

The restaurant and lounge area provide a country-French ambience complemented by a friendly, professional staff dedicated to creating a very memorable dining experience. On display is an outstanding collection of salt and pepper shakers showcased along the wall of the dining room. A seasonal garden patio with outdoor seating offers exceptional respite with a charming waterfall.

This award winning restaurant's continental cuisine features such classics as roast duckling and veal picatta. Daily selections of fresh fish and seafood include such delicacies as lobster, Salmon Wellington, scallops, seafood platter, Dover sole, prawns and pasta, plus that Minnesota seafood—walleye pike.

Other unique dishes will delight the eye and satisfy the palate, as well. Try the Venison schnitzel or lamb penne. Dinners are served with fresh sauteed vegetables, along with a choice of wild rice, potato of the day, pasta or baked potato. Lunch time offers soups, salads, pastas and specialty sandwiches along with chicken and fish.

In addition to the entrées, there is a pleasing selection of appetizers and an extensive wine list to complement any selection. A light Lemon Sorbet intermezzo is served before the main entrée and a chocolate-dipped strawberry is a perfect finish after a memorable meal.

The emphasis is on the details at this Inn, along with a strong people orientation. Lake Elmo Inn can make special preparations for restrictive diets and light appetites. If you have a special need, just ask.

Sunday and holiday brunches offer a culinary extravaganza with a large variety of entrées and desserts, ice carvings and other delights.

Christmas is a special delight at the Lake Elmo Inn. The decorations and the festive mood are not to be missed at this time of year. Lights inside and out are bright and Christmas ornaments from the past ten years hang from the ceiling.

Banquet facilities and catering are also available.

RESTAURANTS

Gasthaus *Bavarian Hunter*	8390 Lofton Ave., Stillwater, MN 55082 **Phone: 612-439-7128.** Hrs: Lunch M-F, 11 a.m.-4 p.m. Sat. noon-4 p.m. Dinner M-Th, 4-9 p.m., Fri, Sat. 4-10 p.m., Sun. noon-8 p.m. Major credit cards accepted.

Enjoying good food is a year-round event at the Gasthaus Bavarian Hunter restaurant. Authentic in every detail, the Gasthaus offers traditional Bavarian specialties such as sauerbraten, jaegerschnitzel, schnweinshaxe and sausages. Even the wait-staff wears beautiful Bavarian dirndls and lederhosen. Visitors enjoy a wide selection of Munich beers on tap, as well as an extensive array of liqueurs in a rural country setting.

In September, it's time once again for Oktoberfest here in the beautiful wooded countryside of eastern Minnesota, just as it is in Germany. The sights and sounds of this outdoor festival welcome guests to this time of taste treats and fun.

Since 1966, Karl Schoene and his son, Carli, have built upon the traditions of their native Bavaria to create a tradition in Minnesota every bit as interesting and colorful as the real thing. Raise a stein of Munich beer, Prosit! and sing along. You are warmly welcomed to the centuries-old German tradition of great food and fun!

◆ ◆ ◆ ◆ ◆ ◆ ◆

Vittorio's	402 S. Main St., P.O. Box 437, Stillwater, MN 55082. **Phone: 612-439-3588** Hrs: Sun.-Thurs. 11 a.m.-10 p.m. Fri, Sat. until midnight. Major credit cards accepted.

At the base of the bluffs in Stillwater is Vittorio's restaurant, serving the St. Croix Valley for 25+ years with fine northern Italian cuisine. The restaurant is located at the former Joseph Wolf Brewery site, and has been enhanced over the years to provide a distinctive atmosphere for your dining experience.

The circa 1840 sandstone and limestone caves once used to store beer provide the ambiance for the "Grotto Blue" Dining Room, "designed for lover's at heart." Anyone seeking a quiet, leisurely dinner in elegant surroundings will certainly enjoy this area. More casual dining is offered in the Family Room, but both dining rooms feature a fine selection of entrées including Vittorio's celebrated Canelloni Bianchi, homemade pasta folded around a mixture of special meats and cheeses and baked in Vittorio's famous white sauce.

Other items of note: Capelletti, Lasagne, Ravioli, Spaghetti, oversized Antipasto Salads and mouthwatering pizzas. A great line-up of luncheon entrées along with daily specials are available, too.

RESTAURANT

Mad Capper Saloon and Eatery

224 S. Main Street, Stillwater, MN 55082
Phone: 612-430-3710. Hrs: Mon.-Sat. 11 a.m.-
1 a.m. Sundays noon-Midnight
Major credit cards accepted.

For more than 100 years, people have been imbibing at the same location in downtown Stillwater. Listed on the National Register of Historic Places, the Mad Capper Saloon and Eatery remains the meeting place for Stillwater locals and visitors alike.

This historic building has a beautiful Victorian interior with a sports accent. There has been a bar at the same location for more than a century and at one time, there was even live boxing in the back. Today, a unique assortment of hats adorns the interior walls and there's a fine collection of antiques throughout the restaurant.

A wide selection of both imported and domestic beers is offered and the sandwich selections, available on three different types of bread, are excellent. Specialty burgers are individually smothered in favorites such as sauteed mushrooms and onions, barbecue sauce or cheddar cheese. Other menu selections feature daily luncheon specials, homemade soups and chilis and a tasteful choice of popular appetizers. Great food in a fun, friendly atmosphere.

SHOPPING

Brick Alley

324 South Main Street
Stillwater, MN 55082
Phone: 612-439-7812
Hrs: Open 7 days a week.

It began life in 1874 as the home of the Stillwater Gas and Light Company. Today, like so much of this historic Minnesota river town, the Brick Alley is reborn into a terrific shopping, browsing and dining emporium with a little bit of everything for just about everyone. After serving as the utility's long time home (it later became known as Northern States Power), the Brick Alley was transformed in 1976 after being purchased and renovated by a local architect. Today, it houses a wonderful Greek restaurant as well as shops featuring crafts and gifts, unique jewelry, clothing, cosmetics, books, Stillwater souvenirs and tourist information at the Chamber of Commerce.

Inside this wonderful brick structure, washed in sunlight from a wide row of windows at the top, you'll find high ceilings with solid wooden beams. There are a variety of levels within each floor, each separated by a short set of wooden steps. Convenient parking for Brick Alley patrons is located on the east side with public lots also to the north and south. A Stillwater landmark worth looking into.

SPECIALTY SHOPS

St. Croix Crafts and Gifts, Ltd.

421 S. Main Street, Stillwater, MN 55082. **Phone: 612-439-6928.** Hrs: (Summer) Mon. - Sat., 10 a.m.-8 p.m., Sun., 10 a.m.-5 p.m. (Winter) M-T-T-Sat. 10 a.m.-5:30 p.m., Sun. noon-5 p.m., Wed., closed
Visa and MasterCard accepted.

Minnesota is blessed with many artists and shops which feature their wares. One of the newest editions to this bounty is St. Croix Crafts and Gifts, Ltd., located in historic Stillwater, Minnesota. This unique store is owned and operated by crafters Mike Simat and Debbie Schmidt, who opened the store in 1993.

Located in the Brick Alley Building at the south end of downtown Stillwater, St. Croix Crafts and Gifts combines handcrafted merchandise and gift items so well that it is difficult to tell the difference between the two. With little or no duplication of work and a large variety of items to choose from, visitors are sure to appreciate the talent and hard work represented at St. Croix Crafts and Gifts, Ltd.

Come to shop or just to browse and remember, there's always room for one more.

◆ ◆ ◆ ◆ ◆ ◆ ◆

Ultramarine

421 S. Main Street
Stillwater, MN 55082
Phone: 612-430-0067
Hrs: Open seven days a week.

Ultramarine art supplies and picture framing was opened in 1989 by Betsy and Jim Anderson, Stillwater artists who saw a need for a shop to service the art material needs of St. Croix Valley area artists. It opened initially on Second Street with a few lines of artist's colors and a small complement of essentials.

Slowly, it grew over the years and, finally, Ultramarine moved to its present location on Main Street in the historic Brick Alley building in 1993.

Now they offer a complete assortment of artist's supplies, including items for children and beginners. In addition, Ultramarine carries a large line of stationery, art and literary oriented magazines and journals, and a variety of other items of interest to the aesthetic mind. If you have an interest in the "finer" things of life, stop in. You'll be pleasantly surprised at what you find!

SPECIALTY SHOP

Commemorative Imports Collectors Gallery/Noah's Ark—A Country Store

5901 Omaha Ave, N., Stillwater, MN 55082
Phone: 612-439-4918 or 612-439-8772
Hrs: Mon.-Sat. 10 a.m.-5:30 p.m., Thurs. 10 a.m.-
7 p.m., Sun. noon-4:30 p.m. Extended Christmas hours.
Visa, MasterCard, AmEx and Discover accepted.

Located "On the Hill," off Highway 36, and only minutes from historic downtown Stillwater, this unique emporium is really two shops in one.

Commemorative Imports Collector's Gallery and Noah's Ark—A Country Store, are owned and operated by a family of six brothers and sisters, some who enjoy the day-to-day operation of the store, others who travel the country, seeking out unique and unusual gifts and decorative accessories for their customers. Combined, the two shops total 3,800 square feet. Their goal is to offer as many diverse, unique and unusual gift items as possible and to give their customers the best in service.

Inside Commemorative Imports, the walls are covered with more than 400 collector's plates, scissor-cut and calligraphy prints plus wreathes and floral arrangements that create a homey feeling. Gifts and collectibles are displayed in an open, airy space where the smell of fresh baking often fills the air.

Here you'll find the exquisite Dept. 56 collectibles, music boxes, cookie molds, stationary, Crabtree & Evelyn bath products and Byers Choice Carolers. The shop carries Lenox china, Gorham crystal, collectible bears and bunnies, collectible Christmas ornaments and Precious Moments collectibles. They also have books for children, gardeners, cooks and nature lovers. Throw in a gourmet food section and a collection of rubber stamps and stencils and you have a terrific selection.

Free gift wrapping, convenient parking, custom orders, gift baskets and gift certificates are available plus mail and phone order service.

If you love country, you'll love Noah's Ark next door. It's full of wonderful country treasures and folk art, a unique collection from America's finest artists and craftsmen. Everything is tastefully displayed among antiques, including handmade dolls and animals sitting in an antique bolt cabinet, hand-carved Santas basking in an old tobacco humidor and Christmas ornaments in an elegant old candy carousel. You'll also find beautiful wood carvings, pottery, candles, books, primitive paintings, cotton throws, lamps, herb racks and tinware plus, samplers, hearts, wood signs and bobbins.

Just minutes from a vast array of wonderful bed and breakfasts where you can unwind and enjoy the sights of historic Stillwater, Commemorative Imports and Noah's Ark are a real delight.

SPECIALTY SHOPS

River Rats

233 S. Second Street, Stillwater, MN 55082
Phone: 612-439-3308
Hrs: Tue.-Sat. 10 a.m.-6 p.m.;
Sun. noon-5 p.m.; Closed Mon.

Built in the mid-1800's, the River Rats is located in one of Stillwater's oldest buildings. The high ceilings, bare brick walls, and hardwood floor make visitors feel like stepping back in time.

River Rats has a fine selection of domestic and imported natural-fiber clothing at very reasonable prices. The cut-loose and "real clothes" clothing lines feature a wide range of colors and quality styles for mixing and matching wardrobes. Accessories such as hats, belts, scarves, boots, shoes, and imported jewelry and ladies' totes from Africa, Indonesia, and Thailand complement a clothing selection. River Rats offers fresh styles from season to season to help create comfortable ensembles for any occasion.

But River Rats is more than just clothing. There is also a wide assortment of imported, hand-crafted baskets and pottery items displayed by local craftsmen. After shopping, discover and enjoy historic downtown Stillwater. When hectic shopping malls and "trendy" fashions won't do, River Rats is the place.

◆ ◆ ◆ ◆ ◆ ◆

Seasons Tique

209 S. Main St., Stillwater, MN 55082
Phone: 612-430-1240 or 800-329-1241
Hrs: Mon.-Sat. 9:30 a.m.- 8 p.m., Sun. 12-5
Major credit cards accepted.

Located in an historic 100-year-old building is Seasons Tique, a Christmas and collectible shop with a magnificent selection of holiday trimmings to ring in the yuletide spirit! It's Christmas all year long at this store.

Visitors receive a cup of spiced tea and an invitation to explore the store with its many Christmas delights. They'll even arrange a guided tour of the store for groups.

A beautiful selection of handcrafted ornaments and miniatures from around the world are offered here. They have the largest collection of handcarved German collectibles in the area. Each wooden character's charming personality is carefully crafted with strict attention to 18th century design and detail.

Seasons Tique is a showcase dealer for Dept. 56 Villages and authorized dealer for Precious Moments, Fontanini, WACO, Annalee, and Cherished Teddies. Russian collectibles can also be found. Free gift wrapping and phone orders.

WAYZATA

The history of this busy suburban town with its many upscale specialty shops is intrinsically tied to the late railroad baron James J. Hill. In the early days, when Wayzata was still a small farming village nestled on the north shore of Lake Minnetonka 12 miles west of Minneapolis, James J. Hill laid his St. Paul and Pacific railroad line straight down the middle of Wayzata's main street, blocking the tiny village's only access to Minneapolis. Wayzata proceeded to sue the Empire Builder, requesting that he move the line to a neighboring street.

Hill, however, was so miffed by this audacity that he not only moved the line—he moved it one mile out of town so the people of Wayzata would have to, as he put it, "walk a mile for the next 20 years" to catch the train. Eventually, the city and the railroad baron came to terms and in 1906 Hill moved the line back into town and built a new depot.

ATTRACTIONS & EVENTS

Today the *Wayzata Depot* is a national historic landmark and the focus for numerous community activities. An ideal way to recapture the mood of the young Victorian town at the turn of the century is a free Wayzata Trolley ride from the depot to town and back to the city beach on Lake Minnetonka. Lake Minnetonka is one of the Twin Cities area's most popular lakes, ideal for fishing, boating, windsurfing and swimming.

Local events focus on the depot, most notably *James J. Hill Days* in September, featuring an arts and crafts fair, children's games, a parade, and athletic events for the entire family. From late June through July, the depot is a venue for weekly, free family concerts featuring a great variety of music and artists.

In the winter, local residents flock to the February *Chilly Open* to enjoy 27 holes of golf on frozen Lake Minnetonka, ice fishing, dinner and cabaret entertainment.

For further information, contact:
Greater Wayzata Area Chamber of Commerce
402 E. Lake Street
Wayzata, MN 55391
Phone: 612-473-9595

ART GALLERY

David Ice Gallery

810 E. Lake Street, Wayzata, MN 55391
Phone: 612-473-3931
Hrs: Mon.-Sat. 10 a.m.-5 p.m. Evenings by
appointment. Visa and MasterCard accepted.

The David Ice Gallery is an unusual collection of fine art, fantastic jewelry, and fun things. Artworks include contemporary fine art, handcrafted and whimsical furniture, pottery, jewelry, and interior accessories.

This is a collection of work of local and regional artists (all proceeds go to the artist) as well as items from around the world. The gallery has an open feeling and invites visitors to feast the eye and visitors can even sit on some of the art. It's a shop of treasures that inspires you to browse, peruse and touch a host of intriguing art for sale, not the usual white-walled gallery.

David Ice has been an artist all his life and his dedication to art is realized at the gallery. Many of his own works are displayed here— paintings, sculpture and many other mediums.

The always-changing displays make the David Ice Gallery a refreshing new experience every time you visit. Custom designed pieces and framing are available.

BOOKSTORE

The Bookcase

607 E. Lake Street, Wayzata, MN 55391
Phone: 612-473-8341
Hrs: Mon.-Sat. 6:30 a.m.-10 p.m. Fri., Sat. open
until 11 p.m. Visa and Mastercard accepted.

The Bookcase has been a community favorite since the early 1960's, drawing a wide cross-section of patrons from near and not so near. This interesting store faces Lake Minnetonka and offers breathtaking scenery year-round. Planters and tables beckon patrons during the summer months to gather their reading material and savor it, like the sunshine, near the lakeshore.

The Bookcase offers an outstanding selection of children's books that occupy one section of the store. In fact, on a monthly basis, the store is filled with stories being related to children by famous local authors. And field trips to the store allow school children to learn how books are made.

Their customers include people from the metro area, of course, but also people from as far away as Japan, France and South America! Special orders and out-of-print services are not a problem, here. The staff is knowledgeable and well-read. Free gift wrapping and shipping services top the list of amenities.

BOAT EXCURSION

Al and Alma's Supper Club and Charters

5201 Piper Road, Mound, MN 55364. **Phone: 612-472-3098 or 612-472-6016.** Hrs: Supper Club—Mon.-Sat. open 5 p.m., Sun. open 4 p.m.-10 p.m., Charter Cruises - May-Oct. Visa and MasterCard accepted.

Cruise scenic Lake Minnetonka aboard one of Al and Alma's fleet of luxurious charter boats or enjoy a fine meal at the Supper Club restaurant. Daryl and Merritt Geyen invite you to take a relaxing and enjoyable cruise on beautiful Lake Minnetonka as you dine on one of the many carefully selected menu specials aboard ship or at their beautiful Supper Club restaurant.

Make your next anniversary, birthday or special group event even more memorable with an unforgettable lake cruise. Al and Alma's Charter Cruises feature both individual and small group charters aboard one of six comfortable yachts including the new "1994" luxury cruiser Avant Garde that accommodates up to 100 people.

All yachts in the fleet are manned by qualified captains and crews and maintained in top operating performance. Weekday rates, group specials and evening charter packages are available and include a wide selection of food and beverage choices. A deposit is required for all group reservations.

Al and Alma's also offers a choice of several affordable public cruises geared for family outings including Sunday brunch and family pizza cruises, a Monday night family pizza cruise, and Friday and Saturday night dinner cruises. Cruises begin boarding 15 minutes before departure. Comfortable attire and soft sole shoes are recommended.

For those who prefer an excellent meal on shore, Al and Alma's Supper Club restaurant offers an exceptional selection of food and beverages. From seafood to choice steaks, the menu has something for everyone including several Mediterranean pasta dishes. The Supper Club's Wine List includes both domestic and imported wines along with several domestic and specialty beers.

Al and Alma's, which was once the Chester Park Grocery Store in 1926, expanded to include a tavern, gas station and eventually a supper club. In 1974, a charter boat service was added and in 1983, purchased by present owners Daryl and Merritt Geyen. The Geyens have added their own unique personal touch to make Al and Alma's Supper Club and Charter Cruises one of the most wonderful attractions on Lake Minnetonka.

RESTAURANT

Sunsets On *Wayzata Bay*	700 E. Lake Street, Wayzata, MN 55391 **Phone: 612-473-5253** Hrs: Mon.-Sat. 6:30 a.m.-1 a.m., Sun.- 9:30 a.m.-1 a.m. Major credit cards accepted.

Residents and visitors alike have gathered at this beautiful spot on Lake Minnetonka for decades. Today, Sunsets on Wayzata Bay is still a popular rendezvous spot for those who desire excellent food combined with a spectacular view. In fact, *Minneapolis/St. Paul* Magazine voted this as one of the top views in the seven-county metro area! Breakfast features Eggs Benedict, Sour Dough French Toast or the Marinaro Special (scrambled eggs with Italian Sausage, peppers and onions). The lunch menu offers a wide selection of appetizers and entrées ranging from Szechuan Spicy Green Beans to Shrimp Linguini, plus an array of delectable chicken and seafood salads. For dinner, guests choose from a variety of steak and seafood dishes or sandwiches.

Whether you come by car, by foot or even by boat, you are sure to experience what the locals have known for years—that Sunsets on Wayzata Bay is the perfect place to enjoy good food, a good view and, of course, good friends.

SPECIALTY SHOP

Blanc de Blanc, *Ltd.*	691 Lake Street, Wayzata, MN 55391 **Phone: 612-473-8275.** Hrs: Mon.-Wed. and Fri. 9 a.m.- 6 p.m., Thurs. 9 a.m.-8 p.m., Sat. 9 a.m.-5:30 p.m. Sunday and Holiday hours vary. Call ahead. Visa, MasterCard, Discover and AmEx accepted.

"Blanc de Blanc" means white to white in French and that's just what this unique shop is all about. It's located on the shores of Lake Minnetonka, west of Minneapolis off I-394, and specializes in white items for very room, for babies or for personal attire.

This gift shop is a treat to see just by itself. It's light and airy to complement the delicate beauty of their merchandise. All items are carefully chosen and exquisitely displayed by a mother/daughter team and their staff. Pride and service are evident throughout. Although the products are top quality, the price range is wide and most visitors can find a special gift or a personal treasure. Many small artists are lucky enough to be accepted here and that creates additional uniqueness in product lines.

So, if you're looking for something white, clean and beautiful, come to Blanc de Blanc, Ltd. They offer bridal, baby or personal gift registries, too.

SPECIALTY SHOPS

Cosecha Designs	746 E. Mill Street, Wayzata, MN 55391 **Phone: 612-475-1945** Hrs: Mon.-Sat. 10 a.m. - 6 p.m. Visa, MasterCard and AmEx accepted.

Exotic. Eclectic. Exquisite. No words better describe Cosecha Designs (pronounced Ko-Say-Cha, Spanish for "harvest"), specializing in beads, jewelry, rare gifts and objects d'art.

They recently completed a facelift by commissioning an exterior mural to reflect the store's ethnic focus. Inside, the atmosphere, too, is exotic, eclectic and exquisite. The handpainted walls, displays and ethnic music set the tone for browsing the folk art, one-of-a-kind masks, sculpture, textiles and ceramics. Owners Gayle and John Liman travel the world in search of rare pieces.

The bead selection is the area's best, including seeds, amber, silver and glass plus a full range of tools, findings and books on beads. They also offer silver, vintage and ethnic jewelry, clothing from Tibet, India, Nepal and Guatemala and folk art and textiles such as hand-carved masks from Zambia and Zaire, carved wooden sculpture, ceramics, handwoven textiles and baskets. Classes in beadwork are available. A second location at 22 S. Fifth Avenue in St. Cloud.

◆ ◆ ◆ ◆ ◆ ◆ ◆

Five Swans	309 East Lake Street, Wayzata, MN 55391 **Phone: 612-473-4685.** Hrs: Mon.-Sat. 9 a.m.- 6 p.m. Extended hours for Christmas shopping. Visa and MasterCard accepted.

Gift shops come and go but few maintain the loyalty of their customers like Five Swans. Housed in an historic food market, Five Swans carries only the finest in home accessories including unique serving pieces, china and crystal, kitchenware, flatware, cookware, table linens, baby items and a myriad of ideas for home and hearth. The bridal registry is a mainstay. At one time, manager Pam convinced the boss to try some colorful inner tubes. The owners agreed reluctantly and sold out on the way back from the gas station where they were inflated! Five Swans still carries them today.

Free gift wrapping, shipping and mailing services are available and they'll special order if they don't have what you're looking for. The longtime staff are creative and caring and they'll try endlessly to honor a request. A Wayzata tradition for gifts and home accessories.

SPECIALTY SHOPS

Crafter's Mall and Long Lake Antiques

2265 W. Wayzata Blvd. (Hwy. 12), Long Lake, MN 55356. **Phone: 612-476-6386.** Hrs: Mon.-Sat. 10 a.m.- 6 p.m., Sun. noon-5 p.m. Seasonally, hours vary. All major credit cards accepted.

The Crafter's Mall and Long Lake Antiques operate in a 7500 square-foot, 2-level building filled with crafts and antiques from over 200 crafters and dealers. There is an enormous selection of hand-crafted items including farm animals, windmills, benches, swings, picnic tables, hand-decorated wearable art, dolls, rugs, jewelry, toys, tools, paintings and a host of other collectibles and folk art to delight the eye and warm the heart.

Their slogan, "Treasures for all," truly describes the nature of this interesting store. There are gifts and decorations for every room and outdoors, too! A Christmas room is open year-round and offers all manner of items for Christmas cheer. A Gourmet Foods Shop is filled with the most unique foods, cook-books and kitchen accessories. The antique shop carries a variety of collectible plates, cups and saucers, crystal, china, glassware, trunks, lamps, toys, linens and much beautiful furniture, as well.

◆ ◆ ◆ ◆ ◆ ◆

Ski Hut

1175 E. Wayzata Blvd., Colonial Square Wayzata, MN 55391 **Phone: 612-473-8843** Hrs.: Mon.-Fri. 9:30 a.m.-8:00 p.m., Sat. 9 a.m.-5 p.m., Sun. noon-5 p.m. All major credit cards accepted.

Ski Hut prides itself on personalized service that can make recreational outfitting choices easier. Owners Jim and Laurie McWethy and their staff offer experience, expertise and a genuine concern for the safety and pleasure of their customers.

At Ski Hut, customers find the equipment and advice they need to enjoy a variety of demanding sports like cross-country and downhill skiing, hockey and figure skating, mountain biking, waterskiing, snowboarding and in-line skating. Always wanted to take up tennis, soccer or softball? Visit Ski Hut for the latest outfits and equipment. And, for those who are between the ages of eight and 18, a winter's worth of fun awaits at the store's Skijammers Ski School. In addition, Ski Hut offers the Ski-A-Way Ladies Program, a series of ski instruction outings for women. The shop offers a variety of special services, too, such as custom-built insoles for boots or skates, custom stone-finished tune-ups for skis, and a balancing service to give the best position and control while skiing.

WYOMING/FOREST LAKE AREA

Forest Lake is a modern, progressive city that's blessed with a beautiful lake and a surrounding area rich in resources for outdoor activities. The land still attracts hundreds of outdoor enthusiasts, who come to the area for fishing, boat races, sailing and water skiing.

Forest Lake takes pride in being the site of one of Minnesota's biggest *Fourth of July* celebrations. The American Legion has sponsored the extravaganza since 1924, and the event usually lasts five days. Main events are a carnival in *Lakeside Park,* a parade 10 a.m. July 4, and a fireworks display at 10 p.m. on the night of the 4th at Lakeside Park. *Masquers Theatre* has provided the Forest Lake area with a summer community theatre using local talent since 1977. The group puts on two shows each summer, with approximately 200 people participating in each production.

For further information, contact:
Forest Lake Area Chamber of Commerce
92 South Lake Street, P.O. Box 474
Forest Lake, MN 55025   Phone: 612-464-3200

BED & BREAKFAST

Greenwood Golf Links/B&B by the Green	4520 E. Viking Blvd., Wyoming, MN 55092 Phone: 612-462-4653 Hrs: 7 a.m.-7 p.m.

Starting their 9th year on the front nine and their 3rd year on the second nine of Greenwood Golf Links is B&B by the Green, an interesting inn with just one three room suite. It's the only B&B located on a golf course in the Twin Cities area!

Naturally, stay and play golf packages are available. After all, golfing is perfect morning activity when you've finished your hearty breakfast. The course has lots of woods and some interesting water hazards, too.

The country setting of the B&B offers guests a natural atmosphere, at once relaxing and quiet. Wildlife abounds in the area. Your three room suite includes a breakfast room, bedroom, parlor and a full private bath. There is a flower-filled deck for morning coffee.

Guests enjoy complimentary beverages, fruit and evening snacks. The inn is air-conditioned and smoke-free for your comfort.

B&B by the Green is located near antique shops and an outlet mall for those who may wish to shop along with golfing.

Prairieland
(& Southern Lakes)

Perhaps the region should lobby for a name change.

The word "prairie," as much importance as it's played on the history of Minnesota and continues to have on its economic life today, doesn't do justice to Minnesota's forgotten corner. Think of Minnesota and you think lakes and rivers and natural beauty.

And that's exactly what you'll find in this vast expanse of Southwestern Minnesota. Despite the name.

From the glorious beauty of the Little Crow Lakes region to the rich, ethnic traditions of New Ulm and New Prague; from the intriguing history of Jesse James and his gang in Northfield and the Dakota Uprising in Jackson and surrounding towns to the modern commerce of Mankato and Owatonna, the Prairieland is an area rich in tradition, culture, landscape and history.

Sounds like the recipe for a good vacation, doesn't it?

Indeed it does!

Although the bison and nomadic bands of Dakota Indians no longer occupy southwestern Minnesota's once ocean-like prairie, it is still a land rich with opportunities for the curious traveller. There are patches of remnant hardwood forest and an occasional lake oasis. But this gently rolling, largely treeless landscape reflects the fact that before the plow, most of the region was covered with a dense carpet of colorful native grasses that grew taller than your head. And it is very fortunate that there are plenty of places you can go to recapture the magnificence of that time.

Virgin prairie. There isn't much left to go around in a modern Minnesota.

What is left you'll find here, at the Blue Mounds State Park near Luverne. The Blue Mounds were formed by a protrusion of quartzite bedrock that burst through the area's fertile soil and was named by settlers travelling west. Approaching families in lumbering wagons could see the bluish hue of the steep escarpment from quite a distance. You can, too.

In the spring, when the wildflowers are in bloom, it is truly spectacular. There's even a resident bison herd to assist you as you conjure up your own images of a time long since past.

And there is so much history to savor.

After all, this was the place where the serenity of the countryside was shattered for six bloody weeks in the late summer and early fall of 1862. It was called the Dakota Conflict and it was one of the most tragic and brutal wars in the history of this country.

It is possible to piece together the many events of those weeks with a trip through the towns and villages of southwestern Minnesota. You can study the many landmarks, explore the historic sites, visit the locations of battles and ambushes and ugly encounters between the Santee Dakota and the soldiers and settlers who fought for what they believed was theirs.

From the Laura Ingalls Wilder Museum at Walnut Grove (depicting life as you knew it in *Little House on the Prairie*) to the End-O-Line Railroad Park at Currie to the many, many wonderful county historical society museums in the region, you can recapture the spirit of the past. Each community has done so much to remember and not just one side of the equation either. At the Pipestone National Monument, you can partake in hallowed Native American cultural traditions which are still alive. And you'll see cryptic evidence of prehistoric life at the Jeffers Petroglyphs.

And then there's the history so many have brought with them to the region. From Czechoslovakia and Germany, from Sweden and Norway, from Scotland and beyond, you'll taste and sample and be part of so much from so far as you make your way through this region.

But do stop along the way, to talk and mingle and be part of this place. Because it is the people of today's Prairieland that make a visit something special.

From the motel owner who scrapes an early frost from your window during a trip to view the fall colors to the smell of homemade pastries and wonderful coffee to the haunting cry of the loon in the shimmering moonlight.

And then there's the sheer beauty of it all. The glorious Minnesota River Valley, from its elbow at Mankato, upstream to Montevideo and all the way along, is a sight to behold. The gentle bluffs of the valley and the floodplain are lush with tall hardwoods.

The gentle river flows provide a break from the vast expanses of agriculture.

At some point, of course, you'll have to leave this land and return from whence you came. But do take with you the memories and the knowledge and the spirit of this place. And do tell someone, somewhere that there's more to the life of any region than just a name.

ALBERT LEA

The city's somewhat incongruous name stems from a U.S. Army cartographer by that name who passed through the unsettled area on an expedition in 1835. Later, Albert Lea grew up to become one of the largest and most prosperous cities in southern Minnesota. This city of 18,000 has attracted companies such as Streater's (a major store fixture manufacturer), Naeve Health Care Association, Mrs. Gerry's Kitchen, and two leading meat processing firms, Seaboard Farms of Minnesota and Hudson's Foods—not surprising since Albert Lea's home county, Freeborn, is in the top three percentile of all agriculture producing counties in the nation.

ATTRACTIONS & EVENTS

The city has maintained scores of historical buildings like the Victorian residences surrounding *Fountain Lake Park.* Four of these, including the *Liquor Rail Depot,* the former *City Hall,* and the *Jones residence,* are listed on the National Register of Historic Places. Two of the most notable sights are the imposing Romanesque grandeur of the *Freeborn County Courthouse* and the unique French classical *Albert Lea Art Center.* The Art Center is an important aspect of Albert Lea's cultural life, presenting monthly art exhibits and regular educational programs. The *Minnesota Festival Theatre,* a widely recognized community theatre, offers a variety of summer performances, from dire drama to fun-filled farce.

In June there is the *Eddie Cochran Weekend & Low Bucks Car Show and Swap Meet,* in memory of Albert Lea's native rock 'n roll legend, Eddie Cochran. Their *Fourth of July Celebration, Rodeo, The Jumpfest, Glider Regatta and Art in the Park* are special events held in July. In February they host the *Black Powder Trade Fair and Gun Show* with fur traders in full costume from throughout the U.S. Other outdoor events are the *Maple Syrup Tapping, White Fox Volksmarch* and cross-country trails at beautiful *Myre Big Island State Park.* The season's most celebrated event, however, is the *Big Island Rendezvous and Festival,* one of the state's largest reenactments of an 1840's fur trader encampment including 200 Indian teepees and lodges, black powder shooting, Native American dances and ethnic foods.

For further information, contact:
Albert Lea CVB
202 North Broadway, P.O. Box 686, Albert Lea, MN 56007
Phone: 507-373-3938 or 1-800-345-8414

ART STUDIO & GALLERY

Adam's Originals Studio and Shop

1322 Fountain Street, Albert Lea, MN 56007
Phone: 507-373-4153. Hours: Mon.-Sat. 9 a.m.-
5 p.m. (Or by appointment)
Visa and MasterCard accepted.

Adam's Originals Studio and Shop provides unique handcrafted merchandise in an affordable price range. A stunning Victorian structure offers the perfect setting in which to display the pottery and paintings of owners Jack and Eloise Adams. The business portion, the attached two-level studio, is fitted with beautiful stained glass decor throughout. Tours of the main house provide an opportunity to view the antiques and artwork that decorate the interior. Demonstrations of how the Adams' craft their art are also included.

Jack and Eloise make items ranging from greeting cards to original paintings and drawings. Eloise also creates beautiful animal sculptures. Custom order work is available on all their wares. A wide selection of stoneware and functional pottery items are also featured in the studio.

BED & BREAKFAST

Fountain View Inn

310 N. Washington Ave., Albert Lea, MN 56007
Phone: 507-377-9425
Hrs: Open year-round
Visa and MasterCard accepted.

The current owners of Fountain View Inn, Dick and Kathy Paul, are happy to share the warmth and charm of this beautiful lakeside refuge. The inn has three guest rooms, all offering a lake view. Each room has a private bath and is air-conditioned. The Jorgenson room contains natural brick walls and a queen-sized bed. The Sullivan room also has a queen-sized bed and a picturesque bay window. The Miskell room is located in a corner of the house providing another angle from which to view the lake and a double sized-bed. The rooms have a charming blend of antiques along with many other cozy creature comforts.

Each morning finds a continental breakfast of fresh seasonal fruit, juice, homemade muffins and breads and coffee or tea, served up hot and tasty on the porch overlooking Fountain Lake.

BED & BREAKFAST

The Victorian Rose Inn	609 W. Fountain Street, Albert Lea, MN 56007 **Phone: 507-373-7602 or 800-252-6558** Hrs: Open year-round Visa and MasterCard accepted.

Built in 1898 in Queen Anne Victorian Style, the Victorian Rose Inn maintains a majestic presence in Albert Lea. The Kensington Suite is reminiscent of the palace of the same name and provides the comfort of a queen-size poster bed, private bath with a shower and sitting room. The Queen Victoria room is decorated in deep, dramatic colors around a marble fireplace and lace canopied queen-size bed. The Windsor room has a flowered canopy over the oak queen-sized bed. The Duchess room contains a double-size antique spoon-carved bed. In the morning a full breakfast is served featuring quiche, fresh baked muffins and breads, pancakes with blueberry sauce, fruit, and coffee.

Darrel and Linda Roemmich have been owners and the innkeepers since it opened in 1990.

BOOKSTORE

The Constant Reader	238 Broadway, Downtown, Albert Lea, MN 56007. **Phone: 507-373-6512.** Hrs.: Mon.-Fri. 9:30 a.m.-6 p.m., Thurs. 9 a.m.-8 p.m., Sat. 9:30 a.m.-4 p.m. Additional evening hours from Thanksgiving to Christmas. Visa and MasterCard accepted.

Step inside the turn-of-the-century building on Albert Lea's main street to find a one-of-a-kind bookstore. New and used books, books on tape, bookmarks, and bookplates make this a reader's delight. The front of the store features new books with strong sections of regional books and nature guides. Children's books, bestsellers, and books on tape are also available.

The back half of the store is a wonderful mixture of used books, slightly hurt books and other book bargains. The atmosphere is informal, with customers sitting on the floor while they look through baskets of craft patterns, sheet music, or school materials. Tall shelves contain half-price paperbacks arranged by genre and author. A children's nook lets children sit and read while parents browse. The values are excellent.

The Constant Reader is a delightful bookstore, one able to satisfy any taste and it provides a great opportunity for readers to browse and find unexpected treasures that stimulate old and new interests.

LODGING

Days Inn	2306 E. Main Street Albert Lea, MN 56007 **Phone: 507-373-6471** Major credit cards accepted.

Conveniently located close to the intersection of Interstates 35 and 90, the Days Inn of Albert Lea provides 129 tastefully decorated rooms, each of which is spacious, clean and comfortable. The motel also features fine family dining in the Courtyard Restaurant with daily specials, a children's menu and a Sunday breakfast buffet. The popular Nite Out Lounge has live entertainment on weekends, dancing and offers a tempting variety of wine, beer and mixed drinks to suit every taste. A relaxing swim in the large, indoor heated swimming pool is a perfect way to end a day on the road.

Albert Lea boasts one million square feet of retail space and hosts many annual events such as Stories from the Heartland and Big Island Rendezvous. The hundreds of miles of groomed snowmobile trails start at the Days Inn doorstep. A favorite outdoor activity is cross-country skiing or nature hiking at beautiful Myre Big Island State Park. Visitors come for many reasons and Days Inn offers them reasonably priced, comfortable accommodations.

RESTAURANT

Main Street Bar & Grill	208 Main Street, Manchester, MN 56064 **Phone: 507-826-3424** Hrs: Tues.-Sat. 10 a.m.-10 p.m. Visa and MasterCard accepted.

You don't have to be big to be among the best. They've proved it in Manchester (population 69) where the award-winning Main Street Bar & Grill serves the finest food and beverages in the area. Located on one of the best snowmobile trail systems in Minnesota, you'll find it just six miles west of I-35 and three miles north of I-90 on Highway 13, near Albert Lea.

Owners and operators Colin and Sue Minehart and Colin's mother, Beverly Blakeslee, started the business by completely remodeling an historic bank building into the best little restaurant around. It has earned a solid reputation and loyal customers by using only the best products available. They purchase fresh-cut steaks daily from nearby Jordahl Meats, another local award-winning business.

Colin is the chef and he's known for preparing your steak just the way you like it. His secret? Great food in a clean friendly atmosphere where bigger isn't necessarily better.

MUSEUM & HISTORICAL VILLAGE

Freeborn County *Historical Museum* *and Pioneer Village*	1031 Bridge Avenue, P.O. Box 105, Albert Lea, MN 56007. **Phone: 507-373-8003** Hrs: Tues.-Fri. 10 a.m.-5 p.m., Weekends 1 p.m.-5 p.m., Closed Mondays

The Freeborn County Historical Museum and Pioneer Village is one of the finest county history complexes in Minnesota. Located two miles south of the intersection of I-90 and I-35, it contains a 13,000 square foot museum and library facility, a pioneer village consisting of the Big Oak country school, 1853 Livdalen log cabin, general store, telephone office, blacksmith shop, woodworking shop, post office, Norwegian Lutheran Church, parsonage, hardware store, shoe repair shop, mill house, and a rural artifact exhibit hall with photo studio, barber shop, city bank, county jail and train depot.

The museum complex interprets the history of southern Minnesota and northern Iowa from more than 12,000 years ago up to the World War II era. Exhibits include such unusual items as a square grand piano manufactured by Georgia and Brown, a 1909 edition of Sports Afield, a mastodon tooth, a salesman's sample of the Kiel Oscillator Washer manufactured in Albert Lea circa 1910, a jicara circa 1890, a sock knitting machine, a wooden clarinet, crazy quilts, a 1936 Buick, potsherds and a log scriber.

The village buildings speak of a time when eight grades were educated in one room, when the general store provided for all of the family's needs not covered by the vegetable garden and farm animals, when emergency needs were met at the blacksmith shop, and when *one* horse power was a luxury.

The library contains a wealth of information—both genealogical and historical—on the people, schools, churches, businesses, entertainment and geography of the area. It's an excellent resource for the researcher, whether amateur or professional.

Highlights of the museum throughout the year include special temporary exhibits, the Living History Day Camp, demonstration days, and guided museum and village tours by appointment. A small admission charge is required to help cover the costs of this unique pioneer experience.

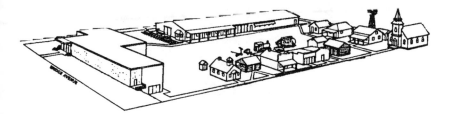

SPECIALTY SHOP

The Heart of the Artichoke	222 East Clark Street Albert Lea, MN 56007 **Phone: 507-373-4258** Hours: Mon.-Sat. 10:00 a.m.-4:30 p.m.

The main attraction on the historical tour of Albert Lea is The Heart of the Artichoke. It has become a favorite tourist spot for bus tours and vacationers over the past 25 years. Stop, visit and sample cappuccino, listen to soft strains of music from the tapes and CD's and browse this beautifully decorated shop with an inviting blend of fine gifts, home accessories, antiques and collectibles.

In this unique store, there are seven rooms chock full of merchandise that is all creatively displayed. The Blackberry Patch is a kitchen area that displays bunnies and bears, pottery, baskets, books and teapots, photo frames, lotions, potpourris, sprays, cards and much more.

The Enchanted Cottage room is home to dolls of every description and price—from porcelain to vinyl and cloth—doll houses and miniature furniture and accessories, reproduction buggies, Dept 56 villages and accessories and snowbabies.

Love Everlasting room has freeze-dried floral wreaths and sprays, baskets and trees, bridal bouquets—every floral item needed for a perfect wedding. Also, many gifts are offered, from garters to guest books, linen and lace.

Antiques and collectibles, glassware, dishes and furniture may be found in the back room, as well as in various niches and corners throughout the store.

Plan to visit the birthday party, their annual event the second week in November for Christmas ideas in decorating. There are trees in every room, from the traditional to the whimsical! Door prizes are given out and the grand prize is a fully decorated Christmas Tree.

Travellers, don't miss the pleasure of shopping and browsing at The Heart of the Artichoke.

BELLE PLAINE

Located midway between Mankato and the Twin Cities on U.S. Highway 169, Belle Plaine, with its wide, tree-lined streets and abundant, inviting parklands, was founded by Minnesota territorial judge Andrew Chatfield. He selected the townsite in 1853 while travelling on horseback from Mendota to Traverse des Sioux to hold court. He selected the name Belle Plaine which, in French, means "beautiful prairie."

How right he was. It remains a beautiful setting, nestled near the woods of the Minnesota River and changed little since it captured the heart of the itinerant judge.

ATTRACTIONS & EVENTS

The *Minnesota River* today provides outstanding recreational opportunities, most notably within the confines of the *Minnesota Valley Trail State Park,* a 21-acre area where people camp, fish, picnic and participate in birdwatching. There are 72 miles of groomed trails in the park for hiking, skiing, horseback riding and mountain biking. In Belle Plaine itself, there are more than four blocks of city parks with playgrounds, shelters, even kitchen facilities.

Although some are loathe to admit it, perhaps the city's most notable sight is an outhouse. That's right. Attached to the *Hooper-Bowler-Hillstrom House,* this two-story landmark may be one-of-a-kind. Also on the grounds of the 1870s Hooper House, with its period furnishings, is a carriage house that has been transformed into the *Carriage House Museum,* with mementoes of Belle Plaine's past.

An *Old-Fashioned Christmas Party* is one of the city's main annual events; it, too, being held at the Hooper House, and featuring sleigh rides through snow-covered streets. *Bar-B-Q Days,* with its parades and entertainment, is a three-day summer festival. The *Downtown Cookout* is held in June, when Belle Plaine merchants set up grills on the sidewalks of the city and serve free food. Showcase features products and displays from local businesses. And in October, the *Scarecrow Festival* is another big event, featuring scarecrows designed by local residents. Or experience the autumn harvest at its finest by visiting *Emma Krumbee's Apple Market* and the many surrounding orchards.

For further information, please contact:

City of Belle Plaine
P.O. Box 6
Belle Plaine, MN 56011   Phone: 612-873-2000

RESTAURANT

Emma Krumbee's Restaurant, Bakery and Apple Orchard	Highway 169 S. Belle Plaine, MN 56011 **Phone: 612-873-4334**

Emma Krumbee's is located just south of Shakopee and is well worth the drive. This restaurant/apple orchard/bakery/deli/country store is truly a "one stop" shop. Started in 1979, this establishment has become a real favorite in the area and has drawn visitors from all over to enjoy the excellent food and friendly atmosphere.

The food and all the bakery items are made from scratch. The restaurant is famous for its baked chicken dinner and BBQ ribs in addition to local favorites like chicken dumpling and wild rice soups. Prime rib is the specialty on Fridays, Saturdays and Sundays. Breakfast is served all day long with a great cup of coffee and conversation.

The new Country Store is located next to the restaurant. Inside you will find apples galore along with Emma's bakery and deli. You can enjoy a view of the apple orchard from the outside deck seating.

Emma Krumbee's Apple Orchard offers U-Pick apples beginning in late August through mid-October. Ride the red wagon through the orchard and select one of 20 varieties of apples among 7,500 apple trees. All ages will have fun feeding the farm animals at the petting zoo.

The Great Annual Scarecrow Festival takes place each fall. Uniquely designed entries provide a charming way to enter autumn and witness the talent of the many contestants. Festival games, pumpkin picking in the Great Pumpkin Patch, and the hay pile jump provide entertainment for the whole family.

BLUE EARTH

Blue Earth is located in the center of southern Minnesota on the crossroads of I-90 and Hwy. 169. A golden portion of concrete can be seen near the I-90 Rest Stops. This is the gold link, the final connecting place where the east and west coast connect I-90. Blue Earth is the birthplace of the ice cream bar and home to the world's largest statue of the *Jolly Green Giant,* overlooking some of the richest farmland in America. *Etta C. Ross Museum,* the historic home of *James B. Wakefield,* and the *Faribault County Courthouse* are just a few of the highlights on a "walking tour" available from the Chamber of Commerce.

Blue Earth hosts the *Minnesota State High School Rodeo, Car Show* and huge *Craft Festival* in June. July brings the old-fashioned *County Fair* and the last weekend in August tourists flock to Blue Earth to observe the *Upper Midwest Woodcarvers, Quilt & Doll Show.* Agriculture tours and other information are available by contacting the *Blue Earth Area Chamber of Commerce,* 111 North Main Street, Blue Earth, MN 56013 or phone 507-526-2916.

BED & BREAKFAST

Fering's Guest House	708 N. Main Street Blue Earth, MN 56013 **Phone: 507-526-5054**

A charming, turn-of-the-century home, Fering's Guest House offers a pleasant and peaceful retreat. There are three guest rooms—the Arizona, the Rainbow and the Minnesota. They are decorated in a contemporary style, with air conditioning, cable TV and private baths. It's an exceptional inn that's reasonably priced.

A homemade continental breakfast is served either in the formal dining room or on the porch. The breakfast consists of fresh fruit, muffins, juice and coffee.

Your hosts are Charlie and Phyl Fering who are anxious to make your stay wonderfully relaxing. Charlie is a retired teacher and Phyl is the mother of their five adult children. The B&B is now a very large "empty nest" to which guests are eagerly welcomed.

Charlie will carry in your luggage, serve you complimentary beverages and top off your evening with an ice cream sundae before bedtime!

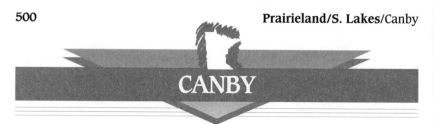

CANBY

Flat as the prairie itself, Canby, "Gateway to the Prairie," is the westernmost city in Yellow Medicine County. It began as a one-person town named after Civil War General E.R.S. Canby. At present, the population is 1826.

The downtown district was rebuilt after a devastating fire in 1893 and is now listed on the National Register of Historic Places. Four city parks provide residents and visitors ample space for camping and other outdoor activities.

A growing hospital, school and vocational college, along with clean air and a low crime rate make Canby an excellent place to raise a family or to retire.

ATTRACTIONS & EVENTS

The historic *Lund-Hoel House* was built in 1891 by John G. Lund, a self-made millionaire land broker. The house now stands like a regal Victorian lady refurbished in all her original finery to invite guests to her door. Tours are conducted upon request.

Two miles from Canby is *Del Clark Lake,* formed by the construction of the state's largest earthen dam. Rainbow trout, walleye, bass and panfish, along with an excellent swimming beach can be found there. Surrounding the lake is *StoneHill Regional Park,* 700 acres of rolling prairie with 36 campsites, modern restroom and shower facilities, picnic shelters, two boat launches and mowed paths for hiking.

"PrairieFest, The Gateway to Music and Arts" is a yearly music and arts festival held the first weekend in July. It attracts visitors from miles around who enjoy a variety of music, art displays and fireworks.

Canby is also host to the *Yellow Medicine County Fair* and its own special summer event, *Celebrate Canby.*

For further information, contact:
The City of Canby
110 Oscar Ave. N.
Canby, MN 56220
Phone: 507-223-7295

ANTIQUES

The I Want Shoppe Antiques

139 St. Olaf Ave. N.(Main St./ Hwy.75 N.)
Canby, MN 56220
Phone: 507-223-7546
Hrs: Mon.-Sat. 10 a.m.-4 p.m.

The I Want Shoppe Antiques is located in one of the few original downtown buildings to survive Canby's Great Fire of 1893. The bank building was built in 1892 and now houses The Shoppe with two floors of wonderful antiques and collectibles. Owner Jackie Nemitz has collected, bought, sold and appraised antiques since 1983. The Shoppe will also take fine antiques on consignment.

You'll find many rooms to stroll and browse through. They're filled with such items as: art, pottery, Watt, cut glass, depression glass, Fostoria, Cambridge, crystal, crockery, linens, frames, prints, postcards, rugs, cast iron, furniture, stained glass windows, toys and wonderful pieces of gold and sterling jewelry, along with costume jewelry. It's a feast for any collector, but don't wait long, the Shoppe has a tremendous turnover!

Jackie is happy to answer any questions or help locate the items you're looking for, so take time out to enjoy a small town. It's where you can bring back memories and make some new ones, too.

◆ ◆ ◆ ◆ ◆ ◆ ◆

CURRIE

Neil and Archibald Currie walked across the prairie in 1872 looking for a site on which to build a grist mill. They found a good location on the Des Moines River near Lake Shetek in southwestern Minnesota and so began the city of Currie.

Fishing at the *Currie Dam* and at *Lake Shetek* attracts visitors all summer while many miles of snowmobile trails add winter fun. Soon, a bike trail will be completed that will run from Lake Shetek into *End-O-Line Railroad Park* in Currie. End-O-Line offers an educational and entertaining tour. In fact, it's growing and gaining national attention for its manually operated turntable, depot, engine-house, section foreman's home, caboose, steam-engine, coal tender, schoolhouse and little general store built by the Currie family in 1872. Currie is also the home of the *Little Red House* antiques.

Currie plays host to an annual *July Celebration* with a picnic, dance, softball and beautiful fireworks to round out the festivities. The Currie area offers visitors a variety of dining alternatives and 4,000 acres of year-round recreation in southwestern Minnesota.

ANTIQUES

Little Red House	R.R. 1, Box 167, Currie, MN 56123 **Phone: 507-763-3504** Hrs: 8 a.m-3 p.m.

The Little Red House in Currie is an antique store that carries all general type antiques, from primitive tools, antique lamps and dolls to whole estates. They sell a bit of everything at this red painted house.

It's located just 2 blocks from Lake Shetek which offers camping, biking, fishing and boating, so you can enjoy your favorite sport right after you go antiquing!

Remember, Currie is home to End-O-Line Railroad Park and Museum. This is where you can still see a manually operated turntable, the device used to turn train engines around in the opposite direction. In fact, the area is filled with historical monuments and information about them.

Antique shopping at the Little Red House is a perfect way to begin any historical trek, but it's not just for the history buff! Many items can be found to add a special touch to your own decor. And items can be bought, sold or traded here.

PARK & MUSEUM

End-O-Line *Railroad Park* *and Museum*	RR1, Box 42, Currie, MN 56123 **Phone: 507-763-3708** Hrs: Seasonally, Mon.-Fri. 10-12 & 1-5, Sat.-Sun. 1-5.

Located on Highway 38 in Currie, MN, End-O-Line Railroad Park offers visitors a chance to experience a working railroad yard as would be found in an early 1900 prairie town. The park and museum started as a 4-H project in community pride and is now a site listed on the National Register of Historic Places.

Its humble beginnings led to the purchases of the depot and the only operable manually powered turntable in the midwest. An engine-house full of railroad exhibits such as a pre-1900 velocipede, a work pit, tools, lanterns, motor cars, baggage carts, and more, provide a hands-on experience on a guided tour of the park. A large variety of other interesting articles from the railroads have been put into the many display cases found throughout the museum.

A model railroad display in HO scale is one of the highlights of the museum. This display is an authentic reproduction of the Currie railroad yards as they were about 50 years ago. The layout features built-from-scratch locomotives and structures, complete landscaping, a full wrap-around mural, complete with sound effects and more.

Hear the old steam locomotive puff and chug throughout the countryside. Hear the puffing and chugging accented by the steam whistle, bell and hiss of steam. You will think that time has been turned back to an age when the great steam engines plied the iron highways throughout this land. The romance and charm are unmistakable!

Walk through the furnished four-room depot, the section foreman's home, the caboose. Be sure to see the newly acquired Georgia Northern #102 engine and coaltender now being restored to their former glory.

Also visit the miniature depot, coal-bunker and tool shed. Wind up your tour with a sample school day in the first country school in Murray county, then reminisce a bit in the Currie Store, the first general store in the area. Projects on the drawing board include reconstruction of the original coal-bunker to be used as a picnic shelter and gift house, plus an addition to the engine-house and restrooms.

End-O-Line Railroad Park and Museum is open from Memorial Day to Labor Day and by appointment. Call for more information.

FARIBAULT

Built at the confluence of the Straight and Cannon Rivers, two tributaries that played an important role in the city's early days, Faribault is rich in history and commerce.

It was the opportunity to trade with the Dakota Sioux that brought Alexander Faribault to the region in 1826. By 1853, the settlement had begun to prosper and the remnants of that prosperity as well as Alexander Faribault's legacy continue to thrive today. The city is home to a vast array of historic buildings and a variety of styles of architecture not to mention institutions that bear Alexander Faribault's mark.

ATTRACTIONS & EVENTS

While each Minnesota city has its own list of historic attractions, Faribault arguably has the state's finest collection. On top of the list remains the *Alexander Faribault House,* a poignant memory of the generous patriarch. The gothic *Shattuck-St. Mary's School,* one of the nation's finest private educational institutions, is another excellent example as is *Tate Hall* on the 1864 campus of the *State Academy of the Deaf.*

Downtown, you'll find a beautifully restored late-18th century heritage preservation commercial district. History buffs will want to explore the *Rice County Museum of History,* which covers both the pioneer and native perspectives. The unique state hospital *Dr. Engberg Museum* is fascinating as is the *Faribault Woolen Mills,* one of the few remaining active woolen mills in the country. The outlet store alone is worth the trip.

You may also be interested in the *Ivan Whillock Studio* with its wood carvings and *Uhlir's Apple Orchards* for some of nature's finest. If the outdoors is in your plans, be sure and visit *Nerstrand Woods State Park,* a rare remnant of the native hardwood forest that once covered this area, the *Sakatah Lake State Park* with campsites and trails and the *River Bend Nature Center* where naturalists are available for guided tours of the 600-acre, carefully protected river habitat.

Heritage Days is the highlight in June when artists, craftspeople and musicians from the area gather. In September, the *Fall Festival* with its hot air balloon rally is another noteworthy event.

For further information, contact:

Faribault Chamber of Commerce
P.O. Box 434
Faribault, MN 55021   Phone: 507-334-4381 or 800-658-2354

BED & BREAKFAST

Cherub Hill	105 N.W. First Ave., Faribault, MN 55021 **Phone: 507-332-2024** Hrs: Open year-round Visa and MasterCard accepted.

Cherub Hill was designed in 1896 by Olaf Hanson, the first deaf architect in America, for Dr. Jonathan Noyes and his wife Elizabeth. Dr. Noyes helped to found the Minnesota Academy for the Deaf in Faribault.

The house, a late Victorian design and on the National Register of Historic Places, reveals Dr. Noyes' affection for children by the cherub accents found throughout. The house was restored as a B&B in 1992.

Guests can choose from one of three charming rooms, each furnished with lovely period pieces and accents. Although rich in antiques, no modern comfort has been sacrificed. One room even features a private bath and a double whirlpool tub.

Weekday continental breakfasts include yogurt, pastries, fruit, juice and gourmet coffee. Weekend guests are treated to a full breakfast which may include waffles, fruit tarts, crepes, egg dishes, juice and delicious coffees and teas. Cherub Hill is also available for special occasions such as weddings or teas.

SPECIALTY SHOP

The Chocolate Drop	228 Central Avenue Faribault, MN 55021 **Phone/FAX: 507-334-3906**

Remember the aroma of mom's homemade candy? That's just one of the many treats awaiting you at the Chocolate Drop, an old-fashioned candy shop in Faribault. Started in 1928, it's a third generation business now and features candy of all sorts made fresh daily by hand.

Taste recipes handed down from generation to generation for Truffles, Cremes, Caramels, Snappers, Fudge, Old-Fashioned Sponge, Heavenly Hash, all Nut Clusters and a large assortment of other candy. They even have sugar-free candy! Their candy is all hand dipped, the way fine chocolate *should* be handled

Want a gift for a friend or a business associate? Mail orders, special packaging and custom gift baskets are easily handled at The Chocolate Drop, with the finest quality chocolate candies to be found anywhere.

GARDEN CENTER

Donahue's
Greenhouse

420 Tenth Street S.W., Faribault, MN 55021
Phone: 507-334-8404. Hrs.: Mon-Sat. 8:30-
5 p.m., (Apr., May, Nov., and Dec.) Sun. noon-
5 p.m. Visa, MasterCard and Discover accepted.

What started as a perennial nursery in 1932 grew in the 1940's, with the introduction of garden mums, and in the 1950's and 1960's with spring bedding plants and the garden center business.

In 1972, Dick and Lois Donahue, along with their family, took over and substantially increased the wholesale and retail businesses. Donahue's Greenhouse is now a seven acre plus greenhouse and grows over 12,000 spring and summer hanging baskets.

The greenhouse has one of the largest displays of spring plants and poinsettias under one roof in the midwest. There are over 100 varieties of clematis, a Minnesota hardy vine, and over 100 varieties of garden chrysanthemums. There is a wide variety of colorful greenery and multi-colored geraniums, petunias, marigolds, fuchsias, hibiscus and bougainvillaea, among many others. Christmas time brings a "sea of red," with over two football fields of poinsettias on display!

Donahue's Greenhouse is a complete garden center offering beautiful flowering and foliage plants, along with a friendly, knowledgeable staff. It is truly a unique and enjoyable experience, one in which visitors can take a little bit of the atmosphere home with them. Donahue's is an international clematis specialist.

RESTAURANT

Lavender Inn

2424 Lyndale Ave., Faribault, MN 55021
Phone: 507-334-3500
Hrs: (Rose Room and Gold Room) Daily 11 a.m.-
10 p.m. Major credit cards accepted.

The Lavender Inn is a famous "little oasis" 50 miles south of the Twin Cities, just off I-35 at Exit 59 and 50 miles north of the Iowa border. It became famous during the 1960's as a drive-in where you could get one-dollar broasted chicken and 25¢ hamburgers. Now, it's a perfect place to stop as you travel in the area.

The Lavender Inn has three different dining rooms, each with its own personality, distinctive decor and elegant furnishings. The classic interior, the aroma of gourmet feasts and the warmth of a family-owned business greet visitors as they enter. Careful selection and preparation of choice meats and seafoods are enhanced by fresh vegetables and fruits.

The menu features favorites like broasted chicken, walleye pike, shrimp, scallops, prime rib and choice steaks. Dinner is complemented by fresh bread and strawberry jam.

Aside from the dining rooms, the Lavender Inn has a beautiful art gallery and gift shop to tempt the discerning shopper. There are gift displays of fine porcelains by LLadro, Hummel, Kaiser, Armani and Royal Copenhagen, plus crystal by Swarovski. Oriental carvings, jewelry, Victorian furniture by Kimbal combine with prints by famous Minnesota wildlife artists and original oil paintings to please the eye and warm the heart.

When you wish to celebrate a special event—birthday, anniversary, graduation—or have a business meeting, or are just traveling through, think of the Lavender Inn as a welcome friend.

SPECIALTY SHOP

Faribault Woolen Mill Store	1819 N.W. Second Ave., Faribault, MN 55021 **Phone: 507-334-1644 or 800-448-WOOL** Hrs.: Mon-Sat. 9 a.m.-5:30 p.m., Sun. noon- 4 p.m. Major credit cards accepted.

Beginning in 1865 with a one-horse treadmill, five generations of skilled craftsmen have developed this family-owned company into a thriving business through pride and motivation. Faribault Woolen Mill Company survived three fires from 1888 to 1892, rebuilding and expanding from selling yarn to producing fine woven cloth.

In an historic brick mill on the banks of the Cannon River, Faribault Woolen Mill Company employees use high-tech equipment to practice an ancient manufacturing process.

In the 125 years that Faribault has been in business, blanket making has gone from hand operation to micro-chip control. One of only a few "fully vertical" woolen mills existing in the U.S., the mill is capable of changing raw wool into woven blankets.

Scouring and blending, dyeing, carding, spinning, weaving and burling all occur under one roof. In fact, the Faribault Woolen Mill manufactures throws and blankets exclusively. These include fine wools, wool blends, cotton and acrylic, designed and woven by its 175 workers.

The Faribault Woolen Mill Store offers these in current first-quality colors, as well as slightly irregular items and discontinued colors. Other items include men's, women's, and children's clothing, toys made from blanket patterns, and hand woven throws and blankets produced by its mill in Houston.

Monogramming and shipping are available. Faribault Woolen Mill invites visitors to their store where warmth, integrity and excellence can be found in every product.

Bus tours are welcome. Mill tours are 10 a.m. to 2 p.m. Monday through Friday. Also, there is a store in Red Wing, located in the Pottery Place.

CORPORATE PROFILE

**Faribault
Woolen Mill
Company**

When the Faribault Woolen Mill Company cele-brated 125 years of continuous family-owned oper-ation in 1990, the mill crew did what it's always done: it went right back to work.

The Faribo team is a dedicated, motivated and highly skilled group of craftsmen. They work in a picturesque brick mill on the banks of the Cannon River. The mill's 175 employees design, weave, and sell more pure wool blankets every year than any other American mill.

But Faribo is more than woven products

It is a living, thriving example of what incentives and motivation are all about. The mill and its workers are a testimony to what hap-pens when an entire company shares a dream and has the motivation to get its job done well. Like millions of American success stories, this one starts with an emigrant in search of the American dream. Carl Klemer, as a 24-year-old German cabinet maker, opened a wood-working shop in Wisconsin. He married, fathered two sons, then packed his family into an ox-drawn cart and headed west nearly 300 miles looking for new opportunities.

He tried farming but didn't like it. He sold the farm, telling a friend he wanted new challenges. He was urged to open a wool-card-ing mill in the frontier town of Faribault, Minnesota. There are plenty of sheep, he was told, but there's no market for the wool. It was 1865 and the Civil War was ending. The upper midwest had 800 woolen mills, but Faribault didn't have one, so Carl decided to fill the need.

He bought a used wool-carding machine and built a one-horse treadmill to supply power. An ad offered local producers a custom wool-carding service. In two years the horse was replaced with a five horsepower steam engine and Carl hired two extra workers. His small mill was carding 12,000 pounds of wool annually and his payroll was $100 a month.

By 1877, Carl had purchased spinning jennies and four looms to weave cloth, flannel and wool blankets. He ran an ad using the name Faribault Woolen Factory and offered his quality wool sheeting and yarns to local families.

In 1883, Carl and his small crew built a new 44'x100' mill along the Straight River and the work force tripled to six. Because the build-ing was unheated, the mill only operated from early May to the end of October. Carl discovered that generating employee loyalty took more than paying 12 cents an hour. Without worker pride, purpose and praise, he couldn't get the quality and productivity he needed. Taking note of this, the weekly *Faribault Republican* said, "the new mill illustrates the virtue of perseverance in the face of obstacles," and pointed out the "good results that flow from enterprise backed by industry and integrity."

A test by fire

The mill grew because Carl Klemer and his small band of workers were weaving an honest, quality product and were overcoming the many obstacles of frontier manufacturing.

But in August of 1888 a fire nearly put an end to the business. Starting in the mill basement, the fire caused $7,000 in damage and shut down production for the rest of the season.

With stoic determination, Carl and his crew replaced machines and raw materials and cleaned up the damage.

The mill reopened the next spring. Then, in 1890, fire struck again. Limited to the boiler room, equipment loss was minimal but smoke damage and cleanup costs cut the short manufacturing season even shorter.

Again the German persistence of Carl Klemer and his team of dedicated employees was tested as the mill was finally put back on line.

By 1892, orders for the quality Faribault products were coming so fast that Carl switched from the traditional 60-hour work week to the demanding pace of 12-hour days, six days a week all summer long. Thirty employees worked the two-set mill in an effort to keep up with the orders and increasing popularity of Faribo products.

Then, in September, disaster struck again

A midnight fire spread quickly through the 10-year-old mill, destroying the building and its machinery. By morning, all that remained were twisted iron frames in a tangled mass of scrap iron lodged in the collapsed basement. Insurance covered only half of the $24,000 in damage.

Faced with a total loss and the beginning of another tough Minnesota winter, it would've been easy for the Klemer family to give up.

But with the help of sons Henry and Ferdinand and the commitment of his family of workers, 68-year-old Carl Klemer straightened his shoulders, stood a little taller and decided to start his mill again.

Up from the ashes

The work began within a few days of the fire. Carl purchased an old water-powered flour mill on the banks of the Cannon River and his crew tore down the old wooden buildings.

By October 26, six weeks after the fire, workers began laying brick. The new mill was to be two stories high. A fireproof iron clad wool warehouse was built next door and several small buildings for storage and waste were added. The same site is still being used today.

Construction continued at a rapid pace through the tough winter.

Equipment was found and more wool purchased. In less than five months the new mill began producing yarn and wool batting. The weaving began in August. Word spread quickly and enough orders came in for the 30-person mill crew to go immediately to a 72-hour work week.

The next generations

A few months before the big fire, Carl gave his sons Henry and Ferdinand each a one-third interest in the mill. With the second generation of Klemers installed, Carl and his wife finally took a vacation, leaving for Germany to revisit memories from their childhood.

For the next 12 years until his death in 1904, Carl Klemer and his sons continued to expand the business. Annual production of Faribo woven cloth grew from 16,000 yards in 1886 to 117,000 yards.

During the pioneering years, other woolen mills faltered and failed. From approximately 800 midwest mills when Carl began, the number had shrunk to only 183 in 1900.

Twenty years later, only 80 remained. Today, just two continue the weaving tradition. Carl Klemer's vision and motivation made the difference.

In 1905, Frank Klemer, son of Henry, joined the company and became the third generation family member to work in the mill. Walter Klemer, son of Ferdinand, was welcomed in 1912 and brought Ed Johnson with him.

Both joined the board of directors and, like the Klemers, there has been a Johnson in a leadership position ever since. The fourth generation of Klemers began with Frank's son Robert in 1932 and brother Richard, who joined the company in 1950. Richard's son, Tom Klemer, represents the fifth generation.

A nice place to work

Faribault Woolen Mill Company always has been a special place for employees. And whatever the magic is, it seems to work.

Original mill workers stayed with Carl through good times and bad, and that tradition remains.

The woolen mill was an early pioneer in employee benefits. A life insurance program for all workers started in 1919. Workers were encouraged to form an independent labor group in 1937. There have been no serious labor problems or strikes.

In 1961, the board funded the purchase of a lakeshore lodge in northern Minnesota as a recreation getaway for employees and customers. The company has a retirement program for all employees.

When workers are motivated and well-trained, the reward is longevity.

In 1960, approximately half the employees had been with the company more than 10 years, and more than half of those had been on the job for 20 years or more.

In the past 30 years, those figures haven't changed much, in spite of America's restlessness. Of the 175 employees today, 78 have been at the mill for 10 years or more. And many of the positions are filled with second- and third-generation workers.

A heritage of excellence

From the end of the Civil War through the development of electric power, central heating, two world wars, a depression, man-made fibers and space technology, Faribault Woolen Mill Company has grown and thrived. For 125 years, quality, innovation and pride are the hallmarks of this quiet Minnesota company.

From the beginning, nearly all mill expansion has been funded internally.

For five generations the Klemer family has lived frugally with a philosophy of stewardship. That means profits are reinvested in the plant and its people and that a company should buy what it can afford and save for the rest.

In an age of leveraged buyouts and junk-bond financing, this strategy of innocence seems old-fashioned and out of place. Yet with virtually no interruption it is at the core of the company's continued success through 125 years.

A company's product is often a mirror of itself. For Faribault Woolen Mill, warmth, quality, integrity and honesty can describe both the company and the products it makes.

For proof, consider that quality control is a part of each employee's job.

All 175 workers make sure what they do is right the first time. Motivated and hard-working, the craftsmen of Faribault Woolen Mill Company get the job done. After all, they've been doing it for 125 years.

FROST

Small towns are a lot like books. You can't tell much about them unless you get into them.

Frost is like that. Passing motorists on Interstate 90 might be lulled into thinking Frost is just another faceless blip on the map. They might be surprised to find the variety of cottage industries located in and around the city of less than 250 people. In fact, visitors from more than 30 states annually visit *Nordic World,* the area's largest Scandinavian gift shop and a country/craft shop.

Main Street Coffee Shop is about as middle America as it gets, the kind of place where area farmers, townspeople and visitors mingle and enjoy the home cooking. A fine restaurant and lounge attracts evening diners from the surrounding area and *The Viking Community Center* provides a place for recreation and gatherings, large and small.

For further information, contact:
Frost Economic Development Authority
P.O. Box 548, Frost, MN 56033   Phone: 507-878-3106

SPECIALTY SHOP

Nordic World	100 Pioneer Trail, Frost, MN 56033 **Phone: 507-878-3110**. Hrs: (May-Christmas) Tues.-Sat. 10 a.m.-5 p.m., (Winter) Tues.-Fri. 1 p.m.-5 p.m. Visa and MasterCard accepted.

Just five minutes south of I-90 on Highway 254 near the edge of Frost sits Nordic World. Sonja Anderson is the owner and she spends her time filling the shop with treasures she has made herself or imported from Scandinavian countries. Nordic World boasts the largest collection of Scandinavian imports and Minnesota gifts in the area. Since 1982 Nordic World has attracted shoppers from all of the states as well as countries outside the U.S. Wooden items rosemaled by Anderson include breadboards, Christmas ornaments, trunks, bowls and plates. Import items include Norwegian sweaters; jewelry from Norway, Sweden, and Finland; a large variety of candleholders, candles, tablerunners; T-shirts and sweatshirts; and Scandinavian records and tapes. Cookbooks and bakeware invite customers to try new and different recipes when setting the table with pewter and crystal atop an imported tablecloth. This intimate and comfortable setting entices customers to browse and thoroughly enjoy the selection and quality provided by Nordic World.

GOOD THUNDER

It's hard to miss the giant mural painted on a scale befitting the prairie landscape of Good Thunder. With Chief Good Thunder as its focal point, it covers the faces of the local grain elevator and adjacent bins and was painted by artist Ta-coumba Aiken of St. Paul. It is but one of many enticing aspects in this Blue Earth County community.

From the charm and friendliness of its midwestern farm village traditions to the fascinating origins of the community, Good Thunder is one of those special places worth searching for.

Bus tours can be accommodated at the *Main Street Cafe* with advance reservations or picnic in the local parks where you'll find playgrounds, tennis courts and barbecue grills. The architectural variety is fascinating, from Queen Anne Victorian to Prairie Plain, Settler's Storefront, and Cape Cod Cottage, making for a great walking tour. Or celebrate with the locals at *Good Thunder Pioneer-Indian Day,* an annual celebration.

For further information, contact: *City of Good Thunder,* County Road 10 & Hwy 66, Good Thunder, MN 56037. Phone 507-278-3730.

BED & BREAKFAST

Cedar Knoll Farm	Route 3, Box 147, 4.1 miles east of Good Thunder off Cty Rd 10, Good Thunder, MN 56037 **Phone: 507-524-3813.** Hrs: Open anytime. No credit cards accepted.

Bring your cello and play Sibelius from the cliffs above the river. Pack your paintbrushes to capture the landscapes. Tote your Audubon Society guides and enjoy the bird-watching. No, the Cedar Knoll Farm, a country bed and breakfast, is no ordinary bed & breakfast. It's a haven—a place where you can meet the countryside on its own terms.

Cedar Knoll, a 138-acre working farm, features an eight-year-old Cape Cod style house. The comfortable combination of traditional and contemporary in the house is enhanced with antiques, art works and accessories. The house contains three guest rooms and is surrounded by a full complement of barns and bins, a lush lawn, tall trees and flowers, and a meandering river.

Breakfasts can range from hearty country fare like ham, eggs, homefries, hotcakes, apple pie, homemade jams or a lighter menu of muffins, pastries, fruit and omelets. And bedtime snacks for children are always available.

GRANITE FALLS

Few communities are as appropriately named as Granite Falls. After all, it's home to the *World's Oldest Rock,* an outcropping of granite 3.8 billion years old and it is on the Minnesota River.

In fact, there is an abundance of granite deposits here. An outcrop is displayed at the *Yellow Medicine County Historical Museum. The Upper Sioux Agency State Park,* complete with horse campground and horse and hiking trails, is another historical site worth a visit. *Western Fest,* where the *Minnesota State High School Rodeo* championships are held, is a must for anyone interested in all the thrills and spills of rodeo.

Of course, the fishing is great, too, with catfish over 50 pounds having been caught in these waters. Canoeing is popular or just be near the water at the *Granite Falls Dam* downtown where you can stroll the walking bridge and feed the ducks in *Rice Park.*

For further information, contact:
Granite Falls Area Chamber of Commerce, P.O. Box 220A
Granite Falls, MN 56241   Phone: 612-564-4039

SPECIALTY SHOP

The Valley Troll

1222 Granite Street, Granite Falls, MN 56241
Phone: 612-564-4041
Hrs: Tues.-Fri. 10 a.m.-5 p.m., Sat. 10 a.m.-4 p.m. Closed Sun.-Mon.

The Valley Troll is a Scandinavian gift shop lovingly created by owner Ann Stensrud with a little help from her family along the way.

The Valley Troll features quality gifts from Norway, Sweden, Denmark, Finland and Iceland. Among the gifts are Scandinavian and children's books, unique greeting cards and napkins, Dale of Norway sweaters, Danish iron candle holders and candles, Scandinavian jewelry, ethnic novelties, foods from Scandinavia and, of course, trolls from Norway.

One of the most popular collectibles in the U.S., the Tom Clark Gnomes are a unique gift that everyone will love.

This unique shop is located 1/2 block north of the Hwy. 212 & 23 intersection in Granite Falls. Watch for the Scandinavian flags welcoming you to The Valley Troll.

HENDERSON

Nestled in the Minnesota River Valley about 55 miles southwest of Minneapolis/St. Paul on State Highways 19 and 93 is historic Henderson. It was founded in 1852 by one of the most important men in Minnesota history, Joseph Renshaw Brown. The community was an early supply, freighting and trading center.

The importance of Henderson to the late 19th and early 20th century is evidenced by the substantial brick buildings that line Main Street. In 1989, portions of Main Street were placed on the National Register of Historic Places.

ATTRACTIONS & EVENTS

The Sibley County Museum, built in 1884, contains many interesting items of historical value gleaned from Sibley County communities and Henderson's earlier boom days. Another interesting building is the *Old Courthouse* (once the Sibley County Courthouse) which was constructed in 1879. Both of these buildings are on the National Register, as well.

The community is surrounded by woods, hills and streams that are beautiful in all seasons of the year. A drive along the country lanes through the woods of the *Rush River State Wayside Rest* or *High Island Park* both offer breathtaking scenery. Primitive camping is available at both spots.

Henderson has many recreational activities. *Allanson's Park* provides campers with electrical hookups, a shelter, hot showers, picnic tables and playground equipment. A 3-mile nature trail offers visitors historic sites and begins on top of the levee in Allanson's Park.

Access to the Minnesota River is available at the boat landing in *Bender Park* and there is ample opportunity to fish from the river bank.

Henderson was first settled by a mixture of ethnic groups dominated by Germans. In an attempt to capture some of this traditional flavor of the town, the local festival is named *"Saurkraut Days."* It is held the last weekend in June. Henderson's *Grand Parade* is held on Sunday of that weekend at 1 p.m.

For further information, contact:
The City of Henderson
Henderson, MN 56044
Phone: 612-248-3234

HENDRICKS

Named after General Hendricks, who served as vice president to Grover Cleveland, Hendricks is located just a mile east of the South Dakota line. It was settled largely by Norwegians whose heritage is celebrated each May during *Syttenda Mai* (May 17, Norwegian Independence Day). Norwegian signage, foods and accents continue to make their mark in Hendricks today.

You can explore the past at the *Lincoln County Museum* or get a first-hand look at the days gone by during the *Two Cylinder Tractor Show* held on the second weekend of June. Or take in a little culture Sunday afternoons in June and July with concerts in the beautiful city park located on the shores of *Lake Hendricks.*

The nine-hole *Hendricks Country Club* is one of the area's best courses. Camping is available on County Road 24 and the lake is a popular recreation spot year-round.

For further information, contact:
Hendricks Business Club
P.O. Box 167-B, Hendricks, MN 56136   Phone: 507-275-3192

BED & BREAKFAST

Triple L Farm **B&B**	Rt. 1, Box 141 Hendricks, MN 56136 **Phone: 507-275-3740**

Ever wondered what a family farm was really like? Or maybe you grew up on one. Joan and Lanford Larson welcome you to The Triple L Farm B&B, a place to come back home. The European style B&B shares hands-on farming experiences like tractor rides, haymows, bike rides on the country backroads, wild flowers along the ditches, and rows and rows of corn and beans.

Though added on to, the original house was built in 1890 and now features unique country furnishings that invite you to sit and relax a bit. Wake in the morning to the smell of coffee brewing in the large country kitchen
and sit down at the round oak table to
an ethnic breakfast or farmer's breakfast served on handmade pottery.

There's a spacious yard with
hammock for adults, a sand pile for
the kids and lawn games for everyone.

HUTCHINSON

In 1855, a trio of singing brothers settled in a scenic river valley that is today named in their honor. To fund an expansion of their frontier church, the Hutchinsons headed east for a fundraising concert tour. The people of Martha's Vineyard, Mass., gave to the cause and a bell they funded still rings at the Vineyard Methodist Church.

Today's Hutchinson carries many reminders of its founders, including the nation's second-oldest park system. The *Wildlife Sanctuary Park,* located on the banks of the *Crow River,* offers excellent opportunities to observe deer and waterfowl. *The McLeod County Heritage & Cultural Center* pays tribute to the past and the *Les Kouba Gallery* features a permanent display with 200 paintings.

A Taste of Hutchinson, the *Water Carnival, Sno Break* and the *McLeod County Fair* are among the many annual events.

For further information, contact:
Hutchinson Convention & Visitors Bureau
45 Washington Avenue, E., Hutchinson, MN 55350
Phone: 612-587-5252

CULTURAL CENTER

McLeod County Heritage & Cultural Center	380 School Road, N., Hutchinson, MN 55350 **Phone: 612-587-2109** Hrs: Mon.-Fri. 10 a.m.-4:30 p.m., Sat.-Sun. 1 p.m.-4 p.m.

Recognized throughout Minnesota as one of the state's finest facilities for the preservation and display of articles related to county history, the McLeod County Heritage & Cultural Center is located on a hill overlooking a beautiful stretch of the Crow River Valley on the west end of Hutchinson.

It is the home of the Les Kouba Gallery, a monument to the internationally recognized work of wildlife artist and Hutchinson native Les Kouba and Kouba's gift to the McLeod County Historical Society. Nearly 200 of his best-known prints hang here along with several original art works, awards and memorabilia, including his early commercial work, cover art for *Sports Afield* magazine, winning designs for the 1959 and 1968 federal duck stamps and a 25-foot mural painted for a local restaurant in 1936.

In addition to the Kouba Gallery, the Center houses a meeting area, facilities for genealogical research and a large exhibit space. The public is welcome 360 days a year.

JACKSON

History hasn't always been kind to the city of Jackson.

Twice in the past, the town was completely deserted after settlers and Indians shot it out among the rickety shacks of the struggling settlement. Even after the Dakota War of the 1860s had settled the conflict once and for all, Jackson was left to suffer, this time through nature's fury via droughts, grasshopper devastations, blizzards and prairie fires.

Today, life is somewhat less challenging. Jackson is a farming town of 3,600 inhabitants where life is good but the past is definitely not forgotten.

ATTRACTIONS & EVENTS

History buffs will enjoy the delightful collection of rock fossils and an *Indian Museum* at the *Jackson County Courthouse*, listed on the National Register of Historic Places. *Fort Belmont* depicts an authentic replica of one of the only upper Midwestern civilian forts built for protection from the Natives. The *Jackson County Historical Museum*, located at Lakefield, is another unique attraction.

For recreation, there are two golf courses to choose from, including the *Jackson Country Club* and the *Loon Lake Golf Course*. There's also fishing and boating at *Clear Lake* and *Loon Lake* or if you prefer swimming, Jackson has an indoor pool at the *High School*. There are six parks scattered throughout the city, most with playgrounds and picnic areas.

Enjoy the beautiful *Des Moines River* or the nature trails of the *Kilen Woods State Park* located 12 miles northwest of town. If auto racing is your thing, you'll love the *Limited Sprint* races at the *Jackson Speedway* including the *Jackson Nationals,* which includes two big nights of racing in late July or early August and attracts fans from all over the United States. The Jackson Speedway has races every Saturday night from Memorial Day to Labor Day.

Jackson County Fair, in July, is always lots of fun. *Fair Village* is worth a visit, as well. And *Fort Belmont Renegade Days* in July is another attraction, featuring demonstrations of old-fashioned spinning and embroidery, lefse baking, butter churning, early blacksmithing and fur trapping.

For more information, contact:
Jackson Chamber of Commerce
1000 Highway 71 N., Jackson, MN 56143
Phone: 507-847-3867

BED & BREAKFAST

The Old Railroad Inn	219 Moore St., Jackson, MN 56143 **Phone: 507-847-5348** Hrs: Open March through December. Major credit cards accepted.

Surrounded by large, old oak trees and woods, The Old Railroad Inn has a quiet, homey atmosphere. The Inn was originally a bustling boarding house for railroad employees. Now a century old, the two-story house has been owned by the present innkeeper's family for the past fifty years.

Don and Joann have taken over the family home and made it into a charming bed and breakfast. To evoke the era of the railroad, they have named the bedrooms after railroad lines and furnished them with antiques, wicker, handmade quilts, lace and embroidered linens. View early railroad history while you enjoy breakfast like Grandma used to make in the unique breakfast room, where the cookie jar is full and the coffee pot is always on. The Inn offers easy access to I-90 and the Iowa Great Lakes Region on Hwy. 71.

Experience the warm and friendly hospitality at The Old Railroad Inn. All aboard!

SPECIALTY SHOP

The Country Cupboard	410 Second Street, Jackson, MN 56143 **Phone: 507-847-5890** Hrs: 10 a.m.-5 p.m., Thurs. 10-8 p.m. Visa and MasterCard accepted.

"Necessities for graceful living"—that's the motto of this interesting home decorating/home accessory store in an historical downtown setting. The store started out mostly offering a line of country decorations, but present owner, Pat Miller, has skillfully blended a more varied stock. Linens, wall hangings, furniture pieces, lamps, bears, dolls, kitchenware, gourmet coffee, candies, Mikasa crystal, silk flowers, candles, wicker, wreaths, jewelry and miniatures can be found along with numerous other items to delight and please. Collectibles include Kitty Cucumber, Memories of Yesterday, Calico Kitty, Cherished Teddy and North American Bear.

A cozy ambiance laced with fragrance and beautiful music await you at The Country Cupboard.

LAKE BENTON

Opera. The mere mention of the word conjures up images of society folks making their way to the great opera houses of the world. It does not make most think of a tiny town in rural Minnesota. Yet in Lake Benton, they take their opera seriously, thanks to the Lake Benton Opera House. Of course, there's much, much more in this community than just high-pitched voices.

Tucked away, high in wooded hills of southwestern Minnesota, at the junction of Highways 75 and 14, Lake Benton is a place to relax and unwind amid the virgin prairie. And enjoy a little culture while you're at it.

ATTRACTIONS & EVENTS

It should come as no surprise that the *Lake Benton Opera House* was the source of great community pride in 1896 when it opened. Fire had destroyed the original wood frame structure the previous December and almost immediately townspeople made plans and raised funds to build another, this a fine brick structure.

It was the heyday of travelling troupes, musicians and actors, many of whom appeared at the opera house. Political gatherings, dances, card parties, dinners, basketball games, graduations and all manner of community gatherings were held here. For a considerable time, it was a movie house known as The Majestic Theatre.

After falling into a state of despair following World War II and being scheduled for demolition in the 1970s, the Lake Benton Opera House was saved, restored and brought back to life. Today, it resides on the National Register of Historic Places and is open March through December.

Enjoy dinner at the *Country House* supper club and restaurant where you'll find steaks, seafood and prime rib. They offer package deals with the Opera House and take great pride in their third-generation family operation. Be sure and visit the *Old Osbeck House*, too, also on the Register.

Other activities in the "Valley of Fun" include fishing, snowmobiling, skiing, hiking and skating. The camping is wonderful in season. Father's Day weekend sees *Saddle Horse Days,* which includes competitive horse events, parades, street dances and trail rides. The food, beverages and entertainment are equally good.

For further information, contact:
President, Service Club
Lake Benton, MN 56149

RESTAURANT

Country House Supper Club	East Highway 14 Lake Benton, MN 56149 **Phone: 507-368-4223** Hrs: Open every night at 5 p.m.

The Country House Supper Club has known nothing but success and growth in its 30-year existence, expanding from a 60-seat supper club to a facility that now holds 190 people. Originally built in 1948 by Gib Williams as a cafe/truck stop, this is a third-generation family business. The supper club features a four-course dinner served by a friendly, courteous staff. Try the prime rib, great steaks, fabulous seafood, BBQ ribs or broasted chicken. The lower dining room offers quick, casual and inexpensive dining in a family atmosphere. Cocktails are served every evening, including Sundays.

The Country House also offers attractive dinner theatre packages for buses and tour groups, in conjunction with productions at the Lake Benton Opera House. Private party and meeting facilities are available plus complete catering services. All dinners are available for take out, but the broasted chicken is by far the most popular.

When you're finished with your meal, take time to examine works on display and for sale produced by local craftsmen.

SPECIALTY SHOP

Christmas in the Valley	106 S. Fremont Lake Benton, MN 56149 **Phone: 507-368-9343** Hrs.: Open year-round

For a charming slice of Christmas year-round, visit historic old Lake Benton hidden away in the hills of Buffalo Ridge, where you'll find a vast array of treasures in a quaint setting.

Step back in time in an old carriage house on the alley behind the 1896 Osbeck House (on the National Register of Historic Places) to find a piece of the 19th century filled with charming antique furniture displaying Christmas items from around the world. Eighteen wonderful trees, all decorated in different themes, await you. Many one-of-a-kind wreaths, garlands and arrangements are available. Tree ornaments of all kinds, hand-carved wooden Santas, Nativity scenes, candles, Victorian cards and wrapping paper are all here in great variety.

The Osbeck House, a Queen Anne home furnished in the period of 100 years ago, is worth a visit and don't miss Burk Antiques at the same site, featuring wonderful Victorian glassware from 1860 to 1910 and many rarities in an 1890s setting.

LITCHFIELD

Litchfield is located 70 miles west of the Twin Cities of Minneapolis/St. Paul on U.S. Highway 12. It's surrounded by farm country as rich as its heritage. The massacre at Acton marked the opening of the Indian wars in 1862 and, later, settlers came to cut the forests and farm the land. Litchfield High School was started in 1879. Litchfield is the county seat of Meeker County.

ATTRACTIONS & EVENTS

Litchfield's *GAR Hall* was built in 1885 by Civil War Union soldiers. This unique building, resembling a fortress, is the only building of its kind in Minnesota. *The Meeker County Museum* is adjacent to the GAR Hall.

When Mrs. Dorothea Kopplin died in September 1970, her last will and testament sought to establish a memorial in memory of her daughter Rosemary who died of leukemia at the age of six. Mrs. Kopplin's wish was finally fulfilled when her Victorian mansion was established as *Rosemary Home* in 1972.

Trinity Episcopal Church is located across from Central Park in Litchfield. This church, built in 1871, is listed on the National Register of Historic Places.

Lake Ripley is located on the south edge of Litchfield and features crappies, sunfish, northern pike and award winning largemouth bass. *Lake Ripley Campground* occupies 1600 feet of lakeshore on the east side of the lake and accommodates 35 recreational camping units. *Anderson Gardens* beautifully decorates the northeastern shore of Lake Ripley. You'll enjoy strolling through this public arboretum. The majestic 18-hole *Litchfield Public Golf Course* adorns the north side of the lake.

The new $4.5 million *Litchfield Municipal Airport* is located a mile south of town and features a 4,000 foot hard surface runway which is 100 feet wide.

Litchfield's *Watercade* celebration is held on the weekend after the Fourth of July. For snowmobilers, there's over 200 miles of groomed and well-marked trails within Meeker County.

For further information, contact:
Litchfield Chamber of Commerce
Box 820-P, Litchfield, Minnesota 55355
Phone: 612-693-8184

SPECIALTY SHOP

Frontier Era Trade Goods by Lietzau Taxidermy	353 Milkyway St. S., P.O. Box 12P Cosmos, MN 56228. **Phone:** 612-877-7297 Hrs: Mon.-Fri. 9 a.m.-5 p.m. Sat. 9-12.

Interested in the frontier period of American history, say 1700 to 1800? Frontier Era Trade Goods by Lietzau Taxidermy is a retail store and showroom that's one of the more interesting you'll discover.

They are not just a taxidermy studio, though that's how they started out back in 1960. Here, you'll find all manner of items related to the frontier period, Native American culture and buckskinning.

Anybody involved with such things as reenactments, museums, schools, interior decorating and historical memorabilia will not want to miss this store. It's an experience you will not forget. They have a very fine selection of furs, a large offering of skulls, teeth, claws, bones and the like. They have prime winter buffalo robes sure to please the frontier history buff.

Buffalo skulls come in all sizes, from the young butcher bull to the old classic herd bull. (You can even order buffalo meat and have it shipped frozen to you anywhere in the U.S.) They also offer a complete line of skulls from most North American game animals and fur bearers.

They carry one of the finest selections of buffalo leather in the country. Buckskin, elk, moose, and leather from domestic cattle round out the leather line. They can help you with whatever leather you need.

The store offers authentic reproductions of the Native American culture like quillwork, beadwork, rattles, spears, dance sticks and more. One-of-a-kind items are added regularly. Most of these works are created by Native American craftspeople. They also carry some of the finest reference books on early American history.

With all these items, it's not surprising that the store has supplied many of the requirements for movies set in that era of history. *Dances With Wolves, Red Headed Stranger, Last of the Mohicans* and *Iron Will* are some of the movies they have supplied.

The store offers mail order and a catalog plus group tours. Call for information. When you stop for a visit here, be sure to bring this book along. They will sign it and give you a copy of the illustrated story of the epic film, *Dances With Wolves*, plus a sample of the leather that was supplied for the film. It's a $16.95 value, FREE!

LUVERNE

Luverne is a most intriguing mixture of farming tradition, prairie wilderness and industry. Of interest to travelers and just four miles north of Luverne is *Blue Mounds State Park,* one of the few remaining untouched areas of prairie left in the country.

Along with The Palace Theatre, the *Hinkly House* is another fascinating historical site that was built in 1892. *The Rock County Court House* built in 1887 and the *Carnegie Cultural Center* provide historical outlets for those interested in history and beauty.

Luverne is the site of the *Tri-State Band Festival,* attracting bands from the tri-state area on the last Saturday in September. The first weekend in June, the Chamber hosts *Buffalo Days,* with a parade, Arts In The Park, buffalo chip throwing contest and free buffalo burgers.

For further information, contact:
Luverne Area Chamber of Commerce
102 E. Main, Luverne, MN 56156
Phone: 507-283-4061

PARK

Blue Mounds State Park

R.R. 1, Luverne, MN 56156
Phone: 507-282-4892
Hrs: Year-round, 8 a.m-10 p.m. daily.

Blue Mounds State Park is one of the largest prairie parks in Minnesota. It features 1,500 acres of prairie grasslands with an array of rare and common plants, including native prickly pear cactus! A small bison herd grazes peacefully on a portion of this virgin prairie.

Most of the park's prairie sits atop a massive outcrop of rock known as Sioux Quartzite. The rock outcrop slopes gently up from the surrounding countryside but terminates abruptly in a spectacular cliff line that had appeared blue to settlers going west. The cliff provides a panoramic view of the countryside.

Miles of hiking and snowmobile trails take you along the cliffs, around the park's two lakes, into the oak woods and through the prairie. Blue Mounds offers you the opportunity to see, hear and feel a real prairie environment, one of the last in existence. Here, visitors experience tall grasses and colorful wildflowers swaying in the wind, or see the power of a summer prairie thunderstorm rolling in from the west. This beautiful land exists much as it has for thousands of years.

MANKATO

There's no doubt that the city of Mankato is surrounded by the blue earth that inspired the name of the county it's located in. What isn't certain, however, is the real story behind the name Mankato. Legend has it that the name resulted from the misspelling of the Dakota Indian word for that dirt.

Mistake or not, few things have gone wrong since. It is actually two cities, Mankato and North Mankato, and is home to a number of institutes of higher education and a host of highly successful companies including Carlson Craft (stationery), Johnson Fishing (rods and reels) and Hubbard Milling (world's largest producer of private label pet food).

And the beautiful location on the bluffs of the Minnesota River remains as stunning as it's always been.

ATTRACTIONS & EVENTS

If you grew up reading *Betsy and Tracy* stories, then you know the city is home to the famed children's author *Maud Hart Lovelace* who created the characters. Some of the city's unique attractions are tours of the various homes and sites described in the series.

Equally important contributions to the cultural life of the area are made by the *Mankato Symphony Orchestra,* the *MSU Theatre Arts Department,* the *Merely Players* and the *Cherry Creek* theatre, located in the lovingly restored *Carnegie Library.* Besides the Carnegie, there are five other significant historical buildings of note: the *R.D. Hubbard House,* the *Judge Lorin P. Cray Mansion,* the *Blue Earth County Courthouse* and the *Seppmann Mill.*

The annual visit of the National Football League's *Minnesota Vikings* is the highlight of the year for sports fans. The team holds its training camp at *Mankato State University.* When in town, the football players spend time on the golf course and the new *North Links* is the best around. In winter, *Mount Kato* inspires downhill skiers from around the region.

The Makhakto Mdewakaton Pow-Wow is a colorful celebration. The 1800s Historic Festival features fur traders, historic artifacts, music and family fun. And the final event of each year, the *Celebration of Lights,* makes for a bright Christmas.

For further information, contact:
Mankato Area Convention & Visitors Bureau
P.O. Box 999
Mankato, MN 56001
Phone: 507-345-4519 or 800-426-6025

ANTIQUES

Earthly Remains Antique Mall	731 S. Front Street, Mankato, MN 56001 **Phone: 507-388-5063** Hrs: Mon.-Sat. 10 a.m.-5 p.m. Visa and MasterCard accepted.

It seems appropriate that a place where people come to latch on to a piece of the past, to take home a living memory, once began in the old carriage house of the Johnson-Bowman Funeral Home; hence the name. Those were the rather humble beginnings of the Earthly Remains Antique Mall.

It has since moved to another historic location, the old Bargain Center on the corner of Byron and Front Streets in Mankato, where its special look and vast collection of antiques and nostalgia have made the area's largest antique store very popular.

Earthly Remains features the wares of some 20 antique dealers, everything from 1950's nostalgia pieces to furniture, jewelry, vintage clothing, fine glassware and china and thousands of books. They also have dolls and toys, holiday items, quilts, fancy lacework and doilies and a selection of primitives, collectibles and memorables. The setting is an old-fashioned general store with room settings and streets filled with quaint shops.

BED & BREAKFAST

The Butler House	704 South Broad Street Mankato, MN 56001 **Phone: 507-387-5055** Visa and MasterCard accepted.

An English-style mansion, The Butler House offers turn-of-the-century elegance to the B&B fan. Owned and perfectly maintained by the Butler-Clements family for 70 years, the mansion still has its original fumed-oak, cypress and birch woodwork, coffered ceilings, leaded glass and walls covered with hand-painted murals.

A choice of five rooms is available to suit any guest's desires, all beautifully furnished with antiques. Large suites with canopy beds and sitting areas are available. One has a fireplace and another has a double whirlpool.

The palatial front porch is the perfect spot for an evening refreshment or a leisurely cup of coffee over the morning paper. A three-course gourmet breakfast is served on weekends and a two-course breakfast is served on weekdays.

HISTORIC SITE & TOURS

R.D. Hubbard House	606 S. Broad Street. Mankato, MN 56001 **Phone: 507-345-5566 or 507-345-4154** Hrs: (Summer) Tues.-Sun. 1-4 p.m. (Winter) Hours vary, call ahead. Admission charge.

The residence of Rensselaer D. Hubbard, founder of Hubbard Milling Company, was built in the second French Empire style and has long been recognized for its historical and architectural significance. Both the house and the carriage house are on the Minnesota State Historic Register and the National Register of Historic Places.

The house is constructed of local red brick painted white on a Mankato Stone foundation. The maid's call register on the pantry wall still lists the room designations as they were in 1888 and the green silk brocade wall fabric, Tiffany light fixtures, and marble fireplace transport visitors to an earlier time in Mankato's history.

The R.D. Hubbard House gift shop offers handmade items from the area as well as period gifts and books on the history of the area. Admission is $2 for adults, $1 for students and seniors, and free to children under six. Family admission is $5, providing the opportunity for an inexpensive trip through time. Tours and other visits by appointment.

LODGING

Best Western Garden Inn and Conference Center	Highway 169 - 1111 Range St., North Mankato, MN 56003. **Phone: 507-625-9333** or Best Western national reservations (800) 528-1234. Hours: Open daily year-round. Visa, MasterCard, Discover & AmEx are accepted.

The Garden Inn, nestled in the valley of the other Twin Cities (Mankato/North Mankato), offers gracious lodging for business or pleasure.

A complimentary continental breakfast awaits guests Monday through Friday, 6 a.m. to 9 a.m. There are 147 spacious rooms from which to choose, as well as meeting, banquet, and convention space for up to 500 guests. An enclosed recreation area with pool, whirlpool, sauna, and video games is also available for the ultimate in relaxation. Bus tour groups may choose from many entertaining packages available.

The Garden Inn dining room features a Heart Healthy menu for the diet-conscious guest. The lounge is completely stocked and ready to serve your beverage of choice. The Best Western Garden Inn is a full-service advantage motel offering fine accommodations, a professional staff and much, much more.

EATERY & SPECIALTY SHOP

The Coffee Hag

329 N. Riverfront Drive, Mankato, MN 56001
Phone: 507-387-5533. Hrs: Tues., Wed., Thurs. 9 a.m.-11 p.m., Fri., Sat. til midnight, Sun. 11 a.m.-6 p.m. Closed Mondays.

Coffee? Yes, they've got cappuccino, espresso and gourmet coffee beans from around the world, teas and many different hot and cold drinks besides! And they've got a lot more at The Coffee Hag. A variety of reading material is available and you can order a sandwich, salad or soup with your favorite cup of java. You can buy such items as incense, candles and hand-crafted jewelry while you munch a cookie, muffin or other sweet goody.

This is a place to relax, unwind and soothe the spirit. The aromas are fantastic! On weekend evenings, this comfortable coffee house turns into an excellent music club featuring local groups and some well-known talent.

But whatever you're looking for in southern Minnesota, you won't find fresher coffee or a wider selection than that offered in the warm atmosphere of The Coffee Hag.

SPECIALTY SHOP

Henny Penny Shoppe

1720 Madison Ave., River City Centre, Mankato, MN 56001. **Phone: 507-625-6360** Hrs: Mon.-Sat. & Sun., by appointment. Visa, MasterCard and Discover accepted.

If you're looking for the best selection of both children's and maternity wear in southern Minnesota, look no further than the Henny Penny Shoppe in Mankato.

The Henny Penny Shoppe was started in a private residence back in 1970 and has since grown and moved into the Mankato hilltop area to better serve a discriminating clientele. They offer a complete range of children's clothing ranging from newborn to 10 in 100% cotton. Specialty children's apparel include such distinctive items as bibs, bonnets and bows. They also carry brother/sister companion pieces featuring Hartstrings and Kitestrings. There are some great gift ideas for a special child, too.

Henny Penny's full line of maternity clothing includes swimsuits, sleepwear, lingerie, careerwear and something for those special occasions. There's always plenty of free, up-close parking available at the Henny Penny Shoppe, and there's toys to entertain the tots while you shop. Gift wrapping is also available.

SPECIALTY SHOP

Harpies' Bazaar

605 N. Riverfront Drive, Mankato, MN 56001. **Phone: 507-387-2736.** Hrs.: Open Daily Mon. & Thurs. 10 a.m.-8 p.m., Tues., Weds., Fri., Sat. 10 a.m.-5 :30., Sun. 12 noon-5 p.m. (Nov.-Dec.) Mon.-Fri. 10 a.m.-9 p.m., Sat. 10 a.m.-5:30 p.m., Sun 12 noon-5 p.m. Discover, MasterCard and Visa accepted.

Tucked away by itself in the Old Town area of Mankato, Harpies' Bazaar occupies three connected storefronts with nine rooms of gifts, home accent ideas and seasonal decor. Harpies began in 1971 as a tiny craft shop but has evolved into nearly a mini-mall. Merchandise in Harpies includes items from area artisans to items imported from around the world.

The fragrance of potpourri and the strains of relaxing music provide a backdrop for creative displays that are a visual delight. The coffee pot is always on for customers to sample a gourmet flavor while browsing through greeting cards, books & journals, a rubber stamp area, Department 56 collectibles, gift foods, clothing and home decorations that can be found in every nook and cranny. Selections vary from Crabtree & Evelyn soaps to irresistible t-shirts as well as unusual jewelry and a Mary Engelbreit collection.

Harpies has always been a little off the beaten path so the staff firmly believes in good customer service. Pictures and lamps often go home with customers for a trial run. Tapes & CD's can be heard before being purchased. The goal at Harpies is to give visitors many reasons to return. Staying in business for over 20 years indicates that Harpies' Bazaar certainly succeeds in turning customers into friends.

SPECIALTY SHOP

The Lighthouse

860 Madison Ave., Mankato, MN 56001-6140
Phone: 507-345-3200. FAX: 507-345-7616
Hrs: Mon.-Fri. 9 a.m.-8 p.m., Sat. 9 a.m.-5 p.m.
Visa and MasterCard accepted.

The Lighthouse's main function is to be a full-service Christian retail store providing churches, families and the community with products that will deepen and enhance their spiritual needs. The store has been in operation for 14 years and is now housed in a large, new facility.

On the main strip in Mankato, The Lighthouse is located in a unique building, custom-designed for its purpose. Approaching this free standing store, customers notice the floor-to-ceiling bay windows, post lamps, and a 100-year-old maple tree that distinguish the exterior.

Inside they find a well-lit interior decorated with antiques and oak fixtures. Ice-blue walls and blue tweed carpet add to the homey atmosphere. "Some of my customers tell me that they wouldn't mind living here," says owner/manager Catherine Bristol.

The Lighthouse has grown from a 1,200-square-foot store in a strip center to its current 4,500-square-foot prime location. "We were in the strip mall for 10 years, from 1979 to 1989," Bristol says. "We went through two expansions at that location before we decided to design and build a free-standing store."

Nearly a quarter of The Lighthouse's floor space is dedicated to children's products—both Christian and classic secular materials. It's a great selection of Christian toys and novelties for children. A listening center attracts local high school and college students.

One change Bristol has noticed at The Lighthouse is an increasing number of male customers. "I think publishers are becoming more sensitive to men's issues and needs and are responding by providing more high quality products for men," she says. When asked about her goal for The Lighthouse, Bristol says, "I want to get a Bible in every home in this community. I want to serve all denominations. To me, the Bible is the ultimate communications tool; it should be used to open the doors of conversation and communication."

The store offers a large selection of Christian music and books, CD's, tapes, and printed music. Christian gifts, jewelry and home decor abound.

The Lighthouse, it's "Where Shopping is an Inspiration."

CORPORATE PROFILE

Taylor Corporation   To many, the Taylor Corporation is synonymous with the state of Minnesota. In reality, it reaches much farther, to many corners of the globe and in many different businesses. In fact, the Taylor Corporation, from its headquarters in North Mankato, is the holding company for more than 45 operating divisions in 12 states, four Canadian provinces, the Netherlands and the United Kingdom.

In Mankato alone, Taylor Corporation employs more than 3,000 people. Around the world, the many and varied enterprises that make up Taylor total more than 7,000 employees.

A Variety of Ventures

The Taylor companies are the nation's largest printer of wedding and business stationery. Always an innovator, Taylor is proud of having the country's first on-site day care center; Golden Heart Care Center located in North Mankato. There, the children of Taylor employees spend their days in a safe, comfortable and stimulating environment.

But there's more

Also in the Taylor family is Taylor Bancshares, which owns six banks in Minnesota, including Valley National Bank in North Mankato. Although the names may be different, there is a long list of Taylor Companies that call the Mankato/North Mankato area home.

They include:

■ Carlson Craft. Through an extensive network of dealers in every state, Carlson Craft fills and ships thousands of orders every day, from wedding invitations to business cards.

■ Fine Impressions is a paper-converting company that manufactures wedding invitations, envelopes and napkins.

■ Corporate Graphics International is the leading national stationery printer for the Fortune 1000 companies.

■ National Recognition Products, the premier manufacturer of graduation announcements and accessories, serves high schools and universities nationwide.

■ Royal Stationery serves the retail stationery, card and gift markets throughout the United States.

■ Thayer Publishing manufactures greeting cards and calendars for businesses throughout the United States.

MAPLETON

It may be thousands of miles removed geographically from Scotland but there is a feeling of closeness to the old country that continues today in Mapleton. In fact, tribute is paid regularly in this Southern Lakes community to its heritage.

Mapleton is known as Southern Minnesota's curling capital. The sport, with its origins in Scotland, has been played winters at the *Heather Curling Club* for decades. Youngsters still learn highland dancing as they always have and tribute is paid each January to the famed Scottish poet Robert Burns.

At *Daly Park,* there are 135 camp sites, swimming, fishing, bike paths, tennis courts and playground facilities. *Lake Lura* offers excellent walleye fishing. *Solie's Castle* is an attraction found on the National Register of Historic Places. *Town and Country Days* is an annual summer festival. For further information, contact:

Mapleton Area Chamber of Commerce
Hwy. 22 South, Suite 200, Mapleton, MN 56065
Phone: 507-524-3358

ANTIQUES & TEA ROOM

Solie's Castle

101 2nd Ave. N.E., Mapleton, MN 56065
Phone: 507-524-3033
Hrs: Friday, Saturday, Sunday, Monday, 11 a.m.-6 p.m.; Tea Room, 1 p.m.-5 p.m.

Take a Queen Anne-style mansion, add period furnishings and antiques, toss in gourmet foods and a tea room, and you have the magic of Solie's Castle, Victorian elegance at its best.

Solie's Castle brings romance, tradition, fantasy and enchantment to its visitors. The experience starts with the Victorian Tea Room, offering gourmet desserts, specialty coffees, and wonderful tea, all served in a beautiful sunlit garden tea room complete with heirloom paintings, white linens and fresh flowers.

The house, listed on the National Register of Historic Places, is home to an ever-changing assortment of antiques, along with gifts and estate jewelry. The items are displayed in theme rooms that mix the traditional and the offbeat. A mermaid room features Amanda, the life-size mermaid floating from the ceiling, and a dungeon in the basement contains Mapletooth (the mechanical dragon) and a barking dog. And no one leaves without a sample of their fabulous homemade fudge.

MARSHALL

The Big Bend of the Red River was a well known spot to the Native Americans who once inhabited these lands. So, it's not surprising that white settlers arriving in the summer of 1869 found the same advantages and settled there, also. In 1872, the railroad came through, securing Marshall's position as a thriving community. The county seat of Lyon County, Marshall now boasts a population of over 12,000.

ATTRACTIONS & EVENTS

Marshall is home to *Southwest State University,* a unique technical and liberal arts university built to accommodate handicapped students. The school plays an active role in the life of the community by providing numerous artistic and cultural activities as well as a variety of athletic events. In addition, Southwest State University houses the *Natural Sciences Museum,* the *William Whipple Art Gallery* and *Southwest State Historical Center.*

In the middle of flat prairielands, a sudden drop into beautiful, steep slopes finds visitors in *Garvin Park* with lush, wooded hillsides and valley meadows. Located 10 miles southeast of Marshall is *Camden State Park* with 1,500 acres of river valley wrapped up in maple-basswood forests, prairie meadows and clear, bubbling springs.

The *Lyon County Historical Museum* is located at 116 N. 3rd Street and includes an original 1928 courtroom, Indian artifacts, county historical records and prairie plants.

A Festival of Kites celebration is held on the 4th of July at Independence Park, Marshall's newest 52-acre park which has many family activities available.

The Lyon County Fair is held in August, with rides, exhibits and grandstand entertainment. The *International Rolle Bolle Tournament* is held in conjunction with the fair.

Each summer, a *Celebrity Golf Tournament* is held as a fund raiser event for the university athletic program. In and around Marshall can be found tennis, golf, swimming, boating, hunting, camping, fishing, skeet shooting, bowling, dancing, snowmobiling, movies, ice skating, hockey, horseback riding, baseball and softball.

For further information and brochures, contact:
Marshall Visitor and Convention Bureau
1210 E. College Dr.
Marshall, MN 56258   Phone: 507-537-1865

LODGING

Best Western Marshall Inn	Junction Highways 19 and 23, Marshall, MN 56258. **Phone: 507-532-3221 or 800-528-1234** Hrs.: Open year-round. Major credit cards accepted.

The Best Western Marshall Inn provides the finest in lodging and dining for this bustling campus community and has for more than a decade. Located adjacent to Southwest State University, it often serves visiting parents and opposing teams. One hundred tastefully decorated rooms are available; two suites feature private whirlpools. An indoor pool, sauna, whirlpool, and game area provide recreation and relaxation.

The popular Camden Country Inn Restaurant in the hotel serves breakfast, lunch and dinner. Dine on Fridays and Saturdays, when prime rib is the specialty or try the international buffet on Fridays. A full menu is featured every night. The Camden Country Inn Lounge is the perfect retreat for socializing and unwinding. Meeting rooms are available for groups from 10 to 500, as well as banquet facilities for up to 400 people.

Camden State Park, Lake Shetek State Park, Garvin Park, and popular Pipestone National Monument are within driving distance.

◆ ◆ ◆ ◆ ◆ ◆ ◆

©MARTENA R. RICHTER

MORTON

It's not so unusual for cities and towns, small and large, to make their mark on the world. But to carve it in stone the way Morton has? Now that's unusual!

The stone in question is *Rainbow Granite* and it has been the building material of choice in hundreds of significant public and private buildings across the United States for decades. One of the oldest and hardest stones available, it comes from Morton. Appropriately enough, the two monuments east of town which commemorate the Dakota uprising of 1862 are also made of the home-grown granite. Memories of the *Dakota Wars* come to life at the interpretive center at *Lower Sioux Agency. The Renville County Historical Museum* maintains extensive exhibits on Dakota life and the pioneer tradition, as well. *Jackpot Junction,* complete with hotel and convention center is one of Minnesota's most popular casinos.

For more information on Morton, contact:
City of Morton, P.O. Box 127
Morton, MN 56270-0127   Phone: 507-697-0127

BED & BREAKFAST

The Simon's House	P.O. Box 238 370 Main St. North Morton, Minnesota 56270 **Phone: 507-697-6918**

The Simon's House is a unique historical landmark located in Morton, just five minutes from Jackpot Junction. The house was constructed of Morton brick produced in a local brickyard. The original foundation and exterior were constructed of local Morton granite.

It has five beautifully decorated rooms, each with cable television and air conditioning.

The Dakota Room features Native American decor throughout. The Celebrity Room is a whimsical and nostalgic room with autographed movie star photos. The Garden Room has a second story, antique furnishings and a view of the bluffs. The High Rollers Suite is luxurious and elegant with its oval whirlpool and french glass doors. The Beckman Room is wheelchair accessible and has its own private entrance.

Guests are invited to lounge in the living room, dining room or relax on the front porch. An enticing continental breakfast is included with your stay.

CASINO

Jackpot Junction

County Rd. 24, Box 420, Morton, MN 56270
Phone: (800) WIN-CASH (946-2274)
Hrs: Open 24 hours, 7 days
Must be 18 or older to gamble

Jackpot Junction gives you the best of two worlds—Las Vegas-style attractions and warm midwestern hospitality. Located just east of Redwood Falls, Jackpot Junction offers outstanding gambling, entertainment and dining 24 hours a day, seven days a week.

Owned and operated by the Lower Sioux (Mdewakanton) Community, it features two floors with 130,000 square feet of gaming area. There are more than 1,700 coin drop Video Slot Machines from nickels to $25, plus Poker, Keno, Craps and Live Video Blackjack. Or choose from 57 Blackjack tables with minimums ranging from $2 to $1,000, daily bingo and pulltabs plus Blackjack tournaments and million dollar Mega Bingo. Choose from fast food or fine dining and everything in between. Alcoholic beverages (for those over age 21) are available throughout. Top-notch entertainment is featured regularly in the Dakota Room. Motels, motorhome parking and full hook-up sites are available with 24-hour security.

Group trips and tours are offered throughout Minnesota.

HISTORIC SITE

Fort Ridgely

A Minnesota Historical Society Site. In Fort Ridgely State Park, 7 miles south of Fairfax on Hwy. 4. R.R. 1, Box 32, Fairfax, MN 55332. **Phone: 507-426-7888.** Hrs: May 1-Sept. 5 Tues.-Sat. and Monday holidays, 10 a.m.-5 p.m., Sun. noon-5 p.m. State Park Fee.

Constructed in 1853 on a high plateau near the Minnesota River in southwestern Minnesota, Fort Ridgely lacked a stockade and was built mostly of wood. In the opinion of many soldiers banished to this western outpost, the fort was impossible to defend.

Nine years after its construction, after a period of peace and routine to the point of boredom, the soldier's assessment was put to the test. On August 20, Dakota Indians attacked the fort but withdrew after five hours. Two days later they returned but fire from the fort's five cannons prevented them from organizing an effective assault.

Today, little is left of the fort. After the war ended and the Indians were forced to relocate to the Dakotas or Nebraska, the fort was closed and settlers tore down the buildings to use the materials for homes and barns. Only a restored stone commissary and a handful of scattered stone foundations remain. Here, the Minnesota Historical Society has historical exhibits and a gift shop to help visitors remember the last Indian war in Minnesota.

LODGING

Granite Valley Motel	400 West Ledge Morton, MN 56270 **Phone: 800-245-9800** Major credit cards accepted.

The Granite Valley Motel is located in the heart of the beautiful Minnesota River Valley. It has 41 rooms and features a courteous staff and extra clean lodging. The motel offers color TV's with in-room movies, monitored security, meeting facilities and lots of parking no matter what you're driving.

Guests enjoy many amenities including a free continental breakfast, free coffee available 24 hours a day, free cable TV, free FAX machine, free copy machine, free local phone calls and a toll-free reservation number.

Nearby is shopping, Native American exhibits and sites, nature trails and parks, the Minnesota Inventors Congress, Walnut Grove's Little House on the Prairie, and, of course, Jackpot Junction gambling casino.

The motel offers a free shuttle service to the casino and to Redwood Falls. Jackpot Junction is one of Minnesota's most popular casinos.

There are a variety of sights in the area. Rainbow Granite, found in Morton, has been the building material of choice in hundreds of significant public and private buildings across the United States for decades. It is one of the oldest and hardest stones available. The two monuments east of town which commemorate the Dakota uprising of 1862 are also made of the home-grown granite. This is where visitors can both view the stone and get an education on the history of the area.

Nature trails and parks offer visitors the experience of the natural scene in and around this interesting area.

MOUNTAIN LAKE

Minnesota's earliest known human dwelling, dating back to 100 B.C., was discovered just three miles southeast of Mountain Lake. In the 1800's, it was slated to be named "Midway" because it was mid-way on the railroad line between St. Paul and Sioux City, Iowa. However, the current name was finally chosen, after a tree-covered island rising from a shallow lake southwest of town.

Mountain Lake is rich in culture and history. Many Russian Mennonite families and German Lutherans settled the area in the early days. These surnames abound in the local telephone directory today. Though now more ethnically diverse, this heritage is still cele-brated during the year.

ATTRACTIONS & EVENTS

Mountain Lake is home to many unique shops and restaurants, including the *Ayte Shtade Restaurant,* featuring Mennonite and German cuisine. *Conestoga Wood, Inc. and the Mountain Lake General Store* offer free furniture factory tours and an adjacent outlet store with gift shop. The Mennonite-run *Care-&-Share Shop* sells exquisite items handmade in third-world countries. *The Carnation Cottage* is a beautifully decorated 19th Century home with an antique, gift and floral store.

Mountain Lake hosts several fabulous celebrations throughout the year, drawing thousands of visitors from far and near. Many come for the fun and festivities, while others—from larger cities—come to experience the hoopla of a small-town all-American gather-ing. *Heritage Fair* is held the second Saturday each September and features food, entertainment, exhibits and activities reminiscent of the town's Mennonite and German culture of the late 1800's.

The annual *Pow Wow Celebration,* held each June, is Minnesota's oldest continuing community celebration. It offers a grand parade, midway rides, food and lots of entertainment.

Christmas in the Park transforms the park into a brilliantly col-ored Christmas wonderland.

For further information, contact:
Mountain Lake Chamber of Commerce
925 Second Avenue
Mountain Lake, MN 56159
Phone: 507-427-3002

SPECIALTY SHOP

Conestoga Wood, Inc., and the Mountain Lake General Store	1050 Second Ave., Box 523, Mountain Lake, MN 56159. **Phone: 507-427-2028** Hrs: Mon.-Sat. 9 a.m.-5 p.m. Visa and MasterCard accepted.

Many companies can boast of celebrity clients or high profile CEOs, but few—if any—can say its president has done what Conestoga Wood, Inc., owner and president has: Outfitted with helmet, goggles and eight-foot long ski jumping skis, Jon Denney has climbed the 250-foot tower of a ski jump, crouched in an "egg" position while gaining momentum down the slide (and speeds in excess of 70 miles per hour!), and jumped the length of nearly two football fields! That was Jon's life for more that eight years as a member of the U.S. National Ski Jumping Team and 1984 U.S. Olympic Team.

Now Jon and his wife, Susan, operate their thriving furniture business known as Conestoga Wood, Inc., a wholesale manufacturer of items like wood cedar chests, benches and desks. The company is housed in a turn-of-the-century lumber building that's been remodeled for modern factory use. Furniture factory tours are offered free of charge Monday through Friday from 9 a.m. to 5 p.m.

Just lately, they received a great honor from the U.S. Olympic Committee. Conestoga Wood was granted an exclusive licensing agreement to manufacture and market cedar chests bearing the U.S. Olympic Team logo. They are the only chest manufacturer in the country to have been granted such a license.

The Denney's also operate The Mountain Lake General Store adjacent to the factory. The outlet store offers furnishings by Conestoga Wood, handmade Mennonite quilts and wall hangings, locally handcrafted wood novelty items, quality sweaters and blankets and many other unique gift items. The store is open year-round and the company hosts an annual open house and anniversary sale each fall.

The U.S. Olympic Team spirit is alive and well in this quaint factory on the plains of southwestern Minnesota. Jon, Susan and the employees at Conestoga Wood invite you to visit and catch the spirit!

SPECIALTY SHOPS

Care & Share Shop	208 10th Avenue North Mountain Lake, MN 56159 **Phone: 507-427-3468** Hrs: Mon.-Sat. 9 a.m.-5 p.m.

Care & Share Shop is a unique international gift and thrift shop filled with gift items imported through SelfHelp Crafts, a job creation program and non-profit marketing agency. The name, SelfHelp, comes from its main goal: to help people to earn a living from their own traditional crafts. The shop has exotic jewelry, carvings and folk art, expressive stationery, collectibles and personal accessories, engaging toys, holiday decorations and home accents, ecologically friendly baskets, bags and tableware.

This non-profit, volunteer-staffed shop, sponsored by Mennonite Churches in the area, offers gift ideas at affordable prices and an opportunity to "make a world of difference" for needy people in 35 developing countries. The Thrift Department offers a wide selection of donated, recycled clothing, household goods, books and miscellaneous items. All proceeds of sales are designated to MCC, the worldwide relief agency of Mennonite & Brethren in Christ Churches in the U.S. and Canada.

◆ ◆ ◆ ◆ ◆ ◆ ◆

Carnation Cottage	404 10th Street Mountain Lake, MN 56159 **Phone: 507-427-3830** Hrs: Hours vary, call ahead.

Safely nestled among large shade trees is one of Mountain Lake's oldest houses, an historic structure which has now become the home of the Carnation Cottage.

Brian and Carol Harder purchased this piece of historical property and lovingly restored its original beauty, leaving all of the original architecture entirely intact. It has now become one of the most popular tourist attractions along Highway 60, offering each visitor a unique experience in shopping for gifts, viewing Mennonite art, contemplating antiques or just absorbing the wonderful aromatic atmosphere of the flower shop.

Feel free to inquire about the Mennonite people during your visit and pick up a complimentary informational brochures to learn more. From the antique pump organ in the wedding room, the Mennonite dolls in the dining room, the deacon's bench in the parlor, to the bronze sculpture in the men's room, the Carnation Cottage opens its door to an enchanting experience to remember.

HISTORIC VILLAGE

Heritage Village	County Rd. 1 & Mt. Lake Rd., Mountain Lake, MN 56159. **Phone: 507-427-3612** Hrs: Mon.-Sat. 10-12 a.m. & 1-5 p.m., Sun. 1-5 p.m. (May 15 - Sept. 15)

Heritage Village is a collection of 18 historic buildings depicting a turn of the century village established in the 1870's by Mennonite and Lutheran immigrants from Russia. Each building is furnished with historic items representative of its function as a pioneer business. A building of special interest is an 1884 Mennonite house-barn combination which houses many items originally brought from Russia. The Minnesota State Telephone Museum is also located at Heritage Village. Tour groups are welcome and a special ethnic dinner is served if reservations are made two weeks in advance of the tour date.

A festival, "Utschtallung" or Heritage Fair, is held each second Saturday of September. On this day, ethnic foods of Russian Mennonite origin are served. There are demonstrations of pioneer activities and hand-crafted items are offered for sale. Special entertainment is provided on the village stage for the afternoon program. A pioneer dress-up contest is open to all who attend the festival.

◆ ◆ ◆ ◆ ◆ ◆ ◆

© MARTHENA R. RICHTER

NEW PRAGUE

Accidents will happen but few as successfully as the mistake that led to the formation of one of Minnesota's most charming towns, New Prague. The original settlers from Bavaria and Bohemia had intended to travel by ferry to the St. Cloud area, where they would make their way in the new world. Instead, they ended up on the Minnesota River, south of Shakopee.

Today, visitors like what they see, from the award-winning charm of *Schumacher's New Prague Hotel* to the many quaint and traditional shops. Each September, they come to celebrate *Dozinky,* a tribute to the ethnic and agricultural heritage of the area, complete with Czech dancing and singing, arts, crafts and historic demonstrations. Of course, there's a beer garden.

Be sure to explore the many historical murals throughout the town and the *St. Wenceslaus Church,* one of Minnesota's largest.

For further information, contact:

New Prague Chamber of Commerce, P.O. Box 191
New Prague, MN 56071   Phone: 612-758-4360

ANTIQUES

New Prague Antiques	104 Columbus Ave. S., New Prague, MN 56071 **Phone: 612-758-2746** Hrs: Summer Mon.-Sun. 10:30 a.m.-5:30 p.m. Closed Mon., Tues. in winter.

Dip deep into your memory bank with a stop at New Prague Antiques, just a half block off the main street in New Prague.

Do you remember those wonderful gasoline globes? There's a terrific collection of them here. Do you cherish your days as a teenager hanging out at the soda fountain? Perhaps you can rekindle your memories exploring another of their specialities, the early soda fountains. And what about those classic advertising signs of days gone by? New Prague Antiques has one of the largest selections around.

Located on Columbus Avenue, opposite St. Wenceslaus Church, New Prague Antiques has been in business at the same location since 1979 and is owned and operated by the mayor of New Prague. Located in a building once used to house horses that delivered milk around town back in the 1930's, they offer antiques, primitives, collectibles and commercial collectibles are their real forte.

HISTORIC HOTEL

Schumacher's *New Prague Hotel*	212 W. Main Street, New Prague, MN 56071 **Phone: 612-758-2133** Hrs: Open year-round. Restaurant, Bar and Gift Shop hours vary. Major credit cards accepted.

To arrive at Schumacher's New Prague Hotel is to step into the warmth and charm of a Central European inn. Set in a lovely Georgian revival style building, the hotel features a nationally renowned restaurant and provides personal touches that guests will fondly remember.

Superb cuisine established the hotel's reputation and owner John Schumacher's quest for excellence has resulted in a menu featuring fabulous ethnic food with an emphasis on homemade freshness. Schumacher, the hotel's executive chef, makes his creativity evident in all the restaurant's offerings. The staff of 60 prepares Czech, German and Polish sausages from Schumacher's own recipes, de-bones and dresses all meats and bakes over-size cinnamon and caramel rolls, kolacky, and rye rolls. Diners can feast on delicious entrées like sauerbraten in gingersnap sauce, wienerschnitzel, venison steak saute, creamed rabbit, pheasant in heavy cream, fresh trout with shrimp in dill sauce or the house specialty—roast duck.

Choose from two dining rooms: The Prague features 150-year-old imported Bavarian wainscotting, hand-carved chairs and Bavarian chandeliers. The Garden is equally charming with its brick fireplace and white linens. Imported Czech and German beers are available in Cully's Bar. The hotel's charming gift shop reflects Kathleen Schumacher's determination to acquire exclusive handcrafted gifts and glassware from central Europe. Furniture, lamp shades and dolls from the Menzel workshop in Bavaria create an authentic setting.

Of course, Schumacher's New Prague Hotel is more than a restaurant. Its 11 guest rooms, each styled in a unique Central European theme, feature Bavarian hand-carved furniture and lamps, original paintings and imported eiderdown comforters, pillows and linens. Overnight guests receive a complimentary half-bottle of German wine. Gas fireplaces and a private bath with whirlpool adds to the romance of this luxurious Bavarian hotel, winner of numerous awards, including being named the favorite restaurant in greater Minnesota by *Minnesota Monthly* and one of the best 10 inns in the country.

Schumacher's is a consistent winner and a wonderful choice.

NEW ULM

They call it the city of "Charm and Tradition" and the moniker is most appropriate.

Unlike many communities that spring up in a haphazard fashion, New Ulm was a carefully planned colonization venture, an idea conceived in the minds of some farsighted German immigrants who came to this region in 1848. Before settling and building, they platted a townsite dotted with park areas, market squares and public squares. Combined with the natural beauty and terrace-like elevations at the confluence of the Minnesota and Cottonwood Rivers, New Ulm is indeed a special place.

ATTRACTIONS EVENTS

A taste of Germany smack-dab in the heart of Minnesota.

That's what New Ulm was and is. And what good German city would be without its own brewery. The *August Schell Brewing Company* has long been an integral part of New Ulm. Founded in 1860 and family-operated ever since, Schell Brewing is one of the nation's most successful specialty brewers. A tour of the brewery and the *Schell Mansion* is an absolute must as is a tour of the *John Lind Home,* home of Minnesota's 14th governor.

The Glockenspiel, with its animated figures, is popular with visitors. At 45 feet high, it is one of the few free-standing carillon clocks in the world. *Hermann's Monument* is a 102-foot tall testimonial to the industriousness of early residents. Other points of interest include the *Harkin Store,* the *Doll House Museum,* the *Holy Trinity Cathedral Church* and the *Brown County Historical Museum.*

Golfers will love the 18-hole *New Ulm Country Club* while baseball fans will admire the magnificent 1,800-seat *Johnson Park. Flandrau State Park* is great for nature lovers with two campgrounds, a natural swimming pool, skiing and hiking.

The biggest and best celebration of the year is *Heritagefest,* held each July. A four-day extravaganza, it is considered one of Minnesota's top festivals. *Oktoberfest* is an all-German celebration in the fall while *Fasching,* New Ulm's own Mardi Gras, heats up the town in February. In April, the *Minnesota Festival of Music* features Minnesota music-makers of all descriptions.

For further information, contact:

New Ulm Convention & Visitors Bureau
P.O. Box 862C
New Ulm, MN 56073
Phone: 507-354-4217

Holiday Inn of New Ulm

2101 S. Broadway, New Ulm, MN 56073
Phone: 507-359-2941 or 800-HOLIDAY
All major credit cards accepted.

The Holiday Inn of New Ulm, "Home of Oktoberfest," provides its guests the finest German cuisine in New Ulm, with exceptional accommodations and meeting facilities.

Designed in a manner befitting a community known far and wide for its German heritage, the Holiday Inn is decorated in a Bavarian theme, offering a charming ambience of old Germany throughout. The hotel's accommodations include singles, doubles, king, king executive, poolside, and the famous Burgermeister Suite.

For banquet parties, the German Cafe offers informal dining for breakfast or lunch in a relaxed outdoor courtyard atmosphere. Meeting rooms and banquet facilities are available for up to 300 people. And each evening from 5-7 p.m. Monday through Thursday, complimentary cocktails are provided for hotel guests.

For breakfast, lunch, and dinner, relish fine dining in Hermann's Heidelberg and Stein where the German cuisine is authentic and the atmosphere is, too. To top off the evening, there is live entertainment and dancing in Hermann's Stein.

The Holidome Indoor Recreation Center is terrific for the whole family and includes a heated pool, whirlpool, sauna, exercise room and large game room.

While staying at the Holiday Inn of New Ulm, you will be at the heart of this wonderful city's many attractions and events. A visit to the area's Glockenspiel, Hermann's Monument, and August Schell's Brewery is a must. You can relive and celebrate New Ulm's European heritage and be sure to partake in New Ulm's Oktoberfest festivities the second and third weekends in October. Also enjoy Fasching—the German version of Mardi Gras —on the weekend before Lent.

For a memorable and affordable experience, the Holiday Inn of New Ulm offers "Gemutlichkeit," the charm, hospitality, and enjoyment of good things in life.

SPECIALTY SHOP

Lambrecht's Gift Shop and Christmas Haus

119 N. Minnesota Street, New Ulm, MN 56073. **Phone:** 507-354-4313. Hrs.: Mon. and Thurs. 9 a.m.-9 p.m., Tues., Wed., Fri., and Sat. 9 a.m.-5 p.m., Sun. noon-4 p.m. Visa, MasterCard and Discover accepted.

Lambrecht's Gift Shop and Christmas Haus offers over 8500 square feet of unique gifts from around the world and is recognized as one of the largest gift shops in the state.

Throughout the store are an assortment of greeting cards, nutcrackers, beer steins, leather goods, collector dolls, T-shirts, beautiful linens and placemats. There is a large variety of glass, crystal, china and brass. For the bride-to-be, there is a large wedding registry.

The Lambrechts are also dealers for these limited edition collectible lines: Departments 56 lighted Christmas villages, Snowbabies, All Through The House, Carin Studio Gnomes, Precious Moments, Possible Dreams Santas, Byer's Choice and porcelain dolls.

The Christmas Haus on the upper level is separated into eleven beautifully decorated rooms: the Scandinavian Room, Victorian Room, Christmas Village Room, German Christmas Room, Santa Room, and the Northwoods Room, where items like large Santa figurines, treetops, Nativity sets and nutcrackers are creatively displayed. Many more selections of gifts for the home and every occasion imaginable are available. Free gift wrapping is offered.

This attractive store also has an interesting history. It was built in 1898 as a harness shop. Numbered hooks still hang in the rafters of the basement where farmers hung their harnesses after they had been dipped in oil vats. It has been owned by several different families and evolved from the harness shop to the first gift shop in the New Ulm area. Purchased by Curt and Donna Lambrecht in 1983, it is located on the main street of New Ulm. The Christmas Shop was added to the upper level in 1988.

This is an exceptional store with many items not found in other shops. The staff is very knowledgeable, helpful and extremely friendly. Willkommen to New Ulm! There's great shopping here!

SPECIALTY SHOP

Domeiers, ***New Ulm's*** ***German Store***	(10 blocks south of downtown) 1020 S. Minnesota St., New Ulm, MN 56073 **Phone: 507-354-4231.** Hrs: Hours vary. Closed Wednesdays. Major credit cards accepted.

Like an enchanted corner of the Black Forest, Domeiers, New Ulm's German Store, somehow appears to be spirited straight from the Old Country. That's because a rich assortment of German treasures bursts from the shelves in the tiny shop and an army of bright wooden nutcrackers stand guard over it!

Hand-painted wooden Christmas ornaments, Bavarian blown glass decorations, dancing dolls, clocks, Old Country recordings and a delicious selection of marzipan, pfeffernuesse, chocolates and other sweets have attracted tourists from around the world. A foreigner's guestbook contains signatures from every continent, including dignitaries and statesmen of many European countries.

Pride and delight in her German heritage has prompted Marlene Domeier to keep the family business flourishing by purchasing rare merchandise on annual trips abroad. Started by Agatha Domeier as a neighborhood store in 1934, the combination of authenticity and warmth has kept a steady stream of customers coming.

There's even a Gnome to greet people from the shop window (unless he's hibernating at the time!). Heinz—that is, Professor Wichtel—brings good luck, good cheer and smiles as he plays German Folkmusik on his accordion. European blown glass ornaments include a rosy-cheeked forest elf sitting on a log, playing an accordion; a grinning black cat; a dour, pot-bellied gnome; and a green-and-red village chapel with a gold onion dome, its roof crusted with glitter snow. There is so much to see that visitors return again and again for new surprises. Thousands of items adorn the store, including smokers, steins, Swiss music boxes, records, tapes, greeting cards, imported cookies, candies and other food, German books and magazines, and more wonders to delight and amaze.

During festivals in the city of New Ulm, 13 flags representing the different areas in Germany color the residential street where the store has stood for more that 60 years.

Domeiers has been the subject of articles appearing in *Midwest Living, Home and Away,* and several newspapers and books. Part of a nationally televised Christmas Special was filmed there with local townspeople performing.

A trip to Domeiers is like a trip to the Old Country. Don't miss it if you go anywhere near New Ulm.

SPECIALTY SHOPS

Der Ulmer Spatz, Inc.

16 S. Broadway, New Ulm, MN 56073
Phone: 507-354-1313
Hrs: Tues.-Fri. noon-5 p.m.,
Sat. 10 a.m.-5 p.m.

A trip to New Ulm would not be complete without a stop at Der Ulmer Spatz, Inc., where you'll find the works of more than 120 artisans, each producing a unique, high quality, handcrafted item. Located just one-half block from the Brown County Historical Museum, this castle-like house intrigues tourists and locals alike.

 Visitors are sure to find something special in this unique gift and craft store. Discover original paintings, pottery, wood carvings, quilting and needlework, wheat hearts, other locally crafted gifts and unusual imports from around the world. There are many one-of-a-kind gift ideas not found anywhere else, including the famed "Ulm Sparrow." In the first two weeks of November, they hold a special Christmas Open House and fill the whole house with Christmas decorations and gifts.

Tour groups are welcome with advance notice. Gift wrapping and shipping available.

◆ ◆ ◆ ◆ ◆ ◆

Fudge and Stuff

208 N. Minnesota Street, New Ulm, MN 56073
Phone: 507-359-5272 or 800-2 FUDGE O
Hrs.: Mon. 9 a.m.-9 p.m., Tues.-Sat. 9 a.m.-5 p.m.,
Sun. 12:30 p.m.-4 p.m. Visa and MasterCard accepted.

This structure has a long and varied history with the town of New Ulm, which probably accounts for those frisky little gnomes, "Otto," "Hans" and "Fritz" who live in the basement of the building and make fresh fudge daily. This "Gnomemade Fudge" includes at least 10 varieties and is always made with the very best ingredients like real cream and butter. Of course, the gnomes will ship any combination of flavors of fudge anywhere you want because they want to make you happy!

Fudge and Stuff is a whimsical store of interesting items arranged in an imaginative way. Besides the creamiest fudge in the world,

 there's pasta, gourmet coffee, tea, herb vinegars, and a most unique selection of gifts.

Visitors also enjoy coffee, iced cappuccino, ice cream or fudge, inside or in front of the store.

SPECIALTY SHOP

Nadel Kunst, Ltd.

212 North Minnesota, New Ulm, MN 56073
Phone: 507-354-8708
Hrs.: Mon. 10 a.m.-8 p.m., Tues.-Sat. 10 a.m.-
5 p.m. Discover accepted.

Nadel Kunst loosely translates as Needle Arts Cottage, and that's just what you'll find there. It's a store that specializes in teaching and supplies for such crafts as knitting, crocheting, cross-stitch, hardanger, tatting, stamped art, klöppeln, basketry and beading.

The store stocks a full line of items including DMC and Kreinik, basket reed, imported fabrics, glass beads, ceramic buttons, crochet hooks, knitting needles and thousands of pattern books. Yarn types include mohair, angora, wool, acrylics, cotton, silks and blends, all in a full array of colors.

Cindy Hillesheim, owner of the store, offers a friendly, relaxed atmosphere. She's proud of her selection of novelty and imported fabrics for cross-stitch and hardanger.

The store gives lessons in any craft that they stock and offers free shipping for pre-paid orders.

BREWERY & TOURS

Schell's Brewing Company

Schell Park, New Ulm, MN 56073. **Phone: 507-354-5528.** Hrs: Tours Available Memorial Day-End of October. Mon.-Fri. 3-4 p.m., Sat.-Sun. 1 p.m., 2 p.m., 3 p.m. (Nov.-May) By appointment only.

If local history fascinates you, the Schell's Brewing Company should not be missed. And if you like beer, then you will be equally delighted.

August Schell, a young German immigrant, founded the brewery in 1860. Once the third largest brewery in the United States, it has remained in continuous operation at this same historic site for 130 years. Today, brothers George and Marti Schell continue the family brewing tradition.

Schell's Brewery offers a distinctive line of beer in eight varieties, an accomplishment unmatched by any other domestic brewery. Its Pilsner and crisp, citrus-tinged Weiss beers are sold across the United States and have won many national awards.

The museum exhibits original operating equipment, brewer's tools, and other interesting memorabilia. The unique gift shop offers many items bearing the Schell logo. The buildings and grounds provide visitors a true step back in time.

NORTHFIELD

Northfield likes to bill itself as the home of "Cows, colleges and contentment." It was not that way on September 7, 1876.

That was the infamous day when terror reigned on the streets of Northfield, courtesy of the famed Jesse James and the James-Younger Gang who had come to rob the First National Bank. It was the beginning of the end for one of America's most celebrated outlaws. It was also the beginning of a rich heritage that lives on in Northfield even today.

The town purposely honors the citizens, not the outlaw, each year in its annual celebration for it was Joe Heywood, a bank employee, who resisted the gang's threats and paid for it with his life, who proved to be the real hero of the day.

ATTRACTIONS & EVENTS

Today's Northfield has much to offer for residents and visitors alike. Home to not one but two outstanding universities—*Carlton College and St. Olaf College*—Northfield is a vibrant community with a host of boutiques and cafes, restaurants and bars.

The site of the bank raid, today known as the *Northfield Historical Society Bank Museum,* has been restored in fastidious detail. It is one of no less than 65 intricately carved stately buildings in the historic preservation district, a list that includes the *Archer House,* a wonderful historic hotel. *The Northfield Arts Guild Gallery* is a must for art lovers as is the *Steensland Gallery,* the *King's Room Corridor* at St. Olaf College. *Willingers Golf Club*, 10 miles west of Northfield, is one of the midwest's finest public golf facilities. *Northfield Golf Club* is no less scenic but not nearly as difficult.

Just down the road is Dundas with attractions of its own. The *Archibald Mill* on the Cannon River is listed on the National Register of Historic Places as is *Martin Oaks,* a wonderful bed and breakfast.

Of course, the *Defeat of Jesse James Days,* held just after Labor Day, is the highlight of the calendar. It regularly draws 100,000 people and is a five-day celebration that includes an arts fair, theater, a kiddie parade, carnival, grand parade and six exciting raid re-enactments that even Hollywood couldn't equal.

For further information, contact:
Northfield Convention & Visitors Bureau
P.O. Box 198
Northfield, MN 55057
Phone: 507-645-5604 or 800-658-2548

BED & BREAKFAST

Martin Oaks

107 First Street, P.O. Box 207
Dundas, MN 55019
Phone: 507-645-4644
Visa and MasterCard accepted.

Located less than one hour south of the Twin Cities, Martin Oaks Bed and Breakfast is listed on the National Register of Historical Places. Guests will find all the ambiance of bygone days at Martin Oaks, hosted by gracious owners Frank and Marie Gery.

Of course, the house is furnished with antiques and features double beds and a comfortable sitting area in each room. Enjoy the parlor

after an elegant, candlelight breakfast of waffles, egg dishes, fresh breads and hot muffins, ice cold juices, lots of wonderful hot coffee and dessert. Listen to the train rumble through town as it has for the past 125 years. Explore the gardens filled with nasturtiums, flax, lavender and mums. Or, like the resident cat, just sit on the porch, waiting for something to happen. Peace and quiet abound at Martin Oaks.

BOOKSTORE & COLLEGE

Carleton College Bookstore

One North College Street, Northfield, MN 55057
Phone: 507-663-4153. Hrs: Mon.-Fri. 8:30 a.m.-5 p.m., Saturdays 10 a.m.-2 p.m. (Sept.-June). Visa, MasterCard and Discover accepted.

Located on the campus of Carleton College, a private, highly selective four-year liberal arts college with 1,800 students and a history dating to 1866, the Carleton Bookstore occupies space on two floors in Sayles-Hill Campus Center.

"Sayles" used to be the college gymnasium before a 1979 renovation transformed it into the crossroads of Carleton, the perfect place for the Bookstore, snack bar and post office. The former basketball court is now "Great Space," recognized architecturally as a unique and innovative reuse of an existing building, and now the town square of Carleton.

Visitors will find a general book department with 15,000 titles on the first floor, the largest selection between the Twin Cities and the state of Iowa, plus magazines and art cards. The lower level (formerly the college swimming pool!) contains office supplies, personal care items, snack food and more greeting cards plus a fine selection of Carleton clothing, gifts and textbooks.

COLLEGE

Saint Olaf College	1520 Saint Olaf Ave. Northfield, MN 55057-1098 **Phone: 507-646-3002** **FAX: 507-646-3921**

Saint Olaf's 350 acre campus—considered one of the nation's most beautiful—crowns a wooded hill in Northfield. As a college of the Evangelical Lutheran Church in America, St. Olaf has maintained a firm commitment to the Gospel, challenging its 3,000 students to strive for excellence within a framework of high academic standards, Christian faith and moral sensitivities. Its mission today is to provide an education committed to the liberal arts, rooted in the Christian gospel and incorporating a global perspective.

The college is recognized nationally and internationally for its strong science, mathematics, English, economics and music programs, among others. Its students come from virtually every state and throughout the world and most are ranked among the best in their high school classes.

The National Review ranked the college among the 50 best colleges in the United States. *U.S. News and World Report* also ranks St. Olaf among "the nation's very best liberal arts colleges."

RESTAURANT

L&M Bar— *Grill—Patio*	224 Railway Street N., Dundas, MN 55019 **Phone: 507-645-8987** Hrs: Mon.-Sun. 6 a.m.-1 a.m. Sun. noon-9 p.m.

It began life rather inauspiciously as a horse barn some 114 years ago and two blocks away. But the building that today houses the L&M Bar-Grill-Patio has been serving drinks in Dundas ever since.

Now you'll find much more than just beverages (although you'll find a great selection of those) including breakfast, lunch and dinner, all at a price that's just right. Dinners include shrimp, chicken, cod or steak, all served with salad, potato or baked beans and grilled Texas toast. Fridays feature the seafood platter. Be sure and try the excellent chef's fresh salad daily while you eat in the smoke-free splendor of Marguerite's Patio. Or try the many munchies, from mozzarella sticks with pizza sauce to breaded mushrooms or the excellent fresh ground hamburgers.

For the oldest bar and the hottest grill in the area, check out L&M Bar-Grill-Patio in Dundas where good times are guaranteed. Full beverage service, game room, pull tabs and lottery.

HISTORIC HOTEL

The Archer House | 212 Division Street, Northfield, MN 55057
Phone: 507-645-5661
MN Watts 800-247-2235.
Visa, MasterCard, and AmEx accepted.

The Archer House was built in 1877 by James Archer in the French Second Empire architectural style. It was renovated in the 1980's by owners Dallas and Sandra Haas. The hotel is located in historic downtown Northfield, a bustling town on the banks of the Cannon River.

Visitors are first greeted by the casual elegance of the lobby with its amber-stained glass portal, pressed-tin ceiling, and carved winged-back chairs. This elaborate hotel captures old-fashioned, homespun graciousness in its 36 rooms. Quaint wallpapers, hand-made quilts, and dried flowers add elegance to the atmosphere. Lavish suites offer the luxury of a whirlpool and a continental breakfast is available upon request. Arrangements for conferences, banquets, or other special occasions are also available.

The first floor of the Archer House provides a haven for a variety of specialty shops and restaurants that guests and visitors alike frequent. The Tavern restaurant is located at the riverfront entrance of the Archer House, providing excellent menu selections for breakfast, lunch and dinner.

While in Northfield, stop at the Northfield Historical Society Museum located in the former Northfield Bank where in 1876 the notorious Jesse James and his gang attempted a robbery. Relive the excitement during the town's celebration dedicated to the event called, "Defeat of Jesse James Days." Northfield is rich in past glory and future promise. The historic downtown or the area parks are definitely worth a visit. Visitors enjoy biking, canoeing, fishing, and nature walks on the riverfront.

Midwestern hospitality awaits at The Archer House, where guests step into the warmth and comfort of an old country inn. It's "One of Minnesota's Oldest River Inns."

HISTORIC SOCIETY

| *Northfield Historical Society* | 408 Division Street, Northfield, MN 55057
Phone: 507-645-9268. Hrs: Tues.-Sat. 10 a.m.-4 p.m., Sun. 1-4 p.m. Closed Mondays.
Also available by appointment. |

The Northfield Historical Society is located in the Scriver Building which is situated on Bridge Square and Division Street, Northfield's main street. The First National Bank of Northfield was located in this building at the time of the attempted robbery by the James-Younger Gang on September 7, 1876.

The bank has been restored to its 1876 appearance both inside and out and is now a museum. Restoration of the 1868 vintage Scriver Building continues, as well.

The Great Northfield Bank Raid is reenacted at the bank museum several times during the Defeat of Jesse James Day celebration the weekend after Labor Day every year. Eight members of the James-Younger Gang attempted to rob the bank on September 7, 1876. The townspeople interrupted the raid and two of the Gang were shot and died in the street.

A pursuing posse killed a third member and captured the three Younger brothers. Jesse and Frank James escaped. No money was taken, but the acting cashier, Joseph Lee Heywood, was killed in the bank and another Northfield citizen died outside. Jesse James' legendary career never recovered from his Northfield defeat. Guided tours are available and admission is charged.

The museum Store is located in the Scriver Building adjacent to the bank. Books, T-shirts, gifts and souvenirs can be purchased there.

Scriver Building
Northfield Historical Society
Northfield, Minnesota

RESTAURANTS

The New *Ideal Cafe*	317 Division Street Northfield, MN 55057 **Phone: 507-645-7641** Hrs: Mon.-Sat. 11 a.m.-9 p.m.

In an era when eating establishments change as often as the weather, The New Ideal Cafe is indeed a rarity. Because food has been served in that same location now for the better part of a century. Constructed in 1873, three years before Jesse James' infamous bank robbery, the building is truly a part of Northfield's historic past.

Inside, you'll find an unusual selection of heart healthy food, from cajun chicken salad to grilled chicken sandwiches, from pasta dishes you can customize to your liking to stir fry and genuine jambalaya. And in the summer months, you can enjoy your meal in the sunshine, with sidewalk seating.

Owner Scott McMillan has created a truly eclectic emporium with everything from homemade bread to tempting desserts. It's all available for takeout, too.

Delicious specials daily and the price is right.

◆ ◆ ◆ ◆ ◆ ◆ ◆

The Ole Store	1011 St. Olaf Ave., Northfield, MN 55057 **Phone: 507-645-5558.** Hrs: Mon.-Fri. 6:30 a.m.- 2 p.m., 5 p.m.-8:30 p.m., Saturdays 8 a.m.-2 p.m., 5 p.m.-8:30 p.m., Sundays 8 a.m.-2 p.m.

Some newcomers are fooled by the name but don't be among them. The Ole Store may have started as a general store in 1889 but today, it is a terrific restaurant offering the finest in homemade breads, fresh pies from scratch and great conversation.

From its beginnings, The Ole Store evolved into a grocery and dry goods store complete with meat locker plant. The cafe was added in 1932. It hit the map with the introduction of the Ole Roll in 1950, acclaimed by the *St. Paul Pioneer-Press* as the "world famous Ole Roll" and Bob and Sue Stangler, who took over the cafe in its centennial year, have maintained the tradition of quality that has made this one of Northfield's favorite places to eat.

Since 1889

RESTAURANTS

Rueb 'N' Stein

501 Division St., Northfield, MN 55057
Phone: 507-645-4405
Hrs: Open 7 days a week 11 a.m.-1 a.m.
Major credit cards accepted.

Located in the historic Kelly Building, which dates to 1907, the Rueb 'N' Stein has been serving great food to Northfield since 1969. From their famous rueben sandwich to the soup and salad bar, Joe Grundhoefer's Rueb 'N' Stein is a local favorite.

It features a huge selection of imported and domestic beers, fine spirits and wines to go along with a menu that includes everything from corn beef sandwiches and burgers to house specialties like London Broil and charbroiled chicken breast.

In 1988, doorways were opened into the Kelly Building on either side. To the north is Grundy's Corner Bar and Grill where you'll find great sandwiches plus excellent desserts and the best burger in town. And on the south, it opens to the Henderson Building, where a big screen TV and complete game room has been added. The Upstairs continues as usual with dancing, occasional live music, a complete bar and private parties. For good food, good fun and good friends, it's the Rueb 'N' Stein.

◆ ◆ ◆ ◆ ◆ ◆

Treats, Ltd.

214 Division Street
Northfield, MN 55057
Phone: 507-663-0050
Hrs: Mon.-Fri 7 a.m.-8 p.m., Sat, Sun 8-5 p.m.

Located in the historic Archer House, Treats, Ltd. is a delicatessen and cafe providing a cosmopolitan continental atmosphere and menu selection. Treats offers specialty ethnic cuisines and authentic Indian curries. Daily specials feature hot entrées such as chicken and leek pie, steak pie, lasagna, moussaka, shepherd's pie, plus curry and pasta dishes. Bakery items include muffins, caramel rolls, croissants, baklava, scones, shortbread and much more. There is a full range of intriguing beverages that include fruit juices, beers, wines and seltzers. Stupendous desserts of French Chocolate Mousse, Black & White Espresso cake, Irish Cream bash and Tiramisu will sate the palate. Imported and domestic cheeses, meats and patés provide a tempting selection from the deli.

Treats offers everything from coffee to a banquet. For the adventurous diner and those hosting special guests, friends or colleagues, Treats, Ltd. offers superb quality and service combined with unique and exceptional cuisine.

SPECIALTY SHOP

Crystals & Wolf Gift Shoppe	414 Division Street, Northfield, MN 55057 **Phone: 507-663-7720.** Hrs: Mon. - Sun. 9 a.m.- 6 p.m. Open Thursdays until 9 p.m. Visa and MasterCard accepted.

More than just a store, Crystals and Wolf is an experience!

It seems an unusual combination but then this is an unusual store, inhabited by every manner of rock, crystal and mineral you could imagine, and by a domesticated wolf named 'Woofey'.

Actually, Woofey stays home now that Northfield's city fathers have determined he doesn't belong in town, but the crystals and the mystique surrounding them remain.

Step through the door and you'll hear music playing softly on a tape or compact disc from a delightful selection of classical, meditation and Native American flute music.

In this peaceful, calming place, you'll also find marvelously unique and unusual jewelry, gifts, cards, limited edition prints, posters and sculptures, Native American handcrafted artifacts and jewelry, including Hopi and Zuni Silver, Navajo Turquoise, Ojibwa beadworks and Lakota leather medicine pouches. An amazing array of wolf artifacts and artworks grace the shelves and walls, honoring these elusive and magnificent creatures—perhaps just a little reminiscent of Woofey's presence.

You may spend time browsing through books on ancient religions, Native American cultures and legends, spiritual and herbal healing and health, Astrology, Tarot, Gemology, children's books and even some on wilderness and backpacking! Or you may find yourself adding a new T-shirt to your wardrobe, perhaps of Native American design, or one graced with wolves, bears or earth-friendly messages.

Proprietor Beverly Rudolph has created this unusual emporium, complete with handcrafted cedar and birchwood flutes by nationally known Lakota flute maker and musician "Lakota George" Estes, half-foot-high wooden cowboys created by master woodcarver Riney Kleinhans, hand-tuned energy chimes and windchimes by J. W. Stannard, and even hand painted Russian lacquer treasure boxes.

Nestled among all of this creativity, flash rainbow light-rays of sparkling crystals, gemstones and semiprecious gems and healing stones from all over the world!

An enchanting place well worth a visit, even in Woofey's absence.

OLIVIA

If you're looking for a landmark that depicts what life in Olivia is all about, you don't have to look far. Just up. Way up. To the Giant Ear of Corn located in Memorial Park.

Yes, Olivia is Minnesota's corn capitol.

Built on the strength of agriculture and recognized as a Minnesota Star City for economic development, this town of more than 2,600 citizens is located 100 miles west of the Twin Cities and is an excellent example of the typical small farming towns that dot the landscape in this part of the world. In that way, it is a choice representative for a calm and peaceful way of life that has long existed in this region and continues to exist that way today.

ATTRACTIONS & EVENTS

If you've got something special in your neck of the woods, why not celebrate it. Sounds logical.

Well that's exactly what they do in Olivia, during a four-day celebration every summer called (appropriately enough) *Corn Capitol Days.* Held each year in late July, the festival features street dances, arts and crafts shows, parades and a free corn feed. There's also a *Junior Miss Pageant,* an aerial show, a softball tournament and a whole lot more. Another July celebration is *Polka Fest,* which takes over the town with its traditional, fun-filled music and dance.

While you're looking for the *Giant Ear of Corn,* you'll probably want to explore *Memorial Park* or the other six spacious parks in Olivia. Most feature attractive, sheltered picnic areas plus tennis courts, softball fields and basketball courts. Memorial Park also offers free overnight camping. Golf, bowling, roller skating and swimming in the indoor municipal pool located at *Olivia High School* are some of your other options.

If history is more your thing, the rather imposing *Renville County Courthouse* is a fine piece of architecture. Also check out the *St. John's Historic Church* or explore the retail center of the county and its many arts and crafts stores.

For further information, contact:
Olivia Chamber of Commerce
P.O. Box 37
Olivia, MN 56277
Phone: 612-523-1350

LODGING & RESTAURANT

The Sheep Shedde Inn

2425 West Lincoln, Olivia, MN 56277
Phone: 612-523-5000.
Hrs: Open year-round.
Major credit cards accepted.

The Sheep Shedde Inn at Olivia has a long tradition offering deluxe accommodations and superb dining for travelers. All rooms are custom decorated to provide a comfortable atmosphere and a complimentary continental breakfast will help start your day off right.

A variety of other amenities include direct dial phones, complimentary casino and airport transportation, handicapped facilities and even room service. Bridal and anniversary champagne suites are also offered.

The Sheep Shedde Restaurant, open 7 days a week, offers American cuisine at its finest. Their special prime rib is served at noon and evenings. Also, with seating for up to 400 guests, the attached meeting rooms offer excellent facilities for meetings, seminars, banquets, reunions, rehearsal dinners and weddings, or just about any group need you may require.

SPECIALTY SHOP

Cindy's Craft Chalet

Rt. 2, Box 150, Bird Island, MN 55310
Phone: 612-365-3591
Hrs: Tues.-Fri., 9:45 a.m.-5:45 p.m.,
Sat., 8:30-noon, Sun.-Mon., closed.

Cindy's Craft Chalet is an interesting store located at the east end of Bird Island on Hwy. 212 and just across the highway from the Lion's Park. You can't miss it because it's a long blue building with decorative shutters and a chalet A-frame at the doorway.

The inside is packed with hundreds of craft supplies, baskets, thousands of "how-to" books for crafters, silk flowers, frames, figurines, candles, Christmas figurines and ornaments, wooden plaques, cut-outs and paint.

The store is literally "Bursting with Goodies," an apt slogan given by owner Cynthia Dresow. Cynthia started the store in 1977 and it is now quite a testament to the success of a small town business.

They stock over 4,000 frames, 6,000 mats and enough silk flowers to design 50 weddings! They will custom design silk and dried arrangements to match or coordinate with swatches brought in by customers. They will also go to your home or office and create a framed photo or print grouping.

OWATONNA

Legend has it that Owatonna was named after the offspring of the great Dakota Chief Wabena, who brought his sickly daughter to drink the water from curing mineral springs that are now part of one of 20 city parks.

She recovered beautifully!

Perhaps there's still something in the water that makes this a special place, particularly for entrepreneurs, because many great commercial enterprises have grown up here. An international manufacturer, Josten's was founded here in 1897 by the Gainey family and is among the many going concerns that still find their home in this community of 20,000.

Federated Insurance still has its headquarters at the center of town. Others include the Owatonna Tool Company, another business of long standing, fitness manufacturer Cybex, glass fabricator Viracon, and the Truth Hardware Corporation, leaders in window hardware. Wenger Corporation is a pioneer in music equipment. Of course, there are farm equipment manufacturers like Gandy, along with a company like King, producing air handling and cooling equipment.

Out of this tremendous manufacturing base has grown a prosperous community which boasts the third-highest per capita income in Minnesota after the Twin Cities and Rochester. Such wealth has also spawned a city that cares about the arts and culture, that brags about its educational institutions and meticulously maintains a variety of green spaces.

ATTRACTIONS

It's a rarity in any town, no matter how big or small, that a bank would be the most noteworthy attraction. Yet, Louis Sullivan's 1908 architectural masterpiece, then the *National Farmer's Bank* and now the *Norwest Bank,* is an outstanding example and impeccably preserved at that, of the little-known Prairie School of architecture. This fascinating edifice is listed on the National Register of Historic Places. It and the *Adair House* are "must-sees" for architecture buffs.

Other historic sites include the Romanesque *Steele County Courthouse,* the *Union Depot* where Old Engine 202 driven by legendary Casey Jones now sits. The *Village of Yesteryear*—one of the top ten attractions in southern Minnesota—is complete with a collection of 11, mid-1800's Steele County buildings now relocated to the site and set up as an actual working village.

The *West Hills Complex,* once a state school for orphaned children, has served since the early 1970's as Owatonna's City Hall. The Romanesque structure was built in 1887 and it, too, is listed on the National Register of Historic Places. Among its features is the *Owatonna Arts Center,* the *State School Museum* and the *Sculpture Garden* as well as constantly changing displays of the works of local artists, two day-care centers, a senior center, indoor pool, gymnasium and indoor tennis courts. The West Hills Complex is also home to local theater, where the *Little Theater of Owatonna* presents an eclectic series of drama, comedy and music several times a year.

Nature lovers will be enthralled by Owatonna's 20 parks. The largest of these, the 225-acre *Kaplan's Woods Parkway,* is a natural paradise with added creature comforts that include trails for hiking, biking, jogging, cross-country skiing and in-line skating. There is also a swimming beach with fishing pier, playground and picnic area.

Among the best of the rest are *Morehouse Park,* where you can share a tranquil lunch hour with the ducks, the 38-acre *Mineral Springs Park,* where the legend of Owatonna was born, and *Rice Lake State Park,* a natural oasis just seven miles east of town.

Also located at Mineral Springs is the outstanding *Brooktree Municipal Golf Course* which, along with the highly acclaimed *Owatonna Country Club* and *Havana Hills* par-three course, make the city one of Minnesota's best for golf.

Also try the 175 miles of groomed snowmobile trails known as the *Great Southern Trails.* Owatonna has over 11 miles of groomed cross-country ski trails.

EVENTS

Central Park is the venue for *Festival of the Arts,* held each July. *The Historical Society Extravaganza* takes place in the Village of Yesteryear each July and features blacksmiths, weavers and spinners plying their traditional trades.

Also in July is the *Car Nuts Antique and Auto Show* and the *Gopher 50* stock car race. *The Steele County Fair* is held each August. Also in August is the *"I Can Fly"* event, with vintage planes, military planes, hang gliding, hot air balloons, sky diving and a pancake breakfast.

The *September Music Festival* features arts, music, booth displays, games and good food. *RPM Classic Car Race* is held in September and is a family oriented event with classic cars, the race and, of course, good food.

For further information, contact:
Owatonna Convention and Visitors Bureau
320 Hoffman Drive
Box 331, Owatonna, MN 55060
Phone: 507-451-7970 or 800-423-6466

ART CENTER

Owatonna Arts Gallery	436 Dunnell Drive, Owatonna, MN 55060 **Phone: 507-451-0533** Hrs: Tues.-Sat. 1-5 p.m., Sun. 2-5 p.m. Closed Mon. and during Aug.

The wide variety of artwork at the Owatonna Arts Center is both delightful and astonishing. Even the century-old Romanesque building housing the Center is an unexpected treasure.

The Center's main gallery features rotating exhibits of regional artists using a variety of media, while the outdoor Sculpture Garden highlights the efforts of Minnesota sculptors.

Works of music and drama are performed regularly in the Performing Arts Hall—a sound-balanced room decorated with six 12-foot stained-glass panels. This room is available for rental for receptions and recitals.

The Center also includes the Marianne Young Costume Collection of over 100 costumes from more than 25 countries. Owatonna Community Education and the Mankato State University Extended Campus often hold classes in the Center's working studios.

The Gallery Shop offers for sale the works of area artists and craftsmen.

LANDMARK

Casey Jones Locomotive and the Union Depot	655 Eisenhower Dr. Owatonna, MN 55060 Interstate 35, Exit 42A

Casey Jones Locomotive and the Union Depot are located on the property of OTC Division of SPX Corporation, a major manufacturer of vehicle special service tools, diagnostic instruments and shop equipment.

Yes! It is one of the actual engines operated by the famous Casey Jones. Old No. 201 was build in 1880, operated for 46 years in the Chicago area and was then put on exhibition for many years before finding its final home in Owatonna. Together, Casey and 201 carried more than 100,000 passengers!

Located right next to the engine is the Owatonna Union Depot, built in 1887. For ninety years, the stately depot served midwestern rail passengers and became a landmark in Owatonna.

If you have a yen for the past, there is no more romantic age than that of the railroads and the big steam engines that plied them. Here's a place where you can relive that bygone era.

RESTAURANT

| *The Kitchen, A Cedar Avenue Eatery* | 329 N. Cedar
Owatonna, MN 55060
Phone: 507-451-9991
Hrs: Mon.-Sat. 6 a.m.-9 p.m. |

If fast food has got you down, do not despair. Away from the hustle and bustle of the big city there are still those special places where the locals gather to gossip, where the home cooking is as good as Grandma's and where the price is still right. In Owatonna, that place is The Kitchen, featuring homemade soups, gravies and dressings.

Long a gathering place for the locals, The Kitchen has gained a reputation among travelers, too, largely because of its consistent quality and old-fashioned goodness. The menu is full of old-style specialties like grilled country ham steak, traditional roast beef dinner and BBQ ribs. You can also eat heart smart or grab a burger and fries before finishing with a slice of fabulous homemade pie. Or come Friday for the weekly fish fry. The Kitchen has a coffee shop-style area in front, complete with horseshoe counter, and a 60-seat dining room in the back. For a home-style atmosphere with service to match, check out The Kitchen, where happiness really is home cooking.

SPECIALTY SHOP

| *Country Treasures* | 143 W. Broadway, Owatonna, MN 55060
Phone: 507-451-6384. Hrs: Mon.-Fri. 9 a.m.-5:30 p.m., Thurs. 9 a.m.-9 p.m., Sat. 9 a.m.-5 p.m. Visa and MasterCard accepted. |

Country Treasures is an exceptionally charming gift shop filled with gifts of every shape and size. The store is designed with different display areas so clients can see how a particular item would look in their own home. The inventory is constantly changing with an influx of new merchandise arriving daily. A wide assortment of country-related items occupies the shelves, including pottery and stoneware made in Northfield. Heritage curtains and table lace provide an elegant accent for the floral designs on dis-play. Wall hangings and Amish, country, and Victorian prints are featured eye catchers. Reproduction country furniture and bath accessories including soaps and gift packages are favorite items always in stock. Minnesota-related items such as clothing, coffee cups, greeting cards, jams and jellies are included. Wicker baskets, porcelain dolls, kitchen accessories and candles complete the inventory.

CORPORATE PROFILE

Federated
Insurance
Every story has a beginning, but the story of Federated Insurance is unique because it has two beginnings.

In 1904, a small group of Minnesota businessmen, concerned about the high cost of fire insurance, decided to form their own mutual fire insurance company. Organized in New Ulm and later moved to St. Paul, the company developed financial problems after about two years of operation. In 1906 the office closed and the Minnesota Mutual Fire Insurance Company became inactive.

Meanwhile...

In 1905, a group of farm equipment dealers had organized the Minnesota Implement Dealers' Association (MIDA) to deal with the common problems they encountered in their businesses. Those problems included the high cost, and often the unavailability of fire insurance. A committee had investigated the possibility of organizing their own mutual insurance company and reported that it was, indeed, possible. MIDA members felt that selecting only loss-conscious, safety-minded members to be insured through a mutual company would result in reduced losses, thereby saving on their insurance costs.

After the governor vetoed legislation giving them the right to organize such a company, MIDA members took over the inactive Minnesota Mutual Fire Insurance Company in 1907. Fate took a strange twist at the Ryan Hotel in St. Paul where the first meeting was to be held but where no meeting room had been arranged. Mr. Charles I. Buxton, a partner in the Buxton & McClintock Implement Company in Owatonna and a charter member of the MIDA, happened to meet these men in the lobby and upon learning of their predicament, offered his room as a meeting place—a gesture that would change his entire career.

Mr. Buxton was invited to sit in on the director's first official meeting and during the meeting was elected to the board of directors. L.C. Pryor was named secretary and the company's name was changed to Retail Implement Dealers Mutual Fire Insurance Company. Immediately after the meeting, Mr. Pryor moved the home office to Minneapolis.

Mr. Buxton was asked to run the company in 1910. At first he declined as he was concerned about his responsibilities in the implement dealership. But after discussion with his partner, W.E. McClintock, Mr. Buxton decided he could take on the added responsibility as secretary of the fledgling insurance company. He moved all the company files and records, in one suitcase, from Minneapolis to Owatonna. He held the position of secretary until 1929 when he became president of the company. During this time, he also served as secretary of the MIDA.

From 1919 to 1939 the company was one of three mutual fire insurance companies in an operating partnership known as the Federal Group. In 1939 this partnership was dissolved and the Federated name began.

John A. Buxton, son of C.I. Buxton, became President in 1941 and in a bold step in 1948, made Federated the first multiple line (property and casualty) company in the United States. He became Chairman of the Board in 1951.

C.I. Buxton II, son of John A. Buxton, became president in 1957, and Chairman of the Board in 1966. Under his leadership, Federated Life Insurance and Federated Service Insurance Companies began. The total Federated organization has now grown to a leadership role in the industry and to a top 60 ranking.

Architecture

Architecture is a language written in stone, wood, metal, glass and myriad other materials, but the message speaks of the intangible. Whether communicated well or poorly, all buildings express human ideas and feelings about life.

Where are the foundations of heritage? How are courage and worthiness portrayed? What does hope for the future look like?

When Charles Buxton moved the company to Owatonna, his space requirements were minimal. After all, there was only he and one other employee.

They took space in the newly completed National Farmers' Bank building. It was commissioned by banker Carl K. Bennett, someone C.I. Buxton had known since childhood. Although the insurance business soon outgrew the space available there, Buxton became convinced that the architectural principles in the bank building reflected his own beliefs.

Designed by Louis H. Sullivan and his chief draftsman, George Grant Emslie, this Owatonna bank represented an entirely fresh vision of a purely American architecture. For Sullivan and a small but dedicated group of Midwestern architects, this style of building proudly celebrated the hardworking and independent lives of the people who brought forth unprecedented wealth from the rich earth of the prairie. In fact, the progressive buildings they designed would in time become known as Prairie architecture.

Buxton, like Sullivan, believed that architecture expressed human ideas and feelings about life. For Sullivan, a master architect often called the father of American architecture, the most important discovery to be found in the story of any building was how clearly the values and purposes of those who built it could be seen at work. Simply, he meant that through architecture, people share the meaning of their community.

Bennett introduced Buxton to architects William Gray Purcell and

George Grant Emslie, whose firm of Purcell & Emslie in Minneapolis was producing some of the finest Prairie architecture.

By 1912, Buxton had commissioned a small house or "bungalow" from Purcell & Emslie, in which he and his wife Grace raised their children and lived for the rest of their lives. A year later, longtime friend Dr. John Adair had the same architects build another, larger dwelling nearby.

During the first decade of its life in Owatonna, the company moved its offices several times, each time quickly outgrowing the new quarters. It was becoming apparent that no existing structure in the town was large enough to house the growing requirements of the business. There were two possible choices: leave town or remain in Owatonna and build a permanent structure.

In 1919, the commitment to remain in Owatonna was made. Lots in the center of town, near the Sullivan-designed bank and adjoining the house where Mr. Buxton lived as a boy, were purchased for $12,000. On April 21, the board of directors voted to erect a building on the site.

Without question, C.I. Buxton wanted a building which reflected his progressive views of architecture. Unfortunately, the architects whose works Buxton had come to admire, Louis Sullivan and Purcell & Emslie, were no longer available.

The changing conditions of American society after World War I had brought the virtual end of business for the Prairie architects. Most of these firms were either disbanded or were responding to the demand for classical, European-styled buildings.

Buxton turned to two local men, David L. Jacobson and his brother Nels, who had only recently returned to Owatonna from studies at the University of Pennsylvania. Perhaps it was because they were from the same Midwestern background that they could so clearly understand the goals Mr. Buxton wanted to achieve.

The new Home Office for the company was ready for preliminary occupancy at the end of 1922, at a cost of $200,000. During the dedication ceremony in June of 1923, Nels Jacobson recognized Louis Sullivan and his principles of design as the inspiration for the building. The result was acknowledged a triumph and the building, though somewhat altered in form, stands today as one of the last major examples of Prairie architecture to have been built in the Upper Midwest.

In the 1920's, the new home of the Minnesota Implement Mutual Fire Insurance Company was one of the most complete office buildings in the United States. Adhering to Sullivan's "form follows function" concept of architecture, the features of the building combined utility with comfort and beauty.

The unique features include an exterior facade of Indian Bedford stone and oriental brick, polychrome clay fired tiles lavishly displayed above the main entrance, hand-molded terra-cotta, an agricultural mural in the entryway and a three-story hall featuring marble, ornamental wrought iron and a leaded glass skylight forty-one feet above the floor.

The John A. Buxton building was added in 1968 and the Charles I. Buxton II building built in 1985, both complementing the beauty of the original. Federated currently occupies almost 500,000 square feet in the city of Owatonna, employing 1,000 people there and another 1,700 at various locations throughout the United States, including division offices in Atlanta and Phoenix.

PIPESTONE

An intriguing combination of Native American heritage and Midwestern farm culture makes Pipestone unlike any other town. For centuries, Native Americans quarried the soft, red stone found here and fashioned it into ceremonial pipes. Tribes from across the country coveted the stone, thus making the Pipestone area one of the last pieces of Minnesota land to be ceded to white settlement. The city was officially founded by settlers Daniel Sweet and Charles Bennett in 1876, 40 years after noted artist George Catlin visited the area and spread the story about the quarry around the world.

ATTRACTIONS & EVENTS

The major attraction in Pipestone is, without doubt, the renowned *Pipestone National Monument.* The monument includes a fascinating culture center exploring Native American heritage of the area as well as the art of pipemaking plus a visitors' center with interpretive displays, films and other information. Try the beautiful, 3/4 mile circle tour past quarries, waterfalls and the fantastic Sioux quartzite stone formations. Near the entrance to the national monument is a pioneer fort replica of *Fort Pipestone. The Pipestone County Museum* features local history exhibits, as well as an impressive Native American exhibit and an extensive collection of paintings by George Catlin. The county museum is located in the old *City Hall* which, along with the *Calumet Hotel,* the magnificent *Pipestone County Courthouse* and 17 other buildings, forms the Pipestone Historic District. Most district buildings are built with hand-hewn Pipestone quartzite and all are listed on the National Register of Historic Places. The new *Pipestone Center for the Performing Arts* is constructed of Sioux quartzite and boasts a "state of the art" theater.

Watertower Festival in June features a huge art and craft show, ethnic foods, sidewalk sales, and a street dance. The top event of the summer is the July *"Song of Hiawatha" Pageant. The Civil War Festival* in August is a celebration in a truly historic setting. The final event each season is the *Festival of Trees.* Starting after Thanksgiving, it features a large number of decorated Christmas trees, sleigh rides, antique toy displays and more.

For further information, contact:
Pipestone Chamber of Commerce
P.O. Box 8, Pipestone, MN 56164
Phone: 507-825-3316

HISTORIC HOTEL

Days Inn *Historic Calumet*	104 W. Main, Pipestone, MN 56164 **Phone: 507-825-5871 or 1-800-535-7610** Hrs: Open year-round Major credit cards accepted.

The Days Inn Historic Calumet is located in one of the largest historic districts in Minnesota. Originally built in 1888, this exquisitely decorated hotel is a three-star, three-diamond hotel facility and is listed on the National Register of Historic Places. There are 38 rooms that are richly designed to provide the utmost in comfort and charm for each guest. The original Victorian furnishings come from period mansions in Louisiana, Boston and England.

In addition to the attraction of the hotel itself, The Days Inn Historic Calumet hosts the Pipestone Festival of Trees each year. This festival starts after Thanksgiving and runs through New Year's. This has been rated one of the best 25 annual festivals in the state, featuring sleigh rides, music and dinners. The nearby Performing Arts Center offers a wide variety of entertainment.

The hotel restaurant serves some of the best meals in the area. House specialties include the seafood platter, prime rib and fresh Canadian walleye pike. The mouthwatering steaks served are hand-cut from certified Angus beef. Tasty lunches are also served, highlighting a different dish daily. The gift shop in the hotel features handmade Native American crafts, including pipes made from stone taken out of the local pipestone quarries. Pipestone is a wonderful and friendly community. Visiting this historic town is like taking a step back in time.

INTERPRETIVE CENTER & GIFTS

Fort Pipestone

104 Ninth Street N.E., Pipestone, MN 55164. **Phone: 507-825-4474.** Hrs.: (May 15 - Aug. 15) Mon -Sat. 9 a.m.-9 p.m. (Aug. 16 - Sept. 30) Mon.-Sat. 9 a.m.-7 p.m.; Sun. 10 a.m.-8 p.m. Visa and MasterCard accepted.

The settlers' era lives on at Fort Pipestone, replica of an historic Minnesota fort. The original fort was built as a refuge from the 1862 Sioux uprising. Today, the fort carries gifts and souvenirs reminiscent of century-old times.

Upon entering, visitors can't help notice the authentic mounted trophy-size buffalo head. Less intimidating items include Indian-style gifts and souvenirs. Minnetonka moccasins, Minnesota-grown wild rice, and Carlson dolls are all famed Minnesota originals available here. Replicas of Indian bows and arrows, hand-painted shields, and Man-del-las interest visitors. Hand-painted buffalo and cow skulls are available, too.

Enjoy a beautiful selection of Navajo and Zuni turquoise and silver jewelry. Authentic Indian-made baskets and pottery thrill souvenir shoppers. Craft-making demonstrations are scheduled throughout the season, as are buffalo feeds, which feature grilled or barbecued buffalo as the main entrée.

LODGING

Arrow Motel

RR 1, Box 212, 600 8th Ave. NE
Pipestone, MN 56164
Phone: 507-825-3331
Major credit cards accepted.

The Arrow Motel offers travelers clean, quiet rooms, a friendly welcome and a good night's rest. That's because it's located away from the downtown noise and is hosted by people who really care about their guests.

The Arrow offers 16 comfortable rooms—double, single or triple; smoking or non-smoking. Rooms have cable color TV, touch tone phones, soft water and air conditioning.

They have a gift shop featuring Native American items and a conference room is available for meetings or parties seating up to 25. A continental breakfast is served each day consisting of good hot coffee, juice and rolls, plus hot chocolate in the winter.

Attractions near the Arrow Motel include: Pipestone National Monument, Pipestone County Museum, historic sites, Harmon Park, the Pipestone Golf Course and Fort Pipestone.

LODGING

Super 8 Motel

Corner of Hwys. 23, 30 & 75
605 8th Ave. SE, Pipestone, MN 56164
Phone: 507-825-4217
FAX: 507-825-4219

This modern Super 8 Motel is located in the midst of ancient tradition and mystery. Here, countless Indian ceremonies of the sacred pipestone played themselves out against the big prairie sky.

Today, visitors are greeted by a friendly smile at the motel, with 39 comfortable guest rooms, all with telephones and color remote-control TV's. The rooms feature either one queen size bed or two full extra-long beds.

No pet, non-smoking rooms are available upon request and pets are allowed with permission and a $20 refundable deposit. For the convenience of guests, a washer and dryer are available. Each day complimentary coffee is available at the front lobby.

Located next to the motel is a fine steakhouse, restaurant and lounge. In the summer, visitors enjoy the city tennis court, swimming pool and park located across the street.

RESTAURANT

Gannons Restaurant and Lounge

Junction Hwy. S., 23, 30 & 75
Pipestone, MN 56164
Phone: 507-825-3114

There's lots of options at Gannons in Pipestone because they offer a coffee shop, a sports bar and a steakhouse lounge. The coffee shop is open daily at 6 a.m. and serves breakfast anytime. Menu items range from burgers and steaks to salad and chicken. They have five varieties of chicken breast sandwiches! A specialty is their homemade soups like chicken dumpling. It's served up hot and delicious each Thursday. Homemade pies round out the full menu.

The steakhouse is open at noon weekdays with a buffet luncheon. Evenings feature some of the finest steaks you'll ever taste, charbroiled to your taste. Other temptations include slow cooked Bar-B-Q ribs with their own special sauce, fresh walleye, orange roughy, crab and scallops for seafood lovers, and several varieties of chicken.

Want to catch a sporting event or test your luck at a game of pool? Try the sports bar with three large TV screens, pool tables, darts and video games. The sports bar opens at noon daily and Gannons does have Sunday liquor.

REDWOOD FALLS

Incorporated as a village in 1876 and as a city in 1891, Redwood Falls is located in an area that was opened to settlers in 1851 after the government signed a treaty with resident Dakota Sioux Indians. The history of Redwood Falls is also influenced by several colorful figures including Army Colonel Sam McPhail, an opportunist with varied skills who financed the entire county of Redwood for a period of two years while the county government was being organized.

ATTRACTIONS & EVENTS

Visit the fascinating *Redwood County Museum,* housed in the 1908 former poor farm, and enjoy hundreds of relics, photos, tools, machinery and much, much more. For more Native American history, don't miss the *Lower Sioux Agency Interpretive Center* and the *Lower Sioux Pottery Workshop and Retail Outlet.*

The main attraction in Redwood Falls, however, is not a historical site, but the magnificent *Alexander Ramsey Park*—nestled in the heart of the Minnesota River Valley where the Redwood River and Ramsey Creek meet. As Minnesota's largest municipal park and affectionately known as "the Little Yellowstone of Minnesota," Ramsey Park sports 217 acres of hiking trails, campground, picnic areas, vita course and the Ramsey Park zoo.

Redwood Falls plays host to the nation's oldest and most successful inventors fair, the *Minnesota Inventors Congress,* held during the second weekend in June. If your interests include arts and crafts, visit Redwood Falls the first Saturday of October for *Old Fashioned Fall Festival,* one of the finest arts and crafts fairs in the area.

The Redwood Falls area is also proud to be the present home of *FarmFest,* a huge three day extravaganza held yearly on the first Tuesday, Wednesday, and Thursday of August. FarmFest is a colorful celebration of agriculture held at the historic *Gilfillan Estate,* which was recently taken possession by the historical society with the goal of establishing a "living history farm."

For further information, contact:
Redwood Falls Chamber of Commerce
Redwood Falls, MN 56283
Phone: 507-637-2828

ANNUAL EVENT & WORKSHOP

Minnesota Inventors Congress	1030 East Bridge St., P.O. Box 71, Redwood Falls, MN 56283. **Phone: 507-637-2344 or 800-468-3681 (MN)** Hrs: Mon.-Fri. 8 a.m.-5 p.m.

Each year, over 10,000 visitors from around the world travel to Redwood Falls to view the hundreds of inventions on display at the Minnesota Inventors Congress' convention. Manufacturers, marketers, inventors, licensees seeking new products and people who are fascinated by innovative ideas wouldn't think of missing this annual event the second full weekend in June.

The convention begins on Thursday with an inventor's workshop focusing on successful invention management, including licensing and marketing. The world's oldest annual invention convention, open Friday through Sunday, allows visitors to view the inventions and provides inventors a common meeting ground with business resources, publicity, seminars and one-on-one consultations on invention development.

The convention includes activities for everyone...

The MIC Marketplace features successful inventions from previous years for sale;

K-12th grade students showcase their inventions at the Minnesota Student Inventors Congress;

Display and induction ceremony of the Minnesota Inventors Hall of Fame and,

Various community events—parade, Pow Wow, arts and crafts.

When the MIC isn't hosting its annual convention, it is serving inventors worldwide through its Inventors Resource Center (IRC). The IRC provides helpful literature, educational seminars and workshops, referrals to businesses, a "hotline" for invention-related guidance, and much more. These services are offered year-round.

Some of the inventions developed with MIC's assistance have given birth to new companies, new jobs and handsome profits for inventors and investors alike. Here's a look at just a sampling:

● Gripper—device to secure rope without tying a knot. Sold over 1 million internationally.

● Rolite Trailer—$3 million idea that was the beginning of the fold-down camper-trailer industry.

● Quad cane—four-pronged cane led to development of rehabilitation company employing 40.

● Nada-Chair (Back Sling)—legless chair for perfect posture and back support with annual sales over $2 million.

BED & BREAKFAST

Stanhope Bed & Breakfast

RR 4, #14, Redwood Falls, MN 56283-9310
Phone: 507-644-2882
Hrs: Check in by 6 p.m. Check out at 10 a.m.
Credit cards not accepted.

Nestled in a beautiful valley amidst the serenity of country life is the Stanhope B&B. Here, a cordial welcome awaits each visitor and quiet, restful bedrooms invite guests to relax and enjoy. The living room even has a baby grand piano, where you can play your favorite tunes. You can commune with the natural setting of the Minnesota River Valley just outside the front gallery or enjoy the old-fashioned kitchen with fireplace, TV and VCR. Stroll outside in season and enjoy a mini-fruit orchard, flower gardens or the nearby woods. There is an Arabian in the south pasture and if you're up early enough, perhaps

you'll see a family of deer grazing there, too! A continental breakfast is served and includes toast, rolls, coffee and tea, juice, jams and cereals. Evening beverages are served, as well.

SPECIALTY SHOP

Geri's Palace

230 S. Washington
Redwood Falls, MN 56283
Phone: 507-637-3023

Geri Dahmes is a certified ceramicist, qualifications that have made Geri's Palace in downtown Redwood Falls a pleasant haven for many in the area and for visitors, too.

Hundreds of her unique creations line the aisles in this spacious store. Geri provides custom work when asked, teaches ceramics classes, and maintains a product line of Duncan paints and supplies for those who prefer supplying much of the personal touches themselves. There's more to Geri's Palace than ceramics, however. She also travels around the state to numerous locations to market her unique resin figurines, button covers, woodworking, board paintings and other special doo-dads for your decorating enjoyment. Additional literature can be obtained by requesting Geri's catalog. Just give her a call and she will send one out to you.

Geri also puts particular care into satisfying custom orders for special events and occasions; her one-of-a-kind pieces reflect the personal touch often lacking in franchised gift shops.

LODGING

Dakota Inn Motel	410 West Park Road Redwood Falls, MN 56283-1416 **Phone: 507-637-5444 or 1-800-287-5443**

Strategically located in the heart of "Dakota" country is the Dakota Inn Motel. "Dakota" means friend and that's just what you can expect here. The spacious 120 room motel welcomed its 100,000th guest in 1993, after only 26 months of operation!

Visitors come from far and wide to visit the Redwood Falls area and, when they do, many stay at the Dakota Inn Motel. That's because the Inn offers free HBO and ESPN, pool and jacuzzi, and a free shuttle to Jackpot Junction Casino, the area's Indian gaming mecca. Mini-suites are offered with special amenities including a refrigerator. A free gaming package to the casino is also offered. The Jackpot Junction Casino is open 24 hours and offers entertainment, restaurants, a gift shop, convenience store and a new bingo hall.

Snowmobilers especially like the Dakota Inn Motel because of 120 miles of groomed trails in the area. But, if you don't snowmobile or gamble, there's a host of other activities to be enjoyed by one and all.

Of course, Alexander Ramsey Park, located in Redwood Falls, is 217 acres of all-season, wooded beauty. The city of Redwood Falls holds its annual Old Fashioned Fall Festival in October, a unique collection of hand-made crafts, art, antiques and a farmer's market. It's a fun tradition that even has live entertainment.

Visitors to the area also enjoy an outdoor Nativity Pageant in December put on in the local community of Springfield, Minnesota.

The area is home to a rich Indian heritage, as well. Travelers enjoy visiting the Lower Sioux Agency and Interpretive Center. The Center provides visitors with an introduction to the history of this site and the cultural differences that led to one of the largest battles between European settlers and the Native Americans of this country. Don't forget to visit the trading post, offering many beautiful items crafted by native peoples.

This area is also home to Farmfest, an annual extravaganza dedicated to agriculture and the family farm.

There are many other historical sites in the area, as well. The Redwood County Museum houses many historic treasures, not the least of which is the Sears room honoring Richard Sears who started the famous mail-order business in North Redwood.

Whatever your reason for visiting this interesting area, be sure to stay at Dakota Inn Motel. You'll love the Dakota—friendly area, the heart of Sioux country!

SPECIALTY SHOP

A&W Furniture and Gifts

1501 E. Bridge, Redwood Falls, MN 56283
Phone: 507-644-3535. Hours: Mon.-Sat. 9 a.m.-
5 p.m., Thurs. 9 a.m.-8 p.m.
Visa, MasterCard and Discover accepted.

A&W Furniture and Gifts is a unique store and the talk of the area around Redwood Falls. It's a store so big, you'll need a map to find your way around! It's 1 1/2 acres under one roof with the largest selection of oak furniture in the upper midwest, including dining, bedroom and occasional furniture.

The owners, Mary Ahrens and Bob Wetmore, show in their selections a true love of the business. Mary was formerly an English teacher and Bob was a farmer. (Mary's family has been residents of the area for 132 years!) Obviously, the career changes resulted in an interesting and thriving business.

The huge furniture store also houses "Beaver Falls Mercantile," the gift store. Here, owners Bob and Mary have carefully selected unique and beautiful decorating accessories. They have original floral arrangements by Robin Even, collectible gifts like Terry Redlin plates and a year-round Christmas area with lots of interesting items. This store draws buyers from the five-state region.

A&W Furniture provides in-home consulting for decorating needs and they ship everywhere in the U.S.

Jackpot Junction casino is a mere 5 miles away. The Redwood Falls City Park is home to the largest municipal park in the state, with 200 acres of beauty and the famous Ramsey Falls.

The coffee pot is always on at A&W Furniture and they welcome visitors with lovely taped music. Some customers stay all day! With all that amount of space and inventory, there's bound to be something for everyone on your gift list, even yourself!

SPECIALTY SHOPS

Books and Gifts of Joy

231 East Second Street, Redwood Falls, MN 56283. **Phone: 507-637-3732** Hrs: Mon.-Sat. 9 a.m.-5:30 p.m., Thurs. 9 a.m.-8 p.m. Visa and MasterCard accepted.

Half a block from Highways 19 and 71, in the Armory Square Mall, is the Books and Gifts of Joy store. It's a wonderful store that is light, clean, homey and offers a great selection of books and gifts.

Many visitors like the inspirational books which abound in the store, as do general titles, children's books and many others. Or, shoppers come to find that special gift for a child, a friend, or for themselves!

The store offers contemporary, classical and religious CD's and tapes, as well. They will special order a book for you using a computer data base with over 1.5 million titles. And they will ship books and gifts anywhere.

So, whether you're passing through on your way to Jackpot Junction or stopping to see the magnificent Alexander Ramsey Park, be sure to make a stop at this interesting store filled with the best kind of treasures—books and gifts!

◆ ◆ ◆ ◆ ◆ ◆ ◆

Simple Pleasures

Armory Square Mall, 231 E. Second Street, Redwood Falls, MN 56283. **Phone: 507-637-5270.** Hrs: Mon.-Fri. 9:30 a.m.-5 p.m., Sat. until 4 p.m. Visa, MasterCard and Discover accepted.

Simple Pleasures is co-op owned and operated by members who specialize in and are knowledgeable about a specific craft. Its wide selection of craft and gift items will satisfy most needs, ranging from the budget-minded to the extravagant. Items include wood or cloth bunnies, pigs and dolls, candles of varied shapes, sizes and colors, nostalgic tin signs, doilies, stoneware, canisters, accent pieces, painted resin figures, pins and buttoncovers, a large selection of brass items, Austrian crystal, rainforest butterflies, windchimes, masks, Dreamsicles and collectibles and more.

The quality of the merchandise is very high. The store is bright and well lit, the sound of chimes greets you and the smell of potpourri is unmistakable as you enter Simple Pleasures.

ST. PETER

Life in St. Peter could be very different today if not for an unusual twist of history. Destined to become the state capitol of Minnesota, the bill that would have implemented that change in 1857 was prevented from receiving the governor's signature by a renegade politician named Joseph Roulette. Concerned it would be too far to travel from his Pembina home in what is today North Dakota, he hid out in a St. Paul hotel with the bill in hand until the signing deadline had passed.

Still, St. Peter, whose original name was Rock Bend, has had an inordinate amount of influence on the politics of Minnesota anyway. No less than five governors have come from here. It has also had a real impact in health and education, thanks to the success and reputation of Gustavus Adolphus College and the Minnesota State Hospital.

ATTRACTIONS & EVENTS

With so many interesting people having come from St. Peter, the town is ripe for history buffs.

The Julian Cox House, for example, was home of St. Peter's first mayor who later became a county representative and state senator. It is maintained by the *Nicollet County Historical Society* which also has a *Museum* containing more than 3,000 objects including artifacts from the local Sioux uprising in the 1860s. *The Regional Treatment Center Museum* traces the history of the first psychiatric treatment facility in Minnesota. The *St. Peter Arts and Heritage Center* is also worth visiting as is the *Nicollet House.*

St. Peter has eight city parks built on 650 acres. Most have picnic facilities, playgrounds, ball fields and rest rooms. *Shoreland Country Club* offers 18 holes of golf. *The North Star Summer Theatre* features professional comedy productions at *Gustavus Adolphus College* where you'll also find the *Minnesota Valley Sommerfest* and its classical performances in July and the *Nobel Conference* in October attended by scholars from around the world. *Christmas in Christ Chapel,* a Scandinavian music festival, is another special event on the campus. And music of a different type is featured during the *Rock Bend Folk Festival* each September.

For further information, contact:
St. Peter Area Tourism and Visitors Bureau
101 S. Front Street
St. Peter, MN 56082   Phone: 800-473-3404

ANTIQUES

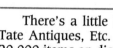

Tate Antiques, Etc.	817 N. Minnesota, St. Peter, MN 56082 **Phone: 507-931-5678** Hrs.: Mon.-Sat. 9 a.m.-8 p.m., Sun. 10 a.m.- 5 p.m. Visa and MasterCard accepted.

There's a little bit of antique collecting in everyone's blood and Tate Antiques, Etc. has something for everyone. The store has over 20,000 items on display and always offers a new selection.

Located in a new building in historic St. Peter, Tate Antiques, Etc. features a diversity of items including furniture, glassware, advertising material, collectibles, china, crocks, pictures and more.

They will buy almost anything that is old, from entire estates and collections to individual pieces. They also feature reproduction furniture hardware, Aladdin lamp parts and collector books. If you like to browse for antiques or just look for some remembrance from a childhood past, definitely stop at Tate Antiques, Etc.

BED & BREAKFAST

Engesser House	1202 S. Minnesota St., St. Peter, MN 56082 **Phone: 507-931-9594 or 800-688-2646** Hrs: Check-in 4 p.m. - 6 p.m. Or by arrangement. Check- out 11:30 a.m. Visa and MasterCard accepted.

Built in 1880 by brewer Joseph Engesser, the Engesser House is today a charming bed and breakfast, offering the elegance and tranquility of an earlier time complete with all the modern touches.

Innkeepers Julie and Chuck Storm have created a wonderful eclectic setting, a blend of antiques and contemporary furnishings and their own art collection, all set in a lovely Victorian atmosphere with original walnut woodwork, stained glass and a carved black walnut fireplace. Choose from four rooms, from the cozy peaches and pastels of Anne's Room to the walnut antiques and canopy king-sized bed in the Governor's Suite, all with private baths.

A large formal dining room welcomes you with homemade breads, a delightful choice of either full or "quick start" breakfast weekdays, a country breakfast Saturdays and a sumptuous Sunday repast. The Engesser House has a wine license, too. Stay in touch with the real world with computer, copier and fax machine available for guests, plus TV-VCR, video and paperback libraries.

BED & BREAKFAST

Park Row Bed & Breakfast	525 W. Park Row, St. Peter, MN 56082 **Phone: 507-931-2495** Hrs: Open Feb. 1-Dec. 31

Park Row Bed & Breakfast is a beautiful Victorian home in a picturesque setting with four charming rooms. The English Room and the French Room downstairs share one bath. The German Room and the Scandinavian Room are upstairs and share a second bath. The decor of these rooms reflects the 1870's, the era of the home's construction. Large windows look out upon the charming city of St. Peter.

In the morning, guests are greeted by a homemade breakfast prepared by owner Ann Burckhardt who is also a food writer. The hot and hearty breakfast includes blended fruit juice, an egg dish, hot bread, a fruit dessert and all the hot coffee you can handle. Newlyweds are always served breakfast in bed. A cozy retreat close to the Twin Cities, Park Row is close enough for comfort.

BOOKSTORE

The Book Mark	Gustavus Adolphus College, 800 College Ave., St. Peter, MN 56082. **Phone: 507-933-7587** Hrs: Mon.-Fri. 8:30 a.m.-4:30 p.m. (Spring and fall semesters) Sat. 10 a.m.-1 p.m. Visa, MasterCard and Discover accepted.

The Book Mark is located on the campus of Gustavus Adolphus College. It has occupied several different places throughout the years but has remained in its Student Union location since 1960. In 1972 a contest was held to find a distinctive name, thus "The Book Mark" was dubbed.

All the required and recommended textbooks and supplies for classes can be found here as well as a large selection of general books. A large selection of adult books and children's titles are also offered.

Books with regional and Scandinavian titles also line the shelves, offering a complete history of the area and its roots. Gift and card items and a variety of college imprinted clothing round out the inventory. The King and Queen of Sweden have managed to make several stops at the college—chances are they couldn't resist taking home a souvenir for themselves!

SPECIALTY SHOP

Mary Lue's At The Woolen Mill

101 West Broadway, St. Peter, MN 56082
Phone: 507-931-3702
Hrs.: Mon.-Sat. 9 a.m.-5 p.m. Most Sundays
noon-4 p.m. Most major credit cards accepted.

The Brinker family continues the tradition of four generations in the woolen mill business, specializing in manufacturing custom-made comforters and wool mattress pads. The St. Peter Woolen Mill is believed to be the first in Minnesota and the oldest business in St. Peter, providing custom wool carding services for the last 127 years. This mill is one of about five of its kind in the country.

Mary Lue's Knitting World has an extensive selection of hand and machine knitting yarns not often found today. They carry a large variety of supplies for other handcrafts such as cross-stitch, needlepoint and quilting. Knitting machines, weaving looms and spinning wheels are also available.

You won't want to miss the unique experience of their gift shop, "Sheep Delights," with one of the largest collections of sheep items you'll ever see. Treasures of all kinds for children and adults are on display. You'll find woolen blankets, jackets, socks and hats, stuffed animals and baby gifts, figurines, collectibles and music boxes, prints and cards, afghans and much more.

After a tour of the mill, visitors should explore the town. Rich in historic heritage, St. Peter is often referred to as the "Williamsburg of the Midwest" for its prominent preservation of colonial homes and churches with 13 sites on the National Historic Register.

SPECIALTY SHOPS

| *Chameleon Connection Craft Supplies and Gifts* | 308 S. Minnesota Avenue, St. Peter, MN 56082
Phone: 507-931-4910
Hrs: Mon. & Thurs 9 a.m.-8 p.m., Tues., Wed.,
Fri. 9 a.m.-5:30 p.m., Saturdays 9 a.m.-5 p.m. |

Housed in a turn-of-the-century building in downtown St. Peter, the Chameleon Connection has everything crafters need to create their special projects. They also have many custom made gifts.

They pride themselves on their commitment to customers and on that personal touch that's not always easy to find. Chameleon Connection features everything from dried flowers to beads, paints, stencils, craft books, wreaths, small wood parts, creative twists and friendly plastics. They have a full line of Fimo and Sculpey clays, plus all the necessities for making unique jewelry.

They also have a great staff committed to helping you find just what you need for your special project.

Classes are offered Saturday mornings and Monday evenings and special orders are always welcome. The chameleon may change constantly but the commitment to customers does not at the Chameleon Connection.

Handicapped accessible. Front and rear parking.

◆ ◆ ◆ ◆ ◆ ◆

| *Swedish Kontur Imports* | 310 S. Minnesota Avenue, St. Peter, MN 56082-0127
Phone: 507-931-1198. Hrs: Mon., Tues., Wed.,
Fri., 9 a.m.-5:30 p.m., Thurs. 9 a.m.-8 p.m., Sat.
9 a.m.-5 p.m., Sun. noon-4 p.m.
Visa, MasterCard and Discover accepted. |

Since its opening in 1962, Swedish Kontur Imports has held the distinction of being the oldest Scandinavian gift shop in all of Minnesota. Located in St. Peter, it is a gift-giver's delight featuring only the highest quality imports from Scandinavia.

Swedish Orrefors and Kosta Boda crystal is known the world over and is a treasure as a gift for that special someone or as a gift to oneself. Dansk dinnerware is the perfect wedding gift and can be found in abundance at Swedish Kontur Imports. Sterling silver jewelry from Denmark and Norway are also on display for a more personal gift selection.

Christmas ornaments and Brio toys bring an Old World quality to the holiday season. Scandinavian jams and ginger cookies are tempting treats year-round and are extra tasty when accompanied by the imported Swedish coffee.

All of the items in Swedish Kontur Imports are authentic and add a special touch to every gift given.

SPECIALTY SHOP

St. Peter
Food Co-op

Hwy. 169, St. Peter, MN 56082
Phone: 507-931-4880
Hrs: Mon.-Sat. 8 a.m.-8 p.m.,
Sun. 9 a.m.-7 p.m.

Not just another grocery store, the St. Peter Food Co-op is a grocery store with a mission.

That mission is to promote the health, dignity and well-being of all. It's a rather lofty goal but one that is achieved through cooperation with customers, members and the environment.

Grocery selection includes fresh produce plus bulk and packaged foods. They offer foods that are natural or organic as well as various international and gourmet items.

But the St. Peter Food Co-op is more than just a grocery store. Located within the co-op is the Sandwich Shop. It features a complete deli with delightful meals, beverages and snacks.

Shopping here is a unique experience. Whether you're after a fast yet healthy meal or it's time to replenish your kitchen's grocery supply, explore the St. Peter Food Co-op.

RESTAURANT

Holiday House

Hwy. 22 South, St. Peter, MN 56082. **Phone: 507-931-4654.** Hrs: Mon.-Thurs. 11 a.m.-9 p.m., Fri.-Sat. 11 a.m.-10 p.m., Sun. 10:30 a.m.-9 p.m. Visa and MasterCard accepted.

Perhaps it's the fine food. Maybe it's the splendid setting. More than likely, it's a combination of the two that has kept people coming back again and again to the Holiday House in St. Peter.

Set in a Japanese Garden with water fountain, where you can see the river if you look out the window, Holiday House features a terrific lunch buffet Monday through Friday from 11 a.m. to 2 p.m. Dinner begins at 4 p.m., 2 p.m. on Sundays, and is equally good, with entrées like walleye and "House" shrimp complemented by "House" pasta. Or try the herb grilled chicken breast or your choice of steaks from filet mignon to club steak. Finish with a hot cappuccino or a drink in the lounge.

The Holiday House also serves a Sunday brunch from 10:30 a.m. to 2 p.m. With the soothing sounds of an baby grand player piano in the background, the atmosphere is excellent. Banquet facilities are available along with small private rooms.

This is a "must stop" in St. Peter.

SHERBURN

Sherburn is a proud city that many visitors have enjoyed over the years. Hunters know it as a place for excellent goose, duck and pheasant hunting. (More than 5,000 geese winter there each year.) Fisherman go to Fox Lake, 1/4 mile north of the city, for walleye, bass, crappie and northern fishing. Many have enjoyed the fine businesses in Sherburn.

The city is located on I-90. In fact, if you're going to Minneapolis from Sioux Falls, there is a shortcut at Sherburn. Take Highway 4 to 169, then go north for a great drive.

ATTRACTIONS & EVENTS

The city's historic main street has fifteen buildings listed on the *National Register of Historic Places.* The buildings were all built in the late 1800's and early 1900's. Also, Sherburnites tell of *The White Squaw of Fox Lake,* a Romeo and Juliet type true story about a lost love, an attempt at suicide and then a life with an Indian chief.

Sherburn offers a variety of activities and events for all visitors. Camping, dining, golfing, swimming, tennis, snowmobiling and cross-country skiing are a few of the activities enjoyed by both residents and visitors. The Sherburn *"Pig Patch Daze"* in September celebrates Martin County's claim to the largest corn and hog area in Minnesota. Many events fill the day including a car show.

Former *astronaut Dale Gardner,* who travelled in space aboard both "Challenger" and "Discovery" shuttles, claims Sherburn as his birthplace and early boyhood home. In fact, the *Dale A. Gardner Aerospace Museum and Learning Center* is located there. The center has numerous artifacts on display including Dale Gardner's flight suit from a Discovery flight, space tiles from a Challenger mission and many videos describing the NASA Space Program. Other displays include a heat shield and model rocket collection. The center has become a teaching resource center for education. A recently acquired "starlab" enhances visitors' understanding of space, stars and planets.

For further information, contact:
Sherburn Area Chamber of Commerce
Box 108-A
Sherburn, MN 5617-0108
Phone: 507-764-2607

BED & BREAKFAST

4 Columns Inn

Rt. 2, Box 75
2 miles N. of I-90
Sherburn, MN 56171
Phone: 507-764-8861

Built as a guest house in 1884 and reconstructed to suit the needs of a 20th century Inn, this very popular bed & breakfast serves its guests in charming country style. Hosts Norman and Pennie Kittleson offer four antique filled rooms. A hideaway Bridal Suite on the third floor features a pulldown entrance to the roof! You can relax in the Walnut Paneled Den as you sit in front of the fireplace. Or, you may go to the Music Room and listen to 45's played on a 1950's Seeburg jukebox, pump the player piano or experiment with the many other musical instruments. You will enjoy a full breakfast at the round oak table in front of the brick fire-place in the Great Room, or, have your meal served in the 19th century style Victorian Gazebo located on the lawn of the Inn. The Innkeepers can help you plan a getaway for a special day.

MUSEUM

Dale A. Gardner Aerospace Museum & Learning Center

Exit 87 from I-90 and MN #4 on Main St.
Sherburn, MN 56171
Phone: 507-764-2607
Hrs: Mon.-Fri. 1 p.m.-4 p.m.

The museum is a "Dream Come True" for many Sherburnites who for years have longed for a "Special Place" to honor their home town hero. Dale A. Gardener was born in Sherburn on November 8, 1948, where his father worked for Interstate Power Company's Fox Lake generating plant.

The Museum & Learning Center has numerous artifacts on display including Dale's flight suit from a Discovery flight, tiles from a Challenger mission and many videos describing the NASA Space Program. Other displays include a heat shield and model rocket collection.

The center has become a teaching resource center for education. A recently acquired "starlab" enhances visitors understanding of space, stars and planets.

Today, Dale Gardener works in the Aerospace Division of TRW in Los Angeles, California, but his early childhood and distinguished career will live on in Sherburn for all to see and know.

Settlers came to Slayton for the very best Midwestern farmland. Today, visitors take advantage of wonderful recreational opportunities, primarily centered around *Lake Shetek State Park.* Located just eight miles north of town on Highway 59, the lake attracts fisherman and hunters. Camping, hiking, cross-country skiing and snowmobiling are also available.

In town, you'll find all the services you need plus some interesting diversions, like the *Murray County Historical Museum,* featuring an old fire hall, railroad and Indian artifacts plus a country store. *Slayton Country Club* is a nice nine-hole layout or you can cool off at the *Slayton Swimming Pool.*

Power Days Farm & Home Show features some of the rowdiest demolition derbies around plus antique tractor pulls and somewhat more restful parades and exhibits.

For further information, contact:
Slayton Chamber of Commerce, 2438 26th Street
Slayton, MN 56172   Phone: 507-836-6902

SPECIALTY SHOP

| *The Hut* | 2620 Broadway Ave., Slayton, MN 56127
Phone: 507-836-6800. Hrs: Mon.-Sat. 9 a.m.-5 p.m., Thurs. 9 a.m.-6:30 p.m.
Visa and MasterCard accepted. |

For more than 25 years, The Hut has brought the finest in gifts and collectibles to Southwest Minnesota and to the visitors passing through. Collectors can find Precious Moments, Memories of Yesterday, Cherished Teddies, Calico Kittens and much more. Pottery, baskets, pine cupboards and shelves, cozy afghans, yankee candles, potpourri and dried wall decor attract the country lovers. Bridal registry features Noritake china and stoneware, Phaltzgraff stoneware, Oneida flatware, crystal, Heritage doilies and curtain lace, table linens, picture frames, rugs and framed prints.

Souvenirs include Minnesota sweatshirts and T-shirts and Minnesota made Minnetonka Moccasins. A Christmas Showcase features many decorated theme trees, assorted ornaments and special holiday gift items.

The Holiday Open House is held the first Sunday of November and offers hot cider and cookies to celebrate the coming of the holiday season.

SLEEPY EYE

Sleepy Eye was established in 1872 when the railroad came through on its vast journey across the wilderness. The village was named for a beautiful lake which itself was named for the chief of a band of Sisseton Dakota, "ISH-TAK-HA-BA," Chief Sleepy Eye, friend to all men. His bones lie beneath the granite obelisk monument erected in his honor beside the historic railroad depot now restored as the Depot Museum by the local historical society.

White settlers began a community in this Indian territory around 1860. During the Indian War of 1862, major battles were fought at Fort Ridgely just ten miles north of Sleepy Eye. The Interpretive Center there houses displays and provides a slide program explaining the history of the site. From 1883 until 1921, the flour mill at Sleepy Eye drew many people to the area. The promotional items given away by the mill have been a favorite of collectors. The "Old Sleepy Eye Collectors Club" has over 1000 members nationally.

ATTRACTIONS & EVENTS

Sleepy Eye is located in the rich agricultural heartland of America and is home to the nation's largest manufacturer of specialty advertising calendars. Sleepy Eye Lake lies within the city limits and boasts two swimming beaches, two parks containing playgrounds and picnic shelters, a boat landing and free campsites. There are several other parks in Sleepy Eye with shelters and playgrounds, also.

Visitors are welcomed at several special events in Sleepy Eye. An old-fashioned 4th of July celebration is an annual event along with fireworks over the lake. On the fourth Thursday in August they hold *Buttered Corn Day.* Steamed sweet corn is dipped in tubs of butter for a gigantic FREE corn feast. The last Sunday in September, thousands of people gather for the *Great Grassroots Gathering,* a flea market and craft show. The first weekend in March is the annual *Farm City Days,* a two day trade show featuring business displays, seminars, and entertainment.

For further information, contact:
Sleepy Eye Area Convention
and Visitors Bureau
108 West Main
Sleepy Eye, MN 56085
Phone: 507-794-4731

LODGING

Best Western Inn of Seven Gables

1100 E. Main (Hwy. 14)
Sleepy Eye, MN 56085
Phone: 800-852-9451 or 507-794-6553

Rich in pioneer and American Indian history, the Best Western Inn of Seven Gables offers a cozy country inn with gracious hospitality. Kenneth and JoEtta Doolittle built this unique 37 room inn in 1992. There are seven gables on the roof, thus the name, Inn of Seven Gables.

Nestled in the heart of Brown County, the Inn features a spacious lobby with a stone fireplace, heated indoor pool and whirlpool. Visitors will find clean, comfortable rooms with queen size beds and remote control color TV with HBO. Suites and conference rooms are available, as well.

The Laura Ingalls Wilder pageant, Heritagefest and Jackpot Junction casino are a few of the attractions that bring visitors to the area.

The Best Western Inn of Seven Gables has been recognized for excellence in facilities and customer service.

◆ ◆ ◆ ◆ ◆ ◆ ◆

The Orchid Inn and Motor Lodge

500 Burnside SE
Sleepy Eye, MN 56085
Phone: 507-794-3211 or 800-245-4931

The Orchid Inn and Motor Lodge is centrally located in southwest Minnesota and is perfect for travelers who need a clean, comfortable room or a meeting place for a group. It offers a combination of large and small meeting rooms, excellent dining facilities and, of course, comfortable motel rooms.

Meeting rooms accommodate from 10 to 1,000, including full meals prepared and served by the highly qualified staff. Even a dance floor is provided following banquets or receptions.

The main dining room offers a variety of items that will satisfy the most discriminating taste. The full menu features chicken, steaks and seafood, as well as daily specials and an hors d'oeuvre table with delicious salads and soups. Friday and Saturday nights feature a smorgasbord, a variety of delectable foods at one reasonable price.

SPICER/NEW LONDON

Renowned Minnesota writer Sinclair Lewis once compared New London to a quaint, Cape Cod village. While that's high praise and a fitting description of these twin towns, it's difficult to do justice with words to both Spicer and New London, two of Minnesota's most popular destinations.

The reasons are obvious.

Located in the midst of the Little Crow Lakes region, Spicer and New London are located in rolling, wooded terrain surrounded by more than 50 lakes in all. With their friendly atmosphere and quaint, restful attitude, Spicer and New London have much to offer.

ATTRACTIONS & EVENTS

Winter, spring, summer or fall, Spicer and New London are well worth a look-see. Golfers will be familiar with the *Little Crow Country Club,* a championship layout and home to numerous competitive golf events. It is but one of many outdoor recreational opportunities in the area. The 2,400-acre *Sibley State Park* features excellent swimming, canoeing, hiking and camping.

The Monongolia Historical Society is located in the old *Lebanon Church* where you'll discover an historical newspaper office, country store and antique farm machinery. You can even be a part of the past yourself by staying overnight at the *Spicer Castle,* long a local landmark and now an elegant bed and breakfast inn.

On the Fourth of July, thousands flock to the area for one of the largest *Independence Day Celebrations* around. It includes a flea market, street dance, road race, arts and crafts fair and music in the park. The usual crowd is between 12-15,000.

New London hosts the *Mt. Tom Tour* in May and the giant *Antique Car Run* between New London and New Brighton, a race patterned after one in Britain and annually attracting racers from the Old Country as well as the locals. *New London Water Days* in late July features fabulous water skiing shows and the *Little Britches Rodeo* offers teenagers an opportunity to try their hand at this distinctly American sport.

For further information, contact:
Spicer Commercial Club,
P.O. Box 244, Spicer, MN 56288   Phone 612-796-0066
or *New London Chamber of Commerce*
New London, MN 56273   Phone 612-354-2011

BED & BREAKFAST

Spicer Castle	11600 Indian Beach Road, P.O. Box 307, Spicer, MN 56288. **Phone: 612-796-5870 or 800-821-6675.** Hrs: Everyday in season. Sept-May, Fri, Sat. only. Major credit cards accepted.

Spicer Castle is a most unique B&B. It was built for John M. Spicer back in 1893 and is now owned by his grandson, Allen Latham, and operated by his great-granddaughter, Mary Swanson.

In those early days, it was a home where friends, relatives and business associates frequently visited and has been used in much the same way since then. In the 1930's, fishermen began identifying this landmark as Spicer Castle as a means for locating their favorite fishing hole. Eventually, the name stuck and it showed up on fishing maps as well as other printed matter.

On the National Register of Historic Places, Spicer Castle has managed to survive with much of its original furnishings and charm intact. That's because the descendants of John Spicer have contributed to the effort over the years, in particular, Eunice Spicer Latham, youngest daughter of John. In fact, each guestroom is named after one of the family and has memorabilia from their careers and interests. All guestrooms have a private bath and a comfortable queen-sized bed. Some rooms come with fireplaces and double whirlpools. There are two cottages on the grounds and these are available, too.

Tea is served in the afternoon and provides an opportunity for guests to meet and learn about castle history. Later, the sun sets over the lake, providing a spectacular view in a relaxing atmosphere. Breakfasts are elegant and hearty, in the tradition of the home, and meals are made from scratch.

Three thousand feet of common area include fireplaces, porches, nooks and many other relaxing havens. The Spicer Castle makes a perfect setting for receptions, seminars or other get-togethers. Special packages are available including murder mystery dinners, dinner cruises on the lake, holiday and anniversary packages. There are many diverse attractions in the area.

RESORT

Dickerson's *Lake Florida* *Resort*	13194 2nd Street NE, Box 94P, Spicer, MN 56288 **Phone:** 612-354-4272 Hrs: Open May through September

Window boxes overflowing with flowers and a plate of fresh-baked cookies on your kitchen table tell you this resort specializes in homeyness and hospitality. Fourth-generation owners Bob and Connie Dickerson want guests to "build sand castles and memories."

Accommodating from 1-8 people, 13 nicely decorated cottages come with full kitchens and are just steps from a beautiful 450' sand beach and the clean water of Lake Florida. Free to guests are sailboats, canoes, rowboats, kayaks, paddleboats, funbugs and bicycles for riders of every age. Motors and a pontoon can be rented.

The resort is located on the east side of the lake for spectacular sunsets. The Dickersons create additional fun for guests by serving homemade doughnuts at Sunday morning "mixers" and by hosting beach pizza parties, hayrides and marshmallow roasts.

BUILD SAND CASTLES & MEMORIES

SPECIALTY SHOP

Minnesota *Country*	12011 Highway 71 N.E., Spicer, MN 56288 **Phone:** 612-796-2199 Hrs: Mon.-Sat. 10 a.m.-5 p.m.; Sun. noon-5 p.m. All major credit cards accepted.

For the elegance and charm of traditional country gifts, look no further than Minnesota Country, conveniently surrounded by 15 lakes and 30 resorts and campgrounds. It represents 75-90 artisans and craftspersons, providing hand-crafted or gift items and accessories from the five-state region.

The store is attractive and inviting, displaying merchandise on unique shelving. The Christmas Room features Christmas tree skirts in patchwork or star design, stockings and applique designs; ornaments, string Santa dolls and much more. Victorian hand-crafted items and accessories are elegantly displayed in the Victorian Room. Other gift items include wreaths and floral arrangements, quilt items, a wide selection of handmade dolls, Amish string dolls, rugs and blankets, cabinets and spice racks, hand-crafted pottery, porcelain figurines, and that's not all. Customized special orders and shipping are also available. It's no secret that Minnesota Country offers only the best quality in all of its hand-crafted gift items.

SPRINGFIELD

Like all of the great northwest before the coming of the white man, the Springfield area was a wild land occupied by a scattered population of Sioux Indians. Some of the early settlers were massacred in the Indian uprising of 1862. Settlers started arriving in full force around 1869 and in 1872 the railroad built a line through the town.

Today Springfield is a rural community with a happy blend of agriculture, business and industry. The population is very diverse with many nationalities represented.

ATTRACTIONS & EVENTS

For those traveling through, Springfield offers many parks, churches, and recreational facilities. In *Riverside Park* there is a new outdoor swimming pool with a figure 8 waterslide, sand volleyball court, horseshoe court, tennis courts, baseball and softball complex, hiking, biking, and ski trails, canoe landing on the *Big Cottonwood River* and a new campground with 10 electrical units, showers, bathhouse and dump station. There are also several other parks to choose from. If golfing is your thing, there is a beautiful 9 hole golf course located on the Cottonwood River.

A short distance from Springfield, you will find the *Mounds Creek Watershed.* This conservation project has a 70 acre lake and park, picnic, hiking and biking area.

During the month of June, *Riverside Days* are held with lots of fun events including a barbecue pork chop dinner in the park, kiddie parade, flight breakfast, street dance, fun run and walk and softball tournament. *Christmas in July* is held on the fourth Wednesday of the month with all of the sights, sounds and scents of Christmas. If you visit on this day, you might start by touring the craft fair, having some refreshments, listening to the musicians and then stay for the Christmas dinner and the talent show.

In December you may travel to see the *Nativity Pageant* which is the Christmas story told outdoors under the stars. Featured are a 75 voice community choir, a live manger scene and many live animals including camels. The pageant is staged each year with 200 community and area volunteers.

For further information, contact:
Chamber of Commerce
P.O. Box 134, Springfield, MN 56087
Phone: 507-723-6240

BED & BREAKFAST

Sod House *On The Prairie*	1 mile east, 1/4 mile south of Sanborn Corner Junction Hwys. 71 & 14, Sanborn, MN 56083 **Phone: 507-723-5138** Hrs: Open year-round.

Rising like ghosts from the prairie, Stan and Virginia McCone's twin sod homes pay homage to the spirit of the 19th century pioneers who settled these parts.

Surrounded by carefully restored tallgrass prairie, today they serve as a bed and breakfast dwelling, a place for visitors to explore the ways of the past and a spot to buy cherished gifts reminiscent of the era. Constructed in 1987 utilizing some 300,000 pounds of sod, the two houses are located just 20 miles from Walnut Grove, the childhood home of Laura Ingalls Wilder of "Little House On The Prairie" fame.

They make a unique bed & breakfast, where you'll find two double beds, a fainting couch, a cook stove and a pair of rocking chairs. Oil lamps provide light and an old-fashioned pitcher and bowl serve as a sink. In the morning, guests enjoy fresh coffee and a full, hearty breakfast.

Summertime at the sod house means early morning sunlight, the sounds of chattering birds, dew on the prairie grass and a delicate prairie flower here and there. Although not air-conditioned, it's cooler inside than outside because of the two-foot thick walls.

Some historians estimate that during the settlement years in the high plains states, more than a million sod homes were built by the homesteaders. Sod houses are gone now, but visitors can see what it was really like to live in one by visiting this interesting attraction. It's not unlike going to a museum as you open the heavy plank door, step inside and walk over to the cook stove, then examine the quilts on the bed.

Bed & breakfast open year-round. Tours May through Labor Day, 10 a.m. to 5 p.m. A unique experience for young and old.

TRACY

Much of the world knows about pioneer life in Tracy thanks to Laura Ingalls Wilder's *Little House on the Prairie* television show. It was based on the life of her family and is paid tribute to in nearby Walnut Grove at the *Laura Ingalls Wilder Museum.*

But there's plenty more history to go around in this community at fascinating places like the *Wheels Across the Prairie Museum,* a vast collection of settler-era machines and equipment. Then there's the *St. Mark's Church Museum,* a restored country church, and a must for railroad fans, the *End-O-Line Railroad Park and Museum.*

Lake Shetek State Park is nearby for outdoor recreation. *Fragments of a Dream* is an annual historical pageant based on Wilder's children's books. *The Pioneer Festival* is held in Walnut Grove. Tracy also hosts *Box Car Days* in August, featuring parades, a teen dance and a concert in the park.

For further information, contact:
Tracy Area Chamber of Commerce
Masonic Building, Tracy, MN 56175   Phone: 507-629-4021

SPECIALTY SHOP

Calico Ribbon Gifts and Ceramics	257 South Street, Tracy, MN 56175. **Phone: 507-629-3092.** Hrs.: (Summer) Tues., Wed., Thurs., 10 a.m.-noon, 1-4:30 p.m. Or by appointment (Winter) Mon.-Thurs., 10 a.m.-noon, 1-5 p.m. or by appointment.

The Calico Ribbon Gifts and Ceramics specialty shop offers quality gifts made to customer specifications. For those who like to finish their own projects, The Calico Ribbon boasts the largest supply of greenware, bisque (fired, ready-to-paint ceramics) and other ceramic supplies. Or if you have a special request, the shop can make quality accent pieces to match the decor of any room of your home or office.

Located in Tracy (on Hwy 14, southeast of Marshall), the Calico Ribbon features more than 7,000 molds, ranging from Minnesota loons and a variety of other wildlife to Native American pieces and kitchen and bathroom items. Holiday decorations exist in abundance from Easter, Halloween and Thanksgiving to more than 100 different Santas and six different Christmas village sets.

Joan and Larry Lanoue opened The Calico Ribbon in 1975, and it's been expanding ever since with the newest ideas in quality gifts. Hours vary so call ahead to make sure the store will be open when you arrive. It's worth the effort.

TYLER

Primarily a farming community, Tyler is a picturesque town located in the southwest corner of Minnesota. Like many prairie towns, it has its roots in the railroad when, in 1879, the Chicago Northwestern Railroad Company sent a crew to complete laying track nearby. A permanent depot was built and the settlers did the rest.

Tyler's Danish heritage makes it home to the *nissemænd,* tiny elves, akin to Irish leprechauns, who can be helpful or mischievous depending on how much food is set out for them!

ATTRACTIONS & EVENTS

One of the most outstanding sights visitors enjoy in Tyler is the *Danebod* complex, an architectural jewel consisting of the *Danebod Lutheran Church,* the *Stone Hall,* the *Gym Hall* and the *Folk School.* The complex is rich with Danish tradition and beauty. Danebod hosts a *Creative Discovery* weekend in September, an event that features old world crafts, workshops and other activities. The Danebod Stone Hall is listed on the National Register of Historic Places.

Babette's Inn Bed & Breakfast is located in Tyler and nearby attractions include *Pipestone National Monument* and *Lake Benton Opera House.*

One of the many activities visitors take part in is known as *"Æbleskiver Days"* held in June every year. The "æbleskive" is a Danish pancake that is ball-shaped instead of flat. This Danish treat is, of course, served at Æbleskiver Days as are other traditional Danish foods. Danish dancers perform, local artists display their wares and a grand parade and street dance are all a part of the cultural activities.

For further information, contact:
Tyler Area Chamber of Commerce
Tyler, MN 56178
Phone: 507-247-3905

BED & BREAKFAST

Babette's Inn/Bed & Breakfast	308 S. Tyler St., Tyler, MN 56178 **Phone: 507-247-3962 or 800-466-7067** Hrs: Open year-round every day by reservation only. Visa and MasterCard accepted.

Owners Jim and Alicia Johnson opened this AAA recommended Inn after returning home to Minnesota from ten years of corporate life. Babette's Inn offers peace, privacy and luxury in a brick Prairie-architecture home built in 1914 by a Danish bricklayer. Three guest rooms upstairs, all with private bathrooms, are decorated and appointed in rich colors and subtle, European flair. Great care in detail and guest comfort is the rule of this house.

A solarium downstairs greets the morning sun or lets you curl up with a book at the fireside. Free videos and books for guest use encourage a relaxing stay. On top of it all, gourmet evenings can be scheduled featuring European cuisine which Alicia prepares with zest and a love for elegant, yet casual, dining.

Breakfast features Scandinavian specialties that are hot and delicious, punctuated by the smell of European roasted coffee! A gift shop in the Inn called 'A Touch of Europe' features stoneware, antiques, gourmet foods and one-of-a-kind luxury items.

The brick home stands on Tyler's main street, just a five-minute walk to Danebod Folk School. The nearby Pipestone National Monument is where Native Americans still quarry red clay for ceremonial pipes.

Lake Benton is just down the road and Camden State Park, just 15 minutes away, is one of the treasured natural gorge parks in the Upper Midwest.

If golf is your game, try the municipal course. It's a classic 9-hole rolling course adjacent to the airport. If you use the airport, it is unattended, but quite charming.

Babette's also offers special-occasion gourmet dining in the European tradition. Call ahead for information about this small place of beauty and style.

WALNUT GROVE

Walnut Grove is another one of the many towns whose history is inextricably tied to the European settlers who came here in the last century and the Native Americans displaced by them. It is located in the southwestern part of Minnesota amid the beautiful prairielands of the area and got its name from a grove of trees just outside of town.

Most will recognize Walnut Grove as the childhood home of author Laura Ingalls Wilder. Her classic books on pioneer life were the basis for Michael Landon's hit television series, "Little House on the Prairie." Over the years, four stars of the show have visited Walnut Grove. Remember nasty Nellie Oleson on the show? There really was a Nellie and, no, she and Laura did not get along. Alison Arngrim, the actress who played Nellie on the show, visited the Walnut Grove area in 1992 and was pleased to hear stories that Nellie really wasn't so nasty after all!

Laura's first home in Walnut Grove was a sod-roofed dugout on the banks of Plum Creek. The Ingalls family survived oxen crashing through the roof and flood waters lapping at the door, but they could not overcome the crop losses caused by grasshopper plagues. So, Pa Ingalls worked in hotels and a butcher shop. Even Laura waited on tables at the Master's Hotel.

ATTRACTIONS

Today, Wilder fans enjoy visiting the former site of the Ingalls' dugout. It is easy to imagine Laura splashing in *Plum Creek* and absorbing prairie sunsets. Displays at the *Wilder Museum* include Laura's quilt, the spinning wheel of the Ingalls' closest friends, the Eleck Nelson family, and memorabilia from visits by Little House TV series stars. A self-guided driving tour includes locations Laura described in *On the Banks of Plum Creek.*  Handcrafted gifts and souvenirs are available from the museum and local merchants.

The flatness of the prairie may be deceiving to visitors, but there is much to do and see in the Walnut Grove area. *Plum Creek County Park,* site of the original Walnut Grove, has a fishing and swimming lake, wooded campground, hiking trails and playground. The *Wahpeton Prairie* preserve is similar to what the Ingalls family experienced more than a century ago when they first arrived in a wagon.

Gentle slopes are covered with lush, native prairie grasses. Bluestem and Indian grasses grow more than four feet high on rich soils deposited along the Cottonwood River. Here, one can almost imagine Laura Ingalls stopping to pick flowers on her way home from school. This preserve was acquired in 1971 by The Nature Conservancy and is named for one of the seven major bands of Dakotah Native Americans who inhabited these lands—the Wahpeton.

Wheels Across the Prairie Museum, located west of Walnut Grove in Tracy, is a tribute to those hardy settlers shown through wheels—wheels of all types from the early days. There's a 1915 railroad steam engine and a variety of other fascinating items from the past. The *Lake Shetek State Park* is a beautiful, wooded oasis on the barren prairie. A 3,600 acre lake is the largest in southwest Minnesota. *End-O-Line Railroad Museum* in Currie tells the story of the early railroads, so important to opening up this country to the settlers. A unique feature at the museum is the state's last remaining hand-operated turntable—the device used to turn steam engines around for the return trip when they reached the end of the branch line.

On virgin prairie, near Jeffers, Minnesota, there are slabs of red rock with some 2,000 pictures carved on them. The *Jeffers Petroglyphs* were created by Native Americans over thousands of years and attest to the actions, thoughts and beliefs of the these ancient peoples. (Note: the Jeffers Petroglyphs may be closed due to construction of a new visitor center.) Nearby, *Red Rock Dells Park* is a gem of a park with a waterfall and the same red quartzite rock found at Jeffers Petroglyphs. A mile east is the *Wellner-Hageman Dam* and lake.

In Sanborn, to the east, is the *McCone 1880 Sod House Exhibit.* The prairie had relatively few trees and lumber was scarce, so early settlers turned to building material that was plentiful—prairie sod. Unfortunately, sod homes and dugouts deteriorate quickly. Almost none of the estimated 1,000,000 sod houses exist today. However, the McCone Exhibit features two sod houses furnished as if someone lived there. These are open for touring and one is a bed and breakfast.

EVENTS

The *Wilder Pageant* offers an outdoor pageant, based on Laura Ingall's childhood, that brings to life the good times and the hardships of pioneer life. It's one of Minnesota's top 25 events. The elaborate technical effects are a show in themselves. A pioneer festival offers demonstrations, crafts, children's activities and live country/bluegrass music.

For further information, contact:

Plum Creek Tourism
P.O. Box 222
Walnut Grove, MN 56180   Phone: 507-859-2358 or 2155

BED & BREAKFAST

The Victorian Lady B&B	RR 2, Box 109-1A, Wabasso, MN 56293 **Phone: 507-747-2170** Hrs: Check in at 5 p.m. Check out at 10:30 a.m. Visa and MasterCard accepted.

Located just up the road in Wabasso, the Victorian Lady is one of those rare, elegant homes that has lots of original features. Your B&B hosts are Gene and Sandy Rogotzke, loving caretakers of this 100-year-old house. They've made it truly a treasure on the prairie!

Hannah's Room features a large, beautiful fireplace, walk-in closet and relaxing furniture. Augusta's Room is large, airy and sunny with four windows. It features a blue canopy queen-size bed complemented with off-white and blue wallpaper, blue skirted vanity and wicker chair. Lillie's Room offers an inviting south-facing sun-porch that has a relaxing love seat and chairs. The high-standing bed and lace curtains make it perfectly charming. The Van Dusen Room is complemented with a masculine green paisley wallpaper, chest of drawers and comfortable bed.

A full, homemade breakfast is served in the formal dining room under the chandelier. Visitors also enjoy the large front porch with a porch swing and wicker furniture. Soothing music, a bookcase full of books, a beautiful fireplace and TV await in the parlor.

WASECA

In the ancient Dakota language, the name "Waseca" meant "fertile." How right they were, not only in the literal sense with the riches of agriculture, but in almost every other sense as well. The early settlers who chose to homestead here made an excellent choice, indeed.

Today's Waseca continues to prosper with a wealth of recreational activities and a host of industries, including electronics giant E.F. Johnson and one of the country's largest printers, Brown Printing. Both are home-grown enterprises that now operate on a global scale.

There's no better place to get a taste of rural Minnesota life than at

ATTRACTIONS & EVENTS

Farmamerica in Waseca. Here you'll find 120 acres of restored farm-steads from different eras (the 1850's, 1920's, and 1970's), each operating as they did complete with costumed interpreters. It's a wonderful place for children and offers rare insight into the lives of Minnesota's settler families. The *Waseca County Historical Society* is also dedicated to farm history. It has a number of interesting collections, including a rural school house, a reconstructed log home and agricultural implements from yesteryear. Be sure and see the *Ward Home* and the distinguished *Waseca County Courthouse* while you're in town.

Recreation in Waseca is centered around *Clear Lake* where you'll find wonderful opportunities for boating, sailing, swimming, fishing and water skiing. On the north side of the lake is the *Lakeside Golf and Country Club,* an excellent 18-hole layout that is suitable for all levels of golfer and is always in beautiful condition. Or for something a little less testy, try miniature golf at *Kiesler's Campground* on the south side of Clear Lake followed by a root beer and a burger at *Barney's.*

Whatever the season, Waseca finds a reason to celebrate. Summer brings *Happy Days* complete with hula hoop, goldfish eating and bubblegum blowing contests. *The Waseca County Fair* features a carnival and blue-ribbon farm animals. When autumn arrives, heavy draft horses turn the earth in old-fashioned plowing contests at *Farmamerica's Fall Fair.* And in winter, the annual *Sleigh and Cutter Parade* is a tradition that dates back more than 40 years.

For further information, contact:
Waseca Area Chamber of Commerce
Department 3, 108 E. Elm
Waseca, MN 56093
Phone: 507-835-3260

CAMPGROUND

Kiesler's Campground on Clear Lake

Highway 14 (East edge of Waseca), P.O. Box 503P, Waseca, MN 56093. **Phone: 507-835-8787 Ext. 2 or 800-533-4642.** Hrs: Open Apr. 15-Oct. 15. Visa, MasterCard, and Discover are accepted.

Nestled in southern Minnesota's quiet farmland near the Iowa border is one of the most exciting and entertaining RV parks to be found anywhere. The owners take pride in their high campground guide rating.

Since 1972, Kiesler's Campground has enjoyed a prestigious location on the 700-acre Clear Lake, situated in the friendly community of Waseca in the "Deep South of Minnesota." The park boasts 250 spacious sites with water and electric hookups, 132 with sewer, free cable television, and picnic tables. Recessed fire pits and graveled parking pads are surrounded by manicured grass. Landscaping includes plenty of shade trees.

Kal and Barb Kiesler play host and hostess to a summer full of activities for the whole family. Children enjoy the playgrounds and activities planned by "Jolly Jon," the recreation director. There is also volleyball, basketball, shuffleboard, horseshoes, and softball. Special events include bingo, kite flying, camper's auction, teen sock hops, bike parade, mini-golf tournaments, tug-o-war, kiddie carnival, fireworks, and much more. Plenty of prizes are awarded for outdoor contests.

For the avid golfer, there is Kiesler's 18-hole mini golf; next door is the Lakeside Club and 18 holes of golf. Water sports enthusiasts enjoy waterskiing and swimming. A large heated pool is on the campgrounds surrounded by loungers for your comfort and convenience. The camp store and recreation hall provide additional conveniences and activities. Fishing licenses, bait, tackle, and boat and motor rental are also available.

Without a doubt, Kiesler's Campground is a vacation center for the entire family located in the middle of the Southern Lakes region of Minnesota.

INTERPRETIVE CENTER

Farmamerica

County Roads 2 and 17, P.O. Box 111, Waseca, MN. **Phone: 507-835-2052.** Festivals every second Sunday, June-Sept. Hrs: 11 a.m.-4 p.m. Visa and MasterCard accepted.

Farmamerica has some of the qualities of a museum, the spirit and fun-filled environment of a rural festival and the educational quality of some of the most enlightened schools. It's a place where serious forums are conducted for professionals in agriculture and for rural community preservation.

Farmamerica is where history comes alive because it's the state agricultural interpretive center. Located four miles west of Waseca in southern Minnesota on a 120-acre farm, Farmamerica brings to life the history of farming in Minnesota from the pioneer days of the 1850's to the present. The land, the people, and the future they made for themselves on the vast open prairie are shown through historical reenactments and restored buildings.

Visitors to the non-profit center start their journey at a restored school that serves as an admission center, then on to the circular "Time Line Trail" where the first stop is a true replica of a pioneer homestead. Built from rough-hewn logs, the diminutive buildings echo the sounds of the early pioneers, acted out by the Farmamerica staff. Across from the settlement farm, a nine-acre swath of original prairie waves in the wind, just as it did a hundred and fifty years ago.

Meanwhile, in a nearby blacksmith shop, a smithy reenacts the centuries old craft, while a complete farm from the 1920's and furnished with authentic period furniture lies further along the trail. Finally, a modern farm completes the circle.

In addition to enjoying historic reenactments, visitors note the vegetables grown at the settlement farm; they are the same varieties as those grown by the settlers. Also, Farmamerica hosts a rambunctious corn-shucking and horse-plowing contest that's fun for all. These are all part of the educational fun that makes Farmamerica a must for anyone interested in the heritage of Minnesota.

Farmamerica was commissioned by the governor and Minnesota state legislature in 1978 as an independent, not-for-profit educational institution administered by a volunteer board of directors and a staff of professionals who work at keeping history accurate and alive.

SPECIALTY SHOP

A Touch of	41830 150th St., Waseca, MN 56093
Country Class	**Phone: 507-835-4163**
	Hrs.: Last two weekends in May & September.
	MasterCard, Visa and Discover accepted.

If you want an out-of-the ordinary shopping experience for antiques, crafts and gifts, you'll want to come to an extravaganza known as A Touch of Country Class. It's a semi-annual show staged at a farm with ten different buildings displaying the handiwork of more than 200 craft persons.

The buildings includes: The Old Barn, The Chicken Coop, The Stable Down Yonder, The Tool Shed, The Farm House, The Garden Shed, The Old Seed Shed and The Milk House.

The show is the work of Jack and Delores Boerigter and began in 1989 on their small rural farm. When the Boerigters first arrived in Waseca more than six years ago, they owned a beautiful hitch of Belgian show horses, necessitating the purchase of a small rural farm. The Belgians are gone now and the show has grown every year since then and is now a display for artists from as far away as Texas.

Thousands of items are either brought to A Country Touch of Class or are sent from crafters around the country for the shows, which are held the last two weekends of May and September. If you like crafts, antiques and gifts, you won't want to miss this very special place. Food is also available.

Visitors may wander from building to building and from level to level examining the seemingly boundless items which are displayed in every possible nook and cranny of the refurbished farm buildings.

Here's the directions: 4 miles north of Waseca on Highway 13, then 2 miles east on Cty. Rd 22 (410th Avenue), then 3/4 mile north on Cty Rd. 10 (150th Street). 2nd place on the right . . .

or . . . from the Medford Outlet, go 11 miles west on Steele Cty. Rd. 12 (8 miles blacktop, 3 miles gravel), then left on Waseca Cty. Rd. 10 (150th Street), first place on the left.

CORPORATE PROFILE

E.F. Johnson

To the police officer on patrol, it's more valuable than any sidearm. To the firefighter inside a burning building, it's the lifeline that keeps everyone in contact, and safe. To the maintenance supervisor, it's the tool that coordinates workers scattered throughout a huge job site.

Radio communications. It's one of the hottest, fastest-growing technologies around. But long before anyone coined the terms *high-tech* or even *electronics,* the E.F. Johnson Company was busy producing the components and products that helped create the radio industry.

Today, E.F. Johnson is one of the largest *two-way land mobile radio* manufacturers in the world. It builds everything from tiny, gold-plated cable connectors, to simple "walkie-talkie" style handheld radios, to complex communication systems that cover thousands of square miles. And millions of people depend on E.F. Johnson products every day, to help make their jobs efficient, productive and safe.

Minnesota roots

In 1923, a young University of Minnesota electrical engineering graduate named Edgar F. Johnson opened a radio parts business in his hometown of Waseca.

Radio itself wasn't much older than Edgar. When fledgling amateur and commercial radio stations couldn't find the parts they needed, Edgar filled their mail orders by designing and making the parts himself.

E.F. Johnson Company grew quickly. By the time World War II broke out, E.F. Johnson had its own factory in Waseca. Johnson® components were designed into all kinds of military equipment, and the company even built complete radio transmitters and receivers. In 1949, with the manufacturing experience gained during the war, E.F. Johnson launched a highly successful line of amateur radio equipment. But during the 1950s, E.F. Johnson management steered the company toward the growing land mobile radio market.

E.F. Johnson began engineering and manufacturing a long series of two-way radios for business, industry and public safety.

A new factory was built in Waseca for both components and radio products. By the end of the 1960s, E.F. Johnson had successful product lines in FM land mobile and citizens band two-way radio. There were hundreds of E.F. Johnson dealers across the country.

The company was perfectly positioned for the coming explosion in radio communications.

Land mobile leadership

It was a new twist on an old idea. For years, telephone companies had designed their networks around the idea of *trunking.* They discovered that, with the right switching equipment, a huge number of customers could be served by carefully allocating a much smaller number of phone lines.

When the demand for two-way radio service grew in the early 1970s, there simply weren't enough radio channels to go around. So the radio industry created a new two-way technology based on the old telephone switching idea and called it *"trunked radio,"* or simply "trunking."

E.F. Johnson developed its own trunked radio system and called it Clearchannel LTR® Logic Trunked Radio. The system was a hit not only with Johnson customers, but with other radio manufacturers as well, several of whom began building radios to work on the LTR signaling protocol.

In the mid-1980s, LTR technology served as the basis for more advanced trunking: the Multi-Net® system. Multi-Net trunking offered more sophisticated features than an LTR system. It ushered E.F. Johnson into the large radio systems market, attracting customers in public safety, business and industry, both in the United States and around the world.

Multi-Net systems are at work in all kinds of situations. A system in Puerto Rico, for example, provides communications for emergency and government services throughout the island. Another Multi-Net system links dozens of offshore oil platforms and onshore support bases across thousands of miles in the Gulf of Mexico. And police departments in China depend on their Multi-Net systems as much as their American counterparts do.

Growing applications

While radio products and systems have been the driving force behind E.F. Johnson's growth over the past several decades, there's more to the company than two-way radio.

To fully appreciate the scope of E.F. Johnson's activities, take a walk through its operations center in Waseca. The facility was built in 1960 and has expanded over the years to cover 250,000 square feet. This is the home of the company's engineering, manufacturing, customer service and administrative support groups; about 700 people in all. (Another 100 work at E.F. Johnson corporate headquarters in the Minneapolis suburb of Burnsville, 60 miles to the north. And about 50 Johnson people serve in field positions around the world.)

At one end of the manufacturing plant is Johnson's Components Division, the direct descendant of Edgar Johnson's original radio parts business. Thousands of different electronic components are made here such as electronic circuit hardware, RF coaxial connectors, and cable assemblies. Each one is machined to exceptionally precise tolerances, down to one ten-thousandth of an inch, to meet a wide range of industry and military standards. Johnson components are known for their high quality, which is why you'll find them in hundreds of products, from copiers to aircraft.

Electronics production fills most of the manufacturing space in the Waseca plant. But not all of the products built here are Johnson two-way radios. E.F. Johnson also has a thriving Custom Manufacturing Division, which helps other companies design and build their own electronic products.

Custom manufacturing really is customized to each client's individual needs. A company can bring a product idea to E.F. Johnson for full engineering development, manufacturing and distribution. Or it can contract for specific services, such as circuit-board assembly or environmental stress testing.

Custom manufacturing grew out of E.F. Johnson's long history of special projects work. Over the years, Johnson has helped bring several new products to market. In 1979, for example, E.F. Johnson was on the team that designed and built AT&T's first cellular telephone test in Chicago. Johnson engineers developed a revolutionary remote reading system for gas and electric meters. And the company designed and manufactured equipment for one of the first aircraft-to-ground public telephone systems.

Data telemetry is another spinoff from E.F. Johnson's special projects work. Packaged in small, modular units, Johnson's data telemetry radios are the building blocks of a huge variety of remote sensing and control applications. Data telemetry products are often used under hazardous conditions, checking for leaks in gas pipelines or operating valves in chemical plants. But they also help track shipments through warehouses, and monitor growing conditions in farm fields.

Dedicated service

E.F. Johnson's radio products come with a two-year parts and labor warranty. But no matter how advanced or reliable E.F. Johnson builds its radio products and systems, they eventually require human attention. That's simply the nature of high-tech electronic equipment. And that's why E.F. Johnson has put a lot of effort into building one of the best customer service organizations in the business.

For most E.F. Johnson customers, customer service is provided by their authorized Johnson dealer. More than 700 E.F. Johnson dealers around the world sell and support a line of Johnson radio products and LTR systems, including telemetry products.

Just as dealers work hard to give their customers great service, E.F. Johnson serves its dealers through a large staff at the Waseca operations center that's dedicated to dealer support. Answers to dealer technical questions are just a phone call away, 24 hours a day, every day of the year. Dealer equipment repairs are backed up by E.F. Johnson's own depot service and service parts departments. Dealers can even link their computers to E.F. Johnson's ACES™ on-line computerized information service for the latest product pricing, technical updates and radio programming software.

New beginnings

In the summer of 1992, E.F. Johnson management made significant new commitments to increase research and development funding, expand international markets, expand custom manufacturing and streamline company operations.

Two new radio product lines were rolled out: the Summit™ family of digital trunked radios for Multi-Net system customers, and the Viking® family of LTR and conventional radios for dealer markets. And as E.F. Johnson engineering teams worked on the next generation of digital radio networks, company executives took a more active role in the FCC and industry discussions which will shape the wireless communication regulation of the future.

But welcoming change and planning for the future have always been part of E.F. Johnson. The company is filled with people who love radio, who enjoy applying its power to solve communication problems, and who can't wait to see what's coming next. That enthusiasm, combined with exciting new radio technology and 70 years of experience, makes E.F. Johnson's future brighter than ever.

EFJohnson™

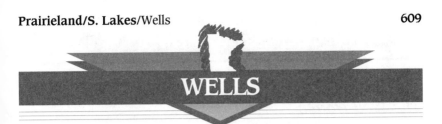

WELLS

Wells is a community of 2,500 people located in Faribault County, just 90 miles south of the Twin Cities. Surrounded by some of the best farm land in the nation, Wells is the commercial, industrial and agricultural center of eastern Faribault and western Freeborn counties and boasts a number of successful, thriving businesses.

A nine-hole golf course, municipal swimming pool, ball diamonds, playground equipment, fitness equipment, tennis courts, picnic facilities and more are all available in the Wells city parks.

In 1994, Wells celebrates its 125th anniversary. Numerous events are planned, highlighted by a production of "A Common Feeling," a musical about Wells' own music man, Harry Gillam. The city's annual *Kernel Days* celebration in late August will offer carnival, giant parade and tons of free sweet corn to thousands of visitors.

For further information, contact:
The Wells Area Chamber of Commerce
125 South Broadway, Wells, MN 56097
Phone: 507-553-6373

BED & BREAKFAST

Siebert Inn	500 2nd Avenue SW, Wells, MN 56097 **Phone: 507-553-3788** Hrs: Open year-round. Visa and MasterCard accepted.

A step into the Siebert Inn is a step into the grace and ambiance of the Victorian era.

Located in Wells, a south central Minnesota town of 2,800 situated between Mankato and Albert Lea, the Siebert Inn has four large bedrooms, all beautifully decorated with charming antiques. Relax in queen-size comfort and soak in the whirlpool after a day in the beautiful rural countryside. Innkeeping sisters Dawn and Nona will serve you a splendid breakfast of Mom's favorite homemade specialties to start the day off right.

Wells is a farming town where you can play golf, cross-country or downhill ski, play tennis, swim, conquer the fitness trail or explore a wildlife reserve and go fishing. It's located six miles off I-90, about two hours south of the Twin Cities. The Siebert Inn has its own charming antique and collectible shop, as well, where you can browse at will or take home a favorite piece of your own. Experience home town quiet at the Siebert Inn in Wells.

RESTAURANT

The Well House

Hwy. 109, Wells, MN 56097
Phone: 507-553-3170. Hrs: Tues.-Fri. 11 a.m.-
1:30 p.m., Tues.-Sat. 5 p.m.-9 p.m., Sunday
brunch 10:30 a.m.-1:30 p.m.

Tired of the fast food jungle? Try a hearty feast at The Well House in Wells, on Hwy. 109 just six miles off I-90. With informal dining, down-home hospitality and generous portions of homestyle cooking, this restaurant has won the raves of both the locals and travelers.

It's a family owned and operated establishment with a touch of country and featuring a wide variety of favorites. The complete menu includes lunch and dinner specials, salad bar, homemade soups and pies. Chicken is a real specialty at The Well House but don't miss the prime rib on Friday and Saturday evenings.

You can have a complete meal in the dining room or catch a quick snack as you watch the game in the sports lounge. A children's menu and banquet facilities are available, too. Their slogan is "Let our house be your house," a commitment that's carried through in the fine food served up by a friendly staff.

For all you die hards, take-out is available!

Eli Lewis came to the Winsted area in 1857 with the intention of starting a soap and potash factory. He purchased the land around the lake for $2000. plotted the site and named it Winsted after his hometown of Winsted, Connecticut. Unfortunately, the potash factory failed, but the town grew and prospered to its present population of 2,000.

In 1886, a fire destroyed the main business section of town, causing the inhabitants to incorporate into a town in 1887 so that they could have fire protection. The Winsted Roller Mills was the source of power for the waterworks system installed for fire protection.

ATTRACTIONS & EVENTS

Winsted boasts a number of park and recreational facilities. *Mill Reserve Park* offers a picnic shelter with tables and benches, playground equipment, bathrooms/showers, swimming and fishing. *Softball Park* is a summer favorite with equipment, bleachers and a fenced playing field. *Southview Park* offers playground equipment and a fenced backstop. *Westgate Park* has a fenced backstop.

Luce Line Trail, maintained by the Department of Natural Resources, is perfect for a summer stroll or snowmobiling in winter. *Athletic Complex* provides a lighted baseball field and football field, lighted tennis courts, dirt track and bleachers. *Hainlin Park* offers a volleyball court, regulation horseshoe court, picnic shelter with power and playground equipment. *Northgate Park* has playground equipment and a basketball hoop.

Several annual events grace this lovely town. Among them are the *Winsted Legion Days* held the second weekend in August. The Legion sponsored event features music, dancing, parade, refreshments and good food. *Agri-Preciation Day* in mid-June has a fun run of 5K and 10K.

There's an *Easter Egg Hunt* in the spring sponsored by the Winsted Civic and Commerce Association and the Jaycees. Of course, what would *Christmas Holidays* be without sleigh rides, apple cider, caroling and a winter parade, all of which just happens to be found right in Winsted!

For further information, contact:
Winsted City Hall
181 1st St. N.
Winsted, MN 55395   Phone: 612-485-2366

CORPORATE PROFILE

Sterner Lighting Systems   Sterner Lighting Systems is a commercial lighting manufacturer that specializes in short-run custom and unique lighting products. Today it manufactures 12 different product families, ranging from custom lighting, flood, area and roadway lighting, prison lighting, landscape and walkways, poles, plastic shapes, lighting controls and more.

The name Sterner originated from the Sterner family that owned and operated a local manufacturing company. The lighting company began with the idea of attaching a hinge base to a lighting pole, which could be lowered for fixture service, greatly reducing maintenance costs. At that time, the plastics industry was rapidly developing one-piece globes and other shapes in a wide range of colors. Sterner exhibited its revolutionary hinge pole with red, white and blue globes at the New York "Lightfair" trade show in 1960. Sterner was the star of the show, capturing New York headlines on what had been up until then a rather unimaginative industry.

Sterner Lighting went public in September of 1961, and it was shaped into the company it is today through a series of seven acquisitions of other lighting companies.

Sterner now employs 250 people and has a broad range of products that generate annual sales of $35,000,000 worldwide. Noteworthy projects in Minnesota include the Nicollet Mall, Minneapolis Convention Center, Metrodome, Norwest Bank Building, Williams Arena, City of Duluth, City of Bemidji, City of Wayzata, Lindberg Terminal, Internal Revenue Building (St. Paul), Mall of America, Carlson Headquarter Properties (Minnetonka) and the Mayo Education Center in Rochester.

Sterner's strength continues to lie in its ability to design and manufacture custom light fixtures to the customer's design criteria for those not satisfied with off-the-shelf products, while incorporating energy efficient lamps. Sterner can duplicate existing lighting fixtures, as it did with the Brooklyn Bridge fixture when it developed a replica of a hundred-year-old gas lantern that now sports energy efficient metal halide lamps.

Other notable projects in the United States include the U.S. Capitol, the Statue of Liberty, Library of Congress, United Terminal at O'Hare Airport, Disney World and Disneyland.

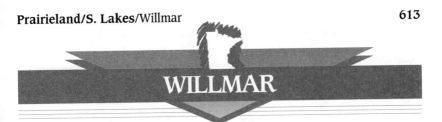

Every town has its own unique traditions and celebrations but few are as inviting as Kaffe Fest in Willmar celebrating the great Scandinavian tradition of "have a cup of coffee." But Willmar is as warm and friendly as that coffee tradition all year-round.

Willmar is the gateway to the Little Crow Lakes of the Central Lakes Region. From the rich prairie farmlands to the south and west, the changing landscape of glacial lakes that begin within Willmar's city limits, and the rolling hills and hardwood forests that stretch to the north, Willmar is both geographically unique and serenely beautiful.

One of Minnesota's fastest growing cities, Willmar is home to a number of major industries, most connected to agriculture, including Jennie-O Foods. The city is a regional shopping center and features a wide variety of accommodations.

ATTRACTIONS & EVENTS

The Glacial Ridge State Trail makes for fascinating exploration over the hilly landscape formed by retreating glaciers. The hiking is excellent. But there are also trails for cycling, snowmobiling and cross-country skiing, all three on the 18.5 mile state *Glacier Lakes Trail* as well as on the trails of *Sibley State Park.*

Golfers will enjoy the *Willmar Golf Course* overlooking scenic *Swan* and *Willmar lakes.* Snowmobile buffs will love the *Mid-America Snowmobile Museum* on Highway 71. The *Kandiyohi County Historical Society Museum* celebrates the past and features Great Northern Steam Locomotive No. 2523.

If you like your coffee as much as the Scandinavians, you'll love the month of June in Willmar. That's when *Willmar Fest* is held, really a combination of four celebrations, including *Kaffe Fest, Frameries Fest, Aqua Fest* and *International Fest.* The result is one rather extravagant week of parades, fireworks, carnival rides and other family fun. The *West Central Concert Series* offers a variety of professional concerts. The *Kandiyohi County Historical Society* sponsors area folk entertainment on Tuesday evenings during the summer. October features an arts and crafts fair. *Sonshine* is an outdoor Christian music festival held each July and drawing more than 10,000 people to hear nationally acclaimed performers.

For further information, contact:
Willmar Convention & Visitors Bureau
518 W. Litchfield Avenue
Willmar, MN 56201   Phone: 800-845-8747 or 612-235-0300

INDEX

Let's Travel Pathways Through Minnesota
Reader Survey

To make our next edition even better, please take a minute to answer the following questions. Mail the completed form to the address shown for a chance to win one of many travel related prizes to be given away over the life of the book.

1. How did you obtain your copy of *Pathways?*
a) Bookstore
b) As a gift
c) At a gift or specialty store
d) Other_____
          (PLEASE EXPLAIN)

2. How many people including yourself, plan to use this copy of *Pathways?* _____

3. How many businesses in this book do you plan to contact or visit during the next 12 months?
a) 1-5
b) 6-10
c) 11-15
d) 16 or more

4. Rank in order of frequency the types of businesses in this book you plan to contact or visit. (1 to 5, with 1 being the most frequent)
a) Specialty Shop
b) Restaurant
c) Bed & Breakfast
d) Lodging
e) Resort
f) Antiques
g) Attractions
h) Art Gallery
i) Museum
j) Recreation
k) Chambers or Visitors Bureau
l) Other _____

5. What are the three features you like most about *Pathways?*
a)
b)
c)

6. Please list any features you would like to see added to our next edition of *Pathways?*
a)
b)
c)

7. On average, how many books do you read per year?
a) 1-5
b) 6-10
c) 11-20
d) 21 or more

8. How many trips, in Minnesota, do you take per year?
Business_____ Pleasure _____

9. How many times per month do you dine out? _____

10. Which area(s) of Minnesota do you visit most?
a) Arrowhead
b) Bluff Country
c) Heartland
d) Metroland
e) Prairieland & Southern Lakes

11. Which of the following recreational activities do you enjoy?
a) Fishing
b) Camping
c) Boating
d) Hiking
e) Skiing
f) Canoeing
g) General pleasure traveling
l) Antiquing
i) Snowmobiling
j) Golfing
k) Other_____

12. Age
a) Under 20
b) 21-35
c) 36-50
d) 51-65
e) 66+

13. Household income
a) $10,000-20,000
b) $21,000-30,000
c) $31,000-45,000
d) $46,000-60,000
e) $61,000-99,000
f) $100,00+

14. Education level
a) High school
b) Trade school
c) Some college
d) College graduate
e) Masters degree
f) Doctoral degree

15. As a result of using this book, do you or other readers plan to telephone any of the listed businesses for brochures, information or reservations?
a) Yes If yes, how many?_____ (approximately).
b) No
*When you call, let them know you read about them in *Pathways!*

16. What are your favorite places you feel should be added to this book?
        <u>Business Name</u>   <u>City</u>
1)
2)
3)
4)
5)

Send completed survey to: Clark & Miles Publishing, Inc.
                            1670 S. Robert St., Suite 315
                            St. Paul, MN 55118